# Striptease

# Striptease

The Untold History of the Girlie Show

RACHEL SHTEIR

OXFORD
UNIVERSITY PRESS
2004

# OXFORD
## UNIVERSITY PRESS

Oxford   New York
Auckland   Bangkok   Buenos Aires   Cape Town   Chennai
Dar es Salaam   Delhi   Hong Kong   Istanbul   Karachi   Kolkata
Kuala Lumpur   Madrid   Melbourne   Mexico City   Mumbai   Nairobi
São Paulo   Shanghai   Taipei   Tokyo   Toronto

Copyright © 2004 by Rachel Shteir

Published by Oxford University Press, Inc.
198 Madison Avenue, New York, NY 10016
www.oup.com

Oxford is a registered trademark of Oxford University Press

Library of Congress Cataloging-in-Publication Data
Shteir, Rachel, 1964–
Striptease : the untold history of the girlie show / Rachel Shteir.
p. cm.
ISBN 0-19-512750-1
1. Striptease—United States—History—20th century.  I. Title.
PN1949.S7S55   2004
792.7—dc22   2004014760

1 3 5 7 9 8 6 4 2

Printed in the United States of America
on acid-free paper

For Lee Siegel, who writes in a way that matters

# Contents

## Part Four
# Striptease Goes to War

## Part Five
# After the War

## Part Six
# Sexual Revolutions

# Striptease

Edward Hopper, *Study for Girlie Show*, 1941. Whitney Museum of American Art,
New York; Josephine N. Hopper Bequest.

# Introduction

A young woman appears upon a darkened stage, her movements picked out by a colored spotlight. She is fully clothed, usually in an evening gown. Moving with a curiously characteristic undulation, swaying hips and shoulders to slow jazz rhythm, she walks back and forth across the stage. Hesitatingly, her hands go to one shoulder to undo a strap. It falls, she catches it. Suddenly, she is off the stage and the stage is dark. The beat of the music increases and she is back in her colored spot, the shoulder strap now hanging undefended. Always moving, usually smiling, her hands release another catch, the dress falls, there is a fleeting glimpse of undergarments, the stage is dark again. And again she reappears, another barrier surrendered, beginning again her disrobing where she left off before the blackout. Between the movements of the dance the audience applauds, demanding more and more insistently. How far she will go depends upon the city, upon the theatre, even upon the performance in which she is appearing.[1]

This is a description of striptease, a distinctly American diversion that flourished from the Jazz Age to the era of the Sexual Revolution. I began thinking about striptease ten years ago, when an otherwise ordinary school friend of mine named Jane became an exotic dancer—a stripper—a descendant of the performers I write about in this book. Jane's transformation seemed improbable at the time, but of course it was not, given the extraordinary instabilities of America right before the last millennium.

What began to intrigue me the more I thought about Jane's apparently radical change in career was how stripping inspired a series of expectations about all the paradoxical things women are supposed to be: chaste amazon, lustful sovereign, sweet gamine emerging from nowhere, comic hag, coy femme fatale. It occurred to me that one thing that stripping stands for is a possibility that women could reinvent themselves as desirable creatures every night. That possibility tantalized, for it seemed to me to both appeal to women of my own era and be part of an American dream.

When my friend Jane switched careers, "classic" striptease had been extinct for three or four decades. Born in the Jazz Age, striptease persisted to the Sexual Revolution. In the late fifties, the "tease" part vanished, as it outlived its usefulness, and having been ravaged by time was shortened to "stripping" or traded in for the euphemistic "exotic dancing." As I discovered through Jane, by contemporary industry standards, striptease was demure. It was a world away from the spectacle in today's strip clubs, where whips, chains, and poles often serve as props and where no sooner have the performers pranced onstage than they rip off whatever shreds of fabric count as clothing. Today, gentlemen's clubs and strip joints feature topless and bottomless lap dancing and pole dancing. They are part of the pornography industry: big business, not show business.[2]

But the striptease existing from the Jazz Age to the Sexual Revolution, which the press agent Louis Sobol once described as "scampishly indecorous," was not really pornography. It claims an allegiance with the American popular theater. Striptease, another writer observed, was "a combination of posing, strutting, dancing, and singing, punctuated from time to time by thrusts and twists of the abdomen called 'bumps' and 'grinds.'" One of the genre's most famous performers, Gypsy Rose Lee, advised: "a woman doesn't take it off like an onion skin. That would make me cry." Gypsy meant that not anyone could be a stripper—a stripper needed artistry, or what Gypsy called "illusion." [3]

> At the age of 16, I knew the value of keeping on something flimsy when the rest of the gals at Minsky's were working on the third layer of skin. . . . Why? Because the naked skin to the naked eye is just so much epidermis, but when it's hinted at, rather than hollered about, it allows for illusion.[4]

Gypsy was hardly the only stripper to believe in illusion. Other strippers began their numbers dressed as debutantes, society dames, schoolteachers, housewives, movie stars, or lion tamers. Sometimes they cracked elaborate jokes while taking it off and ended up holding a velvet curtain in front of them or wearing only a spangled G-string. They captured a mischievous spirit and occasionally a patriotic one. Irreverent or vulgar, they toyed with the straps of their gowns and then removed their clothes while singing a mournful song, or dancing to one.

The writer Alison Lurie has suggested that "people done up in shiny colored wrappings and bows affect us just as a birthday present does: we're curious . . . ; we want to undo the package." In this book that present is, for the most part, female. Male strippers came on the scene in the 1920s, and male strip joints, of course, are now ordinary. But this book focuses mostly on women taking off their clothes, with all of the ambiguities, contradictions, and confusions that act contains.[5]

For a half-century, female strippers evoked, as the art historian Denys Chevalier writes, "an elusive social expression of modern eroticism." [6] The word "striptease" alluded to taking it off: as an "automatic vaudeville,"[7] as a spoof of aristocratic American culture, with unexpected grace. Mostly striptease occurred in burlesque theaters—the bottom of the entertainment food chain, where performers took it off next to slapstick comics. But in nightclubs and vaudeville houses, striptease, though often silly or crass, could also strike a sophisticated or subversive pose. Almost from its inception, critics complained that the elaborate eight- or ten-minute striptease performances, mostly done to ragtime or to jazz standards, seemed ossified or obsolete. But nonetheless, much striptease contained a distinct, thrilling presence in mid-twentieth-century American culture, where it presented a startling erotic quiddity.

TODAY, THERE IS A VOGUE for "retro" striptease—an updated version of the striptease I write about in this book. And much of the pleasure Americans take in stripping of all kinds—as well as the anxiety it provokes—echoes the emotions elicited by striptease a half-century ago. Documentaries like HBO's *Strippers: The Naked Stages* and *G-String Divas*, a serial about strippers in a Pennsylvania gentleman's club, reiterate many of the same myths that began in the Jazz Age. Rated-PG stripping emerges everywhere: It occurs onscreen and off in Hollywood and in silly new Broadway musicals. Legal scholars cite stripping in cases aiming to stretch the definition of the First Amendment to bodily expression; producers cheerfully feature stripping on Internet porn sites; on late-night cable TV shows and in the *New York Times*, stripping functions as proof of gender discrimination, a last stop for troubled women and a testament of the return, at a national level, to decadence. Stripping also accrued its own importance in California, where exotic dancers at the Lusty Lady peep emporium pioneered efforts to unionize sex workers.[8]

As for the emergence of "retro" striptease, it began in upscale nightclubs in Los Angeles and New York and continues to stagger forward. At the Velvet Hammer, a semiannual event at the El Rey nightclub, at Moulin Rouge Nights at Jumbo's Clown Room in Hollywood, and at the Blue Angel and the Va Va Voom Room at the Fez club in New York, women are resurrecting acts from old-fashioned striptease. Tease-O-Rama, an annual festival of retro striptease now in its third year, continues to acquire publicity and crowds. The Burlesque Museum in Helendale, California, attracts attention every year with its national striptease contest. And there are now several amateur historical societies devoted to burlesque striptease and its performers.[9]

To some contemporary women, performing retro striptease is a feminist act and a social obligation, a way to wrest the art of stripping from the world of pornographers. These women argue that their work is a political reaction to twenty-first-century reform forces seeking to foil female sexual expression and that by giving the striptease acts of the fifties an ironic tone, they are updating them, doing a kind of performance art. Of course, critics do not always agree. As Adam Gopnik noted in the *New Yorker*, mingling performance art and old-fashioned striptease can either yield provocative results or implode into a sad, dull evening.[10]

Still, the fact that women continue to be interested in striptease provides an important clue to striptease's identity and meaning. It might seem quaint that we denizens of this worldly age find an erotic charge in the act of one person's slowly taking off her clothes. But there is also an unexpected gravity to the act. Then too, even if the Sexual Revolution has rendered it obsolete, somehow, striptease hangs on. Its sexiness is an insult to some feminists—in current political wisdom it is considered misogynist—while its irrevocable sleaziness complicates the claim of third-wave feminists who maintain they're doing it to empower themselves. (One reason why striptease continues to flourish at all may be that it reminds Americans of a time when male and female roles were more stable.)

THIS BOOK BEGINS in the nineteenth century with the appearance of modern theatrical trends that allowed striptease to be born. But it concentrates on striptease's golden age—the years between the Jazz Age and the Sexual Revolution—when strippers performed in burlesque theaters, nightclubs, vaudeville houses, carnivals, and fairs, and on the silver screen. Although part of striptease's appeal emerges from the taboos surrounding it, its full meaning reaches beyond those taboos to embrace a series of contradictions. In the Jazz Age, striptease became a powerful symptom of twenties decadence and the New Woman's sexual liberation. It was at once a warning about the effects of commercialized vice's takeover and a testament to women's newfound economic freedom. At a moment when male and female ideals seemed to become more distant from each other, striptease appeared to mark a distinct gender identity for women. At a time when women were entering the workforce and making strides in public social life, it is no accident that striptease emerged as a form of entertainment mostly directed at men.

By the 1930s, much of what striptease referred to had shifted. In that decade, the rise of Literary Striptease—elegant acts complete with Algonquin Round Table–style songs—expanded women's self-conception while becoming the focus of the moral panics shaking the nation. The onset of World War II made striptease patriotic, like the pinup girl—although striptease remained a threat to anti-vice reformers at home. After the war, striptease animated a sector of the economy and continued to inform women's everyday proclivities. Fashion, Broadway, and advertising borrowed from striptease's style, as did Hollywood in films like King Vidor's *Gilda*. Striptease provided one answer to the question "Should women seek glamour as usual?" by invading bebop clubs on Fifty-second Street and in Hollywood. The new centers for striptease, Dallas, Miami, Los Angeles, and Las Vegas, linked strippers with gangsters and deviance. The road show burlesque film spread striptease throughout the country as burlesque theaters closed.

In the 1950s, adult movie houses replaced burlesque theaters while new men's magazines like *Playboy* made images of naked women widely accessible. Television sharpened competition between the remaining forms of live popular entertainment. Striptease continued to flourish in nightclubs, at the state fair, at the carnival, and at Coney Island, but it was less respectable. Carnival pitchman Fred Bloodgood recalls that in the 1950s, "The minute a guy started flashing with a girl show, then he was no longer a showman."[11]

By the sixties, the "tease" was vanishing as women's roles changed irrevocably. Nudity in the theater became both a symbol of free love and a mark of men's oppression of women, and topless and bottomless dancing made striptease beside the point. The increasing presence of the mob in the nightclub industry also played a role in the disappearance of striptease from American culture, as did the diminishing amount of fabric in everyday fashions. The introduction of the miniskirt accelerated this process, as did the scanty garments movie stars began to wear in public. In 1962, when Marilyn Monroe stood in Madison Square Garden in her sheer, sequined dress and sang "Happy Birthday, Mr. President," she referred to striptease without actually stripping.

After Monroe, the modern pornography industry gathered strength, and cultural attitudes toward sex loosened. In the most tumultuous decade of the century, Americans were too impatient to sit in a dark theater and wait while strippers teased them. Thus, this book more or less concludes its tale around 1969, the year that the theater critic Walter Kerr dubbed New York's off-off-Broadway scene "the theater of nudity."[12]

SCHOLARS HAVE ALREADY done a lot of work connecting the rise of other forms of American popular entertainment like vaudeville and jazz to the Jazz Age abandonment of Victorian mores. I argue that, as part of this broader cultural revolution, striptease worked to undermine Victorian culture's puritanical bent and confirmed and celebrated a visual separation between men and women, whatever their class. Striptease epitomized modern attitudes toward sexuality. In Americans' shift from an obsession with duty to an interest in what individuals wanted, striptease, the most ribald form of popular entertainment, turned pleasure into a victorious mode of self-expression.[13]

Striptease endured for so long in part because it reveals both pleasure's long reach in the public realm and the limitations of that reach. Striptease straddled the arenas of vice and popular entertainment. I think of this as the principle of "near." For most of its history, striptease was never exactly prostitution, but it was "near" prostitution. It was not pornography, but "near" pornography, not exactly about the consummation of the sexual

act, but about its "near" consumption. When reformers attacked striptease, they did so in a way that always "nearly" eradicated it. In an essentially puritanical society, striptease's relationship with commerce—the
combination of intractable flesh peddling and jostling, jesting sexuality—
made the quest for pleasure nearly as much about the sybarite's failure as
her success. This tension made many Americans uncomfortable.

Striptease also made Americans uncomfortable because it presented
women as erotic objects. It offered a maverick brand of fantasy in Western
culture, one that held out the possibility of redefining—and refining—
American ideas about women, sex, and gender. In Jazz Age society, where
identity could be reduced to a purchasable style, striptease offered women
a bolder medium of self-expression than other forms of popular theater.
Striptease allowed women to be more direct and modern about their sexuality, advancing past the coy, nineteenth-century idiom of the era's theatrical revues. And like other forms of popular entertainment, striptease as a
career gave some women a chance to realize the American dream. By presenting a sexual self outside the realm of ordinary experience, women could
overcome their working-class origins and make it.

The essential character of golden-age striptease lay in its raunchy combination of sexual display and parodic humor. Striptease grew up alongside
archetypal American forms of popular entertainment such as vaudeville
and variety and also anticipated the sexualized culture of the sixties. If striptease counts as its antecedents the Broadway revue and the Folies Bergères,
the French spectacle that casually undraped women for dramatic effect, it
counts among its descendants the lap dance and the peep show, which dramatically undraped women for casual effect. The historian Robert C. Allen
points out that whereas the Broadway revue "elevated" the female body by
connecting it to Paris and rootless cosmopolitanism, burlesque striptease
did the opposite, lowering that body by connecting it to nothing except its
own appetite.[14]

GIVEN ALL OF THIS, how to explain the fact that there is no serious book
about striptease? One reason is that strippers performed in diverse, out-of-
the-way working-class venues that are difficult to research; another is that
striptease so differs from any extant form of popular entertainment that
historians have not really known where to look or what to look for. Until
the rise of cultural studies departments in universities, striptease seemed
too close to pornography to deserve scholarly treatment. And after that, to
many anti-pornography feminists, striptease seemed like rape.

This book seeks to restore the world of striptease to history, to chart
its geography, and to recall its culture and social representation. One of its
projects is to determine who strippers were and to distinguish them from
women in other realms of show business, as well as from prostitutes. An-

other distinction considers the stripper's body. Beginning in the Jazz Age, the popular press described the stripper as more curvaceous and fleshy than Jazz Age Hollywood movie stars and svelte, androgynous Broadway chorines. Thus the stripper's body both allied her with ladies of the night and made her appearance comic.

The historian Susan Glenn argues that many early-twentieth-century female vaudeville and cabaret performers used their appearance to mitigate their dangerous sexiness and to distinguish themselves from real-life fallen women. They became "both spectacles and personalities." She quotes the writer Caroline Caffin describing these performers as "personal and unashamed." And then Glenn goes on to elaborate something that Caffin observed as being distinctive to popular performance. Female vaudeville performers greeted the spectators "straight in the face" and said, "Look at *me!* I am going to astonish you!"[15]

Strippers did this too. But whereas the popular press sometimes celebrated female vaudevillians, it disliked the stripper's "in your face" attitude and often dismissed her as a prostitute. Beginning in the Jazz Age, the convention in journalism was to show how a life in the world of striptease led more often to impoverishment and obsolescence—and sometimes death—than fame. A stripper languished one step below showgirl, an impression strippers themselves sometimes fueled by expressing a desire to be something else—a legitimate actress, for example. Meanwhile, newspaper theater critics dwelled on the fact that striptease required neither talent nor real good looks. "[Strippers] try to be show girls, but they aren't, they hop, stumble, and gallop," a typically contemptuous critic wrote at the beginning of the Depression.[16]

Strippers' power lay in another arena than that of the showgirl, however. The stripper deployed a combination of cool eros and wisecracking bacchanalian humor. In the twenties, when Americans were taking sex lightly, striptease served up a volatile mixture of the erotic and the comic, a satiric supercocktail meant to explode onstage. As a response to modernity's high seriousness, some striptease parodied the trajectory that American women movie stars make when they descend from ingénue to character actor. And comedy allowed striptease to reduce sexuality to its smiling essence. But against the horizon of the Depression, striptease became grotesque, irreverent, parodic, and antiauthoritarian.

We make a distinction today between the words striptease and undressing: undressing mostly involves taking off one's clothes in private—awkwardly, comfortably, or however one wishes. Striptease is a spectacle. Undressing occurs casually, sometimes without style and grace, and probably lacking in costume and prop, while striptease implies ritual and performance, allure, tension, and, generally speaking, an audience, as well as exhibitionism, with all of the flagrant come-hither posturing that that word implies. Even today, striptease is more about the relationship of being dressed to being undressed than about mere nudity.

The best stripteases spoofed sexuality. Some of the most inventive performers—like Gypsy Rose Lee and Carrie Finnell—sent up desire's inconstancy instead of merely reproducing it. In the forties and fifties, strippers skewered the role of the femme fatale while also using excess to puncture postwar complacency. Though striptease of these years was in general less funny, it dramatized the female entertainer's pathetic, savage plight. Many strippers eventually became comedians, tousled prestidigitators of eros and funny stuff, conscious of and scoffing at mortality's fragility.

Through its history, striptease tossed laughter and desire into the air, challenging conventional ideas about gender roles. Striptease often measured women through the lens of men. Sometimes it illustrated what women wanted those measures to be, and other times it seemed more like a male rebuke of what women lack. But the history of striptease is one of men and women failing together and apart.

Filled with racial and gender stereotypes, striptease, some scholars argue, resembles a freak show.[17] But this strikes me as a limited way of looking at a phenomenon that responded to a craving for the fabulous in life. In the thirties, Jean Cocteau suggested that the vogue for larger-than-life striptease performers might be an index of our desire to see a goddess rather than a flesh-and-blood girl: "in the long run, the Americans suffer from a craze for the colossal."[18]

Ultimately what is interesting about striptease is that it flaunted female sexuality—and male sexuality too—in spectacular forms, along the way making fun of those forms. Striptease could be boring, uneven, contradictory, puzzling, and extraordinary. It told stories about identity, fantasy, drive, and passion and evoked sex in a strange, essential way by mocking desire's absurdity. Confronting Americans with a private act in a public space, the best stripteases wove together the mask of humor with corporeal unmasking, intellectual dazzle with physical prowess. At its most archetypal, striptease embodied great theater's antic spirit—albeit in a limited way—with the "polymorphous perversities" and roguish transgressions that all great theater contains.

# Part One

# Undressing

In Berlin, she was allowed to remove her stays but was obliged to keep them on in Vienna.

—Paul Derval

# "A Startled Fawn upon the Stage"

S triptease begins with the rise of romanticism and its passions. In Europe before the Second Empire, the advent of that movement first inspired audiences to feel envy and dazed admiration as well as repulsion at the sight of a scantily clad ballerina. After three decades of shock generated by the French Revolution and Napoleon, political Europe settled into a calm suggested by the restored Bourbon monarchy in France. But in the arts, a revolution emerged in full transforming force. Rejecting classicism's harmony and order, writers, composers, and artists led a movement that valued spontaneity and disdained convention. Although these men—for they were all men—shared romantic tendencies that sometimes contained a taste of the absurd, as often they embraced an imaginative elegance.

Many of these tendencies burst into women's dancing. As the dance historian Lynn Garafola points out, romanticism transformed ballet into an art performed by women for men.[1] The ballerina seized the stage from the male ballet star and stretched into dances with big lines, arabesques, jumps, poses, and drama, and in general began to be both freer in dress and more active onstage. The rise of pointe as a universal symbol for feminine display and of the adagio as a sensuous female motion meant female performers could spread their legs, turn out their toes, throw back their heads, and dance with abandon. There were limitations, of course. Choreographers generally cast romantic ballerinas not as real bourgeois women, but as weird sylphs or fantastic heroines who leapt through scenic highlands and over misty landscapes, or swooned into the waiting arms of men. When Mme Francisque Hutin, the first solo ballerina to appear in New York, neglected to do these things, she became an immediate figure of controversy.

Hutin arrived in New York in the winter of 1827, when the city was already a theater town in the most literal sense of the word. Whereas London housed two theaters, downtown New York boasted six. There was room for all different kinds of entertainment. On Lafayette Street and on Grand, two circuses drew crowds to see girls dancing, horses racing, jugglers, musicians, and acrobats. Black-face minstrels made New Yorkers laugh.

The most important theater in the city was the Park Theater on Park Row near City Hall. Built in 1798, the Park sought mostly to entertain the city's elite with serious British drama and tragedies. In 1827 the Park's largest rival was the Bowery. A year before Hutin arrived, Charles Gilfert,

Madame Francisque Hutin as she appeared at the Bowery
Theatre, 1827. Billy Rose Theatre Collection, The New York
Public Library for the Performing Arts, Astor, Lenox, and
Tilden Foundations.

a young entrepreneur and former pit musician, built it on the site of the Bull's Head tavern on Bowery Street just below Canal.[2]

The Bowery's architectural splendor at first drew the fashionable crowd. Edwin Forrest performed there. Imitating the Park, the Bowery presented abridged operas and light versions of Shakespeare. But to make ends meet, Gilfert raised prices in the boxes and then, thrashing around for a success, somehow discovered Hutin. There is no doubt that Hutin and her French dancing saved Gilfert and the Bowery financially. But Hutin also made an artistic sensation and erased in one evening the American taste for genteel English dancing with hornpipes, jigs, and reels. The night Francisque Hutin premiered at the Bowery, February 7, the theater was full. Hutin was billed in between a pantomime of *Much Ado about Nothing* and a farce titled *The Family Jars or the Bull in the China Shop*. She flew onstage and did a ballet called *La Bergère Coquette*—The Coquettish Shepherdess—to an English romantic song, "I've Been Roamin'."

What she was wearing made as much of an impact as the way she moved. In the European romantic fashion, Hutin was costumed in a semitransparent Grecian robe reaching her calves. As she spun around, her skirt "floated up," revealing her betighted thighs and hips. Her dance lasted a mere three minutes and she took one encore. But in those few minutes, she elicited an alarmed response from the audience. As the critic Joseph Ireland described it: "The graceful danseuse came bounding like a startled fawn upon the stage, her light and scanty drapery floating in the air, and her symmetrical proportions liberally displayed by the force of a bewildering pirouette. . . . [T]he cheeks of the great portion of the audience crimsoned with shame and every lady in the lower tier of the boxes immediately left the house."[3]

A number of observers, including Mayor Phillip Hone, found Hutin graceful. Mrs. Bunell Hoffman, the wife of a prominent criminal attorney, defended the dancer in a letter to one of her friends: "I suppose you have seen a great deal about Mme Hutin, the opera dancer in the papers. She dresses in trowsers loose from the knee up and sometimes loose all the way down to the ankles. Over that she has a light silk frock which, when she makes her 'pirouettes' . . . to be sure . . . [the dress] becomes . . . inflated with wind and flies up like a parachute, displaying her person to the waist."[4]

In 1827 only prostitutes and "waiter girls"—the quasi-prostitutes who toiled in working-class concert saloons—bared their ankles in public. Some newspapers were outraged and others pretended to be. The *Statesman* suggested that she don petticoats and the *New York Observer* attacked her: "The exhibition is to all intents and purposes the public exposure of a naked female."[5]

Some of the brouhaha arose because at a moment when the idea of a lady's going to the theater remained in question, women seemed transfixed by Hutin. One reformer wrote that "even" women in the audience appeared to be admiring her "gross and scandalous display of her person."[6]

In other words, Hutin was a hit. Ceding to public opinion, she briefly donned gauzy Turkish trousers underneath her skirt. After a few weeks of audiences' demanding to see her legs uncovered by tights, however, Hutin returned to the tutu she had worn on opening night and, sans trousers, continued at the Bowery until it burned down on May 26, 1828. She was on the bill that evening as well.[7]

IN PARIS, changes in fashion continued to undress dancers' bodies. After the ancien régime crumbled, the innumerable muslin petticoats ballerinas wore became shorter as daring Continental designers like Alfred Grevin dreamed up skimpier costumes for the stage.[8] Romantic ballet costumes such as the white, uncorseted, below-the-knee, diaphanous gown that the ballerina Marie Taglioni wore in 1832 in the Paris ballet *La Sylphide* revealed, for the first time, a woman's leg and pelvis onstage.[9] Taglioni initiated other sartorial changes, such as donning pink tights beneath her skirt.

In New York, however, another prima ballerina, Fanny Elssler, lengthened her skirts by a foot when she performed at the Park Theater in 1840. After Hutin, the ballet for the most part became a respectable form of entertainment for the American aristocracy even as new forms of working-class theater—most notably the dime museum and the concert saloon— made the undressed woman into a spectacle for a roiling working-class audience. As these men poured into the city in the 1830s, they demanded their own forms of entertainment, and the Bowery Theater—indeed the neighborhood itself—ceded its briefly gained respectability to a grittier atmosphere. The strip stretching from Chatham Square to Cooper Square became a mecca for vice seekers.[10]

Reminiscing about the Bowery Theater many years later, Walt Whitman recalled it as a democratic man's leisure paradise:

> [The theater was] pack'd from ceiling to pit with its audience mainly of alert, well dress'd, full-blooded young and middle-aged men, the best average of American born mechanics . . . the whole crowded auditorium, and what seeth'd in it and flush'd from its faces and eyes, to me as much a part of the show as any—bursting forth in one of those long-kept up tempests of hand-clapping peculiar to the Bowery—no dainty kid-glove business, but electric force and muscle from perhaps 2000 full sinew'd men.[11]

Seated in the pit, these men indulged in vociferous call-and-response by throwing vegetables, singing, cheering, stamping, and applauding. They ate oysters, drank beer, and sang along with the performers, sometimes forcing them to repeat the same stanza over and over. But by 1840, as Whitman points out, the standard of theatrical performance at the Bowery had declined. "Cheap prices and vulgar programmes came in," he wrote that year. Several years later, in one of his newspaper columns for the *Brooklyn Evening Star*, he asked: "What person of judgment, that has ever spent one hour in the Chatham or Bowery theatres in New York, but has been completely nauseated with the stuff presented there?"[12]

A diversion promoted with increasing frequency to this audience was *tableaux vivants*—spectacles in which naked or partially clothed women posed as statues, painted portraits, or historical figures. After the French Revolution, the *tableau vivant* (or living picture) had begun to appear in two places in Europe: the brothel and the salon, where it embodied a semi-chaste aspect of the German obsession with classicism.[13] In the brothels of Restoration England, madams such as Charlotte Hayes, Louisa Turner, and Miss Falkland had used living pictures of Greek figures, Old Masters, and the world of the East to display their prostitutes favorably. Apparently inspired by the voyage of Captain Cook, Miss Hayes once sent an invitation to regulars announcing the "famous feast of Venus" at her "Cloisters." This feast included a pageant supposedly based on the account of one of the explorer's traveling companions. Hayes encouraged avid clients to take part in it if they so desired.[14]

For several decades, as women's clothing and mores changed, living pictures vanished. When they reappeared, they did so at the moment when newspaper barons were democratizing the industry. In 1833 the first penny paper, the *New York Sun*, started to report on human-interest stories and stole readers from old-fashioned broadsheets like Horace Greeley's *New York Tribune*. Thus in the ensuing decades, other penny papers arose to compete by focusing on local news and scandals, especially those revolving around women. Subsequently, papers like the *Tribune*, which until that moment focused on politics and national news, began to cover theater, crime, sports, adultery, suicide, rape, and undressing acts.[15]

ALTHOUGH LIVING PICTURES arrived in New York in the 1830s, the first all-female versions of the genre appeared a decade later, managed by a former animal trainer named Robert H. Collyer. British and well versed in Barnumesque strategies, and the author of his own sensational account of the city's underworld, *Lights and Shadows of American Life*, Collyer went to some trouble to "reveal" the fact that his troupe was so authentic that it "rehearsed" in front of the great romantic painters in Rome and England. Half sly satire, half homage to populist democracy, "Dr." Collyer's living pictures became popular in part because in sending up high art, they mocked the British, who were by this point much hated in New York.[16] Ridiculing Renaissance paintings such as *Venus Rising from the Sea*, *The Three Graces*, and *Suzanna in the Bath*, living pictures sent up the official culture held dear by the aristocrats uptown. But living pictures also achieved a raucous

appeal because they were performed in the dark grog shops and dingy concert saloons springing up along the back streets of downtown New York.

The concert saloon—a theater bar established sometime in the early
1840s—further linked the undressed woman to commercial vice. So-called
to distinguish themselves from regular saloons, concert saloons appeared
along the Bowery and Broadway and offered crude theatrical presentations
and food. These rough, sex-and-booze emporiums could be recognized by
the silhouettes of women hanging over their doors. Inside, the floors were
covered with sawdust. Sometimes a lunch counter or bar served sandwiches
and beer delivered by "waiter girls" who pranced around wearing red
boots with bells on the toes and a knee-length skirt—the uniform of prostitutes. Vice-society reformers perceived these girls as abandoned waifs
and/or as mercenaries, luring rubes or bourgeois clerks to ruin through
any number of inventive cons. The reality was that the waiter girls often
worked on a percentage basis, ripping off clients for watered-down beer or
rot-gut liquor.[17]

George Foster described one concert-saloon living-picture act he saw
as nothing less than a vivid scene from Dante's *Inferno*. On a small revolving
stage erected in the middle of the room sat a voluptuous woman—Suzanna—
who had already appeared as Venus and Psyche. Eager to establish himself
as able to distinguish between "real" theater uptown and the "theater" taking place in concert saloons, Foster noted that Suzanna was no "model in
the European academy," but rather an "old crone."[18]

In one hand, the "crone" held an opaque piece of fabric against her
body. The elders stood behind her chewing tobacco, which, Foster pointed
out, detracted from the tableau's verisimilitude. After the stage revolved once,
allowing the audience to see Suzanna from all angles, the curtain dropped
and Suzanna-Venus-Psyche "rearranged" herself to interpret the next great
master.[19] Elsewhere, though, Foster described living pictures as being less
depraved than comic. Here is "Venus" being arrested for obscenity:

> . . . A squad of naked Olympians . . . wherein Venus was trundled off to
> the Tombs in a wheelbarrow, minus her chemise, and Bacchus had a
> narrow escape through the back window, leaving his trowsers to the vigi-
> lante guardians of public morals—while the three graces—as naked as they
> were born—made an unsuccessful attempt to scramble, most ungracefully,
> out of a back basement.[20]

By contrast, descriptions of legitimate actresses of the era relate their
beauty, elegance, and charm. During the same period when Foster was reporting on living pictures models' depravity, Jean-Léon Gérôme painted
the great French actress Rachel as Tragedy and Alfred de Musset addressed
her as "chère muse."

IN THIS ERA, undressed women also turned up in P. T. Barnum's American Museum, a dime museum that opened on lower Broadway near the Bowery in 1842. So-called because entrance cost ten cents, dime museums displayed the human body—particularly the female body—as a scientific curiosity. The historian Timothy Gilfoyle notes that the result of this was that the American Museum quickly became a known place of erotic assignation, primal mischief, and fantastical female display—a peep show before peep shows existed. The American Museum, one reporter observed, was "worthy to be immortalized by the pencil of Caravaggio."[21]

Barnum was a pioneer in attempts to disguise living pictures' prurience behind a mask of virtue, an effort that only aggravated the anti–living pictures moralists of the era. The penny press railed against the living pictures whose very popularity as a comic and erotic entertainment demanded an explanation. The one that was usually forthcoming was contemporary society's excessive sensuality. "Grey-headed men who passed in the community for moral and upright men, were found side by side with the most depraved."[22]

Critics could dismiss depraved taste when the audience was, as George Foster characterized it, "impotent and dilapidated old letchers and precociously prurient boys."[23] But by the late 1840s, white-collar patrons increasingly attended living pictures. The interest of the Knickerbocker crowd explains why sometimes the penny press response to living pictures did not altogether or exclusively condemn such "depravity," but rather seemed to want to have it both ways, wallowing in living pictures' Rabelasian particulars while pretending to warn visitors off.[24]

In antebellum New York, hysteria about living pictures, ballerinas, and other forms of female display accelerated alongside an explosion in prostitution. As early as 1838, at Tyrone Powers' performance at the Park Theater, at least eighty prostitutes had roamed the galleries searching for clients.[25] A well-known brothel in New York, the Seven Sisters, punned on the title of a popular musical review. By the 1840s, the Five Points—the area south and to the west of the Bowery, which was then the theater district—became synonymous with prostitution. The prostitute Lucy Brady, who worked in New York during that time, reported picking up customers in the theater, as well as in a brothel and a concert saloon. (Many theaters stood conveniently next door to brothels.)[26]

As the second half of the nineteenth century began, New York became a metropolis, and anxiety over prostitution sharpened. As the historian Christine Stansell has documented, working-class women began to adapt some aspects of prostitutes' costumes, and the aristocracy and middle class began to identify certain occupations, such as theater jobs, with "working women."[27] Strong complained that it was difficult to tell the difference between prostitutes and ordinary women. "They come up the same stairs as our wives, and into the same lobby," he wrote.[28] In 1850, George Foster bemoaned the fact that "within a few feet and under the same roof where our virtuous matrons with their tender offspring are seated, are . . . painted, diseased, drunken women, bargaining themselves away to obscene and foul faced ruffians." Foster estimated that a quarter of all theatergoers were prostitutes.[29] And thus the stage was set for more undressing.

# Legs

Shortly after the romantic ballet had introduced Americans to female sexuality, impressionism, photography, and the cancan would blur that distinction by showing undressing women as real. The change in the way women were represented without clothes began around the time that Edouard Manet created his *Déjeuner sur l'herbe*. First displayed at the Salon of 1863, that painting shows two fully clothed dandies apparently oblivious to the naked woman sitting in front of them. A pile of clothes lie at her feet as if she has just undressed. In the background, a clothed woman wades in the stream. The naked woman in the foreground is neither a religious figure nor a mythological one—she appears to be a real woman in an awkward pose. The debate that ensued revolved around the second woman, who possibly was undressing. Before *Déjeuner*, while the undressed woman—the nude—could still be counted as art, the undressing one—caught undressing or with the suggestion of removed clothing—was generally considered a whore. Any artist who depicted a woman in the act of undressing automatically demoted himself to the status of a pornographer. "Art," Maxime du Camp had written in 1860, "should have no more sex than mathematics."[1]

*Déjeuner*, though, suggested how dramatically representations of undressing women were changing. It was only a short step from there to Edgar Degas' and Henri de Toulouse-Lautrec's being inspired by the women of the nineteenth-century music hall. Their images—disenchanted, clumsy, anything but ideal—show women sometimes caught in the everyday fact of undressing. These depictions were not really about nudity, just as striptease was not really about it, at least not until the Sexual Revolution.

Artists were about using real clothes to make undressing erotic and Oriental ones to make it fantastic. This epoch of undressing introduced dresses and undergarments that real women ordinarily wore as well as fantasy garments borrowed from mythology and the courtesanal life. But sartorial innovation failed to dissuade contemporary critics from complaining that undressing in painting made it similar to pornography. To these critics, however props and costumes softened or varied the female body's vulgarity, in the end, undressing would always be a prelude to prostitution.

Meanwhile, the increasing importance of commerce in show business played a role in putting the undressing woman center stage. In 1854, P. T. Barnum had attempted to market women's bodies by staging the first beauty

contest. A decade later, the commercialization of women's bodies accelerated as a trend of women's selling ordinary household goods took shape.
Innovations in retail like the department store used the undressed woman to
sell all manner of products on a mass scale. The modern department store
used versions of living pictures—undressed and undressing mannequins—as
a marketing tool. The rise of shopping whetted the public's awareness of
intimate life. Men and women could see what both sexes wore in the windows, and both sexes undressed in public dressing rooms, a subject for many
scurrilous cartoons showing drunken or half-dressed female shoppers.[2]

Outside of the department store, a vogue for women's legs had been in
full force since the romantic ballet became popular. In Paris in the 1840s
and 1850s, travel guides, memoirs, and essays relished the undressed leg,
which sometimes stood for an antibourgeois theatricality and other times
represented the era's new commercial spirit. Legs could be seen everywhere—
in ballets, living pictures, photographs, novels, the theater, and fashion.
Second Empire intellectuals and writers worshipped legs, devouring them
like the great feasts that were being eaten everywhere in the city at midnight.

Some critics condemned the leg as pornographic and others elevated
it as artistic. To be the latter, the leg needed to be somehow covered since
a naked leg was too obscene to appear in bourgeois public life. In his 1857
essay "The Painter of Modern Life," Baudelaire describes how the dancer's
legs, being nakedly sexual, need cosmetics to transform them into respectable, classically sculpted limbs.

> The use of rice-powder, so stupidly anathematized by our Arcadian phi-
> losophers, is successfully designed to rid the complexion of those blem-
> ishes that Nature has outrageously strewn there, and thus to create an
> abstract unity in color and texture of the skin, a unity which, like that
> produced by the legs of the dancer, immediately approximate[s] the hu-
> man being to the statue, that is, to something superior and divine.[3]

Even rice powder could fail to make the leg "divine," as an anonymous
dance critic celebrating the limb's ubiquity suggested: "Whenever we hear
that a danseuse is coming out we white-waistcoat, pantaloon, and double-
opera ourselves up to the hilt . . . so that nothing may interrupt our study and
contemplation of the 'new gal's legs.' . . . [T]he opera is a bazaar of legs."[4]

The rise of photography as a commercial art form helped bring this
bazaar to the world. In 1856 photography arrived in Paris, New York, and
London—cities where the *carte de visite*, a small card with a photograph on
one side and nothing on the other, had already been patented for two years.
The *carte de visite* multiplied the image of the undressing woman and made
her available to everyone. By the mid-1860s, these *cartes de visite* were exchanged all over the world like baseball cards. In England alone in that

decade, three to four million were sold. Appealing to all classes, other genres of *cartes* presented the private lives of theatrical and political celebrities, and family and individual portraits, as well as slices of life from the demimonde. Into that last category fell women undressing.[5]

Photographers generally portrayed women undressing by imitating the "woman at her toilette" style of certain impressionist paintings. This bought them respectability and the approval of censors. But like the lithographs of ballerinas in the previous generation, these photographs clearly contained an erotic dimension. "Woman at her toilette" also suggested prostitution. And yet early on, some women tried to control the way they were represented. A more complicated way of explaining photography's impact on undressing can be understood from the story of the Countess de Castiglione, one of the first women to take control of her image through photography. Born in 1835, Castiglione was a legendary, eccentric beauty and one of Napoleon's paramours. From the 1850s to the 1880s, she commissioned a series of evocative, demimonde-ish photographs of herself in a variety of states of undress. In one, she wields a passe-partout as if it were a fan. Apocryphal stories depict the countess doing a striptease for her portrait takers.[6]

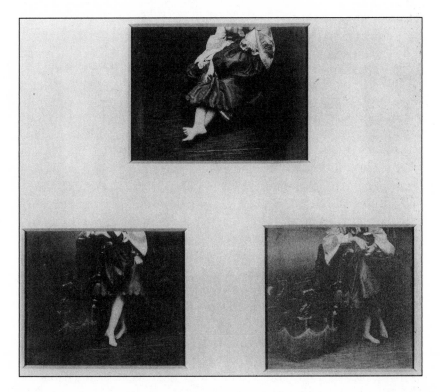

Pierre-Louis Pierson, *Study of Legs, II, The Countess de Castiglione* (1861–67.)
The Metropolitan Museum of Art, New York City, David Hunter McAlpin Fund, 1975.

Unlike the *cartes de visite* of actresses and dancers, which early photographers took almost solely for mass consumption, these aggressive portraits seem to have been shot either for the countess's own personal amusement or, as some historians suggest, to appease her insatiable narcissism.[7] Many of the pictures portray her as an eccentric, by, for example, showing her real legs, with all of their veins and imperfections, instead of dancerly or pristine marble ones. Some viewers considered the photographs to be blatantly pornographic; others thought they were repulsive.[8] But the countess's social status allowed her to get away with a kind of representation that remained taboo for lower-class women.

While the countess's self-portraits allowed her idiosyncrasy, the pioneer photographer A. A. E. Disderi's *cartes de visite* of half-naked ballet dancers and music hall stars demonstrated the undressing woman's stability as a commercial, erotic icon. Disderi's portraits are not about the individual, as the countess's were: they show flirtatious, otherwise forgettable music hall stars at ease, personally accessible, lifting their skirts to reveal shapely betighted calves, thighs, and sometimes behinds. In other words, they reveal woman as mass object. But Disderi's pictures also epitomize the way photography commercialized legs in the Second Empire. One photo, taken in 1864, shows a montage of the ballerinas of the Paris Opera. It reveals women's betighted lower limbs in different ballet poses, and the types of legs are various: knobby knees and bony ones, baggy tights and fitted ones. The legs display differing physiques, but lack the countess's attention to individuality. Ultimately the photographs resemble Irving Penn's 1950s nudes, in which the upper bodies and faces of the women remain outside of the frame, reiterating the idea that female body parts are a product.[9]

BY CONTRAST, the cancan emerged in the same era and animated the undressed woman by representing her as an individual with keen sexual desires. She was Olympia in 3-D. In keeping with the Belle Époque's sharpened emotions about intimate life, the cancan put the undressed woman in motion and gave its dancers a sexual power previously held only by prostitutes. Part of this power resulted from shifts in attitudes towards lingerie, which in turn affected the parts of the body cancan dancers could display. In the 1840s and '50s, doing the cancan threatened to show the sheer lacy pantaloons then in vogue, as well as the dancer's bare legs between her pantaloons and garters.[10]

During this era, Courbet, Degas, and Manet celebrated the prostitute as representative of modern life's vitality in oil and pastel. In Émile Zola's novels *L'Assomoir* and *Nana*, the heroines wear the crotchless pantaloons favored by cancan dancers and prostitutes. In fiction and in real life, the cancan dancer became a high-kicking devil with the potential for revolution—even if it was only sexual revolution. She did all of this to Offenbach's devilish music.[11] Here is the music hall singer Yvette Guilbert recalling La Goulue, who began as a cancan dancer during the Second Empire, later became the subject of unsentimental Toulouse-Lautrec lithographs and was the first woman to dance the cancan at Paris's Moulin Rouge:

> La Goulue, with her black silk stockings, one black satin foot held in her hand, would whirl her sixty-odd yards of black lace petticoat. On her knickers, she had mischievously embroidered a heart which would be revealed on her little behind when she disrespectfully bowed to the audience. Bunches of pink ribbons at her knees and a delicious froth of lace down to her slender ankles would hide and reveal those lovely agile, witty, enticing legs of hers. The dancer would flip off her partner's hat with a smart kick, sink into the splits with her bust straight and her body slim in its sky blue satin bodice.[12]

The elements of Guilbert's description: the ebullient anticipation of the split, felt palpably by the working-class audience at the Moulin Rouge cabaret; the outrageous heart embroidered on La Goulue's pantaloons; and her sending her partner's hat flying with a kick that theatrically and erotically expressed *épater la bourgeoisie*.

Part of the appeal of La Goulue and performers like her was the venue where they performed. Like America's Bowery Theater, the Moulin Rouge was located in a volatile working-class neighborhood, in Montmartre. While Baron Haussmann's modernizing trends—wide, large boulevards—had already altered other areas of Paris, Montmartre continued to look like the medieval city. The winding, colorful cobbled streets, home to the Medrano Circus, brothels, fence joints, con men, and thieves, implied a seraglio.

No star would embody the Belle Époque's overheated populism or its indifference to bourgeois convention more than La Goulue. Her cancan demonstrated female sensuality in direct, physical terms. But she was more than just a dancer. To high-minded revolutionaries and romantics after the Paris Commune, La Goulue became emblematic of the era's irreverent salaciousness and the authentic voice of the populace. "The can can dancers pour scorn on all those things that are held to be noblest and holiest in life," wrote Heinrich Heine in his political analysis of the dance.[13] "The can can ignores . . . all that recalls rules, regulations, and method. . . . [I]t is absolutely a dance of liberty," asserted Rigolboche, another blonde high kicker of the era.[14]

Some of La Goulue's force came from her apparent ability to overturn established rules about female decorum. Her moniker—"the Glutton"—was given to her either because she was capable of knocking back one glass of champagne after another, or because she was the mistress of a young aristocrat named Goulu-Chilapine. She is reputed to have danced in the streets of Montmartre with her breasts outside her corset. Even more strik-ing than La Goulue's many erotic escapades was the casual indifference with which she treated her parade of aristocratic lovers, a behavior that accrued its own political meaning. She supposedly once asked the prince of Wales, with whom she was dallying, "So, are you paying for champagne, or is it your mother's account?"[15]

Depending on their political affiliation, observers loved or hated La Goulue. To liberal commentators, she signified both the near-religious abandon of romantic female performers and a girlish revolutionary fervor. "You are the wickedness of Paris on a very good pair of legs," her spurned prince of Wales allegedly once wrote. Bourgeois reformers and conserva-tives, however, saw La Goulue as a vulgar performer responsible for de-stroying the city's elegance. The arts critic Gustave Coquiot noted, "she had an ugly face, the profile of a bird of prey, a menacing mouth and hard eyes."[16]

IN CIVIL WAR AMERICA, the leg became scandalous, not only because it was exposed but because it had a "masculine" character. Indeed, the women who exposed their legs often appeared *en travestie*—dressed as boys or men. These female performers, who played French spies, pirates of Savannah, and other lusty cross-dressed roles, made male dancers obsolete. The first of such shows occurred in 1861, when the char-ismatic writer and travesty performer Adah Isaacs Menken—"the Menken," as she was known—played Mazeppa in a theatrical adaptation of Lord Byron's eponymous poem. The theater critic Robert Grau called her the most "sensa-tional" of Mazeppas.[17]

Carte de visite showing Adah Isaacs Menken in travesty costume, c. 1863. Author's personal collection.

The Menken arrived at Smith's Green Theater in Albany on June 13, two months after the Civil War began. She was already controversial. Amid na-tional turmoil, newspapers cast asper-sions on her marauding character, many marriages, questionable femininity, and dubious ethnicity—in short, she was per-ceived as a *femme fatale avant la lettre*.[18] Conservative critics speculated that she played male roles because she was unfit for female ones. (The evidence lay in her life offstage: the Menken smoked on the street and wore crimson lipstick.)

The Menken's friend and press agent Ed James, editor of the theatrical newspaper the *Daily Clipper*, described her in sensational terms by focusing on her voracious and therefore unfeminine appetite. She ate, James said, "with the gusto of a working man." Before the theater, she devoured "a dish of raw clams, a thick soup of chicken, a hearty steak and a deep dish pie, and a compote of fruits." She followed her performance with three portions of Charlie Pfaff's New Orleans stew, which contained prawns, oysters, and vegetables, and after that, a "slab" of roast beef.[19] Her gluttony implied "masculinity," and the contrast with her voluptuous body swept audiences in.

Even in its day, *Mazeppa* was no gem. A hack melodrama, a "horse drama" in contemporary parlance, it offers a trivial story of a Polish nobleman and his girl trouble: The nobleman Ivan Mazeppa falls in love with a beautiful, innocent woman who is betrothed to an evil count; the evil count loses to Mazeppa in a duel; Mazeppa nobly spares his life. Of course, the count does Mazeppa dirty and, in a moment the audience would have been waiting for, he strips him of his noble robes, binds him to a wild stallion's back, and releases the horse and rider into the wilderness. In the logic of melodrama, Mazeppa returns on horseback to save the day.

The Menken's take on *Mazeppa* differed from previous ones in two aspects: First, in most earlier productions, a male actor played the hero. Second, the majority of prudent stage managers either strapped a dummy to the horse or chose a broken-down nag to ensure the actor's safety, as the convention of the day dictated that in the fifth act, Mazeppa should ride down a steep runway, which sometimes was as tall as the theater itself. In her inimitable bravado, though, the Menken, who played the title role, insisted on making the ride on her own stallion. The poster for the spectacle capitalized on the derring-do of this choice by displaying an apparently nude Menken strapped to the horse's back.

In the saloons, salons, and newspaper rooms of the city prior to June 13, the literati debated whether Menken would ride as Lady Godiva, costumed only in her hair. In a scathing editorial, the labor reformer and newspaper editor Horace Greeley condemned her salacity, especially during wartime. "We cannot believe that the actress scheduled to play Mazeppa would revolt the audience by appearing in the nude," he wrote.[20]

The Menken was unfazed. Like the Countess de Castiglione, she created her own publicity. Counting among her friends Walt Whitman and Edwin Booth, as well as members of such New York society families as the Schuylers and the Astors, she flouted bourgeois morals and manipulated her image in a Barnumesque fashion. Even before the Menken appeared onstage, she redesigned the tights or "fleshings" that actresses traditionally wore to make them cling to her legs more tightly. When the curtain rose, the Menken wore a man's shirt open to the waist, calf-high boots, and a flesh-colored body stocking.

The first provocative moment occurred in the duel scene, when her enemies gathered around her onstage and stripped her of her "noble" robes, causing one reviewer to exclaim, "Parts of the body of this actress were exposed that God never intended to be seen by any other eye than her mother's."[21] The other sensational event occurred in act 5. The curtains closed after act 4. When they opened, the Menken was already onstage strapped to a live horse galloping down a runway into the theater. The audience could only see the blur of a horse and a human body. Lightning flashed, thunder roared, music blared, and many in the audience were confused as to whether the Menken was naked or wearing a body stocking.

It was not simply the Menken's nudity—or alleged nudity—that made her the talk of New York and earned her immediate fame, launching her on a theatrical career that included triumphs in Paris, London, and Vienna. It was the way she embraced the travesty or breeches role. At a moment when Amelia Bloomer was trying to convince women to don pants, the Menken cut her hair to look more like a man. At a moment when the Civil War was introducing throngs of soldiers to New York, the Menken exploited her androgynous appeal. The woman who would later be Alexandre Dumas' lover understood or intuited that the point was not to pretend to be a man but rather to play up her femaleness while dressing in a masculine style.

The Menken was hardly the only artist to demonstrate sexual fluidity by appearing undressed in this era. She was, though, one of the first female performers to declare her cross-dressed costuming, or lack of it, to be in the service of her vocation. "I am an artist," she frequently and loudly announced to defend her nudity.[22] Attempting to explain the Menken's success, some historians turn to demographics, asserting that in June 1861, two months after the Confederate Army fired the first shots at Fort Sumter, immigrants, carpetbaggers, and former revolutionaries flooded urban centers and created a large audience for female spectacles of all varieties.[23] Other historians have linked the explosion of the leg show to a shift in the perception of the self. Until the leg show era, many Americans believed that the undressed woman, though she threatened bourgeois identity, could ultimately be contained in the brothel and the theater. After the Civil War, this perception abated.

A new group of reformers emerged to respond to the rise of the undressed woman. Representing the second wave of reform in the nineteenth century, these men and women were variously called purity-campaign reformers and vice-society reformers. Unlike the first wave, which was primarily religious, this one was composed of elite men, doctors, and suffragists. Gaining strength

alongside commercialized popular entertainment, purity-campaign reformers focused on prostitution and its associated activities—including undressing acts. Their goal—the modern solution to these vices—was regulation.[24]

AT THE SAME TIME, after the Civil War ended, the leg show became a fixture on the New York theatrical scene. What is sometimes called the first
Broadway musical—*The Black Crook*—opened at Niblo's Garden in September 1866; it presented legs more sensationally than any previous spectacle, in part by demonstrating self-consciousness about its intentions and
in part through excess. According to Joseph Whitton, the production's
stage manager, *The Black Crook* was a "grand ballet . . . designed to make
even the surfeited New Yorker open his eyes and his pocket and hold his
breath in excitement."[25]

*The Black Crook* outdid all financial expectations. With a cast of one
hundred female dancers, it ran for sixteen months and made almost a million dollars. The plot, a variation of the Faust myth, turned Faust into a
smart hunchback named Herzog. But *The Black Crook*'s outrageousness lay
in two dances done by the entire chorus: the cancan, which few Americans
had seen outside the brothel, and a number called the "Pas de Demons," in
which the dancers wore tights without the ballerina's tutu.[26] This last dance
inspired adulatory reviews from both the penny press and respectable newspapers. The *Tribune* swooned over the amount of female leg on view. The
*Clipper* called *The Black Crook* an "undress piece" and joked that "these
demons at Niblo's have scarcely a rag left upon them to take off."

Reform-minded critics saw *The Black Crook* as a serious infraction of
decency. The crusading newspaperman James Gordon Bennett wrote an
editorial in his paper, the *New York Herald*, calling for the police to arrest
everyone in the cast, a move that producers may have concocted to boost
ticket sales. "The model artists are more respectable and less disgusting,
because they are surrounded by a sort of mystery—something like a veil of
secrecy which women do not look behind and which men slip in stealthily
to see." Preaching against the show in a sermon called "The Nuisances of
New York, Particularly the Naked Truth" at Cooper Union, Reverend
Charles B. Smythe recoiled against the women's indecency even as he
dwelled on their scanty costumes.

> The immodest dress of the girls with short skirts and undergarments of
> thin, gauze-like material, allowing the form of the figure to be discern-
> ible . . . the flesh-colored tights, imitating nature so well that the illusion
> is complete; with the exceeding short drawers, also of thin material, al-
> most tight-fitting, extending little below the hip; arms and neck appar-
> ently bare, and bodices so fitted as to show off every inch and outline of
> the body above the waist. . . . The attitudes were exceedingly indelicate.[27]

But Smythe's proselytizing only enhanced *The Black Crook*'s scandalous allure, and the show continued to spawn sequels and prequels, including *The White Crook*, *The Red Crook*, and *The White Faun*. *The Black Crook* also set the stage for Lydia Thompson and the British Blondes, the first burlesque show to conquer America.

IN SEPTEMBER 1868, only a few months after *The Black Crook* closed, the British Blondes arrived in America. Popular in the British music halls, burlesque had emerged in New York in the 1840s as a biting working-class parody of high culture or as an extravaganza full of fairies and mythical creatures. Burlesque sent up Shakespeare and fashion, marriage and women's suffrage. This version of popular theater, which incorporated wacky song-and-dance numbers, marches, silly attacks on fashion's frivolities, and zany parodies of Offenbach, delighted audiences of all kinds.[28]

Dressed *en travestie*, Lydia Thompson and her troupe of young, attractive women, all refugees from Lord Chamberlain's edicts against drama, first performed the burlesque *Ixion* at Wood's Museum, an enormous, Barnumesque museum-theater on Thirtieth and Broadway. They made a hit. The show brought in around thirty thousand dollars in the first month, an amount that was unprecedented.

When the curtain rose at Wood's, the four Blondes pranced onstage in knee-length skirts, thin body stockings, and flesh-colored tights layered on top of short pants. Their bare necks and arms glistened in the lights. They did a parody of the cancan and an Amazon march. They sang a satiric psalm and performed a lampoon of the Ixion myth, which was about a jealous husband. They did one elegiac skit sending up a restrictive style of dress called the "Grecian bend" and others making fun of divorce and suffragists.

But the Blondes were not radicals. They appealed to the male appetite on a visual level. As one reviewer put it, they were "optically edible."[29] Unlike the performers in *Mazeppa*, they were not playing roles. They were showgirls, singing and dancing and making fun of life. The blonde, voluptuous British women, on the surface less brazen, less charismatic and androgynous than the Menken, inspired the diarist George Templeton Strong to call them "uncommonly handsome." As for Thompson, her publicity upon her arrival in New York involved in equal parts the string of lovers she abandoned in Europe and her untarnishable virtue.[30]

In February, the British Blondes opened a new spectacle at Niblo's Garden, the theater where *The Black Crook* had succeeded. To protect New Yorkers, city authorities, after witnessing a private presentation, insisted that the Blondes lengthen their skirts by two inches before opening.[31] Just as the Menken endured criticism when she moved from Albany to New York City, so the British Blondes, upon their arrival "uptown" on Canal

Publicity photo of Lydia Thompson, leader of the British Blondes, in another one of her successful burlesque shows, *Robinson Crusoe*, 1870. The Museum of the City of New York.

Street, felt the force of Victorian disapproval. One minister avowed that the dances suggested ancient orgies. Mark Twain wrote, "The scenery and the legs are everything. . . . Girls—nothing but a wilderness of girls . . . stacked up, pile on pile, away aloft to the dome of the theatre . . . dressed with a meagerness that would make a parasol blush."[32]

The Blondes also incited outrage at Niblo's because the American public continued to harbor resentment against the success of British female performers, especially at upscale venues. But a more interesting reason put forth by some scholars links the Blondes' ability to outrage to their transvestitism. William Dean Howells wrote that the blondes were "wanton excesses: there was nothing of innocent intent in any of their productions. . . . [T]hough they were not like men, they were in most things as unlike women, and seemed created of a kind of alien sex, parodying both. It was certainly a shocking thing to look at them with their horrible prettiness, their archness in which there was no charm."[33]

While male purity-campaign reformers were objecting to—and reveling in—the leg show's transvestitism, in the newly formed suffragist camp, women argued that this art form was inimical to achieving equality. Among the most vociferous members of this campaign was Olive Logan. Actress and daughter of an actress, fashion plate, journalist, and female reformer— a vocation the writer Thomas Beer called a "Titaness from the Midlands"— Logan, after seeing *The Black Crook*, found her destiny.[34] At the 1869 American Equal Rights Association Convention, sponsored in New York by Susan B. Anthony, Logan spoke on the subject. Dressed in a gray silk dress trimmed with scarlet and wearing a pompadour corsage, she talked for eighteen minutes about the leg show's atrocities. Subsequently, in two books and countless editorials, she denounced leg show performers by asserting that they offered no talent—only their bodies.

> They are neither actresses, dancers, pantomimists, nor ballet girls but enjoy a celebrity more widely spread than any of these could hope to attain. . . . Stripped as naked as she dare—and it seems there is little left when so much is done—she becomes a prize to her manager who knows that crowds will rush to see her, and who pays her a salary accordingly.[35]

Not everyone agreed. In Chicago, Thompson stalked and then horse-whipped the editor of the *Chicago Times*, Wilbur Storey, who a few days earlier had accused her of double entendres and "lascivious actions." When the British Blonde appeared at court the following morning, a crowd gathered around her cheering.[36] But when the British Blondes returned to New York in 1870, the theatrical climate had changed. They no longer played to middle-class men and women, but to a mostly working-class all-male audience. Moreover, the reform movement that had begun to emerge at the time of the Civil War took a more concrete shape in the institution of the New York Society for the Suppression of Vice (NYSSV).

FOUNDED IN 1872 by Anthony Comstock, NYSSV, a private society, devoted itself to eradicating commercialized vice and to upholding the morals of young people. The following year, Comstock successfully lobbied for a federal anti-obscenity law, confiscated mail, condemned books and pamphlets, began to arrest pimps and gamblers, and persecuted abortionists and madams. Generously supported by New York City elites and philanthropists, including J. P. Morgan, NYSSV provided Comstock with an institutional base from which he was able to work.[37]

One area of vice Comstock targeted was brothels, where undressing acts regularly took place. Although brothels were not legal, they were ubiquitous. Comstock was interested in brothels both in New York City and all over the country for several reasons. First, he was attempting to get contraception declared illegal. Second, the brothels themselves, having become similar to theaters in terms of the entertainment they offered, were perceived as a greater risk to society.[38] In 1878, working undercover, Comstock visited Elizabeth Williams's Greene Street brothel and inquired about the act called the "Busy Fleas." Comstock paid five dollars to see three women pretending to be looking for the flea in their undergarments, disrobing, and having oral sex while piano music played. Nor was this an isolated phenomenon. Next Comstock entered another brothel and watched a "French act," as this kind of mischief was called, and then proceeded to have the French act arrested.[39] Shortly after these arrests, Comstock seems to have realized that he could not police live undressing acts as effectively as he could control the printed word. For the remainder of his life, he focused on the mail.

By the Gilded Age, the concert saloon reemerged as a mysterious place where, for a few quarters, anyone could see women do the cancan or take off their clothes. Annual masked balls, in some years held at the Metropolitan Museum of Art or at Madison Square Garden, allowed men and women to throw themselves (undressed) into each other's arms. Also, thanks to two impresarios, in the 1870s burlesque, with a generation of peripatetic leg shows modeled after *The Black Crook*, came into vogue.

Borrowing conventions from blackface minstrelsy and the innovations of Lydia Thompson, the American impresario Michael B. Leavitt, focusing on women's bodies, institutionalized burlesque.[40] Whereas minstrelsy had used male performers, burlesque used female ones. In 1870, Leavitt launched the first of these burlesque troupes, the Rentz Santley Novelty and Burlesque Company, which promised to deliver "gay life" in Paris.[41] When Mabel Santley, a star of the company, lifted her skirts and showed her ankle in San Francisco, a riot broke out in the theater. "The entire audience hollered whoooo!"[42] So successful was this troupe that the following year Leavitt renamed it Mme Rentz and Her Female Minstrels, to emphasize the fact that women made up the company. Anything was possible: Another lesser-known troupe presented a number based on a sexual pun—*Ben Hur* became "Bend Her."

A mania for zaftig female performers emerged. May Howard, the star of her own burlesque troupe and the first performer to be crowned a "burlesque queen," bragged that she would employ no woman who weighed less than 150 pounds. In 1899, when Billy Watson, the manager of Billy Watson's Beef Trust, acknowledged that all of his performers were over 200 pounds, he meant to be satiric as well as descriptive. The popular press was full of "comical" stories about the great lengths would-be burlesque performers went to in order to enlarge themselves to the required voluptuousness, such as padding their costumes, only to be discovered on the road as ninety-eight-pound weaklings.[43]

By contrast, white producers began to cast black women in burlesque musical revues in a way that focused, at least partly, on sophistication, svelteness, and ambiance. In 1890 in Chicago, the black producer Sam Lucas convinced Sam T. Jack to hire a chorus of sixteen black women for his spectacle *The Creole Show*. This marked the first time in theatrical history that black women appeared as female minstrels. Though it titillated white audiences, *The Creole Show* made some feeble strides toward presenting black women as real people.[44] It discarded the plantation setting used in blackface minstrelsy and advertised black women playing well-rounded characters. But as James Weldon Johnson would later point out, the restrictions of race in the era's theater nonetheless kept black women in exotic roles.[45]

White female burlesque groups outdid themselves in prurience, reworked old conventions, or struck a moral pose. A few years after *Ixion*, the British Blondes concluded a performance in San Francisco by kicking their legs in a cancan and trying to provoke the audience by chanting, "How's that for high?" During one particularly high kick, May Howard let her anklet fly into the crowd. But shocking the audience had been easier during the Civil War. "When a man can go out in Central Park and see a dozen pairs of well-shaped legs in tight-fitting knickerbockers for nothing," complained an anonymous performer, "he won't pay to go to the theater until he can see a good deal more."[46]

IN THE LAST TWO DECADES of the century, a revolution in the American popular theater increased competition among theaters and created a demand for more female flesh. One important event here was the rise of "refined vaudeville" in the 1880s. This vaudeville emerged out of working-class diversions— variety shows, concert saloons, and dime museums of the mid-nineteenth century. From a formal perspective, there was little difference between variety and vaudeville: both strung together skits, jugglers, singers, minstrel acts, gymnastics, fancy dancing, and short sketches. One difference was class. Variety had appealed to the working class, and although Robert C. Allen calls vaudeville the first American mass entertainment, its impresarios sought a more "respectable" audience. In 1881, Tony Pastor banned drinking, smoking, and swearing from his Fourteenth Street vaudeville theater. Sometime in the 1890s, other impresarios followed suit and by 1915, vaudeville was king of popular amusements.

The burlesque show was composed of more or less the same three parts from the end of the century until World War I: All performers appeared onstage at the beginning for a stock comic patter. In the second part, a solo performer sang or danced; the third part featured a melodrama, or "afterpiece," satirizing the aristocracy or celebrities like Jenny Lind or P. T. Barnum by making fun of their latest fashions and vogues. The idea in burlesque comedy was to bring those who had risen too high down to earth; as Douglas Gilbert observes, in burlesque, the humor "centered about the apertures of the human body." Ralph Allen describes the burlesque comic as "the child of nature" able to overthrow rules and through blundering succeed.[47]

In the nineteenth century, the lines between vaudeville and burlesque blurred. The impresario B. F. Keith, who is thought to have invented "continuous" vaudeville—vaudeville playing between 10 A.M. and midnight—opened the Union Square vaudeville house with the burlesque opera *Ship Ahoy*. Some performers moved freely between burlesque and vaudeville: in the 1880s, the musical comedy actress Lillian Russell worked in both venues, as did Fay Templeton, and the slapstick comics Weber and Fields, whose act revolved around the latter's beating up the former. In the first decade of the century, grotesque female comediennes Fanny Brice and Sophie Tucker began in burlesque and then graduated to vaudeville. Indeed, for the most part, early burlesque and vaudeville gave female performers more opportunities than variety and the concert saloon.[48]

And yet by the first decade of the twentieth century, vaudeville and burlesque evinced distinct qualities—the most prevalent of these being their audience. Although burlesque presented a less diverse entertainment than variety, it directed its humor and content to a working-class audience, as variety had in the 1840s. By contrast, vaudeville catered exclusively to the middle class and, importantly, to middle-class women. To that end, impresarios built vaudeville theaters with palatial facades to distinguish them from seedy concert saloons and storefront burlesque theaters. And yet while vaudeville replaced burlesque's slapdash numbers with wholesome acts, it maintained some of variety's risqué and ethnic identity.

DURING THIS ERA, Broadway, also on the rise, provided another place where women could display their legs. In the 1900 season, there were fifty shows on the boards. Some of these were melodramas and action spectacles; others were comic operas. The audience here also represented a wide spectrum of American life. The center of the theater district in New York was Herald Square, where the Shubert brothers and a few other families were beginning to take over.[49]

In part as a result of the theatrical explosion, the demand for undressed women on Broadway and in vaudeville increased. That in turn increased the amount of leg burlesque performers needed to show. By 1900 only a quarter-century after purity-campaign reformers bemoaned the appearance of tights, the front page of every newspaper extolled the variety performer Frankie Bailey's legs, which she insured for one million dollars. After the actress, who had danced in the burlesque show *The Boston Belles*, appeared in the vaudeville revue *Whirligig*, newspapers referred to legs all across America as "Frankie Baileys."[50]

# "Yvette Goes to Bed": The First Undressing Acts

The first true undressing act emerged in Third Empire Paris, where unrivaled economic prosperity competed with unrivaled social unease. The city was trying to recover from the German invasion of 1870 and the brutal events at the Paris Commune the following year. In the Banquet Years, Paris saw wealth, but also bombs, assassinations, and student anarchy, as well as general unrest and an unrivaled attention to pleasure. But the first undressing acts liberated the imaginative vitality in the fin de siècle in part by advertising themselves as a category of theater. Thus, the undressing act can't be understood without reference to the general importance of theater in fin-de-siècle culture.

In the early 1890s, theatrical visionaries such as Aurélien-François-Marie Lugné-Pöe, André Antoine, and Paul Fort introduced French audiences to Ibsen and Strindberg. Alfred Jarry's *Ubu Roi* premiered at the Theatre de l'Oeuvre in 1893. Undressing acts flourished in the great theatrical brothels, such as the one on rue des Moulins frequented by Henri de Toulouse-Lautrec. Since 1880, the year that Émile Zola's sensational novel *Nana* was published, *tableaux vivants*, *poses plastiques*, *danses du ventre*, *cartes de visite*, and the cancan, all of which started, more or less, as courtesanly enticements, had insinuated themselves into the boulevard theater.

Still, the first undressing act created a sensation. In 1893, at the Bal des Quatz' Arts—the four arts ball—a half-impromptu, half-staged, after-hours procession, a woman undressed not to solicit but to celebrate the Left Bank. Designed to be an annual event at the Moulin Rouge, the Bal counted among its participants Parisian art students from all of the various ateliers in the city. But these dazzling, populist fetes—frenzied, lavish, sensual occasions, both publicity stunts and spontaneous local gatherings—also drew Montmartre artists and writers. The *bals* sometimes acquired humorous tones and sometimes avant-garde ones, and sometimes a messy, irreverent combination of both. An annual event staged the fake wedding of the political caricaturist Francisque Poulbot. Another was part of the "Enraged Cow," an absurdist parade in which students took ersatz vows of poverty and marched through the streets renouncing their possessions. According to La Goulue, Degas, Rodin, Zola, the Goncourt brothers and Dumas fils attended the historic *bal* where the undressing act was invented.[1]

As was typical of much of Montmartre's street and café life, the scene that night of February 9 was bacchanalian, a swirling, urban feast. Jules

Roques, one of the ball's organizers, stationed himself at the top of the stairs of one of the buildings the ball had taken over en route to its destination—the Place Blanche, a square at Montmartre's center. There, Roques tried to keep nude students from entering. The ball's theme that year was Cleopatra, and a float resembling a barge, carried by strong and enterprising students and bearing the naked "queen," paraded through the streets into the Place Blanche, where it stopped next to the Moulin Rouge.[2]

Near midnight, the hilarity increased. Several of the models and students decided to stage an impromptu beauty contest. Two dancers dressed *à l'Orientale*—Manon LaValle and Sarah Brown—ignored the cold, jumped on the float, and began taking off their clothes "down to net," according to Guy Peron, and started a riot in which at least one student "had his silk hat cut open by a police saber."[3]

One reason that the *danse du ventre* became popular is because its performers wore face veils, which set them apart from ordinary women. A couple of years before the first undressing act, the idea of the exotic in undressing was set against the horizon of progress, reason, and technological advancement at the 1889 International Parisian Exposition, the fourth such spectacle to be open to foreigners. Held on the centennial of the French Revolution, the exposition celebrated French achievements, such as the Eiffel Tower, then under construction; machines; and photography. The "Algerian Village" was an apogee of a fin de siècle Paris in the throes of orientalism. With its smiling erotic voluptuaries who may or may not have been Algerian, the village encouraged erotic fantasy and flirted with ordinary existence in an oasis of costume and gesture. The "barbaric" village contained an entire rare and foreign world that included sword swallowers, acrobats, and men who mysteriously appeared to slice their tongue in two. Dark-haired female performers gyrated in the *danse du ventre*.

IN HER JOURNAL recounting the events of the night of February 9, 1893, La Goulue worried that Manon LaValle's undressing act was so dynamic it would render the cancan obsolete. "We thought that it was finished with the can can, with its lace and quilted red garters," she wrote.[4] But the real effect of that fateful night was both more and less dramatic than La Goulue could imagine. The next morning, LaValle's cancan came to the attention of Senator René Berenger. One of the most outspoken reformers of his day, the so-called father of decency, the *bête noire* of Montmartre, the enemy of Toulouse-Lautrec, Berenger had become unpopular in the district by, among other things, championing a statute that would have made it illegal for dogs to urinate in Haussmann's boulevards. He also forced women to wear flesh-colored body stockings onstage. Now, Berenger settled on the *bal* as a political problem. He demanded that a trial be held and the undressing women pay fines.

In a climate where anarchy was rife, Berenger got his way. On June 14, the Eleventh Court heard the plea. Manon and Sarah Brown and one of the ball's organizers, a man named Henri Guillaume, were fined a hundred francs each. In protest, students hung effigies of Berenger throughout Montmartre and proclaimed their right to see nudity. Berenger grew angry, condemned the students, and summoned the police. There was a riot, the Prefecture of Police was besieged, and troops were called in from the provinces. A young man who sat drinking in a café near the Sorbonne was fatally wounded. The chief of police was dismissed.

Although in retrospect the police reaction seems extreme, it was not so extreme as all that. Berenger was part of a Paris police force worried about the political element in Montmartre. Populist, slangy language and wild undressing could easily, in the eyes of the Paris authorities, slide into radicalism. At the same time it is equally easy to romanticize the genesis of the undressing act as part of a radical Montmartre still innocent of commercialism. Certainly, one could say that the undressing act came out of a fin de siècle spontaneity, by artists given to dramatizing the irregular aspects of their lives. It was this self-conscious visibility and theatricality that led many to describe Montmartre and undressing in public as bohemian. And yet the separation between that innocence and its corruption was never complete, for the extravagant gesture of undressing owed much to the world of publicity. Commerce and marketing were important elements from the start. And although there are no records of how it happened, it is easy to imagine that theatrical impresarios all over Paris immediately seized upon Manon LaValle's spontaneous act and began to scheme that it would be profitable to move it to the popular stage.[5]

Only thirteen months later, undressing acts exploded into the music hall scene. The first one appeared at what had been, until 1892, Le Divan Japonais, a small, decadent Asian-themed music hall at 75 rue des Martyrs. Two years earlier, Le Divan Japonais had featured Yvette Guilbert, the singer, one of the first performers to be more phenomenon than actress. She described the café as "an after hours nightclub" done up like a Japanese brothel, with bamboo poles, red and blue billiard tables, and overstuffed Louis Phillipe chairs, and "as seen in certain magazines, large silk panels" on the walls.[6]

The owner, an olive merchant, sold olives during the show. The cafe's ceiling was so low that performers raising their hands could touch it. Perhaps it was as an homage to Guilbert or as a way to capitalize on her name that the first undressing act was called "*Le Coucher d'Yvette*" (Yvette's Going to Bed), even though the honorific Yvette had gone on to sing her pathetic songs elsewhere.[7]

Le Divan changed hands twice and changed its name to Concert Lisbonne. Nonetheless, mentioning the singer would have been in the exploitative spirit of Montmartre. Listed in the program as a pantomime, "*Le Coucher d'Yvette*" told the story of a woman's toilette as she got ready for bed. Its star was one Blanche Cavelli, about whom little else is known. When the curtain rose, a chair and a bed were onstage to represent an ordinary room. Piano music began to play, and Cavelli entered, wearing everyday clothes. She took off her gloves, her hat, and a corsage and threw them on the chair. She took off her skirt and then she removed her petticoat, her corset, her stockings, and finally her chemise, leaving her in some sort of nightgown. Finally, she climbed into bed and the lights went out.[8]

It is not known how long the act lasted, but since lingerie was cumbersome and voluminous in nineteenth-century France, "*Le Coucher d'Yvette*" must have gone on for longer than a couple of minutes. Some critics say that at each stage Cavelli stopped to check on the spectators' sangfroid, as though she were posing for a photographer.[9] The fashion historian Cecil Saint-Laurent describes "*Le Coucher d'Yvette*" as "ingenuous." Apparently, spectators liked her, for "*Le Coucher d'Yvette*" swept through Paris and inspired at least thirty similar "tales" of undressing, many of which starred "Yvette." These included "*Le bain de maid*," "*Suzanne et la Grande Chaleur*," and "*Liane chez le médecin*." By 1896 a short film of Yvette made by the Gaumont film house circulated in Paris, at least privately.[10]

FASHION HELPED shape the undressing act yet further. Saint-Laurent argues that the undressing act arose as a protofeminist response to restrictive Belle Époque undergarments, particularly the corset. In the eighteenth century, under Louis XIV, he writes, "Orgies . . . would never have led to a daily show available to anyone. . . . *Le Coucher d'Yvette* played the reassuring role of an initiating ceremony, designed to show schoolboys that as a woman took off her clothes she revealed a body that differed in certain ways from a man's, but was not as radically different as it seemed."[11]

Certainly the increasing importance of the corset might have made the naked woman seem strange. As the nineteenth century went on, corsets had become more restrictive and ornate, and tight lacing came into vogue. By 1845 the wearer needed assistance lacing them up. The ones being worn at the end of the century shaped women's bodies into an S: S-shaped metal stays flattened the stomach, and the bottom of the corset cut into the groin, giving women large behinds and breasts, as though they were "bound and sealed." Jean Cocteau described two courtesans in a restaurant of his youth as warriors wearing "suits of armour, escutcheons, ironyokes, girdles, whalebone, piping, pauldrons, greaves, thighpieces, gauntlets, corselets, pearl natters, feather bucklers, satin, velvet, and gem-studded shoulder belts, coats of mail."[12]

By the time Blanche Cavelli was undressing, an anticorset move was under way. Sarah Bernhardt and Ellen Terry abandoned the corset, and both Zola and Renoir argued that the garment defied nature. To Thorsten Veblen, it was a "mutilation."[13] Thus perhaps the undressing act was a kind of sartorial liberation.

AFTER CAVELLI, the Parisian demand for novelties created as many new styles of undressing acts as the market could hold. Audiences seemed willing to pay to see glitzier costumes, more scantily clad singers, and, above all, more sparkling antics. At the Casino de Paris, another one of the Left Bank's music halls, an otherwise unknown auburn-haired pantomimist named Angele Herard one night launched into her version of the scurrilous brothel act "The Flea." Herard feigned an insect bite, which compelled her to jump anxiously from one foot to another in the style of a tarantella. This jumping won her an international tour. According to Paul Derval, Folies Bergères director, how much she took off depended on the city in question: "In Berlin, she was allowed to remove her stays but was obliged to keep them on in Vienna."[14]

The undressing act that captured the public imagination in fin-de-siècle France maintained its place in that country's fantasy life well into the twentieth century. The year after Angele Herard's debut, the Folies Bergères opened as a theater and began to produce undressing acts annually.[15] By the end of the century, the Folies, previously known by all Paris as a "permanent fair for prostitutes," had been transformed into a site where the French brand of glamorous, barebreasted revue took place. Half-nude performers did colossal *tableaux vivants*, undressing acts of all kinds, and other decadent types of nude entertainment until the 1920s.

A TRANSFORMING REVOLUTION in the history of undressing was the emergence of film, which erupted in France and the United States during the 1890s and then quickly caught fire in America. The first films seemed to reveal women's bodies in a more real way than theater, and they also encouraged spectators to see undressing as ubiquitous, and as a drama they could follow and perhaps even shape. At the same time, many of them depicted the comic consequences of taking it off with more verve than the theater.

These films were introduced by Thomas Alva Edison. In 1893, Edison, inspired by Eadweard Muybridge's still photographs of horses and people of three decades earlier, invented a device called the kinetoscope—a kind of "peep show" machine—on which he looped short films, most of which lasted less than a minute. The films mostly depicted vaudevillians, and they were shown in kinetoscope parlors—storefront parlors not unlike concert saloons. The first such parlor opened in 1894 in the vice district of New

York's Union Square. It housed ten machines; customers could pay a nickel to peer into them. The following year, every major city in America boasted its own kinetoscope parlor. In the next several years, these parlors appeared in gold rush towns and other out-of-the-way sites, as well as in vaudeville theaters.

Just as the *carte de visite* had made woman at the toilette a mass image thirty years earlier, so now the kinetoscope expanded the possibilities for the expression of undressing. Onscreen, undressing could reach a wider audience—and sometimes a more respectable, middle-class one. Many of the first kinetoscope films featured female vaudeville performers doing sinuous dances revealing their knees and thighs. Some of these were hand tinted, like that of Annabelle Whitford, the former Little Egypt, who performed a serpentine dance. And many of the films were censored. A film of the Spanish dancer Carmencita, a regular at Koster and Bial's Music Hall in Manhattan, was banned in several states, and a kinetoscope exhibitor in California was arrested for showing it.[16]

One of the most interesting things about these films is that even though they revealed the performers' bodies, they also showed the undressing act's awkward qualities. The medium of the camera forced undressing acts to abandon some of the pretense that art had given them, but it also seemed to encourage undressing women to adopt comic personas. By 1894 a number of these films had shifted from portraying solo performers undressing in theaters to "real" women undressing as part of a comic narrative. But not all were comic: a random survey of the films depicting female undressing acts reveals such variation that it must have seemed to contemporary audiences that undressing was everywhere. One such act, for example, took the viewer on a tour of the illicit backstage world of burlesque; another, *The Trapeze Disrobing Act*, did the same on the flying trapeze. *Birth of a Pearl* shows a girl in tights crouching in an oversized oyster shell, while *The Betsy Ross Dance* reveals a young girl in a frilly, above-the-knee skirt skipping around, doing a cancan, and climbing up *en pointe* so that the camera can zoom in on her garter. The most daring of these films juxtaposed daily life with close-ups of previously hidden parts of women's bodies. "The immorality of living pictures is nothing compared to this," wrote a contemporary observer.[17]

These kinetoscope films, essentially burlesque comedies, focused on ways the undressing female body affected male viewers. In *What Happened on 23rd Street, NYC* (1901), a strong wind blows a woman's skirt up over her knees and thighs, anticipating by fifty years Marilyn Monroe, and in general testifying to the undressing woman's elemental force. In other films, lascivious men trying to peep under women's skirts discover, to their horror, that the women are prostitutes, or else these aspirational men get their comeuppance thanks to a spinster chaperon. In *What Demoralized the Bar-*

---

*ber Shop* (1897), the camera zooms in on a ground-floor barber shop, where distracted male patrons gaze up through a window at two women—possibly prostitutes—on the street adjusting their garters. The frame obscures the women's faces and upper torsos. A few years later, *The Gay Shoe Clerk* (1901) showed an enterprising clerk helping a female customer try on a high-heeled shoe while her chaperon reads the paper. The camera wanders onto a close up of the clerk's hand fondling the customer's foot and bestockinged ankle. When the chaperon discovers the clerk copping a feel, she hits him with a newspaper and begins beating him on the head with her umbrella.[18]

All of this undressing on camera happened alongside of the first cinematic kiss between two actors, May Irwin and John C. Rouse, in 1896. Prior to that year, spectators had been able to watch kissing and undressing in brothels and (sometimes) in the popular theater. But with the advent of the cinema, immigrants and the middle class, men and women, could, on any day of the week, for the first time in history, see women disrobing and disrobed and men and women kissing on-screen. Still, to modernize undressing ultimately required a force more immediate than the uncertain work of technological and social change. The one offering itself at the time was the harem girl of orientalist dreams.

ACCORDING TO the vaudeville historian Douglas Gilbert, the first "oriental" dancers appeared in 1876 at the Philadelphia Centennial wearing short skirts and silken bands around their breasts. As would many of the dancers who followed them, they did the cancan, and their popularity catapulted them to the theater at Eleventh and Wood streets in Philadelphia. But oriental dancing took off about twenty years later, after a young American named Sol Bloom sailed to the City of Light to see the International Exposition, where the Algerian Village and its native dancers captivated him.[19]

Bloom imported the Algerian Village to the 1893 Chicago World's Fair, also known as the Columbian Exposition. Designed to celebrate the four hundredth anniversary of Columbus's discovery of the New World, the exposition, officials hoped, would enlighten the working class by celebrating Chicago and America. Businessmen in Chicago, including real estate promoter Potter Palmer, gathered to applaud the city and America's cultural contributions to the world. The exposition's main fairgrounds housed scientific, architectural, and technological advances, and the fair drew many of Chicago society's finest members. It proposed the most progressive idea of what a city might be. But touring the White City, landscape architect Frederick Law Olmsted complained of the exposition's sterility: "More incidents of vital human gaiety wanted." He suggested, "Why not hire exotic figures in native costume?"[20]

Thus the fair came to present the Midway Plaisance, a popular sideshow eschewing progress for pleasure. Set apart from the White City proper, the Plaisance, a colossal sideshow, housed entertainments that were supposed to delight the working class: "ethnographic" spectacles such as Dahomey, Samoa, and Lapp Villages; "dog-eating" natives; Egyptian swordsmen and jugglers; Javanese carpenters; Hungarian gypsies; Eskimos, Chinese, and Laplanders. Inside the Persian Palace of Eros, a tribe of be-corseted dancing girls "swayed gently, as if lifted from a brothel." The World Congress of Beauty offered "40 ladies from 40 nations." This was where the Algerian Village fit in.[21]

When the fair opened in May, the Algerian Village, the Persian Palace, and their dancing girls with their *danse du ventre* made the fair a hit. According to his memoir, Bloom was soon collecting a thousand dollars a week—more than the president of the United States at the time.[22] But a less significant thing about the *danse du ventre* than the money it garnered—for all erotic spectacles reap the coin of the realm—was the mysterious identity of the performers. In some publicity photos, the female performers look less "native" than French and cosmopolitan. Whereas dog eating and the other spectacles taking place at the other villages could be dismissed as ethnographic and therefore ultimately remote, the *danse du ventre* sounded too reminiscent of the brothel to dismiss as Other. The music accompanying the dances sounded not unlike ragtime, the syncopated African American music that also made its first appearance to the white community as "coon singing" at the World's Fair.[23]

The impresario of evoking, Bloom made the *danse du ventre* American by giving it a new name. To capitalize on the American fascination with Paris, he initially publicized it as the *danse du ventre*, but in a drunken songfest at a piano bar early in the fair's run, Bloom pounded out some lyrics in which he dubbed it "the hootchy cootch."

In July, though, the hootchy cootch became not just bizarre and comical, suggesting carnal mischief and folklore, but dangerous. The association of dancing masters denounced it and called for the closing of the exhibits where it was practiced. A minister described the dance as "a muscular contraction of the abdomen with certain peculiar motions wholly improper." As the popular song acknowledged, "The dance that they do is called the hootchy cootchy koo / They do it in France and it's not really a dance."[24]

The "invention" of the hootchy cootch set the Algerian Village and the Persian Palace of Eros apart from the rest of the amusements on the Midway. Purity-campaign reformers singled out the forward and backward movement of the hips that the dance required. Sometimes called "the muscle dance," it threatened the progress the fair promised. Journalist Marian Shaw observed that the dances at the Cairo Village were "not of a nature to suit refined tastes. . . . [H]ideous dances . . . are carried on at almost every corner, accompanied by ear-torturing music." Another described the dance in the Algerian Village in hushed, sexual tones: "A girl dressed in a soft, clinging, transparent skirt sways. She trembles with violent emotion, the orchestra plays with furious fervor, she undulates and quivers in what might be called an ecstasy of delirious delight."[25]

EVERY EROTIC DANCE conjures its primal figure that becomes mythical because she allows us to reimagine ourselves in a new and different way. Little Egypt emerged, in true American style, from nowhere, and yet she managed to become the putative grandmother of modern striptease. Upon being named, she came to stand for more than just one loose woman: she also conjured the Nile Delta's fertility. In addition, she was said to have given Mark Twain a coronary and to have invented the zipper.[26]

The fair's producers promoted Little Egypt as an appealing blend of domestic naughtiness and sexual aggression. According to the pop culture

Little Egypt at the 1893 Chicago World's Fair. Newspaper Microfilm Collection, The New York Public Library.

historian Robert Toll, a carnival barker at the Columbian Exposition announced: "When she dances every fiber and every tissue in her entire
anatomy shakes like a jar of jelly from your grandmother's Thanksgiving
dinner. Now gentlemen, I don't say that she's that hot. But I do say that
she is as hot as the Fourth of July in the hottest county in the state."[27]

Little Egypt, the "once and future New Woman," was hardly the only
female performer who shifted her hips to an oriental tune. At the turn of
the century, European and American capital cities were full of women whose
dances took their cues from the East. In 1886, Loie Fuller had appeared at
New York's Standard Theater in an evening she called "The Arabian
Nights," a composite of several different oriental dance numbers, including the "Dance of Light," which was done with electricity, and the "Veil of
Vapor," done with clouds of steam instead of fabric. Like Little Egypt,
Fuller was more than a performer: she was an erotic force capable of transforming her environment. Fuller, whose nickname was "La fée lumineuse,"
whirling her garments around her, turned the *danse du ventre* into a modern art as vibrant as the electric light now radiating from the Eiffel Tower
and on Broadway.[28]

Performers like Fuller and Little Egypt made money. But they also
embodied fin de siècle anxieties about women's changing roles. Quivering
behind her veil, Little Egypt brought the courtesan's hard yet unknowable
quiddity into the public eye, encouraging purity-campaign reformers to
rise up against her. Anthony Comstock denounced her as being "one of
the most outrageous assaults on the sacred dignity of womanhood ever
endured in this country." Even the souvenir book of the fair condemned
the dance's "suggestive, lascivious" contortions, which it characterized as
both ungraceful and "shockingly disgusting."[29]

But nothing could quash the oriental dancer's popularity. Shortly after
the fair ended, the hootchy cootch burst into vaudeville, burlesque, the
carnival, and silent film, and Little Egypt herself gave birth to "Little
Zelika," "Little Zelima," Stella, and others like her. Little Egypt in drag
performed in burlesque. In New York, some "Little Egypts" were arrested,
fined fifty dollars for "immoral conduct," and released on the condition
that they clean up their acts.[30]

By 1896, two years after the fair ended, the stock character of Little
Egypt was a fixture at Coney Island, a fast-growing resort destination for
the nabobs and con men of the Gilded Age. The dance that she did was
now simply called the cootch—it had shed its oriental pretensions and some
of its veneer of respectability. With her torso sometimes exposed, Little
Egypt also did the cootch in burlesque theaters, which now catered to an
exclusively male audience.[31] The burlesque entrepreneur Sam T. Jack
brought the cootch to the St. Louis Exposition of 1896 and then to the
Chicago burlesque theater he ran with his wife at State and Madison, where

a dancer named Omeena took off enough of her clothing and undulated enough "to satisfy the most blasé old roué. She execute[d] the couchee-couchee or tootsie-wootsie . . . in the presence of men only."[32]

In New York that same year, right before Christmas, one Little Egypt became the centerpiece of one of the period's explosive society orgy scandals when she performed the hootchy cootch in "gauzy and diaphanous apparel" on the tabletop at a raucous bachelor party given at Sherry's, a lobster palace at the Waldorf Astoria Hotel. This particular party was for Herbert Barnum Seeley, the beloved, portly, roguish nephew of P. T.

Memorialized as "the Awful Seeley Dinner" and also as the "Silly Dinner," the affair was summarily broken up in the early hours of the morning by a crusading reformer and policeman, Captain George Chapman, and it immediately became a hot news item in the *National Police Gazette* and the *Tribune*. The Seeleys subsequently used their family connections to bring Chapman to trial before a police board for "conduct unbecoming a police officer." The trial became a media circus as reformers attempted to use the Seeley Dinner as a window into "what transpires in the highest circles." It was only then that Little Egypt acquired a name—Annabelle Whitford—and that details emerged, such as her exchange of photographs with Captain Chapman, and descriptions of what she wore—and did not wear.[33] The *National Police Gazette* wrote that she stripped until she had on "nothing except her jewels" and asserted that Whitford was the exact same person who had done the hootchy cootch at the Columbian Exposition.[34] The *Tribune* noted that she spoke French "half the time."

Even before the trial concluded and the charges were all dismissed, Whitford took her Little Egypt act to New York's Olympia Theater, a vaudeville house, and to "engagements in Philadelphia and Boston." In burlesque, one act named itself after the dancer and recreated the events of the Awful Seeley Dinner, including the moments when Whitford testified in court.[35]

> The Little Egypt Burlesque Co., headed by the sensational dancer of that name, is the attraction this week. . . . "The Silly Dinner" was first on the bill. . . . A dance by two girls, in indecently suggestive costumes, was one of the "specialties." The olio includes several good numbers. . . . "Silly in Court," in which Little Egypt made her appearance in the final scene, closed the bill.[36]

The next phase in the history of undressing began with the Salome fad, which had roots in Europe. In 1892, Oscar Wilde wrote his one-act play, transforming the heroine from a dutiful daughter to passionate creature obsessed with vengeance. But fascination with Salome started years earlier, in Second Empire France, where, sparked by Gustave Moreau's Salome paintings, Stéphane Mallarmé's dramatic poem *Herodiade*, Joris-Karl

Huysmans' novel *À rebours*, Gustave Flaubert's novel *Salammbo*, and the like, she inhabited the realm of the decadents.

To the French, Salome was not a woman at all, but a brute, insensible force: Huysmans refers to her as "the symbolic incarnation of undying Lust . . . the monstrous Beast, indifferent, irresponsible, insensible"; and Mallarmé describes her as being inscrutable: "the veil always remains." Huysmans' hero Des Esseintes characterizes her as a "weird and superhuman figure he had dreamed of. . . . [I]n her quivering breasts, . . . heaving belly, . . . tossing thighs . . . she was now revealed as the symbol incarnate of old world vice."[37] But if in France Salome stood as a symbol of women's inexpressible, raging desire, in America she crashed into puritanism and became both funny and obscene.

In the first decade of the twentieth century, "Salomania," as it was called, was a craze touching virtually every aspect of American popular and "high" culture, from opera to burlesque, from nightclub revues to department store fashions for women. Part of Salome's appeal was her strange allure: she always wore the same costume—breast plates, ropes of pearls, diaphanous skirt, and white trunks underneath. Sometimes she wore a jeweled snake in her hair, but she generally went barefoot. Her costume was scant. (The vaudeville performer Eva Tanguay boasted that she could carry her Salome costume in her closed fist.)[38]

When respectable stars like Tanguay performed Salome as a burlesque, critics applauded. But when a vengeful Salome appeared in Richard Strauss's eponymous 1907 opera, which was first staged at the Metropolitan Opera, its backers, J. P. Morgan, W. K. Vanderbilt, and August Belmont, engineered her withdrawal from the stage. According to *Theatre Magazine*, Salome's dancing "sickened the public stomach." The issue was the fervor with which Salome kissed John the Baptist's head. Sam M'Kee, theater critic for the *New York Telegraph*, described Gertrude Hoffman's sensational "A Vision of Salome" with a mixture of awe and horror:

> Suddenly, she turns and sees the head of John the Baptist. She takes it with a combination of eagerness and aversion . . . places the head before her and in wild abandon, as if to conquer her loathing, begins a tempestuous dance. She is garbed with draperies and gewgaws of a bloody age . . . but the effect is that she is naked.[39]

With her ferocious appetite, this Salome threatened the Victorian sensibility. Psychological theorists who associated movement with women's lesser brains and unstable sexualities seized upon Salome as an example of the worst modern trends. "One reason women love dancing is because it enables them to give harmonious and legitimate emotional expression to this neuromuscular irritability which might otherwise escape in more explosive forms," Havelock Ellis wrote in *Man and Woman* in 1899.[40]

As if to fill the dangerous void opened by this creature, even more popular performers rushed to treat Salome parodically. Oscar Wilde had already impersonated Salome; now the cross dresser Julian Eltinge followed suit, and the vaudevillians Bedini and Arthur tried their hand at a blackface version. In Irving Berlin's "Sadie Salome Go Home," a rag inspired by the Strauss opera and the scandal and the imitators of "the dance of the seven veils," would-be Salome dancer Sadie Cohen performs the number, much to the chagrin of her loyal boyfriend Mose. Using a thick Yiddish accent, Fanny Brice sang the song at the Arvene Theater, hamming it up by rolling her big green eyes and waving her arms around. The moment that won her a standing ovation, however, was when her sailor suit goosed her. In other words, slapstick comedy earned Brice a starring role in Florenz Ziegfeld's 1909 *Follies*. In a few short verses, "Sadie Salome" celebrated the new freedoms that she could enjoy as long as she remained disguised as Salome. Thus this figure defines her identity not just through vivacity and fearlessness, but through her not being Salome. "Most Everybody Knows. I'm your lovin' Mose. Oy, Oy, Oy, Oy where is your clothes? Sadie Salome, go home."[41]

At the same time, the idea of Salome acquired some aspects of contemporary feminism. To women artists of modernist leanings, Salome represented a much-needed escape from Victorian ideas about the restricting qualities of the intellect. In the first decade of the century, the "barefoot modernism" movement borrowed Salome to get back to a more primitive— and therefore more real—form of expression. To the performers who championed her, Salome suggested something savage and above all real. Anna Pavlova and Mikhail Fokine both choreographed themselves in stark ballets centered on the theme of Egypt. Denied permission to mount Oscar Wilde's play in St. Petersburg in 1908, Ida Rubenstein commissioned the dance scene from Fokine. Isadora Duncan used Eastern gestures in her work and performed nude at the Kroll Opera, although she refused to play the role of Salome in the music hall. In Berlin, Ruth St. Denis took on the role of Isis and then proclaimed, "I'm going to be Egypt."

Loie Fuller did the role twice in impassioned if abstract solos, once wearing peacock feathers; and Maud Allen, who is often considered to be an imitator of Isadora Duncan, enacted her own "A Vision of Salome" in London and Vienna. Even Colette attempted her Salome moment, in her 1907 *Rêve d'Egypte*, where she played a mummy coming back to life by slowly unwinding her bandages until she fell into the arms of a loving Egyptologist.

Although these dancers varied in approach and in tone, their critics inevitably accused them of vulgarity. No matter how loudly Allen, for example, claimed to be expressing Salome's spirituality, critics noted her salaciousness, pointing to her "shuddering, quivering flesh." Even a sophisticated dancer like Ruth St. Denis inspired hysterical headlines such as "Dancers Shed Clothing and Put on Ideals" and "Line Drawn between the Nudity of Woman and the Undraping of the Artists."

Salome hung on, continuing to adapt to whatever the zeitgeist required. In the teens, Alla Nazimova's Salome in her silent film looked very much like a peroxide blonde flapper. During the Jazz Age, mulatto prostitutes performed "the Salome dance" and its cousin, "the Zulu dance." Later, the insistent vogue for women doing glamorous and exotic "oriental" dances in striptease suggested how forcefully Americans needed relief from the everyday restrictive qualities of their lives, even if that relief was itself born out of a commercial spirit.[42]

# From Ziegfeld to Minsky: Respectable Undressing and the Rise of Modern Burlesque

I t was in part thanks to the impresario Florenz Ziegfeld, who had started his career in show business at the Columbian Exposition in Chicago, that the undressing acts became part of "legitimate" popular entertainment on Broadway and in vaudeville. Indeed, Ziegfeld's first big American hit, in 1898, Joseph Herbert's adaptation of a Parisian divorce farce, *The Turtle*, was also the first Broadway play whose dramaturgy turned on a disrobing act. Having abandoned her husband (the "turtle") because he is too old-fashioned, actress Sadie Martinot's character finds herself in love with him on the eve of his wedding to another woman. To convince him that she really does love him after all, Martinot sneaks into the marital chamber and begins to take it off. Also, the apotheosis of respectable undressers was Anna Held, Ziegfeld's saucy first wife. The peppy French star, whom critic Brooks Atkinson once called "five feet of sizzling personality," embodied the nineteenth-century "floral candy box sweetheart." Held was a child-woman, a guileless yet clever mechanical doll. Although suffragists tried to enlist her as a New Woman, she demurred, instead rejoicing in the virtues of marriage and nineteenth-century womanhood, giving girlish tips like "how to flirt with a parasol."[1]

When she burst onto the scene shortly before *The Turtle* opened, Held's personality, put forth in flirtatious songs like "Won't You Come and Play with Me?" or "Would You Like to See a Little More of Me?" suggested the pleasure women and men might take in female undressing. Performing in "Big Time," as the high-end vaudeville houses of the day were known, Held expanded the prototypical end-of-the-century female star's repertoire. Mixing comedy and eros, she managed to be playful, not raunchy. When she asked her audience if they dared to see more flesh, she did so with a sweetheart's friendly wink. She flirted in a million and one ways: many of them borrowed comic techniques from ethnic comedians or from black styles of performance then in vogue.

Some of Held's appeal came from her status as a Frenchwoman. When she flailed her arms in the style of a blackface comedian, rolled her eyes spastically, or spoke in thick Gallic argot, she drew attention away from her wiggling bare shoulders or the fact that she was pitching her charms to an unsuspecting patron from the "bald head" row. Thus her undressing seemed less a display of aggressive female sexuality than of her charming, if wacky personality. She turned what might in other hands be scandalous undressing

numbers into whimsical ones. In one particularly strange number, she offered patrons the opportunity to come up and lick her as if she were a human
ice-cream cone. In a burlesque theater, a cootch dancer might have done this
number in a corset and tights. But Held performed in an outrageously jeweled, tightly corseted costume that drew the eye to her hourglass figure but
never exposed it. And although Held's tiny but voluptuous shape replicated
the Beef Trust burlesque queens in miniature, she was ultimately too deli-
cate to ever be lumped in with them.[2]

Keeping the undressing act respectable in this era meant linking it to
trends like conspicuous consumption and the fitness vogue. When Held got
dressed and undressed behind a screen, she did so for the purpose of reap-
pearing in an even more lavish costume. In the 1906 extravaganza *The Parisian Model*, the female performers wore lush rose and green velvet before
they disrobed. Ziegfeld also used the language of suffragism to lure in audiences. He capitalized on the appeal of bicycling, which, as the fitness craze's
most successful form of exercise, by the turn of the century had become an
acceptable fad for women.[3] When Ziegfeld allowed his young wife to ride a
bicycle, it projected a healthful modernity and a girlish hint of suffragism.

Not all Ziegfeld's undressing acts bespoke such healthful, "clean"
modernity, however. In 1899, in Ziegfeld's lifelessly plotted divorce comedy *Mademoiselle Fifi*, Fifi tried to entice her former lover by lying on a sofa
and shamelessly and gratuitously displaying her black betighted legs. Instead of announcing its modernity or displaying lavish clothing, undressing here announced a purely vampish purpose.

A zingier dose of naughtiness emerged in *The Parisian Model*, which first
exposed Americans to the Folies Bergères version of the undressed female
body. A modern sex comedy, *The Parisian Model* tells the story of a model,
Ann (Held), who gets embroiled in a variety of show business scandals and
then saves her boyfriend's reputation by posing in a living picture. Borrowing from the "kaleidoscopic" feminine tableaus favored at the Folies Bergères,
Ziegfeld multiplied the number of scantily clad women onstage and allowed
the creative, positive force of female sexual fantasy to emerge.

In *The Parisian Model* two sensational disrobing numbers shocked audiences: the "Gown for Each Hour of the Day" and the "Parisian Model."
In the former, Held dressed and undressed six times—or, as one review
put it, revealed her "lack of gowns behind a cluster of chorus girls." From
there, wearing only a corset and flesh-colored stockings, she launched into
one of her signature songs, "I'd Like to See a Little More of You."[4] The
most scandalous foray into undressing, though, was the "Parisian Model"
number, which occurred halfway through the show.

The curtain opened on an artist's studio, where six girls in long cloaks
stood partly visible behind six easels. The painter walked onstage, the girls
threw off their cloaks, and the audience saw only gleaming bare shoulders

and curving bare legs, making it seem that behind the easels, they were naked. But when the easels were removed, the nakedness was revealed to be a trick: the girls wore strapless evening gowns with the skirts and trains pinned up.[5]

Predictably, some critics responded with outrage. But the outrage circled around the fact that Ziegfeld had promised more nudity than he delivered. The *Herald Tribune* critic took the most jaded approach, arguing that *The Parisian Model* never achieved the sensational reputation it craved: "The audience is led to believe that six of the handsomest show girls have taken off all their clothes only to have its expectancy disappointed by finding that what appeared to be nudity is only décolleté dressing."[6]

That same year, *The Parisian Model*'s financial success enabled Ziegfeld— egged on by Anna Held—to produce the first daring edition of the *Ziegfeld Follies* at the Jardin de Paris in New York. The *Ziegfeld Follies* multiplied satiny, glamorous nudity, and thus stretched the limits of New York law, which stated that women could be unclothed onstage if they remained stationary. More sophisticated than any prior female spectacle, the Ziegfeld tableaux elevated the betighted body into a sublime, abstract object. Shorn for the most part of the irrelevancies of plot and character, the *Follies* for the next decade undressed women while respecting their beautiful nudity.

AT THE SAME TIME, vaudeville continued to draw middle-class women into the theater in large numbers. In 1898 the vaudeville mogul B. F. Keith had announced, "The stage show must be free from vulgarisms and coarseness of any kind so that the house and entertainment would directly appeal to the support of ladies and children."[7] Vaudeville-goers of the day considered undressing acts anything but vulgar and coarse. In 1903, William Dean Howells, who had chafed at Lydia Thompson's state of undress a few decades earlier, describes a "refined" vaudeville undressing act in a sporty, know-it-all tone that nods to Victorian gentility but acknowledges an erotic edge.

> Twin sisters appeared in sweeping confections of white silk, with deeply drooping, widely spreading hats, and long-fringed white parasols heaped with artificial roses. The sisters sang a little tropical romance, whose burden was under the bamboo tree. . . . [B]efore you could tell how or why, they had disappeared and reappeared in short green skirts, and then shorter white skirts, with steps and stops appropriate to their costumes, but always, I am bound to say, of the refinement promised. I can't tell you in what their refinement consisted, but I am sure it was there.[8]

The historian Robert Snyder calls vaudeville's combination of Victorian purity-campaign reform and twentieth-century modernism "respectable thrills."[9] While vaudeville domesticated undressing acts, another kind of performance—the circus—cast these acts into the realm of magic. In fin de siècle America and Europe, soaring above the audience on the flying trapeze softened the salacious nature of taking off one's clothes in public. For the androgynous figure of the acrobat seemed closer to a supernatural being than a real man or woman. In the late-nineteenth-century novel *À rebours*, the hero Des Esseintes observes, "Miss Urania's graceful simpering and womanly mincing became effaced while in their place the agile and powerful charms of the male began to develop."[10]

Through their derring-do, acrobatic and equestrienne undressing acts ventured not simply that women could act as men or vice versa, but that the genders shared more than many observers acknowledged. These acts required strength and agility, grace, and brute force, not simply nakedness. The modern, self-referential quality of undressing acts begins here on the flying trapeze, and a number of female acrobats undressing in the air during this era display a new physical awareness. The acrobat Charmaine—a British performer also sometimes billed as Charmion or Princess Chemise— was one of them.

In Britain, Charmion performed a classic music hall act beginning with her "accidentally" discovering the trapeze and ending with her hanging upside down in a nightgown, which fell over her head to reveal an acrobat's leotard. In New York, she performed at Koster and Bial's rough variety house, on Thirty-fourth Street west of Sixth Avenue. Koster and Bial's had started as a dive on Twenty-third Street after the Civil War, but by the 1890s, the theater also welcomed young dandies in search of a good time. It was one of three theaters producing European music hall acts such as Yvette Guilbert, Marie Lloyd, and Albert Chevalier, as well as burlesque acts such as "An Affair of Honor," in which two women dueled topless. The theater was arranged like a music hall, with boxes for the rich people located in a square balcony and chairs and tables for the hoi polloi on the floor.[11]

George Jean Nathan describes seeing Charmaine with his father:

> Charmaine, clad in a long black satin cloak and with a large feathered black hat on her head, emerged elegantly from the wings. . . . [S]he deposited herself daintily on a lowered trapeze and was raised aloft. The lights faded except for a spotlight and the orchestra began to play. . . . [W]inking and murmuring seductively, she dropped her hat and her cloak to the sawdust below. She wore a black silk dress and long black gloves. She discarded the gloves, the bodice of the dress and the skirt. Under those garments, she wore a pink petticoat and petticoat cover. And under the petticoat, she still wore black net undergarments, stockings, and satin slippers. She discarded these to reveal slightly scantier black underthings [and] tossed a lace handkerchief to the audience. She removed her stockings and unfastened her garters and tossed one to the audience. The lights went out.[12]

Strongwoman Charmaine (or Charmion) flexes her muscles (date unknown). Billy Rose Theatre Collection, The New York Public Library for the Performing Arts, Astor, Lenox, and Tilden Foundations.

To some observers, Charmaine was respectable because she made a museum exhibit of her body. A photo of her in 1901 showed just her back, in the style of bodybuilders. Although she deviated from prescribed gender conventions of the day (women were dainty, men athletic), she did so in part by referring to the circus. The vaudeville critic Caroline Caffin called her "the perfect woman whose muscles are not only wonderfully developed but also perfectly controlled so that her enormous strength adds grace and defines." Another reviewer described her act as if she were a racehorse "at the start, at the quarter; the half, in the homestretch at the finish."[13] When Charmaine disrobed at Koster and Bial's in 1901, she attracted the disapproval of the president of a purity-campaign reform organization because of "the way she did it." In the vernacular of the time, this was code for jiggling one's hips with a burlesque cootch dancer's authority. But the reformer forgave her, even though her garter fell into the box where he was seated. He took no offense because she disrobed as if she did not know that she was doing so.[14]

BURLESQUE WAS CHANGING quickly. In the nineteenth century, burlesque, composed of three parts, had both satirized the upper class and displayed women's bodies for a working-class audience. By the turn of the century, though, burlesque had already begun its downward spiral into a venue focusing on raucous skits and the solo female performer. "Burlesque queens," "lady athletic acts," and cootch dancers inspired by Little Egypt trotted across the burlesque stage. Scenes gave way to male comics' telling ribald jokes. Burlesque of this era boiled down to gags expressing class and sexual anxiety and to a brand of female sexual display that was essential and crude.[15]

By 1900, Americans could see burlesque shows in Manhattan at Miner's and at the London Theater, in Brooklyn at Hyde and Behman's, the Star, and the Empire. Philadelphia offered burlesque at the Trocadero, at the Fourteenth Street Opera House, and at the Arch, Kensington, and Lyceum Theaters. Even staid Boston featured burlesque at the Lyceum, Palace, and Grand Theaters, as well as—famously—at the Howard Atheneum. Shortly after the new century opened, burlesque turned the cootch dancer into its most important solo performer. Purity-campaign reformers condemned "the cootcher" as a prostitute. Collecting data in 1913 for a survey of commercialized vice, the anti-prostitution advocate George Kneeland wrote, "[I]t may be said that practically all of the women in burlesque shows are prostitutes."[16]

But until 1910, the burlesque industry continued to expand, albeit less so than "Big Time" vaudeville, which dominated the country's popular entertainment even as many small-time vaudeville theaters folded or became storefront burlesque houses. In 1905 the two major burlesque "wheels," or circuits, that would divide the industry for the next ten years emerged: the western or Empire circuit and the eastern circuit, also known as the Columbia circuit. Patterned after the rising theatrical syndicates in vaudeville and Broadway, the burlesque wheels, composed of a string of theaters, allowed a performer to work continuously for forty weeks. This made burlesque a steadier form of employment than either vaudeville or

Broadway. In 1912 there were seventy burlesque shows, a hundred theaters, and about five thousand people working in the industry.[17]

Although the wheels stole material from each other, as well as from
vaudeville, variety, and the Broadway revue, they displayed from the start
fundamental differences that would characterize them until their respec-
tive demises. Founded in 1902 by the reform-minded Sam Scribner, the
Columbia (eastern) wheel promoted "cleaned-up" burlesque. By contrast,
the Empire (western) wheel, established in 1897, was immediately pegged
as the "rough" circuit, with Empire theaters resembling honkytonks and
concert saloons. While the circuit offered convenience to the performers,
allowing them to commute fairly easily between midwestern cities such as
Pittsburgh, Louisville, St. Louis, Minneapolis, St. Paul, and Chicago, in
the early years managers had to bribe respectable audiences with free gifts
just to get them to attend.[18]

A popular turn-of-the-century burlesque number known as "Orange
Blossoms" reveals undressing's importance on the western circuit. Undressing turned "Orange Blossoms'" hackneyed premise—a virgin gets married
to an older, experienced man—into a scandalous event. Set in the boudoir,
the number began as a maid removed the new bride's wedding dress and
undergarments. Somehow, the bride's union suit fell off at the same moment as the bridegroom appeared in his bathrobe. Clad only in a thin body
stocking, the bride kissed the bridegroom and the curtain dropped, allowing the audience to imagine the rest. "Orange Blossoms" lasted only a few
minutes. But it referred more explicitly to the sex between newlyweds than
vaudeville, Broadway, or the Columbia wheel ever dared.[19]

The explosion of these undressing acts in burlesque theaters and illicit
nightclubs corresponded with an explosion of vice districts in immigrant
slums. In New York, these districts spurted up on the Lower East Side and
on Irving Place; occasionally out at Coney Island and in Harlem at spots
like the Uproar House. As two writers for *Variety* would later say, burlesque "was doing very well for itself."[20]

Built in 1888, the Moorish-style Irving Place Theater was among the
most famous of theaters producing the new generation of burlesque
queens—solo performers who combined intentional cootch dancing and
undressing. Exiled from respectable Big Time vaudeville, these performers lewdly shifted their hips and undressed. At Miner's Eighth Avenue
Theater, Dainty Marie "stripped down to champagne tights"; Truly
Shattuck advertised "an entirely distinctive specialty in which is introduced
an instantaneous change from full costume to tights"; and Rose Sydell and
"Madame Cleo" vamped and posed in extravagant wardrobes.[21]

An infamous burlesque theater of the day, Miner's Eighth Avenue stood
on Manhattan's Rialto, a new vice district in the twenties near the old Koster

and Bial's Concert Hall. Miner's catered to both a working-class audience and to "blades," or dandies. Before World War I, Miner's, part of the racy western wheel, moved the idea of undressing forward by introducing amateur night. Miner's offered shop girls and housewives an opportunity to take it off and introduced "getting the hook," which put a stop to ill-conceived undressing acts. In 1911 the Miner family bought two other theaters—one on the Bowery and one in the Bronx—which the most enterprising of the sons, Thomas, took over. A few years later, the Miners abandoned burlesque for silent films, which were then making vaudeville obsolete.[22]

Even more down-and-out than Miner's was the Gayety in Brooklyn, whose crowd a writer for the *Atlantic Monthly* described as "a sadly questionable array of artisans, cheap drummers, petty clerks, temporarily opulent malefactors, [and] certain daring souls from the rural glades . . . [and] a little farther back, a glummer and less decent company, though more at ease. Beyond them a noticeably viler herd. In the balcony, a blend of pickpocket, day-laborer, and unwashed, ne'er do well. Thronging the topmost gallery . . . a rabble of tramps, thugs, jailbirds and noxious urchins. The higher the lower!"[23]

For the most part, when cootching stayed in variety, small-time vaudeville, and burlesque, the group Douglas Gilbert calls the "tst-tst-ers" left it alone. But when it spilled into the "respectable" Columbia circuit and into Big Time vaudeville, purity-campaign reformers and journalists condemned it as obscene. Touring in the revue *A Florida Enchantment* in 1911, Mae West played a French adventuress who did an undressing act to seduce a German woman-hater. *Variety*'s critic praised her, writing that she "made several changes down to full tights with good effect." When West broke into vaudeville the following year, *Variety* took the opposite tack, criticizing her for being too vulgar for mainstream audiences. "The burlesque stage is her place and she can make a name there."[24]

ONE COOTCH DANCER to become a star in prewar burlesque was Millie De Leon, "the Girl in Blue," or the "Odalisque of the East," as she was sometimes also called. De Leon's first moniker referred to the obscene, as in "blue movies" or language, and her second referred to her mysterious brown eyes. Some photos of De Leon show her as corpulent, jolly, and bespangled. She is not highbrow feminine in the wispy beauty standards of the day. She is cheery, takes up a lot of room, and lacks the Gibson girl's cherubic neatness. But when De Leon undressed, she manifested a bad-girl erotic power.[25]

Like many female burlesque performers, De Leon began her career in the hinterlands. Although her name is French (Millie looks suspiciously like Mlle), she built her early career in Cincinnati and was first tutored by western circuit manager James Fennessey. Some early descriptions of her

Millie De Leon, "the Girl in Blue," or the "Odalisque of the East," kicks up her heels, 1916. Billy Rose Theatre Collection, The New York Library for the Performing Arts, Astor, Lenox, and Tilden Foundations.

sound respectable. One reporter noted that her hat "fram[ed] her expressionless face like a Quaker bonnet."[26] By 1903, however, De Leon presented a saucier persona. There is no other way to describe De Leon's act than to say that she impersonated a prostitute. She sauntered onstage swaying her hips and paused, flashing her bare or bestockinged calf. She touched her throat "as if to display her person," as one reporter put it, by which he meant that she suggested she was for sale. She tossed garters from a basket and sashayed into the crowd, kissing one man after another on the head. Sometimes she teased the men by saying, "Come on sport, get my garter."[27] (At this point if the police were in the audience, they would arrest her, hold her for indecency, and release her the next morning, since legally they could not keep her.)

De Leon mixed cootching and undressing to present a vice-tinged sexuality. She tore through the borders of convention and broke the fourth wall. In another version of her act, De Leon entered from the house, near the rear exit of the theater—where prostitutes often waited for clients. She wore a flounced and ruffled dress. Parasol in hand, she strolled through the audience as if she were cruising the Rialto. She circumnavigated the stage and paused dramatically before beginning to pass her clothes to her black attendant.[28]

But like Lydia Thompson and other burlesque performers before her, De Leon was as dangerous offstage as on. A series of articles in the *Chicago Herald* in 1904 sounded not unlike Theodore Dreiser's *Sister Carrie*, which had been published a few years earlier. A certain Mr. Haas, auditor of the Corn Exchange National Bank for four years, had disappeared from Chicago the previous May. At the time of his disappearance, sensational rumors were in circulation that he had become infatuated with a music hall singer. At one performance, he threw "greenbacks" to her as she stood on the stage. After he had left town, his books were examined and a shortage of about twenty thousand dollars was discovered. Asked about the case, Haas denied everything.[29]

After the Haas scandal, De Leon toned down her act for a while. Touring on the western wheel, she wore a spangled dress as she waited for men to parade in the aisle and then shone the light on their bald heads before throwing her garter, *Variety* reported. But a few years later, she elicited outrage from a reporter for the *Philadelphia North American*, who lamented her "undulations," compared her to a "horse," and noted her body's "wave like motion."[30]

> Finally, Millie De Leon became unspeakably frank. Every muscle became eloquent of primitive emotion. Amid groans, cat calls and howls of approval from the audience, she stopped. Standing suddenly erect, with a deft movement, she revealed her nude right leg from knee almost to waist. A strut to the right, a long stride back, and the abdominal "dance" was resumed. The large pink rose in her belt nodded confusedly, and her hands clasped and unclasped spasmodically under the strain of the stimulated emotion. Streaked and sweaty, her face took on the aspect of epilepsy. She bit her lips, rolled her eyes, pulled fiercely at great handfuls of her black, curly hair.
> Indescribable noises and loud suggestions mingled in the hot breath of the audience. Men in the orchestra rose with shouts. A woman—one of six present—hissed. Laughter became uproarious. And then, sensing her climax, Millie De Leon gave a little cry that was more a yelp, and ceased.[31]

This description, both quaintly seamy and cruelly dismissive, marks De Leon as a pioneer who, through cootching and undressing, depicted sex onstage more graphically than any previous performer. De Leon became a working-class folk heroine by distinguishing her scandalous undressing act in burlesque from her Victorian morality at home. She recalled that when a masher followed her from her sick mother's house, "I struck him in the face so that it knocked his hat off and the blow made my comb fall out." Not only was De Leon satisfied with rough street justice, she didn't hold a grudge. A policeman asked if she wanted to file a complaint, and she replied, "[H]e's been punished enough."[32] Quips like these endeared De Leon to her working-class audience and made her seem like one of them—a rough girl on their side trying to make it in the rough city. (When the police arrested her in Brooklyn, a crowd gathered around her and spit at the policeman who had dragged her offstage.)

Then too, the Girl in Blue did cross over to vaudeville. Around 1909, she performed at the respectable Hurtig and Seamon's Music Hall right after being released after one of her arrests. According to *Variety*, she went on to sell out theaters nationwide, proving that no matter how forceful the performance, if the act was lively enough, and the publicity well enough managed, a cootch dancer could succeed. Managers adored her, perhaps because she defined herself in opposition to reformers. In one of many newspaper columns that she wrote, she asked, "Can every self-appointed censor determine what is moral and immoral for his fellow man?"[33]

ON BROADWAY, the *Ziegfeld Follies* continued to present an old-fashioned approach to undressing. In part to conform to the law, the *Follies* hewed to the idea of posing undressed as a delicious mistake rather than adopt undressing a self-conscious device for seduction. But when, in the 1913 *Follies*, ingenue Ann Pennington, wearing nothing but a sheer cape with some leaves strategically pinned on it, posed as the woman in Paul Chabas' *September Morn*, she created a furor.[34]

The French academic painter's romantic nude standing in a lake created a sensation when it was exhibited in America. In May 1913, displayed in the window of a Manhattan art gallery, the portrait caught the eye of Anthony Comstock, still head of the New York Society for the Suppression of Vice. Horrified by what he saw, Comstock stormed into the store, flashed his badge, and roared: "There's too little morn and too much maid. Take her out!" The gallery manager, however, refused. The press gave the ensuing controversy wide publicity, and the painting was simultaneously denounced and defended across the country. Curious crowds filled the street outside the shop straining to see the painting that had caused such a stir.[35]

Soon enterprising entrepreneurs were reproducing *September Morn* on everything conceivable: calendars, postcards, candy boxes, cigar bands, cigarette flannels, pennants, suspenders, and bottle openers. Purity leagues tried to suppress the painting. Postcard reproductions were forbidden. The painting became the object of stock show gags and cartoons, and it even inspired an anonymous couplet that swept the country: "Please don't think I'm bad or bold, but where it's deep it's awwful cold."[36]

Pennington's pose and Millie De Leon's cootch suggested a general loosening of Victorian mores. New forms of dance followed. By 1910 the whole of America fell under the spell of the dance craze: a twitching, thumping national energy to move. While Ziegfeld's scantily clad chorus girls continued to stand still onstage to conform to strict obscenity laws, the dance craze made it possible for women to shake their bodies to music in dance halls and in burlesque. The impresario Jesse Lasky observed that in 1911, "it was still scandalous to dance in a public place. Only a year or two later, the prejudice was mostly swept aside."[37]

In the nineteenth century, formal dances like the waltz had pressed the human body into constrained, stiff, angular motions. But the twentieth century brought an opposing trend. Frenzied dances influenced by black culture, folk dancing, prostitution, and the "back to nature" movement became all the rage. The turkey trot, the grizzly bear, the tango, the monkey glide, the Charleston, and the Apache all eroticized the body through their savage rhythm and volatile beat. The dances predictably elicited outrage from reformers worried about the breakdown of classes, the mingling of the sexes, and, of course, the act of sex itself. But to many women—who were increasingly consumers of leisure entertainment—these dances were sources of pleasure.[38]

Among the most powerful new dances were those whose roots came from the cootch. Many of these first appeared in New Orleans brothels in the first two decades of the century, along with ragtime and honky-tonk music. Stressing syncopated rhythm more than melody, the piano rag became an ideal backdrop for dances like the shimmy. And these dances caught on elsewhere as well. Having grown up in the red light district in Philadelphia before World War I, Ethel Waters recalled that the whores' "unmistakable trade-mark was their hip-wriggling walk." Waters stole that walk for her own early numbers. "When the boys played that [shimmy music] I'd put my hands on my hips and work my body fast without moving my feet."[39]

Meanwhile, changes in fashion freed the body to dance. Women discarded old-fashioned clothing like petticoats, stays, and buns. In 1913 whalebone corsets disappeared for good, replaced by wide elastic girdles and straight-fronted corsets. The shimmy required women to roll down their stockings and throw away floor-length skirts and bustles for split skirts; shorter, loose skirts; or even bloomers. The new tango corset freed women's bodies to move horizontally as that dance required. By World War I, thanks to youth culture's growing importance, many observers ridiculed women wearing the nineteenth-century corset for being old-fashioned.

Hemlines had begun to rise in 1912. In Germany shorter dresses were called "the naked mode." The skirt continued to rise, reaching the knee around 1916, and then returned to mid-calf for ten years. Fashion's turn to boyish appeal during this era pushed burlesque to become more outrageous in its female display. "With the advent of short skirts on the street, leg shows began to lose their sex appeal and in self-defense, the operators of burlesque shows introduced the strutting strips . . . as far as the police permitted," *Billboard* opined in 1915.[40] Shortly after that, female chorines and showgirls began to discard tights. This move had started around 1909, in burlesque with Millie De Leon, but it would take wartime for tights to be flung off in respectable forums. When they were, around 1917, that act contained a taste of immediate emancipation.

The rise of the cabaret propelled the undressing female performer into greater proximity with the audience. The first cabaret appeared in New York the spring of 1911, when Henry B. Harris and Jesse Lasky, two vaudeville entrepreneurs captivated by European cabarets, opened the Folies

Bergere Theater on Forty-ninth Street, then the heart of the theater district. Unlike Broadway theater, the cabaret allowed, as Irving Berlin's wife Ellin Mackay once put it, wealthy Americans to rub elbows with the riff raff as opposed "to dancing at an exclusive party."[41]

The cabaret borrowed burlesque's tough-girl performers and charged Broadway ticket prices for them.[42] Ziegfeld's cabaret number "Midnight Frolics" swaggered onto a transparent glass runway above the audience, which watched as a series of fans stationed at ground level blew the performers' skirts above knee level. The upscale setting made undressing "legitimate" and "fun" rather than dangerous.

In contrast to burlesque, such safely thrilling exchanges encouraged male audience members to reach out to the "vivacious creatures" they admired. The numbers took place on a stage that was on the same level as the audience instead of raised. The same everyday props used in burlesque lured the audience to the performers. In one number, male patrons were given hammers whose purpose was to summon the girl-waiters to their tables. In another, the chorus tossed balloons into the audience and invited its members to "catch the ball" and "throw it back," an act that would prove that the thrower and the throwee were meant to be each other's "affinity."[43]

The sheer amount of undressing in the theater as America approached World War I impelled theater critics to pay increasing attention to women's bodies. *Variety* complained that "the producers dress [the women] up rather than undress them."[44] The theater critic John Corbin noted that "no piece is complete without an undressing or disrobing scene" and that the number of games of strip poker and scenes portraying men and women undressing on their wedding night had reached "absurd" levels.[45]

THE ARRIVAL of the Minsky family into the burlesque industry raised those levels yet further. The Minskys were not totally responsible for transforming undressing into striptease—many other forces contributed—but the family did help what the sociologist and parole officer David Dressler would, twenty years later, call "modern" burlesque to emerge.[46] And what was modern burlesque? It involved women undressing more fully, more quickly, and more frequently, than the Victorian variety.

The Minsky story begins in 1883, when the paterfamilias Louis Minsky arrived in New York. In the space of about a decade, he worked his way up from peddler to loan shark, finally becoming a real estate mogul and an alderman in Big Tim Sullivan's administration.

By 1890 the Lower East Side population had doubled; this surge in population, plus the tearing down of the old brownstones and the building of tall tenements, created a demand for dry goods stores and made the foot peddler irrelevant. Louis already owned one dry goods store on Orchard

Street, and around 1890 he bought the Grand Museum, formerly a freak show and waxworks museum on Grand Street, and turned it into a second store. Considering his sons' destiny, perhaps it is prophetic that Louis bought the museum, which had been owned by a downtown gangster known as Broken Nose Burke, who himself ran it as a seedy living picture emporium.[47]

But despite this purchase, there is no evidence that Louis, whom the *Yiddish Forward* called "powerful" in 1903, wanted his sons to follow in Broken Nose Burke's footsteps. At first the Minsky fils nurtured legitimate aspirations—Mort attended City College, Herb went to Columbia Law School, and Billy briefly worked as a society reporter at the *World Telegram*, which may be where his love of the high life gathered strength.[48] In any case, show business was in the Minsky blood. By 1912, like many other Jews of his generation, the oldest brother, Abe, with Billy's help, began dabbling in it. They convinced Louis to buy the building at 111 Houston Street, situated under the elevated trains at Houston and "the Yiddish Broadway," Second Avenue. The building housed a Lutheran church. But the Minskys leased the first floor to Boris Thomashevsky's National Theater troupe, which performed serious plays and spectacles in Yiddish. It did well.[49]

Louis Minsky, who "loved Yiddish theatre," first let his sons install a second nickelodeon on the sixth floor of the Houston and Second Avenue building that same year. Decorated in gold and rose, this theater sat a thousand. Initially, the brothers made money showing risqué kinetoscope films and in general deploying their public relations savvy by making the titles racier to attract more patrons. But it became harder and harder to turn a profit, and the Minskys were soon wiped out by competition from Ben Kahn, who for a time ran the Union Square Theater on Irving Place as a movie palace, and by Loew and Albee, vaudeville kingpins.[50]

In 1914, Kahn switched to burlesque and began to buy up theaters under the name "Big Ben." He made a profit. By the fall of 1917, the Minsky sons, casting around for something to do with the Winter Garden roof, saw that Kahn had the right idea. They replaced the nickelodeon with a legitimate theater. To get around the problem of carrying the sets up and down six flights of stairs, they housed their own stock burlesque company in the building.[51]

The Minskys distinguished themselves by upgrading burlesque. They charged more for tickets than Ben Kahn and the circuit burlesque theaters did. At the same time, they pitched the simple idea of making the workingman's show slightly upscale—but not as upscale as cabaret—and they connected their burlesque shows with the way women looked and sounded in silent films and on Broadway. As circuit burlesque began to flounder, owing to competition from Broadway musicals, which were becoming more and more risqué, the field was wide open for the National Winter Garden to distinguish itself.[52]

Getting to the National Winter Garden was not for the faint of heart, but the interior contained enough luxurious appointments to remind observers of the vaudeville palaces uptown. On the first floor, Thomashevsky and his troupe performed Yiddish melodramas such as *Hello New York*. The audience for Minskys' Burlesque rode up six floors of the tenement building on the freight elevator. Harold Minsky warned that these folks should "watch their pockets on the way up."[53]

It was easy to get distracted, with the Lower East Side skyline glistening through the windows. Besides the door, the other major exit was down the fire escape. Inside the theater, the legend "The play's the thing" hung over the proscenium arch, with due credit to Shakespeare. Other quotations from great authors including Dante adorned the walls. But these quotations sometimes blurred, since both lobby and theater were filled with smoke and talc, as well as the smell of perfume and greasepaint. The Minskys fixed up the theater by painting some of the walls red and others with murals from *Othello*, and hanging silk curtains on the remainder. They laid multicolored tile on the floor and installed simple brown wooden seats—no plush velvet for downtown.[54] The poet Harry Roskolenko describes visiting a burlesque theater with his Orthodox father one Sunday afternoon.

[There were photographs] of half dressed girls at the left side of the entrance. My father, very frum-religious, his eyes, staring at the right. Soon we were crowding up an elevator to the top floor. Old women in shawls, older men in fur hats and coats, red-cheeked girls, and young boys in yarmulkes! What were we going to see? The girls, when done with their burlesque, left one floor and went to another. They divided their animations between Yiddish shund and an early American strip-tease, doing erotic minded dancing for both mid-cultures in the making at the National theatre. . . . [W]e were watching the living shikses dance and prance. Jewish girls did not do what we were seeing, said my father. They were showing this and that; derrieres, a bit of tit, all of their thighs.

Finally, the burlesque chorines sang a song.

A song: in the torah it is written
With a shikse you cannot sleep
Oh, the best piece in the world.[55]

Over the next several years, the Minsky brothers—the Robin Hoods of show business—sold "shikses" and Jewish women wholesale to their mostly immigrant audience. They also stole theatrical techniques, some of which caught on more quickly than others or else acquired different uses than their original ones. European designers at Ziegfeld's used a dazzling array of lights, but the only light at Minskys' shone from a footlight trough and occasionally gave the performers an unhinged look, illuminating the calves—but not the thigh—and sometimes doubling their chins. Then Abe got the idea to experiment with light—blue, pink, and especially magenta being his favorite colors: the last may have reminded patrons of a brothel. The Minskys also popularized one lighting innovation that Ziegfeld never needed: the warning light, which would in the Jazz Age become crucial to burlesque's survival. When the stage manager spotted a policeman in the audience, he turned on the red light backstage and the performers did the so-called Boston or clean version of their acts.[56]

In those first years, the Minskys never limited their thievery to American institutions.[57] The silliest and most obvious example of this was their claim that their work was equal to the great Parisian theater's: the brothers hung signs on the front of the building with the legends "What the Folies Bergere is to Paris, Minskys' is to New York" and "The Poor Man's Ziegfeld Follies," messages that both solidified and ridiculed the Minskys' highbrow aspirations.[58] It also angered Ziegfeld sufficiently to threaten a lawsuit, although he never followed through.[59]

The biggest difference between Ziegfeld's and Minskys', though, was the female performers. The prewar *Ziegfeld Follies* had overflowed with women, jokes, and elaborate dance and production numbers. As Marjorie Farnsworth noted about Ziegfeld, "[H]e would have 120 girls whose figures would be as provocative as their faces; tall, stately girls, radiant with youth and draped in priceless costumes of furs, gems, laces, ribbons, and flowers, who would need only to walk with patrician grace before the footlights."[60]

THE MODERN ASPECT of Ziegfeld had first emerged with the 1907 *Follies*, in which lines of kicking, silk-stockinged chorus girls posed as so-called precision dancers who moved in synchronized motion like an army. Ziegfeld imagined female nudity as a progressive, modern, independent, mechanized force—a girl nudity without girl nudity's danger. To Ziegfeld, the only "un-universal" type was the one that appealed to burlesque. "One type is missing," he wrote, "because the public has eliminated it. Time was when big women were admired onstage. They were so tall and broad that skirts were imperative. One sees them on the boards no more."[61]

Downtown, Minsky also featured girls—but on a budget. The Minskys mounted fifty-two shows a year for about $3,500 each, whereas one *Ziegfeld Follies* cost $30,000 to produce.[62] Like Ziegfeld, the Minskys used enormous casts, sometimes as many as eighteen principals, over half of whom were women. Sometimes the chorus numbered thirty. But Billy Minsky rarely pretended that any of his performers offered romance. Typical revues were "Razzle Dazzle of 1918," and "Sinbad," both of which *Variety* praised for their comedy. Some of these revues also featured boxing matches.

Sometimes the entertainment recalled the brothel. One Minsky soubrette of the era, Edna De Lillis, under the moniker "Edna Dee, the Redheaded Sunshine Girl," sang, danced, twirled, and, back to the audience, lifted her dress. A "narrow strip of colored ribbon" displayed her bare buttocks, which she shook to whatever tune was playing.[63] Among the most famous Minsky comedians, Jack Shargel offered a raucous series of slapstick jokes. As E. E. Cummings later described him, Shargel played a character who was "super-Semitic, black-derbied, misfit-clothed, keen-eyed but ever-imposed-upon."[64]

Billy Minsky aspired both to get a laugh and to make audience members gasp at his near-naked women. He attempted two opposing tasks: by sending up the female body as an art object, he managed to turn the National Winter Garden into a fantasyland. At the same time, by parodying Ziegfeld, he remained close to class and elegance, but never constrained by it. The Minskys inspired other burlesque theaters to join in this orgy of boisterous Ziegfeldolatry. The Irving Place Theater, on Fifteenth Street near Gramercy Park, and the other major stock theater of the day, the Union Square Theater, which was run by Ben Kahn, produced burlesque revues for the same working-class audience. This gave birth to competition and to competing claims about who invented burlesque striptease. According to Mort Minsky, it began with his family's stealing soubrette Mae Dix from the Union Square Theater in the 1916–1917 season. As he tells the story, at the National Winter Garden, Dix revved up the old Anna Held numbers with a cootch. One night, as she exited, she pulled off the cuffs and collar of her costume so as to get them dry-cleaned. Someone in the audience saw her and mistaking the gesture began to applaud. Dix came back and unbuttoned her bodice until the manager turned out the house lights and threatened to close the theater.[65]

WHATEVER THE VERACITY of this story, cootching thrived downtown in prewar New York, but it remained too hot for the Broadway stage. And yet the patriotism accompanying World War I did much to lift the stigma against the undressed woman. This trend was neither solely political nor solely cultural, but coincided with dramatic changes in Ziegfeld's production team, most notably his addition of the Viennese designer Joseph Urban and the choreographer Ned Wayburn to his team. Both of these men, urbane devotees of the new female glamour business, worked hard to package the undressed Ziegfeld girls as being either as smooth and slick as boxes and tubes or as flat and stepped as geometric designs.

In the 1917 *Follies*, which Wayburn choreographed and Urban designed, the most memorable number, the "Garden of the Girls," displayed beautiful girls representing different kinds of flowers "sprouting" through trap doors on the stage floor and "blossoming" onstage. Behind them hung an opalescent backdrop resembling thousands of pearls. A "Chinese Lacquer" scene depicted a rooftop in which fifty young women in Chinese dress climbed up and down the ladders in unison.

As the war intensified, posing undressed began to be considered patriotic. If a woman stood naked posed as the Statue of Liberty, she was doing her duty for the American troops. Indeed, a record number of women volunteered to be "undraped" in the 1917 edition's centerpiece. In the *Ziegfeld Follies of 1918*, which opened after the United States had joined the war, the curtain opened on a darkened stage to reveal a huge, revolving globe with Kay Laurell perched on top, breasts exposed. Little French girls in rags, a dying soldier attended by Red Cross volunteers, and a trench over which doughboys charged amid devastating gunfire completed the scene. Gazing down on a Ben Ali Haggin set piece designed to look like the world burning, Laurell was supposed to represent the spirit of France, strangely inspiring the choreographer Ned Wayburn to dub her "the American Venus." But for all of these embryonic forms of undressing to explode into striptease, the war would have to end and the Jazz Age begin.

# Part Two

# The Invention of Modern Striptease

-Out—&
steps; which
flipchucking
.grins
gRiNds

—E. E. Cummings, "Sh estiffl"

# After the Doughboys Returned: Nudity in Burlesque and on Broadway

Shortly after World War I ended, the advent of Tin Pan Alley and its distinct sound expanded the surprising possibilities of female sexuality. In the teens, immigrant songwriters had reinvented American popular music with songs ritualizing emotion. Now, these writers' sentimental versions of romantic love burst into an enduring mythology. The hits of Irving Berlin, Rodgers and Hart, Cole Porter, and later, Johnny Mercer, appeared in all varieties of popular theater, including the *Ziegfeld Follies* and the National Winter Garden burlesque, where they were, as Edmund Wilson put it a couple of years later, "thrown on the screen between the acts."[1]

Tin Pan Alley songs took on their most fluid and liberating meanings when female performers sang them. Like girl pirates, these performers seized upon these songs to layer irony on top of sentimentality in a process not unlike today's sampling. The Tin Pan Alley sound—especially in what was called the novelty song—presented a witty figure who, prizing versatility, speed, and sheer chutzpah, gave city living an even more sensuous cast. These songs, although sometimes romantic, ultimately diminished the force of romantic love by pitting outrageous heroes and heroines against an old-fashioned Victorian morality and sensibility. The heroes and heroines mostly won. The heroines, mostly stock melting-pot characters from the vaudeville and burlesque stage, were often sex-seeking sybarites.[2]

Sometimes, when Tin Pan Alley offered a female narrator, she announced a previously unimagined female devotion to pleasure. She drank, smoked, flirted, consumed, and, above all, had sex. But instead of ending up weeping and alone, as she would have in a nineteenth-century ballad, this "good-time" figure could, through lyrics and delivery, transform herself into a girl trickster.

In the nineteenth century, early Tin Pan Alley had allowed risqué burlesque performances to remain respectable. As Bert Lowry wrote in his reminiscence of a night in early vaudeville, a female performer could wear a short skirt (or a shorter one) if she sang "something sentimental" like "Mother Was a Lady."[3] Written in 1896 by the songwriting team Edward Marks and Joseph Stern, that song told the story of a woman on her own. The "Irish" vaudeville comedian Lottie Gilson, who Marks noted could "draw tears from an audience with a perfectly vapid song," popularized it. Trying to defend herself against a rude customer, a single waitress claims that her mother is a lady. It turns out that the customer, a friend of her brother Jack, offers to marry her. By the early twentieth century, though, parodies of that song sent up its good-girl lyrics and the good girl herself.[4]

> My Mother was a lady
> Like yours you will allow,
> And you may have a sister,
> Who needs protection now.[5]

The Tin Pan Alley song that would become synonymous with strip-tease after World War II, however, was Irving Berlin's 1918 "A Pretty Girl Is Like a Melody."[6] Like so much else that came to pass for tradition in striptease, the song's life began on Broadway, in the 1919 *Follies*, where Florenz Ziegfeld used it to glorify the American girl's beauty. As showgirls ambled by, the popular tenor John Steele stood onstage and sang:[7]

> A Pretty Girl
> Is Like
> A Melody
> . . .
> She will leave you and then
> Come back again . . .

The song inspired Ziegfeld to come up with the *Follies* motto "Glori-fying the American girl" three years later, even though his extravagant re-vues had by then already begun their slow decline. In 1920, though, Billy Minsky hired the downtown version of John Steele—a "tit serenader"— the tenor who stood offstage crooning the era's most sentimental ballads. At other burlesque theaters nearby, Tin Pan Alley ballads like "You Were Meant for Me," "Ah, Sweet Mystery of Life," and "Yes, We Have No Ba-nanas" sent up and referred to the big Broadway revues. Especially at the National Winter Garden, played during the head-waggling, arm-whirling, racy, big-mouth moments of Minsky girl acts, these numbers, contrasting with burlesque comedy, provided raw sex and laughs.[8]

Billy Minsky aspired to more than just raw sex and laughs, however— he wanted raw sex with class. He renovated the National Winter Garden by adding rosy drapes and flowers and by modernizing the elevators so audiences could get up to the roof easily. By 1921 the *New York Times* would announce in the "News of the Rialto" section that the Minskys were moving to Broadway. Describing the Winter Garden of that year, the *Times* wrote: "The Minsky Brothers show finds a counterpart in Europe but is unique in New York. Beautiful girls with stage ability and talent are the backbone." The shows were "tuneful" and "spectacular."[9]

Billy first expanded uptown the following spring, when he signed a lease for the Park Theater at Columbus Circle. The previous owners had just finished renovating, and to Billy's mind, it was a perfect venue for "highbrow" burlesque. At the Park, Billy tried out some of the strategies that would make the National Winter Garden a burlesque mecca later in the decade. He envisioned a Hawaiian octet and a twenty-piece orchestra as well as performers imported from Europe. Billy also changed the Park from a "theater" to a "music hall," a name that summoned up an old-fashioned flair. On opening night, a woman sang "I Am Miss Musical Comedy" to prove that Minsky had left downtown. Billy held women's matinees and priced top tickets at $2.20, which was about 100 percent more than he charged at the National Winter Garden, but less than the $6.60 that uptown theatergoers might pay at the *Ziegfeld Follies*.[10]

Also, at the Park, Billy first ventured that he wanted his performers to weigh less than what the *New York Times* called the "hulking" 170 pounds, which remained the typical weight in stock theaters and on the circuits. Reacting against the nineteenth-century burlesque troupe Billy Watson's Beef Trust—and not for the last time—Billy hired performers resembling the svelte chorines of uptown entertainment. Accordingly, Billy called the Park show "Burlesques," which alluded to the *Ziegfeld Follies* and separated it from working-class "burlesque."[11] But Park audiences did not want to see upscale burlesque or thin performers: they wanted to see either *Ziegfeld Follies* glamour or its opposite. After a mere thirty-eight weeks, Billy closed the Park because of low ticket sales.

ON BROADWAY, visual consciousness of nudity—and nudity itself—was increasing exponentially. Some historians see the vogue for nudity as part of a general liberalizing principle erupting out of the same decade that introduced Americans to the flapper and Edna St. Vincent Millay, the burner of the candle at both ends. Americans now wanted to separate themselves from the Victorians in large part by attributing a positive value to sex. This liberalizing principle was further reflected in the figure of the aggressive New Woman and her pursuit of the vote, which she gained in 1920. It was also reflected in the American woman's pursuit of her own pleasure: in ebullient, tragic Zelda Fitzgerald, sassy, brash Mae West, and vampish "It Girl" Clara Bow; in dramatically raised hemlines; in the birth of the modern cosmetics industry; and in the triumph of gossip over news. In the so-called era of wonderful nonsense, everyone was "doin' it."[12]

Prohibition also played a role in making these nude acts more acceptable. Once the Volstead Act was passed and drinking could no longer take place in public, Americans went to speakeasies where one of the things they could do was see women take off their clothes. At the same time,

theater owners, who had previously depended on selling alcohol to supplement their incomes, were forced to devise new ways of bringing in money.[13]

Meanwhile, in serious theater, modernist playwrights like Susan
Glaspell and Eugene O'Neill "undressed" their subjects to critique the
hypocrisy by which society governed the individual. Competing with this
theater, the splashy Broadway revue showed more flesh, spangles, and glitter. Borrowing from decadent European spectaculars and louche Harlem
nightclubs, the revue made the modern woman nude. And on taste's margins, burlesque inspired Broadway to further eroticize the body while
Broadway's commercializing impulse asked burlesque performers to bare
more. The demise of the Columbia burlesque circuit—formerly the eastern wheel—and the ascent of a new wheel, the Mutual circuit, accelerated
this process.

Between 1913 and 1922, the Columbia circuit dominated burlesque.
Led by Sam Scribner, Columbia boasted forty-four of the most prosperous
shows and exercised a virtual monopoly from New York to Kansas City,
Missouri. The circuit's borders were the Missouri Valley, the Atlantic
Ocean, the Ohio River, and Canada. Like P. T. Barnum, Scribner courted
female audience members to gain respectability all the while pandering—
sometimes with startling bluntness—to his male audience. In 1921, Scribner
mandated that all Columbia burlesque shows would arrive at theaters with
their own orchestras, since, by suggesting vaudeville, more instruments
lent respectability to undressing.[14]

Scribner successfully prohibited smoking in Columbia theaters and,
less successfully, the double entendres that burlesque comedians deployed
as their stock in trade. He served on civic and philanthropic commissions
and became a pillar of the community. He outlawed runways in an effort to
keep the performers on the stage and out of audiences' laps, and he thun-
dered publicly that Columbia stood for "legitimacy."[15] The Jazz Age, however, was hungry for the illegitimate. In 1922 a *Variety* reviewer expressed
disappointment that the Columbia show *Lid Lifters* was "one of the first
shows where bare legs were not all over."[16] Thus Scribner compromised.
Having acquired the western circuit after the war, Scribner pushed bare-
breasted, cheaper shows onto it, leaving Columbia to be the clean circuit,
at least in name. And even though the western limped along for years after
Scribner purchased it, the plan seemed to work.[17]

In 1922, however, the success of stock burlesque theaters such as the
Minskys' National Winter Garden forced the western circuit to fold. Stock
burlesque theaters rotated their own companies and performers, many of
whom did more risqué acts than Columbia would allow. That same year, a
disgruntled Columbia manager named Isidore Herk abandoned the "clean"
Columbia circuit and began to build another "dirty" counterpart—the
Mutual circuit. At first dismissed as "the minor league of burlesque," the

Mutual circuit quickly proved its major-league status.[18] Headquartered in New York, Mutual began to buy Columbia theaters all over the country. Rushing to compete with the escalating nudity on Broadway and in film, the mutual circuit promoted bare legs, cootch dancers, and double entendres. *Billboard* wrote that it "polluted public morals."[19]

But Herk called it the "jazz of American entertainment" and noted that burlesque was not "musical comedy." The small, dark, plump "Izzy,"

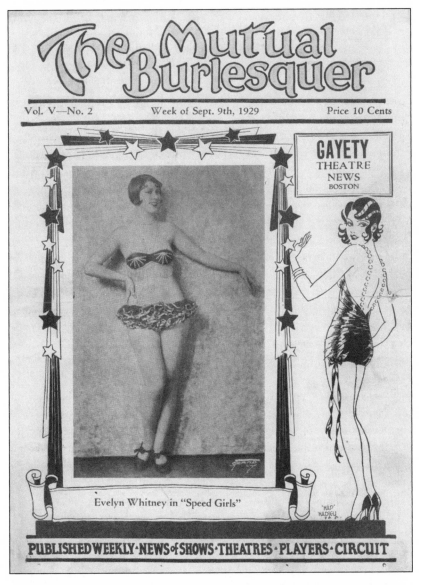

Cover of *The Mutual Burlesquer*, September 9, 1929. University of Las Vegas, Jess Mack Collection.

or "Napoleon," as he was known, was a complicated figure. One half-step above a gangster, the cigar-chomping Herk, who would later also be known as the "Henry Ford of burlesque," claimed experience in every theater on the western circuit.[20] He began in the early teens as treasurer of Toledo's Valentine Theater, then moved to Chicago, where he was briefly the "personal representative" of the midwestern producer Herman Fehr. During the Great War, Herk produced burlesque shows on the Empire circuit such as *Pacemakers*, whose most memorable feature was a bawdy, on-stage game of strip poker.[21]

Like Billy Minsky's, Herk's ambitions extended upscale when it suited him. In 1922, Herk wanted to get into vaudeville, which remained the "voice of the city." In its palaces uptown, vaudeville presented respectable undressing as well as clowns, jugglers, and family acts like "talking dogs." The two big vaudeville circuits, the Keith circuit and the Albee circuit, both controlled monopolies.[22]

Herk tried to vault out of burlesque by allying himself with the Shubert brothers, who were then creating the Time vaudeville circuit—a third vaudeville circuit intended to compete with Keith and Albee. A year later, the Time circuit folded. Herk, bankrupt, jumped to the Mutual burlesque circuit, then to the short-lived American circuit. When the American folded, Herk found himself back at Mutual, which he subsequently built from nothing to fifty franchises in a few short years.

Herk had learned in his youth how to appear to be promoting clean burlesque all the while producing the raunchy version. But he achieved this balance with a pugilist's one-two punch. He would announce to *Variety* or *Billboard* that his shows were "without a blush, working man's comedy, cleaner and cleverer shows," all the while pumping shimmy girls and cootchers. Occasionally, when reformers pushed him, he would come out more frankly: "We're not producing Sunday school shows."[23]

NO ONE WAS. After World War I, the appearance of the shimmy and other hip-swinging Jazz Age dances on Broadway prepared Americans for the curvaceous shape of the female body as burlesque striptease would later present it. The shimmy offered a different shape from the ideal one then being pushed on Ziegfeld's stage, where chorines were slender and androgynous and leaned slightly forward as they walked. An upscale version of the cootch, the shimmy forced dancers to stress the mobile rear end, which lacked grace but demonstrated both a modern erotic authority and an improvisational wriggle. According to jazz historian Marshall Stearns, in contrast to the cootch, which involved the hips trembling, the shimmy added "hair-raising quivers and shakes" of the shoulders, and often the entire body. The shimmy dancer exaggerated her femininity onstage, flirted boldly with the audience and sometimes extended into comedy.[24]

No performer was more adept at the shimmy than the young Mae West, who first performed the dance on Broadway in 1918 and even appeared on the cover of the sheet music for the song "Everybody Shimmies Now." Three years later, in the Shubert revue "Mimic World of 1921," she wore a dress with a "detachable" strap and shimmied dressed as an Oriental dancer, "Our Lady of Fatima." Like many popular dances of the Jazz Age, the shimmy was stigmatized by its link to African American culture. Indeed, the scholar Jill Watts argues that West's lack of success on Broadway and in vaudeville was due to the shimmy's racial taint. It was only many years after West's appearances on Broadway that she admitted that she first saw the dance in the teens in the Elite #1 Club, a black-and-tan speakeasy on Chicago's South Side: "There was a sensual agony about it . . . and if you ever saw it performed, you would know that no white woman could create such a dance."[25]

EVEN WHEN white women shimmied, many Jazz Age Americans continued to associate the dance with the compelling myth of "black" sexuality. In 1922, Gilda Gray sang "It's Getting Dark on Old Broadway" at the *Ziegfeld Follies*. "Getting Dark on Broadway" paid homage to female ecstasy—and particularly to black female ecstasy. Ziegfeld had bought radium paint in Paris, and in this number he required the white performers to slather it onto their costumes. Against a rack of electric lights and a canvas drop depicting Longacre Square, as the lights faded, the performers appeared to be "getting dark" while their white costumes and hats gleamed and their bodies jiggled to piano rags. The popular press described the number as commemorating Harlem's invasion of white New York. The critic Gilbert Seldes reports that Gray shimmied "with delight" as the curtain went down.[26]

The shimmy was just part of the Jazz Age revolution. A year after "It's Getting Dark on Old Broadway," a new generation of Broadway impresarios transformed the American revue girl into a whirling sensual force. Whereas status-obsessed Ziegfeld for the most part promoted "wholesome," classy sensuality through his immobile and unattainable "glorious girls," these young Turks—George White, the Shubert brothers, and Earl Carroll—saw the nude revue girl as lusty, lawless, and intimate. A key player in the nudifying of the Jazz Age revue was Carroll, whom W. C. Fields once described as a "preacher with an erection."[27] Tall, gangling, and soft-spoken, with a love for beautiful white shirts and beautiful white showgirls, Earl Carroll, the son of a farmer, was born in Pittsburgh in 1900 and came to New York to write songs and produce shows. His claim to fame, the *Vanities Revue*, ran from 1923 to 1931 and put undressing on the Broadway stage. "Look at Flo Ziegfeld!" Carroll told a *Variety* reporter in 1923. "The tremendous success he's had in presenting beautiful girls bedecked in jewels and furs. Let Flo spend money dressing them. I plan to undress them."[28]

In June 1923, Carroll advertised his first revue as "exalting the female form." But he also often pitched it as "unusual," which, to contemporary audiences would have suggested a deviant appeal.[29] Unlike Ziegfeld, Carroll saw women neither as unreachable Madonnas nor as abstract Mona Lisas, but as living, breathing girls with sex appeal—marketable girls. Carroll was prone to equating girls to food: they were "bananas, pork chops, or a lot in a suburban development. [Girls] are the most fundamental of all commodities."[30]

Carroll combined burlesque tactics with Ziegfeld's scope more daringly than any other American impresario. Some editions of the *Vanities* contained over a hundred women, and although few of these undressed onstage, they appeared more naked—often half nude—and in more elaborate tableaux than at Ziegfeld's. Even more than Ziegfeld or Minsky, Carroll, influenced by the Folies Bergères—which he had seen in France during the war—filled the stage with bubbles, marble statues, rainbow lights, mosaic glasses, friezes of metal, bars of gold, revolving flowers, subterranean fog, feathers, chandeliers, and bejeweled ruffles. Carroll also used clear plastic— which led people to call his showgirls "virgins wrapped in cellophane." Carroll's first edition of the *Vanities* featured the "Get in a Bathing Suit" number, in which women took off long fur coats to reveal daring one-piece swimming costumes.[31]

Carroll changed Broadway. To compete that first year, the Shubert brothers dragged Ziegfeld's old undressing number from *The Parisian Model* out of the closet and turned it into a revue displaying the first topless women on Broadway. *Artists and Models* might have been, as *Daily News* theater critic Burns Mantle quipped, a ploy to make sure that no one was late for the theater, but it was also the show that solidified J. J. Shubert's reputation as a flesh merchant. The spectacle hit a nerve. Heywood Broun wrote that the longest line he had ever seen was outside the Shubert door backstage after the show's opening night.[32]

When *Artists and Models* opened at the Shubert Theater, like most revues of its day it provided a kaleidoscope of entertainment: twenty-four scenes in two acts, Samoan dancers, a send-up of the melodrama *Rain*, a vaudeville comic, and a blackface comedian. But the topless number in the first act accounted for the then record-setting 312-performance run. Prior to *Artists and Models*, topless women had posed onstage, but because of anti-obscenity laws, they had never moved.

Here, the curtain rose on two "artists" cleverly named Arthur Poor and Frank Famous in the middle of teaching painting to six eager flappers. Stage center, a topless model stood on a dais. A chiffon scarf swathed her lower torso like a diaper. After a few minutes, about twenty other models, also naked to the waist and under the glare of a spotlight, paraded onstage from the back of the theater across the stage. They wheeled around and

*Artists and Models Revue*, 1923. The Shubert Archives.

exited to the left. Burns Mantle wrote in his review that he thought the flappers might have been singing. But Mantle professed to be so distracted by the spectacle of topless women moving onstage that he couldn't remember. "I had been told to watch the models," he wrote.[33]

Confronted with bare breasts, the audience failed to act politely, as they were supposed to do on Broadway. A few people guffawed. A fistfight erupted in the lobby. And then the audience fell self-consciously silent, as if in a cathedral. *Artists and Models* incited the attention of some of New York's anti-obscenity societies. But the critical response was largely favorable as journalists fell over each other trying to prove their sophistication. Some even displayed a Gotham City pride in the idea that New York had surpassed Paris in déshabillé: "There is more female nudity displayed there at the Shubert Theater than ever before on any stage in the city," wrote one critic, who then went on to reflect upon how the endgame of undressing women on the Broadway stage affected men. "In the last ten years, the American male has seen so many female legs that the sight of it excites him as much as the sight of a carrot on a vegetable stand."[34]

The most jaded response leaked from the pen of the critic George Jean Nathan, who epitomized the era's "Broadway wisenheimer" spirit. "This show is offensive to the sort of critic who wears white socks with black shoes—in this Sunday's rotogravure section of the newspaper that has made the loudest howl, I count six photographs of six women without as much clothing as is worn by the least-dressed girl on the Shubert stage theater."[35]

In the early twenties, reformers, the police, and the license commissioner were able to close theatrical performances for indecency only by proving the audience's criminality. Since the audience for Broadway shows was primarily composed of the carriage trade, it was almost impossible to get a conviction.[36] Still, the topless revue signaled a crisis to many in the theater community. Arthur Hammerstein, the impresario who in the teens had introduced the girl show to Broadway, complained, "Something more than blonde dolls with divorce court reputations, something more than plucked eyebrows and dimpled knees, something more than the endless procession of bare backs, curved shoulders and bobbed hair is needed."[37] The reporter interviewing Hammerstein, though, countered with box office grosses: "All of the girl shows in New York are flourishing and there is no surface sign, at least, of a dwindling of public interest in this form of entertainment."[38]

# The First Strippers and Teasers

mmediately after *Artists and Models* and the *Vanities* opened, theater operators downtown, in Brooklyn, and in the hinterlands—most of them on the Mutual circuit—vied to compete. On Fulton Street, the Star Theater installed a runway, as did the Prospect in the Bronx and the Olympic on Fourteenth Street. Edmund Wilson would later describe these runways as "hollow bowling alleys." Many other theaters followed suit in an attempt to move female cootch dancers, "jazz dancers," and "specialty numbers" closer to the audience.[1]

Morton Minsky claimed that the "first runway parade in American theatre history" had emerged several years earlier from his brother Abe's visit to Paris and the Folies Bergères. "[Abe] remarked: 'Ya know, if we could only get the lights somehow, there's quite a stunt they pulled at the Folies Bergères in Paris. They paraded girls on a runway.'" Abe explained that the audience "went crazy" when the Folies performers strutted down the raised platform from stage into the theater. The next day, the brothers built a runway from the orchestra pit up the center of the house to a point just under the rim of the balcony. House lights illuminated the women since the Minskys declined to purchase spotlights. Mort described it: "And what a parade! We had six girls . . . and the audience, mostly male, could look right up their legs. Our audience howled . . ."[2]

Like much else on Houston Street, the runway quickly acquired a nickname from uptown: "Varicose Alley," after Shubert Alley and *Variety* reporter Jack Conway's description of the legs of an old burlesque performer. Billy's brother Mort wrote that when some burlesque cootch dancers got so close to the audience that "they could smell their perfume and hear their heavy breathing, it was sensational!"[3] It was generally acknowledged that the best seats were the ones in "the alley," and by the 1930s many burlesque theater operators installed three runways—one for the general audience and two for the boxes.[4]

Whatever its origins, the runway inspired many burlesque theater operators to encourage their female stars to go bare-legged for the first time. Desperate for audiences, even some theaters on the Columbia circuit featured performers posing tableau vivant style with bare breasts, and although many theater operators tried to get them to cover them, fearing that the trend would cause a reform crackdown, it was too late. At Christmas 1924, in Hurtig and Seamon's in Harlem, a theater manager got the idea to use "border lights" to illuminate the runway and the performers' scandalously bare legs. Thus, on both the Mutual and Columbia circuits, two new acts— the "teaser" and the "stripper"—emerged.[5]

A popular teaser in New York was Isabelle Van, "the Queen of the Runway," whose Christmas show at the Apollo dragged on for upwards of three hours because of "fervent" calls for encores for her performance. A teaser exited after discarding each garment. She appeared the first time baring as little as "a square inch" of collar bone. Then she reappeared eight or ten times after that until she wore her girdle and brassiere or a union suit—a skin-tight one-piece garment designed to simulate nudity and some-times adorned with lace. Since most teasers started out fully clothed, the encores could last for some time. At the end, Van would sometimes "flash" or reveal one of her breasts, a stunt that arose as a way to get around New York Statute 1140a—the provision making it illegal for a female performer to reveal her breasts while she was moving. In general, the teaser undressed with a lot of sashaying, winking, and cavorting in between dressed and union-suit states. As the Chicago journalist and nightlife expert Jack Lait put it, the teaser "sustained suspense."[6]

By contrast, a strip produced a more abrupt removal of clothing. A stripper worked in a straightforward manner. Although the amount she could take off varied from city to city, the stripper started fully dressed and disrobed onstage hook by hook, or clasp by clasp. Sometimes she also un-dressed to her union suit. In burlesque it was not until the early thirties that strippers and teasers would undress to pasties and a G-string.[7] A fuller way of distinguishing between stripping and teasing originated from the performer's intention, at least as the popular press perceived that intention. "To strip" suggested a resolute quality—a focused intent on disrobing— whereas "to tease" alluded to the provisional nodding and flirting that ac-companied it.[8]

ACCORDING TO MOST SOURCES, the first "stripper" was Anne Toebe (some-times also spelled Tobie). Born in Rochester, New York, Toebe began performing there in 1914 in the shows of putty-nose comedian Billy Hagan, whom she would later marry. She continued in traveling Columbia circuit shows for a decade, then switched to the racy Mutual circuit under the pro-duction of Sam Kraus. She also performed in stock burlesque at the National Winter Garden. In shows such as *The Broadway Belles* and *The Moonlight Maids*, the chubby, auburn-haired Toebe became known for "cayenne" and for her "rough" flirtation with the audience. She played stock comic char-acters with genial names like Anna Pep.[9]

One of Toebe's songs went, "My face isn't much to look at: I gotta shape like a frog; but I can make boys in the gallery sit up and yell hot dog!" In a number reminiscent of Millie De Leon, Toebe ambulated down the runway and leaned into the aisle, where she "implant[ed] plenty of lipstick on the dome of a baldheaded jewelry salesman," as *Variety* put it. In another popular number, Toebe turned the graceful "bathing suit" number from the *Ziegfeld Follies* into a gymnastic strip.[10]

In Toebe's bathing suit number, the chorus girls strode onstage and posed wrapped in floor-length cloaks. When they reached the middle of the stage, the orchestra launched into Anna Held's old song "Do You Want to See a Little More of Me?" Each performer sang one line from the song and threw open her cloak, giving the audience a view of her one-piece bathing suit. A few bars and many cloaks later, Toebe herself entered. She threw open her own cloak and revealed her one-piece union suit. After the audience "broke their arms" in approval," she exited.[11] In 1925, Toebe gave the Minskys the idea for featuring female performers' names above comics'. The fact was, women were the ones who sold tickets.[12]

AS FOR THE FIRST "TEASER," she was Carrie Finnell, who inaugurated her tease act in September 1923 in Cleveland and then made it last for twenty weeks. Born sometime in the last years of the nineteenth century, in Covington, Kentucky, Finnell spent her youth performing in midwestern burlesque theaters. She made her first stage appearance with the Le Roy Guy Players, a burlesque troupe in Covington. Subsequently, she became known as "Minneapolis's sweetheart," and she performed in that city at the Gayety Theater wearing blue silk and rabbit-fur boots.[13]

In the late teens, Finnell took herself and her expensive boots to stock burlesque around the country. In 1919 and 1920 she played at the Minsky brothers' National Winter Garden Theater, which the brothers had just finished renovating. Attending the 1920 opening were numerous journalists, socialites, and Broadway producers, one of whom said, after her performance, that he would come to Minskys' to steal ideas for his shows uptown.[14]

Finnell's manager claimed she also toured England and France during this time. But in 1921 she returned to the Midwest. In Chicago, she met her first husband, Charles Grow, then the manager of the State Congress Theater. She performed at the Cincinnati Gayety Theater, where manager Noah Schechter called her "the girl with the $100,000 legs," presumably borrowing the nickname from the turn-of-the-century burlesque and vaudeville star Frankie Bailey, although Bailey's limbs were valued at ten times Finnell's. (Eventually inflation caught up with her—Finnell's obituary lists her legs as being worth a million dollars.[15]) In Cincinnati, the same year that Finnell became "the girl with the $100,000 legs," she broke into an improvised dance to "quiet the audience" while the roof of the theater she was performing in collapsed due to a fire.[16]

# COVINGTON GIRL WITH $100,000 LEGS WEDS

### Miss Carrie Lee Finnell Was the Heroine of a Cincinnati Fire Several Years Ago

Miss Carrie Lee Finnell, 22, former Covington girl and possessor of $100,000 pair of legs, has become the bride of Charles J. Grow, 26, musical director at the Haymarket Theater, Chicago, where the bride has been playing.

Dispatches from Waukegan, Ill., Wednesday, stated the marriage took place in that city Monday.

Members of the company were "in" on the secret, because the bride told the justice who married them there's a barrel of rice and old shoes waiting me at the theater."

The bride is a former New York Winter Garden girl.

Her first stage appearance was made with the Le-Roy Guy Players in a Covington theater. She was the heroine of a Cincinnati theater and "dancing on the stage by the light of candles to quiet the audience when the roof collapsed."

Her legs were considered so beautiful her manager recently had them insured for $100,000.

Miss Finnell is the daughter of Mrs. Martha Fox, 3322 Watson st., Latonia. Mrs. Fox said her daughter met Grow when in Chicago two years ago.

MISS CARRIE LEE FINNELL AND HER $100,000 LEGS.

"The girl with the $100,000 legs," aka the first teaser, Carrie Finnell, makes the cover of the *Kentucky Post*. Archives of the *Kentucky Post*.

Once Finnell arrived in Cleveland's Empire Theater in September 1923, the *Cleveland Plain Dealer*, comparing her to the long-running Broadway tear jerker, dubbed her the "Abie's Irish Rose of burlesque."[17] She was initially also billed as "the girl with the $100,000 legs" and as "Gilda Gray's real competitor."[18] *Billboard* noted that she did an act reminiscent of "Old State Street in Chicago." Over the course of the fall, the Empire extended and reextended Finnell's act. In December, the theater added midnight performances because the earlier shows sold out.[19]

That was the year that the Jazz Age was rousing Cleveland from its Victorian slumber. Only two years earlier, the Cleveland police had allowed the Columbia circuit burlesque theater to stay open on Sunday. In 1922, a year before Finnell's debut, the police arrested the Empire Theater's publicity agent William Dowdell in a downtown hotel for bringing an "allegedly scantily clad" chorus girl to do a private dance at a dinner for the Republican caucus members and their wives and children.[20] The Empire capitalized on the scandal, promising burlesque-goers that "she will dance for you too" and running a half-page photo of the dancer for the entire city to see.[21]

In 1923, Cleveland boasted five burlesque theaters—more than any other city in the country. Four of them were run by the same man—a local theatrical equipment provider named Sam Manheim. The most lavish, the Miles Theater, had opened in 1913 as a two-thousand-seat vaudeville palace at a cost of nearly half a million dollars. Decorated in Louis XIV style in a color scheme of rose, ivory, cream, and gold, the Miles boasted DuBarry damask on the walls and lavish murals on the ceilings. Candy dispensers were attached to the backs of the mahogany seats. In 1920, though, the Columbia burlesque circuit bought the Miles and turned it into what one critic called a "flophouse with a soundtrack."[22]

Two years later, the competing Mutual circuit had taken over the Empire, which was located nearby on Ninth and Bolivar, and turned it into a burlesque showcase. With its less lavish interior and prurient reputation, the Empire needed to find more daring acts to attract audiences. The theater quickly raised the censor's ire. The police shut down its very first show, *The Footlight Frolics*, for indecency. In August 1923, when the Empire needed a "peppy" hit, it hired Fatty Arbuckle. In September it got one in Finnell.[23]

As Finnell told a journalist years later, she went onstage with "a costume I designed, trunks with only a front and back with straps at the side." She described the genesis of her tease as accidental. "So I got the idea of taking off one strap each week; there were ten of them and it took ten weeks," she said shortly before her death.[24] In the 1940s the costume designer Irene Sharaff would describe Finnell as a "kewpie doll." A picture taken around the time of her Cleveland run reveals this quality—she grins and, exuding Jazz Age spirit, bursts out of her semitransparent bra and short pants.[25]

AFTER FINNELL AND TOEBE, stripping and teasing—thrust out on the runway—began to look different from other burlesque numbers. Women revealing their bodies with a combination of giggling verve and coy brashness demanded not just a new vocabulary, but new methods of publicity and marketing. In 1923 in St. Louis, at the Liberty Music Hall, local theater owner Oscar Dane staged "shapely ankle contests" in which he invited ordinary women onstage, lowered the house lights, and pulled up the curtain about five inches. The best ankle received a prize.[26] That same year, Chicago's Rialto Theater for the first time displayed nude photos of performers in the lobby and on its facade.[27] In the City on the Make and across the nation, stripping and teasing demanded a risqué style of advertising. "Pictures stimulate business," said Sam Scribner, the head of the Columbia circuit.[28]

It was also around this time that the candy butcher—the man who gave the spiel about strippers in between numbers and sold cheap gifts, like French postcards and food—became an integral part of the burlesque show. The sexual allusions of his pitches, generally delivered at the beginning of the show and during intermission, contributed to the general atmosphere of salaciousness.

While photographs and candy butchers advertised burlesque strippers and teasers more boldly, American song became still less sentimental. This was in part due to the rise of jazz and blues. When the Jazz Age stripper or teaser sang Tin Pan Alley standards, she sang "out" to the audience—a tradition that also drew from the blues torch song. Her story, when told in this manner—having less to do with melody than spontaneity, syncopation, and improv—came out of the tradition of Afro-American sacred and secular music, in which exchanges between a leader and a chorus were common. It created a feeling of intimacy between the audience and the performers. In burlesque, the rag and polyrhythm that first appeared in popular music in nineteenth-century saloons and dancehalls heightened this erotic sing-speaking by supplementing it with double entendres and gestures.

The use of these songs in burlesque is no surprise. In the early and mid-twenties, many black jazz and blues musicians supplemented their nightclub work by selling songs to white performers or playing in burlesque or both. The blues musician Perry Bradford closed his act with "The Bullfrog Hop," a song describing the shimmy, when he worked on the Columbia circuit.

Like so much other popular entertainment of the era, stripping and teasing enlivened both burlesque theaters and speakeasies across the nation. In Boston's Scollay Square, near City Hall, the Old Howard Theater began to produce raucous burlesque shows full of comics and undressing women. Douglas Shand Tucci referred to the Old Howard as "the center of the Boston Rialto." At 34 Howard Street, the theater sat near a litter of cheap hotels, penny arcades, saloons, and shooting galleries. The Marx Brothers and Fred Allen performed there. "Always something' doin'" was the theater's slogan.[29]

Built in the 1840s, the theater seated thirteen hundred and resembled a supersized speakeasy. Outside, the granite facade boasted an arched front with huge stained-glass windows. Inside, the loges came all the way around the house like a giant horseshoe, and the end boxes hung over the stage. The faded rosette ceiling contained several bullet holes, and a policeman preserved order in the balcony by hitting his billy club on the rail.[30]

During World War I, the Old Howard had attracted sailors on leave, Harvard professors, and Boston Brahmins. Wags often repeated that "the Harvard curriculum includes Howard Athenaeum I, II, III, and IV." But not everyone was fond of it. In 1922, seeking to make a name for himself before he went to the *New York Times*, the young theater critic Brooks Atkinson found the entertainment at the Old Howard "conventional" and the theater itself "ill smelling."[31]

In New Orleans, nude dancing and bawdy singing flourished in whorehouses next to Storyville jazz even after 1918, when the navy shut down the district. Jelly Roll Morton, who claimed to have played in whorehouses in the French Quarter and in Biloxi, recounts that at Gypsy Schaeffer's, a high-class Storyville joint, the pianist Tony Jackson "would dig up one of his fast speed tunes, and one of the girls would dance on a little narrow stage, completely nude. Yes, they danced absolutely stripped, but in New Orleans the naked dance was a real art." In 1902, Jackson had even composed a piano solo, "The Naked Dance," to prove it. [32]

The columnist Westbrook Pegler described a prewar burlesque show on Chicago's State Street in which, after the performance, the comedian auctioned off the girls to members of the audience, "who claimed them then and there and took them, still in costume, to the beer hall in the rear."[33] On the West Coast, burlesque emerged in Seattle, thanks to the manager John Cort.[34]

Kansas City jazz and blues influenced the style of some strip and tease acts. In the "most wide-open town in America," nude or half-dressed waitresses improvised at the Chesterfield Club on Ninth Street. With its gaudy red carpet unfurling along the sidewalk like a great tongue, the Chesterfield Club catered to jazz musicians and tourists, and became widely known for the extraordinary economy of dress of its black and white waitresses, some of whom shaved their pubic hair in the shapes of hearts, diamonds, spades, and clubs. According to Kansas City torch singer Julia Lee, the waitresses "wore nothin' if yo'd overlook the slippers 'n' a cellophane apron."[35] Pegler, outraged by K.C.'s "indiscreet" eating house, described the Chesterfield as the "public restaurant in which the waitresses stripped to their high-heeled shoes."[36]

Undressing performers showed ingenuity in a number of other establishments in the area. "Nude lunch" was also possible at Twelfth and Vine streets in a "businessman's" joint called the Ship. Or one could see four striptease acts costing less than a dollar. The Spinning Wheel offered strippers as well. In the basement cabaret of the Jefferson Hotel on West Sixth Street, jazzmen and tourists watched burlesque shows, gambled, drank, and practiced the other usual rackets.

Nearby, a few burlesque theaters competed with this sideshow. At Martin Regan's Fountain Theater, the "Free and Easy" burlesque lived up to its name, as did Valentine's Love Theater. Run by Joe Donegan, a friend of Boss Pendergast, the Century Burlesque Theater for a brief time housed mutual circuit cootch dancers. Before the summer of 1925, when it burned to the ground, the Gillis Opera House, located at Fifth and Walnut streets featured nude dancing. A bowling alley on top of the theater made it difficult to hear the jokes, so audience members, according to one observer, "contented themselves with watching the female performers in their g-strings." These performers always wore shoes, the observer speculated, for fear of disease.[37]

The extraordinary proliferation of both music and vice activity in Kansas City may explain why the city remained a burlesque wheel hub so late and so long.[38] Geography helped, since K.C. was the westernmost point for many theatrical circuits. Gypsy Rose Lee debuted in burlesque at the Missouri Theater, the former Century Theater, on the cusp of the Depression. Sally Rand, from nearby Elkton, performed her fan dance there in the forties, as did another native, Rosita Royce. Although the Missouri closed in 1932, it reopened during World War II and continued to present striptease until 1969, after many burlesque theaters on the East and West Coasts shut their doors.

ALL THROUGHOUT THE TWENTIES, strippers' and teasers' use of the burlesque runway increased the number of songs that writers could sell per show. The runway allowed the stripper or teaser to both sing the song many times during her encores and plug the songs more directly to the audience. In 1928, *Variety* reported that the average burlesque show needed six songs, as opposed to the four it had needed pre-runway.[39] Many of these were blues tunes. Finnell's colleague on the Mutual circuit, the "peppy" yet demure soubrette Kitty Madison, belted out two songs about sex's merciless ebb and flow: "I Ain't Givin' Nothin' Away" and "How Can I Get It?" In Madison's *Jazztime Revue*, Hinda Wassau and Ann Corio both started their careers bopping to blues numbers.

Some women used music as comedy. In her Mutual circuit show *Girls from the Follies*, the versatile Gladys Clark—who began one strip act in a tuxedo—sometimes came onstage playing either the clarinet or the accordion. In the former, she impersonated the musician Ted Lewis, the "high hat tragedian of song," by performing his languid standard "Just Around the Corner." In all, Clark played five instruments.[40]

Nor was the music for stripping and teasing limited to the blues and jazz. It ventured into ethnic song and also touched the realm of high culture, the way vaudeville did by booking an opera performer. The raven-haired Margie Pennetti, whom *Variety* called "the sizzling Senorita of burlesque," catered to an Italian audience, especially when she performed at the Prospect Theater in the Bronx. Pennetti stripped to "O Sole Mio" and to a brassy version of the Harry Reser and the Six Jumping Jacks' song "Where Do You Work-a Johnny?"[41]

Composed by Neapolitan songwriter Edoardo Di Capua, "O Sole Mio" had attracted immigrant audiences since Enrico Caruso recorded it in 1916.

The romantic ballad expressed longing for home and the old country, and relied on a graceful, "arietta" style. "Where Do You Work-a Johnny," on the other hand, drew from the "coon song" tradition, and used call-and-response to tell the story of two men competing for a woman. The slangy first verse, about a guy working on the rails, left a lot of room for Pennetti's bumping and grinding, "wrestling" with the audience, and "promiscuous kissing," as *Variety* put it.[42]

> 1: Where do you work-a, John?
> 2: On the Delaware Lackawan.
> 1: Oh, yeah, say, what do you do-a, John?
> 2: Oh, I push-a, push-a, push.
> 1: Oh, what do you push-a, John?
> 2: Bimbo: I push-a, push the truck.
> 1: Yes, but where do you push-a, John?
> 2: On the Delaware Lackawanna—
> Chorus: Wanna-wanna-wan, the Delaware Lackawan!
> Ah-ah-ah; ah-ah-ah,
> Oh, Viva la Lackawan! Hey!
> Ah-ah-ah!

Of course, there was more to stripping and teasing than music: teasers prolonged their acts by deftly flinging a Spanish shawl or another imaginative covering around their bodies. Or they ripped papier-mâché cherries from a bunch between their legs and tossed them into the audience, a gimmick Mae Dix pioneered in Chicago at the State and Lake Theater in 1926.[43] Dix's red hair and hefty frame appealed to audiences, as did her "devilish, dynamic dancing" in another of her acts, in which she wore a union suit and a "lonely handkerchief wrapped around her middle."[44] *Variety* described her as an "energetic Amazon" and noted that she impersonated Tex Guinan, the nightclub owner whose tag line was "Give the little girl a big hand."[45] But at New York's Hurtig and Seamon Theater on 125th Street in Harlem, Isabelle Van anticipated the 1930s by doing a smooth tease, working from an ostrich feather cape all the way down to a lacy white union suit. And when the woman *Billboard* described as "the Sex Seeker" stopped, she garnered as many as seven encores.[46]

WHILE TEASE ACTS became longer and more complicated, women's roles were shifting. An important element in this shift was the rise of the New Woman. The Jazz Age strip and tease acts expressed similar impulses to the ones that gave birth to this protofeminist figure. An icon in American feminism since the 1890s, the New Woman, more assertive than the female models before her, drew attention to herself. She forged two major goals after 1910: in contrast to Victorian-era women, she demanded freedom to express her sexuality, and, by emphasizing herself as an individual, she made claiming a "self" distinct from a man possible. Although some feminist critics dismiss this figure, arguing that she failed to garner important political and social advances, her presence inspired strip and tease numbers—and maybe a broader range of ideas about female sexuality itself.[47]

Strip numbers in the early twenties often involved women "being stripped" by an event or series of events beyond their control. In the *Band Box Revue*, a Jazz Age Mutual circuit burlesque show that originated in Kansas City, Eva Bradford starred in a version of the number "How to Get Arrested." In the male version, the straight man, who always played the average guy, steals one item of clothing after another from the comic, the foil, until he is nearly naked. In the female version, Bradford was, as *Variety* described it, "stripped of her clothes piece by piece until she [had] but little left over her union suit."[48]

By being stripped, Bradford remained connected to Victorian-era morality. She was not responsible for stripping herself, the act seemed to say. By the mid-twenties, though, the female version of this act waned in popularity. Stripping became both more dynamic and more forthright. Reviews of strip acts in the popular press shifted from describing performers as "Dresden dolls," after the cute dolls produced in Germany during World War I, to depicting women "flinging off" or "discarding" their lingerie, language that communicated the idea that undressing, though it appeared unselfconscious and intimate, was a woman's choice. If on the surface such reviews maintained the fiction that audience members were just peeping into women's bedrooms, with the promise of voyeurism that that implied, it also put the woman in control.[49]

A NEW LITERARY CULTURE embraced burlesque as an American ritual, one necessary for sexual adventurers. In *This Side of Paradise*, F. Scott Fitzgerald's hero Armory Blaine goes to a burlesque house before he discovers that he knows himself and "that is all." Indeed, going to the burlesque house becomes part of Blaine's process of self-discovery. In 1920, *The Dial*—the preeminent modernist journal of its day—emerged as a voice championing the American scene with what Frederick Lewis Allen called "raucous and profane laughter." In one of its first issues, *The Dial* published four of E. E. Cummings's doodles of burlesque figures. Two of these depicted the baggy-pants burlesque comedian Jack Shargel, and two were female teasers who, with arms akimbo, posed half-undressed and displayed a joyful charm.[50]

Three years later, the *American Mercury* appeared. Edited by H. L. Mencken and George Jean Nathan, the acid green magazine ridiculed what Mencken called "the bilge of idealism." In an article written early on, the photographer, Harlem Renaissance supporter, and chronicler of the Jazz Age Carl Van Vechten dismissed burlesque's working-class audience as "childishly leering and sensual."[51]

E. E. Cummings, "Burlesque Show III," *The Dial*, 1920. Liveright Publishing Company.

Cigars are fixed tightly between the teeth, while greedy, ingenuous eyes devour the scene and estimate the flesh, but slightly concealed by the fleshings. The ladies in these entertainments may be overplump, a trifle seer [*sic*] and yellow, but they suggest sex, in a sense that the ladies in our over-refined and musical comedies do not.[52]

However condescending, Van Vechten's article demonstrated the intelligentsia's growing interest in burlesque as a form of primitivism. And if the male moderns exploited burlesque for their salvation, the exploitation was not altogether one-sided, since the performers themselves could sometimes gain enormous publicity thanks to the attention.

Popular journalism caught on to Van Vechten's excitement about bur-lesque, capitalizing on the enormous emerging market for sex. Launched in 1924 by Bernarr McFadden, the health nut and would-be president, the *Daily Graphic* relentlessly converted news into first-person stories. The *Graphic* was widely considered to have debased journalism, not just for the sex stories appearing on every page, but for its pioneering of the composograph—a picture in which one person's head was grafted onto another's body. Articles told endless tales of mayhem and debauchery, as opposed to local and na-tional news. Nor was coverage of backstage scandals limited to the *Graphic*. During this era, three papers—*Variety*, *Billboard*, and the *Clipper*—all cov-ered the burlesque industry and its correspondent gossip and news.

In these rags' pages, Damon Runyon and Walter Winchell set the stage for the invention of striptease. Vulgar, savvy moniker makers, these men created the mythical Great White Way. The slang they fashioned there in-tended to grab America and rouse it from slumber. Runyon and Winchell wanted to hype up, jack up, and sex up the language. Broadway slang pro-vided a verbal shorthand whose purpose was to separate the suave sybarites who used it from the staid country bumpkins who lived by nineteenth-century rules. Broadway was "the Incandescent District," "Mazda Lane." One didn't impress the audience, one "wowed" them. The term "s.a." meant sex appeal, a whole new concept for the era. The appearance of the word "striptease" was one result of this Jazz Age obsession with hype.

The word "tease" appeared as a show-business term in the early 1920s. It was established by 1925, when a movie called *The Teaser* portrayed its heroine as a manipulative minx who "believed in uttering untruths when they help her out of a difficulty even if they do reflect on other persons."[53] In burlesque, "teasing" translated into a sophistication about sex, thanks to the moderns' emphasis on the word as a metaphor for Jazz Age excess, pleasure, and extravagance.

Some male modernists found stripping and teasing's direct connec-tion with the audience appealing. In 1932, the critic Gilbert Seldes re-called teasers' innovation and variety with affection. "One personable young woman used a double sheet of newspaper, tearing it column by column for each exit, while the men in the audience shouted for her to 'get a tabloid'; another concocted a 'wow' finale by covering herself with stop, go, and detour signs."[54]

But burlesque teasing also made Seldes uneasy in a way that other popu-lar entertainment never did. In *The Seven Lively Arts*, Seldes wrote: "The great virtues of burlesque as I (insufficiently) know it are its complete lack of sentimentality in the treatment of emotion and its treatment of appearance. The harsh ugliness of the usual burlesque make-up is interesting—I have seen sinister, even macabre, figures upon its stage—and the dancing, which has no social refinement, occasionally develops angular positions and lines of exciting effect."[55]

The "exciting effect" of stripping and teasing also resulted from a decrease in the number and size of women's undergarments. As the costume historian Cecil Saint-Laurent put it, striptease could only have arisen in a generation that had "not known the restrictive forms of pre-1914 underwear."[56] By 1924 a decade passed since women traded whalebone corsets and petticoats in for the new "easy" lingerie—pieces women could slip on or off in one gesture. Unlike the whalebone corset, these foundation garments allowed the Jazz Age woman to get undressed in a matter of seconds and without the assistance that she needed for the corset.

Thus stripping and teasing got easier. At the same time, these acts' emphasis on female sexual desire and the female body continued to distinguish burlesque from other kinds of popular theater. The historian Albert McLean writes about how, long before the cinema became a mass art, vaudeville reflected immigrants' hopes and manifested the belief in progress, the pursuit of happiness, and the hope for material success basic to the American character: "It arose in an era of crisis . . . to put man back in the center of the world."[57] Because stripping and teasing from the onset so singularly stressed the sexual, they would never become part of this aspirational equation.

# Pansies, Reformers, and a "Frenzy of Congregate Cootchers": The Birth of Modern Striptease

A

lthough four Minskys worked in burlesque in the mid-twenties, the stripping and teasing that made the National Winter Garden celebrated arose mostly because of one man. This was Billy Minsky, the second-oldest brother. No more than five feet tall—dark, flashily dressed, prematurely aged, but not heavy like the oldest brother, Abe, whom *Variety* would later call an "enstripreneur"—Billy was the brains behind the operation, and the ambition. He walked through the National Winter Garden chain-smoking cigars with an air of certainty about him.[1]

In 1925, though, Billy Minsky's empire was in trouble. This was in part due to his expansion. The previous year, Billy had opened another burlesque theater, "the Little Apollo," "Minskys' Apollo," or as it was sometimes known, "Minskys' Uptown," on 125th Street between Seventh and Eighth avenues in Harlem above Brecher's Opera House. It was a crowded block. The Columbia circuit already owned one theater, run by the team of Hurtig and Seamon, in the same neighborhood.[2] (This would later become the Apollo Theater.) Additionally, the Prospect Theater, across the river in the South Bronx, produced Mutual burlesque shows for "families and parties."[3]

When Billy took over the Little Apollo, he rotated mostly white performers between there and the National Winter Garden. The audience was also primarily white. Billy counted on the fact that the Apollo could offer "progressive burlesque"—wild cootch dances, but more highly produced than that of the Mutual circuits—to draw these audiences. A typical Minsky Apollo number featured Mlle Fifi (aka Mary Dawson), previously a "permanent drawing card at the Olympic" and a well-known oriental dancer. Fifi stepped onstage in a shimmering gold cape only to discard it seconds later, giving the audience a glimpse of her body from head to toe. She then did what *Variety* described as "a dash of the delsarte with a few cooch movements thrown in."[4]

Minskys' Apollo faced increasing police scrutiny. The trade newspapers complained about it, and the police made several highly publicized arrests.[5] Indeed, the most famous arrest in burlesque history—"the night they raided Minskys'"—occurred, according to Roland Barber, when Fifi migrated from the Apollo to the Winter Garden and invented striptease.[6]

One thing that's striking here is not the particulars of Barber's madeup tale, but that he identifies a central factor in striptease's birth: the rivalry between burlesque promoters and purity-campaign reformers. In his first ten years in burlesque, Billy had more or less succeeded in assuaging reformers' fears about his shows. Inspired by late-nineteenth-century vaudeville impresarios, he claimed to transform the straw of rough, working-class burlesque into the gold of Broadway by drawing middle-class women into the audience and banning drinking, smoking, and swearing. But as the Jazz Age went on, to attract audiences, Billy needed to add increasingly larger dashes of the prurient to his burlesque soup.

At the same time, during these years, purity-campaign reformers turned their attention away from literature and toward popular entertainment. One powerful reform group, the Committee of Fourteen (COF), focused on theater and film. Founded in the nineteenth century to address the rise of Raines Law hotels—hotels doubling as brothels—the COF drew members from every economic class, but contained an especially vocal group of police officers and politicians. The organization saw itself as filling a gap where the government had failed to police vice and also as protecting young people.

Where working-class entertainment was concerned, purity-campaign organizations had the law on their side. In 1915 judges had decided that movie censorship did not violate the First or Fourteenth amendment because movies were not art but popular entertainment. Burlesque also fit into this category, and by 1921 the COF had set in motion anti-burlesque campaigns as part of its larger anti-indecency drive against the legitimate theater. One area where the COF focused was the Rialto, the commercial area along Fourteenth Street near Tammany Hall and surrounding Union Square, where no-holds-barred stock burlesque houses like Sam Kraus's Olympic Burlesque Theater thrived.[7]

An essay in the *New Yorker* described the Olympic as presenting burlesque that was "too lurid . . . jocose, lugubrious, on the rampage." Articles like this certainly fueled the reemergence of another reform group, the New York Society for the Suppression of Vice (NYSSV). In 1915, John Sumner had inherited NYSSV from Anthony Comstock. Sumner had attended NYU Law School, and he presented himself as a determined literary man who was at the same time, as he described himself in a 1927 article for *Smart Set*, a "plain, ordinary, everyday, hard-working American daddy."[8]

But Sumner ultimately displayed as much moral stringency as his predecessor. In 1920 he had tried to prevent *Ulysses* from being published in America. In 1926, a year before he tried to close down Minskys', Sumner would argue that much American literature was pornographic. Indeed, beginning in the early twenties, Sumner sought to expand the power of NYSSV by tightening the organization's bonds with the law. In this way, he would ferret out vice and crime, which many Americans regarded not only as sins, but as barriers isolating citizens from the American Dream.

Unlike the Committee of Fourteen, whose membership was dominated by police officers and politicians, the NYSSV was composed of prominent citizens. But what the organizations shared was that they tracked down
"criminals" and, by taking this task upon themselves, implied that the police were ineffective. And yet under the law, no reform organization could
arrest burlesque theater operators—they could only bring them to the
police's attention.[9]

WHILE REFORM ORGANIZATIONS gathered strength, Jazz Age burlesque became a hangout for homosexuals—and a place where these gay men could
perform drag striptease. As burlesque theaters evolved from being sites
where comics and soubrettes performed to being "vice dens" where stripping and teasing happened, they became known as a meeting place for gay
prostitutes and their clients. The historian George Chauncey describes a
generation of drag performers arising in the Jazz Age, when gay men first
became distinguishable from straight men in public life. In general, this new
gay scene reflected the emerging bohemian culture and appeared most dramatically in the nightlife of Harlem, Greenwich Village, and Coney Island—
all neighborhoods where burlesque theaters stood.[10]

Jimmy Durante recounted watching both striptease and "pansy" acts
at a Coney Island nightclub in the late twenties.[11] In Jazz Age burlesque,
some men "passed" as female strippers and teasers, a fact that *Variety* reported in a blasé tone.[12] Indeed, even into the early 1920s, few Americans
expressed alarm at the presence of male cross-dressers, whom they considered to be comedians—artists of their own heft and ingenuity. Costumed
in hyperfeminine fashion, nineteenth-century female impersonators had
parodied showgirls like Loie Fuller and La Belle Otero in refined vaudeville, and no one questioned their "real-life" masculinity. Common wisdom about these female impersonators tended to contrast their onstage
femininity with their offstage masculinity, as if, once undressed, they simply reverted to their biological gender.[13]

But with the addition of strip and tease acts, some alarmed observers,
conflating performers' onstage and offstage identities, declared New York
to be in a "pansy craze." A new breed of female impersonators stripped and
teased on the burlesque and vaudeville stages. Two men pioneering this
flamboyant style of undressing and sexual display, the brash cross-dressing
team of Bert Savoy and Jay Brennan, inspired Mae West. But newspapers
described Savoy and Brennan as illicit, smutty, dirty, sexual, and openly
gay, as "fairies" or "pansies." Savoy "reeked of the corrosive cocktails of
the west fifties," Edmund Wilson commented.[14]

Such documentation of audience responses as exists about male strip
acts of the era suggests that they titillated and outraged in equal doses. As
usual, the theatrical venue played a role in determining whether female

impersonators' taking it off was perceived as witty or obscene. It was more acceptable for female impersonators to remove their clothes in drag parades, balls, and same-sex clubs in Harlem, the Bowery, and Greenwich Village than in mainstream nightclubs or on Broadway.[15]

The career of Barbette, a Jazz Age male stripper, demonstrates how American audiences recoiled from these performances on Broadway. Born Van Der Clyde in 1904, Barbette grew up in Texas and made his debut with the Alfarette Sisters, a female acrobatic act that played on the orpheum vaudeville circuit. He subsequently developed a solo act, "The Exquisite Barbette," and moved to Europe, where he performed in Paris and London, was photographed by Man Ray, and written about by Jean Cocteau. He even appeared in Luis Buñuel's film *Blood of a Poet*.

Barbette's popularity hinged on his glittering parody of a Jazz Age strip act. Like all *travestis*—boy-girl acts—he emphasized his sexuality by borrowing the other sex's trappings. Barbette entered the theater in classic music hall style. When the curtain rose, "she" stood in a spotlight, at the top of an enormous stairway, wearing a feathered headdress and a silver cape, with a train of silver lace. Mincing down the stairs and across the stage, Barbette dropped her headdress on the floor, one floating feather at a time, and finally settled on an oriental couch covered with a white bearskin rug. She did a little striptease to reveal her gymnast's unitard and pastel ballet slippers. Cocteau noted Barbette did "a real masterpiece of pantomime, summoning up in parody all the women he has ever studied, becoming himself the woman—so much so he eclipses the prettiest girls who have preceded and will follow him on the program." Janet Flanner described his ethereal drop as a *"chute d'ange."*[16]

Rising from the couch, naked except for a jeweled bra and G-string, Barbette walked over to a steel tightrope strung between two poles. Leaping onto the wire, to the strains of Wagner or Rimsky-Korsakov, she moved from pole to pole, staging a few girlish mishaps, shrieks, and gimmicks like reapplying her lipstick in the air. As a finale, she dropped the balancing pole she had been holding, leapt onto the stage, and tore off her wig to reveal a bony male acrobat's head. To Cocteau, Barbette was a magician making fluid gender's static qualities by appealing to both men and women.

> Imagine what a let-down it would be for some of us, if at the end of this unforgettable lie Barbette were simply to remove his wig. You will tell me that after the fifth curtain call . . . he does just that and this let down does take place. But watch his last *tour de force*: simply to rebecome a man, to run the wheel backwards, is not enough. The truth must be translated, if it is to convince us as forcibly as did the lie. That is why Barbette, the moment he has snatched off his wig, plays the part of the man. He rolls his shoulders, stretches, flexes his hands, swells his muscles, parodies a golfer's athletic walk. And after the fifteenth or so curtain call, he

gives a mischievous wink, shifts from foot to foot, mimes a bit of apology and does a shuffling little street urchin dance—all of it to erase the fabulous, dying swan impression left by the act.[17]

By "revealing" his gender onstage, by becoming "more feminine" than the biological woman, Barbette introduced a camp sensibility into striptease avant la lettre. But he did more than that. Able to shift effortlessly from female to male without embodying the "natural" state of either, he defined the newly articulated, visible homosexual identity. In Paris, this remained acceptable. But on Broadway, sartorial and erotic borrowings from the other sex become frightening when they suggested sexual pleasure defying static male and female symbols. When Barbette headlined in vaudeville at New York's Palace Theater, the show flopped.[18]

IF CROSS-DRESSERS heightened the burlesque in burlesque comedy by stressing opposing genders, African American performers contributed to the striptease's appearance through a heightened theatrical sensibility. Josephine Baker's 1925 appearance in the Revue Negre in Paris seems half striptease, half female-impersonation act. Wearing a G-string slung with bananas, Baker waddled onstage, her knees bent and spread apart, did a split, splayed her arms and legs as if she were a marionette, and shook and shimmied throughout her whole act. Janet Flanner, who would later praise Baker's "splendid thighs," describes her shimmying as full of flamboyance, shine, and vitality, lacking femininity and undressed.

> She made her entry entirely nude except for a pink flamingo feather between her limbs; she was being carried upside down and doing the split on the shoulder of a black giant. Midstage, he paused, and with his long fingers holding her basket-wise around the waist, swung her in a slow cartwheel to the stage floor, where she stood like his magnificent discarded burden, in an instant of complete silence.[19]

In the black floorshows, revues, and nightclubs of Harlem, male and female performers performed in burlesque shows parodying and celebrating sex with lightning-quick shimmies. *Variety* reports that Stringbean tossed off "violent" pelvic spasms. At Connie's Inn, one of the Harlem nightclubs on Lenox Avenue, Earl Tucker sent up female glamour by shimmying to Duke Ellington's "East St. Louis Toodle-OO." He sashayed onstage in a loose white silk blouse with large puffed sleeves, tight black pants with bellbottoms, and a sequined girdle with a sparkling buckle in the center from which hung a large tassel. He did a belly roll and his shirt fluttered and quivered so fast that, according to dancer Henry Frankel, "that man moved every muscle in his body, and he seemed to move every one of them at the same time."[20]

In the early days of the Columbia circuit, white male performers doing strip and tease acts rarely got to writhe in a way that was erotic and funny. In a popular male undressing number, the "auction" number, a comic auctioned off one item of clothing after another until he stood naked and shivering onstage. But after 1925, on burlesque's raunchier Mutual circuit, white female strippers and teasers borrowed from black and gay style to send up conventions of sexual identity. Gladys Clark started out as a "man," wearing a tuxedo, waistcoat, and top hat, and after caning the chorus girls ripped off her tuxedo, button by button, revealing a skimpy chorus girl costume. Her sharply articulated suit suggested male nudity underneath until she "came out," as it were, to display her "true" identity.[21]

The early twenties' first teaser, Cleveland's Carrie Finnell, used speed to send up sex in a very different way. Finnell toured with her own troupe, a Jazz Age version of the British Blondes named Carrie Finnell and Her Red-Headed Blondes. Sometime after 1926, Finnell invented a second signature tease act: the comic "tassel twirling" that she did with what she called her "educated bosom."[22] Finnell tassel-twirled to "Shave and a Haircut, Two Bits" and, apparently having developed her pectoral muscles, was able to make tassels attached with spirit gum to her nipples twirl in time to the music. *Variety* called this "acrobatic heaving," and Ann Corio likened them to a propeller revving up on a World War I plane.

> Faster and faster it [the first tassel] would spin while its fellow tassel lay limp and neglected on the other bosom. Then the other tassel would come to life. It would start spinning slowly, while the first tassel was at full speed. Carrie looked like a twin engine bomber. She would walk across the stage with the tassels swirling in front of her and applause would ring out.[23]

Tassel twirling became Finnell's trademark, and she took a modern moniker reminiscent of the machine age—"the Remote Control Girl"—to match. Over the years, she added other ordinary songs to her repertoire, such as "Pop Goes My Heart." When she got to the refrain, she would "bosom pop," or "pop" her breast out of her bodice. In burlesque lingo, this was known as a "bust in the eye."[24] Like certain female vaudeville performers, particularly Sophie Tucker, Finnell allowed Americans to laugh at sex even as sexual style in the theater grew more savage. Critics, praising Tucker for singing the blues because she was physically too heavy to conform to the ideal of a desirable woman, conferred upon her a modicum of respectability; likewise, many critics praised Finnell for her comic stunts, as though making fun of herself was the main event and alluring the afterthought.[25]

On Broadway, dance styles continued to become more sensual. The evocatively named Black Bottom, for example, announced not only that women moved with pleasure, but that they would continue to do so. The

Black Bottom gave the female dancer a chance to go crazy, shimmying, slapping her buttocks, and slinging her shawl around her legs and body. Reformers accepted the dance when the petite, vivacious Ann Pennington performed a refined version for white audiences on Broadway in 1926. And they accepted the shimmy when Ethel Waters did it in rathskellers and theaters in Harlem. "I sure knew how to roll and quiver, and my hips would become whirling dervishes. It was those completely mobile hips, not my voice, that won me friends," Waters remembered.[26]

By contrast, Mae West attracted police attention that same year when her shimmy resembled a prostitute's strut a little too closely in her play *Sex*, a "comedy-drama" about the underworld.[27] Unlike many similar plays on Broadway that year, *Sex* was set in Connecticut, not the tropics. And it lacked a tragic finale for the lead character, the prostitute Margey Lamont, played by West herself. But of all the things West did to outrage, the most outrageous was her encore shimmy to W. C. Handy's "St. Louis Blues." The *New York Daily Mirror* observed that West, who herself had toured in Mutual circuit burlesque from 1922 to 1925, "seems to enjoy undressing."[28] Zora Neale Hurston described West's moves as having more "flavor of the turpentine quarters" than of the white bawdy house.[29]

Mae West's shimmy in *Sex* played an important role in transforming strip and tease acts into "striptease." For one, she linked burlesque moves with African American culture. Also, the strip act had already begun to spread into the mainstream as female burlesque performers' aggressive sexuality appeared more widely in the musical and on-screen. But it was in part under the influence of West's parodic dance style and her commitment to singing the blues on Broadway that modern striptease emerged in burlesque.

THE THEATER BOOM of the late Jazz Age helped accelerate the process. The theater historian Mary Henderson estimated that in 1926, 750,000 people moved through Times Square theaters and that the following year, there were 257 Broadway shows and 71 theaters in operation—more than ever before or since.[30] Americans were searching for more vibrant, modern amusements, and burlesque fell into the grip of a new awareness of female sexual expressiveness, which itself reflected a middle-class theater-going public's decadent fashion and taste.

On the languishing Columbia circuit, theater owners competing with stock burlesque and Broadway bombarded their audience with shimmies, bumps and grinds, and strips and teases. In the early Jazz Age, capitalizing on the craze for black performers, the Columbia circuit had competed by producing mixed revues like *Jimmie Cooper's Black and White Revue*, in which Octavia Summler, "the Tiger Lady from Harlem," in a tiger-skin costume, sang a blues number backed by eight black dancers.[31] By 1927, though, both the Columbia circuit and the Mutual circuit were using few black performers. Some burlesque shows alternated black and white companies. But the combination of undressed white women and black performers was mostly considered a novelty and failed to survive the end of the Columbia circuit. Indeed, the final blow to the old-fashioned circuit came that year, when Izzy Herk bought the flagship Columbia Theater in New York and forced the cleaner Columbia to merge with his own Mutual circuit.[32]

Two years later, Mutual was able to offer performers forty-four weeks of straight employment. Until its demise in 1931, Mutual remained the "girl" circuit, first devoted to "a frenzy of congregate cooching" and later to strip-tease itself.[33] Once Mutual demolished Columbia, however, critics began to

Ann Corio, headliner of the Mutual circuit burlesque show *Girls in Blue*, c. 1929.

dwell more intently on the performers' infelicitous appearance. Satirizing Ziegfeld's slogan about glorifying the American girl, *Variety* dismissed the Mutual circuit as glorifying "the shovel and the American cow."[34]

BILLY MINSKY RESPONDED to Mutual's rise in influence as quickly as he could. As late as the summer of 1925, Minsky had still relied on Beef Trust–style female performers such as Carrie Finnell. Edmund Wilson noted in the *New Republic* in July that this performer was a far cry from the "slim legs and shallow breasts the modern American taste for which has been so successfully exploited by Ziegfeld and the other uptown producers."[35]

A year later, audiences clamoring to see a more svelte physique onstage had forced Minsky to hire women closer to Ziegfeld's ideal. Some scholars have observed that female performers on Broadway at the end of the twenties not only needed more boyish figures than their prewar counterparts, they needed, for the first time, to be physically stunning. Indeed, the number of complaints in the theatrical press about female burlesque performers' weight escalated as the decade wore on. This points to a sea change in what women could look like in burlesque, in how they fit into male fantasies, and how newspapers could talk about them in public. Some of these reviews reveal how a new ageism, brought on by the Jazz Age youth craze, separated strippers and teasers from other "legitimate" female performers such as Ziegfeld's showgirls.[36]

The National Winter Garden, where Edmund Wilson reported hearing someone say that he came because he liked hearing "sincere dubble entendres," still advertised "plenty of short girls, tall girls, fat girls." But many *Variety* and *Billboard* reviews of burlesque shows in the late twenties express a heightened level of revulsion toward such physical variety. One review condemned "bare legs, especially when they develop flabby-fleshed flanks, varicose veins, liver spots and hair," and welcomed "the wearing of tights and hose that camouflage the symbols of advancing years, thereby carrying out the illusion of youth."[37] *Variety* criticized Anna Toebe as "not waxing petite."[38] Carrie Finnell, the paper complained, should lose weight or look for another profession: "No woman of her lines can coquet, even in United Burlesque."[39]

The negative critical response to early strippers and teasers illustrated the limited and rising idea that women should look smooth and flawless, promulgated by popular theater and myths of the time. The Broadway idea—that women were expected to look like boys or like shadings of an androgynous projection of male fantasy—trickled down to burlesque. The stripper, comedienne, and manager Kitty Madison quit striptease at age thirty because she felt "too old." As she put it, "Why in show business you're an old hag already. . . . Do you want them to say, 'look at that old hag'? Competing with those girls, are you crazy?"[40]

BILLY MINSKY WANTED to compete. Shortly after Edmund Wilson wrote his first review of the National Winter Garden in 1925, Billy stepped up his efforts. He made some changes in personnel, notably hiring Mildred Cozzier, "the Beale Street Mama," a blues singer and teaser from the mutual circuit. He hired vaudeville comics and pugilists. He also put into place an array of other innovations, which ultimately cemented the National Winter Garden and burlesque in the hearts of the "high lowbrows." He redecorated in an "oriental" color scheme and put life-sized pictures of the principals in the lobby. He took a page from cabaret and Broadway by encouraging the principals to step off the runway, sit in the audience, and flirtatiously applaud their colleagues.[41]

Billy's most important innovation, though, put the strippers and teasers center stage. He was the first to pay women two dollars extra weekly for the "take-off," as *Variety* sometimes called the breast flash. Billy gave these performers thirty-five dollars a week, which was unheard of at that time, a fact he explained by saying that he recruited them from a professional dancing school. Moreover, to make up for the high salaries, he charged audiences $2.20, which was still about $2 more than tickets at many other burlesque theaters.[42]

Billy also made the female performer central by changing her position in the burlesque show lineup. Before World War I, the soubrette or prima donna had appeared anywhere on the bill. She could get lost in a sea of comics and straight men, skits and scenes. Billy reckoned that placing her either directly before the act 1 finale or directly before the act 2 finale could work to make the audience anticipate her.[43] Also, the pint-size Barnum started the "warm up," or advertising process, long before the audience ever got into the theater. To convince the intelligentsia that Minskys' was the place to be, Billy's brother Mort invited the faculty from New York University, which he briefly attended. Playing up the amateur quality of his girls, Billy staged "fun" promotional contests: shimmy contests, Charleston contests, and living-picture contests. "Curls Mason for Queen" ran an advertisement for the stripper who styled her curls like Mary Pickford's. On another evening, the girls themselves would vote for the best shimmyer. An advertisement teased by printing the first line of choreographer Maisie Harris's "campaign speech"—"Up with Maisie, down with Prohibition and off with union suits!!"[44]

Courting favor at the daily tabloids, Billy gave journalists Robert Garland and Walter Winchell lifetime passes to all Minsky theaters. He also sent hundreds of scented notes to the Princeton, Harvard, Yale, and Tennis and Racquet clubs with suggestive messages printed on them, like "When will I see you honey? Same time same place—corner of Houston Street and Christie. Your sweetie Madame Lazonga." Billy pasted posters on the subway that provocatively stated, "*She* is dancing today."[45]

These gimmicks gave the National Winter Garden a sporty quality and helped convince the intelligentsia that the strippers were primitives— not low-class whores. Meanwhile, Billy Minsky and his family continued to expand their empire. In June 1926 the Minskys bought the Fulton Theater in Brooklyn. They installed "the latest" in novelties and scenic devices, including a vertical running board and phosphorescent lighting.[46]

BY THE END OF THE SUMMER, Billy's strategies had attracted tabloids' attention. Both Robert Garland—the drama critic for the *Herald Tribune*—and Walter Winchell, the powerful columnist for the *Daily Mirror*, became enthusiastic promoters. In column after column, Winchell sang the National Winter Garden's praises, and Garland sent a telegram congratulating the brothers on their success. What *Billboard* called a "classic clientele"—rich New Yorkers from uptown—began to frequent the theater: at the matinees, a group of NYU faculty, doing what became known as "the Minsky Sneak," mingled with salesmen, Wall Streeters, and debutantes.[47]

The "new" clientele initially convinced some anti-vice reformers that the National Winter Garden had cleaned up its act. Committee of Fourteen vice investigator Harry Kahan visited the theater and tried to solicit a "soubrette" undercover. To his great surprise, he was rebuffed.[48] But some modernists bemoaned the National Winter Garden cleanup. George Jean Nathan wrote that burlesque in general lacked its old vital punch. Edmund Wilson complained that the theater, having been "subjected to a renovation" that included thinner women, new costumes, and "more elegant" sets, lost its authenticity. "The poets, the artists, and the smart magazines" were making the National Winter Garden fashionable.[49]

On September 4, the theater's season opening, the New York literati, including members of the Algonquin Round Table, converged on Second Avenue in formal dress for the first time. A line of expensive limousines stretched down the block outside the theater, and theatergoers streamed from the National Winter Garden to Manny Wolf's, a well-known Yiddish speakeasy of the day.[50]

A list of theatrical, publishing, and Hollywood luminaries who went to Minsky's includes Hart Crane, Mary Pickford, Chaliapin, Norman Bel Geddes, Mark Hellinger, Brooks Atkinson, Irvein Cobb, Condé Nast, Frank Crowninshield, John Erskine, John Dos Passos, Reginald Marsh, Robert Benchley, and Otto Kahn. By the end of that year, the trade papers were swooning. "We have never seen choristers as young . . . as we did at the Minskys'," *Variety* proclaimed.[51]

Wilson notwithstanding, creative artists and writers continued to flock there. And although the obsession with the prurient was unique to neither burlesque nor New York, Minsky strippers and teasers represented to these artists and writers a unique mix of rawness and redemption. Male modernists, at least, believed that burlesque comedy, strip, and tease acts might liberate them from the tyranny of melodramatic theatrical formulas onstage and in the boudoir. Uptown, much legitimate theater—dramatic plays—grappled seriously and boringly with issues like love. Many of the moderns, however, saw burlesque, and particularly striptease, as redolent with the excitement, as well as the limitations, of sex. Perhaps they took to heart D. H. Lawrence's suggestion that American literature strip off "the idealistic clothes" and see the "dusky body" underneath.[52]

Others continued to see the allure both as an appeal to their masculinity and as a chance to ally themselves against the tyrants of anti-vice reform. E. E. Cummings recalled that the National Winter Garden and the Old Howard of this era proposed a "human, masculine" aura and also wrote about burlesque as a kind of liberation.[53] In *Him*, a Jazz Age riff on Strindberg's *Dream Play*, the poet satirizes both the Old Howard and John Sumner, who is "John Rutter," "president for the contraception of vice" who wears "tortoiseshell glasses" and tries to stop the show. In an essay published in *The Dial*, Cummings also praised burlesque's "primitivism" and the "excessively mobile" shimmy of the Minsky cootch dancer Cleo, who, as she finished, exclaimed, as if congratulating herself: "Burn my clothes! I'm in heaven!"[54]

Gaston Lachaise used a burlesque teaser as a model for his monumental female sculptures, and Henry Miller paid homage to Cleo, whose real name was Vivian Clio. Miller liked the fact that Cleo stared solemnly back at the audience and in the last moments of her act ground her hips against the curtain at the stage's edge. But Miller too admired more than just Cleo's stare. As he describes it in his essay "Burlesk," the gritty and at times "grotesque" National Winter Garden was more authentic than and therefore preferable to the artificial fare uptown. "Moving toward the National Winter Garden in a yellow taxi . . . poverty walking about in fur coats. Turkish baths. Russian baths, sitz baths . . . baths, and no cleanliness."[55] In the twenties, Miller considered writing two essays on the National Winter Garden for the *Menorah Journal*, an important Jewish journal of the era, and although the essays never appeared, a decade later, in a letter from Paris to his longtime friend, the artist Emil Schnellock, he would write of returning to New York to visit the theater because he thought it would "renew" him.[56]

As for Edmund Wilson, though he now found the National Winter Garden too polished, he continued to view burlesque as revealing the woman's power in the modern relationship between the sexes. He referred to the burlesque shake as "the orgasm dance," and in an essay on the Olympic Theater on East Fourteenth Street, he depicts teasers toying with the patrons in a hushed and brutal courtship ritual.[57]

In one of the numbers the girls come out with fishing rods and dangle pretzels under the noses of the spectators; the leading ladies have lemons. The men do not at first reach for them; they remain completely stolid. Then, suddenly when the lures have been played for some minutes, a few begin to grab at the pretzels, like frogs who have finally decided to strike at a piece of red flannel or like cats [that have] simulat[ed] apathy while watching a cork on a string. . . . [T]hey have come for the gratification that they hope to derive from these dances, but this vision of erotic ecstasy, when they see it unveiled before them—though they watch it with fascination, it renders them mute. . . . [G]littering and thick lashed seductresses . . . stand on a level with the audience [and] address them with so personal a heartiness . . . [T]hey have come to the theater, you realize, in order to have their dreams made objective, and they sit there each alone with his dream. . . . [T]heir decorum, is not undermined by this brazenly sexual exhibition; on the contrary, it makes them solemn.[58]

The solemnity added to the glitter entranced Wilson, and he returned to burlesque as both a cultural diversion and a fictional device to reveal class difference. In Wilson's 1920s novel *The Higher Jazz*, the composer Fritz Dietrich drags his girlfriend and another couple to the National Winter Garden.

Caroline I could see, didn't like it when we got out in the winter mud and were confronted by the cheap and sordid entrance. She had never been in this part of town. . . . I knew that all the men we saw were the kind she would describe as "queer-looking," and in the theater itself, where the show was already on, there seemed to be nothing but men. The rest of us were tight enough to be indifferent to, even perhaps to rather enjoy, the attention we attracted as we got to our seats, the ladies in their evening cloaks; but Caroline was a little scared and chilled, and I couldn't help resenting it, because going with a lady to a burlesque show is something you both have to be brazen and superior about or you can't carry it off at all.[59]

Other writers imagined the National Winter Garden less as a place for revealing how upper-class women behaved in difficult situations than for observing how the strippers and teasers glimmered. In "National Winter Garden," a section of *The Bridge*, his fantastic epic poem about New York, Hart Crane names the Minskys' as the honorific burlesque theater. Crane's description lends the strippers a spiritual aura, but it also suggests that they are bereft of romance and pinioned by morose imagery.[60]

Outspoken buttocks in pink beads
Invite the necessary cloudy clinch
Of bandy eyes . . . no extra mufflings here:
The world's one flagrant, sweating cinch

And while legs awaken salads in the brain
Lead to ecstatic nights of passion elsewhere as
You pick your blonde out neatly through the smoke.
Always you wait for someone else though, always
(Then rush the nearest exit through the smoke.)

We wait that writhing pool, her pearls collapsed
All but her belly buried in the floor;
And the lewd trounce of a final muted beat!
We flee her spasm through a fleshless door.
Yet to the empty trapeze of your flesh
O Magdalene, each comes back to die alone
Then you, the burlesque of our lust—and faith,
Lug us back lifeward—bone by infant bone. [61]

WHILE MODERNISTS were hoping strip and tease acts would remove them from the confines of Victorian mores, anti-vice reformers and the police became increasingly antagonistic toward the theater in general. In 1925, New York district attorney Joab Banton had met with the Boston police censor to gather new ideas about curtailing prurient theater. Although Banton ultimately found Boston's strategies too draconian for sophisticated New York, his journey to the place where the phrase "Banned in Boston" defined the city suggested the new aggressive approach toward shutting down "obscene" theater.[62]

The increase in attention to the theater was driven in part by the 1925–26 Broadway season. An unusually large number of plays treated sexual subjects: The French writer Edouard Bourdet's *The Captive*, which starred the glamorous Helen Menken, told of a lesbian love affair; *The Shanghai Gesture* narrated the travails of Mother Goddam, a corrupt Chinese madame; *Lulu Belle* presented the story of a mulatto hooker who cruelly seduces everyone she meets. Finally, Mae West's incendiary play *Sex* opened in April 1926 to media sensation.[63]

Sex in the theater did not only erupt onstage or on Broadway. A well-publicized sex scandal involving prominent members of the theater community had already occurred in February, when Earl Carroll staged his famous "champagne bath" party. According to reports, chorus girl Joyce Hawley ended up naked in a bathtub full of champagne. By June, a burlesque performer "played" Joyce Hawley on 125th Street. But the police released her when she claimed that, unlike Hawley, she had worn a "silky" union suit while "bathing."[64]

The tension between reformers and burlesque theater owners worsened. In January 1927, a couple of months after the National Winter Garden season premiere, West's second play, *The Drag*, premiered at Poli's, a stock burlesque house in Bridgeport, Connecticut. *The Drag*, about a young woman married to a gay man, sent up female eroticism and presented what was, for the time, a sympathetic view of gay men. It featured a drag ball with male performers doing campy oriental dances. West hoped to find a theater for the play in New York.[65]

The 1926–27 season's offerings were as prurient as those of the previous year. But this time, reformers acted. One reason the reformers had held back at all was then Mayor Jimmy Walker, the author of "Will You Love Me in September as You Do in May" and several other musical flops. Walker was hardly a friend of reformers. He once quipped, "A reformer is a guy who rides through a sewer in a glass-bottomed boat." While the mayor was on a tryst with his girlfriend in Florida, the reformers and the district attorney set about getting the police to stage raids on a number of the offending Broadway revues for nudity, as well as on Eugene O'Neill's *Desire Under the Elms* for its use of "hell" and "damn."[66]

On February 10, New York police chief Joseph V. McKee, a devout Catholic whose nickname was "Holy Joe," raided *The Captive, Sex,* and *The Virgin Man.* A trial over *Sex* began. It was widely understood that both raids and trial came about because of the threat of the *Drag*'s opening on Broadway.[67] But vice-society reformers were not indifferent to the Minskys. They raided the National Winter Garden on February 26, accusing twelve performers—including Cleo—of giving indecent performances. While the police ushered the performers into patrol cars outside the theater, Abe Minsky rushed outside and offered to send them in taxicabs. But the police refused to allow it.[68]

IN NEW YORK, at this moment, reformers' main tool against theater was the state anti-obscenity statute, Section 1140a of the penal code, which stated: "Any person who as owner, manager, or agent, or in any other capacity, prepares, advertises, gives, directs, presents or participates in any obscene, indecent, immoral, impure scene, tableau, incident, part or portion of any drama, play, exhibition, show, or entertainment, which would tend to the corruption of the morals of youth or others . . . shall be guilty of a misdemeanor."[69] The statute, however, lacked teeth. Earlier in the decade, reformers had tried to coax theater producers to form their own censorship committee. But this strategy failed.

Thus in March 1927, reformers enlisted the governor of New York, Al Smith, to pass the Wales Padlock Bill, which would allow the district attorney to padlock a theater if it produced an "indecent" production featuring "sex degeneracy" or "sex perversion." The bill also would allow the DA to prosecute everyone associated with such a production and allowed him to close that theater for up to one year. Essentially, the bill treated theater as an offshoot of the underworld. As critics would point out in the following decade, the bill was technically unconstitutional, because the district attorney was neither obligated to prove his case in court nor forced to justify to anyone why he considered the shut-down play objectionable.[70]

To the New York theater community's surprise, Al Smith, who entertained presidential aspirations, signed the Wales Padlock Bill into law late that month. City officials promptly shut down *The Virgin Man* as well as Tex Guinan's, the eponymous illegal nightclub owned by the female impresario. Vice-society reformers defended themselves against charges of censorship by claiming that they were protecting audiences from unscrupulous producers. In an editorial in *Theatre Magazine*, John Sumner wrote, "During the past five years, seemingly under the impression that every resident or visitor was itching to spend much good money for an evening of insane or salacious stage display, theatre buildings . . . have been rushed to completion."[71]

The Padlock Law devastated burlesque. In the months following its passage, at least four burlesque theaters closed in New York and others "toned down." The burlesque industry lost $125,000 by June. In what *Variety* called a "follow the leader effect," police and anti-vice reform organizations across the country conspired to get burlesque out of their cities by using the law. Milwaukee would even marshal it to try to close a theatrical hotel where burlesque performers "clad only in teddies . . . hosted parties that lasted from midnight til dawn."[72]

Yet as Morris Ernst, one of the founders of the American Civil Liberties Union, noted, vice-society reformers and elected city officials quickly discovered that enforcing the law was difficult. Bringing a burlesque show to trial in front of a jury—as required by the law—made reformers look like prudes since public opinion generally ran against reformers in the Jazz Age. Moreover, conviction was difficult and sometimes the police who made the arrests failed to show up. Most of the theaters reopened the following season.[73]

Also, to vice-society reformers' dismay, the publicity from these trials not only attracted media attention, it increased burlesque ticket sales. At the obscenity hearing for the National Winter Garden cast held in March 1927, Lady Astor, the lawyer Clarice Barright, and the socialite Mrs. Charles Dana Gibson sat in the front row. Mrs. Gibson left shortly after the proceedings began. Still, there was hardly an empty seat in the courtroom, even though the only crime that the DA could discover was that Abe smoked a cigar in the theater, thus violating fire laws. The case against the National Winter Garden dragged on for months. On June 1, the judge dismissed it for lack of evidence. The Minskys never even testified.[74]

WHILE THE RASH of vice-society reform activity increased stripping and teasing's illicit allure and widened its audience, the advent of the talkies changed the way the acts looked and sounded. After 1927, with the appearance of *The Jazz Singer*, the first talkie, women increasingly began to sing-speak while performing. Their acts also continued to use ragtime, blues, and jazz, and incorporated the African American style of singing known as coon shouting, as well as the street slang beginning to be used by certain female movie stars. These vocals rejected posh, midlantic vowels and celebrated Brooklynese and midwestern and southern patois. Stripping and teasing acts elevated the beating of drums and the haunting cacophony of saxophones. It was, as much as any modern music, twentieth-century *bruit*. When critics describe the ragtag voice of striptease, they use the same snobbish tone with which they dismissed jazz.[75]

> The musicians creep from beneath the stage . . . drums roll. Instruments clear their throats with experimental melodies. The longhaired director swings his violin to his chin. The overture bangs out. The cymbals clash a brazen welcome. The conductor fiddles valiantly. The curtain rolls up and twenty chorus girls prance uncertainly about the stage singing "We are the chicks from gay Paree!"[76]

The blues provided both the stripper and the teaser with an assertive voice. That development seemed natural in a decade in which Ethel Waters and Bessie Smith sang domestic sex arias like "Kitchen Man" and "Handyman"—numbers speaking frankly about female desire. Played while white performers stripped, the blues increased strip and tease acts' risqué quality. In one such song, the stripper—or sometimes several strippers—strolled onstage carrying a pillow and sang a few innocent, sweet lyrics recalling childhood: "Would you like to lay upon my pillow? Would you care to, would you dare to? Would you keep a secret?"

After this coy beginning, the tempo revved into double time. The stripper winked, crooked her fingers, and did a hootchy cootch. She threw away the pillow. And sometimes, in a variation on this number, she ripped off her dress and tossed it into the wings, as if to throw away the old Victorian shackles constraining her sexuality. In this version, she placed the pillow in front of her G-string and, bumping and grinding, turned going to sleep into foreplay. Thus sending up the nineteenth century, while acknowledging the twentieth's erotic superiority with song and gesture, she sang-shouted before the blackout: "Would you like to lay your head upon my—er—pillow?"[77]

Blues numbers allowed strippers to invoke, freely allude to, and play with the rawest possible ideas about sex, but from a female perspective. "Somebody Sneakin' in When You Been Sneakin' Out," one stripper at the Olympic sang.[78] Another popular number strippers used to accompany their take-offs, "Ride, Jockey, Ride," when sung by male Memphis blues greats, alluded to their own sexual prowess. Blues women also made this number popular and when strippers adopted it, they dared men in the audience to approach them:

> If you want to be my jockey,
> Then get by my side,
> Stick your whip in my socket,
> And let 'er ride.[79]

THERE IS ONE performer remembered for putting together the prolonged teasing with the onstage disrobing that was stripping: Hinda Wassau. Indeed, the arrival of the word "striptease" occurred after Wassau burst onto the scene. Like the birth of stripping and teasing, the birth of striptease takes place not in New York, but in the Midwest. Also, this event happened accidentally, when Wassau, née Hinda Warshaw, aka the "Blonde Bombshell," entered a shimmy contest at one of Chicago's burlesque theaters.[80]

Born in Milwaukee around the turn of the century, Wassau had by the spring of 1927 already acquired a reputation and a police report. Arrested a year earlier for indecency at the Empress Theater, Wassau left Milwaukee before she could stand trial. She performed as a headliner on the mutual circuit show Kitty Madison's *Jazztime Review*. It's entirely possible that Wassau did the first striptease in Chicago at this time, even though no newspaper heralds her innovation.[81]

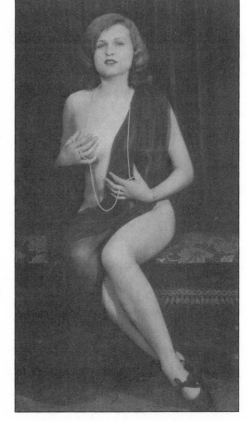

Wassau's appearance in Chicago—even if apocryphal—is significant, for it came about at the same time that jazz and blues musicians began fleeing New Orleans and the South after Crescent City shut down its vice district in 1917. Between 1925 and 1929, the City with Big Shoulders was home to a healthy jazz scene alongside of a burlesque industry rivaling—some say surpassing—that of New York. According to French jazz critic Hugues

Hinda Wassau, the "Blonde Bombshell," headliner of the Hindu Belles, Mutual Burlesque Troupe, c. 1929. Author's personal collection.

Panassié, "brilliant" Chicago jazz featured Louis Armstrong cornets, clari-
nets, saxophones, strength, subtlety, melody, and intensity.[82]

You could say the same about Chicago striptease. Strip acts in Chicago focused on teasing instead of cootch dancing, although according to
*Variety*, the teasing was just as dangerous.[83] In 1928 the Chicago burlesque
scene employed five hundred people, and new burlesque theaters seemed
to open every day. Chicago offered its citizens "the Midnight Shambles," a
wild party of stripping and teasing exploding at midnight in different theaters all throughout the city.[84] By 1925 the two South Loop burlesque
theaters named in the story of Wassau's take-off act—the State-Congress
and the Haymarket—had acquired nefarious reputations. Of the two, the
State-Congress was slightly more upscale. Owned by former circus men
Arthur Clamage and Warren B. Irons, the Haymarket stood at the corner
of Madison and Halsted streets. Its motto was "Shake it up" and its audience was working-class men. "The main qualification for a job in this house
. . . seems to be an ability to perform with the hips," *Variety* wrote.[85]

According to most versions of the story, Wassau's striptease occurred
by accident. Wassau wore a regular chorus girl costume on top of a short,
beaded, fringed dress. When it was her turn to exit, remove the regular

chorus costume, and reappear in her
undercostume, the chorus costume
got caught on a clasp backstage. The
music was playing and Wassau ran
onstage with the chorus costume
half on and half off. At her number's
climax, it came loose and so she removed it. The crowd—of course—
went wild. When Wassau returned
backstage after her encores, the stage
manager, worried that she would attract the vice squad, yelled at her.

In her memoir, Ann Corio claims
that Wassau's strip got her promoted
to headliner and then signed by Tex
Guinan, the most powerful female
speakeasy owner on the New York
nightclub scene. Although there are
no records documenting the rela-

Hinda Wassau, with reindeer,
Washington, D.C., c. 1947. The Kinsey
Institute for Research in Sex, Gender, and
Reproduction.

tionship between the two women, in December 1928 both were in New York: Wassau and her burlesque troupe the Hindu Belles arrived in the city to play the Columbia Theater; Tex opened Club Intime, a new speakeasy in the basement of a hotel on West Fifty-fourth Street. By April, though, Club Intime had shut its doors.[86]

Even if Wassau and Guinan never crossed paths, by 1928 Wassau had become the first "upscale" striptease success. The Shuberts asked her to be in *Artists and Models*. She resurfaced with the Hindu Belles in August and began a yearlong tour on the Mutual circuit. Toledo adored her. When Wassau played in New York, though, *Variety* ridiculed her "hifalutin'" style. "It was a laugh to see blondine Polack trying to give them that oriental stuff," Sime Silverman, the lead critic, wrote.[87]

"That oriental stuff," in this case, was an American version of ballet. After her Chicago debut, Wassau studied with the Viennese-born choreographer and ballerina Albertina Rasch, who had choreographed many Ziegfeld Follies shows and other musicals and films. In 1923, Rasch had founded a dance studio in New York to teach the combination of ballet and precision dancing for she became famous.[88] From Rasch, Wassau developed the elegance she displayed in the early thirties.

In one number from this era, Wassau, with her shining gold hair and white skin, walked onstage wearing a white-fringed negligee. Later, she changed to a transparent, floor-length black or white gown. She swayed her hips back and forth. She giggled. She walked around, stood still, looked out at the audience. And giggled. She said, "It's naughty—but oh gee, I like it," while the orchestra played the Mamie Harris song "Sweet Sue."

> Every star above, baby,
> Knows the one I love:
> Sweet Sue—just you!
> And the moon on high, baby,
> Knows the reason why:
> Sweet Sue—is you!

Wassau sometimes did a kind of anti-striptease. For the entire time she was onstage—about eight minutes—she never revealed more than her head, hands, and feet, although she occasionally flashed her ankle. When she sang, she lisped in singsong baby talk and sometimes paused to shriek, "My name is Hinda Wassau, now don't you think me nice?"[89] During this era, Wassau developed other versions of her babydoll act. In 1930 she whirled across the stage to the Harry Akst, Sam Lewis, and Joe Young Tin Pan Alley song "Dinah," which Ethel Waters had turned into a blues number in Harlem nightclubs in the mid-twenties.

Dinah
Is there anyone finah in the state of Carolina?
If there is, and you know 'er,
Show her to me.

Akst, Lewis, and Young originally wrote the song to introduce white
New Yorkers to the Black Bottom. But instead of shaking her hips as that
dance required, Wassau glided across the stage. At the refrain, she threw her
gown over her shoulders and let it hang from her back like a cape, revealing
her naked body covered only by a fig leaf. Indeed, Wassau did not let her
modern dance training prevent her from doing scorching take-offs. According to Irving Zeidman, by the late thirties, under the tutelage of her husband, burlesque comic and onetime baseball producer Rube Bernstein,
Wassau was the first women to run her hands over her body while stripping.[90] In the fall of 1931, when Wassau headlined at the Star and Garter in
Chicago, *Variety* described her number as a "modernist" sex act.

> Hinda Wassau hasn't a knock out set of measurements. She's flat in the
> wrong places. But she has something the other teasers haven't. She gets
> dramatic, where others are posers and flesh-disclosers. Other strippers
> are coy and make a great fuss over tossing the brassier and then trip
> mincingly into the wings. Hinda Wassau wears more clothes than the
> average stripper. Her forte isn't stripping. It's sex showmanship. She
> makes only one strip and that's where she ditches the brassiere early in
> the works. But even then she works with her back or her side to the
> audience. At no time do the boys get as much flesh from Wassau as they
> do from others. But one thing they do get from Wassau is action, hot
> action. She gives a cootch, but dressed in modern, rhapsody-in-blue wah
> wah style. She pants, darts, spasmodically, lets her hands glide over her
> body; she exerts herself full of sex movement.[91]

Wassau's story—like the earlier origins myths about stripping and teasing—reveals something essential about striptease's history. For one, the
romantic idea that striptease arose accidentally, which allows it to be an
eternally feminine, artless, natural act, continued to be popular. The woman
is simply dancing and she seizes the moment, she becomes erotic through
her dance. Also, the idea that striptease was "made" by an appreciative
audience suggests that it comes out of the male imagination. Then too, it
seems that most audiences prefer to think of the stripper taking off her
clothes in a mad rush, out of impulse, as if she had no control over it.
      It was in a slightly less spontaneous fashion that the word striptease
emerged. According to one of the most appealing legends about the word's
origins, Mike Goldreyer and the improbably named George Alabama
Florida, two of Billy Minsky's front men, concocted it in 1931.[92] The words
strip and teaser first appeared together in print at the end of 1928 when

*Billboard* described Mae Brown: "Sex seductive stripteaser stops the show."[93] Plain old "teasing" hinted at the Jazz Age woman's sudden sexual availability but also reminded the object of that teasing that Victorian limits were at hand. "Sex teasing," on the other hand, evoked scarier emotions, as it contained fantastical desires and lurid fears.[94]

Striptease presented a threatening figure—the epitome of the modern, take-charge New Woman of the Jazz Age. This woman commanded her own sexuality. At a time when women were cutting their hair and wearing makeup in greater numbers than ever before, *Billboard* and *Variety* increasingly remarked on the prevalence of strippers with "marcelled" or bobbed hairdos as a shorthand way of reporting on their aggressive sexual display.[95] By the end of the twenties, many Mutual circuit strippers were doing as much as they could to be "sex seductive": some were even taking off their bras onstage. Gladys Clark "stripped to a strap," *Variety* wrote. "When Miss Clark is showing she's just showing, walking around like a queen wondering if the tub is full."[96]

# A Pretty Girl Is Like a Melody, Sort Of

### Alice Blue Gown

I once had a gown it was almost new,
Oh the daintiest thing, it was sweet Alice blue
With little forget me nots
Placed here and there. When I had it on, I walked on air.
And it wore and wore and it wore
Till it went and it wasn't no more

The little silkworms that made silk for that gown,
Just made that silk and then crawled in the ground,
for there never was anything
Like it before
And I don't dare to hope there will be any more
But it's gone 'cause it just had to be
Still it wears in my memory.

—Harry Tierney, *Irene*

The American actress Edith Day first sang Harry Tierney's Tin Pan Alley song "Alice Blue Gown" in the popular 1919 musical comedy *Irene*, a rags-to-riches story that ran for a record-breaking 617 performances. "Alice Blue Gown" told the story of a woman who loved a special dress. But after 1928, burlesque strippers made a specialty out of transforming Tin Pan Alley numbers like "Alice Blue Gown" into racy, jazz and blues–influenced ones. The blue gown became a prop the enterprising stripper could literally take off while the song played.

In burlesque, many strippers adapted a lightning-quick, super-dramatic style of vocal accompaniment increasingly discarded by performers in more refined genres of popular entertainment who continued to base their own singing on that to be found in the movies and on the style of other performers. Since most late Jazz Age strippers either sang as they disrobed or were accompanied by singing, the differences and meanings in form could be great. But from burlesque striptease's beginning, critics rarely considered the sound strippers made onstage to be a form of legitimate music. A well-known joke about strippers went, "Fable: once upon a time there was a stripper who could sing. The end."[1]

Bernard Sobel provides one answer to the question "Did burlesque serve as a training school for the young composer, give him a chance to experiment and develop?" The answer is no.[2] And yet according to Sobel, in the teens, burlesque did shape the development of ragtime by giving composers a working-class theater in which to try out different arrangements. Leonard Bernstein wrote, "Meanwhile, just across the street, the vernacular was booming away in the plotless musical theatre"—vaudeville, burlesque, and the revue.[3]

From World War I to the sixties, though, most critics dismissed music in burlesque as contributing little to the American scene. In a review of the 1955 LP *Burlesque Uncensored*, the *New York Times* made fun of the music strippers used:

> Striptease music is not quite like any other kind. It is invariably in two parts, a slow section (during which in the theater a purple spotlight is thrown on the performer) followed by a passage in quick time. The combination reminding burlesque fanciers irresistibly of the cavatina-cabaletto form which occurs so frequently in the operas of Bellini and Donizetti. This part of the performance is managed by an orchestra under the direction of Harold Rausch. The artistes are Marie Voe and Patti Waggin.[4]

But there was more to it than that. There was the paste-up. Gypsy Rose Lee was one of the first strippers to sing a paste-up, in which she "pasted" dirty words on to "clean" music. Many other strippers danced to blues numbers like "Sugar Blues" that told tales of betrayal and desire accompanied by a growling trumpet. Maybe the most prevalent mode of stripping in the Depression used music to parody sentimentality and mimic decency with zeal.

Onstage, the most brazen strippers sometimes abandoned singing and instead shouted beguiling, irreverent phrases like "Oh daddy!" "Clap if you want to see a little more of me!" "Didja see it fellas?" or even "Look what the good lord gave me!" in the style of a street-smart call-and-response that harkened back to African American traditional forms of entertainment. Margie Hart, "the Poor Man's Garbo," brandished her Bible and shouted, "If I shake it's for my mother's sake!"[5] (As it turned out, this was true—she later bought her family a 120-acre farm in Missouri.[6]) Elsewhere in Brooklyn, Mimi Lyne sang "I'm Hungry" and the audience replied, as if on cue, "You'll never go hungry, baby."

Sometimes these songs did lack the verve and complexity of jazz and blues standards. H. K. Minsky wrote "I'm Umpa Bumping All the Way from Gumpa" for Georgia Sothern in 1935. As Sothern pointed out, Minsky was no Irving Berlin.[7] Rose La Rose, "the Original TNT Girl," sang "Who Will Kiss My Ooh La La?" La Rose, whose trademark was what she called "dignified savagery," arrived onstage in a long, flowered dress with three cutouts and hardly undressed at all as she slapped her "ooh la la" plenty of times.[8]

But when critics dismissed strippers' dancing as not being real and their singing for the same reason, there was something a little too eager in their tone. *Time* noted in 1934 that, for a stripper, "the ability to sing is by

Margie Hart in her hula costume, c. 1934. Billy Rose Theatre Collection, New York Public Library for the Performing Arts, Astor, Lenox, and Tilden Foundations.

Rose La Rose on the hood of a Dodge automobile, New York City, 1941. The Hulton Archives/Getty Images.

no means essential."[9] A few years earlier, the critic John Bakeless had described the musical chaos accompanying a teaser routine:

> The band strikes up and there emerges a coy and charming lady. . . . [S]he is here to sing and dance. Of course no one knows what she is singing. The programme says it is a ditty called "O-kay baby," but you have to take that on faith. . . . The audience doesn't know what the lady is singing. It is doubtful whether the lady does. Only the orchestra leader . . . seems to have the least idea. He has the music before him; but his men seem to be largely improvising.[10]

Perhaps because of striptease's proximity to prostitution, music critics were all too eager to find fault with the aesthetic qualities of its music—a pattern resembling the one that reformers had pitched against jazz a few years earlier. But as with jazz, the critics' disdain inspired the great strippers' search for innovative ways to use music. From around the time of her first performance in 1929 in Toledo, Gypsy Rose Lee milked sound for comedy by plinking dressmaker's pins into the tuba in the orchestra pit. Here she describes the gimmick's genesis:

> Musicians in their shirt sleeves, with racing forms in their pockets, played Sophisticated Lady while I flicked my pins in the tuba and dropped my garter belt into the pit. Then my petticoat. When it fell, it covered the tuba player. He struggled to get it off and the audience laughed. I thought, I'll keep that in.[11]

Gypsy's soundtrack was a far cry from the heavy orchestration prevalent elsewhere in American popular theater. This was the era when great musicals and revues were being written and great lyricists were emerging. And yet, although striptease demanded a more impromptu sound, it also demanded that that sound fit the strip. Although musician Art Hess, who played in a burlesque orchestra in the late 1930s, described playing for strippers as a "dogcatcher's" job—steady nightly work—drummer Charles De Milt said, "Ad-libbing to the stripper's bumps and grinds and kicks [was] the most important function of the drummer. If you didn't do that, you might as well stay home."[12]

From the late 1920s, strippers also took it off to Tin Pan Alley classics like "Alexander's Ragtime Band," which by this point reminded the audience of a more demure era, and a less syncopated one. Also, of all the American genres strippers cottoned to, ragtime resembled military music and allowed the stripper to march back and forth across the stage. As the French art critic Denys Chevalier put it, "[C]omings and goings, lefts and right indicate a prisoner in her cell."[13]

By the time striptease was born, jazz had already eclipsed ragtime and Tin Pan Alley in the popular imagination. From that moment, strippers were drawn to it for what Chevalier calls its "physiological" quality and also its wildness.[14] Recorded in 1928, Duke Ellington's "The Mooche" attracted strippers for its so-called jungle or rough sound, which included brass, noise, and cries. As jazz historian Marshall Stearns writes, "The cry and the field holler did yeoman service."[15] Henk Niesen describes "The Mooche" as being about two conflicting forces, featuring three tunes, and caroming from clarinet to piano and back. Another song popular among strippers, "Mood Indigo," in Niesen's words, described a "state of mind in which fury, melancholy, and resentment have disappeared, leaving only room for lonely meditation."[16]

"Caravan" and, in the 1930s, "Sophisticated Lady" also presented jazz that seemed designed for mournful stripping. Ellington may have even shaped striptease by writing music that contained a range of mood in one piece. "Sophisticated Lady" offers, as the Ellington scholar James Lincoln Collier says, "the flavor of the decadent lady nursing her wounds in an expensive café. . . . [N]onetheless it maintains the air of subdued melancholy."[17]

The orchestration of the forties eluded striptease. It would be the 1950s when jazz standards like George Shearing's "Lullaby of Birdland" and Peter DeRose's "Deep Purple," written in 1934, caught on because of their swingy lyrics. "St. Louis Blues" had another effect: it made the stripper seem more isolated than any Tin Pan Alley song ever had. Written in 1952, "Lullaby" suspended the stripper in an Archimedian landscape. Perhaps the combination of soulful music and vulgar gestures captured Americans' fear about the type of sexual aloneness that striptease might propagate. More than ragtime or Tin Pan Alley, many reformers associated jazz with a state of nervous stimulation, not unlike that of big cities behind the lines of a war.

Indeed, most of the cities associated with the origins of striptease were midwest jazz strongholds like St. Louis, Chicago, and Kansas City. At night on the prairie, striptease and blues or striptease and jazz, combining syncopated rhythms with a steady bass, slurred sex and sound and created a cacophony of music. The typical five-piece strip bands—as they came to be called—were the smaller bands of hot jazz. They contained piano, cornet, trombone, clarinet, and trap drums, with a decided emphasis on the brass, which provided the precise razzmatazz that striptease needed.[18]

As the appearance of big band encouraged theater owners to add more musicians to burlesque orchestras in the thirties, the number of striptease acts on a bill increased. In 1931 *Variety* reported between six and twelve in one single evening. Eventually, the number of musicians and the number of strippers contributed to the closing of burlesque theaters. In Chicago the Rialto shut its doors in 1946 in part because theater owners could not pay the nine-piece orchestra the strippers then required.[19]

ALL OF THIS MUSICAL tomfoolery coincided with changes in the way strip-tease looked on the burlesque stage. In Jazz Age strip numbers, the performer sang her song fully dressed. At the end of the song, she left the stage, slipping off a shoulder strap or toying with her buttons. When the audience applauded, she returned, minus one article of clothing. She perhaps sang another chorus, left the stage again wearing less, and so on, for up to six or seven encores. At the last moment, she stood onstage, her arms spread wide to embrace the audience. By 1932, although strippers still performed this type of "staggered" strip, they developed the more presentational style that would be the hallmark of the Depression-era genre. Now a stripper took off her clothing while she was onstage. She might or might not sing to the accompanying music, but like earlier performers, she responded to applause by undressing further. (Exceptions immediately introduce themselves—Gypsy Rose Lee began and ended at her own allegro pace.)

In 1933, Americans cottoned to Harold Arlen's "Stormy Weather." Saccharine ballads and swing were in vogue. But Tin Pan Alley standards remained striptease's first soundtrack and a drummed-up Irving Berlin its anthem even into the late fifties, as bebop and rock and roll gained ground. Berlin songs, elsewhere gentle and even sometimes morose, continued to demand a flamboyant, satiric presentation in striptease.

To heighten the irony, these songs were sometimes sung not by the stripper herself, but by the man known colloquially as the "tit serenader" or "bust developer." Robert Alda, actor Alan Alda's father, who in 1950 created the role of Sky Masterson in *Guys and Dolls*, began as a tit serenader.[20] The old-fashioned crooner would stand offstage or in the wings warbling a ballad like "The Sweetheart of Sigma Chi" or "Mother Machree"—the song about the Irish matron and her long-lost son—in falsetto while the stripper removed her clothes. E. E. Cummings noted burlesque's devotion to the matriarchy as early as his 1925 poem "Humanity, I Love You" in which he observes, "songs contain the words country home and mother when sung at the old howard."[21]

On the surface the Depression pushed striptease and sentimentality closer together. But the stripper's act provided an ironic contrast to the saccharine songs. When Louise Fraser made her specialty taking it off while singing "Mother Machree," she pushed striptease into a parodic realm. The lines "There's a spot in my heart which Colleen may own, / There's a depth in my soul never sounded or known, / There's a place in my life that not 'til other own . . ." won Fraser the coveted next-to-last slot at the Irving Place.[22]

ANOTHER WAY SOUND satirized and defused striptease's erotic aspect in burlesque was comics' adding jokes to a ballad while a woman undressed.

Connie Ryan and Steve Mills did this in the number "Sandman." As the straight woman stripped upstage, Ryan and Mills, downstage, kidded each other about the beautiful girl the "Sandman" could bring them.

> Mr. Sandman
> Yes?
> Bring me a dream
> And make her complexion like peaches and cream
> Oh go to hell![23]

From a distance, it looks like such routines contain a trace of envy for the new female self-reliance that was appearing in other spheres of life in the Depression. The theater historian Robert C. Allen suggests that the appearance of boisterous male comics alongside (silent) undressing females makes striptease misogynist. By separating the ability to speak and the ability to express sexuality along gender lines, striptease is "silencing" women. [24] Allen's point of view, though, strikes me as an incomplete way of describing the dynamic between men and women during a striptease performance. Rather, striptease, by pushing men onto the sidelines, elevated women's bodies into the realm of the fabulous. Even women's silence could not detract from striptease's potency.

THE ADVENT OF BIG BAND sound in the 1930s inspired some status-conscious stock burlesque impresarios to hire their own orchestras to accompany striptease, the idea being that the sound of strings and horns would help elevate undressing to respectability. In the early days, Big Band meant anything more than four instruments. Thus Ellington and others helped move striptease up the entertainment ladder. Glamorous striptease receded in the first years of the Depression, but returned after the New Deal, and, assisted by the smooth shock of big sound, taking it off regained some of the respect it had enjoyed in certain circles during the Jazz Age.

In the late thirties, as striptease became even more glamorous and subsequently more mainstream, more a part of the world of popular theater, its soundtrack for the most part followed suit. In burlesque houses, striptease was performed not just to jazz's hot, atonal tempos and lyrics or to swing's triumphant strut and the candid sexuality of the blues, but also to the witty, sophisticated "smarty verse" of the Algonquin Round Table writers and Cole Porter's 1934 "You're the Top," not to mention variations of "Tschaikowsky," Ira Gershwin's improbable list song, which used the names of fifty-one Russian composers. "You're the Top's" flip, ingenious rhyming of "Mahatma Gandhi" and "Napoleon Brandy," its razor-sharp turns of phrase, deliberately bad grammar, and genteel French may have inspired Gypsy Rose Lee's own list song, "I Can't Strip to Brahms."

IN 1922, MARY CASS CANFIELD had observed the "unforced and happy communion" between artists and audiences in vaudeville houses. The vaudevillian, she wrote, was a democratic American performer:

> He jokes with the orchestra leader, he tells his hearers fabricated confidential tales about the management, the other actors, the whole entrancing world behind the scenes; he addresses planted confederates in the third row, or the gallery and proceeds to make fools of them to the joy of all present. He beseeches his genial, gum-chewing listeners to join in the chorus of his song; they obey with a zestful roar. The audience becomes a part of the show and enjoys it. And there is community art for you. A vaudeville comedian in America is as close to the audience as Harlequin and Punchinello were to the Italian publics of the eighteenth century.[25]

In burlesque striptease, the business between performer and audience carried a more ambiguous value. Although striptease might, as the comedian George Jessel said of vaudeville, have "lived by the reaction of the audience," vaudeville demanded that artists tailor their craft to put together a genial familiarity and intimacy designed to appear spontaneous. Vaudeville was not "highbrow," as Caroline Caffin once said, and its music was often less "highbrow" than that of the philharmonic. But vaudeville was nonetheless family fare. Striptease took all of vaudeville's elements and eroticized them through music and form. In other words, the sound of striptease carried audience members from their neighborhoods into a world of eros, comedy, danger, and rhythm.[26]

# The Burlesque Soul
# of Striptease

can't sing, I can't dance," Gypsy Rose Lee—whom Mike Todd called one of "the two greatest no talent show business queens"—once bragged.[1] Gypsy offered something else. Indeed, when the best strippers came onstage, they excited the audience not—as in vaudeville—with beautiful songs, amazing feats of skill, or precision dancing, but with what Jazz Age Americans called "it" or sex appeal. The most dazzling of these strippers deployed wit, charm, vivacity, and versatility as they walked across the stage. Others just knew how to walk. Set against the horizon of their sexuality, these qualities, which might be considered assets in Paris, inspired more complicated responses in an America still struggling to free itself from Victorianism.

But striptease was just one half of "modern burlesque." The other half began as ethnic and "grotesque" or low comedy. Here comics employed the crudest of stereotypes. Burlesque cast Jews as miserly, Irishmen as drunk, Germans as stupid, men as licentious, and women as willing to do anything for two bucks. As one observer put it, burlesque was a "kindergarten for comics." Burlesque trained Fanny Brice, Sophie Tucker, and Al Jolson, as well as slapstick comics Joey Faye and Steve Mills and teams like the Marx Brothers and Laurel and Hardy. Abbott and Costello did their celebrated routine "Who's on First?" there. Into the fifties, these comics labored, telling old jokes, dirty jokes, and clean jokes, and doing skits—really, as Irving Zeidman writes, "anything for a laugh." Ralph Allen describes it as "brutal and naïve" and a "mechanical parody of sexual desire." Much of this comedy celebrated the underdog, attacked the upper class, and focused on sex. It was sometimes absurd and always unsentimental. *New York Times* theater critic Brooks Atkinson wrote in 1927 that burlesque was "a riotous whirligig of clumsy entertainment—coarse and immodest—with intimate glimpses of immodest girls."[2]

After burlesque traded the three-part structure of the nineteenth-century minstrel show for the looser one of the Broadway revue, "bit comedy" and sketches became the major idiom of its humor. In bit comedy, the comics served up numbers, or bits, that had been passed down from one generation to another, some of them since the minstrelsy days. There was the doctor bit, the judge bit, the editor bit, the bit where the woman crossed her legs, "Floogle Street" . . . Certain words, such as "scrutinize," became double entendres. Sometimes a "straight woman" acted as a foil for the two comics. "You will wish you hadn't heard them," *Fortune* wrote about burlesque jokes in 1935. But as early as 1908, *Variety* complained that burlesque bits were old.[3] Sketches were just pieces of bit comedy.

> Waiter: Would the lady like some tongue?
> Talking woman: Sir, I'll have you understand that I never eat anything
>     that comes out of an animal's mouth.
> Waiter: Then how about a couple of eggs?
> [The waiter fries eggs.]
> Woman: Waiter, I want one order of chicken soup.
> Waiter: One order of chicken soup!
> Woman: Listen, I changed my mind. Make that pea soup instead.
> Waiter: Hold that chicken, make it pea![4]

In another typical joke, a waiter was asked to fry eggs first on one side and then on the other. A third involved getting squirted in the ear with a seltzer bottle.

BY THE TWENTIES, a typical burlesque show might include a dance team or a "prima donna" in addition to bits and "girl" production numbers. True to its origins in the Yiddish theater, the National Winter Garden sometimes interpolated melodramas into the burlesque mix. But for the most part, bits and production numbers alternated with the strips, which, in the thirties, became the main event. Unlike vaudeville, burlesque, almost totally improvisatory, was rarely refined.

This heightened the contrast with the female performers since the majority of strippers stripped without speaking, much less cracking jokes. And the majority of burlesque fans considered comedy to be a male activity anyway. E. E. Cummings wrote, "I've seen in the past thirty years of my proletarian life, a lot of burlesque shows (and I hope to see a lot more). . . . [B]urlesque appeals to me."[5] That same year, in an essay in *Stage*, Cummings conjured up June St. Clare's sober striptease in rapturous tones.

> When Miss St. Clare walks, she walks. But when she does something else, she very easily becomes all the animals who ever came out of the ark, rolled into one. Most people move by not keeping still; a very few move by moving; she does neither. She propagates—that is perhaps the word for it—a literally miraculous synthesis of flying and swimming and floating and rising and darting and gliding and pouncing and falling and creeping and every other conceivable way of moving; and all these merely conceivable ways are mysteriously controlled by an inconceivable way which is hers alone.[6]

Many other writers, in fact, observed that striptease inspired the opposite of laughs. Taking it off could not possibly be funny because it was sexy.

Bernard Sobel's Depression-era history of burlesque, *Burleycue*, blames the death of "clean burlesque"—by which he means the slapstick comedy and singing popular before the Jazz Age—on strippers' lack of talent and never mentions their comic appeal. Sobel argues that if these "dirty" women could do anything besides taking off their clothes, burlesque would have been considerably enriched and reformers would have failed in efforts to wipe it out. This is an interesting argument in that it neatly reverses the usual one having to do with female stars and the entertainment world. That story goes that Mae West "saved" Paramount and Marilyn Monroe "saved" Hollywood with their raw sexuality. But in Sobel's account, the female actually destroys the great institution of burlesque instead of saving it, as if she were Helen of Troy or Medea, making the rivers run backward.[7]

In reality, few strippers saved anything. But also, it seems to me that Sobel misses the point. Like La Goulue and other music hall greats, the stripper holds a unique place in our feverish imaginations: this figure presented America with a mysterious and sometimes funny image of itself. What makes her do what she does? At best, she is a tarnished national heroine—the Statue of Liberty with her crown askew—who embodied amiability and freshness that Americans find appealing. At worst, she epitomized failure and disgrace. At the same time, striptease was rarely about stardom. It involved more than taking off clothes or revealing a sculpted body. It presented a radically democratic array of shapes and sizes. It was modern and fluid.

Moreover, sometimes striptease celebrated the comic because it raised up a tiny human triumph over absurd circumstances. Perhaps it is absurd to bring Samuel Beckett into a discussion of striptease at all. And yet in one aspect at least, the best strippers are not so unlike Beckett's clowns, for they combine the whisper of copious eros with the pathos of missed opportunity. Just as burlesque comics performed a kind of anti-comedy from which no redemption could emerge, so many strippers did antisexual acts. Onstage, strippers often seemed barely able to take off their clothes and finally did so only under extreme duress or the intervention of a natural element, which itself became ridiculous in contrast to a naked woman.

In Georgia Sothern's premiere at Minskys' Republic, she rode onstage on an elephant. Clad in an evening gown, Rosita Royce stood helpless onstage while her seven trained doves flew around her and carried off pieces of her gown while she fed them birdseed from her mouth.[8] Sally Rand and Faith Bacon for the most part effortlessly manipulated enormous fans that weighed around twenty-five pounds each. Zorita cavorted onstage with a snake, which disappeared while she took off her clothes. Zorita said she liked the idea of a beautiful woman's performing with a hideous beast. Perhaps she also liked terrifying the audience. In another number, Zorita impersonated Mae West emerging from a spiderweb. As a finale, the spider "groped" her. Before she settled on a black panther, Blaze Starr thought about adding an alligator to her act, but then rejected the reptile as too expensive and too high maintenance for her take-off.

Mitzi Sinclair did a fire-eating striptease, transforming herself into a sequined human inferno as she took it off. Starr became known as "the Panther Girl" and tied small pieces of steak to her bra and panties and then lay supine on a red shag carpet so that her great black cat (Midnight) could slink onstage and pull them off—the pieces of steak, that is. In another act, Starr reclined on a velvet couch as the teepee she had crawled out of minutes before burst into flames. "It's hot!" she screamed.[9]

Rose La Rose invented a cartoon number, with life-size replicas of well-known characters, including Woody Woodpecker. This may have been to honor the Donald Duck cartoon in which Donald chases bandits into a burlesque house and gets so distracted by La Rose that the bandits get away.

Strippers designed these tricks to make audiences laugh and to astonish, as at the circus. More than a few of them were accidents, or appeared to be. In Philadelphia, Georgia Sothern forgot to put down her hand mirror before she walked onstage. While she stripped, the mirror's reflection glared in the audience's eyes. Roars of laughter shook the theater.[10]

WHEN STRIPPERS FAILED to capitalize on their humor, they did rely on mystery. Comparing strippers on his trip to New York in 1936, Jean Cocteau wrote that the difference between them lurked in their approaches. "One star holds the audience quickly spellbound, another works them into a fever. One . . . freezes the public in a terrible ice-block, another sets light to the tinder, another hurls arrows and daggers. Each has her own line of genius."[11]

Cocteau singled out Lillian Murray as the apotheosis of striptease. Other reviewers described her as stripping with a "placid serenity," but Cocteau saw in her a pagan quality. Murray's act began on a fan-shaped dais behind a transparent curtain. A group of naked girls stood downstage with their hands in ermine muffs trimmed with Parma violets. Murray walked in front of the audience and little by little "flaked away" her dress. After a few bars of music, she exited into the wings and came back wearing less. She looked vaguely Latin, with what Cocteau called square, "Mexican idol" features and thick, shoulder-length hair. She was built like a Diego Rivera or Gaston Lachaise figure with huge breasts and buttocks and sturdy limbs. She did not walk but "loomed" into view and then "crab wise she scuttled naked across the stage."[12]

VARIATIONS IN STRIPTEASE ultimately relied not just on sexiness or comedy. Burlesque striptease sometimes presented an innocence all the while implying the weight of adult sexuality. Robert Toll described burlesque as "grasping" like "violent sports." The stripper always lay just out of reach.

Also, striptease brought the female personality into focus. To be sure, by the twenties, female celebrities in general were on the rise, first in vaudeville, then in silent films, and finally in the talkies, where new female characters such as the Madcap Heiress, the Independent Girl, and the Vamp wrested the stage and screen from the Victorian sentimental woman and from the male stars who captivated audiences in the nineteenth century.[13]

Beginning in the twenties, no other type of performer was expected to rivet the public the way the stripper was. A stripper was a sex symbol on whom all eyes focused. Like Houdini, she mesmerized the audience to the point of hypnosis. She set the mood of an evening the moment she entered, and she could make or break the show by what she was able to communicate in the first seconds onstage. The *New Yorker*, in one of the first "Talk of the Town" pieces devoted to striptease in the 1930s, dismissed the importance placed upon this special virtuosity. "The difference between a mediocre stripper and a great stripper is between $35 and $400 a week. . . . [W]hen a stripper does not get her usual encores, it never occurs to her that she is losing her genius. She accuses the orchestra leader, piano player, and first fiddler of having been bribed to ruin her by playing too slow or too fast for her strip rhythm."[14]

But in a celebration of Mike Todd's 1942 Broadway extravaganza *Star and Garter*, a newspaper critic celebrated the amount and variety of striptease onstage: "How will you have it? In the style of Georgia Sothern, with the bricktop hair and the gyrations of a whirling dervish? Or in the manner of Carrie Finnell, who, as rumor goes, once gave blush to a salesman in the front row? Or would you prefer to witness the most specialized of all arts as it is interpreted by the star of *Star and Garter*, Gypsy herself, who puts a little quality into her work that has been touched by critics?"[15]

In the first few seconds of her performance, the "standout" stripper—the one commanding four hundred dollars a week in the Depression—exerted enough power over her audience to win it over. She broke down the psychological barrier between performers and spectators with the mystery of her personality, with her bubbling vitality, with gimmicks and sometimes laughs. Only through the force of these often incongruous elements could the stripper become legendary.

Both Gypsy and Ann Corio coyly protested, "I'll catch cold if I take that off!" even as they hung behind the curtain, dangling their bras in front of the audience. The carefree "typical American homegirl" Mary Sunde popped a bottle of champagne and threw the cork into the audience, capturing raunchy sex and goofy elegance; Margie Dix sailed onstage with a nonchalant swanky glide.[16]

Georgia Sothern, "the Human Dynamo," stripped to the "Tiger Rag," the New Orleans Dixieland jazz number recorded by Louis Armstrong and Jelly Roll Morton. While the "hold that tiger" refrain played, Sothern shook her hips so ferociously that she needed one hand to steady herself against the wall. Before the musicians had even finished playing the first eight bars, she grabbed onto the curtain and threatened to rip it from the proscenium arch; combed her fingers through her long, red hair; ripped off her clothes; and began whirling them around her head. Critics called her "the tiger girl."[17]

Sometimes at a midnight show, Sothern would interpolate popular jazz dance steps from the teens and twenties into her strip. She would do the Texas Tommy, the fly away, walking the dog, the toe punch, and falling off the log. These were all complicated exhibition steps that Broadway had appropriated. Caroline Caffin described the Texas Tommy as "fierce" and "acrobatic." Sothern would get so excited that she would put on and take off her clothes several times in one number. She would do difficult dance steps from musical comedy such as the muscle kick and the fan kick. Sothern could also do the hitch kick, in which the dancer thrust her leg perpendicular to the floor and hopped across the stage. (Ann Pennington had made this famous.) As Joseph Mitchell put it, "After a blackout on a Sothern strip, the customers fall back into their seats, exhausted." Emmett Callahan, a burlesque impresario, observed, "She strips just like she had dynamite for lunch."[18]

Sothern had this effect on audiences even into her forties. In 1966, Wallace Markfield described her performance at a Times Square burlesque house. After a short tease, Sothern began

> moving at 32 frames per second . . . in flipping and flapping, in spinning, and in the sustaining of the spin . . . she pulls her hair, and rips her cheeks, she spins up and down, back and forth as though haunted by dybbucks.[19]

Dorothea Maye strutted with peppy baby steps, fell to one knee, and displayed her garter. Evelyn Myers strode across the stage "sweetly." They all evinced charisma. According to the theater manager Kitty Madison, the young burlesque star Ann Corio stripped "like a whirlwind . . . [J]ust like a magnet she drew them in." Joseph Mitchell described Corio as a "sweet and slow" stripper who "wears a lot more than most strippers when she begins and when she ends, and she is more feminine than tigerish in her strut across the stage. She is not addicted to the bump . . . nor is she expert with the grind."[20] In the 1950s, when production values rose to compete with Las Vegas, Corio appeared onstage between two smoke bombs wearing chiffon and a white boa, as if emerging from a war zone.[21]

In striptease, as in jazz, strippers put great faith in originality, even if that faith sometimes lay on the surface. "I learned early on not to steal," said the stripper Kitty Oakes.[22] And yet of course, everyone stole and catfights arose over who actually invented the "cool" fan dance or the "hot" striptease. As in jazz, which the French jazz critic Hugues Panassié first divided into two categories in 1934—sweet and hot or straight and hot—a mythology grew up around the techniques of striptease: the "fast worker," the "slow worker," the "parade strip," the "society strip," the "dramatic."[23]

But all of these styles of striptease are shorthand for comic types the way commedia dell l'arte's Pantalone and Harlequin are. And it was the choice of this style that allowed for certain kinds of unconventional emotion: disabused tolerance, for example, sexual hardheadedness, lack of false modesty, simple high spirits, outright salaciousness. A line from the anonymous early-twentieth-century song "It's All in the Way She Does It" became a euphemism for striptease's improvisatory quality, which was at once an homage to American vitality and a witty way of alluding to sex's raw, elusive energy.

Beginning in the 1930s, striptease evoked emotional and physical comic excesses that could not be contained in civilized life. Striptease provided a relief from and a counterpoint to burlesque's raunchy, violent clowning. It erupted in the forest in *Midsummer Night's Dream*. As for the women who only did comic strips, they pushed comedy further than many female comedians dared by using it to deflect the threat of anarchic sexuality and to make a claim for distinction. The parade of short bald men in mismatched coats and tall, beautiful women wearing few clothes set spectators on edge but made them laugh, relieving them of most anxiety associated with women's taking off their clothes in real life.[24]

In a modern context, some of this seems cruel, and it also draws on the stock publicity campaigns carnivals used to lampoon domestic tranquility. Billed as "the Queen of the Amazons," or "the Eyeful Eiffel" Lois de Fee married a midget as a publicity stunt; a joke circulating on the occasion of their divorce a few days later went:

Q: How did the midget make love to Lois de Fee?
A: Someone put him up to it.[25]

Height was also a practical asset. In the cavernous burlesque theaters, many of them former vaudeville palaces, a stripper, like a Greek performer in fifth-century Athens, needed to be tall to be seen. As *Variety* put it, "Short teasers never get anywhere."[26]

FANNY BRICE DID ONE of the most famous numbers spoofing striptease in 1934. No one excelled at making fun of sex more than Brice, who started as a burlesque comedian in the first decades of the twentieth century. After seeing Sally Rand in Chicago in 1933, Brice's then husband Billy Rose wrote "Countess Dubinsky" for her to perform in the *Ziegfeld Follies* the following year. Wearing a black velvet strip gown, Brice marched onstage and talk-sang the story of her tumble from the Russian aristocracy to strip-tease and Minsky, all the while taking off her clothes. Brice told how she came from old Russia, where "Nicolai and his princes nibbled nightly on my blintzes."

Upon her arrival in New York, billed as "the Dirty Duchess" and "the Vulgar Boatman," "the Countess Dubinsky, right down to her skinsky, [was] working for Minsky now." Brice didn't stop there, however. She went on to make fun of the puritanical response to striptease, conjuring up a robust and phony sorrow. Dropping her Russian accent, she parodied a New York showgirl.

> I can't show my face
> Can't go any place
> People stop and stare
> It's so hard to bear
> Everybody knows you left me,
> It's the talk of the town.

Brice flashed and then proceeded to an equally absurd fan dance. When she teetered "naked" on high heels behind two large ostrich-feather fans, the audience broke into peals of laughter. As Brooks Atkinson put it, "none of the moral Catos of this town has delivered such a blow to the lascivious mummery of burlesque." A Stieglitz photograph in *Vanity Fair* shows Brice, naked except for a few stray feathers, posed as Rodin's *Thinker*.[27]

Reviewers seemed divided about Brice. Andrew R. Kelley, in a review of the 1934 *Follies* in the December 5, 1933, *Washington Times*, called her "pa-thetic": "Her fan dance belongs on Ninth Street, where the competition would be perhaps ruinous. All of the Brice songs are filthy." But an uniden-tified review praised her: "Brighter than any other of its highlights are the songs of Fannie Brice. . . . 'Countess Dubinsky' a burlesque of a burlesque 'strip' number . . ." And in the *Washington Star*, E. de S. Melcher wrote:

> Fanny Brice's fan dance is the hit of the new Ziegfeld "Follies." In frank and unashamed and extremely diverting imitation of a young lady who had all of Chicago's swains talking this summer, Miss Brice trips onto the stage sandwiched in between two fat feather fans and thereupon does a job which even Egypt's Cleopatra might envy. Although Ninth Street burlesque patrons may claim that they have seen such a dance before, they have never seen Miss Brice do it. She accomplishes it with that sly look in her left eye, that sudden thrusting forward of the lower lip, and that slight knee-bending which ends in nothing save a mild panic.[28]

In burlesque, strippers endowed with fewer comic possibilities than Brice could inspire ridicule as well as acclaim. For one, whereas in real life, physi-cal aberrance often caused sorrow, in burlesque striptease, it more frequently impelled laughter. This was especially the case in literary depictions of strip-tease, where sometimes the laughter was at the reader's expense. In Damon Runyon's 1938 story "Neat Strip," the snooty burlesque-goer falls in love with a stripper, and then discovers that his mother used to be . . . a stripper.

But other times, laughter occurs at the stripper's expense. In John Cheever's 1937 story "The Teaser," Beatrice, a woman "of a certain age," marches onstage, takes off her white evening gown, and stands naked. "She is no great object of beauty," Cheever writes. To draw attention to her unattractiveness and to the incongruity of her nevertheless being onstage, on her rear end she has painted—or has had painted—two red handprints. The house "goes wild" with laughter. Like other female comedians of the day, Beatrice is making fun of her own girth and age—deliberately culti-vating her own unattractiveness to be funny. The scarlet hands mark her as a "fallen woman," and also perhaps remind the audience that she is alone.

The feminist historian June Sochen has pointed out that, unlike the streamlined chorines on the vaudeville and Broadway stage, many female comics of this era, by sacrificing a conventional ideal of femininity, acknowl-edged their sexuality as threatening even as they pointed to it. In vaudeville and film, women "screwball" comics—those who existed—primarily used language to be funny while men continued to bop each other over the head. In burlesque skits, women often played the ingénue to the male comic's lecher. But when strippers did comic acts—some of which used the gross, pie-throwing vernacular, and others of which relied on ethnic or, even worse, sexual comedy—they broke rules. During the Depression, the increasing stress on humor in striptease goes a long way toward explaining why women continued to watch it alongside of men.[29]

# Part Three

# The Golden Age of Striptease

Striptease . . . is based on a contradiction.
——Roland Barthes

# "Minskyville"

n 1930, *New York Times* theater critic Brooks Atkinson wrote a profile
titled "Burlesque with a Ph.D.: Those Up and Coming Entrepreneurs,
the Brothers Minsky Finally Tell All." Atkinson treated the Minskys
as legitimate impresarios on the level of the Shubert brothers and detailed
not simply how the "first citizens of Second Avenue" brought burlesque to
Houston Street, but how they ennobled it.[1] The trade papers followed,
telling a similar story, complimenting both of the Minskys' downtown burlesque theaters—the National Winter Garden and the Irving Place. "Manager Charlie Burns gives his patrons something for their money just as the
management of the National Winter Garden, another high class stock burlesque house does," Atkinson wrote.[2]

One aspect of the "high class" burlesque newspapers remarked upon
was the audience. The Minskys had renovated the National Winter Garden
again the previous year, and as the 1929–1930 season opened, the theater

Herbert and Morton Minsky chatting, 1938. Time Life Pictures/Getty Images.

attracted "some high class Broadwayites and many lovers of burlesque from all over the city." *Billboard* called the National Winter Garden a "roof garden," using the elegant word frequently applied to Ziegfeld for the sixth-story theater downtown.[3]

In other words, burlesque continued to draw the uptown crowd and striptease continued to amuse it. In 1931, when Gypsy Rose Lee arrived in New York with her comic striptease, she didn't lack work. She first stripped in New Jersey, with *Girls from the Follies* at the Empire Burlesque Theater in Newark. She was about eighteen years old.[4] *Zit's* review of Gypsy's "Powder My Back" strip describes her as "a striking beauty of the Ann Corio type . . . a brunette of unusual beauty in face and form. She has a charming personality. She knows how to use her flirty eyes. We like the way she offers her numbers, working with grace, and she was warmly received every time she appeared."[5]

THAT WINTER, when the Depression overtook New York City, Billy Minsky turned twenty-eight. Despite—or because of—the National Winter Garden's success downtown, he was restless, eager for Broadway acclaim. In February, Billy moved burlesque out of the Lower East Side and onto Broadway, to the Republic Theater on Forty-second Street. This was almost two years after Wall Street had "laid an egg," as *Variety* described Black Tuesday.[6] The rest of show biz was in a slump. But, undeterred by the economy, Billy Minsky teamed up with theater operator Joseph Weinstock, and the pair beat out Isidore Herk for the Republic's lease—by their success emboldening other burlesque impresarios to join them on the Great White Way. "Times Square to Be Scene of Probable Combat," *Zit's* wrote to describe the scene.[7]

It is practically impossible to overestimate the impact of Minsky's taking over the Republic. Built in 1901, the Republic until that winter had been best known for housing the long-running tearjerker *Abie's Irish Rose*. Noel Coward's Anglophile satire *Private Lives* was playing next door and Fred and Adele Astaire were dancing cheerfully at the New Amsterdam down the street. Still, the Astaires and Coward were remnants from the past, from Broadway's heyday, when the street generated a different kind of excitement. As theater historian Mary Henderson puts it, "By 1930, the boom that had engulfed New York for nearly thirty years was over. . . . [I]n no sphere of urban life was the depression more accurately mirrored than in Times Square, the center of its theater and entertainment world."[8]

A year later, half of the ten remaining legitimate theaters on the block had abandoned live performance. Billy's arrival hardly elevated Forty-second Street. When he moved into the Republic, the number of honky-tonk businesses on the street, especially on the block between Broadway and Eighth Avenue, exploded. Near Eighth, Hubert's Flea Circus featured sidewalk exhibits such as a two-headed suckling pig. According to Alva Johnston, along the street skulked "Indian herb doctors, Gypsy seeresses, lecturers on golden medical secrets, strongmen, and living statuary," as well as phrenologists who could read the bumps on people's head for personality traits such as sex drive, which at that time was called "amativeness."[9] A few blocks north, Johnston observed, the "Salon des Arts" displayed a good collection of female nudes. In the beginning, these were stolen from hotels, but later they were painted by the Salon's own "artist" of the Salon's own "models." There was also what Mort, the youngest Minsky, called a "pretty hot" nude in the lobby of the Hotel Marguerey and in that same lobby a peep show where one could see odalisques moving by turning a crank.[10] In other words,

Marquee advertising Billy Minsky's Republic Theatre on Forty-second Street (1930s). Museum of the City of New York.

Forty-second Street, not for the Little Old Lady from Dubuque, shared more with Coney Island than the rest of Manhattan.

When Billy opened his Republic Theater on February 12, he implemented his "highbrow" ideas about how to put burlesque striptease across. At a time when most other burlesque theaters offered shabby interiors, Billy tempered honky-tonk with luxe by redecorating the Republic's interior in red and gold plush in the style of an upscale movie palace. Whereas most burlesque theaters smelled of antiseptic and old newspapers, Billy called the Republic's burlesque "intimate" to liken it to cabaret and to separate it from the ungainly spectacle elsewhere in the industry. Male ushers wore braided uniforms in the style of French gendarmes, mustaches, and capes with red satin linings. Female ushers in frilly skirts and black silk stockings showed patrons to their seats. The lobby was adorned with gilt and velvet and a velvet drape hung over the hot dog concession. Tickets were $1.50, three times as much as downtown.

But although Billy was interested in glamour, what he envisioned owed equal parts to honky-tonk and tongue-in-cheek sheen. He ripped out at least a hundred seats from the Republic auditorium and installed not one, but two illuminated runways to give the strippers more intimate access to the audience (and vice versa). He added more seats and installed a modern lighting system. He repainted the theater's austere facade in a checkered pattern onto which he pasted enormous, near-naked likenesses of the headlining strippers.[11]

Whereas the competition used predictably tell-all names such as "Cuddling Cuties" and "The Girls from Paris," Billy tried for a more ironic tone, and one reminiscent of his own downtown immigrant neighborhood. He called his first show *Fanny Fortson from France*. Many of the subsequent titles of the Minskys' shows insinuated ethnic identity or "deviant" sexuality, and each was more comically obscene than the next: *Sarah Neigh from Belmont, Tillie Pipick from Peru, Countess Schmaltz from Capon, Ada Onion from Bermuda, Carrie de Booze from Canada, Mind over Mattress, Ima Pansy from Central Park, The Sway of All Flesh, Panties Inferno,* and *Dress Takes a Holiday.*[12]

There was more advertising, Minsky style. In the ensuing weeks, months, and years that the Republic was in business—less than a decade in all—the marquee always listed the strippers' name above the comics'. Billy hired a stilt walker to walk up and down Forty-second Street wearing a billboard with the strippers' names on it. The stilt walker's shirt buttons, cigar butt, and nose lit up as he moved.[13]

The carnival attracted the American aristocracy. On opening night, the audience in evening clothes watched a mix of raw and rawer stripping. While the scenery was second-hand Ziegfeld, Billy imported some first-class bump-and-grind experts from Chicago. One of these midwesterners,

Frances Parks, stripped to nude. Apparently others pranced far out on the runway, lay down on their backs, and shimmied—this was called "horizontal cootching" and was unheard-of in New York outside of the brothel. The horizontal cootch resulted in a good deal of negative publicity.[14]

"They go to see the teasers," *Variety's* Sime Silverman wrote, attacking the highbrow audience and going on to compare the Minskys' strippers to slaves.[15] *Billboard* described the show as "spicier," "more vulgar," and with a "more lavish cycle of . . . stripping" than other burlesque theaters. Gilbert Seldes asserted that the Republic's success meant that old-fashioned "clean" burlesque was finished.[16] The *New York Times* sneered, "The first show is christened 'Fanny from France,' to use the abbreviated form, but the program is franker in describing it as 'Burlesque—mostly girls.'"[17] Yet despite— or because of—the negative publicity, the house sold out and Billy become a celebrity yet again. The *New Yorker* would run a "Talk of the Town" piece "renaming" the Broadway district "Minskyville."[18]

The Republic opening inspired some journalistic hand-wringing on the subject of the audience, and in particular, women in the audience. Sime Silverman and other anti-burlesque columnists, accustomed to characterizing the burlesque audience as composed of criminals, homosexuals, and prostitutes, made fun of the presence of the upper class. "The audience is funnier than the show," he wrote.[19]

Sime was not the only one counting the number of women in the audience. That same year, *Zit's* reported a "large" number of women at the Irving Place and up to 50 percent at Fox's Jamaica. In 1932, Joseph Wood Krutch noted that the number of women at a Times Square burlesque show was "a scattering" of women in a "languid but large" audience. A few years later, the parole officer and sociologist David Dressler would observe that burlesque had succeeded in making women think about sex as much as men. That was a revolution.[20]

To musical revue and comedy producers, the female presence at the Republic reminded them not so much of changing gender dynamics as of their own economic failures. While Billy Minsky profited, their box offices slumped. George White, whose *Scandals Revue* had flopped, punched out the king of Burlesque for this reason a few months after he opened the Republic.[21] And to Depression-era vice-society reformers, there was more at stake than money or changing demographics. The Republic's success was a wake-up call. It meant that organized vice had succeeded in penetrating mainstream society's fabric. At the forefront of these doomsday prophets was Minsky's nemesis from the Jazz Age: John Saxton Sumner, the president of the New York Society for the Suppression of Vice. Even before the Republic opened, Sumner was trying to use striptease to censor burlesque in other theaters in the city.

Back in January, for example, Sumner had helped organize the arrests of eight burlesque performers at the New Gotham Theater in Harlem. The women "carr[ied] their undressing in the strip numbers too close to nudity."[22] But as in the Jazz Age, the charges mostly failed to stick.

On Forty-second Street, burlesque continued to make inroads. One month after Billy Minsky opened the Republic, Max Rudnick, a former operator of Brooklyn nickelodeons, opened a burlesque show at the Eltinge down the street.[23] In April, Gypsy Rose Lee premiered at the Republic in "Yetta Lostit from Bowling." This revue included a production number with a horse on a treadmill and chorus girls dressed as cowgirls and Indians shooting paper bows and arrows into the audience. After Gypsy's strip the tenor sung "The Bells of St. Mary's," and twelve girls in G-strings congregated onstage to hum "Angelus." Gypsy got rave reviews from the trade papers. *Zit's* complimented her "stunning" "flaming tight" red dress and broad-brimmed hat. The audience applauded Gypsy all through the following number.[24]

It's worth mentioning that after her debut, Gypsy made the first significant change in her appearance: she straightened her hair. In her memoir, she attributes this decision to Billy. But it would've been in line with black and Jewish performers' trying to make it in mainstream popular entertainment. Fanny Brice, after all, had had her nose straightened.[25]

GYPSY'S ARRIVAL ON BROADWAY coincided with another surge in vice-society reform activity against burlesque. On April 9, John Sumner engineered what would be the first of many Depression-era raids at the Republic. In court Sumner testified that there was no actual nudity in "Yetta Lostit from Bowling," and that most of what he objected to was the "double entendres" in the burlesque comedy.[26] Sumner also used the opportunity to declare himself the unofficial burlesque censor and to draft the first of many guidelines attempting to restrict what strippers could wear. In his notes he suggested a minimum size for the G-string—three inches in the front and four in the back. (It is interesting to note that at a time when bras were for the first time in history becoming more malleable, more able to be molded to a woman's breasts, Sumner required the old-fashioned kind of bra—hard, static cones.)[27] Sumner also suggested that strippers be forbidden to touch their bras or any other part of their bodies. Posing onstage was okay, but the act of undressing itself was unacceptable.

An unspoken reason for Sumner's focus on Forty-second Street striptease was the deteriorated economic situation. Burlesque as a cheap entertainment had profited from the economic slump. Burlesque theaters in Times Square remained open from ten A.M. until midnight, making them havens for hobos, migrants, and out-of-work men. Unlike vaudeville and

Broadway, burlesque, which still cost less than those forms of theater, did not require a reserved seat, so instead of waiting on breadlines, thousands of out-of-work Americans distracted themselves from hard times by watching comics and stripteasers. In *Starting out in the Thirties*, Alfred Kazin described unemployed men waiting to get into the Republic the same year that Clifford Odets' political play *Waiting for Lefty* gave voice to American dissatisfaction about workers' rights. "In the unnatural blaze of lights over Times Square marquees at eight in the morning, there were already lines of men waiting. . . . Those same men wound up in the smoky balconies of Forty-Second Street burlesque houses."[28] Or, as Harold Minsky put it much later: "Wives would turn their husbands out into the streets in the mornings to look for work. The husbands knew there was no point in looking for jobs that didn't exist, so they passed their time as best they could."[29]

At the end of the spring, a burlesque zone flourished on Forty-second Street. Even before Billy had moved uptown, *Billboard* worried about a "record number stock burly houses in [the] metropolitan area."[30] But Billy's success encouraged others to join him. After Max Rudnick leased the Eltinge, Isidore Herk, formerly the president of the racy Mutual circuit, rented the Central Theater from the Shuberts; he was about to open it as a burlesque house when the Minskys bought him out.[31] In 1934, Max Wilner, then the owner of the Irving Place, would open the Apollo, formerly the home of George White's *Scandals*, as a grind house and begin producing four burlesque shows a day there.[32]

If the increase in the number of burlesque houses alarmed vice-society reformers, it also lent striptease a kind of minor theatrical legitimacy, at least in the trade papers. Critics reviewing striptease sometimes summoned up great national sports games, populist leisure pastimes like vaudeville or destinations like Coney Island, or primitive cultures. Even *Variety*'s Sime described one stripper displaying "hot hips" and a second wearing a "mysterious skirt," as if she were a Polynesian icon.[33] At some moments, striptease seemed to be cut from the same cloth as these democratizing activities—a source of if not good clean fun, at least pleasure. This was especially true of Gypsy, who struck *Variety* as "being a sentimental, old-fashioned sort of a strip-dancer."[34]

According to the urbane *Herald Tribune* journalist Stanley Walker, the Minsky family changed the molecular structure of Forty-second Street itself. "The street, its people, and its character, resemble something conceived by those *entrepreneurs* of burlesque, the Minskys."[35] Indeed, like all showmen, Billy continued to dream up new ideas each week. After he opened on Broadway, he announced a plan for a new "glorified" burlesque circuit. (This never came to pass because of the weak economy.) Another scheme involved producing a sidewalk cootch show to lure customers into the Republic, but neither the police nor the Forty-second Street Association, a businessman's group, liked the idea. So Billy eased up and subsequently announced that he would "eliminate" striptease. He died of Paget's disease in the summer of 1932, while still tussling with the authorities, and the National Winter Garden closed that year. As Stanley Walker noted, the women were less pretty, although Broadway "continued to stage a peculiarly excited condition of fourth rate emotions."[36]

Billy's death produced a number of changes in New York burlesque, the first and most dramatic of which was to release the brothers from each other. It seemed that for some time an animosity had roiled between them, based in part on the fact that H.K. had married a chorus girl and Abe slept with strippers behind his wife's back—as well as other family squabbles. A month after Billy died, Abe opened the Gaiety on Forty-fifth and Broadway. A year later, Abe split from the family business entirely and devoted his attention to the New Gotham on 125th Street near Second Avenue, just down the block from the other Minsky-run theater in Harlem, the Little Apollo. In midtown, H.K. took over the Central, which Isidore Herk had been managing. The brothers' animosity would push burlesque striptease to new extremes in style and form, as well as force reform to articulate new strategies to crush it.

IN THE THIRTIES, as in earlier eras, vice-society reformers targeted not only burlesque, but comic books, movies, novels, and legitimate plays. Of course, many Americans also continued to find burlesque reprehensible, and the legal system continued to reject First Amendment arguments that might have allowed burlesque to be performed. As late as 1941, a judge noted, "Regulatory power is at odds with freedom of speech, but the alternative is social anarchy, and oppressive license."[37] At the same time, however, throughout the thirties, opposition from the Left toward vice-society reformers became more pronounced. An article published in the *Nation* advised "permitting grown ups to decide for themselves what books they shall buy, what plays they shall see, and even what pictures of undressed females they shall look upon."[38]

Thus if the Depression promoted sexual conservatism, it also nurtured a kind of freedom of speech. By 1931 the freewheeling Jazz Age was over; to the vice-society reformers, just as the freefalling economy indicated a lack of financial leadership, so the rise in burlesque indicated a lack of moral leadership. At the same time, as Paul Boyer notes, these reformers never regained the power they had lost in the twenties. The Victorian era was behind America. The popular press perceived Sumner to be splenetic and irrational. But Sumner continued to forge ahead in censoring burlesque striptease and other popular arts, just as in Hollywood, Will H. Hays created and enforced the Motion Picture Production Code, thus ensuring that a generation of Americans would not see any kind of sexuality displayed on the silver screen.[39]

One explanation for reformers' objections to burlesque and striptease is that it was driven by class anxiety, as it had been in earlier eras. In other words, had burlesque remained in Harlem and downtown in the immigrant ghetto, reformers would have ignored it.[40] Certainly the police were less likely to make a fuss over the scantily clad women parading in the *Ziegfeld Follies*. But the objection to striptease cannot be reduced to reformers' preference for luxuriously appointed chorines. The fact was that many Americans—even theater people—believed that striptease reflected contemporary immorality and posed a moral threat. Published late in 1931, Bernard Sobel's *Burlycue* blamed striptease for the decade's social ills and yearned for the Victorian era, when "we didn't have to talk about sex."[41]

But *Burleycue* was ambivalent about sex. In the chapter "Social Significance," Sobel posed a rhetorical question: how has striptease affected Americans psychically, smothering them with images of naked women every day? The answer: striptease has contaminated American life. At the same time, under the pretext of warning readers against the horrors of striptease—which Sobel connected to Sigmund Freud's popularity—he presented, following a chapter describing the success of the anti-burlesque crusade, a saccharine afterword about strippers with hearts of gold. While Sobel argued for strippers' essential virtue, the photos of beckoning girls presented them as hoydens.[42]

In the 1930s, on the burlesque stage, striptease gave women more agency than other forms of popular entertainment by acknowledging their sexuality and allowing them to connect directly with the audience. As Denys Chevalier later put it, striptease revealed the female erotic imagination. In doing so, striptease stepped away from Victorian conventions that told women how to behave in public. Whereas torch singers sang about sex, and movie stars sometimes found themselves in highly charged sexual situations on-screen—even if those were left on the cutting-room floor—strippers went so far as to perform sexual acts in public. Taking off their clothes, strippers looked at the audience and welcomed—or seemed to welcome—its presence. At the very least, they acknowledged it.

Also, like burlesque comedians, strippers never took sex seriously. The continued presence of striptease in the thirties proved that these changes were not simply a facet of the Jazz Age. In 1930 the Mutual circuit stripper Gladys Clark either spewed forth obscenities or brazenly flirted with customers: "Hey, you're a big boy, take your hands out of your pockets now." Clark even leapt into the audience and grabbed a man by the front of his pants.[43] For such stunts, theater managers paid strippers handsomely. In 1931 *Variety* reported that "high priced strippers" were leaving the Mutual circuit for stock burlesque.[44]

DURING THE FIRST YEARS of the thirties, the political climate was becoming less hospitable to burlesque—indeed to all the forms of commercial vice that had emerged during the Jazz Age. In 1930, as he prepared to run for president, Franklin D. Roosevelt, then governor of New York, created a reform commission to investigate municipal corruption in Manhattan. As counsel for this commission, he named a retired judge from a patrician family—Samuel Seabury. The hearings opened in October, and initial affidavits and interviews revealed fifteen thousand pages of transcripts about graft and fraud. The first hint that burlesque might be involved surfaced in 1931, when the commission investigated the murder of Vivian Gordon, a stripper turned prostitute turned witness, at the same time as Billy Minsky moved burlesque to Times Square.[45]

In the spring of 1932, Seabury found that "good time" Mayor Jimmy Walker was guilty of fifteen counts of corruption.[46] During his tenure, Walker, a wit and a dandy who wore garish Broadway clothing and had written a Tin Pan Alley song, had supported all genres of show business. Walker himself had attended the grand opening of the Minskys' Republic Theater on Forty-second Street in February 1931. Nor was he the only man accused by Seabury with his hands in burlesque: District attorney and former Supreme Court justice T. C. Crain and his two sisters owned a piece of the Irving Place Theater. In 1932, when this news first hit the tabloids, it caused Crain some political discomfort.[47]

A playboy who eloped with a chorus girl, a charmer who took too many vacations, Walker was beloved by the entire city. He was also, however, fatally indifferent to graft. It was hardly a surprise to anyone when, in September 1932, Walker resigned and sailed for Europe to join his girlfriend, the showgirl and former beauty queen Betty Compton.[48]

Even before Walker left New York, support for other reforms had gained ground. Back in the spring of 1931, a few months after Minsky's Republic opened, Walker himself had made some gestures toward a crackdown, perhaps anticipating the tsunami of Seabury's commission. Walker's license commissioner James Geraghty had initiated hearings to evaluate whether burlesque theaters' annual licenses should be renewed. But the result of these hearings was business as usual.[49]

By April 1932, however, as Walker was taking the witness stand, the New York Society for the Suppression of Vice (NYSSV)—still the leading anti-vice association in the city—gained a new ally: the Forty-second Street Property Owners Association. Throughout most of the 1920s, the NYSSV had failed to make obscenity charges stick against burlesque theaters. After the Republic opened, the organization had jumped on Billy Minsky, asserting in its annual report that burlesque "consists almost entirely of a series of salacious sketches separated by chorus numbers wherein the featured female performers engage in stripping."[50]

The report complained about the paucity of legal support the organization's reform efforts received. Although the NYSSV was able to get arrests made, it was unable to make them stick. It was also unable to raise support for imprisoning theater managers and impresarios. Moreover, Roosevelt approved a bill that protected performers from arrest. But in its 1931 annual report, the NYSSV agitated against such protection. "We should like to see the police arrest actors who engage in indecent performances and we should like to see the District Attorney stand squarely behind such a prosecution."[51]

A year deeper into the Depression, the NYSSV was in a much stronger position. It allied itself with the Forty-second Street Association, pushed the mayor's office into action, and significantly expanded the license commissioner's power, giving him the ability to close theaters more or less without explanation. Until then, the commissioner's powers had been limited to revoking theatrical licenses after hearings, a privilege the city granted him in 1927.

IN APRIL 1932, right before Walker testified before the Seabury Commission, Geraghty began a new round of hearings on obscenity and burlesque. No distinction was made between revoking a theatrical license and refusing to renew one. The city called a spectacular array of witnesses to convince Geraghty that burlesque theaters—in other words, striptease—had single-handedly caused Forty-second Street's disintegration. Religious leaders—including Cardinal Hayes—condemned burlesque. Office girls who worked at McGraw-Hill on Forty-second Street attested that burlesque did indeed attract "undesirables."[52]

How did they know? Because, they complained, men loitering around the theaters frequently called out to them, "Hello baby, can I take you out to lunch?" Some female passersby were even goosed. A bank president testified that he would never loan money to any business foolish enough to buy a store on Forty-second Street. Real estate agents contended that burlesque brought down real estate prices and frightened tenants. Others complained that the signs used to advertise burlesque brought an unattractive element to the area. A rabbi was swore that he had sent a special envoy to beg the Minskys, for the sake of the Jews, to cease producing burlesque striptease. (The Minskys refused to back down, instead expressing their outrage at being singled out.)[53]

When the defense called its witnesses, the trial took a more sensational turn. The theater owners invited Geraghty to visit their theaters and see for himself how tame burlesque and striptease actually were. (Geraghty declined.) The defense cited the artist Reginald Marsh as an example of a sophisticated person who loved burlesque but who was not a degenerate. (His work was found in the Museum of Modern Art.) Falling back on the class argument, Louis Fehr, the *New York American*'s drama critic, swore that there was nothing one could see at Minskys' that one couldn't see at a Broadway revue such as George White's *Scandals*, and that there was not that big a difference between ballet and striptease. In short, Fehr did everything he could to make a fool of the tough-minded assistant district attorney Ferdinand Pecora, who was prosecuting. When Fehr described striptease as ballet, Pecora said: "Did you say bellies?" Fehr replied: "Ballets and bellies also."[54]

All of the defense witnesses maintained the same irreverent tone. Among the sassiest was ninety-three-year-old Mother Elms, the Republic's avuncular wardrobe mistress. Asked how old she was, she said, "I never notice years; that is why I am 93." But Elms proved a savvy witness as well as a jokester. Asked if she liked the dances the strippers did at Minskys', Elms, who had been a burlesque queen in the 1890s, quipped, "I wish I could do [them] myself. There was a time when I could." Moreover, refusing to fall into the prosecution's trap of damning Depression-era morals and sanctifying Victorian ones, Elms, when asked if women wore more clothes in the old days, replied, "They could lift them just as high." And Elms seconded Fehr's testimony that nude women were everywhere—even in the eminently respectable Noel Coward's *Private Lives*. Like Fehr, Mother Elms believed that for the mayor to be singling out burlesque meant that something else was at stake.[55]

More and more dramatic—or at least comic—evidence piled up. The testimony would eventually reach over one thousand pages. Probably the most damning accusation was that burlesque was a front for prostitution. This accusation would have been especially explosive in light of the Seabury Commission's as well as decades of reformers' trying, with mixed success, to ferret out vice in the city. And the newspapers wanted to have it both ways. On the one hand, there seemed to be a consensus that burlesque—with its dirty jokes and striptease—had gone too far. On the other, watching fascism rise in Europe, left-leaning forces feared that the impulse to censor would curtail not just the theatrical culture of the city, but democracy itself. The *New York Times*'s avowedly anticensorship drama critic Brooks Atkinson quoted Kurt Weill as joking that he went to a striptease show and came out a misogynist. When in court Geraghty asked Atkinson how he would remedy things, Atkinson smugly replied, "Only by improving the human race."[56]

In its zeal to wipe out striptease, the city did not exactly play fair. In May it was established in court that a telegram from the actress Jane Cowl supporting the anti-burlesque crusade had been forged.[57] The editors of the *New York Times* opined that burlesque was "pornographic" but warned against attacks on civil liberties.[58] Thus the 1932 trial ended in early May with a kind of compromise: the theater owners agreed to phase out striptease by decreasing the number of strippers and persuading them to wear brassieres, and Commissioner Geraghty agreed to temporarily return their licenses.

But in the fall it was clear that if reform was to "work," reformers needed another strategy, as the theater owners had done little to tone down striptease. Thus Geraghty summarily closed the Republic and the Eltinge until they agreed to promote themselves as something less "insidious" than burlesque. The Republic became known as "Billy Minsky's Frolics Theater" and the Eltinge took the name "the Eltinge Follies." Then Geraghty trotted out a "burlesque czar"—the old Columbia circuit warhorse Sam Scribner—to police the striptease shows. Bad feeling between the city and the theater owners lingered, as each side suspected the other would soon renege on their promises.[59]

Many headlining strippers used the restrictions to focus on getting laughs. In October, *Billboard* reported that Gypsy performed a modified striptease at the Republic that "held the interest of the patrons as closely as tho the lid were off. An actress of considerable charm, it seems impossible for her to make a single move that could be called objectionable. She added a touch of comedy in one of her specialties by dropping bits of raiment on the bass player's dome."[60]

# "I Never Made Any Money until I Took My Pants Off": Fans and Bubbles around the Nation

I t is easy to imagine that if Billy Minsky had lived after 1932, old-fashioned burlesque striptease might have lived longer in New York. None of the other brothers could conjure up his flair, his panache, his silver-tongued success at placating the authorities. Of course, as the Depression worsened, mayors became harder to please. The man who followed Walker, interim mayor Joseph V. McKee, one of the few New York political figures to emerge stainless from Seabury's investigations, cracked down on burlesque the minute he took office in 1932. Back in 1927, McKee, then police commissioner, had been a driving force in raiding Mae West's *Sex*; now he showed his support for civic and business leaders' efforts to censor burlesque on Forty-second Street, all the while loudly declaring that he was most definitely not a censor.[1]

Nor were any of the concessions the frères Minsky made enough for John O'Brien, who replaced McKee in the winter of 1933. O'Brien, a bombastic former Supreme Court justice, was as eager as McKee had been to distinguish himself as a reformer and so, upon taking office, immediately announced, "Hereafter there will never be tolerated the removal of clothes on any stage in New York City in an indecent manner."[2] But the removal of clothes by strippers in an indecent manner continued.

As spring came around again, License Commissioner Geraghty again felt compelled to take strong measures. He warned theater managers that if strippers continued to "flash," or reveal their breasts, he would revoke their licenses. Adapting Sumner's idea from the previous year, Geraghty told managers that the only way he would let theaters stay open was if strippers refrained from touching their bodies and from discarding their garments onstage. But now Geraghty added a time limit to his ukases—he demanded that the changes be put into effect in twenty-four hours.[3] This sent the burlesque impresarios into a panic. For there was no question but that striptease was filling theaters and putting money in their pockets. Still, Minsky and the rest of the managers had no choice but to comply, at least for the moment.

Outside of New York, vice-society reformers faced greater opposition. In 1932, Americans elected Franklin Delano Roosevelt president. Shortly after that, FDR presented his New Deal, which he promised would lift the country out of the economic slump. The following year Roosevelt rescued American banks and restored hope among many. Too ebullient to be thinking about the nation's moral fiber, Americans flocked to burlesque theaters to hear funny jokes and see pretty women. Also, by 1932, vice-society reformers across the country, though sometimes as aggressive as their New York counterparts, had been discredited by a number of abortive investigations and met mixed success in efforts to shut down burlesque. The passing of the Eighteenth and Twenty-first amendments in 1933 distracted Americans, who had been denied legal liquor for fourteen years.[4]

In Boston, when the Watch and Ward Society —the New England version of the New York Society for the Suppression of Vice—petitioned Mayor James Michael Curley to close the Old Howard, the mayor replied with his stubborn tendency to mischief: "I would like to honor your petition, but do you realize the historical significance of the Howard Athenaeum? You may think the Howard is well known, but the Old Howard is known in every port of the world. It is one of Boston's great institutions."[5] After seeing one of the Howard's burlesque revues, Curley blamed its success on tourists: "They had a full house, but all of the people there seemed to come from Maine, New Hampshire, and Vermont." The Watch and Ward Society managed to padlock the Old Howard for thirty days. But subsequently the theater reopened to tourists, to Bostonians, and to its prior infamy.[6]

In Philadelphia opposition to striptease would not reach the fevered pitch it did in New York until the 1950s. In 1932, Max Wilner and the choreographer Allan Gilbert opened a new burlesque circuit—the wonder wheel—which presented smooth striptease routines sans burlesque comedy. *Variety* and *Billboard* praised these routines for their "refinement."[7]

Chicago played dogcatcher to strippers whom other cities had run out of town. That spring, as Mae West's comedy *She Done Him Wrong* sold out at movie theaters in the loop, strippers streamed to Chicago, where the burlesque business boomed in time for the 1933 World's Fair—the Century of Progress Exposition. Back in the twenties, Chicago burlesque theaters had exported raw strip numbers to New York. Francis Parks's "You Can't Believe My Naughty Eyes," in which she wore a mask with two eyes over her breasts, began there. But an unexpected consequence of the Chicago burlesque boom of the Depression era was the perfection of an altogether different "refined" mode of nude entertainment: the fan dance.[8]

The fan dance as it emerged in the early thirties presented the female performer as a showgirlish blend of child and vamp. Instead of doing the bump and grind, the fan dancer maintained an elegant presence, at her best recalling the mythical Philomel. Shards of Depression-era class consciousness found their way into her act. The oversized fan poked fun at wealthy women who, to protect themselves from the elements, carried enormous ostrich feather fans. Moreover, unlike Broadway chorines, fan dancers never wore headdresses. Their heads were unencumbered by the battleships, crowns, tiaras, and other paraphernalia that might have turned them into abstract physical presences, so they remained concrete and dangerous.[9]

As much as any of these numbers can be linked to one performer, the fan dance begins with one of Earl Carroll's "vaniteasers"—Faith Bacon—who first did it in a New York nightclub in 1930 in an effort to circumvent the legal restrictions against nudity. "We tried veils but the idea was too tame. We tried the French tights, but these seemed too ordinary. Finally, we hit on the fan dance," Bacon told reporters.[10]

The dance was so successful that Earl Carroll hired Bacon to do it in the 1930 *Vanities*, at which point she was arrested but not convicted, although a grand jury determined that she should leave the show. "She was absolutely naked," Captain James J. Coy said. Bacon's infamy got her a booking in the 1931 *Ziegfeld Follies* the following year, and in the 1932 edition of the *Vanities*, Bacon passed two fans back and forth in front of her body; in a chorus number called "Fans," a hundred women paraded up and down a giant staircase, waving ostrich plumes over their bodies like semaphores and suddenly turning around, as *Billboard* put it, and "treating" the customers at the sides of the house "to a vista of big, bare buttocks reaching up almost to the flies."

Even worse, Bacon's pasties "came loose," and the ubiquitous Coy, who had also—by testifying in the Mae West trials in 1926 and 1927—helped shut down the show, once again served Bacon with a warrant and called "Fans" offensive.[11]

IT WAS IN CHICAGO, though, that the fan dance became a national fad, thanks to Sally Rand, who first made a sensation with it at the *Streets of Paris* concession at the Century of Progress Exposition in 1933. Several years later Bacon sued Rand for $375,000 for stealing her act. "She used to hold my fans at the Valencia nightclub in New York," Bacon said, adding that "the only thing that hurts is that Sally goes around boasting that she originated the dance and that all other fan dancers are cheap and vulgar imitations."[12]

Of the two women, Rand was shrewder and more ambitious. Born Harriet Helen Beck in Elkton, Missouri, in 1904, Rand ran away with a traveling carnival at age fourteen. Taking the stage name Billie Beck, she worked in a German beer garden in Kansas City and with Adolph Bohm's Chicago Ballet Company. In Chicago, she also studied modeling at The Art Institute, where a painting of her won a prize.[13] Rand moved to Hollywood in 1923 to pursue dancing. At first, she made a success as a Mack Sennett bathing beauty, but when sound arrived, her Ozark twang failed to amuse producers. (Some say it was her lisp; she herself explained that she could not light a cigarette while acting.) She worked as a stagehand, was a WAMPAS (Western Association of Motion Picture Advertisers) baby, and did cameos in Cecil B. DeMille films. In *King of Kings*, she played a

Sally Rand doing her fan dance. Folly Theatre Archives, Kansas City.

handmaiden to Mary Magdalene. DeMille gave her her stage name after seeing a Rand McNally map one day.[14]

Exiled from Hollywood in the late twenties, Rand dabbled in vaudeville and for a time traveled on the Orpheum circuit with an act called Sally and Her Boys. After the Stock Market crashed, she found herself adrift. She worked briefly in New York and arrived in Chicago in 1928 in a touring burlesque show, "Sweethearts on Parade."[15]

Rand was almost thirty. Out of work in the months before the fair opened, she slept in alleys, rented yachts to newly rich bootleggers, and tried to convince Charlie Weber—the county commissioner who owned concessions at the *Streets of Paris*—that she should perform there. Initially she did not succeed. In the fall Rand began to perform her fan dance at the Paramount Club, a Gold Coast speakeasy whose patrons included Machine Gun Jack McGurn, one of Al Capone's men. (Rand told a reporter that she got the fans from a "fan manufacturer" in New York.[16])

According to Rand, when she did her first fan dance, no one was interested. In the Depression, audience members awaited ethnic songsters to serenade them at their tables. Weber continued to be uninterested in her act, and the fan dancer concluded, like many Chicagoans, that the fair was a spectacle for the upper classes. "The Streets of Paris was sponsored by the high and mighty of this town," she told Studs Terkel much later.[17]

Her class consciousness gave birth to an idea. Rand decided to try to sell herself by crashing Mrs. Hearst's "milk fund" party the night before the exposition. She snuck out to the Hearst yacht in a long blonde wig and white velvet cape and rode naked across the stage at the invitation-only dinner for Chicago's elite. (The man at the gate let her in.) The emcee shouted, "And now Lady Godiva will take her famous ride." Amid the chiffon and frogs' legs, speeches and prayers, supposedly a man from Evanston shouted, "My! My! It's years since I've seen a white horse."[18]

But Rand explained her piece of street theater as arising out of a left-leaning political conscience. She had seen a woman wearing a dress made out of money and thought it was in bad taste. She asked Studs Terkel, "How dare you have a dress of $1,000 bills when people are hungry?"[19]

After the Hearst yacht party, the *Streets of Paris* concession hired her. On May 27, the day the fair opened, Rand performed her sophisticated fan dance, to the consternation of Mayor Edward J. Kelly. The self-proclaimed classically trained dancer began to make money at the *Streets of Paris*. Her act was a hit.

What did the dance look like? "I attempt to prove the Rand is quicker than the eye," she quipped. Wearing a peroxide blonde wig, naked (or mostly naked) under a blue light, behind two pink ostrich feathers, Rand undulated to Claude Debussy's *Clair de Lune* and a Chopin waltz. "It is just my interpretation of a white bird flying in the moonlight at dusk," she said. "A white bird flying up. It flies up into the moonlight. It is dusk. It flies low. It flutters. Then it begins to climb into the moonlight. Finally it rests." The writer Frederick Lewis Allen depicted her as a media event: "The crowds surged to see her coming down the velvet covered steps with her waving fans (and apparently little else) before both she and Chicago profited."[20]

As THE FAN DANCER herself noted, though, the fair made money, but Chicago did not: in 1933 the number of unemployed there equaled the number of employed. In his first novel, *Somebody in Boots*, Nelson Algren, using a fictional paper, *The Tribute*, to stand in for the *Chicago Tribune*, described how the press magnified the inequity: "The *Tribune* gave glamour to its World's Fair reportage, but said nothing of hundreds of thousands living in shelters . . . not a word of women forced into prostitution."[21] Years later Rand said, "They planned this fair to bring business to Chicago, into the Loop. But you could have fired a cannon down State Street and hit nobody, because everybody was out at the fair."

According to Rand, she grossed over five hundred thousand from the fair.[21] And so, like Little Egypt forty years earlier, a woman undulating saved the day; she also inspired other stripteases, managed by the Capone faction, to offer "special" performances. Hot-Cha San did a number in gold paint. At the Berlin Cabaret, Alexianne danced wearing a star-shaped G-string. In its first month, however, the fan dance's morality came into question, thanks to Mayor Kelly and a reform-minded lawyer named Mary Belle Spencer. Spencer brought a lawsuit against the fair for violating the Illinois anti-obscenity law that forbade "lewd" and "lascivious" exhibitions. Fair officials responded with immediate action, raiding Rand while she was making a thousand dollars a week. (The same week reporters discovered that Mayor Kelly was dipping into city funds, reformers condemned Rand for performing a "skin opera."[23])

By July, Rand was on trial. She defended herself in court by saying that she performed naked because if she wore clothes, the fans stuck to them and made her act more difficult. Eventually, Superior Court Judge Joseph

Sally Rand at The Rialto. Author's personal collection.

David dismissed the case by memorably declaring, "Some people try to put pants on a horse." He added, *"Honi soit qui mal y pense"*—in other words, those who saw obscenity in Rand's act were themselves obscenity minded. "When I go to the fair, I go to see the exhibits and perhaps to enjoy a little beer. As far as I'm concerned, all these charges are just a lot of old stuff to me. Case dismissed for want of equity."[24]

David was not exactly taking Rand's side, however. Rather he was arguing that if Spencer wanted to make her accusation stick, she needed to go through the state's attorney and get him to shut down the concession itself. Spencer followed his instructions to the letter. Allied with other reformers, such as the Juvenile Protection Association of Chicago, she convinced Mayor Kelly to turn up the heat. Rand was eventually sentenced to ten days in jail and fined two hundred dollars. "Refusing to shake the prosecutor's hand, she pointed out that her sentence was exactly twice that given Machine Gun McGurn," one paper wrote. (Rand appealed and finally the appellate court cleared her of all indecency-related charges.[25])

When Mayor Kelly visited the fair, though, the *Chicago Tribune* noted that he turned "bashful pink" at the fan dancers' "purely hypothetical costumes." Kelly, who prefaced his crackdown by saying, "I am not a prude," demanded that the dancers cover up—or at least wear G-strings and bras—and ordered a 1:30 A.M. curfew.[26] The performers rose up in sartorial protest. One dancer wore yellow silk pajamas and red lace panties. Hot-Cha San brushed on a thicker coat of gold paint than usual. Someone put "pants" on Lady Godiva's horse.[27]

As for Rand, her infamy brought her success. In August, Rand began performing at the Chicago Theater in the Loop, where she sold out, and at her old hangout, the Paramount Club. She was immediately fined twenty-five dollars for indecent exposure. Still performing at the fair but now under orders to wear clothes, she inspired, according to the *Chicago Daily News*, "yawns."[28] By the middle of the month, Rand left the fair, a decision some newspapers attributed to a salary dispute, others to the political demand that she wear more.

Leaving proved to be a dangerous decision. That very day Rand "fell" off a speedboat into Lake Michigan. Nor was dry land safer. In late September she got into a fight with Sam Belkin, the owner of the Paramount—she bit him on the arm and he clouted her. Charges were dropped. Then she was again dragged into court on indecency charges.[29]

After all this, Rand left for New York, where she did the fan dance at the Paramount Theater—not to be confused with Chicago's Paramount Club—although the police arrested her and insisted that she don "opaque raiment."[30] All of this served to draw her to Hollywood's attention, which, as Louella Parsons noted in her column, was what Rand wanted. "Oh what a different ex wampas baby star returns to play the feminine lead for Paramount in *A Search for Beauty*."[31]

That film never happened. But Rand appeared in *Vanity Fair* opposite Martha Graham and performed a toned-down version of her fan dance in *Bolero*, which starred the gangster-actor George Raft and Carole Lombard. Rand played Arnette, a carnival showgirl. She made ten thousand dollars. *Bolero* was released in the winter of 1934 and Rand got good reviews, although the film itself bombed.[32] Hollywood, in turn, made Rand more attractive to the Century of Progress Exposition, which she returned to in the summer of that year to perform at the Italian Village concession.[33]

In her months away from Chicago, Rand had invented a new act: the bubble dance, in which she handled a giant opaque balloon as if it were a living creature. She danced behind the balloon and next to it. And instead of performing solo, Rand now headed a big show of 24 dancers and 16 showgirls. "I wanted a balloon sixty inches in diameter, which is my height, made of a translucent or transparent material," Rand said, explaining the new act's genesis.[34]

As with the fan dance, several stories emerged about who did it first. Rand claimed she invented the number herself. The challenge was that the biggest balloons available at the time were only thirty inches high. They were heavy red target balloons used by the War Department. Since no one knew how to make bigger ones, Rand traveled to Ohio to talk to the rubber companies making these balloons and fronted six thousand dollars for the necessary experimentation. After numerous tests, she created the superdooper see-through bubble.[35]

But here too imitators plagued Rand. Rosita Royce, age sixteen, whose strip number followed Rand's fan dance in the first year of the fair, also claimed she had invented the bubble dance. Royce was Rand's nemesis. Née Marjorie Rose Lee, Royce might have reminded the audience of the great luxury automobile appearing for the first time in the United States just as Bacon had reminded them of delicious food. Royce told reporters for years that she had invented the bubble dance at age ten. "I had it copyrighted. . . . I had a description of my dance and a photograph sent to the Library of Congress and they copyrighted it. It is No. 157757." Unlike Rand, Royce apparently performed totally nude behind the balloons.[36]

The balloon act presented more problems than the fight over who originated it, though. For the key to its popularity proved to be instability. The wind could blow the balloons away, and disruptive audience members tossed cigarettes at them or tried to pop them with pins. Royce said, "They often burst on me. In a lot of cabarets they use these steel-wool brushes on the floor and sometimes a tiny piece of wire gets caught in a crack and when my balloon hits there is an explosion. Also the spangles from the chorus girls' dresses get caught in the cracks."[37]

In the summer of 1934, one observer noted that the fair authorities ran metal fences on three sides of the stage to protect Rand.[38] But if anything, the possibility of seeing Rand naked behind the balloons increased the fan dancer's popularity, for she performed five shows a day throughout the summer.[39]

Nor was the balloon dance the only daredevil nude act being performed that year. At the *Streets of Paris*, the young impresario Mike Todd, a former soundproofing expert and comedy writer, got his first taste of producing. Todd concocted an entertainment, "the flame dance," that traded on the phenomenon of a moth's attraction to light and, of course, female nudity. A woman wearing a gauzy costume entered and did a short ballet around a huge candle until she got too close to the flame. Her costume burned off, and the seemingly naked woman flapped her "wings" and flew offstage. (The moth actually wore a flesh-colored asbestos body stocking.) About the act Todd said, "I burned up four girls before I got it right."[40] But the flame dance was a hit. According to his memoir, Todd brought the flame dance back to New York and installed it in Billy Rose's Casino de Paree as a featured act and then in one of his less successful revues, *Bring on the Dames*.[41]

As for Rand, when the Century of Progress closed in 1934, she returned to State Street and the Chicago Theater. The authorities convicted her for indecent exposure again, but a higher court overturned that verdict and while Rand stood trial the second time, American popular culture absorbed the fan dance by turning it into a marketing tool.[42]

During the next several years, Rand traveled all over the country selling GE air conditioners and other "family" products. Explaining her success to a group of salesmen in New York in 1935, she said, "There were accidents in the way of publicity, but the wisdom comes in using accidents for your own needs instead of letting them stay accidents. It required quite a bit of maneuvering and sales talk to turn these accidents to my own advantage."[43]

Rand studied acting and performed the role of Sadie opposite Humphrey Bogart in *Rain*.[44] She made a success in the hinterlands and on the West Coast. In 1936 she performed her fan dance at the California Pacific Exposition in San Diego, where she tangled with members of a nudist colony. Like "Sister" Aimee Semple McPherson, Rand made the mistake of declining to visit the nudists when "Queen" Tanya, "the Queen of the Nudists," invited her for tea. Then too, Rand claimed publicly that unlike the nudists, she was an entertainer and that her dance was an art form suggesting flight and idealizing the human body. The nudists took offense and picketed her act: "She probably figures that nudism will sound the deathkiss of sensationalism such as she practices," commented Mary Pomery, one of the nudists.[45]

Four days later, the *New York Times* reported:

Sally Rand, fan and bubble dancer, suffered bruises under her left eye and upon her left thigh from pebbles flung at her as she danced at the exposition last night. Bleeding at the cheek from the injury under her eye, she reappeared upon the stage after a brief retirement, with fans replacing her bubbles, and completed her act. The management announced it would have guards in future crowds about the dancer's stage.

But even when a reporter intent on revealing the "true" Rand described how she covered her "stubby hair" with her beautiful blond wig, Rand continued to make money. She flirted with the idea of using short-wave electricity to take off her clothes. She starred in a "nude ranch" at the 1936 Frontier Centennial Exposition in Fort Worth, and event that Billy Rose produced. The nude ranch featured forty "cowgirls" clad only in big Stetson hats, bandannas wrapped around their necks and middles, belts, and cowboy boots. Behind a glass window, the cowgirls played badminton, shot arrows, swam, and fished. Ticket sellers stood in barrels, the middle of their bodies covered. A Texas journalist wondered how Chicago city officials could ever have ignored Rand's talent.[46]

One aspect of Rand's contribution to striptease lay in the fact that she first brought together the cowgirl and the fan dance, uniting nostalgia for the gold rush with the modern thrill of seeing naked women in leather boots and guns. As the art and fashion historian Anne Hollander brilliantly puts it in *Sex and Suits*, male uniforms such as the cowboy's say "threat or bodily risk." When worn—or unworn—by women, male garb can yield an added frisson. The cowgirl striptease would become one of the most widely imitated numbers during the Cold War.[47] But Rand also established two ideas about stripping in the popular imagination: first, after 1933, no fair producer could consider his programming complete without a "girlie show," just as no burlesque theater operator could consider his show complete without a stripper. Second, undressing in public or performing nude were quick—perhaps the quickest—way for a woman to make money. As Rand put it, "I never really made any money until I took my pants off."[48]

# "Temporary Entertainment for Morons and Perverts": LaGuardia Kicks Striptease out of New York

Back in New York, burlesque continued to entertain the masses until, in January 1934, Fiorello LaGuardia came into office.[1] Obstinate as a bull, LaGuardia, elected on a Fusion or cross-party ticket, burst onto the scene with a Homeric reputation for reform. LaGuardia's career was marked by a fierce hatred of commercialized vice. An intoxicating speaker and an untiring fighter, "the Little Flower" dreamed of a New York free of burlesque, striptease, and organized crime. "I shall not rest until my native city is the first not only in population but also in public health; until it is not only out of debt but abounding in happiness," he said.[2]

One of the first things LaGuardia did was to revive the municipal vice squad, which the Seabury Commission had caused to be abolished by proving that it reeked with graft, that it framed innocent women, and that it had participated in fantastically corrupt schemes. Part of the strength of LaGuardia's purity campaign was that, quite simply, New Yorkers wanted him. Then too, LaGuardia took an active approach to discrediting the forces that had created deviant conditions as well as the previous administration, which had allowed them.[3] But he was also zealous because by 1934, Roosevelt's New Deal had still not ameliorated many of the Depression's woes: LaGuardia needed to give constituents the feeling that he was taking charge.[4]

When LaGuardia was elected, Times Square sagged even more than it had in 1932. The 1933 Warner Brothers movie *42nd Street* called the thoroughfare "naughty, bawdy, gaudy, [and] sporty." Critic Ward Morehouse compared the street to Coney Island: "cheapened and nightmarish . . . offering palm readings and photos while-u-wait, live turtles and tropical fruit drinks, sheet music, nut fudge, jumbo malteds, hot waffles, ham and eggs, hot dogs, and hamburgers . . . and fifty beautiful girls."[5]

It was not just the landscape. Times Square housed an increasingly visible homosexual population. As George Chauncey has documented, in addition to out-of-work men and women, Depression-era burlesque attracted gay men, drag queens, and gay hustlers from the South and other rural areas. Stories circulated about how, in the darkened theaters, gay prostitutes picked up wealthy gay men, and in some cases mugged them. The popular press and reformers began to associate burlesque houses in Times Square with gay prostitution. Thus the "good" notoriety Billy Minsky sought to cultivate at the Republic in 1931 brought about a "bad" notoriety, which increased as the economy continued to drag.[6]

At about this time, copper-haired Margie Hart, who shortly would become striptease exhibit A, arrived in New York. Like a lot of strippers, Hart began her ascent in a relatively unassuming fashion. Sometime in the first year or so of the Depression, she left home in rural Missouri and began posing as the Statue of Liberty at the Old Garrick in St. Louis. She started stripping at the Trocadero in Philadelphia in the winter of 1932, and by the end of 1933, when the Minskys saw her there, Hart was taking it off to her shoes, her G-string, and "two dabs of rouge."[7]

IN NEW YORK'S City Hall early in 1934, LaGuardia cracked down. He put his own man in the license commissioner spot—Paul Moss, a courtly, balding, theatrical type whose brother owned the Criterion Theater on Forty-second Street.[8] Described by one columnist as "sweep[ing] the city from early in the morn until late at night," Moss liked to attend theatrical openings: he himself had once produced a hit called *Subway Express*. He looked at burlesque with "a regretful eye." He won't be a "sissy," the *Brooklyn Daily Eagle* reported.[9] The *New York Times* called Moss "the broom."

A Jew and a bachelor with a seventh-grade education, Moss might have seemed humorless, but at times he could display a demonic wit. When the burlesque managers complained that one of Moss's early embargoes on striptease would run them out of business, the wry license commissioner made a suggestion: why didn't the burlesque men turn to other forms of entertainment—like opera—to support themselves?[10]

No sooner had LaGuardia installed him than Moss said he planned to clean up the city. He told his staff shortly after being appointed, "I don't want to be a censor, but certain indecent performances should not be permitted." He attacked many forms of "dirt," including magazine publishers and racketeers. But he seemed to harbor, perhaps because of his own theatrical background, a particular antipathy toward burlesque, which was bolstered in part by the genre's alleged connection to organized crime. By this time, then district attorney William C. Dodge had received numerous complaints from business establishments in the vicinity of Irving Place that hoodlums gathered in the theater lobby and annoyed the working women in the neighborhood. But Moss also operated with fervor for political reasons: at that moment the Seabury Commission suspected the entire license department of graft.[11]

Even before LaGuardia formally took office, Moss arranged for ten strippers to be arrested at the Irving Place Theater, and the following week he drafted a letter to burlesque managers telling them what needed to be changed so they could avoid being shut down. His demands included dismantling the runways and forbidding "mingling," which involved striptease performers' descending into the audience to flirt. Moss also insisted that strippers only strip down to their bras, and then only "flash"—as insiders called the ultimate brief moment of undressing. Moreover, he wanted to ban the encores, during which strippers grabbed onto the curtain and ground their hips. (The theater managers tore out the runways and nodded toward the rest of Moss's edicts.[12])

The city encouraged Moss's half-restrictions rather than outlawing nudity altogether because while it was not that difficult to padlock a theater and arrest a few performers, it was difficult to keep the theater padlocked and the performers in jail. In 1935, Albany judges would throw a conviction against a burlesque theater out of court and forbid politicians to padlock theaters with no prior convictions on the basis of one obscenity charge. Vice-society reformers' attempts to pass the Dunnigan Bill, which would have given the license commissioner power to revoke a license if he thought a show was immoral (in other words, without evidence) also stalled. While these pro–free speech decisions frustrated vice-society reformers who saw Depression-era New York as a city overrun by naked women, trade papers continued to point out the license commissioner's differing approach to nudity in high- and low-class theaters. "Nudity is no longer considered indecent in uptown night clubs where men and women pay from $10 to $20 for seats and similar performances are given," *Billboard* noted.[13]

NUDITY PREVENTED burlesque performers from creating a strong union and from taking advantage of some New Deal protections. By the time LaGuardia arrived in office, burlesque, like many other industries in the country, needed financial help. Back in the spring of 1933, Congress had passed the National Recovery Act (NRA) to combat the Depression's worst effects and had created an agency, the National Labor Recovery Board (NLRB), to administer it. Among the NRA's functions were to regulate labor abuses, to help various industries recover from the Depression, and to combat unemployment. The act called for industrial regulation and ordered employers to draft codes for fair competition to protect workers. Additionally, these codes were supposed to cover hours of work, rates of pay, and setting of prices.[14]

Abuses against performers in burlesque were legion—worse than in almost any other area of show business. Salaries varied wildly. A popular stripper could make about $60 a week, while Ann Corio earned $5,000 one week in 1932. But most performers made much less, and the work week lasted as long as 70 or 80 hours. Days off did not exist. The performers rarely received extra money for the midnight shows the management called upon them to do. Managers were required neither to notify performers of the show's closing nor to pay for transportation. Sometimes, if money was short, the performer's pay envelope would include an IOU instead of the money owed to her, and for the most part she accepted this treatment for fear of being blacklisted.

Whereas legitimate actors, vaudevillians, Jewish actors from the Yiddish theater, and chorus girls sought protection under the loosely knit organization known as the 4 A's, burlesque had been unable to organize, in part because of its performers' poverty. At an early hearing to support a fledgling burlesque union, Thomas Phillips noted that of 903 members, only 10 percent had paid their dues. But spurred on by the NRA's support, burlesque performers became by the fall of 1933 more aggressive in these efforts. "We feel we are a distinct and separate part of theatre," Thomas Phillips, president of the Burlesque Artists' Association (BAA) wrote in a memo, explaining why burlesque performers should have more autonomy.[15] Phillips wanted to establish a minimum wage—$17.50 a week for stock performance and $20.00 for work on the road.

Right from the beginning the question of whether a union could exist with striptease was raised because no other performers wanted to adopt burlesque. At a hearing in November, Phillips tried to latch on to the chorus girls' union, but that union was not interested. Nor did Equity want to sponsor burlesque. Even a letter from Alfred Nelson, *Billboard*'s editor, failed to convince the chorus girls' union that merging with burlesque would be in its best interest.[16]

By the fall of 1933, burlesque performers complained that without their own union, they would never be able to put into effect the ideas President Roosevelt championed. "We are unable to get near theaters or appoint a deputy to collect dues. This is due to the type of man in control of the burlesque theater," Phillips wrote in another heated letter to Frank Gilmore, the president of Actors Equity. On December 23, an informal executive board was named to oversee BAA. Gypsy Rose Lee was a member. Directly after the new year, the BAA got its own charter, bylaws, and union. The standard for burlesque was defined as "what happened at Irving Place."[17]

The creation of BAA raised as many problems as it solved. Early on, members discussed whether members of other unions could work in burlesque. Phillips resisted this idea. He argued that if BAA made burlesque a closed shop, the industry would clean up, and this would keep reformers and politicians from shutting down burlesque theaters. Taking on the role of industry watchdog, the BAA put together a regulatory list of do's and don't's for strippers and asked LaGuardia to create a self-governing board of censors.[18]

Meanwhile, from Washington, Sol Rosenblatt, deputy director of amusement industries for the NRA, ordered LaGuardia to acknowledge the BAA as legitimate and to use the NLRB to create a wage scale for burlesque performers, as well as allow them to create their own censorship policies. At a pivotal meeting held in the ballroom of the Mayfair Hotel in Washington, Isidore Herk, whom the government had named "code advisor"—a position

designed to mediate between Washington and the burlesque industry—
demanded a bigger raise for performers in small-town burlesque houses
than the BAA had initially requested. Strippers, he argued, should make
$30.00 a week, and chorus girls should make $22.50. Paul Weintraub, the
attorney for the National Burlesque Association, a competing organization headed by Herk and representing mostly managers, described burlesque as "wholesome."[19]

When Rosenblatt countered that striptease was hardly wholesome,
Weintraub shrugged and responded cavalierly, "Some call it nudity, some
call it a strip number. But the more cosmopolitan call it a higher type of
aesthetic entertainment for civilized human beings."[20]

But neither the BAA's efforts to counter an anti-burlesque prejudice
nor those of the NLRB worked, mostly because obscenity trials and arrests
were increasing across the country and making it difficult for the American
public to see burlesque as anything but obscene. In February 1934 the
police raided the Irving Place Theater for seeking to hire "women with no
experience . . . for near nude posing." Among the ten performers they
picked up was Margie Hart, whom theater managers then wanted to blacklist. *Billboard* described her as a "smart parader" and a "clever" and "artistic" stripper. *Zit's* wrote that she looked "sweet" as she paraded around
stage "not even singing. . . . [T]he crowd would hardly allow the finale of
the first part to go on. They wanted more of her."[21]

The BAA responded by both defending Hart and launching "a war
against dirt." Thus the BAA won strippers' support for the first time. By
painting theater operators as the villains, the ones who insisted on nudity,
the BAA became the champion of the "little guy."[22]

Herk's first task was to convince the mayor that theater operators could
turn the dross of burlesque into the gold of vaudeville. Thus, Herk lobbied
for strippers to wear bras and advocated giving theater operators the right
to blacklist strippers such as Margie Hart, who, Herk asserted, took it off
too "strongly." Burlesque, Herk argued, should distance itself from striptease, "clean up," "clamp down," and "rehabilitate."[23]

Eventually, Herk did help burlesque performers by completing the
employment code. And yet Herk continued to struggle to convince politicians that burlesque was theater and not pornography. Many burlesque
performers remained suspicious of Herk: until 1935 the man LaGuardia
chose to be his "burlesque czar" owned part of the New Gotham Theater
on 125th Street, along with the Minskys. *Variety* had long criticized Herk
for being duplicitous. "When Izzy Herk says, 'we are trying to get away
from stripping. We can't yank it out all of a sudden, but we're going to do
it gradually'—that's the cue for more stripping and more strippers."[24]

Also, theater operators crippled by the Depression argued that the wage
codes Herk proposed were too ambitious. In 1935 several Los Angeles op-

Cartoon of stripper from *Zit's Theatrical Newspaper*, March 31, 1934, 7. Billy Rose Theatre Collection, New York Public Library for the Performing Arts, Astor, Lenox, and Tilden Foundations.

erators went before the BAA to argue that if they paid the wages the union required, they would go bankrupt.[25] The NRA began to toy with the idea of shelving a burlesque code altogether.[26] It was clear that because of striptease's role as an art form non grata, the NLRB had decided that burlesque overall did not deserve to be treated on par with other entertainment industries. Thus whereas the other highly effective and articulate theatrical unions founded during the Depression—such as Actors Equity—were able to turn the era's anger and hopelessness into concrete financial gains and rights, the BAA remained stigmatized by burlesque's reputation for "dirt."

The dispute over who the BAA represented would continue into the late thirties. In the spring of 1935, the BAA tried another strategy to project a more positive appearance to the public: the union considered a proposal from IATSE—the stagehands and musicians' union—to join forces. The union also sought to blame theater operators for continuing to put striptease into their shows. At a union meeting on May 20, Thomas Phillips noted that Commissioner Moss objected to striptease, not burlesque.[27]

By June 1935, however, the NRA had abandoned the burlesque code. Theater operators took advantage of this and switched from two-a-day to three-a-day policies, which allowed them to get more striptease for less money.[28] Unable to negotiate the competing demands of the burlesque audience, the performers, and the reformers, the crippled union struck for four days in September. When the strike was settled, one result was that the industry overall was weakened as the two sides, unable to agree on even the most basic terms—such as minimum salary for performers—continued to squabble. A second result was that the NRA refused to police burlesque at all. The managers' association—now called the Eastern Burlesque Managers' Association—continued to promise cleaner shows and say they would "modify" stripping and decrease the number of strip acts in a burlesque show from five to two.[29]

THIS PROMISE WAS hardly kept. Several of the very managers who had sworn to decrease nudity increased the number of strips in each burlesque show. In his memoir, John Sumner, director of the New York Society for the Suppression of Vice, cited 1935 as the year in which "burlesque commenced to run wild."[30] Nor was the striptease explosion limited to New York. Back in 1932 the Minsky family had tried to start their own burlesque circuit—the Supreme circuit—which only lasted a few months. Now they created a kind of franchise, opening Minskys' Music Hall in Miami, with an eighteen-piece orchestra and thirty-six undressed chorines and sending another troupe of burlesque performers to Hollywood's Burbank Theater.[31] In their eternal effort to pitch upscale burlesque, the Minskys traded the word burlesque for "revue-esque" and called the LA show *Life Begins at Minskys*, to send up Harold Arlen's popular musical revue *Life Begins at 8:40*, which starred the burlesque comic Bert Lahr.[32]

H.K. rented an enormous neon sign for the marquee with the legend "Hollywood has gone Minskys / Minskys' has gone Hollywood." Opening night resembled a movie premiere. A crowd stormed the entrance and the police arrived to keep order. *Zit's Theatrical Newspaper*, reporting on the family's westward expansion, predicted that "'Life Begins at Minskys' will do its part to make Hollywood more sex conscious . . . if that's possible."[33] But reviewers complained that ultimately the Minskys needed fewer "tame" strips.[34]

New York, though, was ground zero for striptease. Burlesque theater operators pinched by the Depression and bad publicity added strippers to their shows. In 1935 the Apollo featured twenty-eight bare-breasted dancers onstage—apparently a record. That year, for the first time, theater operators hired black and Chinese strippers, as well as novelty acts such as the "European aerial strip artist," whom Abe Minsky persuaded to take off her G-string at the Gotham. Even the Republic featured bare-breasted and bare-buttocked strippers—and sometimes totally nude ones.[35]

THE EXPLOSION IN STRIPTEASE in burlesque was accelerated by the fact that after Prohibition was repealed at the end of 1933, nightclub owners began to hire showgirls and scantily clad dancers to fill their clubs. Of course, clubs with strippers had existed during Prohibition: Jimmy Kelly's in Greenwich Village specialized in fan dancers, the Club Richman in "practically naked" dancing, and the Embassy Club in a woman "shedding" the glass beads on her dress. The Hollywood, where Nils T. Granlund first emceed, featured "droves and droves" of good-looking girls.[36]

But the new generation of "legitimate" nightclubs disassociated themselves from the gangster image that speakeasies had acquired in the 1920s. Many of these new clubs were enormous places offering naked women, food, vaudeville acts, and liquor to mass audiences. Like their burlesque counterparts, nightclub impresarios wanted to produce both family and adult entertainment. Granlund claimed that his second nightspot, the Paradise Café, which served eight hundred people at "ringside" every night, was a "family" joint. At the same time, he hired Rose Zelle Rowland, a stripper, to appear as "the Golden Girl" in nothing but gold paint and a G-string. She was so successful that Granlund began to hire strippers regularly. But according to Georgia Sothern, when N.T.G., as he was known, hired her for one of his midnight shows in the winter of 1935, he was shocked when she stripped to a G-string while singing "Pardon my Southern accent, pardon my Southern drawl."[37]

A pipeline developed between nightclubs and burlesque. After Sothern's appearance at the Paradise Club, the impresario Billy Rose hired her for a similar number at his Casino de Paree, a spectacular revue-nightclub located in the Gallo Hotel on Fifty-fourth Street. But unlike Granlund, Rose demanded that she stop stripping in burlesque while working for him. Rose also saw the Casino de Paree as being a nightclub for the "working man" with food and liquor: although he varied conventional cabaret entertainment with eccentric variety acts, he was concerned that Sothern would be too wild even in the nightclub the columnist Lucius Beebe described as "delirious." According to Sothern, though, the numbers she did for Rose revealed more flesh than her burlesque strips. Robert Alton, who staged Cole Porter's *Anything Goes* and would later work on the *Ziegfeld Follies of 1936*, costumed Sothern in green paint from the waist down, a G-string, and some beads to cover her breasts.[38]

Writing about the striptease fad in post-repeal nightclubs, George Jean Nathan noted that such clubs were doing a "land office business."[39] But, Nathan complained, the new clubs confused things. It was difficult to tell whether one was "in a night club or a nudist camp, a burlesque show or a girls' shower room."[40] It was an upscale nudist camp, at least. At Mario's Mirador, on Fifty-second Street, strippers developed elaborate, highly produced acts that matched their elaborate, highly produced rags-to-riches stories. Usually these acts lacked humor. Alma Braye, who began as the cigarette girl at Mario's and graduated to striptease, advanced a well-worn tale about her "accidental" discovery of the genre. One week Margie Hart doubled at Mario's and the Apollo Theater uptown, and the columnist Louis Sobol dropped in to catch the act. While Hart was stripping, Braye, who knew Sobol, whispered to him that she could do a better strip on the trapeze. (She had worked with the respected circus family the Renauds.[41])

Sobol wrote a column about Braye, which drew the smart set to Mario's to see her. In it he claimed that she was eighteen years old, that her father was a full-blooded Cherokee chieftain named Whitewings, and that her mother was a descendant of English nobility. Whatever her heritage, she did the acrobatic "butterfly" strip in which she removed her pants in an ankle drop. A second Mirador stripper, Jacqueline Joyce, dropped one fur after another on the floor, and in her press material she dropped a story about aspiring to luxury after relatives in Canada had given her six silver foxes, four white foxes, a silver fox cape, and an ermine cloak worth ten thousand dollars. (The reality, which "slipped" into the press but seemed to make no difference to her career, was that she was Dina Dell from a small town in North Carolina.) By 1936 a headline in *Zit's* read, "Night Clubs to Feature More Daring Nudes."[42]

Nightclubs were also where the B-girl first emerged. B stood for bar, and it was widely understood that B-girls were not so much performers as scantily clad escorts whose job it was to induce customers to drink watered-down liquor.[43]

TO COMPETE WITH nightclubs, the most successful burlesque theater of the mid-thirties—the Irving Place—varied "glorified" striptease with the best production values it could muster and really raunchy disrobing. Thus the popular press wavered between praising the Irving Place as "ground zero for striptease" and criticizing it as a speakeasy where women flashed "both smiles and rear ends at the audience."[44]

Another aspect of the Irving Place's identity crisis came about thanks to a change in management. In the fall of 1935, Tony Miccio, who was reported to have mob connections, took over the theater from the Wilner family, which had owned it since the Jazz Age. After Miccio, striptease, Irving Place style, might feature a chorine in a solo spotlight lifting the flimsy strip of silk covering her breasts or one strutting up and down the runway wearing nothing at all. "The customers expect the limit and get it by applauding," *Billboard* noted.[45]

With Times Square theaters opening and closing, the Irving Place became a destination for the slumming middle class. Its prices were relatively high for burlesque—$1.65 and $1.10—but the theater also attracted what used to be called "deviants." When June Havoc went to see her sister Gypsy Rose Lee perform there in 1935, she reported that salesmen, engineers, students, and the occasional female patron sat in the orchestra. But

Berenice Abbott, *Irving Place Theatre*, c. 1938. Museum of the City of New York.

"perverts sat . . . alone in the balcony with action."[46] Visiting the Irving Place a couple of years later, the English anthropologist Geoffrey Corer described the audience in a repelled tone:

> I think it may be taken for granted that the greater number of men who go to burlesque theaters week after week, year after year—do not go there for purely aesthetic reasons, or for simple entertainment; the extra-ordinary [*sic*] monotony of the performances would exclude both possibilities. They almost certainly go there for sexual stimulation. . . . [T]his is their only dream, and they go by themselves, shut in, intent, determined to exclude the life they know; If they concentrate hard enough maybe they will get the physical illusion of reality.[47]

Havoc, however, also praised the Irving Place's vitality backstage. "There was a sense of energy in the place that rarely appeared in other types of theater," she wrote.[48]

Some of that energy came from twenty-six-year-old Allen Gilbert, a young burlesque producer and choreographer from Cleveland. Slight, bald, and distracted, Gilbert produced striptease numbers for the Irving Place from 1933 to 1938, when the theater closed.[49] In part due to Gilbert's influence, the theater operator Max Wilner ripped out the Irving Place orchestra pit and runway to replace them with a stairway, which allowed for more elaborate Ziegfeld-style choreography.[50]

Gilbert interpolated Broadway dancing with striptease. In one revue, he choreographed a tap striptease, a minuet, a dance featuring six girls in hoop skirts, a military tap number, a French dance, a bubble dance, and a striptease. He encouraged Wilner to hire fewer comics and more strippers, including the then ingenue Gypsy Rose Lee, the tassel twirler Carrie Finnell, and Georgia Sothern.[51] Some reviewers criticized Gilbert for harboring uptown aspirations. "Gilbert's fault just now is a highbrow complex," *Variety* wrote.[52]

But *Zit's Theatrical Newspaper* celebrated the "uptown" aspect of Gilbert's stripteases.[53] Probably the most complex portrait of Gilbertesque striptease at the Irving Place comes from the journalist H. M. Alexander, who describes one night there in a romantic-comic-pornographic tone. Starting the evening is a production number featuring chorus girls imitating horses, an act that, as Alexander points out, hardly interested the audience at all. But then the strippers appear.

> . . . the band plays "La Cucaracha" . . . a little crop-headed brunette appears in a much bespangled white evening dress with a yoke collar. She moves downstage in a jerky, eccentric movement that is neither a walk nor a dance . . . "La Cucaracha" crashes into its final bars. Carmen maneuvers to the wing, and as the song ends, she puts her hand behind her neck, undoes the yoke, flashes her breast, and winds herself in the curtain. There is applause, but no enthusiasm. The spot picks her up again. The band plays "Lady of Spain" in a fox trot tempo. Her left forearm and hand cover her breasts, her right hand holds the dress at her middle. She parades once across the stage, more or less in time to the music, dips, whirls, and returns . . . exposing her breasts. With the same hand, she undoes a row of snappers on the side of her specially prepared skirt. The left cheek of her backside appears, the left thigh, the left calf, the left ankle. As she reaches the end of the stage, the music concludes, the right hand at Carmen's middle whips away what's left of her dress. She is revealed in a g-string, a glittering, tiny triangle.

A song follows and then another production number, with comics firing guns with blanks. And then the next stripper is on. The emcee introduces her as "the sweet, the elusive, the dainty Sylvie Sylvane." Alexander characterizes her as

> what they describe in burlesque as "strictly a blonde." A little red hat sits on her platinum head, and she wears red pyjamas. . . . "Find Out What They Want," she sings, "and give it to 'em ju-ust that way." . . . She does a frank, arm-swinging walk from one end of the stage to the other, dipping with arms extended when she turns. At the end of her trailer, she

slips smoothly out of her pyjama coat, gives it a twist so it will swirl when she drops it and smilingly accepts applause . . . she grasps the curtain and does a grind. There is applause. She turns around and bumps. One arm is extended, wrist flexed, palm towards the audience, the other hand at her middle . . . she takes her bow in her G-string. There is applause, mostly from the first four rows. The white lights go out and the tramp comic and his straight man are on the stage hollering . . . they keep applauding for Sylvie. . . . [T]his time she comes out in only her G-string and little red hat. She does her dips and turns and arm-swinging down the stage and back. She pulls the curtain across her middle with one hand, undoes her G-string with the other, and just before the black out, she whirls it round and round in the spot to show that (underneath the curtain) she really hasn't a thing on.

Another production number provides a break for the audience. Two comics play a hackneyed scene about a traveling salesman, four rooms, and a woman who walks in her sleep. The last stripper is Joan Sanders. A comic fires a shiny, empty revolver and the emcee introduces her.

She is beautiful. It may be the lavender spot on the auburn hair and white skin and a green evening gown with a flowing jacket. The audience is still. The girl moves swiftly downstage. She stands and sways to the syncopated music. Her long bob falls to her shoulders in curly ringlets . . . swings from side to side . . . carves graceful lines out of her forehead and neck and shoulders. She makes dynamic Wigmanesque gestures, left arm extended sidewise, right arm pulled down across the body, the palm passing her face. The effect is rendered somehow childish and yet charming by the full sleeves of her jacket, snug at the wrist. She changes her position. . . . She does three fast bumps as the drummer raps out rim shots. . . . She undoes the yoke of her dress and abruptly drops it. Arms outspread, she looks down at her breast with the frank sensuality of a child discovering her body for the first time. She throws back her head and smiles.[54]

This new wave of elegant burlesque and striptease inspired another generation of artists and writers, many of whom were interested in describing the social significance—and sometimes the despair—of the working-class world. Still swooning over striptease, Cummings, in a letter to Ezra Pound, recommended "the Irving Place Burlesk stripteasers in excelsis and to hell with I.D. ology."[55] Striptease was less attractive in James T. Farrell's *Judgement Day* when, as a young man, Studs visited a Chicago burlesque house and found himself both repulsed and attracted. Frank, the vaudevillian in John Dos Passos' *The Big Money*, would rather be anywhere than on "the filthy stage of a burlesque house."[56]

A more woeful representation of burlesque appeared in the work of Reginald Marsh. Influenced by the Ashcan School and John Sloan, Marsh began to paint and sketch burlesque strippers as "everywomen" around

1927. Along with other working-class entertainments, Marsh continued to sketch burlesque scenes into the thirties and forties in New York and New Jersey. In an egg tempera series based on visits to the Star in Brooklyn and the Gaiety on Forty-sixth Street, Marsh painted burlesque scenes contrasting the strippers' aggressive sexuality and the audience's ordinariness. Marsh crammed the paintings with overripe female bodies bursting out of the few clothes they wear, as if stifled by the excess ardor. The scenes are full of motion. In one of these paintings, *Burlesque*, Marsh clustered the strippers onstage *in medias* undress and celebrated the kinetic casualness exploding from the stage. The strippers are so overblown that they often seem to have jumped from a comic book. Marsh puts the viewer in the audience, which is eternally rapt, in the thrall of the stripper pulling off her dress onstage.[57]

Burlesque striptease fascinated Marsh because of the contradictory qualities he saw in it: crudity and beauty, spontaneity and mechanical drone. He connected burlesque to a rapidly vanishing city and also thought it a "sad" commentary on the working-class man. But he loved burlesque's makeshift quality. "You get a woman in the spotlight, the gilt architecture of the place, plenty of humanity. Everything is nice and intimate, not spread out and remote as in a regular theatre."[58]

Marsh was not the only artist moved to envision burlesque as social commentary. Having returned from Paris, Berenice Abbott photographed the Irving Place Theater in 1938 as part of the Changing New York series she did for the WPA. The building, which would become a Yiddish theater the following year, looks magisterial except for the sign on the marquee. In the foreground, life continues as usual. The muralist Stuyvesant Van Steen also painted burlesque strippers as part of his series of portraits of vanishing American lives.

A more surprising version of striptease is Edward Hopper's. A fan of the theater since his youth, Hopper visited a burlesque show in the late 1930s, and embarked on painting *Girlie Show*, which revealed striptease's corrosive effect on solitude. Hopper examined solitude in all of his work, but in this painting the central figure's solitude is actually emphasized by the presence of an audience. Caught in the limelight, the naked "girlie" strides across the stage alone, a rebuke to her admirers, waiting for pleasure and applause to overtake her. In the painting the woman's back is slightly arched, her arms spread away from her body; and she holds a blue scarf or skirt behind her back. Her eyes are blacked out in shadow. The harsh stage light dulls her chalky skin against her blue G-string, shoes, and scarf; and her brassy hair shines fakely, matching the color of her crudely drawn nipples. Besides the stripper, the viewer can see the men's heads and the drummer in the orchestra.[59]

Reginald Marsh, *Star*, 1935. Estate of Reginald Marsh, 2004, Arts Students League, New York, Artists' Rights Society, New York.

EVEN AS IT ATTRACTED the attention of "higher" art forms, striptease remained under threat. In 1935 burlesque's tenacity begat more reform when McCall-Dooling bill, put forth by reformers in Albany, sought to outlaw nudity altogether. A wry editorial in *Zit's* reminded readers that nudity existed in nightclubs and Broadway revues as well burlesque, but that a ban would outlaw it everywhere.

> Try to imagine the Minsky masterpieces being presented without the benefit of nudity. Or Earl Carroll's presentations without the bare facts

of life. Or Sally Rand with underwear. If these fantastic pictures can be visualized, it should also be easy to visualize the miles of empty seats forlornly glaring at the warmly clad performers.[60]

Taking advantage of the doomsday atmosphere, burlesque theater operators added extra stripteases to their burlesques. At the New Gotham uptown, business tripled. The long-awaited opening of the Triborough Bridge on July 11, 1936, connected Manhattan, Queens, and the Bronx for the first time and made it easier for outer-borough residents to see striptease in East Harlem, where the bridge ended.[61] Nor was the New Gotham the only burlesque theater in New York where strippers of all kinds performed. At the Star in Brooklyn, there were "four specialty numbers, two exotic twists, a military tap, and classical wiggle."[62]

The year-end report in *Variety* described a "sizeable" increase in business and offered for the first time a list of the twelve best strippers. Burlesque theater owners were hiring more strippers—as many as seven a show. At the New Gotham, four women stripped "for an electric moment with nothing on at all." At the Republic, some strippers "peeled right down to their hands." All of this made LaGuardia aware that if he wanted to eradicate burlesque, he needed to take more decisive action.[63]

Thus the mayor turned again to John Sumner and the NYSSV to help create a climate of public outrage about striptease. In its 1936 annual report, the NYSSV noted that striptease performances were "carried to the extreme of nudity," conflated burlesque and "striptease," and stated that burlesque was a breeding ground for criminals. "This type of underworld exhibition should not be tolerated in the city of New York. It may give temporary entertainment to morons and perverts . . . but there is no demand for it in the public in general."[64] In the pages of the *New York Times*, Sumner would challenge the managers' pledge to clean up burlesque. "I hope they can," he wrote.[65]

Sumner's attacks impelled the "living Minskys," as H.K. and Morton had begun to call themselves to distinguish themselves from their brother Abe, to reinvest in the "silk hat" trade.[66] In October, H.K. and Mort purchased the Oriental, a "legitimate" theater on Broadway, between Fifty-first and Fifty-second streets. Once a movie palace, then an Italian film house, the Oriental seemed like the perfect place to revive glamour striptease. Mort and H.K. did everything they could to give the Oriental an upscale air: they asked Norman Bel Geddes to produce; they specified formal dress on the Christmas Eve opening's invitation; they had Phil Silvers emcee the gala; and they invited guests to peruse an exhibition of "original oils" of nudes in the lobby while tuxedoed waiters and women in oriental dress served champagne. But Billy Minsky's ghost hovered in the center of the art exhibit, where a live cootch dancer swayed inside a glass case.[67]

As was the Minsky style, the Oriental also paid homage to Broadway by titling its first revue *Red, Hot, and Nude*, which the Minskys borrowed from the recently opened Cole Porter musical *Red, Hot, and Blue*. Porter protested and the Minskys changed the show's name to *Swing, Baby, Swing*, which sent up the movie musical *Sing, Baby, Sing*. The revue featured black performers, a passel of comics, and four strippers, including Margie Hart.[68] But unlike the Minsky efforts of the 1920s and early 1930s, *Swing, Baby, Swing* failed to sustain an audience.[69] *Variety* pointed to the Oriental's out-of-the-way location and to the small stage and bad sightlines, both of which made live performance impractical. But the newspaper not only condemned the show as dull, it singled out the strips as being tame. "Margie and the other girls are apparently under instructions to get down to the g-string in two walk-ons and no encores. That's going to disappoint Margie's followers," critic Joe Bigelow scolded. Then he added, another stripper "doesn't even wake them up." Neither good follow-up reviews a month later nor LaGuardia's blessing could save the production. The Minskys abandoned the Oriental in April.[70]

As EARLY AS February, the mayor had stepped up his anti-striptease campaign by giving a radio press conference that began with the operatic line "This is the beginning of the end of incorporated filth." Privately LaGuardia mused to Paul Moss that "even the word striptease sounds dirty."[71] The Minskys responded through public relations. They founded a "striptease institute," Minsky University, and supported a burlesque critics' organization whose mission was to get daily newspapers to assign reviews to writers "acquainted with the particular type of entertainment program offered by burly houses."[72]

None of this worked. In the first days of April, a coterie of irate businessmen and religious leaders again met with Moss in a hearing at his office on 105 Walker Street to demand firmer action against striptease, arguing that despite the steps taken in the past five years, stripping still flourished. On April 9, a grand jury hearing was held to determine whether Abe's theater, the New Gotham, which was widely considered to be the most scurrilous burlesque house in the city, had violated the penal code on a night in late August of the previous year. The trial had been delayed for several months. Every time it was scheduled, as *Variety* described, "the corridors of the criminal court building were packed with people hoping for a glimpse of the stripteaser, who, the Minsky press agent announced, would demonstrate that striptease was a classical art."[73] The fact that one of the strippers was Roxanne Sand, the ex-wife of the prizefighter King Levinsky, added to the media circus.

In the end, Moss triumphed. He obtained a conviction to close the New Gotham not just for a week, but until the fall, under Section 1140a of the penal code. Reporting on the event, the *New York Times* headline for the first time included the word "striptease."[74] Leaving the courtroom, Sumner and Moss were in a celebratory mood. "The conviction is a real victory," said Sumner. "At least we have a check on the striptease situation." When asked if he intended to start a campaign against striptease, though, Moss replied that he had been gathering evidence since 1934 against burlesque theaters, but that he was simply doing his job. The district attorney swore that this conviction meant the end of burlesque altogether.[75]

At the sentencing hearing held a week later, Abe got up in court to protest the padlocking of his theater and to accuse Moss of violating his rights. "You think you are running the whole country," he mumbled, then added, "This has been going on for twenty five years and you have been in office for three years . . . and you haven't done anything."[76]

But the results of the New Gotham trial threw all the burlesque theater owners into a panic. They knew that May 1 was the date for license renewals, and if the mayor decided to revoke theirs, they were out of jobs. And so they spent the rest of April trying to clean up their acts, dimming the colored lights that the strippers favored and warning them not to take off their G-strings. Still the strippers continued to take off their G-strings, and the stagehands continued to shine bright lights on them. And the religious leaders lobbying to convince Moss to deny the theaters their licenses knew it. "You cannot make these places decent. You might as well try to freeze hell," said Rabbi Wise of Brooklyn.

In mid-April, under the leadership of Thomas Scanlon, a vigilant Knight of Columbus, the religious leaders had suggested that while LaGuardia could not deny a theatrical license under the Constitution, he could refuse to renew the ones the burlesque theaters already obtained. The reformers were made bold by the sensational contention, advanced by Moss and by Police Commissioner Louis Valentine, that burlesque—in other words, striptease—caused the wave of sex crimes sweeping through the city. Throughout the spring, several ugly sex crimes involving children had been committed, and the city, at a loss as to what do about them, welcomed a scapegoat.[77]

At an annual communion breakfast in the Hotel St. George in Brooklyn Heights, Valentine said that when he dropped in on a burlesque show, he was shocked by what he saw. "Talk about immorality and indecency," he said.[78] The following day, DA William Geoghan announced that of the 350 crimes committed in the Times Square area in the past year, the majority were sex crimes, and of those, a good number—it was never specified how many—were perpetrated by men who watched striptease on a regular basis. Times Square was now a slum, and the LaGuardia administration, concerned about the increase in these crimes, saw denying licenses as a better place to start changing the neighborhood than sterilizing criminals, which was also under discussion.

At the end of April, the police raided three Brooklyn theaters and arrested countless performers. In emotional meetings held in Moss's office, Thomas Phillips, the tall, showy executive director of the Burlesque Artists of America (BAA) played down striptease's role in burlesque and instead made a threat. The fact was, he told the commissioner, that prohibiting burlesque was like prohibiting liquor in the Jazz Age: it would just give rise to more burlesque. When that argument failed to move Moss, Phillips changed tactics and pleaded for the hardworking, decent people suddenly unemployed in the Depression. "What is going to happen to the thousands of people in burlesque if the theaters are closed?" he asked. "Should they, perhaps, go out and commit crimes so that they may have sustenance?"[79]

Still, no one knew exactly what Moss would do. May 1—the day the licenses were renewed—he issued a statement that said he was considering refusing to renew any of the fourteen existing theaters' licenses or giving a license to the three new burlesque theaters petitioning for one. "Clean entertainment pays," he told the press.[80]

The burlesque theaters waited to see what Moss would do at midnight. The following day, a Saturday, Moss refused to renew the fourteen theaters' licenses and refused to grant licenses to the three new theater operators. Initially, a question about his legal ability to do this left the Gaiety and the

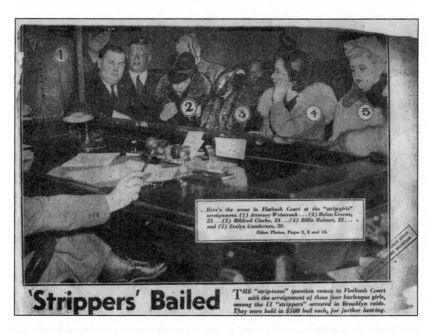

*Here's the scene in Flatbush Court at the "strip-girls" arraignment. (1) Attorney Weintraub ... (2) Helen Greene, 23 ... (3) Mildred Clarke, 24 ...(4) Billie Holmes, 23 ... and (5) Evelyn Gunderson, 20.*
*Other Photos, Pages 3, 8 and 16.*

**'Strippers' Bailed**  THE "strip-tease" question comes to Flatbush Court with the arraignment of these four burlesque girls, among the 11 "strippers" arrested in Brooklyn raids. They were held in $500 bail each, for further hearing.

"Strippers" Bailed, c. 1932. Chamberlain and Lyman Brown Collection, Billy Rose Theatre Collection. New York Public Library for the Performing Arts, Astor, Lenox, and Tilden Foundations.

Eltinge open that night. Long lines stretched outside of these theaters as New Yorkers waited, hoping to get in their dose of burlesque before it disappeared from the city for good. As the *New York Times* reported, some of these eager burlesque-goers were women. The houses were at capacity. "We're doing business as usual," bragged Morton Minsky.[81]

But his optimism was premature. Police Commissioner Valentine installed policemen by the ticket booths. By midnight Valentine had succeeded in getting all of the theaters closed except for the Gaiety and the Eltinge in Times Square. Moss's decision put more than two thousand people out of work in the middle of the Depression, a fact that did not go unnoticed by the press. In the following weeks, letters pleading with Moss to change his mind barraged LaGuardia, but the mayor stood firm while the burlesque operators protested and swore that they would sue for a writ of mandamus. Meanwhile, Moss sent several of them summons.[82]

At the hearings held in early May, the Minskys fell apart. Joseph Weinstock, the brothers' silent partner, who, after Billy's death, wound up owning the majority share of the Republic Theater, made headlines when, at the license renewal hearings, he accused the mayor of a conspiracy against burlesque. "We've been accused of everything except kidnapping the Lindbergh baby," he sobbed, referring to the crime that had shaken the nation and was then being tried. Abe went on to accuse the mayor's left-hand man of being swayed by personal connections. Moss's brother owned the Criterion, a theater on Forty-second Street. The theater was losing money thanks to burlesque striptease.[83] A grand jury was called to determine whether Moss had overstepped his rights. Most of the burlesque theaters reopened for a couple of days, at least. Visiting the Irving Place in early May, Brooks Atkinson praised a stripper who "disrobed with the coyness of a mack truck." "The human body," he wrote, "terrifies some people."[84]

The prospect of being out of work during the Depression terrified the Minskys. To get their licenses back, the brothers agreed to LaGuardia's demands, from removing the word "Minsky" from the marquees to changing the names of the shows from "burlesque" to "follies." Of course, the Minskys above all "eliminated" striptease. Then they abandoned burlesque to produce "Negro" shows, but Moss still refused to grant the Minskys a license, arguing that their very name made any theatrical endeavor they proposed suspect.[85]

Other theater owners struck even more conciliatory poses. Initially, a group of the most disgruntled had demanded a jury trial and threatened to take Moss to the Supreme Court on the grounds that he had overstepped his role as license commissioner. But the judge hearing the appeal thought a grand jury sufficient. That jury ruled unanimously on the side of the city.[86] In June, LaGuardia distributed a statement assuring New Yorkers that "burlesque and its principal recent attraction, the striptease, became a thing of the past yesterday." Brooks Atkinson commented, "[T]he iniqui-tous strip-tease, defiler of youth, has been purified."[87]

On burlesque and nightclub stages, strippers performed their own political satire.[88] At the Republic, Ann Corio put on white, see-through organdy and sang a eulogy for her profession.

> The old days forever are through
> When we showed everything we had to you.
> 'Cause now they've got us with our clothes on
> No more will you see us strip
> We can't even shake a hip
> You'll see a little but that's your loss
> That's by order of Commish Moss
> Mr. Striptease is dead
> And I'm his widow
> He's gone but not forgotten
> I'll just try to be brave
> You should see the celebrities
> Gathered at his grave
> LaGuardia, Moss were in the crowd
> They had come by thousands to see the shroud
> Herk was crying and so was Minsky
> While music on a g-string was played by violinsky
> Mr. Striptease is dead
> And I'm his widow
> How I hated to see the Old Boy go
> But while living, how we made the dough.[89]

Corio exited, as if she were going to launch into one of the stripteases that used the wings to create suspense. When she returned, she wore a sheer black organdy negligee. But for the large padlock slung over her hips, she would have launched capably into her act. Instead, she began to sing another anarchic tune and flashed her shoulder: "I would if I could but I can't. So I won't . . ."[90]

Such comic tributes failed to placate the license commissioner. And the mayor, far from finished with burlesque, instructed Moss to hold onto many of the theaters' license applications until the fall. When he returned them, he had decreased the license tenure from a year to three months and increased the fee theater operators paid fourfold. After that, in Times Square, only the flamboyant marquees remained to call striptease to the attention of crowds of curious passersby. In its year-end report for 1937, the NYSSV noted that it had wiped striptease from the city.[91]

STILL, NOT EVEN MOSS'S most draconian measures could totally squash burlesque. Although LaGuardia's initial success inspired a nation of re-formist mayors to exploit the distinction between revoking and renewing licenses, outside New York no mayor ever matched LaGuardia's success. In Chicago, Mayor Edward Kelly had ordered strippers at the Rialto and the Folly Nickelodeon to put on bras during the 1935 election, as if the sight of women's be-pastied breasts would compromise the city's civic virtue. In Los Angeles, at the Burbank Theater, the police arrested waves of performers on Christmas Day 1937, and while these arrests were an augur of the reform coming to the West Coast, they were no more permanent than those on the East.[92]

Several burlesque impresarios, including Tony Miccio, the most recent owner of the Irving Place, tried to get around LaGuardia's ban by creating a floating striptease nightclub, modeled after the Jazz Age floating speakeasies. These clubs lasted about a week. Elsewhere in New York, women continued to strip in burlesque theaters despite the municipal sanctions. At the Star Theater in Brooklyn, Georgia Sothern's older sister Jewel performed a classic bump and grind, and June Marsh took off her clothes while describing her evolution from a choir singer in Duluth to a torso slinger in Brooklyn. And while some strippers took off fewer clothes after 1937, others remained as salacious as they had been five years earlier. At the Brooklyn Star on Jay Street, Terry King "wasted no time in getting down to a flimsy bra and g-string," and Sherry Britton tore off her clothes as if she were trying to "throw her limbs to the wolves." At the Gaiety, strippers "alternately flipped breasts and buttocks to audience" and used capes to cover themselves only when reformers and police attended. Underneath, they appeared entirely nude. Only uptown, at the Triboro—the former Gotham Theater on 125th Street—did the strippers deploy "extra heavy g-string equipment" to stave off reformers.[93]

"The new variety looks exactly like the old burlesque," Paul Moss complained at the beginning of 1938.[94] Five burlesque theaters remained open, struggling with the censors monthly, and the following year three still survived. The Burlesque Artists Association changed its name to the vague Brother Artists Association, and the three theaters open in 1939 remained so until 1942. But the very reform crushing striptease also unleashed a new pulsating stream of erotic entertainment.[95]

# Gypsy

The career of Gypsy Rose Lee, the woman who in 1936 began to be billed as "the Literary Stripper," abounds in American ironies. Gypsy wound up in striptease because physically she eluded categories. She was what the French call "jolie laide." Gypsy was too lanky to play flapper roles, and her features were too big to meet the Lilliputian standards of Flo Ziegfeld. She exploited humor, not caring to limit herself to being, as she put it, America's "number one stripper."[1] Gypsy stretched her Victorianism into caricature, hoping that what she knew to be publicity stunts others would interpret as virtue. Throughout her life, she would play the diva. In 1936, for example, she declined to participate in a striptease contest held at Columbia University. (Although she did pose for one at the University of Chicago.[2])

Gypsy earned the Literary Stripper moniker not because she was born an aristocrat but rather because she was a self-made one. She attained upper-class status by educating herself. And like many who reach those heights, she made fun of her status at every turn. By the time that happened, Gypsy had been stripping for almost seven years. She began in burlesque on the Mutual circuit, where she became a star in her own right for taking off less— not more.

In the fall of 1929, Gypsy had debuted in Kansas City's Missouri Theater, at Twelfth and Central. Although she had toured in vaudeville since childhood, she got her start as a stripper in a humble theater not far from where Count Basie had played a couple of years earlier. In her memoir, she describes it:

> Greasy make up towels dragged off chairs onto littered floor. Cigarette butts and empty coffee containers and old newspapers were all kicked together with dirty frayed satin shoes under the make up shelf. Gnats swarmed around a half empty container of beer resting on the edge of a filthy sink that was filled with laundry left overnight to soak. Sticky red lip rouge smudges penciled in with eyebrow pencil was an initial. The mirrors were broken. Their jagged edges reached out like claws. Shreds of net and bits of rhinestone and beads hung by thin strings on nails behind the thin rail.[3]

After that, Gypsy appeared at the Baghdad in Dallas, Mounds' Country Club in St. Louis, the Gibson House in Cincinnati, the Club Fortune

Gypsy Rose Lee, glamour portrait, c. 1934. The Shubert Archives.

in New Orleans, and the Cuban Gardens Nightclub in Kansas City.[4] She played at several nightclubs in St. Louis and Miami, and then she joined *Girls from the Follies*, the Mutual circuit review. When Gladys Clark got sick in Toledo, Gypsy did her first striptease at the Gayety Theater there. Compared to Clark, she must have looked positively Victorian. She wore a full-skirted red dress under a lavender net bodice and undressed to "Little

Gypsy Sweetheart." Her second strip number accompanied the nineteenth-century variety hall song "Won't You Powder My Back?"[5]

> Oh won't you powder my back every morn?
> 'Cause honey there's no one can do it like you
> Oh won't you powder my back every morn
> It makes me happy when I'm feeling blue
> And if you'll powder my back every morn
> Then maybe some morn, I'll do it for you.

As the Jazz Age ended, Gypsy applied her vaudeville training to strip-tease. Recycling the turn-of-the-century whorehouse garter number in Chicago and Philadelphia, she pranced into the audience, shone the spotlight on one "baldhead," and tied a piece of his comb-over with a ribbon. "Doesn't he look pretty?" she asked. Then she bent over to kiss his head. A stripper needed to conjure an air of tragedy to become famous, though. In publicity photos from this era, Gypsy's mother, Rose, painted teardrops on her face.[6]

GYPSY WAS ALSO an oddity because her affinity for swathing her routine in literary chat pointed to a brainy masculinity even as she took off her clothes and revealed her undeniable femaleness. Her elegance was similarly paradoxical. Gypsy approached stripping from a genteel angle. She rolled down her garter as she discussed, in rounded tones, why she couldn't "strip to Brahms." She was the Dorothy Parker of burlesque, and although like Mae West she never relinquished her working-class roots, she eagerly embraced society.

Gypsy exploited her seamy striptease past in order to brandish her distance from it. She used elegance as a comic device while taking off her clothes. Her presence and influence in the arena of glamour helped to crystallize the trend. She was the stripper who most successfully capitalized on the mid-thirties nightclub vogue and the American aspiration for glamour even as she sent it up. She wore floor-length designer gowns and orchids and rode in a chauffeured Rolls Royce with her initials painted in gold on the door. This equipped her perfectly to take off her garter and sing risqué songs with impunity.

Gypsy's striptease ditty "A Stripteaser's Education," which she first sang in the *Ziegfeld Follies of 1936*, created and celebrated the ironic image of the Literary Stripper—the character she invented and became. The number also made fun of the slumming literary audience clamoring to understand what she was thinking. Nothing endured like a working-class girl emulating the aristocracy, especially if she did it with style.[7]

AFTER HER TRIUMPH at Billy Minsky's Republic in 1931, Gypsy briefly traded burlesque for Broadway. She performed as a chorus girl in *Hot-Cha*, a 1932 revue produced by Florenz Ziegfeld. Financed in part by mobster Waxey Gordon, *Hot-Cha* was a box office dud. But here Gypsy first attracted attention for sending up her own profession. Billed under her own name, Rose Louise Hovick, opposite Bert Lahr, she gave a "swell characterization of the dumb dame" according to *Zit's*.[8] Although *Hot-Cha* ran for only four months, that was long enough to launch her. Although the *New Yorker* failed to notice Gypsy, the *New York Sun* described her as "a vision in white at the Ziegfeld Glorified Girls Club."[9]

BERNARD SOBEL CLAIMS that Gypsy's literary prowess first emerged at a post-show party for publishers and their wives. For some reason Sobel himself arrived to save her from the mean-spirited Follies girls who were ready to shun her. But he noticed that "she could take care of herself" so he took her everywhere. By the end of 1935, Gypsy "had branched out on her own and was entertaining guests including Carl van Doren, George Jean Nathan, Heywood Broun, Beatrice Kaufman, Claire Luce, Tallulah Bankhead, and Moss Hart."[10]

Still, knowing famous people would not put dinner on the table. In June 1934, Gypsy briefly emceed at Billy Rose's Casino de Paree nightclub. According to her memoir, she got herself fired for flubbing the introductions on the night that Fanny Brice was in the audience. But Billy Rose claims that they fought over money, that Gypsy said that if she was going to strip, she wanted $500 a week, not the $60 that he was paying. She returned to the Irving Place, where *Billboard* celebrated her: "Gypsy was wearing a bridesmaid's gown and looking better [than] at anytime . . . we have seen in the theater."[11]

Indeed, part of Gypsy's appeal lay in the extravagant costumes she brought from Broadway. The following year, when Gypsy wore a dress from the 1890s, *Billboard* wrote that she was "a Park Avenue Mae West type."[12] She had always loved dress-up. While she was performing at the Republic back in 1931, one of her numbers had featured no less than three costume changes. She went from a tight-fitting red costume and red picture hat to a maid's black velvet dress with a white apron, which she partly stripped, to a white velvet gown for her strip number "Lonesome Little Eve."[13]

> I'm a Lonesome Little Eve
> Looking for an Adam
> Gee I wish I had him,
> Cuddlin' me,
> 'Neath the shade of the tree
> And in our garden we would be so happy.

Then she launched into a bluesy double entendre chorus.

> Would you . . . for a big red apple?
> Would you . . . for a piece of mine?
> Would you . . . for a big red apple?
> Give me what I'm trying to find.[14]

Heavy orchestration swelled as Gypsy coaxed the "Adam" planted in one of the boxes to take a single, dangerous bite. After a few more bites, she tossed the apple to the first man, who "fell" out of his box with delight. Gypsy then turned her focus to the rest of the audience and began to talk self-consciously about her act. She promised to keep the "apple" business in and revealed that she dreamt about the Follies. Thus she made a pitch for her ambition and sent it up at the same time. She teased and then revealed that her teasing was just a sham. Such mischievous numbers succeeded because they made fun of and celebrated the public conception of a stripper.

At the Irving Place in 1934, Gypsy began to experiment with talk-singing in the "blue" style of the Algonquin Table ditty writer Dwight Fiske. She used "Mrs. Pettibone," which recounts three failed marriages, and "Ida the Wayward Sturgeon," which tells the story of a "fish's" adulterous love affair.[15]

> Ida was just a little wayward sturgeon.
> She said to herself:
> There must be more to this sex-life
> Than just swimming over each other's eggs.
> "I'm going to find out for myself," she said.
> So she went upstairs
> And put a little badge on her right shoulder
> Which said: I WILL SHARE.[16]

Fiske was not Gypsy's only source for ideas, though. In 1935 at the Irving Place Theater, she entered dressed like the girlish Mary Pickford and stripped with a lot of "sugary teasing" and "audience baiting."[17] According to her memoir, while touring the vaudeville circuit with her mother, Gypsy read a lot. In her adult life, Gypsy cut out "Great Minds"—a newspaper column detailing the lives of the intellectual geniuses of all ages—and put them in her scrapbook, to later be used as the basis for some of her numbers. Witty sayings are attributed to her, such as "God is love, but get it in writing."[18]

But when Gypsy sang Fiske's "Mrs. Pettibone" at the Irving Place, she meant to scandalize by associating herself with gay life. Fiske first rose to popularity during the Jazz Age, when a gay subculture thrived in American cities. In the thirties, although many gay nightclubs went underground, others continued to feature openly gay and lesbian performers. Fiske was

among the most successful of these. Born in 1892 in Providence, he studied at the Paris Conservatoire but became popular at parties for visiting
wealthy Americans. He was supposedly discovered by Tallulah Bankhead
and returned to America for his concert debut at Chickering Hall in 1926.
In the thirties, he performed exclusively on the elite party circuit and became a fixture at the Savoy-Plaza Hotel's Cafe Lounge, where he collabo-
rated with Dawn Powell and with the legendary female impersonator Ray
Bourbon. Fiske cultivated a naughty style: in 1937, Brooks Atkinson described him as "obscene."[19]

After flirting with Fiske, Gypsy continued to bounce between Broadway and burlesque. According to *Variety*, Leonard Silliman signed her into
his annual revue *New Faces of 1935*, which the previous year had starred the
young comedian Imogene Coca, as well as Henry Fonda. That 1935 *New
Faces* never opened. But Gypsy continued to attract attention for the company she kept offstage. Many newspapers ran stories about Gypsy's hanging out with socialite friends such as the Otis Chatfield-Taylors.[20]

OFFSTAGE, GYPSY played up her image of sophistication and class. Reviewers marveled at her elegant hilarity, as if they thought that by elevating
burlesque out of prurience, she could save New York from depravity. She
attracted cognoscenti. In February 1935 the novelist George Davis pro-
filed Gypsy for *Vanity Fair*, which dubbed her "the dark young pet of burlesque."[21] The following fall, plays based on Gypsy's life began to open on
Broadway. *Strip Girl*, which ran for a month, told the story of a burlesque
dancer and a check forger.[22] *The Body Beautiful* ran at the Plymouth on
Forty-fifth Street for four days. Written by Robert Rossen, the comedy
followed the adventures of stripper Lulu, who insisted that she was doing
ballet and even managed to convince the license commissioner and have a
recital in Carnegie Hall.[23]

Sighting Gypsy at the opening of Billy Rose's musical extravaganza
*Jumbo* in December 1935, Cholly Knickerbocker wrote about her in his
*Herald Tribune* society column "The Smart Set," which detailed the goings-
out of the New York 400. In his *Journal American* column "New York by
Day," O. O. Mcintyre described Gypsy as

> an eyeful in a showy way, but not quite the over carmined type one might
> expect. She occupies an apartment, a perfect bijou on the north side of
> Gramercy Park. . . . Gypsy is of an intelligence belying her calling . . .
> quick on the trigger. . . . [A]s she continues her slink through the Park
> Avenue drawing rooms there are not many who do not angle for her, and
> in every instance, to those who have not seen her she proved a surprise
> package. Those who expected to find Miss Lee over rouged and thickly
> veined with a Rabelaisian repartee, discovered instead, a self possessed lady
> with a cough drop voice and a dress suit accent who might have run up

from Bryn Mawr for a prom. She scatters effortless French phrases through her conversation and fits in perfectly with the Dear Noel motif.[24]

The Chicago industrialist Otis Chatfield Taylor, who wrote a society column for *Town and Country*, called Gypsy "the Gene Tunney of Burlesque" after the self-made heavyweight boxer who had defeated Jack Dempsey a decade earlier.[25] To most of the male journalists who wrote about her, Gypsy's comic flair and aspiration made her unique. Later, there would be other strippers who achieved aristocratic status—at a certain point *Billboard* began likening strippers to "society debs"—but Gypsy assumed this role with a monarch's dignity after performing "A Stripteaser's Education," her signature routine in the 1936 *Ziegfeld Follies*.

By 1936 the *Follies* was an enormous entertainment machine. Florenz Ziegfeld had died four years earlier, and the Shuberts, along with Ziegfeld's widow, Billie Burke, commandeered the show. When the 1936 edition opened in January, it starred the musical comedy actress Eve Arden and Josephine Baker, who returned to New York for the first time in ten years, as well as Fanny Brice, Bob Hope, and Judy Canova. Ira Gershwin wrote the lyrics, and the music was by Vernon Duke. Vincente Minnelli wrapped the showgirls in cellophane à la Earl Carroll.

In the spring, the show ran aground. Brice got ill and left. Subsequently, Baker went back to Paris, and the Shuberts, casting around for some "spice," hired Gypsy as well as the burlesque comedian Bobby Clark.[26] According to Gypsy, the Shuberts just wanted the fall edition to make enough money so it could go on the road, so they offered her considerably less than what she had made stripping at the Irving Place.[27] Gypsy lacked the vocal ability and romantic persona to do the number that Eve Arden had done with Bob Hope— the duet "I Can't Get Started." Most of the numbers Gypsy sang at Irving Place were too burlesquey; she needed something fit for Broadway.

THE DARING STYLISTIC CHOICES in a new musical may have helped her make the decision. Back in March 1936, Richard Rodgers and Lorenz Hart's musical *On Your Toes* premiered at the Lunt Fontanne Theater on Forty-fifth Street. Prior to *On Your Toes*, no musical had ever combined ballet and musical comedy. Choreographed by George Balanchine, directed by George Abbott, and starring two dancers, the Russian ballerina Tamara Geva and the tap dancer Ray Bolger, *On Your Toes*, as the musical theater scholar Ethan Mordden described it, "essentialized the show's conflict of ballet and street strut."[28]

According to the dance and jazz historian Marshall Stearns, this strut owes a lot to the fact that the black tap dancer Herbie Harper, who had worked with the black virtuoso dancers of the twenties, assisted Balanchine. One of the musical's two high points was the finale, a satiric but serious dream ballet called *Slaughter on Tenth Avenue* set in a dingy waterfront bar. Geva did a "modified" striptease making fun of ballet and of highbrow striptease. "Geva romps through . . . Slaughter on Tenth Avenue with a completely grim expression," *Newsweek* wrote.[29]

Ostensibly written by one of the characters in the show (a WPA-funded struggling composer), *Slaughter on Tenth Avenue* takes place in a seedy Tenth Avenue strip joint. The number mixes American ballet and jazz vernacular in the story of a customer who falls in love with a stripper. The big boss discovers the stripper's betrayal after closing, and in the violence that ensues, the customer witnesses a murder right before the curtain falls. In the balletic striptease, Geva hardly took anything off, but her dance, a playful hymn to romance, combined love and abandon in a sophisticated, Balanchinian way. In an interview, Geva noted, "Slaughter started as a take off of Gypsy Rose Lee." *On Your Toes* ran for over a year.[30]

WHEN THE *ZIEGFELD FOLLIES* reopened on September 14, Gypsy used her delivery to hype her "aristocratic" past and to establish her present lowbrow pedigree. Replacing Eve Arden in some of the comic scenes, she became the rarity—a stripper who cracked jokes on the Broadway stage. She played the mama to Baby Snooks and, as an entrant in the "Major Bones's Talent Search" act, appeared as a gray-haired dowager who could play the kazoo and bang on cymbals fastened to her knees. She also teamed up with Bobby Clark for a rendition of the Vernon Duke hit song "Words without Music," although, as some critics pointed out, neither performer could sing.

The most striking event of that edition was Gypsy's striptease number. Written by the Broadway script doctor and magazine writer Edwin Gilbert, "A Stripteaser's Education" filled the slot where, in the first edition, the Nicholas brothers, a black tap-dancing team whose spins, flips, and taps had stopped the show.[31] Right before the end of Act I, Gypsy strode onstage in her red picture hat with velvet roses, white Victorian shirtwaist, and floor-length Gibson Girl skirt over four lacy white petticoats. Her hair was done up in a demure coif. Standing facing the audience, she slowly removed one of her white elbow-length gloves, finger by finger. She tossed her head, craned her long neck, and then took off her clothes, as if to suggest that although she was genteel, she was still the woman whom the Minskys had advertised a few years earlier in less prim language. While she stripped, she romped through references to Cézanne and Oscar Wilde. The more she took off onstage, the more erudite Gypsy seemed offstage as she allowed Americans to laugh at the improbability of her upper-class origins even as they respectfully nodded to her rapid rise to fame. That she got rich by her G-string would have been scandalous had she not made fun of herself at every turn.[32]

The number Gypsy used for the rest of her life suggested elegance even as it made fun of the questions everyone was asking about her. She stared down the audience, and began:

> Have you the faintest idea of the private life of a stripteaser?
> My dear, it's New York's second largest industry.
>
> Now a strip-teaser's education, requires years of concentration
> And for the sake of illustration, take a look at me.
> I began at the age of three, learning ballet at the Royal Imperial
> School in Moscow. And how I suffered and suffered for my Art.
> Then of course, Sweet Briar, ah those dear college days.
> And after four years of Sociology
> Zoology, Biology, and Anthropology
> My education was complete.
> And I was ready to make my professional debut on 14th Street
> Now the things that go on, in a strip-teaser's mind,
> Would give you no end of surprise,
> But if you are psychologically inclined,
> There is more to see than meets the eye.

She walked across the stage and handed her hat to the band leader. After that, she raised her dress and petticoat, unfastened her stockings from her garter belt, and rolled them down.

> For example—when I lower my gown a fraction,
> And expose a patch of shoulder,
> I am not interested in your reaction,
> Or in the bareness of that shoulder.
> I am thinking of some paintings,
> By Van Gogh, or by Cézanne
> Or the charm I had in reading, Lady Windemere's Fan
> And when I lower the other side, and expose my other shoulder,
> Do you think I take the slightest pride, in the whiteness of my
>     shoulder?

Here she exposed her shoulder.

> I am thinking of my country house
> And the jolly fun in shooting grouse.

Then the music got faster.

> And the frantic music changes, then off to my cue,
> But I only think of all the things I really ought to do.
> Wire Leslie Howard, Cable Noel Coward
> Go to Bergdorf's for my fitting, buy the yarn for my mother's knitting
> Put preserves up by the jar, and make arrangements for my church
>     bazaar.

The music slowed down again, and Gypsy paraded back and forth across the stage, taking the pins from her blouse and throwing them into the orchestra pit. As each pin fell, the drummer tapped the cow bell. Gypsy never completely took off her blouse. It hung open for the rest of the act over a crooked black bow dangling across her breasts. She continued singing:

> But there is the music, and that's my cue,
> There is only one thing left for me to do, so I do it.
> And when I raise my skirts with shyness and dexterity,
> I am mentally computing just how much I'll give to charity.
> Though my thighs I have revealed, and just a bit of me remains
>     concealed,
> I am thinking of the life of Duce
> Or the third chapter of "The Last Puritan."
> None of these men whose minds are obscene,
> They leave me apathetic, I prefer the more Aesthetic,
> Things like dramas by Racine . . . "Gone with the Wind"
> And when I display my charms in all their dazzling splendor,
> And prove to you conclusively, I am of the female gender.
> I am really thinking of Elsie de Wolff, and the bric-a-brac I saw.
> And that lovely letter I received from Mr. Bernard Shaw.
> I have a town house on the East River, because it's so fashionable
> To look at Welfare Island, coal barges, and garbage scows.
> I have a Chinchilla, a Newport Villa,

She unhooked her skirt, held it in front of her, and said, "and then I take the last thing off . . ."

A plant in the audience screamed, "No!" She and the audience laughed. Gypsy pulled the curtain in front of her, allowing the audience to get a glimpse of her G-string.

> And stand there shyly with nothing on at all.
> Clutching an old velvet drop, and looking demurely at every man.
> Do you believe for a moment, that I am thinking of sex?
> Well I certainly am.[33]

Later, Gypsy embellished the act. Other times, she pasted sprigs of cherries on her breasts instead of oversized bows. But whatever she wore, the number rarely ended at her first exit. In the forties, the music would speed up and Gypsy would reappear onstage in a short gold dress and feather boa.[34]

Gypsy's strip was novel because, as Brooks Atkinson wrote, she worked "from the inside out." In other words, she peeled the inner layers of clothing while keeping on some of the outer layers. But perhaps she also meant that she flashed her brain. "Bare flesh bores men," she said.[35] But perhaps Gypsy's greatest contribution was that she posed as a kind of protofeminist, since she admitted that she was thinking about sex, even though she never told what she was thinking about it. At the same time, her striptease combined the conventional language of femininity, nostalgia for the Victorian era, and double entendre to cover up undressing's prurient nature.

After the *Follies* opened, Gypsy began to manufacture her own story more aggressively. And she was in demand. She sang "A Stripteaser's Education" on Rudy Vallee's radio show. *Collier's* devoted a feature to her. She befriended George Jean Nathan, as well as Jean Cocteau (who upon seeing Gypsy murmured, "How vital!") and *New Yorker* correspondent Janet Flanner.[36] Yet while the literati helped validate Gypsy, she never would have become "legit" without the New York tabloids, which publicized her earnings and also printed hundreds of anecdotes suggesting that her "self-taught"

Gypsy Rose Lee costumed in a polka-dot dress around the time of her appearance in the 1936 *Ziegfeld Follies*. The Shubert Archives.

knowledge made her superior to the elite crowd. "It's said she discusses Joyce and Santayana at every opportunity, although I am at a loss to know just with whom she discussed those fellows at Minskys'."[37]

The *New Yorker* appreciated her less. "Note on ingratitude: Gypsy Rose Lee, mystically translated from 14th Street to 'The Follies,' has a number burlesquing the striptease, which got her where she is. It is almost as if Ernest Hemingway had suddenly begun to kid a bull."[38] And in the *New York Evening Graphic*, Ed Sullivan criticized her hunger for publicity.

> [H]ow does Miss Lee operate? I am not privileged to take you behind the scenes with this distinguished striptease artist but I can reveal her technique for prodding paragraphs. Not long ago, a Broadway columnist, a contemporary, attended the Follies and sat in row a. . . . [T]o the other performers, he was just another customer, in on the cuff . . . but Gypsy Rose Lee was more alert. She sent a note out to him, a shy little missive in which she related that the presence of the great big man was so thrilling that she couldn't give a performance of artistic integrity. The great big man was thrilled, too. . . . [S]ince then, she has been mentioned daily in his columns two and three times.[39]

But many ordinary Americans were in Gypsy's thrall. The 1936 *Follies* ran for twelve weeks. After it closed on December 19, a touring edition kept Gypsy busy that winter and part of the spring.

GYPSY'S SOCIAL LIFE kept pace with her onstage success. At the playwright Carl Van Doren's soiree, the stripper launched into a voluble appreciation of Pearl Buck, whose *The Good Earth* had just been published, and thus "panicked" the ill-read guests.[40] She counted as her friends the editor Carmel Snow and the columnists Burns Mantle and Walter Winchell. Journalists compared her intelligence to that of Amelia Earhart and Eleanor Roosevelt.[41] Reviews of Gypsy praised her sense of humor and tried to divine her sources in making fun of sex. "There is nothing sensuous in her act," the *New York Post* noted.

The same review praised the speed with which Gypsy undressed. The fact was that Gypsy spent nine to ten minutes taking it off in burlesque and in the *Follies* a mere four, ostensibly because the highbrow audience, accustomed to nudity from nightclubs and Broadway, expected it. Later in her career, she was perfectly capable of stretching her strip to twenty minutes.[42]

Gypsy made such a hit in the *Follies* that she attracted the interest of Daryl Zanuck, who began angling to get her in his stable of stars at 20th Century Fox in the winter of 1937. Attempting to make fantastical films dominated by nostalgia—during the Depression Zanuck's three-year-old company was often called "Nineteenth Century Fox"—the mogul knew he wanted to sign Gypsy the minute he saw her.[43] The first step was to steal her away from Lee Shubert, whom Gypsy once described as a "fascinating cross between a wooden Indian and a hooded cobra."[44]

It took a few months, but after Zanuck offered the Shuberts twenty thousand dollars, they gave in.[45] In the spring Gypsy headed to Hollywood to work in the same studio that produced Shirley Temple. "Gypsy Rose Lee to Be a Star," the *New York Post* predicted.[46] But whereas Shirley Temple thrived on sweetness and light, Gypsy was never able—or given the chance—to adapt to Hollywood's demands. She made five musical pictures, none of which used her quirky combination of wisecracking and striptease. *Battle of Broadway*; *Ali Baba Goes to Town*; *You Can't Have Everything*; *Sally, Irene, and Mary*; and *My Lucky Star* all asked her to be a just another musical comedy bit player.[47]

THE ACCRUING POWER of the czar of censorship, former postmaster general Will Hays, prevented Gypsy's Literary Striptease from appearing on-screen. Since 1934, Hays, installed at the Production Code Office, had decided what was and was not fit for American moviegoers to see. Hays and his associate Joseph Breen—the so-called Hitler of Hollywood—rejected anything that struck them as "gross" or "vulgar." In 1936, they cracked down, abetted by the Catholic Legion of Decency's increasing strength.

Representatives of the Legion complained to studio heads that Gypsy was "an exemplar of what has most unfortunately become highly publicized under the degrading appellation of the striptease act." The studio assured the Legion that it had no intention of exploiting Lee's sensational background since, after all, it had decided to award her a contract after her screen test—just as with any other star. Meanwhile, Legion administrators were conflicted—if they succeeded in barring Gypsy from the screen, she would be forced to return to burlesque—hardly their aim.

In the end, though, the studio backpedaled. In the *New York Times*, the chairman of the motion picture bureau of the International Federation of Catholic Alumnae complained that Gypsy was "one of the two headaches the Catholic Legion . . . sought to cure," and to reiterate that studio heads had assured him that "Miss Lee would not appear in roles that would be influenced by her former experience."[48] Accordingly, Will Hays convinced the studio to bill Gypsy under her own name. And in 1937 and 1938, Gypsy could only make those five comedies and movie musicals under a name the public had never heard—Louise Hovick. Reduced to mere acting, she could not perform her signature striptease in any of her pictures. A reviewer of *You Can't Have Everything* quipped that Hollywood gave Gypsy two things she needed least: clothes and another name.[49]

"GYPSY FLOPPED IN HOLLYWOOD," another headline read. Yet even without Hays, it's unclear whether Gypsy would have been a success on film. The list of those who headlined in vaudeville, made a few pictures, and dropped out of the public eye stretched all the way up Sunset Boulevard. A few months after her Hollywood debacle, though, Gypsy headed back to New York on a vaudeville tour, on the surface undaunted.[50]

Of course, by this time, vaudeville was much reduced. Still, that didn't stop Gypsy. Teaming up with Jimmy Durante, she stripped her way back east, stopping in one vaudeville theater after another. She called her number "From Hollywood to Broadway." The number began with Jimmy Durante reading a telegram about Gypsy's being detained in Hollywood and then invited the audience to watch a few scenes from her film. As the projector began to roll, Gypsy burst through the screen, triumphant, to tell the story of her life and do her striptease. But critics thought she was better in the flesh. [51]

Back east, hoping to reestablish her highbrow credentials, Gypsy wrote a book. She had already published an account of her childhood in a 1939 guest column for Walter Winchell, but it was in her dressing room that she discovered how easily she wrote.

"Making the book words," as Gypsy called writing, gave her a "neurotic" stomach; to soothe it—or perhaps to cement her reputation as an author—in the fall of 1940 she moved into George Davis's boarding house at 7 Middagh Street, in Brooklyn.[52] From 1940 to 1945, when the city swept it away, 7 Middagh Street attracted a remarkable collection of writers, painters, composers, and theatrical people. The four-story brownstone with the view of New York Harbor looked like no other on the maple-lined block: its dilapidated facade featured gingerbread detail that made the building resemble a Swiss chalet. Inside, the house was a sort of Yaddo South, a communal refuge where a diverse group of young artists and writers tried to exist on the edge of conventional life, much like Americans in Jazz Age Paris.

The menagerie came into existence thanks to a lost job. In the 1930s, George Davis—who, although gay, would later marry Lotte Lenya and guide her and himself into a second career—was the brilliant, self-destructive literary editor of *Harper's Bazaar*. Davis inserted into that magazine's glossy pages a dazzling array of contributors, including W. H. Auden and Carson McCullers. But Davis was both arrogant and unruly. In the fall of 1940, warned by Carmel Snow (then the magazine's editor) to stop strolling in at noon, Davis quit, assuming he would be rehired. He wasn't.

Davis liked to say that he first saw 7 Middagh Street in a dream. (He knew the neighborhood because he went regularly to nearby Sands Street, then a seamy gay pickup spot where transvestites, sailors, and hookers commingled.) But once he spied his dream in Brooklyn, vacant and for sale, Davis borrowed $125 for deposit money from Gypsy and moved into 7 Middagh's first floor. McCullers and Auden became the first tenants, and then Benjamin Britten and his lover, the tenor Peter Pears—each fleeing his own cramped circumstances—rushed to pay $25 a month in the rough, unfurnished house. When McCullers, who learned she had tuberculosis, temporarily returned to Georgia, Davis invited Gypsy to stay in her room. Gypsy lent the house her cook, a former Cotton Club chorine. News of 7 Middagh spread throughout the literary community, and soon there was a waiting list. Residents included Paul and Jane Bowles; Richard Wright and his wife and daughter; the composer Colin McPhee; the set designer Oliver Smith; the painter Pavel Tchelitchev; and Thomas Mann's son Golo, whose sister Auden married to help her escape Germany. Visitors included the composer David Diamond and the poet Louis MacNeice, the flamboyant Salvador and Gala Dali, and the critic and impresario Lincoln Kirstein. Davis rented empty rooms to a monkey trainer and a midget actor.

Seven Middagh took on a gaudy, even macabre aura that seemed inspired by McCullers's fiction and Tchelitchev's mysterious landscapes. In his own gloomy first-floor apartment, George Davis installed bulky nineteenth-century furniture and a life-size cutout of Gypsy Rose Lee taken from a theater lobby. Benjamin Britten moved a Steinway into the parlor, and to the consternation of many tenants, Tchelitchev painted one of his swirling murals on the wall. Anaïs Nin, who visited in 1943, called the house "a museum of Americana," while McCullers once described it as "campy."[53]

At 7 Middagh, Gypsy exchanged literary chitchat with McCullers, Davis, Britten, Christopher Isherwood, Salvador Dali, and Aaron Copland. Louis MacNeice remembered trying in vain to concentrate while Britten and Pears were rehearsing in their room to one side of him and Lee was on the other side "like a whirlwind of laughter and sex."[54]

Gypsy's bohemian stint resulted in a batch of short stories, which she promptly sold to the *New Yorker*. These would be published in 1943. Over the next several years, she would write many more articles, two detective novels, and a play.[55] When in 1941 *The G-String Murders* outsold all other detective fiction written until that time except *The Thin Man*, Gypsy was elated. Yet because of her burlesque past, many critics wrote off her literary output as an attention-getting novelty, something that was not so far from the truth. The *Daily Worker* called *The G-String Murders* a stunt and others saw it as vulgar. Still, by 1942 the New York tabloids celebrated "strippers who write" and ran articles about her process.[56]

Reworking became a way of life. The success of "A Stripteaser's Education" in the late 1930s allowed Gypsy—or forced her—to continue the same idea in the forties. This resulted in numbers such as "Stravinsky to Minsky" and "I Can't Strip to Brahms," as well as a second murder mystery, *Mother Finds a Body*, and a Broadway musical. All of them told the same story—that of a working-class girl made good through striptease. Throughout the forties and fifties, she was always on the lookout for songwriters who could work with her personality. And although she tried to introduce new characters into her repertoire, she remained the Literary Stripper. The only change in "From Stravinsky to Minsky," which she first performed for Mike Todd in 1940, was that it told the "Stripteaser's Education" story with a little more edge.[57]

> At the age of 9 I sang in the choir
> And did transcriptions for the lyre.
> At the age of 12 my heart was set.
> On doing grand opera
> At the Met.
> I warbled each aria right to the letter
> But Flagstad could always sing it
> Much better.
> I studied in Europe
> 2 years in Milan
> and for what?
> So I could hit high C
> With my clothes on.
> No somehow I just couldn't fit the bill
> Tragic opera was making me ill.
> It was all so discouraging, that learning to sing
> Until the Mess'rs Minsky took me under their wing.
> Now my name is on Broadway, in electric lights.
> Below it says, "Wrestling Thursday nights."[58]

Gypsy sustained her career for almost three decades because she remained a mystery. Perhaps because of her success, other strippers emulated Gypsy's regal persona, challenging common wisdom that a woman who wanted to take off her clothes in public was just a dumb blonde.

# Part Four
# Striptease Goes to War

It might be a good idea to relate strip-teasing in some way . . . to the associated zoological phenomenon of molting. . . . A resort to the scientific name for molting, which is ecdysis, produced both ecdysist and ecdysiast.

—H. L. Mencken

# From Literary Strippers to Queens of Burlesque

At around the same time as Gypsy was rising to fame, other Literary Strippers arrived to tell their stories. Described by Irving Zeidman as "dreamy-eyed, languorous, inspiring," Ann Corio claimed to be reading Spinoza, Pearl S. Buck, and Omar Khayyam backstage and stripping for monarchs. Like Gypsy, Corio threatened to abandon taking off her clothes to be a real actress and volunteered to strip for noble causes such as helping the boys on the front or selling tickets for Roosevelt's birthday ball.[1]

In one number, perhaps referring to Mae West's 1934 film *I'm No Angel*, about a cootch dancer's rise to Hollywood fame, Corio took off her angel costume while her three-year-old nephew played the violin. Faith Bacon claimed to be a descendant of Peregrine White, the first child born on the Mayflower. Sally Rand did her bubble and fan dance to Chopin and Claude Debussy. In 1938, Rand gave a lecture at Harvard titled "How to Be Intelligent even though Educated."

Literary Strippers made an impression, though perhaps not always the one that they wanted. When Rand told freshmen that they could "possibly save this country's democracy by doing something in labor and politics," students responded, "Where's the bubble?" and "What's your phone number?"[2]

By the late thirties, Rand, Corio, and others became not only Literary Strippers but burlesque queens, or, as Corio was often billed, "her Majesty the Queen." This meant, as it did in other realms of entertainment where people were dubbed the "king" or "queen" of their field, that she became the royalty of her profession, although that title might be granted with a leer or a smirk. Florence Cubitt was "Queen of the Nudists" at the San Diego Exposition.[3]

The striptease culture in which "queens" existed, shaped in the late thirties by Gypsy, Ann Corio, and Sally Rand, was maintained by them for twenty years. As burlesque changed shape during the war, achieving stardom via striptease became more difficult, and even more so in the 1950s and 1960s. Queens vanished. The worlds of legitimate show business and striptease, having flirted at a time when it was economically necessary, became divided after World War II in an era of prosperity. The form of celebrity glamour created by Hollywood made achieving legitimacy difficult for many strippers, whose franker sexuality was antithetical to it.

Women conjured on-screen had an elegant presence that strippers could never achieve no matter how many novels they read or wrote.

The success of Gypsy Rose Lee, the increasing presence of striptease acts in nightclubs, and the increasing strength of the censor raised the media's expectations about strippers. To establish her credentials as a queen of burlesque, a stripper could no longer simply take off her clothes and recite ditties. When the Chicagoan Ada Leonard stripped at New York's Hollywood Club in 1937, *Variety* noted that she might "quicken the pulse of visiting firemen" but complained about her imprecise diction.[4] Apparently, Leonard never convinced the magazine of her claim to have studied at the Sorbonne. Accordingly she never became a queen of burlesque. But the war years found Leonard, her now-brunette hair tied back neatly in a bun, leading a successful all-girl swing band, the All American Girl Orchestra. When insistent audiences cried, "Take it off!" Leonard, dressed in an evening gown, began to play. Reviews often credited her for being a good psychologist, as if her skill at conducting emerged out of her previous career's mastery over men.[5]

In the late thirties, part of a queen of burlesque's duty was to decry the vulgarity of other, lesser stars in her profession. Few strippers after the war achieved the stature to take up this role in the same way as Corio, Gypsy Rose Lee, and Sally Rand did. For one, the avenues open to strippers had narrowed. It was no longer possible for strippers to perform in Broadway shows or films. Instead, they worked in road show burlesque films and carnivals. Then too, fewer strippers captured admiration—even spurious admiration—for their erudition. Comparing postwar burlesque queens to Gypsy and Ann Corio, wags and reporters found that the former had abandoned their "art" and focused entirely on creating sexual images onstage.[6] In general, in contrast to prewar stripping, teasing was less necessary in the forties and fifties, so many in the newer generation of performers opted not to perform it.

INTELLECTUALS AND JOURNALISTS continued to try to define striptease as a uniquely American form of entertainment. Published in 1936, H. L. Mencken's *The American Language*, the first book to celebrate words native to the United States, first defined a stripper by noting that she did "bumping and grinding, the striptease's distinguishing feature." Next Mencken compared a stripper to a hoofer, "who grinds, bumps, and strips, i.e. rotates her hips, follows with a sharp, sensuous upheaval of her backside, and then sheds all her clothes save a G-string in burlesque."[7]

Not everyone looked to popular dance to define striptease, though. A year after *The American Language* appeared, H. M. Alexander's *Striptease: The Vanished Art of Burlesque* described it from a hard-boiled, populist point of view. Alexander blamed New York, reformers, and Gypsy Rose Lee's mother for killing striptease. "Five years ago . . . the owners, limiting their advertising to word-of-mouth, tried to avoid attention from the reformers. Their attitude was changed by a certain Mrs. Hovick. She was ambitious; she had a daughter. . . . [P]ublicity made Gypsy."[8]

Alexander was responding to the American public's desire to be confirmed in its misgivings about women who take off their clothes for a living. His particular brand of snobbishness, typical of an era in which movies glamorized the lives of the elite as thousands starved, riled Gypsy, who favored equal opportunity undressing. "The poor man is entitled to depravity as well as the rich. The cops don't try to pull Dwight Fiske away from the piano," she said, referring to the fact that the police ignored lascivious ditties sung in nightclubs uptown while they arrested her.[9]

In fact, the tensions over who owned striptease increased as the number of newspapers covering it grew. In the first years of the Depression, theatrical trade papers such as *Zit's Theatrical Newspaper*, *Variety*, and *Billboard* both reviewed striptease and covered police raids of burlesque theaters and arrests of strippers. *Zit's* especially played a unique role in the rise of striptease. Founded by C. F. Zittel, a former columnist for Hearst and a press agent, back in 1921, the newspaper launched by announcing itself as a competitor of *Variety*. Quickly, though, *Zit's* became devoted to gossip and burlesque. Until 1938, although the back page editorial ran quirky items such as how to find "lamb fries," *Zit's* provided more news and coverage of striptease than any other paper. And it lacked *Variety*'s scorn for burlesque.[10]

By contrast, *Billboard* and *Variety*, as well as some of the tabloids, tended to cover burlesque as a mix of underworld and show business. In the early years of the Depression, *Variety* particularly claimed that striptease "killed" the good-natured, working-class comedy that burlesque had presented before World War I. In 1931, in its year-end column, *Variety* had suggested that striptease was responsible for the Depression itself.[11] The same year, in *Burleycue*, Bernard Sobel argued that before the Crash, burlesque had entertained the family with jokes and pretty women, but now, thanks to Jazz Age excesses, striptease had turned burlesque pornographic.[12]

In the mid-thirties, however, many daily newspapers abandoned this censorious view and covered striptease with amused tolerance, pathos, or even flat-out admiration. The number of essays and feature articles on striptease's stars, trends, and behaviors surged. As a journalist on the *New York Herald Tribune* in the thirties, Joseph Mitchell noted that "much typewritten cheesecake is about striptease girls."[13] Articles in such respected magazines as the *Saturday Review*, *Fortune*, *Time* and *Newsweek*, and, after 1936, *Life*, acknowledged that striptease was worth following. Some of these articles purported to educate women "how to." Indeed in 1937, *Life* ran a titillating feature titled "How a Wife Should Undress." The magazine lectured: "Two excellent purposes are served by rolling down stockings instead of merely pulling them off by the toes. Economically, a husband is pleased by the absence of runs; romantically, he is gratified by his wife's graceful method of displaying her legs."[14] Founded in 1933 as a magazine for men, *Esquire* failed to share *Life*'s pedagogical approach toward striptease. But the magazine did use striptease to aspire toward class. From the beginning, it published the first modern "pinup girls"—scantily clad women—each week. To distinguish itself from other "stag" magazines, *Esquire* called these "pin up girls in good taste."[15]

Serious periodicals also weighed in on striptease's meaning. In *New Theatre*, the esteemed theater critic John Erskine interpreted striptease as being not about sex at all, but about sadism, as well as the "direct physical conflict, assault and battery" that comprised all great theater. In the *American Mercury*, Laurence Bell declared striptease to be a national art. Gossip columnists Jack Lait and Lee Mortimer argued that striptease belonged to the nighttime landscape as much as the Stork Club.[16]

Both the dailies and the trade papers continued to focus on concerns about striptease's reputation. *Zit's* ran at least one article complaining that too many strippers were gangsters' molls looking for a thrill.[17] Not long after he attacked striptease supporter Walter Winchell, the conservative columnist Westbrook Pegler derided it as "pure filth." But novelist, playwright, and noted foreign correspondent George Weller, who wrote principally for the *New York Times* and beginning around 1939 for the *Chicago Daily News*, wrote a short essay on striptease for the *Atlantic Monthly* condemning the hypocrisy of those who attacked striptease.[18]

By creating a new, mainstream visibility for striptease—no matter how ambivalently—journalists helped propel it into everyday life.[19] And with the start of the war in Europe, journalists adapted an even more tolerant attitude toward striptease. As the country began to emerge from the economic doldrums, more and more journalists turned from writing about striptease as entertainment for the common man to celebrating it as a chic— if decadent—spectacle to be seen during a night on the town. The *American Weekly* applauded striptease as proof of Americans' sophistication and reported on strippers' love affairs.

In his syndicated column, Walter Winchell repeated Laurence Bell's contention that striptease was one of this country's only contributions to culture besides jazz.[20] Tabloids such as *Pic* and *Easy Money* published titillating photo essays about striptease, and quasi-serious articles chronicled the genre's history in *Vogue*, *Fortune*, and the *New York Times*. These articles treated striptease, for the most part, like vaudeville's outré cousin— a cousin with a legitimate theatrical past, a rough and dazzling American style, and a gritty future.[21]

After 1937 many newspapers and magazines described the costumes and customs of striptease for the American public as if they were tourists visiting a foreign country. Sometimes this boiled down to describing what strippers took off and to disseminating striptease jargon. So Americans learned that the "parade" referred to the first part of the strip act, when the stripper walked up and down the length of the stage, and that the "flash," the theatrical instant the stripper revealed her breasts, came from vaudeville and jazz dance, where it described any theatrical moment designed to shake up the audience.[22] And Americans also learned that strippers got $2.50 extra for exposing both breasts and $1.25 for one. Those in the know called this a "lung flash."[23]

WHILE JOURNALISTS FUNCTIONED as laymen-ethnographers, in 1937, David Dressler, while a sociology graduate student—he later became a parole officer—wrote the first scholarly thesis on burlesque. "Burlesque as a Cultural Phenomenon" described the acts and audience of burlesque as such, as opposed to a moral blight. Dressler concluded that burlesque presented a modern point of view about sex and that it allowed men to fulfill their "sex urges" without going to prostitutes. "Modern burlesque is a sex show," he wrote. Although the thesis was never published, Dressler became an expert on the topic and testified in the 1937 burlesque hearings in New York.[24]

By his own admission, Dressler had attended a thousand performances to do his study, in addition to interviewing around three hundred people. He frequented burlesque theaters and got to know strippers and comics. He sent patrons audience surveys, which they could fill out in the privacy of their own homes. In other words, he created a series of case studies about burlesque patrons. Dressler's analysis is hindered, to some extent, by the morality of the day. And yet he concludes that burlesque is not a menace and documents the genre's complexity more than anyone else had. He does this, first of all, by distancing himself from everything that had been written thus far. "In the present study, the writer began with the assumption that he knew nothing about burlesque," he wrote in the introduction.

Also, while politicians and moralists sought to tar the burlesque audience as being "deviant," Dressler described an audience composed of various classes. Thus, when he tackles the question of why Americans go to burlesque, his answer is fittingly complex: they go for different reasons. Among his subjects were a hypochondriac stenographer, a radical student from a wealthy family (both women), a journalist, a mechanical engineer, and a reformer. One began going while she was a young woman and continued secretly, to flirt with taboo. Another clearly went to burlesque to rebel against her family. Some men attended for "deviant" reasons, in other words, to pick up other men.[25] In a related section of Dressler's thesis, he interviews women about how they feel about striptease. What he concluded here was that some women identified with the strippers and others experienced homosexual leanings when witnessing them. In other words, some women aspired to be queens of burlesque.[26]

ANOTHER ELEMENT contributing to the queens' continued popularity was the conservative fashions of the 1930s. During this era, women, recovering from the asexual costumes the flapper popularized in the Jazz Age, sought glamour onstage. In everyday life, men wore suits and jackets; women wore long skirts and occasionally pantsuits; and hemlines dropped.[27] By contrast, stripping became easier in the late 1930s due to advances in fashion technology—the zipper, stockings and suspenders, and rayon. Invented in the nineteenth century, the zipper first appeared in off-the-rack wear and couture in 1935. Although Elsa Schiaparelli designed a whole collection featuring zippers or "zips," many Americans continued to associate the zipper with sexual lassitude into the forties.[28] But women liked its convenience. In 1937, H. M. Alexander happened upon the "Gypsy Lee strip dress," with its neck-to-floor zipper, sold in Kansas City to "junior misses."[29]

But queens of burlesque themselves disdained the zipper. Gypsy used old-fashioned straight pins. Ann Corio began one act in a long, black velvet cloak with feathered sleeves and unsnapped it to reveal a diaphanous white gown. A maid did the rest, unsnapping one snap at a time. "I would never appear in a zippered costume," Corio said. "Zipping a zipper would be entirely too obvious for artistic effects."[30]

Stockings and the suspender belts holding them up also allowed strippers to tease by revealing an expanse of thigh. These items really came into vogue during the war. DuPont introduced nylon at the San Francisco World's Fair, which was held at the same time as the New York one in 1939. But since the introduction of rayon in the early thirties, designers had been able to create sheer items that were not silk and strippers wore costumes that would "drip dry" backstage.

Also during this era, the garment known as the "strip" dress or the "breakaway" dress emerged in burlesque. Breakaway tables and chairs—props with folding limbs that collapsed when performers used them—had existed since the early days of vaudeville. Like the zipper, the breakaway dress—designed by an anonymous source and notoriously worn by Margie Hart—made it easier for strippers to be both clothed and unclothed. Hart's dress had detachable panels in front and long, satiny lines. When Hart wore the dress, she ripped off the top and flicked the skirt around her body to reveal glimpses of her legs and thighs. At the end of her act, she ripped the skirt off with one motion, making men lean forward in their seats to see if she was wearing a G-string. As *Variety* put it, "When conditions permit something else being taken off, Margie will take it off." In the words of Ann Corio, Hart was responsible for more "eye strain" in one night than the New York Eye Hospital saw in one year. In 1940 the New York police confiscated Hart's costume.[31]

Women had worn some version of sleepwear, lingerie, or bathing suits on the burlesque stage since the nineteenth century. But in Hart's hands, the strip dress turned underclothes into a carnival tent. While wearing it, she existed to manipulate the slinky material. She expressed physical awareness of the dress against her skin in her lithe stance and confident stare, and of course in the revolutionary way she touched her clothes and herself in front of an audience.[32]

Hart was a pioneer who forced audiences to recognize the two most important garments for a queen of burlesque in the thirties: rosettes, which covered the nipples and resembled pasties, and the G-string, a tiny panel of fabric swaddling the crotch. Statutes about nudity varied from state to state. In most states, strippers wore rosettes attached to their strip dresses. Later, they would paste them on over their nipples and underneath their bras. On top of their G-strings, they sometimes wore what were called "net pants," or nylon underwear. By 1931, except for Gypsy and Ann Corio, who ended their acts partially clothed, the majority of strippers rushed offstage in a G-string as the blackout fell. And in this era, G-strings themselves became an industry staple. Until the Depression, most strippers had either made their own G-strings or bought them from traveling salesmen. But in the late thirties, Charles Guyette, the "G-string King," became the first commercial G-string manufacturer. Guyette made and sold costumes to burlesque performers from Eleventh Street in New York and later from a Midtown showcase.[33]

The origins of the term "G-string" itself are nebulous. Though the garment can be seen in frescos of Pompeiian slave girls and prostitutes, the G-string made its American debut in the costumes of Earl Carroll's showgirls in the Jazz Age. But the G-string's etymology follows a trajectory from practical function to sharp, funny-business allure. According to the *Oxford English Dictionary*, a G-string was a narrow strip of fabric in the loincloth worn by a squaw, until sometime in the early thirties, when it acquired its striptease definition.[34]

Is it a coincidence that the term G-string was in use in the same decade as the term G-men, slang for FBI special agents? In the thirties, a "g" also referred to a thousand-dollar bill, so perhaps it suggested that what the garment was hiding was worth that amount. A "g" also might mean a scam.[35] In burlesque slang of the Depression, the G-string became known as "the gadget," a double entendre referring to a handyman's "contrivance," an all-purpose word for the thing that might "fix" things. The linguist Robert Hendrickson asserts that "g" stood for "groin."[36]

Until the fifties, only the most daring queens of burlesque discarded the G-string—or even gave the illusion of doing so. In the 1930s, Margie

Hart wore a "Chicago G-string"—a G-string made of monkey fur or black wool that resembled pubic hair—while she paraded from one end of the stage to the other.[37] According to the stripper Sherry Britton, who broke into burlesque with an act in which she set two glasses of water on her breasts, in 1939 the red-headed Hart also performed without a discernible G-string at the Republic Theater. "Margie had a detective friend who would warn her when the censors were coming around and she would wear a g-string. Then she started seeing somebody else and he got jealous and didn't warn her and they closed us down."[38]

The term "Chicago G-string" arose because as the center of the burlesque industry shifted out of New York, some of the biggest G-string manufacturers were found in the Second City. Harry Bosen, owner of the New York Costume Company on Dearborn Street, made Chicago G-strings as well as one with fox eyes that lit up when the stripper bumped. Tony Midnight began as a female impersonator, and then sold G-strings in gold and silver lamé, white ermine, and mink. "Standard issue" G-strings cost a dollar, but Bosen sold a rhinestone one for four hundred dollars.[39]

After the advent of the burlesque queen, a popular myth about the G-string's origins—one that played with the allegedly highbrow provenance of striptease—circulated: the G-string acquired its name because of the narrowest string on the violin. The story went that a burlesque comic, searching for a euphemism, hit on "G-string." This is apocryphal, since the e string is the narrowest string. But the explanation continued to appeal. In the 1941 movie *Lady of Burlesque*—based on Gypsy's murder mystery *The G-String Murders*—Barbara Stanwyck, about to do her big strip, sings Sammy Cahn's lyric "Take it off the e string, play it on the g-string" to tell the bandleader to jazz up the music. The following year, on trial for obscenity, Margie Hart referred to her G-string as a "victory garden" to make fun of reformers' zeal.

By the end of the thirties, when "striptease" had become a mainstream word, its vocabulary sometimes sounded like a recipe for Depression-era hardship. Synonyms for stripping alluded to a mysterious and troublesome social force: "grind" intimated hardship, which left-leaning playwrights such as Elmer Rice and Clifford Odets began to be concerned about in this era; "heaving," "shucking;" "tossing," "peeling," and "slinging" described the movements comprising striptease and resonated strongly of women's domestic work.[40] As for the names of strippers, in this era they seem mundane except for Gypsy Rose Lee, which revealed the American obsession with the consolation of glamour. According to one rumor, Ann Corio was derived from "anchor" as an homage to the large number of sailors in burlesque audiences.[41]

Who were these queens of the world of honky-tonk and glitter? Royalty of the fringes, ladies of the underworld, they were queens of burlesque theaters, which, in New York at least, existed in the popular imagination as much as literally. And yet striptease continued to be considered an American art, sometimes in the strangest of places. In 1937, while Gypsy was trying out Hollywood and LaGuardia was shutting down burlesque in New York, Billy Minsky's brothers, H.K. and Morton, traveled to Washington to argue this position at a hearing for the Dickstein Bill, which sought to prohibit foreigners from taking Americans' jobs. In the initial months of the planning of the World's Fair in 1937, New York City officials had worried that the best jobs would go to foreign performers.

In front of the House Immigration Committee, the brothers, following the testimony of some tenors from the Metropolitan Opera, testified in the hopes of restricting the entrance of foreign stage artists into the country. A photo of Congressman Samuel Dickstein and the Minskys ran in the *New York Times*.[42] "Strange as it may seem," H.K. said, "these strip tease artists have to be trained and schooled. They have to be taught rhythm in a manner synchronous with the music. They are taught to strip and unclothe by specialists in the atmosphere and lighting of the stage." He added that foreign performers arriving in the city intending to make it in opera often ended up in burlesque, which made it more difficult for American queens and hopefuls.[43]

BY THE END of the thirties, striptease was becoming, if not international, multicultural. While Gypsy read Plato and posed with coeds from the University of Chicago, black and Asian female performers stripped in many burlesque theaters and nightclubs across the country. Writing about a black-and-tan (mixed-race) nightclub on Chicago's South Side in 1936, the French explorer Henri Champli noted that "women sang, then gradually undressed themselves before their audiences and shimmied in the most suggestive way."[44]

But these women for the most part could not become queens. In the twenties, with rare exceptions, few women of color had stripped or worked in white burlesque. In general, circuit and stock burlesque produced white striptease, although the first black cootch dancer performed at Minskys' National Winter Garden in 1929. All-black female revues such as Irvin Miller's *Brownskin Models* and the *Chocolate Scandals* also sometimes played white burlesque theaters into the 1930s.[45] Although some female troupes such as the Whitman Sisters included undressing acts in their revue, generally the black vaudeville circuit—the Theatrical Organization of Black Artists (TOBA)—eschewed burlesque striptease.[46]

The Depression changed this picture. For one, after the Crash, the renaissance in black theater faltered. Many black entertainers found themselves out of work, and black theater owners lost control of many of their theaters to white entrepreneurs. At the same time, by the middle of the

Depression, the striptease boom made it difficult for white burlesque impresarios to find enough white strippers to fill their theaters. Thus they began to hire performers of color.[47]

Nelson Algren's first novel, *Somebody in Boots*, describes the strippers and the audience at the Rialto Theater in Chicago in 1935 as both black and white. But this hardly meant that the color line had vanished. When the theater hosted its amateur night, only white strippers participated in the "win a lucky garter" contest. Only white men ever got the ticket that entitled them to take the garter off one of the chorines.[48]

In 1937, Valda, a black stripper, performed at the Brooklyn Star, one of two burlesque theaters owned by the Raymond family. An advertisement that year in *Billboard* described her as "positively the only colored strip teaser and dancer in burlesque."[49] During the early thirties, the Raymonds had run the Star, which was located on Fulton Street, as a "grind" house—a raunchy theater churning out four shows a day. But by 1937, under pressure from Moss and LaGuardia, the Star acquired a reputation as a neighborhood "variety" theater.[50]

Still, the presence of women of color in Depression-era burlesque hardly marks progress in racial attitude. With names like Aloha and Naomi Dusk, these strippers' appeal centered on their "exotic" or domestic quality. The popular press described them as "dusky," "brownskin," or "sepia."[51] Aloha, a "Polynesian tinted" stripper who performed with the Hindu Belles in 1940, did her number to the beat of a tom-tom. The two-hundred-pound Aunt Hattie did a "mock" strip in which she revealed "ebony undies." At a moment when Gypsy Rose Lee was popularizing "A Stripteaser's Education," black strippers were limited to doing "torrid dances" or mammy acts.[52]

During the war, the demand for black strippers increased, and two black burlesque circuits stumbled to life in Philadelphia, where a powerful burlesque culture existed. One, called the Metro, lasted only a few months. The other used as its main venue the Lincoln, a former Yiddish theater. Clarence Robinson, the black vaudevillian and the choreographer responsible for introducing tap dancing to the Apollo Theater, was said to be on board and "ready to produce."[53]

Neither of these circuits succeeded at all, perhaps because theater in general during the Depression floundered. Nonetheless, the appearance of strippers of color, who never became as commercially successful as white ones, did represent somewhat of a leap into modern consciousness where the variety of sexual entertainment was concerned. For black women in Hollywood and on Broadway, the possible roles were limited to the mammy and the maid. As in jazz and tap dance, striptease offered women of color an opportunity to appear as equals of white performers, at least on the surface. On the other hand, sometimes being "of color" was as good, if not better than, being of color.[54] A Latina stripper named Chiquita Garcia performed as early as 1934, and Princess Whitewing, a "Native American" stripper, began appearing at nightclubs at the end of the decade. But the most popular ethnic strippers, who also surfaced in the mid-thirties, were Asian women.[55]

The first Asian stripper to perform in burlesque was Ming Toya, a Chinese American who did specialty numbers in San Francisco, and then burst onto the scene at Minskys' Brooklyn in 1935. "She is a real Chinese girl. She worked neatly, is pretty, and has a neat appealing form. She appeared in her native costume, a dazzling costume of bright colors."[56]

Like black women, Chinese American women had begun to venture into white popular entertainment in the twenties. Although the roles they played sometimes broke ethnic stereotypes, mostly they recreated them or else imitated generic ideas about American glamour. Still, these women had few other choices if they wanted to be entertainers, since Asian Americans in general could not succeed in Hollywood. In the late thirties, however, a few Chinese American women leapt from San Francisco's Chinese-run night-club Forbidden City into burlesque circuits and white nightclubs.

At the time, San Francisco housed the biggest Chinese community in the country. Some Chinese Americans wanted their own nightclub along the lines of the Harlem nightclubs of the 1920s. Several all-Chinese night-clubs opened. In 1938, Chinese American businessman Charlie Low founded Forbidden City, the most famous of these nightclubs, on the border of Chinatown. For about ten years, he produced an all-Chinese variety revue, in which Chinese American performers impersonated Sophie Tucker and Cole Porter. At first the audience was Chinese. But after *Life* made Forbidden City famous, Low catered to movie stars and tourists. In a financial crisis in 1940, Low hired Asian fan and bubble dancers and strippers alongside of tap and other acrobatic and animal acts. Low's aim was assimilation. "Chinese women are not old fashioned way all bundled up in four or five pairs of trousers. Why, Chinese women have limbs as pretty as anyone's," he said.[57]

To tourists seeking exoticism, however, Forbidden City disappointed. In 1942, *Collier's* described the club as humdrum. "At first only tourists patronized Chinese night clubs, expecting to whiff opium smoke and maybe see a hatchet or two flying. All they saw was Miss Joy Ching (Home Economics, University of Chicago) doing a striptease as The Girl in The Gilded Cage."[58]

Still, because of Forbidden City, a handful of Asian strippers became striptease headliners in mainstream burlesque. Amy Fong starred in *China Dolls*, a burlesque revue named for her, as well as in a "white" revue called *Modes and Models*, which toured, among other places, to Boston's Old Howard. In both revues Fong's publicity stressed her "authenticity" as an Asian woman. In *Modes and Models*, she also played straight women in burlesque skits.[59] A photograph of Fong in this era provides a sartorial representation of her divided alliances: on top, Fong wears a strip costume that features a traditional Chinese dress's shoulder pads. But she is also wearing a fringed G-string.

None of the homogeneity of Chinese American strippers and fan dancers diminishes the significance of their entering burlesque in the late thirties. Traditional Chinese culture forbade women to show their legs in public, and often women who performed in such clubs broke with their families. Thus a dancer like Fong took considerable risks when she chose her occupation, just as first-generation American Jews did by stripping for Minsky in the twenties. As with black performers, however, cultural expectations about Asian women dictated how they got reviewed and how they stripped. Drawing from stereotypes of the Orient, reviewers either remarked on Fong's "delicacy" and "polite" stripteasing or on her "glitter."[60]

As the demand for Chinese American strippers grew during the war, other women joined Fong. Discovered by Charlie Low in 1939 at the San Francisco World's Fair, Noel Toy became a star at Forbidden City. Billed as "the Chinese Sally Rand" and "the Glamorous Chinese Fan-tasy," Toy did a bubble dance at the Music Box Theater and then moved east, where, although she would perform in many burlesques and nightclubs, she would never be queen.[61]

Noel Toy, "The Chinese Sally Rand," at the Forbidden City Nightclub in San Francisco, c. 1939. The San Francisco Performing Arts Library and Museum.

# "Clamouring for a Table and Pounding for an Encore": Striptease at the World's Fair

In New York, the advent of the 1939 World's Fair seemed to pose a problem. The World's Fair, "The World of Tomorrow," promised to present a glossy, futuristic scenario of life in America. In the *New York Times*, H. G. Wells described its effect on the typical fair-goer, "the fair will cease to look like a collection of things for sale and reveal its real nature as a gathering of live objects, each of which is going to do something to him, possibly something quite startling." Like the fairs of 1898 and 1933, the New York fair also needed a midway full of naked women to make it run.[1]

The brains behind that midway would be the impresario Billy Rose, formerly the brains behind the Casino de Paree and Diamond Horseshoe nightclubs. And yet it is striking to learn that the year before the fair opened, Rose used striptease to convince Grover Whalen, the president of the fair corporation, to let him run the midway. In the weeks prior to the revue, Rose worried that Whalen, a WASP-y official whose nickname was "the Gardenia of the Law" because of his habit of wearing a boutonniere, would turn him down. Thus Rose went to great lengths to make it clear that his striptease—indeed his girl shows overall—were not the "burlesque" version, but rather a "glorified" funny nightclub type. "This is the show which kids Mr. Whalen," the *New York Times* wrote.[2]

Rose staged *Let's Play Fair* at the Casa Mañana, a lavish, family-style nightclub on Forty-fourth Street and Broadway. Like Rose's earlier nightclubs, the Casa Mañana sought to give its customers a thrill without making them sit in a dingy burlesque theater or cabaret. In between acts, patrons could sample the "Palm Beach bar," where private cabanas with sunlamps and attendants offered, in the words of a promotional brochure, "vitamin D with swing music."[3]

*Let's Play Fair* opened on January 8, 1938, over a year before the opening day of the World's Fair. An hour long, *Let's Play Fair* cost $150,000. Rose cast the comic Oscar Shaw as Whalen. It starred vaudevillians, jugglers, and animal acts, as well as the stripper Hinda Wassau and the fan dancer Sally Rand, who had just finished a successful tour of the West with her nude ranch—scantily clad women in cowboy boots, holsters, and hats.[4]

In Rand's number, the vaudeville comic Doc Rockwell played a professor of anatomy hot to convince the Grover Whalen character that displaying women's bodies would bring in big bucks. Thus he launched into a burlesque monologue about Rand and the Chicago Century of Progress

Exposition. "Without her hips," Rockwell quipped, "it would have been a bust." "Would the audience like to see her?" Applause. "The thighs have it, Miss Sally Rand."

Rand did her bubble dance with a globe showing the layout of the fair's grounds. Rockwell commented, "Here we have a bit of astronomy . . . showing that when a globe passes before a heavenly body, we have an eclipse of the moon.[5]

Whereas Rose presented Rand as part of a burlesque comedy routine, he featured Wassau as a solo act. In *Let's Play Fair*, Wassau, "the Midwestern Bombshell," ripped off her dress in a single motion, performing "spasmodic sex movements" and letting her hands glide over her body. She giggled, panted, and flashed her breasts, inspiring reviews of *Let's Play Fair* to incriminate not just the Hindu Belle, but the "low-minded" audience that watched her. Wassau's "torrid, Minskyesque strip," Abel Greene wrote in *Variety*, made the "Minsky minded [to] pound tables and clamour [*sic*] for an encore."[6]

Such reviews attracted police attention, and Rose took Wassau out of the show. But Whalen initially seemed to have no objections to Rand. Shortly after *Let's Play Fair* closed, Whalen made Rose entertainment director. At first, Rose claimed to be planning to produce a patriotic spectacle. It was only after several months of negotiating that Whalen agreed to let Rose change his plan and build an Aquacade, a musical swimming revue that eventually became the most popular and most lucrative exhibit at the fair. The Aquacade, which starred the athlete Eleanor Holm—at the time Rose's wife—as well as many other women in bathing suits, was considered good, clean fun.[7]

The fair was scheduled to open on April 29. But in the months before opening day, Whalen seemed slow to book girlie shows for the midway. Instead, he hired a group of penguins for an exhibit about Admiral Perry's exploration of the South Pole. Whalen had always had a prudish streak. Whereas at the Chicago fair, newspaper columnists had unanimously agreed to call the midway the midway in an homage to the 1893 fair, Whalen named his midway the "amusement area," a phrase that would amuse some of the performers enough to don underwear with the words on the front.[8] In the publicity material for the fair, Whalen focused on the area's organization, not what would be inside. A mere two months before, *Variety* had reported that the amusement area "looked bleak." Some old-time fair experts from Chicago speculated that the New York planners' strategy was to wait until the last minute and overwhelm the fair with sex shows.[9]

Asked whether he would hire Sally Rand, though, Whalen remained evasive: "The Fair will retain the final decision," he said. But if Whalen was willing to hire nude or near-nude performers, he ultimately seemed to have no intention of hiring well-known strippers such as Rand. "There will be no Sally Rand or Sally Rands at the World's Fair," he announced.[10]

As for Rand, she fled to San Francisco to pitch her nude ranch to the 1939 Golden Gate International Exposition, which was about to open. At first she produced the nude ranch at a nightclub while she waited to see if the city would have her. San Francisco mayor Harris Connick quickly gave her a vote of confidence: "We'd like to have Sally with us . . . in any capacity," he said. The official Golden Gate Exposition pamphlet described Rand's nude ranch as a "dude ranch à la 1939." Even after her success in San Francisco, Rand failed to convince Whalen to include her in New York.[11] Illustrated by Maxfield Parrish, Rand's Christmas card that year showed her flashing her behind at New York and a top-hatted Whalen as she strode west across a map of America.[12]

Sally Rand abandons the New York World's Fair for the San Francisco World's Fair, c. 1939. Author's personal collection.

In real life, Rand continued to hope for reconciliation. In February she flew back to New York to make her case in person. But Whalen remained uncharmed. Among burlesque strippers exiled from the fair, a protest erupted. Ann Corio threatened to strike. When asked if strippers deserved a union, she punned that the "present situation called for a 'See I Oh' organization."[13] Pitching the act she wanted to do, "Afternoon of a Faun," Faith Bacon walked down Park Avenue with a two-hundred-pound deer on a leash.[14]

Part of the difficulty may have been money, since Rand announced to anyone who would listen that her "25 cents a head days were over." But in interviews, Rand, who had worked with Billy Rose in Texas in 1936, also blamed the impresario for her exile, arguing that he wanted to make Eleanor Holm, his second wife, the "Sally Rand" of the New York fair. "Very well, let the public decide if anyone can take the place of Sally Rand," she warned.[15]

Still, by the end of March, Rand or no Rand, Whalen was on his way to booking many shows featuring nude women, especially those posing with mechanical devices or in "natural" settings. Unfortunately, few of these were ready on opening day. In its initial review of fair entertainments, *Variety* complained that only 10 percent of the midway was operating. On May 13, two weeks after the fair had launched, the *New Yorker* warned fairgoers, "The amusement section is slowly pulling itself together, but don't expect too much."[16]

It took an entire month for the amusement area to be running at full speed. When it finally lurched into existence, *Variety* described the amusement area as "10 Coney Islands rolled into one." John Krimsky, Whalen's director of entertainment, produced "The Arctic Girl's Tomb of Ice"—in which a scantily dressed woman emerged from a block of ice. Norman Bel Geddes staged the "Crystal Lassies," or "A Peep Show of Tomorrow," an exhibit displaying nearly nude women reflected stripping hundreds of times in fun-house mirrors to rumbas and the music of Camille Saint-Saëns. A nude mannequin stood on the pedestal outside beckoning audiences to touch her. Bel Geddes renamed this exhibit "Classie Lassies." The Cuban Gardens concession advertised a "Miss Nude 1939."[17]

Comparing one of the G-rated entertainments—the penguin show about the discovery of the Antarctic—to the strip shows, Brendan Gill wrote:

> Far more popular than the penguins was a hapless nudie show sneaking into the fair under the sacred name of education. The girls were allowed to go bare-breasted because they were teaching us the customs of the ancient amazon warriors, and so, by extension, giving us a glimpse of that lost classic world so privileged by our elders.[18]

Brooks Atkinson observed, "This is a girl show run with somewhat less versatility than the wicked burlesque shows latterly outlawed in the world of today." Nils T. Granlund did not even pretend to educate. A "Congress of Beauty," which *Life* described as featuring "a whole horde of fan dancers," starred former burlesque and nightclub strippers Faith Bacon, Yvette Dare, Gladys Clark, and many others. The acts were imaginative, extravagant, satiric, and nude. Gladys Clark, for example, impersonated Tex Guinan, the café owner from the 1920s.[19]

With the arrival of the "Congress," the midway—which was open until 2 A.M., long after the other exhibits at the fair had closed—began to acquire a carnival feel. The "giant" stripper Lois De Fee, who first stripped at Leon and Eddie's nightclub on Fifty-second Street that year, paraded at the Glamazon Village, a midway concession starring naked women as "glamazons." The six-foot-four De Fee exploited her height, advertising the number of yards necessary to make the dresses she performed in, and declared that before entering show business, she had been the only female bouncer in New York. Reviews and ad copy compared her to the "Lilliputians" she worked with. "She towered over the . . . other strippers," *Billboard* noted.[20]

Other strippers performing in the fair relied on either birds or animals to take off their clothes, a trick that subverted the injunction against touching one's body while undressing, or alluded to classical dance. Faith Bacon performed "Afternoon of a Faun," parodying Nijinsky's sensational ballet in part by resetting Debussy's music for a dance orchestra. Yvette Dare's parrots disrobed her to the sound of African drumming. But although her parrots plucked off Dare's floral bra, she never could train them to undo her G-string: since the birds only pulled off her sarong, the act retained a G-rating. Rosita Royce, a former Denishawn dancer and headliner at the 1936 California Pacific Exposition in San Diego, performed a similar number with doves for a thousand dollars a week at the Crystal Palace, which the *New Yorker* described as "a resume of peep shows through the ages." About Royce, a carnival and fair favorite, *Variety* wrote that "doves peel her, at the same time returning to rest on her arms and shoulders in a pretty posture," adding that the way the audience rushed to the glass partition she stripped behind would have "made the Minskys cry with shame."[21]

Rosita Royce and her dove act at the World's Fair, c. 1939. Culver Pictures.

In the end, most of these striptease acts made less money for the fair than the planners wanted. Thus in 1940, the fair planners wanted to focus on big names and glamour instead of hordes of strippers. "The fair will have a shot of glamour, the second time around," *Variety* wrote.[22] And yet when the fair reopened in May 1940, the striptease entertainment was more carnivalesque and comic than glamorous. Some of the old standards from the first year, such as Rosita Royce's act, returned. But a host of newcomers to the fair defined the midway. At Mike Todd's Gay New Orleans concession, Carrie Finnell performed a tassel twirl in which she pretended to be Mrs. Henrietta Longstreet, a Daughter of the American Revolution, who, as it turned out, could pop her bosom while she sang a comic song advising young women to stay away from "predatory" men. In that same concession, one of the four bars was called the Carrie's Do Bust Inn, after Carrie herself.[23]

Another one of Todd's contributions was Muriel Page, the flame dancer he had "discovered" at the Chicago World's Fair. And of course Gypsy Rose Lee stripped at the most "glamorous" of Todd's concessions, the *Streets of Paris*, which was a burlesque show. Brooks Atkinson, reviewing Gypsy's act, described the Literary Stripper as "tall, sleek, and mischievous," but in keeping with the new seriousness that the arrival of war in Europe had put on the world, he questioned her "sanitized" style of striptease. "Humor in strip-teasing is in questionable taste. Some things are too sacred to be kidded: the line between things that are serious and things that are frivolous ought to be drawn somewhere and not too high."[24]

The Literary Stripper, however, had the last laugh. Despite the censor's watchful eye, the version of "A Stripper's Education" she performed at *Streets of Paris* was more risqué than the one she did at the *Follies*. Like later versions, it expanded and honed her image as the woman who aspired to class but also needed the blues.[25]

One personnel change reveals how the second year of the fair differed from the first. In July, Royce left the fair and checked herself into the hospital, a decision she attributed to exhaustion. "We did 74 shows a week," she complained. But according to the trade papers, Royce left because a sniper peppered her doves with a bb gun and the management refused to do anything to protect her. Ann Corio contends that "Tirza the Wine Girl," another stripper, was the sniper, and whether this is true or not, a few weeks later, Tirza stepped in to replace Royce.[26]

Tirza reflected the fair's combination of technology and nudity. Before the fair, Tirza had performed a cabaret and nightclub "Apache" dance number she called "The Spider," in which she wore an enormous feathered headdress and glow-in-the-dark radium-covered wings. Sometime in 1939, though, she added to her repertoire a "wine bath" act. According to Tirza, the idea arose when her mother and a friend—a gay dancer—suggested she

Newspaper advertising for Tirza the Wine Girl, c. 1939–1940. Author's personal collection.

fashion her moniker from the Greek name Thryzha. The act was an immediate hit. "It was torn, bleeding, right out of the Greek myth," an excited fairgoer who described Tirza as "intellectual, but hot" exclaimed.[27]

In a nine-minute striptease in a shower of red wine, Tirza told the story of the "festival of Bacchus."[28] The five-foot-four platinum blonde entered wrapped in a pale blue chiffon dress and a short sequined jacket while an offstage narrator explained the Greek myth of Bacchus, the wine fountain, and the Grecian maiden who became so enamored of him that she threw herself into the fountain and then turned into wine. Tirza exited and an actress dressed as a maid entered and handed grapes to the audience. A few minutes later, the "Goddess of the Wine Bath" reentered wearing an evening gown and did a ballet routine. Sometimes Eubie Blake's piano rags accompanied her; sometimes a keyboard solo of the Turner Layton jazz standard "Deep Purple" coyly referred to the wine itself.[29]

After a preliminary spin around the floor wearing flowing robes and carrying a glass of "wine," Tirza mounted the specially built platform located upstage above the bandstand. In this triple-mirrored alcove, complete with tall glass containers of red liquid, a spray of wine came from pipe jets underneath the flooring and dry ice created mist in the liquid. Red and blue lights flashed and Tirza disrobed to a bathing suit. She writhed and danced as the brightly colored liquid flowed over her body.[30]

As with Gypsy, the popular press focused on Tirza's common touch as well as her sex appeal. But tabloids also stressed Tirza's modernity, which dovetailed, in at least a superficial way, with the fair's "World of Tomorrow" theme. "Sexology plus technology," one headline proclaimed. After the fair closed in December, Tirza flourished. Not only a performer, but also an entrepreneur and a member of plumber's Local 2, "the Wine Girl" became a different kind of stripper, as the Blitz struck Poland and France, and England declared war on Germany. While the draft was reinstated, the tabloids ran stories about Tirza's self-sufficiency: when she was traveling across the country, the demands of fixing a shower with five pumps that was so big it took three people to lift it inspired Tirza to get a plumber's license.[31] Along with many other strippers and pinup girls, Tirza was allotted special government privileges during the war, such as a special t-card that allowed her extra gas rations so she could travel from one nightclub to another and entertain as many soldiers as she could.[32]

# Striptease during Wartime

The war buoyed the burlesque industry and striptease. The influx of men in port cities and army bases in the Midwest created a demand for strip shows, just as it had in earlier eras. While politicians continued to suppress burlesque in New York, outside of Gotham it flourished. In 1941 the impresario Isidore Hirst founded a thirty-week burlesque circuit by consolidating the one he had been running—the Independent circuit—with a midwestern one controlled by Arthur Clamage, Dewey Michaels, and N. S. Barger. To discourage reform attention, Hirst limited the number of strips to two per show.[1]

The Hirst circuit was a hit. Strippers and comics working for Hirst toured Chicago, Boston, Minneapolis, St. Louis, Detroit, Milwaukee, Toronto, Cleveland, Cincinnati, Youngstown, Toledo, Indianapolis, Rochester, and Norfolk, Virginia, a naval base. At first Hirst produced shows starring the headliners of 1930s burlesque: Hinda Wassau, Ann Corio, Georgia Sothern, and Margie Hart recycled or updated their Depression-era numbers by adding singing and dancing. "Burlesque, along with aviation and munitions, is experiencing a wartime spurt," Ann Corio wrote in *Variety* at Christmas of 1941, just after Pearl Harbor.[2]

Six months later, it was clear that burlesque strippers alone could not fill a thirty-week circuit with twenty-eight theaters in the Midwest and East.[3] Thus Hirst began to hire striptease acts from Broadway and nightclubs, as well as strippers who made fun of other strippers.[4] One successful headliner, Rosita Royce, the dove dancer from the 1939 New York World's Fair, did "The G-string Quartet," a number sending up Gypsy Rose Lee, Ann Corio, Margie Hart, and Georgia Sothern.[5]

Other strip acts borrowed from Hollywood. After *Gone with the Wind* swept the Academy Awards in 1940, Alice Jewel, the "Scarlett O'Hara of Burlesque," impersonated Vivian Leigh's antebellum character. As America was reinstating the draft, the real Scarlett embodied romantic ideals about southern women and America itself, while the burlesque "Scarlett" lampooned the Hollywood heroine. Billed as being "gustier than *Gone with the Wind*," Scarlett, the ad copy read, "blows up" Friday.[6]

At the same time, intellectuals continued to be entranced with striptease and its gropings towards elegance. As H. L. Mencken recounted in the second volume of *The American Language*, in 1940 he received a letter from Georgia Sothern, asking him to create a word that would mean strip-tease but would contain a more elegant sound and sense.

> I am a practitioner of the fine art of strip-teasing. . . . In recent years, there has been a great deal of uninformed criticism leveled against my profession. . . . I feel sure that if you could coin a new and more palatable word to describe this art, the objections to it would vanish and I and my colleagues would have easier going. I hope that the science of semantics can find time to help the verbally underprivileged members of my profession. Thank you.[7]

Mencken chronicled the difficulty he encountered in searching for a synonym for stripteaser.

> The word moltician comes to mind, but it must be rejected because of its likeness to mortician. . . . A resort to the scientific name for molting, which is ecdysis, produces both ecdysist and ecdysiast. Then there are suggestions in the names of some of the creatures which practice molt-ing. The scientific name for the common crab is *Callinectes hastastus*, which produces *callinectian*. Again, there is a family of lizards called the *Geckonidae*, and their name produces *gecko*. Perhaps your advisers may be able to find other suggestions in the same general direction.[8]

Mencken settled on "ecdysiast." But besides Sothern, many strippers saw Mencken's project as suspect and snobbish—an effort to transform striptease into something refined and therefore inauthentic. Gypsy Rose Lee herself interpreted in Mencken's efforts Americans' desire to ridicule the sexual fantasy of the rich about the poor. In the word "striptease," Gypsy read her own authenticity and connection to her peripatetic working-class roots; in Mencken's "ecdysiast," she saw the highbrow set's bogus claim on her. Just as Mae West continually returned to her working-class roots, so Gypsy, having arrived, now wanted her downtown public to continue to see her as one of them, despite her fame. "We don't wear feathers and molt them off. . . . [W]hat does he know about stripping?" she asked.[9]

Nonetheless, in London, a society for ecdysiasts was formed, and its members sent letters to the Lord Chamberlain to ask if he would revoke the ban on striptease if the person taking it off was called an ecdysiast. (He would not.) "Stripteuse," a Frenchified version of the word stripper, and "striptteuse" also appeared in newspapers and magazines as if making the name more elite would elevate the art into a refined entertainment.[10]

By 1942, American theater operators were inventing their own syn-onyms for stripper. In Baltimore, theater operators coined "beauty flasher." In Philadelphia the word "exotic" described performers who abandoned bumps and grinds for slinking across the stage in a tiny costume. The ap-pearance of these words may have been partly motivated by local censors' attacks on striptease and burlesque, but I like to think that they also re-vealed the genre's variety.[11] Still, language could disguise neither striptease's working-class origins nor its oblique connection to prostitution. In the first years of the war, American reformers and politicians worried that strip-tease, along with the increasing availability of pinups and other forms of commercialized sex, could drive civilians and soldiers to immorality. "Pa-triotism, vast admiration, fervor and precocious sex urge get all tangled up in adolescent bodies that are not yet equipped with the necessary adult intellectual processes with which to make decisions," said one reformer.[12]

Nevertheless, ordinary Americans were less interested in striptease's "dangerous" aspect than in allowing soldiers to take advantage of it as a wartime perk. Soldiers stationed overseas could see women posing naked or nearly naked, but American-style burlesque striptease was less common. In London, for example, the Windmill Theater offered the *Revudeville*—choruses and tableaux of immobile, undressed women and American-style performers such as "the Platinum Goddess," who got around the Lord Chamberlain's edict by allowing her bra and skirt to be torn off by savages. According to Sheila Van Damm, the Windmill Theater's operator, the only time one of these performers moved was during the war when a V-1 bomb exploded fifty yards from the theater. Otherwise, the performers posed like statuary in an Italianate garden.[13]

The Lord Chamberlain notwithstanding, *Variety* reported an American-style striptease vogue in London in 1940.[14] And the British also invented the comic book heroine "Jane," who was constantly taking off her clothing as she saved the country from Nazi depravity. Jane, a curvaceous blonde secret agent and the darling of the British troops, got tangled up with Nazi spies, tumbled down cliffs, and got caught in tree branches in episodes that invariably concluded with her losing her clothes. When Britain went to war, bomber crews painted Jane on Lancaster fuselages. Submarines moved into the Atlantic with weeks of her advance comic panels stored away, and tank crews plastered Jane's undraped likeness on their turrets. Winston Churchill is said to have cited Jane's morale boosting as Britain's secret weapon.[15]

Carnival or sideshow strippers also entertained the troops overseas. The "darling of the American Army in Africa and Italy," the French entertainer Josette, did a stunt that involved her hanging by her teeth hoisted several feet above the ground. She undressed down to her sparkly bikini, then spun around with her leg up in the air and her teeth still clenched. When she returned to the ground, she took off her bra and walked behind a pillar. When she returned, she bent backwards. The petite performer started to look like a figure from Todd Browning's classic movie *Freaks* as she contin-ued to bend around until her head was directly above her rear. She grasped her ankles, did a few more crowd teases, and then took off her G-string.[16]

Thus, at least on the surface, striptease was part of the war's opening the door to sexual expressiveness in mainstream America. *Yank* magazine featured the first pinup—a still of Betty Grable looking over her shoulder—and pin-up magazines and erotic comic strips proliferated. Rita Hayworth posed in lingerie for *Life*. "War aphrodisia"—a live-for-the-moment mentality encouraging sexual freedom—was cited as the reason. In 1940 the red-headed Margie Hart proclaimed to *Life*, "I'm helping the Allies win the war, every time I unhook my brassiere."[17]

Not every American subscribed to belief that undressing in public comprised part of an American woman's patriotic duty. When Hart mailed sixty-two-year-old Major General William N. Haskell, commander of the Twenty-seventh Division New York National Guard, 50 copies of her "most vivacious photograph" with the promise of 4,550 more, he asked, "Who's Margie Hart?" When informed, the General wrote "REFUSED" across the photos and returned them.[18] In Miami, a special report on vice included a visit to two nightclubs army chaplains had condemned for immoral excess in striptease.[19]

Big-name burlesque strippers continued to criticize burlesque. "The art of stripteasing," Corio declared in the *New York Times* in 1941, had declined. "It has been prostituted by cheap performers, cheap managers. They even have strip teasing in restaurants. People don't get any sense of adventure anymore in going to a theatre to see it."[20]

Like Gypsy and Sally Rand, Corio tried Hollywood. Over a period of several years, she appeared in such B-movies as *Swamp Woman, Jungle Siren, Call of the Wild*, and *Sultan's Daughter*. In *Swamp Woman*, Corio plays a saloon singer who returns to her Florida hometown to find her niece engaged to her former lover and a fugitive causing trouble. In *Jungle Siren*, a surveyor and his sidekick battle Nazi agents in a remote African jungle while Corio, a white-woman sidekick, tags along.[21] During this phase of her career, Corio also toured in summer stock productions of plays such as *White Cargo*, which had appeared in the Jazz Age but in 1942 had been turned into a Warner Brothers movie. *White Cargo* starred sex symbol Hedy Lamarr as a seductive savage in a clingy sarong. Playing in vaudeville and burlesque theaters, Corio would sometimes perform the Lamarr role. When she sashayed onstage one night at Boston's Old Howard, the public responded, at least when the stripper referred to *White Cargo* while stripping. Removing her "junior-sized" sarong, she proclaimed, "I am Tondelayo!" the line Lamarr shouts to the men she is about to devour.[22] One night, at that moment, a Harvard undergraduate leapt from his seat and shouted, "What an actress!"[23]

Having Hollywood-ized her burlesque, Corio remained among the most ardent proponents of striptease. She claimed striptease was an art, and, doing Mencken one better, argued that it should be renamed "deciduous kinesthetics." When reporters asked her how to be a good stripper, she always recommended being feminine: "Make yourself as feminine-looking as you can. Go in for a lot of frills, furs, ruffles, and parasols. Always put everything you have into your work to put it over. . . . [D]on't take off your panties; it makes a girl's figure look prettier to have those little gadgets on."[24]

PERHAPS IF burlesque operators had paid more attention to Corio, their theaters would have remained open in New York after Pearl Harbor. In the spring of 1942, only three burlesque houses were in operation there. The mighty Republic had turned into a movie palace. The Irving Place was once again producing Yiddish theater. Under pressure from reformers to quash burlesque striptease, License Commissioner Paul Moss announced, "The mayor has repeatedly stated that war conditions will not be permitted to lower the standards of morals and decency in this city." He added that when the Star's license expired in a few weeks, he planned to close it as well. But the political climate had shifted. After almost a decade of LaGuardia's cleanup efforts, anxiety about overzealous reform contributed to the birth of an anti-reform coalition comprised of left-leaning intellectuals and respected members of the theater community. Worried that the mayor's censorship policies would violate theaters' constitutional rights, the antireform movement united against the Little Flower. The perils of the nude woman were trivial compared to those the war imposed on Americans.[25]

One of this group's main objections circled around the fate of Clifford Odets' *Waiting for Lefty*. Although the censor had allowed *Waiting for Lefty* to be performed in New York in 1935, many other cities subsequently banned it for its politics. And while few members of the Authors' League of America had ever seen a striptease performance, its members issued a statement to LaGuardia demanding to know why he shut down burlesque theaters. Respected performers also took burlesque's side. Helen Hayes opined: "I don't think I'd enjoy burlesque. But I enjoy still less the spectacle of free Americans being robbed of a livelihood without a trial."[26]

After writing *Life with Father* and producing *Arsenic and Old Lace* together, Howard Lindsay and Russel Crouse assailed LaGuardia's forsaking of the democratic procedure in language that seemed stolen from one of their scripts. He is "starting off with the methods of totalitarianism," they said. The two collaborators, whose own Broadway show about burlesque, *Strip for Action*, would open later that year, went on to warn, "We are at Munich. And complacency at this point, just because it involves burlesque, does not mean peace in our time."[27]

Organizations that in the early thirties had avoided siding with burlesque striptease now mobilized to support it. The Women's City Club of New York, traditionally an anti-vice organization, expressed concern that Moss was overstepping his constitutional rights and that he could, at a moment's notice, shut down any theatrical performance. The Actors' Equity Association, which had ignored burlesque for years, voiced its disapproval about LaGuardia's excesses. Frank Gilmore, executive director of the Equity, wrote, "It is our considered opinion . . . that the question of censorship over theatrical performances by any official or group is offensive to us and that we will sustain this policy of ours by every means in our power."[28]

Journalists chimed in, arguing that the mayor should leave burlesque alone because the working man needed it. Brooks Atkinson noted that the mayor's actions "by fiat" were undemocratic. In an impassioned column countering Joseph Wood Krutch's concerns about the vulgarity of "working man's entertainment" of the early thirties, Damon Runyon took a populist view of the controversy. Runyon, unlike Krutch, did not judge. "I think it is a disquieting symptom of the present and perhaps of the future that the poor man has been robbed of his strip tease. It is one of the many social industries that are overlooked in times like these."[29]

INSTEAD OF SLOWING DOWN LaGuardia's anti-striptease crusade, the waning of public support made him intensify his efforts. Whereas during the Depression, he had identified striptease as a threat to young men and women's morality, now he named it as a drain on the morale needed for a nation at war. As his affidavit in the hearings about the Eltinge and the Republic, the mayor submitted a radio address he gave in February on WNYC, in which he swore that he would not "permit the moral standing of a city to be lowered by dirty shows, salacious pictures, and commercialized vice." He denounced what he called "g-string morality and undressing debauchery" and swore that burlesque theaters would be shortly closed.

One of the ACLU's founders, attorney for the Minskys Morris Ernst, declared LaGuardia to be a "grave threat" and compared his methods to those of Hitler and Mussolini. Ernst tried to appeal but could not overturn the closing. Meanwhile, LaGuardia's actions inspired Molly Minsky, Abe's wife and Harold's mother, to scream at one of the city's lawyers, "I'll kill you for this! You're ruining my son's reputation." Her doctor wrote to LaGuardia begging him to back down. But LaGuardia did not back down. The rumor was that Moss would refuse to renew the Gaiety's license. The Minskys eventually filed for bankruptcy, claiming to be $65,000 in debt.[30]

Although the Depression-era crime wave had abated, Americans continued to fear that striptease would cause illicit behavior. In letters to the mayor, mothers from all over the city begged him to shut down burlesque theaters. "Congratulations and thanks to Mayor LaGuardia from a mother of two boys," one reads. Another woman writes that her husband was so aroused by a striptease that he went home and attacked his daughter.[31]

In the end, LaGuardia complied. Moss closed the Brooklyn Star. Authorities hoped the theater would be torn down to make way for an office building, but it somehow survived until December. Critics predicted a new Prohibition. The Gaiety and the Eltinge abandoned burlesque for "colored" reviews. "The American sense of humor has handled striptease more intelligently than moralists," Brooks Atkinson wrote, defending burlesque. "Ann Corio and Margie Hart are as much a part of show business as the circus."[32]

OUT WEST, Hollywood—monitored by Will Hays and the Catholic Legion of Decency—continued to eschew striptease. Although the studios produced a handful of movies about burlesque during wartime, none of them filmed real striptease numbers. Still, the trade papers continued to proclaim that a stripper could "step" from burlesque to Hollywood.[33] And yet when Gypsy Rose Lee's *The G-String Murders* became the film *Lady of Burlesque*, the studio declined to cast a burlesque stripper for the Gypsy role. Instead, they chose the young Barbara Stanwyck to be Dixie Daisie, the stripper with a heart of gold.[34]

Produced by Hunt Stromberg, who in the 1930s was responsible for the Thin Man movies, *Lady of Burlesque* projects a cheery myth about striptease. Its stock characters—the gruff policewoman; the pretty stripper and her arch enemy; the one who speaks with a Russian accent even though she's from the Midwest; the kind, irresponsible comic— give *Lady of Burlesque* a homespun familiarity. Its situations, set as if they had fallen out of the pages of a comic book, borrow shamelessly from other films and situations: the competition between two headlining strippers; the rise and fall of one of them, thanks to her inherent "bad" qualities; the inefficient and sensational police raid; the reconciliation between the two

Lobby card for the film *Lady of Burlesque*, based on Gypsy Rose Lee's novel *The G-String Murders*, 1941. Author's personal collection.

quarreling strippers; the moment at the end in which one of the girls "makes it" to the *Follies*. The killer strangles several strippers with their own G-strings. The *New York Times* criticized *Lady of Burlesque* for an "absence of glamour" but conceded that burlesque demanded this absence.[35]

An equally important influence on striptease emerged during this era on Broadway, where flesh and pizzazz momentarily distracted Americans from the war's savagery. Even before America got deeply involved over-seas, the vogue for casting strippers in Broadway musicals had acquired force. In 1940, Lorenz Hart and Richard Rodgers, who five years earlier had written "Slaughter on Tenth Avenue" for *On Your Toes*, wrote "Zip" for the musical *Pal Joey*; thus they created a Gypsy Rose Lee–like heroine who had achieved literary greatness on Broadway.[36]

Based on a collection of grim stories John O'Hara wrote for the *New Yorker*, *Pal Joey* was the first musical to depict underworld characters in an unsavory—though not totally unsentimental—fashion. Rodgers and Hart imagined their creation to be a prototype for a new "serious" American musical. Set in seedy 1930s Chicago, it narrates the story of Joey Evans, a thug, and Vera Simpson, a wealthy widow and former stripper obsessed with him. There is no happy ending and no likeable characters. "Nobody like Joey had ever been on the musical stage before," Rodgers noted in his autobiography.[37]

A signature number appearing at the top of the second act, "Zip" paro-died Gypsy Rose Lee's "Stripteaser's Education." Whereas "Slaughter on Tenth Avenue" had both parodied ballet and paid homage to burlesque's authentic American roots, "Zip" parodied the Literary Stripper, as well as her ill-gotten celebrity status. It seems a little mean. In the musical, the song is sung by Melba Snyder, a reporter who, before interviewing Joey, tells the story of meeting Gypsy.[38]

> I've interviewed Pablo Picasso
> And a Countess named di Farasso
> Admired by Stravinsky.
> But my greatest acclaim was the interview with the star
> Who worked for Minsky.
> I met her at the Yankee Clipper
> And she didn't unzip one zipper.
> I said, "Miss Lee, you are such an artist
> Tell me why you never miss.
> What do you think of while you work?"
> And she said: "While I work,
> My thoughts go something like this: . . ."

The song then dives into the rat-a-tat-tat listing of the best and the brightest trends of the day—just as Gypsy's song had. The first verse pokes fun at the psychology craze, the journalist Walter Lippman, the writer

William Saroyan. More provocatively, by mentioning gay men and women, it also establishes Gypsy's heterosexuality. It finishes as Gypsy annihilates the other strippers competing with her for the title of "Miss Intellectual." Thus "Zip" both celebrates and ridicules the whole world of striptease.[39]

> Zip! Walter Lippman wasn't brilliant today
> Zip! Will Saroyan ever write a great play?
> Zip! I was reading Schopenhauer last night
> Zip! And I think that Schopenhauer was right
> I don't want to see Zorina
> I don't want to meet Cobina
> Zip! I'm an intellectual
> I don't like a deep contralto
> Or a man whose voice is alto
> Zip! I'm a heterosexual
> Zip! It took intellect to master my art
> Zip! Who the hell is Margie Hart?[40]

Critics liked this number. But *Pal Joey*'s smirking irreverence may explain why it failed to capture as big an audience as *Oklahoma!* Americans were looking for good feeling at the moment the Allies were declaring war on Germany. Still, the musical ran for a respectable 374 performances, even though Brooks Atkinson and some other critics panned it.[41]

Throughout the war, the yen for striptease remained the most powerful on Broadway. One reason was financial gain. After Pearl Harbor, Broadway was experiencing a boom. Cleaned up and buoyed by satire and luxury, striptease could finally really appeal to women. "Burlesque holds a strong appeal for fem patrons who had always been intrigued by such entertainment and in niteries can enjoy it on equal terms with the male," explained *Billboard* in 1942.[42]

In the summer of that year, only months after LaGuardia shuttered the last burlesque houses in the city, striptease had colonized the Great White Way. The stripteases on Broadway fell into two categories—comic-literary and brash-sexy—and both made fun of burlesque. The comic-literary was embodied by Gypsy Rose Lee, the latter by Georgia Sothern. Each type responded to different aspects of American demands for entertainment during World War II. Whereas striptease on Depression-era Broadway had been dominated by Gypsy and her rags-to-riches story, in the forties it needed to strike an upbeat if not patriotic pose, flaunt women's bodies to the sound of a good score, and make fun of burlesque.

The shift in the way striptease looked on Broadway also reflected changes in popular music. Major American lyricists wrote songs about striptease to entertain soldiers. In the thirties, most strippers had performed to Tin Pan Alley numbers or to the blues or jazz song-talks of tough female performers. But after the advent of swing in 1935, composers and lyricists began to write striptease numbers for large orchestras. These numbers—smooth, big in sound, and using vocals to swing—reached an enormous audience. Some of them also "tamed" striptease by drawing from "wholesome" forms of music such as polka.

Johnny Mercer's 1942 "Strip Polka" uses polka's slangy 2/4 rhythm to tame striptease and to draw out its comic aspect. This song, meant to appeal to homesick soldiers stationed overseas, begins with the growling trumpet. But it quickly segues into a polka beat. Then the narrator reminisces about "a burlesque theater where the gang loves to go to see Queenie the cutie of the burlesque show."[43]

> And the thrill of the evening
> Is when out Queenie trips,
> And the band plays the polka while she strips. . . .
> "Take it off, take it off!"
> Cries a voice from the rear,
> "Take it off, take it off!" Soon that's all you can hear . . .[44]

As sung by the fresh-faced girl trio the Andrews Sisters in 1942, "Strip Polka" made burlesque seem a little more innocent. The fact that the Andrews Sisters were female singers helped. Even though the censors allowed the song on the radio for only nine or ten weeks, in that short amount of time, "Strip Polka" climbed to number two on *Variety*'s list of bestsellers and earned Capital Records millions of dollars.[45]

ON THE HEELS of LaGuardia's closing the Times Square burlesque theaters, the first Broadway revue of the decade to hire strippers, *Star and Garter*, opened at the Music Box. In June 1942, *Star and Garter* looked clever and fresh. Originally called *The Gypsy Rose Lee Follies* after its inimitable star and backer, *Star and Garter*, produced by Gypsy and Mike Todd and directed by Broadway hit-maker Hassard Short, aimed to please both sailors on leave and the intelligentsia."[46]

The production team was star studded. The dance numbers were choreographed by Albertina Rasch; Johnny Mercer wrote "Blues in the Night" for a big production number. Harold Rome, the bookwriter for such socially relevant works as the 1937 musical *Pins and Needles*, composed some of the music and wrote "Bunny, Bunny, Bunny." That number began as a chorus of showgirls paraded onstage holding furry muffs in front of their naked midriffs and sang:

> Bunny, bunny, bunny
> Pretty little bunny
> Who'll buy my bunny
> So soft and warm?

Program for Mike Todd's *Star and Garter*, c. 1942. Author's personal collection.

Fiorello LaGuardia objected to this lyric, so Rome changed the refrain to "Money, money, money."[47] In a more upscale vein, Gypsy performed some of her classic comedy numbers. As the headliner in the "Star and Garter Girls" number, she wore a sparkly showgirl costume with a cape and carried a wand. In "I Can't Strip to Brahms," a distilled version of the "Stripteaser's Education" number from the 1936 *Follies*, she wore her trademark Victorian outfit. The *New York Times* wrote that she "gives the technique of striptease without the wickedness."[48]

The fact that all of the costumes in *Star and Garter* were designed by Hollywood and Broadway costumer Irene Sharaff and made by the ballet clothier Madame Barbara Karinska lent the production a sophistication for the most part unseen in burlesque. Georgia Sothern first appeared in a white ball gown, which, as Sharaff put it, "made her look like a blowsy Princess Margaret." As "Hold That Tiger" played, pieces of Sothern's costume flew into the wings at perfectly timed moments. Here, Sharaff describes Gypsy's costume for her "Stripteaser's Education" number, which began with the Literary Stripper wearing her usual long skirt, white blouse, and leghorn hat:

> She shed several starched petticoats and finally stood in a small g-string made of flowers crocheted in wool of pastel colors, with an extra flower on the tip of each breast. . . . [S]he had invented a trick of pasting the crocheted flowers on her nipples in such a way that the tightly woven stem of each flower untwirled at a light tap of a finger.[49]

Having cast Gypsy to please the society crowd, Mike Todd included more "burlesque" stripteases in the show to appeal to more burlesque tastes. Georgia Sothern's "Hold That Tiger" number implored the audience to "clap its hands" if it wanted to see more of her. The *New York Times* described her as "unpretentiously hot stuff."[50] Carrie Finnell did her tassel-twirling number—which *Variety*'s Sime called "a mammary St. Vitus dance." Finnell, now a matron of about forty, wore a pink strapless satin pajama costume underneath a garish corset. On Finnell's head sat a veiled hat with a crescent moon and a star peeping off it. A "civilian" publicity photo of the time shows Finnell wearing a short fox fur coat and weighing about two hundred pounds. "Inflation did it," she joked when asked about her girth.[51]

*Star and Garter* also offered a cleaned-up version of the classic burlesque skit between a beautiful, silent undressing woman and a garrulous, inept man. Professor Lamberti, a Buster Keatonish vaudeville and nightclub comic also known as "the Great Lamberti," played the latter. Lamberti's bald pate, his wild eyes, and the unkempt fringe of hair sprouting from the back of his head made him perfect for the role. He strode onstage wearing a shabby, mismatched tux and red underwear. As the curtain rose behind him, he stood behind a xylophone and announced the first musical number he was going to play, "Wishing Will Make It So." As he tapped out the song, a woman appeared upstage and began to take off her clothes. The audience burst into applause and Lamberti, "unaware" that he was not the one to garner the applause, bowed effusively and said, "How'd you like to hear a couple . . . more bars?"

Each sequence got an increasing amount of applause as the woman stripped.

"You folks appreciate the good stuff, don't you?"

"I once played this in Denver."

The laugh centered on Professor Lamberti as the intellectual bumpkin, ignorant that his inept performance might not be garnering the applause that "the body beautiful" could.[52]

Critics liked *Star and Garter*. It pleased both "old school burlesque fans and the aesthetes in equal proportions."[53] Most of all they cottoned to the jokes. George Jean Nathan noted, "Mr. Todd's deference to License Commissioner Moss's ban on the strip-tease, which took the precautionary form of doing away with it altogether save in the single instance of the intellectual Miss Gypsy Rose Lee . . . helped materially to augment the comedy."[54] The show ran for two years and grossed about twenty thousand dollars a week.[55]

*Star and Garter*'s success encouraged other show business teams to try their hand at a striptease musical. Howard Lindsay and Russel Crouse, who a few months earlier had protested LaGuardia's ban on burlesque, opened *Strip for Action* on September 30. Lindsay and Crouse were not, like Todd, self-made entrepreneurs. They were serious satirical writer-directors. Lindsay attended Harvard and Crouse briefly worked as a journalist. In the thirties, the team assisted Cole Porter with the book and staging of *Anything Goes* and *Red, Hot, and Blue*. They also wrote the long-running hit *Life with Father*. Now they decided that they would create a musical in which striptease uplifted soldiers' morales.

When *Strip for Action*, the lighthearted account of how a burlesque troupe's antics transforms an army base, opened, a headline in the *World Telegram* said, "Mme Burlesque Is Back in Town." In the *New York Post*, Wilella Waldorf wrote about the show, "It probably would have seemed funnier and much more of a novelty if Broadway had not been pretty liberally dosed with burlesque lately."[56]

Though they were intrigued by burlesque's authentic American energy, Lindsay and Crouse wanted to appeal to a middle-class audience. So instead of using a Gypsy Rose Lee or a Georgia Sothern, the team chose an ingénue named Jean Carter to play "Florida," the headlining stripper. (They did, however, borrow Billy Koud, the longtime Mutual circuit dance director, to choreograph the dance numbers and appear as an actor in the show.)

Even more than *Star and Garter*, *Strip for Action* relied on annihilating laughs—on cruelly making fun of burlesque striptease. In one number, a stripper is unable to coordinate her bumps to the drummer's rhythm. In another, strippers entered wearing mess tins on their breasts, the idea being that they were tenacious or desperate enough to build costumes in the unlikeliest circumstances. The critics liked much of that business, but overall *Strip for Action*, which ran for a mere seventy-four performances, was a flop.

TWO DAYS BEFORE *Strip for Action* opened, though, a more daring striptease extravaganza premiered at the Shubert Ambassador, on Forty-ninth Street just west of Broadway. *Wine, Women, and Song* shared a title with Johann Strauss's turn-of-the-century Viennese waltz—a fact LaGuardia would later try to marshal as evidence of the producers' duplicity. But this brainchild of Isidore Herk combined a patriotic revue with raunchy striptease. It was, after all, produced by the man whose distinctions included the announcement, in 1917, that "burlesque is nothing more or less than a mercantile business."[57]

By 1942, though, Herk was no longer the brash man who had made that brash statement. Nor was he the man who in the 1930s helped Fiorello LaGuardia create a burlesque code and a union—the Burlesque Artists Association. At age fifty-nine, suffering from heart trouble, Herk needed a hit. He had been out of a job since the Gaiety Theater closed in the spring.

Like the other Broadway revues and musicals incorporating striptease, *Wine, Women, and Song* loudly asserted its cleaned-up mainstream credentials. Herk advertised it as a "revue-vaudeville-burlesque show," and Lee Shubert and Max Liebman of *Straw Hat Revue* fame agreed to help bankroll it. But Herk also stressed *Wine, Women, and Song*'s burlesque connection by casting Noel Toy, the "Chinese Sally Rand," and Margie Hart, "Garbo of the Lowbrows," in leading roles. *Wine, Women, and Song* also starred the burlesque comics Pinky Lee and Jimmy Savo.

But the revue scandalized audiences with striptease. Of what *Variety* called its many outlandish "take-off" numbers, the ones performed by Hart and Toy stood out. Hart's number "Priorities" especially attracted attention. Brooks Atkinson described Hart as "impersonating wickedness." As John Mason Brown, then the drama critic for the *New York World* and the *Saturday Review*, wittily put it, "Miss Hart has a larger following than a wardrobe."[58] Although Hart began her strip in standard burlesque manner, she added her own topical flair. She entered in a blue evening gown, hat, and muff and strutted up and down the stage while the orchestra began to play "Take It Off." From a box in the audience, three male actors— one dressed as a soldier, one as a sailor, and one as a marine—sang, "Take it off for the army, the navy, the U.S. Marines."

Onstage, Hart coyly refused, and the men implored Hart to take it off for the chairman of the War Production Board, who at that moment was desperate for scrap metal: "Take it off for Donald Nelson. He's anxious to get materials."

Hart took off her muff and tossed it offstage. Then she remarked that the government needed felt and removed her hat. Then the men in the box asked her to disrobe for Harold Ickes, the secretary of the interior, who had just asked Americans to ration gas.

"Take it off for Mr. Ickes, he needs gas." As Hart walked upstage, they added, "Isn't that a pretty little . . . lass?"

The music sped up. Hart suggested the government needed metal and removed her dress, and then offered to take off her petticoat, which she did. Then she said that rubber was needed and took off her girdle, leaving only a bra and underwear. But the line that got her in trouble was the one where she said a girl should take off her bra and "bust" Hitler in the eye; as she did the former, she revealed two blue flower pasties covering her nipples. She took them off and bumped. That left only her panties and the men in the box sang, "Take it off for the defense."

"If I do that, I'll have no defense," quipped Hart. But a minute later, she began to take them off anyway. Someone in the audience screamed, "No!"

Still, the men in the box insisted, and Hart swayed alone onstage in her G-string for a moment. She pulled the stage curtain over her body and then disappeared.

*Wine, Women, and Song*'s other flesh-baring number, Noel Toy's fan dance, seems childish by comparison. Wearing lacquered pigtails with plastic cherry blossoms struck in them, Toy entered wearing a kimono. Two women carrying her fans attended her, waving the fans around body. Behind the fans, though, Toy was naked save for a small moleskin patch over her genitals.

During its first month, *Wine, Women, and Song* attracted audiences but little critical acclaim. *PM Magazine* characterized the show as "a horrible mistake." George Jean Nathan noted that, by focusing on the undressing female form, *Wine, Women, and Song* bored. "[It] is ultimately doomed to go the way of all flesh," he wrote. "Emphasis on strippers and nude women in burlesque revivals at fancy prices cannot . . . be conducive to prosperity in the long run," he continued. Brooks Atkinson agreed. "It is a routine burlesque show with Margie Hart performing a little farther uptown than usual."[59]

But on October 31, Halloween evening, it became clear that the critics had underestimated the show's sensational effect. That evening, License Commissioner Paul Moss sat in row M of the Shubert Ambassador. Apparently Moss was so appalled that he phoned the police immediately, and two days later Herk received a summons accusing him of violating Section 1140a of the penal code by producing an obscene spectacle. Immediately ticket sales soared, assisted in part by Margie Hart's nightly pre-curtain speech describing the "wonders" the audience would no longer see.[60]

From the beginning, the *Wine, Women, and Song* trial differed from those that closed down striptease in 1932 and 1937. For one, emboldened by anti-LaGuardia sentiment and the more liberal feeling of the times, Herk attempted to get the trial moved from a special closed session to a general one, where an audience could witness the proceedings. (He never succeeded.) LaGuardia, whom Bob Hope had dubbed "Mr. Five by Five in a Zoot Hat," used the uproar about *Wine, Women, and Song* to pursue several other "indecent" shows—including *Star and Garter* and *Strip for Action.*

A group of religious leaders including Cardinal Spellman denounced the return of striptease to Broadway. The trial was marked by suspicion on both sides. During jury selection, one of the potential jurors, the sociologist Robert Lynd, suggested that the trial was political and that LaGuardia was singling out *Wine, Women, and Song* to make an example of it. Judge Owen W. Bohan chastised him and said the jury's job was not to make a political judgment but to decide whether Margie Hart had given an indecent performance. Ultimately Lynd was excused from jury duty.

Once the trial started, Judge Bohan allowed Margie Hart and Noel Toy to describe their acts, but not to perform them. When the defense suggested that the jury see the show, the prosecuting attorney ridiculed that offer. "The show you'll see might be entirely different," he yelled, referring to the fact that in the thirties, the stripteases performed in court hearings were tamer than those performed onstage.

Thus, for the first couple of days, the jury did not see the striptease they were being asked to judge. Instead, inside the courtroom, Toy and Hart described what they had worn onstage, and witnesses for the prosecution countered their descriptions with more sensational ones. But after a couple of days, the women would be called to the witness stand. When the prosecution called upon Toy to demonstrate what a fan dance was, she first raised one fan, and then the other, and began to take off what the *New York Times* described as her "flimsy Oriental" dress. "I don't have enough room," she complained, which incited Judge Bohan to bark, "Stay where you are!"

Hart was more circumspect. She displayed as evidence her G-string and the safety pins she used to pin miniscule flowers over her breasts. When asked if they took off their bras, the strippers freely admitted that they "flashed," or revealed their breasts.[61] And yet shortly after the trial began, detectives acting as witnesses for the defense testified that Hart actually wore a body stocking during the performance. In other words, she only appeared to be naked.

In his closing statement, Arthur Markewich, Herk's lawyer, attempted the class argument used in the thirties. He tried to argue that by contemporary standards, *Wine, Women, and Song* was not obscene. Naked and undressing women were ubiquitous in New York in 1942. Wealthy New Yorkers had the opportunity to view undressing woman at every turn and so should the working-class man. "Look at Lily Pons in *Daughter of the*

*Regiment!* She disrobes every night on the Metropolitan Opera stage and there is little comment by the newspapers. Or consider Hedy Lamarr and her picture in the *White Cargo* ads or Dorothy Lamour in her sarong. Or *Life Magazine,*" he noted.[62]

But Markewich's argument about shifting standards and operatic disrobing failed to convince either Judge Bohan or the jury, which, after deliberating for only forty-five minutes, found *Wine, Women, and Song* to be "obscene, indecent, immoral and impure." On December 17, comparing the fifty-nine-year old Herk to a pimp, Judge Bohan sentenced him to six months in jail. Hearing the sentence, Herk burst into tears. Trembling and distraught, he collapsed. A guard ushered him out of the courtroom. "I hope that striptease earns the contempt of those who are still interested in upholding the morality of the stage," Bohan said, apparently unmoved by Herk's plight.[63]

Markewich issued a statement bemoaning the fact that the Shuberts had gotten off free. "The people who really gained are not before the court. They made themselves extremely scarce after prosecution began," he wrote. In an editorial, *Billboard* defended Herk. "The show was hardly obscene. It was just plain dull."[64]

*Billboard*'s defense, though, failed to save the show. At the Ambassador, the verdict was announced during a matinee. Word spread quickly backstage, and, to show support for Herk, the orchestra struck up "Auld Lang Syne" while the company lined up for its final bows. Upon hearing of the verdict, LaGuardia noted that Herk would have to "use some soap, sapolin, or disinfectant, if he wants to stay in business." No one believed Herk would do time, but the Shuberts let him take the fall, and he served several months of his sentence. He died in 1944, a few months after his release from Riker's Island.[65]

THE CRUSHING OF *Wine, Women, and Song* made it obvious that LaGuardia would never tolerate striptease in New York, even if it was performed in a legitimate Broadway theater. Although Broadway shows after 1942 continued to use striptease for what *Variety*'s Joe Laurie called "escapology," few performances resembled the gritty stripteases of 1930s burlesque. The *Priorities of 1943* updated the hokey striptease auction number for a patriotic, wartime era. Chicago-born Sally Keith, playing a stripper clad in a dress made of war savings stamps, auctioned them off until, dressed in "only a smile," she was told to wear panties in "the interest of national dignity."[66]

The same year, Chicago produced *Good Night, Ladies*, an update of the Jazz Age comedy *Ladies' Night at the Turkish Bath*. Written by Cyrus Wood, *Good Night, Ladies* tells the story of a misogynist professor and his playboy friend hiding in a Turkish bath only to be transformed by women undressing. As its *deus ex machina* in the second act, *Good Night, Ladies* featured a

Gypsy Rose Lee–like striptease. Despite terrible reviews, the play ran for over a hundred weeks at the Blackstone Theater, although when it was transferred to Broadway, even out-of-town success could not save it from flopping. In fact, in this era, each attempt to put striptease on Broadway seemed more doomed than the last.

In New York, George S. Kaufman adapted Gypsy Rose Lee's autobiographical play *The Naked Genius* for Broadway. Todd originally called the play *The Seven Year Cycle*, then *The Ghost in the Woodpile*, and finally settled on *The Naked Genius* because he thought the word "naked" would sell. He was wrong. Even with a small role for Georgia Sothern and with Joan Blondell starring as "Gypsy," the story of "Honey Bee Carroll," a stripper who writes a book in order to improve her image, struck audiences as hokey. After weeks of daily revisions, Gypsy asked that her credit be changed to "Written by Louise Hovick." The show got abysmal reviews. The *New York Times* begged Todd to "take it off."

Still, when *The Naked Genius* closed after three weeks, some observers were surprised. "No one expected her to write a first class drama. But no one expected her to miss the bus by a block."[67] Moreover, the flopping of *The Naked Genius* could not quash the striptease tsunami on Broadway. The next week in the *Artists and Models* of 1943, two sisters stripped. In another number, women impersonated "Gypsy Rose Corio" and "Margie Smart." As the war continued in Europe, one musical after another featured stripteases. "This is an act that needs little explaining," wrote a bemused San Francisco critic.[68]

In 1944, *On the Town* romanticized the cootch dancer and turned her into an elusive, yet comic American icon. Betty Comden and Adolph Green invented a fantasy version of this figure for their dream ballet sequence in that musical. "Miss Turnstiles"—aka Ivy—a woman chosen to decorate the subway platform, catches the eye of Gabe, a young, idealistic sailor on twenty-four-hour leave. Her poster advertises her as studying classical ballet and painting, but in real life, she works as a taxi dance hall girl—a woman men could rent for a dance—at Coney Island. Gabe pursues Ivy for twenty-four hours, and when he finally catches up with her, she is doing a bump and grind. He sails from New York having lost his innocence about women.[69] Two numbers in the musical, "The Imaginary Coney Island" and "The Real Coney Island," make Gabe's journey—and its ending—clear.

Meanwhile, the success of many strippers who started their careers at the World's Fair suggested that in some places at least, propriety had relaxed since the war began. Lois de Fee dined with soldiers as part of her cross-country tour. Back in 1941, Gypsy had performed her Literary Striptease in *Stage Door Canteen*, when it opened in the basement of the Forty-fourth Street Theater. RKO released a movie version three years later.[70]

Outside of New York, the war continued to buoy burlesque theaters' business. "Burlesque is dead," *Collier's* announced in 1943. But people lined up around the block in Toronto to see Hinda Wassau, and in Chicago burlesque nightclubs were hiring between six and nine strippers per show.[71] On State Street, the Rialto Theater closed in the summer of 1944, inspiring Abbott and Costello, who performed there, to quip, "The g-strings are finally strung up on the violins."[72] *Life* covered the theater's transformation into a vaudeville house as if it were an event of national consequence: "Burlesque in Chicago sang its raucous swan song."[73]

*Life* blamed the Rialto's closing on the profusion of nightclubs and cabarets where "men could sip beer while watching girls strip almost to the nude." But the Rialto's management attributed the theater's closing to the war, which diminished the number of younger burlesque-going patrons in Chicagoland. After D-Day, the Rialto reopened, and *Billboard* noted, "The end of the war spells the return of the under-38 males whose absence put a dent in burlesque."[74]

Minsky's Rialto Theater on South State Street in Chicago, c. 1953. Chicago Historical Society.

# The Private Lives of Strippers

Increasingly, when describing the private lives of strippers, journalists depicted them as living a shadow version of the myth of Broadway success. This myth contained warnings about the way the rags-to-riches story failed to apply in the world of burlesque striptease. Unlike Broadway, if striptease sometimes made a more comfortable life possible, the strippers hardly ever leapt from it unscarred. In the popular imagination, a woman impelled toward the questionable life of a stripper forewent the usual Broadway or Hollywood happy ending.[1]

There was some truth to this, of course. Describing how they got into the business, strippers themselves summoned up an element of the Broadway rags-to-riches story; like their sisters in Hollywood and on Broadway, strippers cast themselves as starlets poised to dance up the staircase of success in silver tap shoes. And yet strippers were not starlets and often justified their choice by talking about money. Sherry Britton, a Minsky stripper, recounted how she had never thought about stripping until she "failed" as a dancer.[2] In other words, no amount of money could diminish the idea in the popular imagination that burlesque striptease represented a woman's "last chance" before prostitution. As *Fortune* observed in 1935, "The insistent question most men ask is: are the girls moral?"[3]

Gypsy Rose Lee answered this question the way all burlesque theater operators did in court: "Some virgins, no professionals."

But in burlesque striptease's American heyday, when asked what she did, a "peeler" might answer "dancer," thus heading off any suggestion that she was being taken advantage of or that she was part of an industry that was tantamount to prostitution. Or she might avoid the question altogether, focusing instead on the unexpected aspects of domesticity she found backstage. When Kitty Oakes, a stripper who doubled as the cross-dressing jazz trumpeter Billy Tipton's lover, talked about her occupation, she stressed its backstage camaraderie: "There was a magic about our lives. . . . I sang, 'would you like to lay upon my pillow . . . would you care to, would you dare to, would you keep a secret.' I always kept my clothes on. I was never ashamed of what I did."[4]

Unlike the *Ziegfeld Follies*, which journalists described as an avenue for working-class women to meet and marry wealthy men, burlesque, even after it became a destination for urban sybarites, only occasionally provided a way for strippers to do the same. In 1935 one sugar daddy, the

Baron d'Empain, the Belgian financier, spied the stripper Rose Zelle Rowland at the Dorchester Club in London, married her, and, by marrying her, made sure she would never again perform for three dollars a day in splotchy gold body paint. Rose Zelle moved to England to marry him. "The Baron controls the subways of Paris and owns the electric train system of Egypt," tabloids reported.[5] According to Rose Zelle's sister, Betty, the marriage came with a prenuptial agreement: if Rose Zelle had a girl, the baron would abandon her. If she had a boy, Rose Zelle would stay baroness. She had a boy.

But in general, striptease sugar daddies were more likely to be low-level bootleggers and racketeers, bellhops, small merchants, policemen, firemen, federal agents, men looking for adventure, taxi drivers, writers, aspiring artists, sailors, and bookies than titled aristocrats. If they were not all, as Sherry Britton complained, "leeches and pimps and jerks: degenerates," they were certainly not all well-off.[6]

So why would a woman become a stripper, if not to marry well? To make a living? To hypnotize men? To get back at them for some childhood trauma? Because she was a secret exhibitionist? Because she was a lesbian? All hypotheses emerged in the late thirties and early forties as journalists struggled to document the exploding world of commercialized sex. And yet these reasons also seemed insufficient to explain a woman's choice to take off her clothes for money.

Trying to understand why a young girl might fall into this world, Depression-era reformers fumbled, just as Gilded Age reformers had failed to see how grim the alternatives were for immigrant women in the 1890s. These reformers could not understand that besides prostitution, striptease was one of the only ways out of the grueling demands of housework and the toil of the sweatshop—monotonies that reformers, being mostly men, generally only theoretically understood. Time and time again, asked what made them turn to taking off their clothes in public, strippers answered that it was easier than crouching behind a cosmetics counter, wielding a broom, or sweating over a conveyor belt.[7] "I ain't in it for glory, I want to eat," said Carrie Finnell, the "Girl with the Million Dollar Legs."[8] "I didn't want to stand behind the counter and serve people," explained Rose La Rose, who before her death in 1957 owned several burlesque theaters in Toledo, Ohio.[9]

Even without a man, a savvy peeler could achieve a certain degree of independence and upward mobility; and if she faltered, by, for example, succumbing to alcohol or drugs, it was better to do so cushioned by necessary luxuries—furs, evening gowns, and diamonds. On the other hand, the game was not so easy. Burlesque theater operators and nightclub owners were a tough, suspicious lot, easily corruptible, linked to organized crime.[10] Moreover, the world of striptease was an insular one, and once a woman was in it, it was difficult to see a way out. Some women, surely, were co-erced into taking off their clothes on the striptease version of the "casting couch." And still, if a young woman of little education arrived in the city alone in, say, 1937, this line of work might not be such a bad choice. Al-though it might alienate her from her family, it simultaneously presented her with possibilities of a new life.

Which raises a question. Putting aside the cliché of that discovery or the insistent dreams of Hollywood stardom, how did the decision to be-come a stripper happen? What were those final moments like? And who were these women, in the end?

Unlike in many other areas of show business, the majority of adver-tisements for strippers stated that "no experience" was required. Accord-ing to most sources, the majority of strippers came from rural America. A few could boast ballet training, a few more came from other realms of dance. Ann Corio began at Minskys' in the 1920s. The theater operator Kitty Madison saw her in a "pick-out" line, a line where managers came to "pick out" strippers, in 1926. Madison hired Corio and made her a star until the Mutual circuit bosses, seeing how much she was earning, wanted to give her her own show.[11]

Most strippers, though, began in the burlesque chorus and thought stripping could increase their salaries. The majority of them of lacked edu-cation. In the thirties, tabloid journalists sometimes attempted to convince readers that women who stripped poured into the profession from the middle class and the American aristocracy. But as H. M. Alexander pointed out in 1936, the educated stripper was the exception, not the rule.[12]

It was not hard to convince such women to do what in respectable circles might be considered "immoral," especially if they were hungry and "damaged," fleeing an alcoholic or abusive parent, which was sometimes the case. This woman might like to take off her clothes or she might just acquire the taste for it. Or the ingénue could also be persuaded to undress in public by an older sibling who herself left home, as was the case with Tempest and Jewel Storm. She might be talked into it by a lover or a male acquaintance already established in show biz.

In the thirties and forties, tabloids continued to report that women were being tricked into striptease as if it were white slavery. Perhaps this represented a longing for an age when women were more innocent. For six months in the late thirties, Charmaine "practiced" stripping in the Cadillac Theater in Detroit. Only later, according to the National Police Gazette, did she learn that her practicing took place in front of an audience. She de-manded a salary. It is not known whether she got it.[13] Strippers themselves claimed a certain innocence in public. Sherry Britton fainted when she first revealed her breasts at the People's Theater at 165 Bowery, where admission cost ten cents.

Sherry Britton publicity photo, c. 1942. Author's personal collection.

A stripper might be influenced by her own stage-struck mother, as the so-called Literary Stripper Gypsy Rose Lee was in 1929 in Kansas City. "A lot of big stars worked in burlesque. There is not a reason in the world we can't—until vaudeville comes back," Rose Hovick implored her daughter, trying to get her to go onstage. And later Rose stressed that what Gypsy was doing wasn't really stripping. "Of course you won't really strip, but there's no reason why you can't walk around the stage in time to music and drop a shoulder strap at the end."[14]

Or the ingenue would be signed by a fast-talking agent who would ask her, in his office, if she were willing to "pose," by which he meant "pose naked." If she was already a chorus girl in burlesque, she might lunge toward the idea, since taking off her clothes in public was a quick way to at least double her salary. But not always. The amount of money strippers made varied wildly, but it was always more than any other burlesque performer. In 1932 chorines earned $20 a week whereas strippers earned twice that.[15] Headliners made as much a $5,000, although in the early thirties, the average headliner made $125. These inequities guaranteed that how much a stripper made would continue to be a source of tension. In 1940 a group of Seattle strippers filed the first class action suit (for strippers) against management, arguing that they earned about $14 a week and worked twelve-hour days.[16]

Still, the fact was that few working-class girls could afford to turn down an offer to become a stripper. Or to put it another way, as the tough-talking dame impresario Tex Guinan once memorably did, "Virtue only pays if you have a market for it." In the Depression, a girl's lodging at the drab-best, tiniest Broadway show biz hotel would cost five dollars a week, and she would incur other expenses, such as for costumes, which would likely run up to much more than she could afford. And while reformers complained about the low tone of morality among these girls, they rarely considered that a legitimate job seldom paid more than enough to buy lodging in a flophouse. Of all the crusading reformers, only the nineteenth-century Jane Addams worried as much about what would become of these girls as about the "cheap theater" they liked to watch at night.[17]

Nevertheless, a young woman who arrived in New York City after the Great War and found herself without money might do worse than to start in the burlesque chorus at Minskys' National Winter Garden Theater, at the Irving Place, or at the People's Theater.

Ads in *Billboard* and *Variety* promised work for attractive young women. For striptease was a girl's game. Child-labor laws notwithstanding, peeling demanded youth's energy, the newcomer's face. By the thirties, audiences influenced by the great cry for young presences on the stage and screen demanded it, and young, poor girls everywhere obliged. Née Hazel Anderson, Georgia Sothern arrived in Philadelphia at age thirteen in 1929, having named herself after the state and the region, which she misspelled.[18]

Margie Hart came from St. Louis with a friend when she was fourteen; Ann Corio escaped her claustrophobic Italian family in Hartford when she was fifteen; at fifteen Sherry Britton fled the blows of an abusive father and arrived in burlesque after a pit stop in the world of Aunt Bobbi and Uncle Bumpsy—vaudeville performers. Gypsy Rose Lee was, by comparison, an old lady, getting into the business at about sixteen, although she had performed in vaudeville for many years before that.[19]

At first the age of some of these performers is shocking and makes it clear why reformers were so certain that white slavery was afoot. In 1934, *Variety* reported that a pair of thirteen-year-old strip dancers endangered the liquor license of a Philadelphia saloon.[20] Certainly the peeler's youth made her vulnerable, the way Sister Carrie's made her so. It was as true between the wars as it had been in the nineteenth century that youth attracted all manner of adventures in New York. Unless she had a male escort, a young girl alone, and particularly a girl who worked at the National Winter Garden, might be tricked into stripping.

Anyway, if she was working in striptease, the popular imagination would assume her to be a whore, and Stage Door Johnnies might follow her, say, around the corner to Haimowitz's, a performers' haven and speakeasy on Forsythe Street, where the girls ate cheap suppers of steak and herring between shows. It would be almost impossible for her to get work in any of the big revues on Broadway unless she changed her name and lied about her time in burlesque, as Gypsy Rose Lee did in 1932 when she performed in *Hot-Cha*. And it was not so easy to perform night after night in run-down theaters where hecklers regularly threw stench bombs, tomatoes, and pennies. Or where an overstimulated mob might rush the stage. Or where men masturbated behind newspapers. Or drunk customers tripped the performers.[21]

What, then, to do? If the stripper was lucky, she could stretch out her career until she arrived at the ripe old age of thirty or so, at which time she would be demoted to the back row of the chorus. After that she might become a wardrobe mistress or seamstress; she might marry a straight man or a comedian or even the manager. As Sol Goodman, the operator of Baltimore's Gayety Theater, said, "They used up their youth. . . . [S]ome of them went home. Some got married. And some just seemed to fade away."[22]

It could be worse than that. During and after Prohibition, strippers were vulnerable to the underworld. In 1936, Ann Corio's life was threatened by the doorman at a burlesque theater who tried to extort money from her. Gypsy Rose Lee's diamonds were stolen. Sally Rand allowed some Chicago mobsters to lay claim to a big percentage of her earnings, a fact that drove her into bankruptcy. The mob probably determined the fate of Kiki Roberts, a former *Ziegfeld Follies* girl and Legs Diamond's moll. In October 1930 the promise of seeing the titian-haired showgirl lured

Legs out of his hideout. She was next door at the Hotel Monticello in Room 831 when Dutch Schultz tried to kill Legs. And she was also there a year later in a rooming house in Albany when Legs was actually shot.[23]

Kiki knew too much about Legs's death. After headlining at the Irving Place, the Star, and the Gayety, Kiki tried to escape into small nightclubs in Atlantic City. Then, after she embarked on a short, disastrous marriage to a football player and another to an insurance salesman, she tried fan dancing in the *Pepper Pot Revue*. Burlesque could not save her. In 1941, eleven years after Legs's demise, she vanished.[24]

EVEN IF THE STRIPPER stayed clear of gangsters, hers was a precarious livelihood. If she was careless or proud, if she did not plan, she would have other problems as time advanced. For one, she would find herself less and less in demand and have to work in grimy, mob-run nightclubs and two-bit carnivals. As she aged, she would find less and less employment, and eventually she might go broke and then starve. Or she might be crushed by drugs or her audience's disdain or plain old violence. Georgia Sothern's boyfriends beat her. Blaze Starr got into a knife fight with a jewel thief who scarred her face.[25]

At age forty-five, twenty-some years after newspapers voted fan dancer Faith Bacon "the most beautiful girl on Broadway," she jumped out the window of a stairwell in her Chicago hotel, a victim of heroin and misery. "She wanted to get back into the spotlight. She would have taken any work in show biz," said her roommate, a grocery store cashier, who revealed that Bacon was only in Chicago to begin with because her family lent her money to get there.[26]

Bacon's life had been difficult for years. After she danced at the Century of Progress with Sally Rand and in New York at *Earl Carroll's Vanities*, her career declined. In the winter of 1936 in Chicago, while posing nude in *Temptations*, she fell through a glass drum on which she was dancing. She sued the Lake Theater Corporation for $100,000 since the scars on her thighs made it difficult for her to find work.[27] But she spent her settlement of $5,000 on a ten-carat diamond. In 1948 she sued a carnival promoter for putting tacks on the stage where she danced barefoot. She lost. Eight years later, the only possessions found in Bacon's room were "miscellaneous clothing, one white metal ring, [and] one train ticket to Erie, Pa., for eighty-five cents."[28]

Nor was Bacon the only stripper to end tragically. A number of strippers, having moved to Hollywood to get into film, died alone in efficiency apartments or SROs. Buddy Wade's tap shoes caught fire, the sparks ignited her costume, and she burned to death one night at the Old Howard in Boston. Walter Winchell wrote a column about her commemorating her courage for not getting near the other performers. Dixie Evans, the "Marilyn Monroe of Striptease," caromed into poverty after Monroe died in 1962, when no one would hire a stripper whose act made fun of the American Blonde Venus.

In 1954 the "Darling of Burlesque," Loretta Miller, watched one of her fans shoot himself at the LA Follies Theater. A night earlier he wrote her a mash note, saying, "Angel Face, all I can do is worship you." She was fired the next day.[29]

According to some sources, Lilly Christine died of peritonitis. In the late fifties and early sixties, when strippers needed to be giant-sized, many underwent "water" breast implants, which both disfigured them and caused them physical pain. The stripper Mickey Dare killed herself. She was pregnant and a heroin addict and hated stripping. She left a note that read, "Please do not condemn me as I already have been."[30]

But not all strippers lived unhappily ever after. Some of these resilient performers evinced a will to survive that protected them from life's centrifugal force. It was what allowed them to go on with the show. And there is as much evidence that a "torso tosser," in *Variety*'s phrase, might prosper as the other way around. She might become a talking woman comic or make the jump to burlesque movies.

She might be able to pursue a career on Broadway or in summer stock, turning herself into a semi-serious actress, something that Ann Corio and Gypsy also tried, with financial success, if not critical acclaim. These were sort of success stories. Familiar by the fifties was the fate of Sherry Britton, who played the "green-clad woman" in an American National Theater and Academy production of *Peer Gynt*. Or Lili St. Cyr, who performed as herself in Howard Hughes's 3-D porn movie *Son of Sinbad* and Roger Corman's bullet-riddled thriller *I, Mobster*. Or Lois de Fee, who stripped in a carnival.[31]

A STRIPPER MIGHT be lucky enough to get married and settle down in the suburbs, thus removing herself from the struggle of trying to figure out how to live. Or if she were business-minded, she might parlay her talents into management. In 1953, after two Boston policemen got Rose La Rose "banned from Boston" by ingeniously smuggling an infrared camera into the Old Howard, where she was stripping, she left town. Judge Elijah Adlow shut down the theater, which sat empty for nine years.[32] But La Rose bought the Gaiety Theater in Toledo, Ohio, and made a fortune teaching amateurs "how to take it off in front of their husbands." In 1960 she became a pornographer.

Hinda Wassau made around $600 a week in the 1920s, and her salary dropped to around $400 in the 1930s. Margie Hart commanded $400 a week in the early 1940s; Rose La Rose got around $2,500. In 1940, Ann

Corio regularly made $1,000 a week and thus had enough clout to command a contract that included 25 percent of the house take. By comparison, an editor at *Vanity Fair* made $35 a week at the start of the Depression.[33] After the war, strippers' fees skyrocketed, especially those who could work in Las Vegas. Blaze Starr earned $60,000 one year. Tempest Storm could get as much as $10,000 a night. For four years running, she made about a quarter of a million every single year. Lili St. Cyr climbed to a similar tax bracket. But problems with money were common despite success stories. A few years after making $1,000 a week at the World's Fair—at the heart of the Depression—Sally Rand declared bankruptcy.[34]

And although the average stripper made more than what a Broadway showgirl would get paid, it was still much less than Rand, about $125 in her prime in the thirties. Maybe this explains why Carrie Finnell continued to do her tassel-twirling act in Vegas and at other nightclubs until she was a senior citizen. "If you want a real belly laugh drop in at the Galaxie Club and see Carrie Finnell," read an ad in the *Cincinnati Post* a few weeks before she died, at age seventy.[35] But besides Carrie, Tempest, and Lili, the prime of a stripper was limited—for most, no longer than six years. And so she had to think fast, on her feet, all the time.

FOR A FORM of entertainment with such impact, striptease involved a relatively small number of people. In 1929 there were a handful of strippers who performed at around 80 burlesque theaters across the country.[36] By contrast, at its height, vaudeville boasted 1,000 theaters nationwide. Movies had an even larger share of the entertainment pie: in 1930 there were 800 movie theaters in New York alone. In the late twenties, the audience for the movies was between 20 and 30 million.[37]

The anti-burlesque movement of the thirties appeared to encourage growth. In 1935, according to *Fortune*, after the first wave of censorship, the number of strippers grew to 3,300 nationwide, and the number of audience members reached 50,000 a night. In the postwar era, the number of strippers would only dip to 2,500 or so, even though New York venues had supposedly all but disappeared circa 1942. How did this happen?[38]

The burgeoning field of agentry and public relations in the thirties contributed to striptease's tenacity. Agents competed with each other to get into Walter Winchell's column. In the South, the West, and the hinterlands, the demand for striptease swelled as quickly as the North censored it. Indeed, in the early 1930s, the decline of the mutual circuits and the rise of stock burlesque, which needed a supply of independent strippers, first gave rise to the striptease agent, a character even more Runyonesque than the rest of the "pressmen."[39]

The biggest striptease agent of the Midwest, Milt Schuster, a former song-and-dance man, came to agenting in the late twenties. Outside the window of Schuster's second-story office in Chicago's West Loop hung a sign with a corny slogan typical of burlesque: "Be a Booster for Milt Schuster." Schuster's brazenness and popularity spoke to striptease's continued drawing power in the Corn Belt during and after the Depression. His letterhead announced: "If you want people, or if you people want work, phone Milt." From the 1930s to the 1950s, Schuster brought big stars east and toured lesser ones on the Midwestern circuits.[40]

The other principal movers and shakers in the industry, Nat Morton in Philadelphia, who exported Margie Hart from the Midwest, and "Daddy" Pickins in Kansas City and Chicago, trained strippers for the Minskys. In New York, Eddie Jaffe, an orphan, started in burlesque. He briefly worked as a newspaper columnist. In 1933 he became an agent and printed up his own letterhead, which read, "exclusive to Walter Winchell." He found his first client in Margie Hart; he dubbed her "the poor man's Garbo" and came up with the idea that she should write a column, "My Night." The phrase "the poor man's Garbo" appeared in Walter Winchell's column, Hart's earnings tripled, and Jaffe went on to represent others, including Rosita Royce and Zorita, as well as movie stars such as Marlene Dietrich. Some of Jaffe's stories veered into outrage, like the one in which he linked Zorita romantically to her snake and then hired a psychiatrist to get some good copy about what was wrong with her. But Jaffe overlooked one possibility: that the psychiatrist would name the press agent himself as the problem.[41]

GIVEN SUCH TECHNIQUES, it is no surprise that many strippers traded agents as they advanced in the business. After Hinda Wassau dumped one agent for a second, the first tried to sue her, as did Gypsy's first agent, Irving Sherman. Harry Finkelstein, a saloonkeeper and Orthodox Jew, was agent and lover to both Sally Rand and Georgia Sothern. In other cases, friends or confidants played at least some of an agent's roles: George Davis, the gay *Vanity Fair* writer, influenced all areas of Gypsy's life during the forties. In the fifties Gypsy "kept" a handful of agents at once the way that men kept mistresses. "You know you cannot have two or three agents working on a deal," one of them chided her when he discovered that he was just one of the harem.[42]

In fact, Gypsy's agents rarely displayed the savvy or the passion for marketing that she herself did. One of them felt that the day of the stripper was over, although, he conceded, Gypsy could still wring some sales out of her reputation. "Smart women will buy a Gypsy Rose Lee identified dress at Bergdorf Goodman," he observed in a letter.[43]

For most of her life, "the most publicized woman in the world" acted as her own best agent. She was always working on how to sell herself. In the late fifties, she invented "slapstick lipstick" and "peel-off" paper, which she hoped to market. A frequent guest on the Jack Paar television show in the 1950s, she piloted her own talk program in the late sixties.

Agents could hardly save strippers from making less-than-ideal romantic choices—or the tabloids from reporting on these choices as comic or tragic tales. Ann Corio married Mike Iannuci, a former quarterback for the Pittsburgh Steelers, and he became her agent. In one well-publicized incident, after Iannuci engineered a starring role for his wife in a stock production of *Will Success Spoil Rock Hunter*, in Bristol, Pennsylvania, he decided not to pay the cast's hotel bill. A litigious local physician sued.[44]

In 1932, Georgia Sothern's first husband beat her up and then staged a suicide, a fact that, according to her memoir, the Minskys rushed to publicize. "Mate Fakes Suicide Attempt for Love of Stripper," one headline read. Sothern wore a rhinestone eye patch while she stripped that evening and the audience went wild. In the early years of the Depression, the violence in her personal life helped her working-class audience see her as one of them.[45]

In general, striptease and domesticity mixed poorly. Much married, Gypsy Rose Lee, Sally Rand, and Lili St. Cyr ended up alone. Rand stole Thurkel Greenough, a rodeo performer, from his first wife, only to discover that he was prone to paranoia and rage. "The marriage to the cowboy was not successful," she told her mother.[46] St. Cyr complained to *Confidential* magazine that she always wound up marrying men who needed financial support. They all became Mr. Lili St. Cyr. Rose La Rose divorced her third husband when he tried to get her to stay home and eat pasta. "When I was home from tour, he'd try to fatten me up with spaghetti, ravioli, lasagne, and pastafazool. Can you imagine how the customers would have reacted if I showed up fat?"[47] One of Blaze Starr's husbands owned a strip club across the street from the Two O'Clock Club. Their divorce in 1962 after eight years of marriage may have had something to do with the fact that the stripper was succeeding in business.[48]

There was more to these stories than what newspapers printed. And yet such previously private details became more readily available after the war, when journalistic conventions about what to reveal about strippers' lives loosened alongside the expansion of reporting on mainstream America in general. Part of this reflects wider changes in cultural attitudes toward sexuality. World War II brought men and women "unprecedented" opportunities for all sorts of erotic experiences and weakened the control the family had on young people. Writing about the war's effect on sex a decade later, Alfred Kinsey attributed the new erotic freedom in part to the classes mixing. In any case, different rules were emerging about what was acceptable conduct, and after D-Day, American soldiers returned home with a new hunger for striptease.[49]

# Part Five

# After the War

The orchestra went into medium tempo, the lights changed from glaring yellow to soft violet. And then they came out, seven girls wearing horn-rimmed glasses and ultra conservative costumes. They walked primly and altogether resembled the stiff-necked females in a cartoon. . . .

Father o father you have me now, they formed a line and slowly waved black parasols as they sang.

Then that became daddy o daddy. Then the women took off the rest of their clothes.

—*Manhattan Detective Story Monthly*, December 1953

# Stripty-Second Streets

In the first years after the war, strippers continued to take it off at burlesque theaters everywhere except New York. "New Burly Season Finds N.Y. Only Key City Not on List," *Variety* proclaimed at the start of the 1947 season. "Should New Yorkers Give Burlesque Another Chance?" a headline in *PM Magazine* asked.[1] With LaGuardia out of office, Actors Equity lobbied for burlesque's return to the city. But the new mayor, William O'Dwyer, expressed no more support for burlesque than LaGuardia had.[2]

New Yorkers pining for bump and grind could commute to New Jersey, where the Union City Hudson and the Newark Empire delivered "glorified" burlesque, which the Minskys meant to suggest a more upscale entertainment than the Irving Place version. According to Louis Sobol, during this era H. L. Mencken and George Jean Nathan enjoyed the Jersey theaters, which, along with sixteen other burlesque theaters in the East and Midwest, comprised part of the profitable Hirst circuit.[3]

In 1951, Harold Minsky, Abe's son, a former law student, transformed the Adams Theater, then a concert hall, into a burlesque house in downtown Newark. More professorial in demeanor than the other Minskys, Harold wore a cardigan sweater and smoked a pipe. He saw the Minsky Adams as a kind of university, albeit one that taught the secrets of the flesh. According to Minsky publicity, the combined "campus" lure of the Minsky Adams, the Union City Hudson, and the Newark Empire inspired so many New Yorkers to make the reverse commute on Friday and Saturday nights that the already overused tunnels became even more clogged. "We try to give them not dirt-sex, but fun sex," Harold Minsky told *Variety*. For that distinction, *Variety* rewarded him by calling his theater "the Radio City Music Hall of Burlesque."[4]

By all accounts, the two-thousand-seat Adams attracted a mixed audience. Couples, young men, lawyers, and high school and college students all attended. According to one source, 50 percent of the audience was women. Hoping to stave off the legal troubles his father Abe had encountered in New York, Harold encouraged this mix by, among other things, holding a "Ladies Day" matinee at which the performers served the female patrons tea and cookies. In a more raunchy vein, performers also used numbers like Julia Lee's "Spinach Song," a bluesy homage to marijuana and the female sex organ.[5]

The Minsky Adams was hardly the only burlesque theater to lure in women during the late forties and early fifties. In Columbus, Ohio, the Gayety, which opened in 1946, ran ads encouraging men to "bring the ladies—they'll scream!" Some women did attend the Gayety, as well as the Folly in Kansas City. Back in 1941, around the time of Pearl Harbor, along with many other burlesque theaters outside of New York, the Folly—the former Missouri Theater where Gypsy Rose Lee had debuted in 1929—reopened after almost a decade of closure. Until 1969, the Folly flourished as a bump-and-grind burlesque house, employing an old-fashioned tit serenader to accompany its strippers.[6]

Kansas Citians preferred local strippers to national favorites: the World's Tallest Exotic; Miss Perpetual Motion; Marie Antoinette; a Russian Girl Cossack; and Gypsy Rose Lee. Local laws and censors regulated the Folly as strictly as LaGuardia had regulated the Republic in the 1930s. Few strippers took off their bras. A sign on the bulletin board at the Folly Burlesque advised performers: "Women MUST Wear Net Pants & Brassieres—Brassieres Must Have Cover for Nipples—No Bumps or Grinds Direct to Audience—No Hanging on Curtains—Do Not Touch Body—No Extreme Flash—Wear Panels—No Suggestive Lyrics in Any Vocal Numbers!"[7]

Folly Theatre, Kansas City. Folly Theatre Archives.

Showgirl Sherry Shannon told the *Kansas City Star*, "This is the strictest town in the circuit. Positively the strictest. We watch ourselves pretty closely, I can tell you!" The police watched the Folly Burlesque as well.[8]

Rose La Rose got arrested in K.C. because she ignored the red light the theater used to warn performers when police were attending. Or perhaps it was because her act went on for ten minutes, longer than any other stripper's. Then too, she often neglected to wear net pants, as the nylon panties covering the G-string were called.[9] The sultry La Rose, a good tap dancer, started in red velvet; sang, according to one spectator, "abominably"; and dropped her stole at the curtain call at the midnight show.[10]

Other flush midwestern cities hungry for nightlife caught the postwar striptease wave. In Columbus, the Gayety Burlesque at 250 South High Street and in Cincinnati, the Gayety Burlesque on Vine Street opened and closed. In 1951 five burlesque houses were operating in Ohio, more than anywhere else in the country. The following year, an Ohio circuit emerged. Journalist Al Schottelkotte explained: "In the 1940's and 50's Cincinnati was a Mecca for illegal gambling clubs that attracted star performers like Frank Sinatra and Dean Martin. When the casinos moved to Las Vegas in the mid-50's, strip clubs moved in."[11]

Near Chicago, in Calumet City, Illinois, strippers willing to go beyond the legal limit performed in mob-run nightclubs even before the war ended. The smoking steel mills of East Chicago, Gary, and Hammond, Indiana, created a vice district in the tiny city of twenty-five thousand. In 1941 the ratio of people to bars was 46 to 1. No church ever opened. Dubbed the Midwest's "Barbary Coast" by *Life*, Calumet City boasted 308 nightclubs and seven policemen.[12] "There was not much tease in that striptease," wrote Jesse Alson Smith in *Syndicate City*, an exposé of crime in the Midwest.[13]

Other forces drove the industry. Competition with nightclubs inspired burlesque strippers to ask for more money. In 1953, Harold Minsky complained that the performers' union and "minimum wages" would drive the theater operators out of business.[14] And another factor that contributed to the increasing flamboyance of burlesque striptease was the introduction of the bikini. In 1946, after the United States dropped the A-bomb on the Bikini atoll, Louis Reard, a French automotive engineer running his mother's lingerie shop, "invented" a bathing suit he named for the island. Reard called his bikini, which was only thirty square inches of fabric, "smaller than the world's smallest bathing suit." No professional model would agree to wear it, so he hired a stripper to do so. The *Herald Tribune* reported, "The first showing of the bikini suit here today started a chain reaction among the throng of sportswear experts who penetrated the Molitor lagoon shortly after the explosive exhibition."[15] By the early fifties, though, the most daring American women ventured onto the beach wearing it.[16]

ON THE WEST COAST, in New York, and even in some places in the Bible
Belt, supper clubs reinvented striptease as a glamorous act, as if the stripper were a little girl dressing up in her mother's evening gown and shoes.
A descendent of the Parisian cabaret, the Jazz Age speakeasy, and the thirties nightclub, the supper club was upscale. Waiters wore tuxedoes; candle-
light and fine linen adorned the tables. Sometimes the word "supper" was
a mere formality. The entertainment, occasionally daring, more often struck
an uneven note.

In the supper clubs of the 1940s and 1950s, the old trappings of burlesque striptease could no longer satisfy the postwar appetite for glamour.
The new breed of impresarios backing these clubs came from nightclubs
and Hollywood, not burlesque, and when they introduced stripping into
their high-class watering holes, they made it more lavish, anticipating the
floorshows in Las Vegas. Among the ritziest was Lou Walters' Latin Quarter, which Walters had built in New York in 1937, modeling it after the
Moulin Rouge in Paris. But there were many others, including the old
standby, Leon and Eddie's.[17]

In New York striptease returned, as the writer Jan Morris put it, "surviving LaGuardia's dictum that no navels must be shown on stage."[18] A
form of striptease prospered in all of the swank nightclubs on Fifty-second
Street between Fifth and Sixth Avenues and in Greenwich Village, where
the sound of bebop outside anticipated the undressing women inside. The
trend was already on the upswing in 1944, when, as *Variety* put it, America
was on a "national pleasure jag." A year later, Fifty-second Street had acquired the monikers "Stripty-Second Street," "Sexty-Second Street, "Strip
Street," and "Strip Alley," a fact many New Yorkers in love with jazz would
soon bemoan. "You won't recognize the old Fifty-Second Street—which
used to devote itself to swing. Now I call it Stripty Second Street! . . .
Nothing but strippers," griped Louis Sobol, the press agent and nightlife
aficionado.[19]

The number of strippers in these clubs continued to increase. Bebop
disappeared as café owners turned to strippers to bring in money, especially when the economy slumped. "We're being choked by a g-string," an
out-of-work jazz musician said.[20] In his memoir, Miles Davis blamed the
increasing reliance on striptease on hard economic times at the end of the
forties. "Some of the clubs on the street had stopped featuring jazz and had
turned into strip joints," he wrote.[21] The journalist Allen Churchill thought
the takeover was more dramatic: "On any night of the week you can watch
a girl on a 52nd Street stage," he noted.[22]

Some of these clubs imitated the enormous nightclubs of the thirties;
others increased the feeling of intimacy by replacing the burlesque runway
with a flat central area ringed by tables. Because of the proximity to the

audience, a stripper had to work harder to maintain the illusion of glamour. She might enter from the middle of the floor and do her trailer among the tables, but the prolonged blackout restrained her act, as did the audience, which now was composed of a growing number of women and middle-aged couples.

The fanciest of the tiny, street-level warrens, the Famous Door, boasted a shady ambiance in its fifty-five-seat lounge and still sold bootleg liquor, despite Repeal. Next door at the French Casino, Sugar Ray Robinson emceed for a while between fights. The atmosphere there was reminiscent of Nils T. Granlund's 1930s Paradise, where Zorita the snake dancer had punched a drunken customer who dared to slap her snake. After the war, more typical was the nearby Club Samoa, which employed Georgia Sothern and Sherry Britton, who had quit *The Man Who Came to Dinner* to disrobe full-time. Britton did lightning-quick strips and sang feel-good songs such as "Pin Up Girl" and "Rum and Coca Cola," at Leon and Eddie's, which began as a speakeasy cellar in 1928 but by 1936 was holding weekly strip-tease contests, including one to find "the next Gypsy Rose Lee," for a well-heeled tourist crowd. Lois DeFee started there as a bouncer.[23]

Success brought the joint to larger premises next to Jack and Charlie's "21," and there it stayed, offering a postwar version of the thirties mixture of family dining and striptease. In 1945, ads for Britton, one of Leon and Eddie's stars, asked, "Can 2500 servicemen be wrong?" The Lido, the Harem, and the Ha Ha Club all flourished on the same block, and around the corner the old Blue Angel, Le Ruban Bleu, and Le Boeuf Sur Toit offered what *Variety* dismissed as "modernistic" undressing, by which it meant a less prurient, suburban version of the Minskys'.[24]

Fifty-second Street during this era recalls Legs Diamond's quip "It's great to be a sucker if you can afford it." Mario's, Leon and Eddie's, and other clubs sometimes hired strippers who dressed up their undressing acts with exoticism or hardly stripped at all. Noel Toy, the Chinese bubble dancer, "kept her duds on" at the Latin Quarter, as did Princess La Homa, an "Indian tribal dancer." In 1952, before Dixie Evans became the Marilyn Monroe of striptease, she did a cowgirl number at Leon and Eddie's in which she twirled her G-string like a lariat.[25]

Leon and Eddie's and Mario's Mirador, a swanky club full of high-toned fun, contrasted with some of the other, less-legitimate clubs on Fifty-second Street and elsewhere. As the forties wore on, more and more nightclubs, struggling to survive, traded elegance for the confidence game. Newspapers and magazines began to describe these clubs as clip joints, worthless sucker traps with carnival barkers, broads, hustling tables, finger men on the prowl, lookouts for blackmail mobs on steady duty, badger game veterans, and various other dregs of the criminal world. There were a thousand and one scams going on, each more nefarious than the next. In this era newspapers and magazines ran one feature after another to explain to tourists and the ever-present "visiting firemen" how not to be duped while watching naked women.

In the Broadway wiseguy style of the day, columnists Jack Lait and Lee Mortimer described these locales as joints where a rube would see the promise of "naughty displays of undraped female cuticle on the boardwalk." Yet, Lait and Mortimer warned, by the time the rube paid his tab, he'd seen nothing more revealing than a "zaftig performer whose generously proportioned panties and bra (which always remained on) were constructed of material as thick as carpeting and as opaque."[26]

As the clip joint became more prevalent, another wave of reform arose to curtail nightclub striptease.[27] By 1952 that wave had had an effect. Reformers shut down eleven nightclubs. The following year, Leon and Eddie's went bankrupt and closed, and other clubs followed. Developers razed sections of Fifty-second Street and Greenwich Village, where they turned some of the former strip clubs into New York University buildings and others into parking lots. The remaining clubs got seedier and seedier. "Fading 52nd Street Joints Wait It Out for Last-buck Suckers," *Variety* announced in 1954. A year later, *Cabaret* Magazine ran a eulogy for the street titled "The Short, Happy Life of 52nd Street."[28]

THE HINTERLANDS LAGGED a year or two behind New York. Each region of the country became known for one kind of stripping. In Chicago over half the bistros continued to depend on rough peelers. Montreal welcomed American strippers such as Margie Hart and blonde June St. Clair, whose "sleaze" appealed.[29] In Miami, Collins Avenue nightclubs attracted newcomers to striptease and drag strippers, and in Las Vegas the Desert Inn and the Spa drew the crème de la crème.[30] In Baltimore, two supper clubs— Club Charles and Club Chanticleer—as well as "the Block," a seething vice district on Baltimore Street, offered different versions of striptease during and after the war years.[31]

When it opened in 1941, Club Charles, located at the corner of Charles and Preston streets, was swinging. After the war, on the Club's bill was the very young comic Lenny Bruce as well as Yvette Dare, "the gorgeous Balinese half caste and her sarong stealing parrot." Down the street, Club Chanticleer, originally a cocktail lounge, became a luxe nightclub. Recessed fluorescent lights flattered a shell-pink ceiling and blue walls and deep pile carpet covered the floor. Patrons sat in plush white leather chairs and on top of a sunken oval bar in the middle of the club, entertainers sang and danced and told jokes on a revolving-glass podium lit from below. As for "The Block," its fourteen strip joints gave Baltimore the name "Sin City."[32]

*Variety* attributed striptease's success in Sin City (also called Charm City) to the mix of social classes in its audience, to a strong police force, and to the absence of the mob, as well as to the banquets taking place at the nightspots there. "Celebrities from the political, social, sports, and theatrical life of the town and nation gather here nightly. . . . [S]hrimp, oysters, crabs, steaks, herring, or gigantic hot dogs are served."[33]

Striptease flourished in a different way in New Orleans, whose history as a pleasure town dates back at least to the nineteenth century. As A. J. Liebling wrote, New Orleans is less the southernmost point in the United States than the northernmost point of Costa Rica. A fancy residential avenue in the nineteenth century and home to the New Orleans Opera House after the war, Bourbon Street was now dubbed "Harlot's Row." In 1930, Dauphine Street, where many African Americans lived, was the center of the action. The New Orleans–born Madame Norma Wallace described it as "full of hookers and nightspots and dance halls."[34]

At the onset of the Depression, the Dauphine Theater opened as a "naval palace," where strippers paraded onstage wearing only fig leaves. Just as quickly as it gained attention, the Dauphine closed, having collapsed under financial mismanagement. In the thirties, with their laissez-faire attitude, Vieux Carre clubs were characterized by employing an unusually large number of female impersonators, a fact that inspired wave after wave of raids and arrests.[35]

Although Tennessee Williams wrote that the war ruined the city, the history of striptease in New Orleans continued, lifted, as it were, by a wind from the North. In 1942, Izzy Hirst and Harold Minsky opened the Casino de Paree, a burlesque nightclub on Bourbon Street, which became a good-time destination for servicemen as the New Orleans port became a center of wartime activity. "The sharp staccato of riveting has been added to the symphony of indulgent living," wrote *Variety*, announcing the club's arrival.[36]

No sooner had the war ended than the joie de vivre returned. In his 1950 memoir *Weegee by Weegee*, the crime photographer called postwar New Orleans "the Bowery with a cover charge [where] the strippers stripped around the clock." Weegee, who had worked in a burlesque theater in his youth, took photographs of strippers, along with murder victims, transvestites, and the very rich. His portraits of nightclub strippers in the Crescent City seem lifted from B movies. His 1950 *Sonata in G-Strings* catches a stripper in the act of being dressed. Shielding her breast from the camera, she smiles mischievously and turns to her dresser, a thin woman wearing a long-sleeved shirt. Above them hangs a clothesline of G-strings—the sonata of Weegee's title. Other photos, such as "In the Dressing Room," "Mugging for the Camera," and "The Show's Going to Start Any Minute," are, like much of Weegee's work, snapshots of unabashed emotion and ugliness. There is nothing romantic about them.[37]

Weegee, *Sonata in G-Strings*, New Orleans, 1950. Weegee/International Center for Photography/Getty Images.

As industry increased in New Orleans during the fifties, clubs with headquarters in New York and Los Angeles, like Ciro's, opened outposts on Bourbon and Rampart streets and competed with local clubs such as the Silver Frolics, the Shobar, the Poodle Patio, the Hotsy Totsy, Chez Paree, and Prima's 500 Club. Just as Chicago jazz had shaped striptease in the twenties, so New Orleans jazz determined "how" strippers stripped in the forties and fifties. As the jazz critic Henk Niesen put it, New Orleans style is "rapid, filled with notes played legato."[38]

New Orleans strippers undulated to New Orleans jazz with fast and furious bumps and grinds. At Prima's, which was run by Leon Prima, the brother of bandleader Louis, the theme was Southern decadence: a tropical mural embellished the wall and ceiling. The musicians wore fezzes and the saxophone player Sam Butera made strippers dance to music that was all "Jump, Jive, and Wail," as the Louis Prima song went.[39]

Crescent City clubs rotated nationally known performers with home-grown ones who included Alouette Le Blanc, the self-proclaimed "world's greatest tassel twirler." Lilly Christine's savage "Cat Girl" dance, the "Would you like to put your head on my pillow?" number, and her voodoo striptease all started in New Orleans, where she was born. In the last number, which made her a star, Christine played a voodoo priestess guiding two sailors in the quest of love. She feeds them a potion that she herself imbibes and then she goes into violent convulsion that, of course, shakes her entire body.[40]

Other New Orleans veterans included the exotic dancer Kalantan, who later headlined in Las Vegas. At the Casino Royale on Bourbon Street, one New Orleans performer, Kitty West, aka "Evangeline, the Beautiful Pearl in the Half Shell," emerged from an oyster shell and dallied onstage, toying with an oversized pearl. Undulating to a New Orleans jazz number written specifically for her, surrounded by tufts of seaweed, she resembled a latter-day Venus. She even dyed her hair green until she discovered the dye irritated her scalp.

In 1949 the Casino Royale hired a performer from up North known as Divena "the Aqua Tease." Inside a tank holding 550 gallons of water, Divena got undressed and swam around, pretending to be a mermaid. When she played at the Casino Royale, Evangeline the Oyster Girl—ostensibly jealous— shattered the tank with an ax. A *Life* photographer who happened to be in the audience caught Evangeline's show on film.[41]

Following the age-old pattern, media attention to striptease brought reform. Until 1949, the New Orleans police mostly looked the other way when stripping happened. Police would round up forty or fifty strippers and bring them into the police station only to release them for lack of evidence. But a police crackdown on Bourbon Street joints increased along with the nationwide trend and in the wake of a few local nightclub deaths. By 1952 the newly created state liquor board was ordering Lilly Christine and others to add "four inches of fringe to their costumes."[42]

IN CALIFORNIA, striptease thrived in burlesque and nightclubs, many of which were owned and managed by women. This trend started during the Depression and took off during the war as women "invaded" jobs formerly held by men. Sally Rand managed two nightclubs in San Francisco, first the Music Box in 1939 and then Sally Rand's Hollywood Club a year later. This club lent a higher degree of class and glamour to a then rough and tumble neighborhood. Sally's club apartment featured simulated leopard-skin carpeting covering both the floor and the walls. Her stint as manager lasted only through the war years.

Overall, though, the trend of women-owned burlesque clubs continued into the late forties, after many men had returned home from overseas. Lillian Hunt managed the El Rey Theater in Oakland, across the bay from San Francisco, and the Follies on Third and Main in Los Angeles. Stripper Ginger Britton owned the Follies from 1944 to 1946—a wealthy husband bought it for her. Betty Rowland bought the Café Le Maze nightclub and turned it into the Ball of Fire, which also happened to be her moniker.[43]

The increasing number of women managing burlesque theaters and strip clubs may in part account for the rise of the most famous postwar stripper in America: Lili St. Cyr. In the 1940s and 1950s, the peroxide blonde's elaborate production numbers and costumes made Gypsy Rose Lee look old-fashioned. In some of St. Cyr's advertisements for her appearances at the Club Samoa in New York, she styled herself as a Roman senatress; in others she posed as a medieval courtesan with lute. In both cases, she also drew from Christian Dior's "New Look," which promoted a fragile feminine form. In some of St. Cyr's advertisements, her ornately braided hair piled on top of her head and her costumes' soft classical lines suggested decadence and class.[44] Whereas most burlesque strippers of the era were zaftig, St. Cyr was slender. But even though she did not look like a burlesque queen, early on some reviewers found St. Cyr's performances to be vulgar for revealing too much flesh. When she appeared at the Latin Quarter in Miami in 1944, *Variety* wrote, "Gal is as streamlined as a p-38 and equipped with almost as much fire power, but is almost certain to offend many as routine carries beyond the border-line of good taste."[45]

St. Cyr quickly recovered. For unlike the Literary Strippers of the thirties, she neither read from the classics nor self-consciously compared her burlesque past to her stylish present. Borrowing from Gypsy, St. Cyr sometimes teased, as she exited, "That's all you get boys. . . ." But that was as far as her humor went. In fact she more often worked in the opposite direction, emphasizing the idea that desire made her a victim instead of poking fun of it. She performed mostly in silence and in lavish numbers with pulp fiction titles such as "Bedroom Fantasy" and "Love Moods." *Variety* described her: "There's a touch of Liberace in the act. She lights a couple of wall candelabra. She makes her entrance in mink, does her boudoir act, and makes an exit in the swish of silk."[46]

That "swish" allowed St. Cyr to jump from burlesque to nightclubs with an ease few other strippers could manage. At a moment when men were coming home from the war starved for female company and the "feminine mystique" described by Betty Friedan, many of St. Cyr's numbers operated on the theme of waiting for and being rescued by a man. In a number of publicity photos, she vamps on Gloria Swanson's enormous, gilded, swan-shaped satin bed from *Sunset Boulevard*. St. Cyr bought the bed in 1951, a year after the movie was made. On St. Cyr's set, a large snapshot of a good-looking blond man hangs over her, smiling.

BORN WILLIS MARIE VAN SHAAK in Minneapolis in 1918, St. Cyr moved with her mother to California after the Great War. She never knew her father. One of her sisters would become Dardy Orlando, a stripper who married Harold Minsky. In California in the late thirties, St. Cyr worked as a waitress and then began performing at the Florentine Gardens, a theater-nightclub

Lili St. Cyr poses "on set" in front of Gloria Swanson's bed. Kinsey Institute for Research in Sex, Gender, and Reproduction.

taken over by the former Broadway impresario Nils T. Granlund in 1939.[47] One of the most beloved entertainers of the decade, Granlund—Granny to his friends—had run nightclubs in New York until LaGuardia chased him west. On Sunset Boulevard, Granny became the creative director of the 950-seat house, whose name originally was meant to refer to Florence, and which was decorated in a powder blue and gold scheme. Granny provided jazz, vaudeville, song-and-dance teams, and also, as *Variety* put it, many "cuties," "near nudies," and burlesque stars like Sally Rand.[48]

In 1941, St. Cyr moved up the entertainment ladder. She began stripping at the Music Box nightclub in San Francisco, which she described in her memoir as resembling a French chateau with red damask–covered walls and a white marble floor.[49] She did a strip there nightly as "the girl of the hour." Each hour, she paraded around the nightclub wearing fewer clothes. The idea, as she described it, was to keep men in the club longer. Ignoring the owner's advice, she refused to talk to any of the nightclub-goers, instead remaining silent, which, she argued, created an aura of elegance and glamour. Describing her technique, St. Cyr said she created "miniature" pieces of theater in which she never broke the fourth wall to smile and tease, as other burlesque strippers did. Nor did she bump and grind or shake her hips.[50]

Ivan Fehnova, who had worked for Mike Todd in New York before becoming the lead choreographer at the Music Box, taught St. Cyr how to dance. He also convinced her to choose a new name. As with so many name changes in burlesque, though, conflicting stories explain its provenance. St. Cyr says she invented "Lili" after Lillie Langtry and Lillian Russell and St. Cyr after a military school she read about in a magazine. Another version of the story attributes her last name to Rex St. Cyr, a big spender at the club. But St. Cyr is also a homonym for "sincere"—at a moment when she controlled her act with an iron grip, her name promised honesty. Or perhaps she took the name from Johnny St. Cyr, one of Louis Armstrong's Hot Five jazzmen in the thirties.[51]

The Music Box closed at the end of 1941, just before Pearl Harbor, and St. Cyr found herself out of work. Increasing activity at the naval base in San Diego created a demand for burlesque at the Hollywood Theater, which had struggled during the Depression.[52] St. Cyr despised burlesque, but she admired Faith Bacon, whose act she had seen at the Orpheum in Los Angeles a few years earlier. For St. Cyr's strip at the Hollywood, Fehnova created an act that would be as elegant as Bacon's fan dance but would also avoid the censors—he called it "The Flying G." In the first part of the strip, St. Cyr undressed to her G-string, which was painted with radium and attached to a point offstage with a wire. Then there was a blackout. From the wings, a stagehand pulled the G-string off and slid it along the wire into the balcony. The audience could see the G-string dancing offstage.[53]

According to St. Cyr, Fanny Johnson, the Hollywood manager, wanted her to do something more flamboyant. In any case, St. Cyr left the West Coast and went to New York, where the former Ballets Russes dancer and vaudevillian Paul Valentine took up Fehnova's role as coach and muse. After marrying St. Cyr, he taught her all kinds of routines and numbers. "I made her a star," he told a reporter. For her part, St. Cyr dreamed that she and Valentine would become the Alfred Lunt and Lynn Fontanne of burlesque.[54]

That dream eluded her. St. Cyr proceeded to Miami and then to Montreal, the "Paris of the West," a city with a burgeoning Francophile nightlife.[55] During the winter of 1944, St. Cyr headlined at the Gayety, then the city's most lavish burlesque theater. She spent the next several years commuting between New York and Miami nightclubs and Montreal burlesque.[56] Her acts were full of style. She did a slow grind and a decorous bump to "In a Persian Market" at Leon and Eddie's.[57] "The Chinese Virgin" displayed a blonde, icy veneer, embodying the threatening side lurking beneath the perfect fifties homemaker. According to William Weintraub, in the act the curtain rose on a set of a Chinese temple. On an altar sat smoking incense and a statue of Buddha. Orchestra music swelled. In a harem costume dominated by a wide, glittering chastity belt, St. Cyr's first ballet steps on stage "convey[ed] sadness and despair." Then she mimed the story of how her suspicious, wealthy husband had abandoned her with only the chastity belt for comfort. She implored Buddha to free her, so that she could meet her lover. She writhed with desire, the music became allegro, and her clothes fell to the ground. Her undulations became more and more frenzied and "a flash of light illuminated the stage." The Buddha "gave" St. Cyr a large key, with which she unlocked the belt and freed herself.[58] *Montreal Herald* nightlife columnist Al Palmer dubbed the Gayety "the house that Lili built," and the city celebrated her as "La Belle Lili."[59]

Several of St. Cyr's other numbers, such as "In a Persian Harem" and "The Dressing Act," presented similar exotic tales. But in the late forties, St. Cyr developed "Love Moods," a striptease number that traded exoticism for domesticity, albeit a deluxe brand. In "Love Moods," St. Cyr designed an undressing act around a bubble bath, which she called a "crystal" bath to distinguish it from ordinary suds. Tom Douglas, a Los Angeles–based millionaire and society interior designer, paid for the set, which cost over ten thousand dollars. When St. Cyr got dressed after taking the bath, she wore Balenciaga, Balmain, and Dior.[60] As with so many of St. Cyr's numbers, "Love Moods" began with her waiting for her lover. She walked onstage fully dressed. She tried on a hat and took off one bra. (Like many strippers, she wore two.) A maid helped her remove the era's ornate lingerie— and held a towel between St. Cyr and the audience. Then St. Cyr would slip into the tub, apparently naked.[61]

"Bedroom Fantasy" started with a phone call from her lover and showed St. Cyr getting aroused onstage. "Cinderella's Love Lesson" starred the stripper as an ordinary woman transformed by a wand into the fairy tale heroine only to lose her clothes at midnight. Other numbers centered less on flesh than on lovesickness—or lust sickness. In "Jungle Goddess," St. Cyr "made love" to a parrot. In another number, she climbed in and out of a life-sized champagne glass. In "Suicide," performed in Montreal, she played a woman in despair at having been abandoned by her lover. Behind her, the set depicted New York's skyscrapers. Clutching her lover's photograph, St. Cyr slowly divested herself of her clothes. When this ritual failed to entice the lover to appear, she climbed up on a window. The audience shouted, "Don't jump!" A body double jumped and St. Cyr proceeded to dance as the angel of death. The curtain fell.[62]

These numbers replaced the ribald humor deployed by 1930s strippers with a disturbing combination of hard irreverence and sensual vulnerability. St. Cyr's cold, outward elegance brazenly mimicked old forms. She updated Gypsy Rose Lee's "I'm Eve Looking for an Apple" number by dancing around a giant apple as if she were one of Macbeth's witches. She performed elaborate versions of the stories of mythical vamps: Salome, Carmen, Cleopatra, and Leda were hers, as well as Sadie Thompson, the prostitute with a heart of gold immortalized by Gloria Swanson in the Jazz Age play *Rain*. She played a geisha and a cowgirl, a character that was the apotheosis for postwar strippers. She did a Christmas number in which she opened packages. Only a few months after the wedding of Prince Rainier and Grace Kelly in 1956, St. Cyr did "Lili St. Cyr's Royal Wedding Night," in which, by impersonating Kelly, she modernized the wedding night number from turn-of-the-century burlesque. But although St. Cyr changed her act frequently, some critics continued to describe her as "distant" and "cold."[63]

In 1949, St. Cyr returned to Los Angeles to headline at the *Follies*, where, according to Ted Jordan, then Marilyn Monroe's boyfriend and later one of St. Cyr's husbands, Monroe patterned her image after the stripper. Jordan and Monroe watched St. Cyr do her parrot strip and her champagne glass strip at the Follies. Monroe became obsessed with St. Cyr.[64]

More than any other stripper, St. Cyr was influenced by Hollywood's postwar lust for glamour. She strove to emulate Gilda, the title character in the King Vidor movie starring Rita Hayworth in 1946. Called upon to do a striptease, Gilda demonstrated an unstable combination of puritanism and self-indulgence, prudery and licentiousness. *Gilda* presented striptease as both naughty and dangerous, its practitioner at once simple-hearted and sexually depraved. In *Gilda*, the unforgettable striptease sequence occurs at the end of the movie, when Gilda, drunk at Macready's bar, shakes her long, glossy hair in front of one eye and begins to peel her glove from her arm. She smiles. She looks terrific, but some good-intentioned men save her from stripping completely. And so she is rescued from the fate of being a stripper.[65]

WHEN ST. CYR RETURNED to Los Angeles in 1949, besides the nine burlesque houses open on the West Coast, a string of magnificent supper clubs on Sunset Boulevard still attracted A-list patrons in part by presenting striptease. These clubs—which included Earl Carroll's Theatre and the Florentine Gardens—served liquor and thus could make money faster than burlesque theaters. They could also provide a front for gambling and other illegal pastimes. On the surface more up-market than Fifty-second Street, the West Coast clubs drew wealthy Americans and movie stars with their relaxed, seductive allure. At the opening of Earl Carroll's Theatre in 1939, *Variety* noted that one room, reserved for the "inner circle" of celebrities, cost $500 to get in and $1000 for a lifetime membership.[66] To these celebrities, Earl Carroll's presented vaudeville and highbrow burlesque entertainment. Among the 500 guests at opening night were Errol Flynn and Franchot Tone, Claudette Colbert, Daryl Zanuck, and David Selznick. The décor included banquettes made of patent leather.

The following year, Herman Hover, who had been a choreographer and legman for Carroll, took over the management of another "velvet rope" nightclub, Ciro's, which *Variety* dubbed "the swankiest club in glitterland." Before working for Carroll, Hover had managed the Silver Slipper Nightclub in New York, and he had long imagined his own club offering glittering entertainment. Ciro's was designed by Tom Douglas, who painted the walls apple green and the ceiling red. Patrons sat on silk wall sofas. Bronze urns buttressed the orchestra.

Hover dazzled by mixing exclusivity and sex appeal. His club became a franchise with branches in Miami, Chicago, and New Orleans, and the LA club's elite qualities continued to attract the society set, who sat behind the

Publicity postcard of Earl Carroll's nightclub, Hollywood, c. 1945. Author's personal collection.

"velvet rope." As for the onstage entertainment, Hover wanted vaudeville, Earl Carroll style; in the early fifties, he combined Tinseltown figures such as jokester and songster Joe E. Lewis, Sophie Tucker, and Pearl Bailey with Lili St. Cyr and others for a naughty-but-nice flavor that Las Vegas would later emulate.[67]

According to her memoir, at her debut at Ciro's in the spring of 1951, St. Cyr premiered her bathtub strip, "An Interlude before Evening," to music by Rimsky-Korsakov and Gershwin in a number she described as "possessing dignified and base elements." Civic leaders attended, St. Cyr broke all of the club's earnings records, and Las Vegas and Palm Springs nightclubs courted her and offered her upwards of $2000 a week. St. Cyr also returned to Montreal, where she performed as Salome during the week of St. Jean Le Baptiste. The police arrested her and then released her until her trial, although some members of the force attended her performances every night. "I'm afraid to take off my glove, or even move my finger," she complained. A jury acquitted her, and the Chamber of Commerce celebrated her as a tourist attraction.[68]

As on the East Coast, one West Coast supper and jazz club after another was failing. Part of the nightclub shake-up occurred because of changes in the music scene. Less melodic and more improvisatory, "cool" and West Coast jazz were not conducive to stripping. Indeed, strippers sometimes would complain that when jazzmen began to riff, it was impossible for them to do their numbers. In the early fifties, many impresarios and club owners arrived at the same conclusion: they did away with music and focused on striptease. The new nightclubs emerging out of the old ones tried to cater to both the working-class stiff and the American aristocracy: movie stars.

One Los Angeles club that succeeded for a while, Strip City, reflected striptease's West Coast appeal to the working stiff. In 1950 former musician, restaurateur, and jazz aficionado Maynard Sloate bought a former nightclub on the corner of Pico and Western, a black-and-tan neighborhood. Sloate called Strip City "the home of big name burlesk." But unlike Florentine Gardens and Ciro's, Strip City attracted more of the average guy, immigrants and tourists.[69]

Anticipating Hugh Hefner's Playboy Clubs of the late fifties, Sloate imagined Strip City as a "typical" bachelor pad. He hired a five-piece "bump-and-grind" band and produced what were known as "quick-fix" stripteases— where strippers took off their clothes in five minutes or less. Down the street, other clubs did likewise. Chuck Landis's Largo Club drew a similar crowd. At the Colony Club in Gardena, a supper theater-cum-striptease club, strippers burlesqued twenties musicals for middle-class men and their wives.

Arriving in Los Angeles, the soon-to-be emissary of hip Lenny Bruce premiered his scatological routines as emcee at Strip City while his wife,

Honey, did a "classic" strip at the Colony Club in which she hid behind a parasol for her finale. Driven by insecurity and despair at working in the lowest kind of club in the city, Bruce resorted to ridiculing the strippers: "The House of Big Name Burlesque? That means the girls are Polish."[70]

And yet some of Bruce's most brilliant "sick" comedy, his focus on the underdog, his outrage, his rage, his weird riffs and monologues about the underworld emerged as he began to compete with the strippers by committing one wild act after another. Bruce's idea of "talking dirty" reveals roots in burlesque comedy and turned on the fact of Bruce making fun of himself for being stuck in a strip club at all. Bruce did a satire of the "gorilla and the stripper" number that culminated in his being naked onstage. Many of Bruce's early numbers ended with his being naked, or dressed only in strippers' gear, such as a mink stole and stockings. It was also in these clubs that Bruce began to attack religion.

In the mid-fifties, Bruce made two fantastical, semi-autobiographical movies parodying burlesque. In *Dance Hall Racket*, an FBI agent cracks a white slavery ring run from a burlesque theater. In *Dream Follies*, two ordinary guys sneak out of their oppressive office to "peep" at the strippers at a downtown burlesque house. The comedy verged on the bizarre. In *Dream Follies*, one of the guys "removes" the secretaries' blouses, a feat that the Bruce character is unable to see; in *Dance Hall Racket*, Bruce, who played the small time thug, dumps a bowl of spaghetti on his mother's head.

Shortly after completing these movies, Bruce opened his own strip club, Duffy's Gaieties, on Cahuenga Boulevard. His emcee antics became even more outlandish as he cast an unromantic light on burlesque's seedy world. "The strippers in those clubs had four words in their vocabulary: I'll have the same," he said in one routine. After his apprenticeship in burlesque, Bruce moved on to San Francisco, legitimate nightclubs, and fame.[71]

EAST AND WEST, the recession alongside an increase in police raids made it harder for strippers to earn a living in burlesque. Popular opinion about them was hardening. Newspapers began to describe strippers as gold diggers animated only by greed or as dolls articulated only by love of ornament. Strippers played into this trend. "I won't marry a poor schnook for love," the columnist Lee Mortimer quoted Lilly Christine (the Cat Girl) as saying. "I love dough," she added.[72]

As for the Midwest, lacking West Coast opulence, or even access to Hollywood, most of the new "strip" nightclubs opening there appealed to the lowest common denominator. In Chicago the 606 Nightclub at 606 South Wabash and cabarets such as the Liberty Inn on North Clark Street and the L & L Café on West Madison encouraged patrons to sit close to the performers and drink beer. The Red Garter did the same. The Liberty Inn, Chicago's largest strip club, dangled as many as twenty-five strippers in front of an audience in one evening. A little further east, in the increasingly scruffy South Loop, the Chicago, the National, and the State-Harrison theaters continued to offer burlesque striptease, and other clubs began to show pornographic films. Art Hess, a musician who hung out in Chicago after the war, recalled Snooky DeWitt, a glamorous stripper who performed at the Flamingo Club. But he also remembered horizontal cootches—strips women performed lying down on the stage—and men so drunk that they couldn't walk.[73]

IN THE SAME ERA, though, the highbrow nightclub version of American striptease caught on in Europe. Posing naked had flourished in London during the war, and in Paris at the Folies Bergères and elsewhere since the turn of the century. But around 1950 the City of Light added American striptease to its repertoire. According to the impresario Alain Bernadin, American striptease first appeared at the Crazy Horse Saloon as part of the influx of American culture that French chauvinists constantly warned against and that the younger generation, with equal constancy, loved.[74] Around 1948, as Bernadin tells it, he was strolling with several colleagues in the seedy working-class district of Pigalle, where women posed in shop windows to advertise their appearance on cabaret stages. Bernadin realized that he could rejuvenate the nightclub industry by opening a French nightclub where dancers could shake and where, as he would later boldly put it, an audience could see a completely naked woman from the rear.[75]

"The art of striptease is difficult to learn, impossible to teach," Bernadin opined. But Bernadin set about that task with Cartesian determination: he lobbied to get the law against nude performers' moving onstage revoked, collected backers, got costumes and sets designed. Predictably, as inspiration, he summoned the muse of High Art. ("Why did Rodin shatter French sculpture 100 years ago?" Bernadin asked in an interview. "He opened women's thighs.")[76] Once Bernadin had ushered striptease from Pigalle onto Avenue George V, close to the Arc de Triomphe, he went to some effort to transform it into a glamorous Parisian soirée.

Striptease also caught on in Japan, after Shigeo Ozaki, a Japanese impresario, saw Gypsy Rose Lee perform in the late forties. Ozaki produced striptease extravaganzas in Tokyo's Shinjuku district, reforming the indigenous tradition of posing, Ziegfeld style, into a more kinetic burlesque-style dancing and stripping.[77] Japanese "strip shows," as they were called after 1948, developed along the same lines as American ones, with Japanese B-girls and revues. But in a conformist culture such as Japan, striptease could not ultimately hold burlesque's irreverent spirit. Japanese stripping became more and more sexually explicit and finally superseded the American version in the late fifties, when it was transformed into live sex shows.[78]

BACK IN AMERICA, the Korean War broke out in 1950. Again men went off to war. But this time it was a war that no one seemed to want. Mike Todd seized the opportunity to produce another version of his escapist brand of striptease on Broadway. As in *Star and Garter*, Todd capitalized on the fact that, in the popular imagination, soldiers risking their lives on the front deserved to see the unclothed female body. Todd's new show, *Michael Todd's Peep Show*, owed even less to burlesque than *Star and Garter*.

*Michael Todd's Peep Show* opened in June, days after the Korean War began, and offered soldiers and tourists "girly, womanly, female, feminine dames."[79] With lyrics by Jule Styne and Bob Hilliard, and the Harold Rome song "Gimme the Shimmy," it updated the formula of "tall dames and low comedy" for the cool fifties by combining parody of striptease with nostalgia for the Jazz Age. The revue's title number drew its inspiration from pinup magazines. An aquamarine tarp with forty-eight holes and a giant rhinestone keyhole allowed the audience to "peep" through to see hordes of women cavorting in a giant bubble bath. "Violins from Nowhere" began with a parade of women weaving around the stage playing string instruments. But then a nude male violinist—perhaps the first onstage male nude—appeared upstage behind the scrim.[80]

*Peep Show* starred Lili Christine in several numbers: in a heavily orchestrated dance piece called "Desire," in her signature "Cat Girl" dance, and doing the shimmy. The tall, blonde New Orleans stripper brought "animality" to Todd's show. She had already become infamous for the umbrella number—a version of the fan dance in which she entered nude and opened and closed a lace umbrella. *Variety* would later review her as "having feline grace." Another newspaper described her as though she were a tiger: "Miss Christine holds nothing back. Everything moves. And her control is amazing."[81]

Because Todd wanted to contrast the latest in cool culture with the heat of exotic dancing, the music for "Desire" sounded more like a tone poem than Tin Pan Alley. Written by Raymond Scott, the electronic jazz composer and bandleader known for his quirky arrangements, "Desire" borrowed from bebop and from *Looney Tunes* soundtracks, many of which Scott also wrote. But the Act II finale, Lili Christine's shimmy number, which accompanied the singing of Lina Romay, celebrated Tin Pan Alley and old-fashioned bump and grind. "To be up to date, it appears, you've got to go back thirty years," went one lyric while Christine twirled.

In its costumes, *Peep Show* displayed a similar mix of the modern and the old-fashioned. Like *Star and Garter*, *Peep Show* was costumed by Irene Sharaff, who, using the strategy she had undertaken with Gypsy a decade earlier, dressed up Lili Christine by putting her in a Marie Antoinette wig. But Christine, who never spoke while performing, was no Gypsy Rose Lee. Reviewers compared her energy to that of thirties stripper Georgia

Sothern. "She revolved all around," wrote John Chapman in the *New York Times*.[82] Others advised parents to leave children at home and noted that the spectacle was for the tired businessmen—not a family affair. *Peep Show* ran for a respectable 278 performances, perhaps because, as George Jean Nathan wrote, it stressed "sex, ferociously."[83]

Sex, ferociously, it seemed, was what Americans wanted.

# The Seamy Sides of Striptease

F ar from the world of supper clubs, Broadway, and tuxedoed waiters, a tawdry version of striptease ground on at fairgrounds, at Coney
Island, and in road show burlesque movies. Despite a brief period
of Coney Island's being a "family" destination, after LaGuardia chased
burlesque out of Times Square, a seedy Boardwalk full of girl shows triumphed. As on Fifty-second Street, some observers complained that these
shows failed to show enough skin to compete with what ordinary women
were wearing. "The Coney strip tease exhibitions, I discovered, were a
marked anti-climax to anything you could see on the five mile beach free
of charge," wrote George Jean Nathan in 1942.[1]

"Tirza the Wine Girl," former headliner at the New York World's
Fair, began stripping at Coney Island in 1947. A few years later, tired of
performing, she opened her own nightclub at 1500 Surf Avenue, where
she grossed about two thousand dollars a week.[2] Other boardwalk impresarios began to display nudist colonies, which, emphasizing the "natural"
aspect of women's having already taken it off before the show started, theoretically downplayed any titillation associated with burlesque striptease. In
one sideshow Albert/Alberta, a "man/woman," posed partly naked; in another, "Aquagals," a take-off of Billy Rose's Aquacade at the World's Fair,
a group of scantily clad "gals" frolicked, swam, and dove, as if water miti-
gated their nudity. Farther down the boardwalk, the World Circus Sideshow displayed among its main attractions a "Negro girlie show."[3]

Nudity was everywhere, even on the big screen, as a new generation of
moviemakers subverted the Hollywood production code by making cheap
"exploitation" or "road show" films that could be screened in burlesque houses.
Indeed, Sol Goodman, the longtime operator of Baltimore's Gayety Theater, had a simple epitaph for striptease. "Movies spoiled it," he said.[4]

Rather than leave show business altogether, many burlesque theater
operators turned to movies. As burlesque theaters closed in small cities and
towns across America, a market arose for filmed burlesque shows, which
were shown in either theaters or tents. Thus, these "exploitation" film-
makers—as they began to be called—mostly avoided the restrictions of the
Hollywood production code. Merle Connell produced his first burlesque
shorts in 1947, borrowing strippers and chorus girls from the Los Angeles
Follies Theater. Some early films included *Roadshow Attractions*, *Hollywood
Peep Show*, *Hurly Burly*, *Shim Sham Follies*, *French Follies*, and *Ding! Dong!*[5]

Connell, the first exploitation filmmaker to realize that he could shoot one of these films in a couple of days, and ship it around the country cheaply, made a lot of money. Lili St. Cyr recalled that most of these films were finished in the few hours strippers took for breaks each day. By 1949, Connell and others in the first generation of road show producers began to experiment with feature-length burlesque movies. Harry Farros, a West Coast burlesque theatre owner, formed Broadway Roadshow Productions to produce and distribute such films, many of which followed the same bare bones aesthetic as Connell. Farros' *Midnight Frolics*, a filmed version of a Los Angeles burlesque show, continued to circulate for fourteen years and created a market for "shot through" burlesque movies such as *Hollywood Revels*, *A Night at the Follies*, and *Striptease Girl*. Two other "blue" companies—one run by the Sonneys, a carnival family, and the other by Willis Kent—produced numerous feature-length films, as did a third, a Washington, D.C., team with the winning name of Lust Entertainment. *Time* reported on the phenomenon of "old fashioned flesh and spangle shows . . . converted to the screen."[6]

The vogue for burlesque movies extended to black companies as well. In 1949, William Alexander, who would later produce blaxploitation films, directed the first full-length black burlesque movie, *Burlesque in Harlem*. Aimed at both inner-city black markets and white markets, *Burlesque in Harlem* strove to capture on film the variety entertainment of nightclubs in the Harlem Renaissance. *Burlesque in Harlem* starred the comic Pigmeat Markham and his "Markham Dancer" tappers, and alternated exotic strippers such as the "Atomic Bomb" Gloria Howard and a Josephine Baker–ish performer named Princess with comic strippers.[7]

In some of its acts, *Burlesque in Harlem* merely translated white burlesque numbers to a black idiom. One black dancer shuffled and shimmied across the stage wearing hot pants and a short skirt, while another vogued in an Apache duet with slow music and old-fashioned costumes. In a comic routine about the everyday trials of marriage, the wife stripped while the husband wondered aloud why she no longer wanted to make love to him. But *Burlesque in Harlem* also exploited parody in striptease in a way rarely seen in white burlesque. The penultimate number featured the "lovely" Gertrude "Baby" Banks stripping to a fractured version of the smoky Duke Ellington version of Cole Porter's ballad "Night and Day." But the last number both parodied Banks's glamorous sensuality and threw audiences back to the Old Mammy stereotype from minstrel shows. In the song's final moments, as the lyrics swooned, straight woman Mabel Hunter, a hefty comic, sang "Doin' the Best I Can" and stripped to polka-dotted shorts and top.

Earlier in the show, Hunter, then in an evening gown, had talked about how she loved all men. Now she greeted the audience with similar frankness. Referring to the fact that she could never be as lovely as Gertrude Banks, she entered and said, "Hello boys, I'm just doin' the best that I can." Then she dove into a shimmy until she finally turned around to show the audience a sign on her behind: "That's all."[8]

IN THE SAME ERA, drag striptease, more public and more vehement than in previous generations, changed and reidentified its audience. Drag strip-tease flourished in the burlesque theaters and nightclubs that reappeared after World War II, when gay men and women returned from overseas and participated more openly in the nightlife of American cities. Strip bars and nightclubs became places for lesbians and gay men to hang out, along-side straight people. A demand for female impersonators first became pub-licly visible in 1939 in Miami, where straight and gay audiences of both sexes congregated at Danny's Jewel Box on Collins Avenue. Run by Danny Brown and Doc Brenner, a team billing themselves as "boy-ological ex-perts," the Jewel Box strove for glamour.[9]

Brown and Brenner's touring drag show—the *Jewel Box Revue*—swept across the United States and Canada performing campy versions of *Ziegfeld Follies* numbers in drag. The singer Rae Bourbon did his drag burlesque, modeling one number after Gypsy's "Stripteaser's Education."[10] Before Jim Crow laws were overturned in the South, drag clubs there welcomed the kind of black and white drag striptease the *Jewel Box Revue* produced; thus Storme de Laverie, a black woman, emceed in butch drag to intro-duce the various acts.

In Seattle the gay community flocked to the Garden of Allah nightclub, which was located in a tawdry downtown area near peep shows and pawn-brokers. The Garden of Allah was decorated to resemble the Casbah, with white pillars in front of the building and blue and pink lights inside, as well as a Wurlitzer organ. Striptease at the Garden of Allah was flamboyant and expressive, and, as in many straight strip bars of the era, performers dressed as cowgirls, dames, or ingenues offered a nascent form of lap dancing.[11]

In New York, whereas LaGuardia had outlawed female impersonators along with strippers during the Depression, they now performed at the 82 Club at East Fourth Street and Second Avenue. Many in this generation of "glamour" drag strippers cited training in thirties burlesque as being the foundation for their acts. "It's one thing to work nude against a bunch of impersonators, and seem like a real woman. But when you're performing on a stage with the genuine article . . . you have to be faultless," one drag artist said.[12]

Skippy la Rue, a drag headliner, described the tactics he used while stripping "down to nothing." "We'd wear a panel of cloth around our shoul-ders which hung down so us boys could partially cover our small breasts and fake it. In these strip numbers makeup does a lot and you are moving so fast that the customers don't know what is going on."[13] Stealing lines from Gypsy or Sophie Tucker, performers like Skippy both paid homage to and ridiculed femininity.

Like female strippers, each drag artist developed his own style. Ricky Renee began in a silver bra, which, after taking it off, he held to his chest to disguise the absence of breasts. He stripped down to a silver G-string with a question mark on the front. Another female impersonator of this era wore only a transparent cape. The drag strippers paid homage to female entertainers, voguing and stripping to—and sometimes lip synching—pop numbers such as "Let Me Entertain You," "The Stripper," "Song of India," "Dawn on the Desert," and "In a Persian Market."[14]

*Focus* magazine reported that Harold Minsky would hire Christine Jorgensen, the first celebrity transsexual, to strip at the Minsky Adams. Jorgensen was not the first person to seek gender reassignment when she went under the knife in Denmark in 1952, but for millions of newspaper readers in the United States, she might as well have been. Her transformation made international headlines, and for decades she was the best-known transgendered person in the world. Had she agreed to take it off for the Minskys, she might have saved burlesque. (Jorgensen did sing at nightclubs around the country, as well as at the Dunes in Las Vegas.[15])

But Jorgensen's association with burlesque revealed how in this era striptease was linked to deviance. One rumor claimed Jorgensen did a striptease for the young Woolworth scion Jimmy Donohue in his penthouse apartment.[16] Indeed, until the end of the decade, drag bars and nightclubs remained connected to the underworld. At the same time, these bars, as well as burlesque theaters, continued to function as "safe houses" for gay men and women until the early 1960s. Lillian Faderman, later known as a gay historian, did a Lili St. Cyr–style bubble bath number at Big Al's Hotsy Totsy club in San Francisco in 1959. About a year later, while still a college student at Berkeley—albeit one living with her female lover—she went to work as the burlesque stripper Mink Lust at San Francisco's President Follies.[17]

A LESS-ELEVATED venue for striptease was the carnival, which first became financially successful during the Depression. In 1936 more than three hundred shows were in operation, and the only problem critics saw was how producers would divide up the territory. The carnival became a popular venue for striptease in the early forties. The carnival of this era, typically housing a burlesque show, brought strippers and girl shows to rural towns.

Back in 1933, Sally Rand had proven that nude women were indispensable to world's fairs. In the early forties, no carnival producer dared be without a girl show. While urban purity campaigners had prevented the barker from doing his work in front of burlesque shows, at the carnival, he stood outside the tent and sell the show in flamboyant language.[18] Typical pitches treated the audience as sophisticated, modern men: "If you're a broad-minded person, if you're living in the 20th century, the girls will give you the show, and I mean they'll give it to you just the way you want it. It's burlesque as you like it: red-hot, spicy, saucy, sizzling, burlesque entertainment. Get tickets, go now."[19] Or, as another barker announced:

Next comes princess Ila
Every muscle, every fiber, every tissue from the top of
Her head down to the very tips of those
Terpsichorean toes
Will move, throb, quiver, pulsate, vibrate just like a bowl full of jelly in
a Greek restaurant on a frosty morning
This is the show, gentlemen, that makes the old men young and the
young men dizzy.[20]

After the war, when rationing of coal, sugar, and gas ended and trains again began providing reliable transportation, the carnival exploded. When the Hirst circuit floundered, unemployed burlesque headliners began performing in carnivals, where even though they had to do ten to twelve shows a day, they could work for twenty-eight or thirty weeks straight. Taking it off for wide-eyed American country folk differed from an "elegant" nightclub peeler's revealing her semi-nakedness to middle-class customers and minor celebrities. As Sally Rand put it, "Not everyone can be a successful carnival draw. Someone who is successful at 21 may be a bomb at the carnival. You have to love the every day person."[21]

Before the war, the carnival striptease was sometimes more pornographic than burlesque. Its origins included the disreputable "turkey" tent show, one of burlesque's predecessors. At the carnival the oldest "canvas" or tent contained the girlie show—the thinnest membrane separating the strippers from the audience.[22] In the previous century, carnivals had housed itinerant variety shows, animals, freaks, and agricultural contests. Carnivals had always been the home of cons and scams, and this was true of the girlie shows as well as the midway games. In a typical scenario, a spieler promised that one of the carnival "girls" would be auctioned off to the highest bidder, who would win a "dinner date" with her. The "suckers," anticipating a delicious evening, were delighted when the girls suggested that they board their special train, since there was usually no place to go in the small towns. Once aboard, the suckers were further delighted by being taken to the "privilege car," where they could order drinks and play cards. At midnight, when the suckers began to get suspicious, some of the men in the show would stage a fake raid; claiming to be railroad detectives, they ordered the strangers off the train. The suckers went home and the girls went wearily to bed.

After the war, the prevalence of cons continued to give carnivals a seedy reputation. But by the late forties, the highest-end carnivals hired "refined" strippers such as Gypsy, Sally Rand, Sherry Britton, Faith Bacon, and Georgia Sothern, who drew enormous crowds and made piles of money. Harry Hennies, of the Hennies Sideshow, hired Rand to "improve quality." At the Hennie's Sideshow at the Des Moines Fair in 1947, Sally Rand attracted almost 11,000 patrons. At the Minneapolis State Farm Fair in 1949, a record 800,000 people came to see "Sally Rand and Gypsy Rose Lee with their emphasis on s.a."—sex appeal. *Carnival* magazine published state-by-state limits for undressing. "This is as far as you can go in Kansas," advised a handy editorial, complete with pictures.[23]

Influenced by the circus and the nightclub, carnival strip acts also paid attention to the injunctions against nudity that had demolished burlesque. Diane Ross, not to be confused with Diana Ross, the singer, did a striptease act in which her two monkeys, Tweaky and Squeaky, took off her clothes. She varied this by sometimes taking off her clothes while the monkeys took off theirs.[24] But even such attempts to be good could not prevent burlesque strippers from sometimes tangling with the authorities. In Minneapolis the 4-H club objected to girl shows at the state fair, but the management insisted on hiring Sally Rand, as she earned more money than any other act.[25] A similar situation arose in 1951 at the Missouri State Fair, where the governor stepped in to defend Rand from reformers. Georgia Sothern took off too much in a carnival outside of Wilmington, as did Evelyn West in Des Moines, inspiring Democratic Party leaders to describe the Wilmington act as "nudity run riot."[26]

The rise in carnival girl shows made attendance at regional burlesque houses falter. In Columbus the Gayety waited until the carnival left to reopen for the fall.[27] For some strippers, though, the carnival offered steady employment in the summer, when burlesque theaters closed. Gypsy Rose Lee spent the 1949 season with the respectable Royal American Carnival, which described itself as "a slice of Broadway" en route to rural America. Gypsy did her striptease act ten to fourteen times a day, including her own "girl show," composed of about twenty women. She made $125,000 that year, in part because she was able to attract female audience members.[28] A few years later, Evelyn West performed on the Amusement Corporation of America midway and also drew record crowds. These success stories notwithstanding, overall, carnival striptease could not escape its seedy past. Some strippers performed topless and others removed all of their clothes. Pitch artists began to dredge up contests such as "the battle of the strippers" to draw in patrons. According to the circus producer A. W. Stencell, the pole dance—a mainstay of today's strip clubs—started under the big top.[29]

THE ADVENT OF television further challenged striptease. For one, the lure of the small screen made it more difficult to get Americans to leave their houses. But also, the heads of most networks failed to consider striptease a good form of entertainment for such a "family-oriented" medium. In 1948, CBS had "faded out" Gypsy because her costumes were deemed unfit for a Christmas pageant. Although Edward R. Murrow would let her onto his show in 1957 to promote her memoir, in general, executives at major networks remained reluctant to program burlesque strippers.[30]

Television's most powerful role in the history of striptease was as a tool for reformers seeking to eradicate it. In 1950 the Tennessee senator Estes Kefauver and the Kefauver Commission traveled across the country investigating political corruption's connection with the mob. Kefauver visited Dallas, Miami, Chicago, Cleveland, and other midsize cities. The results, broadcast live on national television during the spring of 1951, exposed the connection between strip bars and Mafia kingpins. In New York, Kefauver focused on Irving Klaw, the "movie still monarch," known for photographing pinup girl Bettie Page. In the Midwest, Kefauver targeted burlesque bars, which moved tiny runways where dancers shimmied from behind the bar to about two feet away from the customers.[31] (These burlesque bars advanced stripping toward contemporary lap dancing.)

Still, hundreds of small-time gaudy strip clubs and show bars in the hinterlands continued to present striptease. These clubs, with slick, blazing names like the Top Rail or the High Hat, were often brothels posing as strip joints.

Curtain call of burlesque performers at the L & L Cafe, Chicago (date unknown). Chicago Historical Society.

Here the bar girls, or B-Girls, as they were called, spent most of their time urging customers to drink—for which they received a one-third cut on over-priced items such as two-hundred-dollar bottles of champagne.

Widespread in the Midwest, burlesque bars centered in Chicago on West Madison Street near Haymarket Square. Miles west, in Calumet City, or "Cal City," as it was known, they were a major industry. As nightlife columnists Jack Lait and Lee Mortimer put it, in an industrial wasteland, these bars "made striptease wholesale."[32] A police list from the era names Cal City as home to a fifth of the major burlesque bars of the era. The syndicated columnist Earl Wilson noted that you could see striptease at 11 A.M. there if you wanted to. Indeed, the burlesque bar achieved popularity in Cal City because of that town's longevity as a vice district. Cal City's biggest draw became "continuous action" clubs such as the Rip Tide, the Rainbow, the Ron-da-voo, the 21 Club, the PlayHouse, and the Zig Zag, known for the way the shows were staggered to allow customers to "zig-zag" from one to another.[33]

These often vile clubs provided gambling and drinking in the form of a "set up," an expensive ice-and-mix combination for men who brought their own booze. To that cocktail, Calumet City added the champagne girl—a version of the B-girl whose job was to get men to drink $18.50 bottles of champagne the clubs purchased for $1.50.[34]

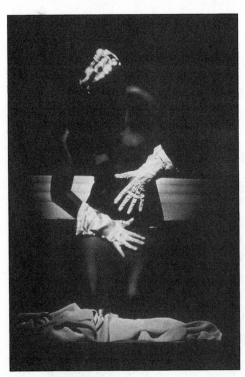

In Cal City, the cheap and tawdry strip acts verged on sex shows. In "The Devil and the Virgin," the "virgin" undressed, coerced by a devil in white tie and tails. Cal City's most decadent act was a stripper named Roszina's "Beauty and the Beast" number. She began wearing a gorilla costume on one side of her body and a strip outfit on the other. As the music got wilder, the "gorilla" would rip the strip costume from the stripper's body. The lights faded with the "gorilla" on top of the "stripper."[35]

Since 1941, Cal City reformers had tried to get the strippers to keep on their bras and G-strings, to no avail. The columnist Robert C. Ruark summed up the town's gold rush cli-

Nude burlesque performer: "Beauty and the Beast" number, West Madison Street nightclub. Chicago Historical Society.

mate at the end of the forties: "A wave of righteousness swept the city but Rush Street and its Strip Row components went on doing business."[36] In 1954 the American Guild of Variety Artists would put Cal City on the "unfair" list—the list of places that flouted union standards. Still, the clubs stayed open and some strippers continued to perform there.[37]

CONCERN OVER THE RISE of such tawdry entertainments was in part responsible for the crackdown on striptease in the upscale world of nightclubs. In October 1951, Lili St. Cyr headlined at Ciro's, following a short stint at the *Follies*. In both venues, St. Cyr performed "An Interlude before Evening"—her bathtub strip. The set, as always, was lavish. The interior designer, Tom Douglas, lent St. Cyr a statue that belonged to Carole Lombard. The bathtub, according to Douglas, was made of pure silver and had once belonged to Empress Josephine. St. Cyr's costumes were by the Hollywood clothier Marusia, and her hats by the society milliner Keneth Hopkins.[38]

On October 18, the police, unimpressed by St. Cyr's accoutrements, raided Ciro's and arrested the woman billed as "the best dressed undressed lady in theatre" for indecent exposure.[39] This was not an isolated incident, but rather the result of a broad, West Coast attempt to eliminate striptease. A few months earlier, the police had closed Strip City and LA county officials had slapped a countywide ban on striptease. At the time of St. Cyr's arrest, Lillian Hunt, the general manager of the L.A. Follies, was serving six months in prison.[40]

St. Cyr, however, fought back. She hired the celebrity attorney Jerry Giesler, who had successfully defended Charlie Chaplin against charges of violating the Mann Act and Errol Flynn against charges of statutory rape.[41] Before and during the trial, Giesler's strategy was to ridicule the prosecution as prudes while declaring St. Cyr to be practicing that great American endeavor—"free enterprise." Giesler first toyed with the idea of getting St. Cyr a jury of her peers. To him, that meant a jury of twelve strippers. That effort failed, although Giesler did manage to get a majority of women on the jury. His real aim, as he reveals in his autobiography was to distinguish between St. Cyr's "art" and lewd striptease. "I can honestly say I succeeded in having her case laughed into a not-guilty verdict," he writes.[42]

The trial began on December 6. In the courtroom, Giesler humiliated the policeman who made the arrest by establishing that he did not even know the difference between bumping and grinding or between a half bump and a full one. Then he put portly Herman Hover, Ciro's owner, on the stand and asked him to define the terms for the jury. Hover settled the confusion. "A bump is a pelvic propulsion," he said. The entire courtroom roared with laughter.[43] Next, Giesler drew a complicated diagram on a chalkboard to show the jury where in the club St. Cyr had stood, where the audience had sat, and where she had removed her clothes. He also drew where the maid who assisted St. Cyr with her clothes had blocked her from audience view.

Giesler introduced a bra and G-string as exhibits A and B. When the prosecution accused St. Cyr of letting her towel slip and revealing her naked body, St. Cyr replied that she was wearing exhibits A and A "throughout." The jury was delighted. Finally, Giesler got St. Cyr to play her trump card. She volunteered to "take a bath" in the courtroom so that members of the jury could see that it was impossible to see her body behind the towel. The judge politely denied her wish. "If it was merely a matter of her exposing her body, she didn't have to invest twelve thousand dollars in stage settings," said Giesler."

Two months after the jury acquitted St. Cyr, *Look* magazine ran a photo spread on her. "Lili St. Cyr, probably the most stylish of the current crop of strippers, takes off with modesty and aplomb," a caption underneath a picture of St. Cyr in a ball gown read. Less than a year later, she headlined in Vegas opposite Joel Grey.[44]

# Striptease Confidential

On tour in Europe in 1952, Gypsy Rose Lee struck a familiar theme when she remarked in her journal that striptease had become more difficult to perform since women on the street were now wearing less than she did on stage. "Audiences watch me with their mouths wide open, but not longing for me. . . . [T]hey seem to be saying 'we show more than this on the beach.' And indeed, with nude sunbathing, they certainly do."[1] But audiences' fatigue with striptease revolved around more than the diminishing proportions of everyday wear. Times were changing. The journalist Albert Goldman described "old fashioned burlesque" as "too leisurely and roundabout" for the modern man. "The elaborate production numbers with eight leopard skinned broads playing off between the top and the bottom banana . . . the whole big deal with the feature strippers and their arty dance acts got to be too goddamned much."[2]

Although Gypsy still did more or less the same act she had in 1936, few other performers could afford that luxury.[3] In the South and the West, a flamboyant striptease was emerging. The woman epitomizing this style was Tempest Storm. Beginning in the early 1950s at the Follies Theater and the El Rey in Oakland, Storm stripped and did highly exaggerated bumps and grinds. Journalists described her as "a force of nature," as they had Ann Corio in the 1930s, but here the phrase was meant to be even less glamorous and more parodic. "The 'Storm' Returns," one of Storm's posters read. Storm wore a leopard-print bra in pinup photos and even considered recording an album, which she wanted to call *Stormy Weather*.[4]

Born Annie Blanche Banks in Appalachia in 1928, Storm escaped into stripping from a turbulent home life. She fled an abusive father at age sixteen and, after a few years' worth of detours and marriages, came to Los Angeles after the war. She first stripped at the Follies Theater at the end of 1951, under the name Stormy Dan. Quickly, she changed it to Tempest Storm. In keeping with the national trend of "oversized" strippers, Storm's appeal relied less on grace or charm than on her dimensions. A 1955 *Playboy* pictorial, "Tempest in a C-Cup," did exactly that.[5]

Agents had advertised strippers as larger-than-life since burlesque's beginnings. But Storm, the first to advance through the size of her breasts, anticipated the advent of modern hard-core pornography.[6] Storm and her managers and agents invoked various strategies to promote her breasts, including the old stunt of insuring them for a million dollars, which she enhanced by making a plaster cast of her torso, an exercise reporters caught on film. In 1956 some publicists and Hollywood gossip columnists invented the Mickey Awards, which they named after burlesque comedian and stripper aficionado Mickey Rooney. Storm received the award given to "the stripper with the best props." Escorted by Jerry Lewis and Dean Martin, she accepted the award on national television. According to Storm, she could hardly get a word in edgewise since Lewis and Martin cracked one joke after another about her breasts. But as she put it, being made fun of on national television didn't faze her. It helped make her a star.[7]

Storm's performances at nightclubs followed similar lines. The same year as the *Playboy* pictorial, she updated Norman Bel Geddes' Crystal Palace exhibit from the 1939 World's Fair at Mr. Bimbo's 365 Nightclub in San Francisco. The gimmick this time around was that a nude girl could be projected, via mirrors, from a downstairs stage, into a fishbowl ensconced in the club's cocktail bar. She would wink and wave to the customers. Part of the appeal was the question asked by radio and TV announcers: Would Tempest Storm fit into the tiny fishbowl? When Mr. Bimbo "cast" Storm, he capitalized on this idea.[8]

Tempest Storm preparing for her fishbowl number, Mr. Bimbo's 365 Nightclub, San Francisco, c. 1955. Author's personal collection.

And yet, to at least some of her fans, Storm projected more than just bawd onstage. Having seen her in Miami in the 1960s, the writer Foster Hirsch recalled: "She was not funny at all. She was stately." She brandished the costume and props of thirties striptease like armor. "She merges voluptuousness with simplicity," said Harold Minsky.[9] Other journalists, though, described her as "animalistic."[10]

It's also worth mentioning that Storm performed onstage with black jazz musicians, an activity that in the late 1950s remained taboo. As in other areas of show business, the color line had been eroding in burlesque since the 1920s, but it still existed. In 1959, Storm married the jazz singer and actor Herb Jeffries, a former front man for Duke Ellington, and musicians such as the Delta Rhythm Boys, Pearl Bailey, and Nancy Wilson became her colleagues. In one of her most memorable numbers, Storm did a playful strip to Jeffries' rendition of the 1924 Gershwin standard "Oh Lady, Be Good."[11]

Storm defined postwar striptease by being a naughty but nice girl, as well as by her physical appeal. At a moment when Hollywood was making glorious pumped-up epics such as *Spartacus*, burlesque was promoting pumped-up striptease, celebrating size as if doing so could liberate Americans from the constraints of Freudian repression. Straining for originality, striptease of this era turned excess and size into a virtue by sending up the burlesque acts of earlier decades. Size also suggested excessive sexual appetite and the fantasy of sexual appetite. Strippers of this era, America's forbidden fruit, became a symbol for the agonized corked libidos of the Cold War. Many strippers capitalized on the vogue for size. Virginia "Ding Dong" Bell, "Miss 48-24-36," made nudie-cutie movies and did a cowboy striptease. Evelyn West, "the Girl with the $50,000 Chest," had, Walter Winchell said, "the most eye poppin' act." Earl Wilson said about her, "[S]eein' is believing."[12]

A vogue for "chaste" striptease went hand in hand with the arrival of these superwomen. Martin Collyer described West as looking akin to a "virgin from early Rodgers and Hammerstein musicals." At the Wedge, a Philadelphia nightclub, Julie Gibson performed "The Bashful Bride," a striptease number reminiscent of turn-of-the-century burlesque. *Esquire*—one of the champions of this trend—wrote, "She emerged coming downstairs . . . in a sequence of emotions, shyness alternating with abandon." The article noted that not all strippers were "on leave from Miss Farthingale's Finishing School." Gibson's demure strip, performed for her "theoretical" husband, attracted not just ardent fans, but police attention. The Philadelphia police raided the Wedge shortly after the *Esquire* story appeared.[13]

At the same time, a version of American striptease flourished in Paris. Visiting Europe in those years, Harold Minsky said, "Europe is one big striptease. Hamburg looks like 52nd Street in the wild days; Paris one strip joint after another."[14] In the City of Light, striptease seemed to acquire special significance. As Denys Chevalier would put it, by the end of the decade, "striptease had conquered the city."[15]

In Paris, the haute, soigné character of striptease distinguished it from its sassy, bare-all, occasionally bargain-basement American counterpart. The founder of the Crazy Horse, Alain Bernadin, recounted how in the thirties, he had toured America in search of striptease acts, but never found anything he could fit into the Crazy Horse.[16] This was a kind of French snobbery. If on the surface French striptease borrowed from performers like Lili St. Cyr, it quickly superseded these performers and drew more from the music hall than American burlesque.

French striptease gave birth to, among others, the slyly named Dodo d'Homberg, Jenny Boston, and Rita Cadillac, all of whom did complicated, highly produced, funny, sexy numbers. In one of her most famous boudoir acts, set in an 1880s Arizona honky-tonk, Cadillac removed her white corset with green polka dots and her black tulle gloves with an agonizing slowness that, according to Charvil, inspired total silence in the theater.[17] Known in Paris as the "tragedian of strippers," the French noir actress and nude model Rita Renoir, who had also acted in plays by Corneille, did "A Curtain Named Desire," a number that she based on Tennessee Williams's play. "Striptease, for me, is a combination of mime and dance. You have to have a reason to take it off," she told *Le Figaro*. Dodo d'Homberg did a Groucho Marx–style act in which she began in a long, leopard-skin coat and nerdy glasses. In Nice, at the Trois Cloches nightclub, the owners experimented with numbers in which a prize was given to the audience member who undressed the stripper in the speediest fashion.[18]

It's worth noting that unlike many American performers, French strippers did cross over into legitimate entertainment in France. Rita Cadillac went on to strip in films, and work in operas. She also recorded witty, racy cabaret songs such as "Don't Count on Me to Show Myself Totally Nude." But more remarkable than the ease with which French striptease crept into French society is that, as with all things they find taboo, the French made striptease the subject of institutional inquiry. On March 2, 1955, the Académie du Striptease, an organization whose purpose was to promote and disseminate information about the genre to the eager public, was founded. Less than two weeks later, the Academie, headed by the French artist and president of the Institut de France Edmond Heuze, held a contest for the first time at the Café Ambassadeurs on the Champs Élysées. In remarks to the press, Heuze, epitomizing the French reverence for conflating the aesthetic and the erotic, characterized striptease as "spiritual" and "chaste."[19] Other members of the jury included the ex-police commissioner Jean Baylot and Maurice Chevalier. An eighteen-year-old Polish stripper won the contest.

The creation of the academy was just the beginning of the French's interest in elevating striptease to a classical art. By the end of the decade, works by acclaimed scholars sought to describe striptease as the archetype in female desire and an act of the female imagination. The first of these, Roland Barthes' 1957 essay "Le Striptease," honors a popular culture phenomena as though it were a painting by Renoir. "Striptease is based on a contradiction: woman is desexualized at the very moment when she is stripped naked," Barthes observed, going on to describe other aspects of the strip, such as the G-string, in similarly elevated prose. "This ultimate triangle, by its pure and geometric form, by its brilliant and hard material, brandishes sex like a pure sword and reimagines the woman in a mineralogical universe, the precious stone being here the irrefutable theme of the total and unuseful object."[20]

Barthes' essay could describe American striptease, as well. Subsequently, when other French intellectuals turned their attention to striptease, they treated it as though it were a cultural phenomenon on the level of the invention of the beret. They paid less attention to striptease's shocking quality and more to the feminine imagination and the libido. With titles such as *Histoire et Philosophe du Striptease*, *Métaphysique du Striptease*, and *Histoire et Sociologie du Striptease*, these books drew on Georges Bataille, Descartes, Kierkegaard, Nietzsche, and Karl Marx, to connect striptease to developments in literary theory and philosophy. Denys Chevalier wrote that striptease presents nothing less than a "universal feminine ideal."[21] Even Umberto Eco chimed in, writing about Marxism and the Crazy Horse and claiming that striptease "oppressed" the proletarian spectator, who, after a semi-"cathartic" experience, returned unsatisfied to his everyday existence.[22]

BACK IN AMERICA, sans philosophers, striptease continued to flourish in Miami Beach, where, as Lenny Bruce put it, "neon goes to die," in a few lavish supper clubs such as Ciro's and the Paddock, as well as in dozens of "low-down" strip clubs. Despite waves of arrests and crackdowns, Miami, a destination for pleasure-seeking Americans, remained a home to strippers fleeing New York.[23] In 1956 the city featured twenty nightclubs ranging from the Red Barn, which was actually a termite-riddled old farm building redone for show purposes, to the Five O'Clock, a smart night club where a few years earlier Martha Raye was both headliner and partner. "Miss Widemouth" moved to the more lucrative field of television, and the strip industry took over. Between these extremes, such clubs as the Rainbow Inn, the Gaiety, the Place Pigalle, the Paper Doll, and the Jungle Club featured "name" headliners such as Brandy Martin and Dixie Evans, and provided opportunities for the newcomers in the trade. At the Paper Doll, Bonnie Bell, "the Ding Dong Girl," attached bells to her breasts, and *Cabaret*

Tampa Striptease Club, c. 1950. Kinsey Institute for Research in Sex, Gender, and
Reproduction.

magazine noted that Jeanne Delta did a torrid dance that "begins on stage
. . . [and] almost ends in a patron's lap."[24]

A hundred miles north, at the Two O'Clock Club in Baltimore, a city
Murray Kempton once described as "Philadelphia, with Sodom," hired strippers whose acts projected a glittering, tawdry spectacle.[25] In 1952 thirteen
"cabarets" existed on "the Block," which stretched to three blocks of tattoo
parlors, penny arcades, burlesque shows, and commercial vice on Baltimore Street, a waterfront drag. The Block first attracted national attention
two years later in an *Esquire* article about the Two O'Clock. The article,
titled "B-Belles of Burlesque: You Get Strip Tease with Your Beer in Baltimore," described the strippers at the Two O'Clock as if they were equal
parts farm girl and starlet. *Esquire* singled out Blaze Starr as "one of the
current sensations. . . . [U]nder the fresh and plump skin she is really the
girl next door, putting on an act while the folks are away."[26]

Starr was hardly the only attraction on the Block, though. Run by John
Hon Nickels, another strip joint on the Block, the Gayety Nightclub—née
the Gayety Theater, also endured. Designed by the theater design firm J. B.
McElfatrick and Sons in the teens, the Gayety, through its baroque and art
nouveau ornament, announced the pulchrutide inside. The façade displayed
male and female figures bearing the name of the theater and two large
breasts. Down the street, two other clubs—the Clover and the Globe—
offered, as one Baltimorean put it, the "meanest, most low down burlesque
in the world." The Oasis, which advertised itself as the "worst" nightclub in
the world, featured a mural of undressed houris on the ceiling.[27]

But the Two O'Clock remained the undisputed king of the Block. It opened in 1936 but did not achieve national notoriety until 1953, when Starr began to perform there at age fifteen. She had arrived in Baltimore from the Appalachian Mountains via Quantico and Washington, D.C. One of eleven children, she was dirt poor. Her family lived in a one-room shack. She went to school until eighth grade and then left home. She got a job at a doughnut shop in Washington, which is where she worked until someone told her she could make it in show business. In her first act, at the Quonset Hut, she stripped as a cowgirl.[28]

According to Sol Goodman, the Two O'Clock's manager, Starr walked in off the street in 1953 and asked for a job. As Thomas Morgan would later paint her in a memorable *Esquire* profile, the young stripper's bouffant hair and zaftig figure made her heart-shaped face look tiny and, more important, made her seem tall. Reporters sometimes described her as looking Indian because of her cheekbones. But what really made her act was the way she danced. The *New York Herald Tribune* wrote, "The motif of her performance seems to be self-adulation and her claim to distinction certain muscular controls, but the total effect is of a routine carried through with deadpan precision."[29]

In part thanks to Starr's "muscular controls" and "deadpan precision," from 1953 until 1969, the Two O'Clock Club, with its Chicago-style "burlesque bar," drew a national audience to Baltimore's Block. Goodman imported national headlining strippers such as Pat "Amber" Halliday, Zorita, and Libby Jones. Goodman also got Starr's sisters to work there, although they never became as big as "the Queen of Burlesque" herself.

Starr became Baltimore's mascot. She posed on a swing in a Baltimore hotel room during Preakness Week wearing a cape, two daisies, and a G-string. She bought a house, which she called "Bella's Little Acre," in the posh suburb of Villa Nova. She decorated it in purple silk and white shag. She toured. "The human heat wave" was in demand. According to her memoir, in the mid-fifties, she had an affair with Frank Rizzo, then a crusading police captain in Philadelphia and later its mayor. Enamored of backroom brawls and wily dames, Rizzo, then known as the "Cisco Kid," fell for the stripper, whose panther act he saw at the Black Cat Cafe. Apparently, he liked the part where her writhings were so sensual that they "set" the stage furniture on fire. Having arrested her, Rizzo carried on with her while his wife languished in the suburbs.[30]

Back in Baltimore, Starr made history in the Two O'Clock Club, which, like many similar clubs, comprised two small rooms. To get to the club, customers descended one flight, as if they were going to one of the circles of hell. In the first room, they could watch TV in an early version of a sports bar. The second room, dominated by a big horseshoe bar, was where the strip show took place. As Morgan describes it, a "runway shaped like a flat propeller" splayed out from a curtain to the audience. Behind the curtain sat the black musicians, playing "stripper" versions of blues and jazz standards.[31]

Among the most outrageous celebrity stripper of this era, Starr recycled one or two acts for her entire career. Like Tempest Storm's, her acts circled around the ideas of heat and tease. She did her first number of the evening after all of the other "walk-around" strippers, as they were known, had finished—sometimes there were as many as seven of these. In the number Morgan describes—the classic number, the one Starr did to woo Earl Long later in New Orleans—she emerged from backstage wearing a gown and cape of "Somalian" leopard skin and holding a single rose and a long, gold cigarette lighter. The set contained a long red couch, three electric candles, and a lamppost/street sign instrucing the audience that it was now on Passion Street.

Starr had sewn the cape so that the leopard's paws clasped her behind. After strutting up and down the runway, she discarded it, turned on the electric candles, and strutted some more, with the rose in her mouth, like Carmen. She bit the rose in half and threw half of it to an adoring fan. She bared one breast and flicked some stray rose petals onto them; they bounced into the audience as well.

Starr stripped further to a black garter belt and bra and commanded a willing member of the audience to "powder her butt." The music sped up. At this point, Starr would use different songs from the top-forty chart, depending on what was popular at the moment. One she played while being powdered was "That's My Desire."[32]

> That's My Desire
> To spend one night with you, in our old rendezvous,
> And reminisce with you
> That's my desire.

Reclining on the couch, Starr crowed "suf-f-fer" to the audience. When powder flew around her body, she shrieked, "That's not dust . . . it's r-r-r-ust!" After various other acrobatics, Starr deployed her secret weapon: she pushed a button that made smoke rise, apparently from between her legs, and pieces of red lingerie wave like flames. Starr pretended to blow out the electric candles. As she exited wearing a sheer baby doll nightie, she teased, in a dim echo of Gypsy Rose Lee, "We must keep covered and be a lady all the time."[33] The drummer went wild.

After her act, in show biz tradition, Starr got dressed and came out to work the room. She would circulate, now talking to visiting conventioneers, now talking to locals. She was a celebrity and aimed to please. (It was later rumored that Baltimore native Spiro Agnew frequented the Two O'Clock after he became Baltimore county executive in 1962.[34])

AROUND THE TIME of Starr's rise, the sexual zeitgeist was changing again. One milestone came in 1953, after Alfred A. Knopf published Alfred Kinsey's second volume on sexuality, *Sexual Behavior in the Human Female*. Describing sex as it was—not as it should be—the first volume, *Sexual Behavior in the Human Male*, had become a best-seller and created a firestorm. In a few weeks, the second volume sold two hundred thousand copies and scandalized reformers, the public, and other scientists. J. Edgar Hoover opened a file on Kinsey. One aspect of the book that bothered many Americans was that Kinsey documented women masturbating and having affairs and orgasms, as well as premarital and extramarital sex. Even more provocative was that Kinsey, having interviewed more than five thousand women, concluded that women who had come of age during the twenties were more promiscuous than those who were born before 1900. The coup de grâce, though, was the way that Kinsey demolished stereotypes of female sexuality. For example, he described a nymphomaniac, who prior to this would have been regarded as demented, as "a woman who has more sex than you do."[35]

After "K-day," as it was called in publishing circles, St. Cyr and other strippers became informal spokespeople for Kinsey's book, as if, by virtue of stripping, they knew more about sex than civilians. Asked about Kinsey in an interview, St. Cyr said, "People have lived by a false set of values for years, but I don't believe in hiding anything." In another interview she touted her own expertise and promoted herself as a female Kinsey: "Dr. Kinsey interviewed a 'sample' of 5,300 males to get the facts of his report,

but as many as Kinsey's whole 'sample' come to see me in a single three-performance day."[36] "Treasure Chest" Evelyn West wrote articles for men's magazines and for her own pitch books, sold in theaters where she performed. She claimed that these told "how I feel about sex"—the idea being that since she took off her clothes in public, she should "feel" more than other people. West became a walking, talking advertisement for a new woman—one who was not afraid of sex. At the same time, when pulp

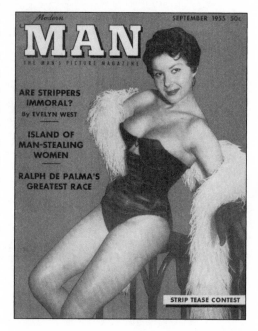

Evelyn West and her article, "Are Strippers Immoral?," on the cover of *Modern Man* magazine, September 1955. Author's personal collection.

magazines were not brandishing strippers' sexuality, they were making fun of them, even when the strippers wrote these articles themselves. "Are Strippers Immoral?" a cover story in *Modern Man* asked, next to a cheesecake photo of West herself.[37]

Strippers were able to become "sexperts" in this era in part due to the explosion of girlie magazines such as *Modern Man* after the war. All of these magazines ran pinup photographs and features of burlesque striptease stars. Founded in the late forties, *Adam, Cabaret, Modern Man*, and *Cavalcade of Burlesque* existed to titillate. *Playboy* emerged the same year as *Sexual Behavior in the Human Female*, and the magazine's demand for strippers—experts on "sexology" or no—put strippers in the public eye even as it portrayed them as silly and craven.[38]

At first glance, *Playboy* seemed to be publishing the same types of pinup photos *Esquire* had made popular in the Depression. But Hugh Hefner, who had worked for George von Rosen, the publisher of *Modern Man*, the previous year, aspired to something of greater magnitude.[39] Early on, Hefner wanted *Playboy*'s pinup photos to be fresh and wholesome, not tawdry, as other pulps' were. In the magazine's first two years, Hef did not always achieve this. As a journalist later put it, many of the playmates "displayed the bored expression and weary pose of the professional stripper."[40]

After 1955, however, the magazine did use fewer strippers and more girl-next-door types as models. Except that physically, these girls were the girl next door times ten. Pitching itself to the "beleaguered" male, *Playboy* presented having sex as a more active endeavor, and a less furtive one, than ever. In the first issue the editor's note read, "We like our apartment. We enjoy mixing up cocktails and an *hors d'oeuvre* or two, putting a little mood music on the phonograph, and inviting in a female for a quiet discussion on Picasso, Nietzsche, jazz, sex."[41]

In general, though, *Playboy* treated striptease and burlesque as an exotic, if slightly old-fashioned, pastime and one that might be dangerous. "We prefer our sex in the bedroom with nary a pig, parrot, nor panther in sight," wrote one journalist.[42] Indeed, during this era, popular culture presented the idea of aggressive female desire—which striptease often suggested—as hostile. Evan Hunter's *Blackboard Jungle* and Mickey Spillane's pulp novel *I, the Jury* both described women stripping but stopped short at the sexual act. Spillane used striptease, though, to prove his heroine was lethal. Mike Hammer, Spillane's macho private eye, kills Charlotte, the femme fatale, in the book's final pages, even after she tries to distract him with a striptease. "Charlotte unzips her skirt and lets it drop to the floor to reveal transparent panties. . . . She was completely naked now, a suntanned goddess giving herself to her lover." But Hammer is unswaying. He will still kill the stripper.[43]

Perhaps this anxiety about femmes fatales explains why so many burlesque and nightclub stripteases of this era traded the previous decade's comedy for a silent but smoldering female desire aimed to please men. In full body paint, "the Silver Goddess" did a reverse striptease, ending up fully dressed, only to undress and dress over and over again. "The Devil Made Me Do It Girl" wore a ventriloquist's dummy who invoked her to take it off as a kind of sinister joke. Other numbers celebrated the exotic. Toni Lamarr's "Dance of the Wandering Hands" combined her strip act with Balinese shadow dancing. Sheeba did a number titled as "King Solomon's Forbidden Love." Chris Owens, drawing from another kind of exotic, was touted as "the Exciting Latin Dancer with Her Maraca Girls."[44]

MEANWHILE, "BURLEY" FILM producers began to test the limits of the amount of flesh that they could reveal in road show films. Often three versions were filmed: a clothed version; a semiclothed version, in which performers wore net bras and panties; and the most risqué version, in which the strippers undressed to a merkin—a flesh colored panty with hair on the front that gave viewers the illusion that they were disrobing completely. Which one was shown would depend on the city and state.

Like burlesque shorts, feature-length road show burlesque films cost very little to make as they were essentially shot from the third row of the theater. If the films bothered with plots at all, they recycled incoherent ones with happily-ever-after endings. For example, in *A Night at the Follies* (1956), a murder provides an excuse to see undressed women backstage. Or the plots revolved around such clichés as the "heroine in trouble": examples included half-naked Cinderellas who need undressing; rich courtesans stuck in see-through bubble baths; quirky, dumbfounded B-girls forced into burlesque; and other undressed ingénues. Another standard plot was a man in quest of naked women. *The Rage of Burlesque* (1950) tells the story of a small-town boy's antics racing from one nightclub to another in search of pleasure as epitomized by the perfect striptease. In other words, these films were not cinematic masterpieces.[45] About *Teasearama* (1953), one of the best burlesque films of the era, *Variety* complained: "Virtually all routines are done on some inlaid linoleum against a background of some yard goods hung on a wall. With the exception of an occasional sofa, there are no sets or props as such."[46]

What these films lacked in ambiance and plot they made up for by staging a post-Kinsey fantasy about female erotic life. Lili St. Cyr, Tempest Storm, Bettie Page, and others announced their sexuality on film by taking off their clothes and staring at the camera, as if to suggest carnal knowledge. In the 1953 filmed version of her nightclub act, *Love Moods*, Lili St. Cyr performs her bubble bath strip while gazing straight ahead at the lens. Although she is waiting for a man, St. Cyr hardly offers a passive spectacle of female sexuality. Nor does Tempest Storm in *A Night in Hollywood*, which features the "4-d stripper," or, as she was alternately known, the "stripper with the fabulous front," guiding audiences through an evening of burlesque striptease, comedy, ragtime and jazz music, and stripping.[47]

Rotating through small towns where burlesque theaters had closed, these films supplemented strippers' incomes from nightclubs. Referring to strippers as exotic dancers, *Newsweek* observed: "The defunct burlesque theater is a pretty lively corpse, and one mushrooming byproduct of burlesque, at least, seems well-set to stay in the entertainment field. This hardy element is what the 1954 billboards call the exotic dancer." Estimates varied, but one put the number of strippers employed in nightclubs and films as high as 2,500. Indeed, although the number of burlesque theaters nationwide had dropped from 60 to 25, the number of exotic dancers had quadrupled.[48]

Since 1947, when the first burlesque short was made, many burlesque managers had joined the exploitation film industry. Lillian Hunt, manager of the El Rey in Oakland and the Follies Burlesque Theater in Los Angeles, directed about ten features and shorts; Pete DeCenzie, owner of the El Rey, made *French Peep Show*.[49] Russ Meyer, the exploitation flick maven, made one film starring Tempest Storm.

Three full-length grind house movies—*Striporama*, *Varietease*, and *Teaserama*, first released in the mid-fifties—did more to spread striptease across the country in this era than any one burlesque short. Produced and directed by Jerald Intrator and Irving Klaw, pinup girl Bettie Page's manager, *Striporama* bombards the audience with one striptease after another, plus comedy skits and songs, as well as a *National Geographic*-style narration, thanks to the exploitation filmmaker David Friedman. In *Striporama*, Page, Lili St. Cyr, Rosita Royce, and Georgia Sothern, as well as some Laurel and Hardy look-alikes, play supporting roles by revisiting an old story: three comics try to "convince" the "New York Council for Culture" at gunpoint that burlesque is a national institution and should be included in a time capsule about the era. Comics and strippers then proceed to show the council "what it would be like" by doing their ten-minute specialty numbers from the thirties and forties. At the end, burlesque triumphs.[50]

Unlike *Striporama*, *Teaserama* and *Varietease*—also directed by Klaw— were photographed in Eastman color. They also abandoned the idea of plot. With more vaudeville acts than either *Striporama* or *Teaserama*, *Varietease* featured only three strippers: Bettie Page doing a harem number ("Dance of the Four Veils"); Lili St. Cyr in "Cinderella's Love Lesson"; and Vicki Lynn, a slim female impersonator of the era, in a contest with a female stripper. After the female performer has finished, Lynn struts up and down, does a striptease, and winds up back at the table where she started. In the last moments, Lynn takes off the wig to reveal her bald head. The effect is more comic than sexy. *Teaserama* starred Tempest Storm, and Page was featured in several numbers, even appearing as Storm's maid in a "reverse strip" boudoir number. Storm gets out of bed and gets dressed, thanks to Page, who is wearing a French maid outfit. As her finale, Page imitates Storm, which causes a catfight.

Often shown in pieces between live strip acts, these movies never presented anything new. What they did was spread striptease, drag strips, and burlesque comedy to a provincial audience. In essence, they were giving these audiences what they might see in Miami, Las Vegas, or some other cosmopolitan city.

If road show striptease displayed all varieties of men and women stripping, Hollywood continued to cast strippers as gold diggers or worse. In the Warner Brothers film *She's Working Her Way Through College*, a watered-down version of the James Thurber play *The Male Animal*, Virginia Mayo played an ex–burlesque queen doing what the title said. At around the same time, in the RKO fantasy *Son of Sinbad*, produced by Howard Hughes, Lili St. Cyr does an exotic dance as the Caliph's favorite dancer. Even more extreme was the 1958 movie version of Norman Mailer's *The Naked and the Dead*, in which St. Cyr plays a selfish, cold, neurotic, sexually omnivorous stripper—a cartoon of a woman. In Mailer's book, the story of America's campaign in the Pacific reveals in the sadistic Sergeant Croft the Cold War era's anxiety about the excess of power. The movie version, directed by Raoul Walsh, with a cast including Joey Bishop, Raymond Massey, and Aldo Ray, pumped up the sex and violence considerably, partly by casting St. Cyr to play Croft's wife. Walsh added some details, though: whereas Mailer simply made the woman unfaithful, Walsh turned her into a stripper named "Lili." In the first scene, an MP raid cuts short St. Cyr's striptease. (A dream sequence in which Croft savagely bayonets her in a quasi-hallucinatory episode never appeared in the movie itself.)[51]

The theater of the day also often presented women taking off their clothes because they were "nymphomaniacs" or desperate. In 1956, William Inge's *Bus Stop* presented a woman who does a striptease because she needs to be rescued. In the film version, the role of Cherie, a hard-living grifter who takes it off out of joy and rage to appeal to the cowboy she loves, was played by Marilyn Monroe, the quintessential good-bad girl. As Cherie, Monroe brought to her striptease rough seduction and cornball antics, hayseed ritual in a noir frame.[52]

By contrast, it seemed that every foreign film streaming into the country used striptease as an erotic weapon. Brigitte Bardot's *Mademoiselle Striptease*, which was released in America in 1956, made striptease less outrageous and more about "natural" sexuality. On one level, *Mademoiselle Striptease* is nothing more than a silly melodrama. When ultrarespectable General Dumont discovers that his nubile daughter Agnes is "A.D.," author of a scandalous under-the-counter novel, he wants her shipped to a convent. But she escapes to Paris, planning to live with her brother, ostensibly a rich artist but really a poor guide in the Balzac Museum. This misunderstanding gets both in serious trouble, and puts Agnes in immediate need of money—just the amount offered as grand prize in an amateur striptease contest that her new boyfriend, reporter Daniel, is covering for his magazine.

Simone de Beauvoir explained that Brigitte Bardot differed from American strippers because she neglected to cast a spell. "Her clothes are not fetishes and, when she strips, she is not unveiling a mystery. She is showing her body, neither more nor less, and that body rarely settles into a state of immobility."[53] But Americans found Bardot's "aggressive" sexuality unsettling. The local production code board banned her in Philadelphia. The vogue for naturalness in American nudity would come a decade later, and when it did, it would be a graceless, hippie naturalness, not the chic French version. During this era, striptease competed with the rising amount of undressing in fifties Hollywood by satirizing it or by going further.

As the decade wore on, Hollywood stars continued to borrow from burlesque striptease's flamboyance. In 1955, the pneumatic Jayne Mansfield posed for publicity shots for *Will Success Spoil Rock Hunter?* in an angora bikini. Jane Russell appeared in the film *The French Line* wearing, in one Legion of Decency inspector's words, a G-string and a "rhinestone harness" revealing the "apex" of her breasts. Mansfield's costume for the 1959 film *Too Hot to Handle* was a sheer floor-length dress with a few sequins in strategic places. In that movie, an updated *Gilda*, Mansfield plays a nightclub singer singing "Too Hot to Handle." But Mansfield's face is too hard to sustain Gilda's wounded innocence. And she is not saved by anyone. Indeed, by the end of the fifties, Hollywood portrayed striptease as being both a morally corrupting force and a daily part of show business life. *Playboy* described a vogue of starlets willing to strip "to the buff" in order to make it. The offer "Would you like to be in pictures?" took on a new meaning.[54]

As Cold War paranoia in Hollywood increased, journalists linked deviance and striptease more tightly. The decade careened toward Camelot and the Sexual Revolution, and the popular press focused more than ever on public figures' personal lives, sometimes singling out strippers as sexual deviants. A part of this trend came from Walter Winchell's reign as kingmaker and reputation breaker and from the rise, in 1952, in Hollywood, of the gossip magazine *Confidential*. Tom Wolfe would later call *Confidential* "the most scandalous scandal magazine in the history of the world," dedicated to "tell[ing] the facts and name[ing] the names."[55]

During its heyday, *Confidential* brought celebrities' peccadilloes to the surface in the most lurid ways possible. A popular tale was that of the powerful man brought down by the gold digger. This tale appealed to a public hungry for scapegoats and exposés. A similar equation was at work when, on national television, Dean Martin called Tempest Storm, who claimed she had had affairs with Sinatra, Elvis, and J.F.K., "his favorite gold-digger."[56]

Another story tabloids centered on in this era involved the wiretapping of strippers' telephone lines to reveal their "deviant" habits. In the political arena, the FBI used wiretapping to "out" communists. However, as reported in the popular press, the wiretapping of strippers' telephone lines uncovered their sexually deviant lifestyles. In 1955 a jealous wife paid a private detective to tap Ann Corio's line. The incident made the tabloids when the wiretap was discovered.[57] Two years later the Dallas Police tapped Candy Barr's line, which was how they busted her for marijuana possession. None of this by itself was remarkable, and yet it heightened the atmosphere of deviance around striptease.

ON THE BURLESQUE STAGE, striptease had been borrowing from Tinseltown and vice versa since the Depression, but in the 1950s, the relationship acquired an edge.[58] Movie stars dressed in costumes that, in earlier eras, strippers might have worn, dabbled in striptease and appeared in burlesque movies.[59] In 1952, shortly before Marilyn Monroe made *The Seven Year Itch*, Dixie Evans, whom Mort Minsky had billed as the "Southern Comfort Girl," arrived at the Minsky Adams for work one day to find that she had a new billing. She was now "the Marilyn Monroe of Burlesque." The moniker caught on. For several years, Evans mimicked the movie star's glide, her gestures and facial expressions, in the nation's burlesque theaters and strip joints. Wearing a peroxide blonde wig and a pink "Seven Year Itch" dress, Evans, whom Harold Minsky once described as "the truck driver's delight more than the college man's," devoted her career to impersonating Monroe.[60]

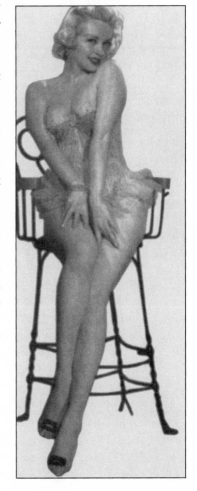

Evans revved up both Monroe's sex appeal and her humor as she "revealed" how Marilyn Monroe got into pictures.[61] In the first versions of this number, Evans strode onstage to the sentimental Nacio Herb Brown ballad "You Are My Lucky Star."

"Who, me?" she would ask.

Dixie Evans, "The Marilyn Monroe of Striptease," publicity photo, c. 1955. Author's personal collection.

The band responded, "Yes, you."[62] Movie camera in hand, Evans ran to one side of the set. As the music changed to the 1938 Johnny Mercer song that Bing Crosby made popular, "You Must Have Been a Beautiful Baby," Evans mimed giving herself a screen test.

> You must have been a beautiful baby
> You must have been a wonderful child
> When you were only starting to go to kindergarten
> I bet you drove the little boys wild.
> And when it came to winning blue ribbons
> You must have shown the other kids how.
> I can see the judges' eyes as they handed you the prize
> You must have made the cutest bow.
> You must've been a beautiful baby,
> Cause baby look at you now—

During the last lines, Evans would take off a few more items and drift center stage, where she would fall down and have a tantrum. Then she would seduce the producer's (empty) chair. The storyline went that she wanted to be a star, but the invisible producer refused her. Evans crawled to the couch and discarded a few final garments. The Sam Coslow song "Just One More Chance" would play.

> Just one more chance
> To prove it's you alone I care for
> Each night I say a little prayer for
> Just one more chance.

Evans crawled back to the producer's chair; having left her panties on the carpet, she finished the act wearing only a G-string. Unlike Lili St. Cyr, she neither played herself nor an exotic "other" like Salome. The "character" she was trying to please was not a lover, but a producer. Evans claimed to be showing the audience Hollywood's underbelly—the Marilyn no one could see while Marilyn herself was self-destructing. Evans continued to tailor her act to developments in the Blonde Bombshell's life. In 1954, when Monroe married Joe DiMaggio, Evans did a number with a dummy DiMaggio, two baseballs, and a Yankees dugout bench. After *The Prince and the Showgirl* came out in 1957, Evans traded DiMaggio in for a dummy prince. In a third act she spoofed Judy Garland singing "You Made Me Love You" to a photo of Clark Gable, and then morphed into a teenage Monroe singing to a photo of Elvis Presley. In 1958, Monroe threatened to sue Evans, but dropped the lawsuit after the stripper agreed to stop performing these acts.[63]

EVANS WAS HARDLY the only stripper to impersonate a celebrity or near-celebrity. In Vegas, Gay Dawn spoofed the Mickey Jelke case, in which the oleomargarine heir Minnot "Mickey" Jelke ran a pinup girl and prostitution ring. The case exploded in 1953, when Jelke's former girlfriend, prostitute Pat Ward, testified against him using names from her little black book, which revealed her clients—ostensibly elite New Yorkers. Eventually a jury sent Jelke to prison, and the press wrote about the case as the little guy's vindication against the wealthy.[64]

In her "Jelke" number, Dawn played Ward as a heroine. She entered brandishing a little black book, which she opened and closed as she struck a number of pinup poses. The act took thirty minutes. Here she describes the audience's disappointment when she delayed stripping to tell her story: "At first they made so much noise, I was in tears. But when I came back in the second act, they cheered," she said.[65]

While many striptease numbers ridiculed Hollywood stars or members of café society, the names many other strippers took alluded to superhuman forces like those in the scary world where scientists were experimenting with the atomic bomb in the Nevada desert. The "Shirley Temple of Burlesque" did a baby doll act complete with a rattle. After the Sonny Liston/Cassius Clay fight in 1964, two eponymous strip acts appeared.[66] Blaze Starr, Crystal Starr, Flame Fury, Electrique, the Wham Wham Girl, the Terrific Turkish Torso Twister, and the Parisian Whirlwind all intimated the uncontrollable power of the stripper's body—a physical force gone haywire. As it had with the outrageous Mae West, the popular imagination perceived these strippers to be maxed-out femmes fatales, superblonde Barbies, Rita Hayworths on steroids. With names like "Irma the Body" and Evelyn "Treasure Chest" West, some strippers broadcast their larger-than-life appeal; others, like Kim Hither and Flesh Gordon, used their names to convey seductiveness.

Some of these names resonated in gay culture. Most acknowledged the humor that emerges from sensual life. As the fifties wore on and America's role as superpower was confirmed, strippers chose names celebrating American products, including Ann Tenna, Apple Pie, Bonnie Bell, Alky Seltzer, and Peppy Cola. In 1955 the rise of rock and roll influenced and was influenced by striptease. When Elvis exploded onto the scene that year with "Don't Be Cruel," he gave teenagers everywhere an excuse to bump and grind with impunity. The *New York Times* compared Elvis's shaking, twisting body to that of a stripper. His pelvis was "a virtuoso of the hootchy-kootchy. His one specialty is an accented movement of the body that heretofore has been primarily identified with the repertoire of the blonde bombshells of the burlesque runway."[67]

Even as striptease continued to influence music, however, theatrical newspapers abandoned it. The only weekly newspaper covering striptease was *Billboard*, where Charles Feldheim, aka Uno, wrote a gossipy column called "Burlesque Bits."[68] Less than a page long, it just told the facts about who was performing where or celebrated a performer. Fewer and fewer of the big monthlies treated strippers like celebrities; more striking was white strippers' appearance in a new generation of magazines for African Americans. The postwar black migration to Northern cities created a generation of black strip clubs, and, for the most part *Jet* and *Ebony*, the new African American magazines, celebrated them.[69]

On Chicago's South Side, Joe's Deluxe Night Club offered events for black and white female impersonators, and many mixed couples danced there.[70] Every city sustained one or two all-black nightclubs featuring black strippers and jazz, such as the Club DeLisa in Chicago, the Riviera in St. Louis, and the Flame Show Bar in Detroit. In 1955, though, *Jet* noted that the racial dynamic was shifting. DeLisa was beginning to hire white strippers, whereas black ones were beginning to work downtown in the Loop's burlesque theaters.[71]

The West Coast remained a home to striptease, perhaps because its Cold War versions of the act continued to be earthy, primal, liberated, and ridiculous all at once. But ironically, the first successful union of striptease artists crippled burlesque in California. The El Rey in Oakland and the President Follies in San Francisco both stood until 1957. The former was a victim of the new freeway. The latter might have survived longer, but the American Guild of Variety Artists (AGVA)—the Burlesque Artist Association's (BAA) descendant—won higher wages for burlesque strippers across the board. The Follies could not pay them.

The fact was that no union had been eager to represent strippers. Since the late 1930s, BAA had operated under the auspices of the Associated Actors and Artistes of America (AAA). In 1957, though, AAA withdrew BAA's charter, complaining that the field was insufficiently organized. The same year, AGVA created a special branch for burlesque comics and strippers. The executive director of AGVA, Manny Tyler, said, "Strippers represent our minority but they're bringing home 95% of the bacon." The following year, a group of strippers in Los Angeles demanded a raise, which put many burlesque theaters out of business.[72]

CHANGING IDEAS about how much flesh was acceptable to show drove burlesque striptease further underground. Back in 1953, after the city of Newark had denied the Minsky Adam a license, the American Civil Liberties Union took the theater's side, appealed, and won. The New Jersey Supreme Court ruled that the city of Newark's ban on stripping was illegal and found stripping to be a form of free speech. "The piece de resistance of modern burlesque is the girl, who disrobes, partially or entirely," Justice William Brennan, then on that court, stated in his opinion.[73] But in February 1957 the ruling was reversed. The U.S. Supreme Court ruled that obscenity was not protected by the First Amendment. In other words, Newark won. On Valentine's Day, the Minsky Adams closed its doors. The ordinance, *Variety* wrote, "has tamed a tornado of torso."[74]

Across the river in New York, a similar battle was taking place. Since 1953, Thomas J. Phillips, the executive director of BAA, had been trying to open a "clean" burlesque revue—i.e., without striptease—called *Welcome Exile*, in Brooklyn. The *Exile* would have featured pre-Depression-era burlesque, which Phillips wanted returned to New York after a sixteen-year absence. The city denied Phillips a license on the grounds that after the 1930s, burlesque's very nature made it impossible to "pre-censor" this form of entertainment.[75] License Commissioner Edward McCaffrey said that the main reason why no one wanted burlesque was striptease.

> From the first lifting of the trailing skirt to display the female ankle to the ultimate disrobing, leaving a more or less adequate g-string, the history of burlesque has been an ever further reaching beyond the pale of community accepted standards of female decorum in dress and action.[76]

The back-and-forth went on for several years. The New York Supreme Court overturned McCaffrey's ruling. The city appealed. In 1957, Phillips finally won the right to bring *Welcome Exile* to New York, as long as there was no striptease. But no one wanted to see burlesque without striptease. *Welcome Exile* closed after four days.[77] Two years later, when the Broadway musical about her life was about to open, Gypsy Rose Lee summed up the impoverished state of the industry when she expressed reluctance to strip in a New York nightclub. "I must not play the Casa Cugat. It's wrong for Gypsy to be shaking the beads in a saloon while the 'myth' is on Broadway. The original must live up to the story."[78]

# You Gotta Get a Gimmick

**I**n 1959, *Miami Herald* columnist and sportswriter Jack Kofoed compared Sally Rand to Harold Stassen, the perennial failed presidential candidate. The startling fact was that Rand was still "campaigning."[1] At the end of the fifties, Cold War reformers anxious about the moral fiber of the nation continued to worry about the tenacity of the striptease industry. Now strippers became characters in a perceived underworld vice empire complete with kickbacks, baby adoption rackets, dope fiends, and Communists. As striptease moved south and west into nightclubs in Miami, Dallas, Calumet City, and Las Vegas—all cities where gambling was rife—it slid into mob territory. Thus the stripper came to be seen as a subverter of official morality—a Commie, a drug addict, and a lesbian.

Candy Barr, the green-eyed blonde kewpie doll whose "sweetheart" look belied her messy personal life, epitomized this "deviant" stripper. Born Juanita Dale Slusher in Dallas, Barr had run away from home at age fourteen and become a prostitute and a thief. In 1951 she had starred in a blue movie, *Smart Aleck*, and by the middle of the decade had begun to strip in Dallas and New Orleans nightclubs. Las Vegas's Second City, Dallas glittered from D-Day until 1964, when Jack Ruby shot Lee Harvey Oswald. The city contained both conservative forces such as the "How Dare You" Squad—a group of Dallas reformers who prosecuted intent as well as crime—and gangsters, showgirls, oilmen, Russian immigrants, and macho journalists. Having arrived there from Chicago in 1947, Ruby opened his own nightclub, the Silver Slipper, and in 1961, he opened a second one, the Carousel, on Commerce Avenue.[2]

One of twelve nightclubs on the block, the Carousel became Ruby's showcase. He referred to it as "a fucking high class place."[3] Located on the second floor, the Carousel, a square, barnlike room with dark red carpeting and black plastic booths, featured strippers on a stage the size of a boxing ring. A five-piece bump-and-grind orchestra played, but no one danced. Men (and sometimes women) sat at the boomerang-shaped bar, which Ruby had finished in gold-plated plastic with gaudy gold-mesh drapes. Above the bar hung a gold-framed picture of a stallion. The Carousel closed after Ruby went to jail.[4]

Ruby wanted to compete with the Weinstein brothers, who owned two other clubs on Commerce Street. In 1963, with the idea of earning a quick buck, and attempting to stave off the IRS, Ruby hired Jada, whom Walter Winchell had called "the hottest exotic dancer" in New Orleans. Jada did mostly what the other strippers condemned as "laying" a tiger skin—a Blaze Starr–ish horizontal bump and grind. Or she pranced onstage in a white tulle and gilt evening gown and in the middle of her act whipped off her G-string and twirled it around her head. She snarled, she laughed. She "made love" to the column in the middle of the club. She bumped and ground with the trumpet player. She got into a pie-throwing fight with the comic and the bandleader. Anxious about censors, Ruby turned out the lights whenever Jada flashed her G-string. In the tradition of making strippers respectable, Ruby tried to promote her, at various times, as the granddaughter of Pavlova or John Quincy Adams. But Jada entertained a less elevated identity: she rode around Dallas wearing a fur coat and high heels, and smuggled in pot from Mexico.[5]

Meanwhile, Candy Barr became the How Dare You Squad's *bête noir*. Abe and Barney Weinstein had given Candy her name sometime in the fifties because "she liked sweets." According to Garry Wills, Barr's guiltless sexual impudence made her appear to be ridiculing Texas pride in downtown Dallas, which is why that she got such a heavy sentence for possessing a minuscule portion of marijuana.[6] In her signature cowboy act, she balanced a ten-gallon Stetson on her chest, cocked her leg and aimed her toy pistols into the audience. She came onstage for encores in nothing more than the Stetson and boots, and she would take the hat off and balance it over her heart. Some observers thought this gesture referred to an event in Barr's real life, a few years earlier, when she had shot her husband in the stomach after he kicked down the door of their apartment. The wound failed to kill him, and Barr later told newspapers that she had been aiming for his groin. The mishaps—highly publicized by Weinstein— helped increase her notoriety, as did *Smart Aleck*. The coup de grâce was when Weinstein wangled her the Jayne Mansfield part in a local production of *Will Success Spoil Rock Hunter?*

On October 27, 1957, the police arrested the wide-eyed stripper for marijuana possession. The defense attorney picked an all-male jury, which ultimately convicted her. During Barr's trial for possession the following February, her mere presence in the courtroom so distracted Judge Joe B. Brown that he momentarily abandoned his role as court official, took out his camera, and snapped pictures of her from the bench.[7]

Barr played ingenuous. "Why, I don't even smoke," she told journalists. The prosecution focused on the fact that the stripper had stashed some of the marijuana in her bra and repeated the word "bosom" over and over. Barr never took the stand. To journalists, she insisted the arrest was a "frame-up." According to most sources, the police had tapped her phone,

# WANTED!

Candy Barr, Alias: Toothsome Hershey, Sweettooth Sadie, or Baby Ruth. Caution: She's loaded with energy and will blow your head off at the least provocation. Her captor will be well rewarded!

Candy Barr with Stetson and handguns, publicity photo, c. 1957. Author's personal collection.

and the search warrant they brought when they raided her house was unsigned. (Around the same time, a man convicted in Dallas on six counts of transporting and selling heroin got five years.[8])

On Valentine's Day 1958, Judge Brown handed Barr an initial sentence of fifteen years. She mounted one appeal after another. As the appeals wound their way through the various courts, the pudgy Vegas gangster

Mickey Cohen took an interest in Barr and the two briefly lived together. The appeal failed and Barr served a sentence of three years and four months in prison. Both her liaison with Cohen and her prison term raised her status as stripper. When she got out of prison in 1961, she returned to Ruby's Carousel Club and played to standing-room-only crowds. Later, she would testify at Cohen's trial.[9]

WHILE ON APPEAL in 1958, Barr stripped at the El Rancho Hotel in Las Vegas. In a postcard from that time, she poses topless in red tights, though it's unlikely she undressed that far in her act.[10] Still, Vegas was a long way from Dallas. Vegas in the late fifties traded on a populist allure. In bringing striptease there, hotel men and mobsters alike wanted to capitalize on sex appeal without dredging up burlesque's sleazy attributes. Bumps and grinds in the showroom encouraged gamblers to drop money at the craps tables. "No one pretends . . . that the shows pay their own way," one reporter wrote.[11]

One allure of the Strip was that visitors could leave ordinary morality behind. From its beginnings, the Strip offered respite from cover charges, state speed limits, sales tax, waiting periods and blood tests for marriages, state income tax, and regulation of gambling. Hotelman Tommy Hull had built the El Rancho as part of the postwar Vegas hotel boom in 1941. With its yellow and blue windmill, El Rancho was more casual than clubs in Los Angeles or New York. On opening night, many guests arrived in formal eveningwear, crisply pressed suits and tuxedos, and lavish gowns, but Hull ambled in late, sporting blue jeans, boots, and a cowboy shirt. By the early fifties, the mob followed with the Sahara and the Sands, the New Frontier, the Royal Nevada, the Riviera, the Desert Inn, and the Dunes. Tourists and movie stars who wanted to gamble and see a glamorous floorshow flocked to the desert. Carrie Finnell and Gypsy Rose Lee both headlined in the Painted Desert Room at the Desert Inn only months after construction ended. "Five big casinos pull talent from New York and Los Angeles," *Look* magazine reported.[12]

In 1950 the Silver Slipper opened. With no hotel—just a casino and nightclub—the Silver Slipper resembled a cross between a supersized dining car and a Pullman circa 1877. A rose patterned carpet and heavy velvet and gold brocade drapes emulated Gay Nineties luxury. Over 1,200 people could be seated in the theater, where a stage 30 feet wide and 27 feet deep offered space for entertainment. The Silver Slipper became the insider club for the Rat Pack.

More and more strippers arrived. Lili St. Cyr performed at El Rancho, fresh from triumphs in Los Angeles, New York, and Montreal. She mingled with Eleanor Roosevelt and the entertainer Joe E. Louis, who then owned the Moulin Rouge Hotel, as well as Dorothy Dandridge and Mae West,

# Minsky's Las Vegas, 1950s

Harold Minsky poses with billboard featuring his star Tempest Storm.

Left to right: Joe E. Lewis, Beldon Katleman, Lili St. Cyr, Eleanor Roosevelt. May 1958. Frank Watts Collection.*

All photos from University of Las Vegas, Harold Minsky Collection (except *).

Nat King Cole, Liberace, Elvis, and Noel Coward. St. Cyr stripped on a swing to Bizet's *Carmen*, Ravel's *Bolero*, and "Temptation," the Nacio Herb Brown and Arthur Freed standard, which Bing Crosby and Perry Como had just recorded. She shared billing with Shirley Bassey.[13]

There was also quite quickly a Minsky presence. Abe Minsky's son Harold came to Vegas in 1952 via Reno, where he produced *Minsky University*, starring Sherry Britton. *Minsky University* presented a collegiate theme with Gallic punctuation, *Variety* reported. The evening ended, as the show's title suggested, with the strippers accepting diplomas. But the highlight was Britton.

> Miss Britton, lush in black and white furs, floats through the chorus line singing "Ma'moiselle du Paris" and slowly strips. With a background of six lovelies, she lets down her hair for the most sensuous, sexy dance Reno has seen in years. Moving slowly, she never quite resorts to the freshman tactics of bumps and grinds, but turns in a master's degree thesis on the art of sex in slow motion. Doll uses her long tresses for an enticing bit of costuming.[14]

Five years later, after losing the battle with New Jersey authorities over the Minsky Adams, Harold Minsky joined his nephew to produce a Minsky revue for Major Riddle, the Dunes' new owner. Riddle was in the process of redecorating the hotel to look like the Arabian Nights, and he needed help. Over 85 acres on Highway 91, the Dunes housed 200 rooms, a shopping center, and several dozen private estates. Perched on top of the main building was a sultan and his harem girl. The Dunes' main buildings centered on an 86,000-square-foot patio, and the main restaurant, the Arabian Room, was the only restaurant in America with equipment similar to that in a Broadway theater. The Arabian Room's 65-by-35-foot stage, its lighting and other technical features made it perfect for a huge Minsky-style revue. Harold's first Dunes show, *Minsky Goes to Paris*, combined Crazy Horse–style production numbers with American bump and grind. "We have something people can't get on television," Harold told *Playboy* a year later, explaining the success of *Minsky Goes to Paris*.[15]

Borrowing from the spectacles Minsky saw at the Crazy Horse and elsewhere, *Minsky Goes to Paris*, the first topless stage show to appear in Nevada, replaced the actual bump and grind with showgirls parading across the stage. Still, when *Minsky* opened on January 10 of that year, the Nevada State Legislature protested with what the press labeled "the bare bosom bill."[16] The bill died in committee, however.[17]

As for *Minsky Goes to Paris*, it was a big hit and enjoyed a four-and-a-half-year run of three presentations a night. Asked how he expected his "Minsky mannequins" to compete with Vegas's celebrity entertainers,

Harold waxed nostalgic: "I asked him [my father] the same question when we were about to open on Broadway. The old man looked at me and smiled, then said, "Don't worry, Harold. We still have first run on tits.""[18]

But the market in what one journalist called "a resolutely Byzantine fantasy in the Nevada desert" was far more competitive than New York in the thirties.[19] Thus the "battle of the tits" began. The Tropicana imported the Folies Bergères straight from Montmartre, the New Frontier produced an "oriental" revue, and the Stardust imported a topless revue from Lido de Paris. Trying to out-Paris Paris, Minsky replaced the G-string with tiny patches strung around the performers' bodies with chains. Minsky described these as being akin to an old-fashioned bicycle clip, "the kind that slips over a trouser leg to keep it from getting caught in the chain."[20] Stripper Jessica Rogers explained the difference between working in burlesque and nightclubs and working in Vegas circa 1957 as one of storytelling: "They no longer holler 'take it off,' they want to see why you take it off." But there was more to it than that: Vegas revues included tons of feathers and rhinestones, and as many as twenty-four beautiful nude models. The Vegas strippers developed highly choreographed gimmicks to compete. In *Minsky Goes to Paris*, Pat Amber Holliday "sinuously" strutted around the stage, striking stark poses. "Satan's Angel" started out in a devil suit, but quickly stripped to a G-string and tassels, which she set aflame and twirled in opposite directions. Taking his cues from Hugh Hefner, who made the "girl next door" safe in the 1950s, Harold Minsky talked about the difference between striptease Vegas style and burlesque another way. In newspaper interviews, he described the strippers as if they were ordinary people. Instead of focusing on their measurements, or sordid personal lives, as burlesque impresarios and pulp magazines often did, Minsky detailed his performers' educations and their husbands. "Four percent return to their home town and marry childhood sweethearts," he said.[21]

And yet despite the success of Minsky's innocent pulchritude, by the mid-sixties, the era of striptease in the big Vegas revues was on the wane. For one, the government was shutting down one palace of desire after another for tax evasion.[22] Most of these clubs were, after all, mob financed or run. Also, competition continued to play a role. As Minsky put it in 1966, "Back east, with burlesque, you usually had the only show in town."[23]

Across America, few strip clubs could sustain anything near Las Vegas's democratic glamour. Girlie magazines and blue films forced nightclub striptease to become more sexually explicit. More strippers began to incorporate "floor work" or horizontal cootches—as shimmying while lying supine on the runway was known—into their acts. (According to A. J. Liebling, floor work—also called "squirming"—originated during Blaze Starr's tenure at Baltimore's Two O-Clock Club.[24])

STARR NOTWITHSTANDING, the number of theaters and nightclubs where women stripped in the burlesque tradition was shrinking every day. In 1960 a handful of burlesque theaters remained open in cities such as Baltimore, Pittsburgh, Cleveland, Toledo, Tampa, Miami, Washington, and Kansas City. The burlesque circuit connecting them was run by the Bryan and Engel firm, whose headquarters were in Boston. Strippers could do "one-night" stands in Allentown and Reading.[25] But on Broadway, striptease became the subject of nostalgia. *Gypsy*, the musical version of Gypsy Rose Lee's memoirs, opened at the Broadway Theater in New York in the spring of 1959. *Gypsy* oozed sentiment for Depression-era burlesque, and yet, at the same time, the musical revealed how far the image of the stripper had come: this stripper was a cartoon. Everything she did proclaimed the fact that all she had was a gimmick. Little in the musical celebrated the stripper's talent or virtuosity—rather it revealed her as a woman deceiving herself about who she was.

"You Gotta Get a Gimmick," which was performed in Act Two, included three strippers—Mazeppa, Electra, and Tessie Tura—each proclaiming a stripper's artlessness and her guile. The strippers performed numbers that shared more with schlocky, fifties nightclub burlesque than jazz age elegance or Depression-era sexiness: Mazeppa took it off while she played her trumpet; Electra swirled electric lights to accentuate her bumps and grinds; Tessie transformed a melancholy ballet into a wild shimmy.[26]

With music by Jule Styne, lyrics by Stephen Sondheim, book by Arthur Laurents, direction and choreography by Jerome Robbins, set by Jo Mielziner, and Ethel Merman starring as Mama Rose, *Gypsy* immediately became a smash hit.[27] But many critics treated the show as a documentary, and saw the burlesque atmosphere as emblematic of show business's tawdry beginnings. Brooks Atkinson wrote: "Backstage at a striptease burlesque house is equally grotesque, especially when bored show girls with spears lazily file by in Roman armor. Without glamour, the symbols of show business are ludicrous."[28]

Still others dismissed the musical for sugarcoating burlesque and singled out Sandra Church, who played the role of young Gypsy, for being vacuous. As Kenneth Tynan noted, Church was "too chaste in demeanor to reproduce the guileful, unhurried carnality with which the real Gypsy undressed."[29] Walter Kerr complained that it was strange that Gypsy's climactic strip number showed such "faltering delicacy" and "reserve."[30] In other words, theater critics were asking, "Where was the va va voom?"

Certainly not on Broadway. But there was plenty of it in New Orleans. The same year that *Gypsy* earned millions, a stripper in Crescent City made headlines on the front pages of national magazines, and she did so neither for faltering delicacy nor reserve. In the winter of 1959, Blaze Starr, aka "Miss Spontaneous Combustion," became "friendly" with Earl Long, whom

A. J. Liebling once described as a "peckerwood Caligula." In his third term, the populist, corrupt governor of Louisiana began acting so erratically that his wife, Blanche, took offense, moved out, and got him committed to Mandeville, an insane asylum. Some of the ensuing controversy whirled around Starr, who had arrived in the Crescent City three years earlier, fresh from her triumphs at Baltimore's Two O'Clock Club, to become a local legend in the striptease scene. She was nineteen years old.[31]

Starr worked at the Sho Bar and at the indelicately named Bourbon Street club Chez Grope. She did all of the numbers she had invented in Baltimore, including the one where she blew rose petals into the audience and "The Heat Wave," in which she "sweltered" onstage. When Long saw "Miss Blaze," as he called her, for the first time at that club, he was sixty-three, forty years her senior. Blanche had moved out, and Long was drinking heavily and taking Dexedrine. According to Starr, he "picked her." That night, as she told it, Starr was doing one of her oldest numbers—the one with the hillbilly theme she had done at the Quonset Hut in D.C. in the early fifties. She played "Dixie" on the guitar and wore a tight, low-cut, red-sequined dress. Long jumped up on a chair and applauded as if she were a diva at the Met, even though he generally never drank anything stronger than Coca Cola in public.[32]

Some say that Starr slipped a publicity photo of herself with some sweet words on it into Long's front pocket. Most observers claim the two began to have an affair. Starr visited him at the governor's mansion; his farm, "the pea patch"; and his Roosevelt Hotel suite. Long showered her with diamonds and furs, and the couple set up residence on the Esplanade. Starr turned down offers of three thousand dollars a week to strip because he wouldn't let her out of the house by herself. Sometimes they went to the Sho Bar, where Starr once met JFK. She adored Long. "He is entitled to a little happiness," she said.[33]

The feeling was mutual. When Charles DeGaulle visited Louisiana, Long, sitting in the lead car of the parade honoring the French president, ordered the driver to swing down Bourbon Street. It wasn't the official route; he just wanted to bring the general past the Sho-Bar so Starr could see him.[34] "He treated me like a Cinderella," Starr said years afterward.[35]

In May 1959, Long was hospitalized, and Starr gave an interview to the *New Orleans States-Item* in which she defended Long's right to pursue his sexual freedom. Her free-wheeling attitude scandalized even laissez-faire New Orleans. After Long got out of the asylum, the story about him and Starr made national news. It was the first time such an affair had done so. "Goddam all because of a woman," Long told *Time* to explain why Blanche wanted him restrained. A picture in *Life* showed Starr running across a field in a negligee. The caption read, "Blaze Starr Dons Gauze for a Bucolic Bump during Weekend in the Country."[36]

The publicity didn't hurt him. Long was released and began traveling across Louisiana and Texas. Perhaps in part to play the working-class angle, Long brought along Starr, whom he introduced in some places as "the future first lady."[37] Long also continued to display erratic behavior. He bought cowboy boots for "an unidentified lady friend." Back in New Orleans, he urinated on live television. Long returned to the hospital in September 1960, and Blanche prevented Starr from seeing him. When he died that month, he left her fifty thousand dollars, which she was never able to collect. "Cinderella bites the dust again," she said many years later.[38]

After Long's death, the media made Starr unwelcome in New Orleans. Writing about her presence at Long's funeral, the *Times Picayune* reported, "An unexpected visitor was Blaze Starr, showgirl friend of Long." But in his political analysis of Long's career, A. J. Liebling offered a more tender motive for the stripper's presence: "I expect Long would have expected her though; she had been on his side when a lot of the political mourners weren't."[39]

Blaze Starr runs across the lawn of Earl Long's farm in July 1959, not long after he was released from the asylum. Time-Life Pictures/Getty Images.

BURLESQUE STRIPTEASE was disappearing from the theater just as half-dressed and undressed women were appearing on the screen. In 1960 the exploitation filmmaker Russ Meyer released a new movie about striptease, *The Immoral Mr. Teas*. Produced by burlesque impresario Pete De Cenzie, the film told the story of Teas, who resembled the baggy-pants burlesque comics of the 1930s. Teas sees women undressing everywhere and fails to pursue them while a voice-over offers wry commentary spoofing cold warriors: "Has the pressure of modern living begun its insidious task of breaking down the moral fiber of our indomitable Mr. Teas?"

The film skyrocketed to cult status. Critics compared Teas, an aging, bumbling delivery boy, to Charlie Chaplin and Jacques Tati's hapless Mr. Hulot. Meyer used undressing as a metaphor for ripping the veil off of

1950s sexual hypocrisy. He was a pioneer. Whereas thirties exploitation films had broached questions of propriety straight, Meyer did so with a diabolical sense of irony. Earlier road show films had showed stripping women under an "educational" guise, but Meyer filmed a "feature" with no redeeming qualities. In a decade when polls suggested that fewer than a quarter of Americans endorsed premarital sex, Meyer, perhaps influenced by Lenny Bruce, pointed to the hypocrisy surrounding men's desire to see naked women.

Part of the reason for its notoriety was that *The Immoral Mr. Teas* was the first exploitation film to play in regular movie houses. "Last Friday evening the peep show finally moved across the tracks from Main Street," a critic for the *Los Angeles Times* wrote. *The Immoral Mr. Teas* also distinguished itself by showing more nude women than any previous film. Moreover, it presented no passion, no actual sex; Teas himself had more in common with the ninety-eight-pound weakling than Casanova. Was Meyer's idea that even a ninety-eight-pound weakling can enjoy striptease? In a long essay in *Show* magazine, the critic Leslie Fiedler contended that Teas was "nobody's dream lover, just a dreamer." Fiedler wrote that Teas's unfulfilled voyeurism "is a metaphor for our unfulfilled consumer desire." To Fiedler, the tongue-in-cheek shots of Teas's salivating reaction to the nudity around him elevated the film above grind-house fare like *Teasarama*, in which the audience witnessed only the woman undressing and not the man's self-conscious pursuit of her.[40] In an interview, Meyer said that he was reacting against European art films. He wanted to show more flesh than they did. Apparently he had the right idea. *The Immoral Mr. Teas* made over a million dollars and spawned several sequels.[41]

THE SAME YEAR, Hugh Hefner's Playboy Club opened on Michigan Avenue in Chicago and extolled "bunnies" as sex objects and the club as "a Disneyland for adults." Just as *Playboy* had tried to upgrade girlie magazines in the previous decade, so the Playboy Club sought to celebrate the exotic without burlesque's ambiance. In contrast to decrepit strip clubs and crumbling burlesque theaters, the Playboy Club had a modern nightclub atmosphere. Taking a clue from strip clubs, Hefner imposed a "look but don't touch" rule in regard to the performers. But although the bunnies were scantily clad in satin leotards, no bunny ever stripped. More important was that the bunnies did borrow from burlesque the idea of being super-sized American women—Hefner allowed only size 34D and 36D bras. Soon Playboy Clubs spread all over the country.[42]

In these clubs, Hefner began to espouse his philosophy of separating sex from "sickness, sin, and sensationalism," which he believed would eradicate striptease. And yet in a year when the birth control pill first became available to American women, the demand for striptease refused to die.

Explaining its longevity, the longtime burlesque agent Dave Cohn fell back on the laws of supply and demand: "The public wants strippers. Not that people are sex crazy, but they want something a little different."[43]

But at the same time, the burlesque industry was experiencing a crisis: a shortage of trained strippers. *Variety* reported: "Chicago, for years a stripper's haven, is now seriously beset by a dearth of peelers. The local AGVA office receives some eight to ten calls a day from strip operators scraping the barrel for peeling talent."[44] Nor was the demand for strip-tease abating on the East Coast, where the agents Lou Miller and Cohn, who began working in burlesque in the Depression, fielded more and more calls from would-be strippers. In his New York office at 165 West Forty-sixth Street, Cohn promised to turn every woman into a blonde bomb-shell. Cohn and Miller were experts of a sort: Cohn had worked as an advance man in burlesque, and Miller had labored as a booker, starting essentially from the other end and rising. Each of them used to supply young girls for the Minskys. For a 10 percent commission, the two-hundred-pound Cohn would teach any woman how to walk, what to wear, and what color to dye her hair. Then he sent her to burlesque theater owners, who would osten-sibly make her a star.

The idea of teaching women "how to undress in front of your hus-band" was hardly new. Ann Corio had first made it popular during World War II. The way Corio's act worked was that a straight woman came on and showed the audience how "not" to strip. Then Corio entered and stripped "the right way." Corio herself may have gotten the idea from an educational blue movie that had been released in the 1930s. But what was new in the 1960s was the openness with which Cohn spoke about his ser-vices being in demand. Perhaps this is because, paradoxically, common wisdom of the era dictated that women, having abandoned traditional femi-nine graces along the route to modernity, needed to be taught them anew by men. "I had a guy call me the other day and he says he wants to know how to make a stripper out of a dame—his wife," Cohn told a reporter.[45]

And yet the unhappily married man alone could not keep burlesque striptease alive. The survival of burlesque into the 1960s hinged in part on how energetically a particular city pursued urban renewal. Burlesque held on until 1958 in Detroit, when the Gayety Theater, also known as the Cadillac, closed. Tempest Storm was the last stripper to perform there.[46] In 1961 a group of preservation-minded Bostonians, along with Ann Corio and other former burlesque stars, began to raise money to save the Old Howard from destruction. Corio intended to stage her revival *This Was Burlesque* there. On June 21, a "mysterious" fire of "unknown" origin swept through the 115-year-old theater. Before the last embers died out, cranes moved in and tore down the Old Howard's walls, making renovation im-possible. After that, Mayor Kevin H. White unveiled his plans to turn Scollay

Square into "Government Center." But the demolition also gave birth to a new vice district in Boston: the Combat Zone.[47]

Other burlesque theaters had already disappeared. In Chicago, the Star and Garter and the Rialto closed in 1953, when Mayor Daley knocked down all of South State Street. The Gayety in Philadelphia burned down that same year. In 1958 the Denver Victory Theater closed. The Gayety Columbus would do the same the following year, lost to dwindling attendance and labor disputes. In Seattle the Rivoli shut down two years later.[48]

THE MOST DEVASTATING BLOW to striptease, however, was neither urban renewal nor fires. It was the federal assault on organized crime. In June 1962, the McClellan Senate Committee Hearings on Racketeering convened in Washington with the intention of exposing connections between the union of performers—the American Guild of Variety Artists (AGVA)—and the mob. Senator John McClellan, an Arkansas Democrat, and his cronies sought to link exotic dancing to prostitution and to prove that the union failed to enforce rules in many nightclubs because the mob was getting kickbacks from these clubs. The AGVA did represent legitimate entertainers such as Bob Hope, but also, as the *New York Herald Tribune* reported, "borderline talents like strippers or exotic dancers."[49]

Due to the coverage they received in national newspapers, the McClellan hearings did much to cement the idea in the public mind that strippers were prostitutes. Much time was spent describing "B-girls"—women who neither danced nor sang, but tricked customers out of their money—to a national audience.[50] Hearings started June 12. The first person to testify was Penny Singleton, who accused AGVA of transforming dues-paying strippers into criminal B-girls. "I charge here and now that the exotic and strip artists have been abandoned and made outcasts by the very union to which they pay dues for representation and protection," Singleton declared. That same day, she went on to charge, "It is a matter of public knowledge that many of these so called strip clubs are managed by people who are fronts for racketeers."[51]

The committee failed to understand the idea of B-girl and spent some time trying to clarify it. Senators suggested to Singleton, perhaps somewhat facetiously, that the union divest itself of B-girls. But this task was apparently more difficult than it appeared. When B-girls began describing their jobs, the testimony sounded like a Mickey Spillane novel. One worked at the Bon Bon supper club in Philadelphia where "you cannot buy so much as a potato chip" and drinks "are watered down or plain water, totally water, or they are sautern and water for champagne."[52]

In the hearings, a surprisingly large amount of time was spent distinguishing between a B-girl and a stripper. As one witness put it, in the old days the Bon Bon club hired strippers who "had nothing to do with any patrons unless [she] cared to." But when strippers and exotic dancers became B-Girls, the specter of prostitution emerged. "Very few of them do more than [walk] around, with some movements I understand are not allowed also, and a few bits of action onstage and a few little leery grins, and [then] they are off stage, as fast as they can, because their little fish that's waiting at the bar might leave," one witness said.[53]

In Calumet City and other vice districts, "exotic" was a code word that suggested prostitution. One witness testified, "A girl who was a legitimate entertainer came into the club and was immediately told that she would have to revise her act and come out in something a little scantier and do a more exotic dance, which she did."[54] Frank Rizzo, the chief of the Philadelphia police, testified that a magnum of champagne in one of these clubs cost seventy-five dollars. The committee blamed striptease's decline on the rise of the B-girl, who spent so much time coercing customers to drink that she could only muster, as one witness put it, a few bumps and grinds.

From 1950 to 1959, witnesses testified, Calumet City's three- or four-block section of State Street full of strip clubs had been a front for crime activity, and, although club owners initially had hired union performers, they forced many of these performers to work in prostitution, be escorts, and dabble in pickpocketing. They also forced some women to strip naked.[55] Erwin Fast reported that from 1956 to 1962, he tried to organize the performers in the Chicago clubs. Mobsters threatened him and asked him to leave the city. (Clubs wanted to avoid paying taxes by treating the employees as independent contractors.) When Fast began to focus on clubs in Cal City such as the Shay Club, the Follies Bergere, and the Brass Rail, which all supposedly hired only union strippers, he found it impossible to make headway. So in 1957, Fast suggested that AGVA stop trying to organize performers in Cal City altogether.[56] Finally, the only way to reform the clubs was to deny them their liquor licenses. In 1959 many Cal City clubs stopped presenting striptease because they could not get their liquor licenses renewed. Even after that, some B-girls got naked, winking while the band played such tunes as "How Dry I Am."[57]

The horrified committee suggested using the Mann Act, which prohibited bringing women across state lines, and calling in the FBI. The most outrageous testimony linked the exploitation of B-girls to "the unwed mother racket" and white slavery. Witnesses testified that performers were beaten up and abused mentally and physically. Others claimed that some of these clubs were connected to a nationwide crime ring. One performer said, "It is a sin to think that any human being has to be treated like an animal, I do not care if it is a stripper, you, or anyone."[58]

Why did women work in these clubs, the committee wanted to know. As had the House Un-American Activities Committee, this committee seemed unconvinced by the simplest answer, which was that, when burlesque theaters closed in the summers, strippers needed to pay the rent. The result of the hearings was to discredit AGVA and make striptease synonymous with prostitution.[59]

AT THE SAME TIME as the McClellan Committee was striving to push striptease off the map, a popular song helped resurrect it as a show business cliché. In 1958, the British composer of light instrumental music David Rose had written "The Stripper" as the theme song for the popular television show *Burlesque*. But "The Stripper" did not become a hit until after MGM asked Rose to record another number, "Ebb Tide," for the film adaptation of the Tennessee Williams play *Sweet Bird of Youth*. "The Stripper" became "Ebb Tide"'s B-side. One night shortly after that, Los Angeles DJ Robert Q. Lewis played and replayed "The Stripper" on his show on WKHJ.[60]

Unlike many of the previous songs women had stripped to, "The Stripper" offered a pounding drumbeat and bass rumble instead of lyrics. The instruments mostly swung, at least as much as light instrumental music could swing. But occasionally "The Stripper" almost sounded like human voices. "The Stripper" was, you could say, a musical version of a striptease gimmick. It quickly became the new soundtrack for striptease, surpassing the Tin Pan Alley and blues standards that strippers had favored. It also acknowledged the downsizing of striptease bands. As it became more difficult to pay them, nightclubs hired fewer orchestras. The tit serenader was long gone. But now, with "The Stripper," lyric and melody faded away too, leaving a burlesque of rhythm.[61]

A FEW MONTHS before the AGVA hearings, Corio, perhaps drawing on *Gypsy*'s success, presented another nostalgic, feel-good spectacle about striptease. *This Was Burlesque* opened at the Casino Theater East on the Lower East Side, not so far from where Minskys had "invented" striptease forty years earlier. Corio herself performed the "how to undress for your husband" number in the show, and she dragged several other ancient performers out of retirement. But she also threw in a few young strippers to make sure that people attended.

*This Was Burlesque* ran for over 1,000 performances off Broadway. It moved to Broadway in 1965, ran for 124 performances, and then toured. On Broadway, columnists and audiences adored the music by Sonny Lester and his orchestra. *This Was Burlesque*, like *Gypsy*, featured "glorified" striptease, while foreign and American-made sex exploitation movies were becoming more explicit. Ann Corio positioned herself as being an entertainer—not a pornographer—by announcing that *This Was Burlesque* featured no topless dancing and that it was "feminine." "I'm really just a prude," she told journalists, repeating the mantra she had invented for herself since the beginning of her career. The show "stir[red] nostalgia for a chapter of show business that is as dead as the dodo in this town," the *New York Times* opined.[62]

Ann Corio's femininity, which had charmed reporters in the 1930s, on the cusp of the Sexual Revolution seemed to do so even more. For this femininity tapped into the popular cultural focus on female desire of the early sixties. In 1962, Helen Gurley Brown's *Sex and the Single Girl* took Kinsey's argument that women could enjoy sex a step further. Admitting that she herself had had affairs, Gurley Brown provided a "how-to" manual for the single woman. She no longer needed to abstain from sex. Following Gurley Brown's advice, women could see striptease as part of women's sexual liberation—something that she needed to learn to take pleasure in life.

One striptease "school" after another opened, showing women "how to do it." Lenny Bruce's mother, Sally Marr, became dean of the Pink Pussycat College of Striptease in Los Angeles in 1961. Joan Collins studied there to prepare for a role in a film in which she had to strip. In Dallas, a year or so later, Barney Weinstein, the owner of the Colony Club, opened Striptease University, which shared the same address as his nightclub. He imagined Striptease University as a place for him to train women to work in his clubs. The Pink Pussycat gave strippers movie star names like "Georgia Raft" and "Peeler Lawford." And its curriculum sounded avowedly pre–Sexual Revolution. The dean of the Pink Pussycat told one reporter that the "education [is] devoted to men" and that "a woman's best weapon is a man's imagination."[63]

In addition to schools for striptease, at a time when many record labels were releasing comedy albums for Americans to play in their living rooms, a whole genre of "music to strip by" emerged. Sherry Britton had narrated *Best of Burlesque* in 1958, and Gypsy released a similar album. But the most famous such album, *How to Strip for Your Husband*, with Sonny Lester and his orchestra, spun off *This Was Burlesque*. Released on the Roulette label, the album included not just music, but its very own G-string and instruction manual. As the *New York Times* writer Herbert Mitgang put it in a round up of these LPs, though, no matter how hard they tried, they failed

In Hollywood, the diminishing force of the production code introduced Americans to a degree of nudity absent from mainstream culture since the thirties. Americans lined up for foreign art films, where they could see more of the female form than they could in Hollywood. In 1960, in Fellini's *La Dolce Vita*, the Swedish star Anita Ekberg jumped bare-breasted into the Fountain of Trevi in Rome; playing a bored aristocrat recently divorced from a millionaire, Nadia Gray did a striptease ending up, Blaze Starr style, on her back on a fur stole. Sophia Loren did one in Vittorio de

Sica's 1963 film *Yesterday, Today, and Tomorrow*, in which she plays a hooker educating a young seminarian about the pleasures of the flesh. Four years later, the French stripper Rita Renoir had a bit part in Michelangelo Antonioni's *The Red Desert*, making her the only stripper to appear in an avant-garde film. Most of these foreign bodies arrived in Hollywood sometime in the early sixties. And it was in part their force that would propel American striptease into the world of pornography.

"How to Strip for Your Husband," pamphlet accompanying the LP record of Ann Corio's Broadway show *This Was Burlesque*, c. 1962. Author's personal collection.

# Part Six
# Sexual Revolutions

Striptease will become irrelevant when naked entertainment becomes ubiquitous.

—Marshall McLuhan

# Topless Dancing

**W**hereas in the Jazz Age the dance craze had worked to create striptease, in the early sixties a new dance craze, go-go, pushed striptease further to the cultural margins. Found in go-go bars, go-go dancing was a West Coast fad. When the first such bar, so named after the 1957 French movie *Whiskey a Go Go*, opened in 1963 on Sunset Boulevard, it was a media event. Go-go was a metaphor for modern life. It meant being on the move. Women in go-go clubs shook their bodies and danced new dances, jiggled in frenzies in cages high above the crowd. The noise in these clubs was deafening. *Esquire* compared the women to "insects in a bottle."[1]

The new dance craze started with the twist, which Chubby Checker introduced in 1960. After that, even more jiggly dances, such as the frug, the swim, the mashed potato, the pony, and the wacky, lascivious watusi became popular. These dances presented the visual opposite of a strip parade. They projected youth, energy, and slimness instead of striptease's voluptuous, languid elegance. Rather than promote the ideal of sophisticated cosmopolitanism, go-go asserted irreverence, a disdain for formality, and more movement than striptease could contain.[2]

Although striptease continued to elevate the curvy female bodies popular in the 1950s, the new dances were best suited to thin, breastless women and long-legged models like Twiggy. The *San Francisco Examiner* described the swim as "an incredible and eyebrow-raising shimmy—the most advanced state of the shakes ever."[3]

IN 1964, a few hundred miles north of the Whiskey a Go Go nightclub, in San Francisco, topless dancing emerged. "Topless" women dispensed with the brassieres and pasties that strippers had worn to conceal their breasts. Once you were topless, it left only one possible garment to take off: the G-string. Thus toplessness was another step toward total nudity—bottomless dancing, naked cootches, and live sex shows.

The road to the disappearing bra was paved by the shrinking skirt. In 1964 the British designer Mary Quant invented the miniskirt, which the Tories claimed revealed women's "ungovernable" sexuality. Quant made quite clear that her design was about sex. "Am I the only woman who has ever wanted to go to bed with a man in the afternoon?" she asked. "Any law abiding female, it used to be thought, waits until dark. Well there are lots of girls who don't want to wait. Miniclothes are symbolic of them."[4]

Rudi Gernreich's monokini, c. 1964.

The miniskirt precluded the wearing of garter belts and stockings—essential props for the postwar stripper. Pantyhose, invented in 1953, became *de rigeur*. Women wore pantyhose on the street and could don garter belts for pleasure, instead of just to keep their stockings up.[5] But the fashion development that led directly to topless dancing was the monokini. Created by the Austrian émigré designer and avowed nudist Rudi Gernreich, the monokini had a normal swimsuit bottom and two skinny, suspender-like straps brushing over—but failing to cover—the wearer's breasts.

Gernreich envisioned the monokini in 1962, when he predicted that "bosoms will be uncovered within five years." He saw it as a kind of "freedom." At the end of 1963, *Look* magazine ran a feature about futuristic fashions, and a version of the monokini appeared in it. The actual bathing suit appeared in 1964 in *Look*. According to the model Peggy Moffitt, author of a book about Gernreich, it was first photographed in the Bahamas on a prostitute in June 1964 since no model would wear it. In San Francisco, Gernreich first sold the monokini to the Joseph Magnin department store, where it became an overnight hit. On June 12, the *San Francisco Examiner* featured a photo of a woman sporting a see-through blouse on the front page.[6]

A WEEK LATER, Carol Doda, former prune picker, file clerk, and cocktail waitress, wore one of Gernreich's monokinis to work at the Condor Nightclub in North Beach. Davey Rosenberg, a four-hundred-pound former burlesque and sideshow impresario, and now the public relations guy for the Condor Club, had seen the photo and rushed to Magnin's to get it for her.

In the late fifties, San Francisco had resembled Greenwich Village or Paris of the 1920s. The rise of gay and beat culture sensualized the city and especially North Beach, which offered a home to all sexual outlaws and mixed old-world charm with new-world outrage. The gay cabaret Finnochio's featured a drag revue modeled after the one the Jewel Box Revue had toured in the 1950s. Lenny Bruce and the savage comic Lord Buckley had performed nearby. Jazzmen riffed and ice cream parlors sold "erotic" desserts named

Pineapple Thunderpussy. As Tom Wolfe later described it, the center of North Beach, Broadway, featured "skin-show nightclubs, boho caves . . . and 'colorful' bars with names like Burp Hollow."[7]

By 1964 the Condor drew a motley combination of beats, jazzmen, Berkeley students, and tourists. The act began with Doda at first invisible to the audience, seated topless on a grand piano suspended from the ceiling. As the piano was slowly lowered, the audience saw her legs, "turning and twisting," while the five-piece band blasted out rock and roll. A round of applause erupted. Then the rest of Doda's body came into view. The emcee shouted, "And now Miss Carol Doda will perform the swim." She moved her arms to simulate a breaststroke while the band switched to the sentimental ballad "I Left My Heart in San Francisco." Doda paused and the emcee announced another dance. Another round of applause. After ten minutes and several dances, she returned to the ceiling.

In one evening, the formula that had defined striptease for half a century became irrelevant. The next day, the Condor erected a nude, neon Doda with blinking red nipples on its marquee, announcing that what was happening now was about nakedness—not undressing. Lines ran halfway around the block, and within days women were baring breasts up and down Broadway. As Wolfe put it, "The whole performance is—it is not a strip tease, it is no kind of *tease*, it is an animated cartoon."[8]

Doda performed topless at an explosive moment in American history, a fact that she never hesitated to emphasize. In Dallas, Judge Joe B. Brown had just sentenced Jack Ruby to death. San Francisco, where the Republican convention was even now taking place (nominating Barry Goldwater for president), was the site of violent protests over civil rights, as well as other kinds of sexual and political turmoil. Students protested at the convention; the free speech movement arose at Berkeley. Indeed, Doda sometimes said that she took off her bra to overturn the sexual oppression of the McCarthy years. "It is the most personal way I can communicate

Condor Club, Broadway, North Beach, San Francisco, 1964. San Francisco History Center, San Francisco Public Library.

with people."⁹ In 1966, Doda would appear at a student protest on the steps of Sproul Hall at UC Berkeley.

Two years after that, Doda played the role of Sally Silicone in the movie *Head*, which starred the Monkees against a psychedelic backdrop of social protest about everything, including the Vietnam War. Written by Bob Rafaelson and Jack Nicholson, the movie, a Hollywood version of social protest, featured cameos by Frank Zappa, Warren Zevon, and Victor Mature. Doda appeared in a boxing sequence as the stripper holding up a card to announce a new round. In other words, she presented a dream version of herself.¹⁰

BUT WHILE DODA tried to unite topless dancing and sixties radicalism, another popular image of burlesque striptease remained stuck to a fifties *Feminist Mystique* aesthetic. The same month that Doda made national headlines for going topless, the *San Francisco Chronicle* interviewed Lili St. Cyr. The headline read, "I'm Really a Housewife at Heart," and St. Cyr provided her recipe for chicken in cream.¹¹ And yet at the same time, an equally powerful image of striptease arising out of its carnival and fairground past began to build force. When Diane Arbus photographed Blaze Starr to illustrate Thomas Morgan's 1964 feature for *Esquire*, "Blaze Starr in Nighttown," she envisioned Starr as the Circe in the hallucinatory dialogue section in *Ulysses* in which the hero ventures into an underworld.

The first of Arbus's pictures showed Starr, then twenty-nine, gazing into the camera. A boa is flung across her shoulders; she wears a G-string and spangled pasties. She is leaning against something—maybe a pole—and although part of her body is hidden in shadow, she looks the viewer full in the face. Her body anticipates the ravages of gravity. The second photo is shot in Starr's living room in her house in the suburbs of Baltimore. The room could be lifted from any bourgeois household except that Starr is cantilevered against a shag carpet decorated with crows' feet. A statue of the Buddha is on a table. Starr's hair is bouffant. A tiny white dog perches on the carpet.

Arbus's photos depicted Starr as a freak and a housewife. At the same time, the photos suggested that there was something old-fashioned, if not pathetic, about the burlesque stripper. Life followed art. A year earlier, to keep up with the times, Starr had released a nudie-cutie movie, *Blaze Starr Goes Nudist*. The film was directed by Doris Wishman, and its gimmick is that Starr tries to get away from it all by visiting a nudist colony. Starr also appeared in *Burlesque on Parade*, a nostalgic Broadway show about burlesque. Reviewing it, the *New York Times* wrote, "Burlesque seems tame, or maybe it needs a man in an overcoat furtively selling French postcards near the entrance."¹²

By 1967, Starr would more or less stop performing in Baltimore, although the mayor's office would use the Two O'Clock Club in tourist brochures until the city razed the neighborhood to build new police headquarters in 1968.[13]

If St. Cyr was cooking chicken and Starr was buying real estate, Doda was the new sex symbol. She openly discussed changing her body for public consumption. She told reporters about her breast implants, which she had had inserted soon after she first appeared at the Condor. As Tom Wolfe recalled, seeing her a few months after her premiere, "Her breasts have grown, grown, grown, enlarging like . . . dirigibles . . . topless, topless, the girl who blew up her breasts."[14]

Doda set off a trend. By the end of June, toplessness had turned into a nationwide craze: topless restaurants, shoeshine parlors, ice cream stands, and girl bands proliferated across the nation. In San Francisco, toplessness seemed to have taken over. "Are we ready for girls in topless gowns? Heck, we may not even notice them," Earl Wilson observed in his column. A real estate ad in the *Examiner* promised potential buyers that "bare top swim suits are possible here." The Soviet government called "toplessness" immoral, as did the pope. The New York City police threatened to arrest any woman wearing a monokini and fine her for indecent exposure. San Francisco mayor John Shelley tried to figure out what legal strategies he could take against toplessness and found that there was "no law under which there could be a successful prosecution." Still, he commented, "Topless is at the bottom of porn."[15]

In the year that followed, Shelley and other reform-minded urban politicians tried to wipe out topless dancing by retreating to the First Amendment restrictions that worked before, as well as by assigning inspectors to check out the clubs' zoning permits, health restriction laws, and fire laws. Club owners responded by testing Shelley. In essence, they asked the question, How much nudity is legal? Lawyers for club owners in Los Angeles contended that the clubs failed to outrage public decency, since nudity for the sake of nudity was not criminally indecent.[16]

Politicians disagreed. In San Francisco, by the middle of April 1965, Shelley was ready to raid the North Beach nightclubs. In a press conference held in the middle of the month, Shelley stated: "I want it understood that our city is not against fun. Fun is part of our city's heritage." But Shelley did want to be able to establish what was indecent and obscene and what was, as the nightclub owners contended, merely entertaining.

On April 22, the San Francisco police attempted to file criminal charges against two nightclubs for indecent exposure and keeping a disorderly house. They arrested fifteen dancers and the managers of twelve clubs. One of the women arrested was Carol Doda. The following day, a crowd of a hundred gathered outside the police station and shouted, "We want Carol!" and "We want Mario Savio!" referring to the Berkeley free speech student activist already in prison.[17]

Doda and the other North Beach topless dancers countered the police raids by hiring as counsel Melvin Belli—who earlier that year represented Jack Ruby in the killing of Lee Harvey Oswald—and the future mayor of San Francisco, George Moscone.[18] And just as in the 1940s when the ban on striptease created the strip clip joint and the exotic dancer, so in the 1960s the ban on topless led to "bottomless," live sex shows, and other latter-day forms of sexual entertainment.

The San Francisco Chamber of Commerce reported that a third of the city's 101 nightclubs were topless. Strippers all but stopped using pasties and flashed their bare breasts in strip bars, go-go bars, and the few remaining burlesque theaters. The first bottomless performer appeared at Big Al's, a club competing with the Condor. Tosha, the "Glo Girl," wore a bathing suit similar to the one Gernreich had designed, but cut out over her rear end and her breasts.[19]

Topless even became fodder for Marshall McLuhan. In August 1965, McLuhan arrived in San Francisco for a festival celebrating his work. By this time he had already published "The Medium is the Message," and his ideas about "participation mystique," a force of energy compelling human beings to complete the picture, had influenced the zeitgeist. He had also created his mot "Advertising is striptease for a world of abundance." *San Francisco Chronicle* columnist Herb Caen describes eating lunch with Tom Wolfe, McLuhan, the advertising executive Howard Gossage, and Dr. Gerald Feigen in a topless restaurant in North Beach in August 1965. McLuhan observed that the waitresses were "the opening wedge of the trial balloon."[20]

While McLuhan's lunch companions fell silent, the waitress arrived at the table. She was wearing high heels, bikini underpants, and blue sequined pasties. After she took their order, Caen said that she was good looking. "Interesting choice of words," McLuhan continued. "Good-LOOKING girl. The remark of a man who is visually-oriented . . . and I further noticed that you could not bring yourself to look at her breasts as she took your order. You examined her only after she walked away—another example of the visual: the further she walked away, the more attractive she became."

"Actually," Caen apologized, blushing, "I'm rather inhibited."

McLuhan nodded. "Another interesting word. Inhibited is the opposite of exhibited," he pointed out. "And what is exhibited causes you to be inhibited."[21]

By the end of the sixties, topless seemed to have unlimited appeal. *Playboy* and other pinup magazines published photos of topless women. But burlesque strippers badmouthed topless dancers at every turn. "They look cheap," said Ann Corio.[22] Harold Minsky insisted that topless was not the end of striptease. In an interview he said, "[F]emmes on the bump and grind circuit do not merely expose themselves. There is drama and interest in what they do, how they do it."[23]

# 1969: Who Killed Striptease?

On the morning of December 28, 1969, one of the last striptease houses in America closed. In Kansas City, at Twelfth and Central, the Folly Theater was no more. It had served a generation of Americans, having opened right after World War II. From Gypsy Rose Lee to Tempest Storm, all of the burlesque stars stripped there. The headline in the *Kansas City Star* read: "Old Grind Gets Bumped at Folly Theater Here." The article reported that "the plan is to replace the show girls with showings of adult art films." Referring to the decline of striptease since the 1940s, Folly Theater manager Mark Stuber complained about the local talent: "These girls they have around here all the time are vulgar, they're cheap. They have cheapened the name of burlesque."[1]

Other theaters were disappearing every day. The Cincinnati Gayety would, it was announced, be turned into a parking lot. Days earlier, on December 20, fire had demolished the Gayety in Baltimore. Fire swept the stage and destroyed the floor and roof. All that was left of the theater was a blackened shell.[2] It was a fitting end to the year that killed striptease.

THE FOLLY and the Gayety were hardly the only burlesque houses in trouble. For the last decade, none of the twenty or so decrepit grind theaters across the country had survived by simply featuring striptease. Forced to compete with X-rated movies, topless bars, and an increasing number of men's magazines, burlesque theaters were scrambling to add 16-millimeter adult movies and peep shows, as well as continuing to hire a few strippers and aging comics.

Strippers, particularly, were expensive. In 1969 a headlining stripper began at $1000 a week. Union wages started at $175 a week, which at the time was more than many other jobs unskilled women could get.[3] And yet even a headliner couldn't always fill a burlesque theater. In 1967, when Tempest Storm opened at the T and T Follies in Oakland, California, sixteen people sat scattered throughout the cavernous theater, staring at the stage.[4]

Another factor in striptease's decline was its monotony. Tempest Storm performed more or less the same number from 1951 until she stopped stripping in the 1980s. To accompany what in the business was called a "boudoir" number, stripping from an evening gown to a G-string, she chose three standards: Harold Arlen's classic "Stormy Weather," Arthur Freed and Nacio Herb Brown's "Temptation," and the Ira Gershwin/Harold Arlen torch song "The Man That Got Away," which the pair wrote for Judy Garland in the 1954 movie *A Star Is Born*.

For "Stormy Weather," Storm walked onstage in a white fox stole, a full-length black fur coat, and white gloves. She shook her red hair and smiled. She was statuesque, what *Variety* used to call a "standout" stripper. As three ancient musicians ground out the first bars of the song, Storm slowly took off her coat. Underneath it she wore a black full-length velvet gown with a zipper in the front. She removed the gown, then her gloves, then a white slip, then a beaded net bra and lacy merry widow. Around her neck, a large rhinestone necklace gleamed. By the time the musicians were playing the last bars, she slipped the bra off her shoulders. She spread out her arms to display her body and disappeared behind the curtain. When she reappeared, she was wearing a filmy negligee. She bowed slightly. "Thank you," said the woman who, in 1956, had won the "Micki," the award for the best "props" that a stripper could want in Los Angeles.[5]

Also, there was the graying of the strippers. At forty, Storm was hardly the oldest one taking off her clothes. Ann Corio, who had started stripping in the twenties, and Sally Rand, who made it at the Chicago Century of Progress Exposition in 1933, remained on the scene. In 1966, Corio performed in a tent show at the county fair on the outskirts of Baltimore. Women in the audience outnumbered men three to two. A photo of Corio from this tour shows her looking somewhat matronly, in chiffon, arms akimbo, giant diamond earrings hanging from her ears. In the background, the faces of countrywomen of all ages, bespectacled and gray-haired, stare up at her in amazement and curiosity. The very same tent, *Life* boasted, hosted summer stock musicals such as *Pajama Game* and *Camelot*.[6] In 1967, Sally Rand did her fan dance in Joey Faye's *Anatomy of Burlesque* in Miami.

Many articles from this era about Storm and other burlesque queens are filled with amusement at their insistence on being undressing divas in an age when nakedness was the province of youth. To some journalists, age became a way to dismiss strippers just as weight had in previous decades. But others also evinced admiration for the performers' tenacity. Ann Corio was an "old timer." Sally Rand was "still sexy at 68."[7]

Then too, a lot of the old-timers and "still sexys" were retired. Gypsy Rose Lee had moved to California and spent time in her garden and selling high-end pet food. More in tune with the changing times, Lili St. Cyr opened a mail order lingerie store where she marketed expensive garments like those she wore onstage. They came in a box that said "intimate secrets by Lili St. Cyr."[8] On the other hand, Blaze Starr retired in 1972, when she was in her forties, although she came out of retirement three years later to strip at the Palace Theater in San Francisco.[9]

These semiretired strippers were anomalies for another reason besides age. They revealed much less skin than the topless dancers who had first appeared in 1964 in San Francisco. Nineteen sixty-nine was six years after Justice Potter Stewart had remarked that he knew pornography when he saw it. But was striptease pornography or, as liberals described it, mere "erotica"? According to many strippers, striptease was comedy, as well as being the only genuine popular art form America had produced.

THERE WAS NO single event that did in striptease. But by 1969, the Sexual Revolution, having used naked bodies in public as political tools, changed the way Americans thought about nudity. Women at Cornell removed their blouses and covered their breasts with jam to protest their status as sexual objects. Nudity in the burgeoning off-off-Broadway theater and performance art scene made Tempest Storm, Blaze Starr, Gypsy Rose Lee, and the other first ladies of striptease seem even more old-fashioned.[10]

The first generation of "nude" plays began to appear in 1961. In Terrence McNally's *Sweet Eros*, the actress Sally Kirkland, who would later become a member of Andy Warhol's clique, sat naked and tied to a chair onstage for forty-five minutes. *Sweet Eros* premiered downtown. According to Kirkland, the show protested the Vietnam War. McNally himself said the nudity provided a "revelation." By the middle of the decade, there were many such revelations on the off-Broadway stage.[11]

In 1967, as the Summer of Love combined politics and culture in a heady mix, writers were parodying the trend. In "The Shock of Recognition," the first of four skits grouped under the title *You Know I Can't Hear You When the Water's Running*, a desperate actor auditions for one of the new nudicals. Written by Robert Anderson and directed by the great American director Alan Schneider, *You Know . . .*, which opened in March 1967, told the story of a playwright who hated four-letter words but wanted to put a naked man onstage, despite his producer's objections. Was Anderson making fun of undressing as Americans' consciously taking off "their old selves" and emptying themselves of their bourgeois status, or did he support it? Critics could not agree.[12]

That same year, *Hair*, an antiwar musical dramatizing a love-in, came to Broadway. In one of the most controversial scenes, some nude hippies emerged from under a blanket and stood facing the audience. This was not striptease; it was just nude people hanging around.[13] *Hair* had begun at Joseph Papp's Public Theater, newly opened in Greenwich Village; was moved to a disco called Cheetah; and then finally moved to the Biltmore Theater. The show was an unprecedented mainstream success, touring for several years despite being banned in many places around the country. After *Hair*, many more downtown playwrights adapted the trope of showing humanity through the naked body, and they eroticized it in a new way.[14]

Critics were ambivalent. "The new nudity needs an 'artistic conscience,'" complained one writer. Martin Gottfried pointed out that this new nudity, unlike burlesque, was not funny.[15] But the downtown gurus of the avant-garde did not care about critics, or humor. They cared about getting the bourgeois audience to shed its inhibitions. Kenneth Tynan's "erotic" revue *Oh! Calcutta!*, the Living Theater's *Paradise Now*, and the Performance Group's *Dionysus in 69* all displayed, in various proportions and combinations, nude actors, actors undressing, and actors simulating sex.

These spectacles invited audiences to participate in a more active way than burlesque did. In *Dionysus in 69*, which premiered in 1968, the Performance Group attempted to break down the barriers between performers and spectators. As Eleanor Lester noted in the *New York Times*, *Dionysus in 69*, "a group grope," was instantly famous for its "dancing, orgies, and whispered secrets." Performances of *Paradise Now* often spurred the audience to undress. In *Che*, which purported to be a "revolutionary dialogue" about America's oppression of Cuba, the creator, Larry Berkowitz, walked onstage naked and shouted, "Take me naked or don't take me at all!"[16] *Che* featured sex of all types and nudity, as well as vaguely political speech, such as when the character of Uncle Sam says, "Your perception illuminates."[17]

*Che*, *Paradise Now*, and *Dionysus in 69* opened downtown. But *Oh! Calcutta!* introduced the new nudity to a mainstream audience. When the revue opened off Broadway in June at the Eden Theater, a former burlesque house on Second Avenue, it presented nudity's liberating, counterculture power to a middle-class audience. Titled after the nude painting by Clovis Trouille, *Oh! Calcutta!* was a pun on the French phrase *"Oh, quel cul t'as"* (Oh, what a nice ass you have). It made bourgeois the Sexual Revolution's slogan "Make love not war." Put together by the theater critic Kenneth Tynan, the revue included "erotic" skits written by Sam Shepard, Jules Feiffer, and Samuel Beckett, as well as lesser-known writers. (Beckett eventually withdrew "Breath," his contribution, from the show after he learned naked bodies were to appear on the stage.)

According to Tynan, *Oh! Calcutta!'s* raison d'être was the absence of "civilized" sex in theater: "I realized there was no place for a civilized man to take a civilized woman for an evening of civilized erotic entertainment."[18] But Tynan had long scorned burlesque for its vulgarity, and he intended *Oh! Calcutta!* to be anti-burlesque, not just anti-bourgeois. The spectacle refuted striptease and thumbed its nose at the conventions of burlesque. "The idea is to use artistic means to achieve erotic stimulation," he said. Tynan initially planned to use some striptease, particularly that of the Paris variety. He wanted to cast a black stripper and use a Lili St. Cyr bathtub number, as well as a number Alain Bernadin created in which a widow strips as the organ plays at her husband's funeral. Tynan even asked the avant-garde Peter Brook to direct. (Brook declined.)

As *Oh! Calcutta!* producer Hillard Elkin put it, *Oh! Calcutta!* was cool, a Rorschach test of hip. "It's definitely not for the uptight," he told *Playboy.* A few days later, in a mock interview between him and an "intelligent person" in the *New York Times,* Tynan added, "It seemed to me a pity that eroticism in the theater should be confined to burlesque houses and the sleazier sort of night club. . . . [A]ll that I hope is that the result will be a few cuts above burlesque in intelligence and sophistication."[19]

The last surviving member of the Minsky family, Mort, wrote in to defend burlesque and striptease: "Was burlesque bad in the days of Minsky? I doubt very much whether the status of the contributors to *Oh! Calcutta!* is above that of the comedy skit writers for Minsky Burlesque in the 20's and 30's, so admired by Nathan, Mencken, Edmund Wilson, and other respected critics of the era. . . . [T]here is an honesty in early burlesque nowhere apparent in the current rash of nudies."[20]

But honesty was exactly what *Oh! Calcutta!*'s first skit—"Taking off the Robe"—sought to celebrate. When the actors walked onstage and removed their street clothes, it seemed for a moment that they were doing a burlesque tease. But then it became something more of the era. The actors undressed indifferently, dropping their clothes sloppily on the floor, making sure that the audience knew that this was not a performance designed to entertain. It portrayed a private, spontaneous moment. The actors ended up in the white light, exposed, naked. "Taking off the Robe" deliberately lacked striptease's artifice. Instead, the actors simply "let it all hang out." Their headshots came into view on a scrim, thus referencing the artifice of undressing onstage. Whereas St. Cyr's elaborate boudoir had challenged

"Taking off the Robe" number in *Oh! Calcutta!,* 1969. Jerome Robbins Dance Division, The New York Public Library for the Performing Arts, Astor, Lenox, and Tilden Foundations.

the coldness of the 1950s, *Oh! Calcutta!* embodied the freedom of the Sexual Revolution. Director Jacques Levy, who would revisit *Oh! Calcutta!* in his testimony at the Chicago Seven trial, wanted "nakedness, not nudity, frankness not sex."[21]

Still, *Oh! Calcutta!* did share one thing with Minskys' burlesque: it attempted to glitter. Its opening off Broadway at the Eden Theater was attended by celebrities, including Joe Namath, Shirley MacLaine, and Hedy Lamarr. New York critics, though, remained skeptical that the spectacle was about more than just flesh. Writing about the trend of "nude plays" that year, Richard Gilman declared pornography to be "sexual writing that fails as literature," and, perhaps summoning up nostalgia for bump and grind, Clive Barnes noted that the stripping in *Oh! Calcutta!* was devoid of eros: "It is childlike when they strip. And the stripping . . . was the only tolerable part of the evening." The *New York Times* gave Barnes's review the headline "A Most Innocent Dirty Show."[22]

But America loved "innocent dirt" in part because it was funny. *Playboy* reviewed the spectacle as a comedy. "*Oh! Calcutta!* satirizes and celebrates contemporary sexual mores, hang ups and diversions." If *Oh! Calcutta!*, heir to burlesque, was using sex as a basis for comedy in a different way from its predecessor, it was also finding humor in sexual desire, which was the same thing that burlesque did. The show was a smash. In July the script was published. A touring company started. By September tickets in the first two rows of the New York production were being sold for $25—the highest ticket price of any show ever.[23] Eventually, *Oh! Calcutta!* grossed $316 million. Charles Keating, chairman of Citizens for Decent Literature, came to see it and dubbed it "pure pornography."[24]

By having both men and women undress, *Oh! Calcutta!* announced a shift in the sexual dynamic between men and women. *Oh! Calcutta!* asserted that civilized men and women, democratically and politically allied, had moved closer together visually. Women no longer needed to strip to tantalize men. Instead, both men and women stripped for audiences. But was this revolutionary or just sensational? "The fact that people from the Midwest loved the show shocked everyone except people from the Midwest," said Jacques Levy, the director.[25]

A YEAR EARLIER, the avant-garde Living Theater had seized on the idea that striptease could be a metaphor for political liberation. Unlike *Hair*, the Living Theater's work never performed on Broadway. And they used more radical theatrical methods to get their point across. Having created a Dionysian spectacle, *Paradise Now*, in Italy, the Living Theater premiered it in Avignon. In the fall of 1968, they arrived in America. They first performed at the Yale School of Drama. In the initial segment of the anarchic spectacle, titled "The Rite of Guerilla Theatre," the members of the theatrical troupe strode onstage and chanted a series of taboos, including "phrase five . . . I'm not allowed to take my clothes off." The stage directions read:

> Even the nearest, the most natural is prohibited. The body itself of which we are made is taboo. We are ashamed of what is most beautiful; we are afraid of what is most beautiful. The corruption of the fig leaf is complete corruption. We may not arouse each other; we may not act naturally toward one another. The culture represses love.

Then the actors stripped down to bathing suits and underwear, or to what Julian Beck, the theater's cofounder, described as "the legal limit."[26]

"If I take off any more, I'll be arrested," Beck shouted as he dashed into the audience, preaching liberation via nudity. In New Haven the Becks were arrested for indecent exposure, which only confirmed their belief in the idea of sexual repression as the root of all evil. Judith Malina, Beck's wife and a cofounder of the troupe, made a distinction between *Paradise Now* and other "nude" plays such as *Hair*. She envisioned *Paradise Now* as stretching the limits of bourgeois society: "*Paradise* is an attempt to break that at every point we know how, including taking our clothes off to the legal limit and then pointing out to you that there is a legal limit and what are you going to do about it and what are we going to do about it together."[27]

*Paradise Now* sought to transform the actors into countercultural holy men. According to Richard Schechner, this disappointed members of the audience who expected a full striptease. Thus, the Living Theater politicized striptease both by dramatizing its taboo quality and by making its ultimate goal—nudity—a source of potential freedom. Taking it off was a step in the road to consciousness, forbidden from Americans because of an unorthodox combination of the law and internalized oppression.[28]

Mainstream critics were skeptical that stripping could overturn the status quo. "What does taking off your clothes have to do with the Vietnam War?" asked Elenore Lester in *Esquire*.[29] Other critics compared the performers' physiques to those of strippers and found them lacking. "You will not be interested in the performers in g-strings," Walter Kerr wrote in the *New York Times*. "Their bodies are scrawny and undeveloped."[30]

But the Living Theater actors' strip show inspired at least one viewer to push "the legal limit." On March 1, 1969, the night after seeing the Living Theater in Los Angeles, Jim Morrison, high on cocaine at the Dinner Key Auditorium in Miami, ripped off his pants onstage. Someone poured champagne over his head, and according to some accounts, he began to masturbate. That was more or less the end of Morrison's performing career. At least where rock and roll was concerned, stripping was still considered going too far.[31]

AROUND THE SAME TIME, feminism burst into mainstream consciousness and, as a movement, encouraged a highly politicized antipathy toward burlesque and striptease. In feminist circles, striptease and female display came to be seen as part of the widespread tyranny against women, something created by a capitalist and patriarchal culture to imprison them without their knowledge. In 1968, New York Radical Women, a feminist group, had united to protest the Miss America pageant in Atlantic City. *Ms.* editor Robin Morgan speculated that women were so incensed that they might burn their bras. Indeed, women did throw undergarments into a trashcan as a symbolic gesture while shouting "Freedom for women!" Out of this protest, the myth of bra-burning women's throwing off the garments that had "restricted" them was born. The story features women stripping angrily, as opposed to seductively.[32]

On January 19, 1969, a day before Nixon's inauguration, women radicals erupted again, motivated by growing fissure between men and women in the Student Democratic Society (SDS), the main countercultural student organization in the movement. Stokely Carmichael, the Black Power activist, famously said, "The only position for women in SNCC [the Student Nonviolent Coordinating Committee] is prone."

Women, beginning to feel like they were adjuncts in the movement, set about fighting what they saw as their male counterparts' bigotry. But they found themselves hurled back into repressive realms. The trouble started in Washington, at a meeting of the National Mobilization Committee, an antiwar forum, when the young radical Marilyn Webb took the podium. No sooner did she begin her speech with the words "We as women are oppressed . . ." than the men in the audience responded by hooting and jeering and shouting "Take it off!" and "Take her off the stage and fuck her!" as though, one observer noted, they were in a burlesque theater. "If radical men can be so easily provoked into acting like rednecks, what can we expect from others?" Ellen Willis wrote at the time. Thus striptease, by standing for the ultimate in antiwomen exploitation, became a conspicuous target for the modern feminist movement.[33]

BY CONTRAST, gay men used striptease as a playful, liberating device. The fashion historian Anne Hollander has observed that traditionally, men have looked "undignified and ridiculous" in their underwear and "not enticingly semi-nude."[34] The Stonewall riots began the end of that sorry state. On June 27, 1969, a group of gay men and lesbians resisted a police raid at the Stonewall Inn off Sheridan Square in Greenwich Village. For the protests that ensued, drag queens went public. When queens marched alongside of more acceptable "butch" homosexuals, they announced that it was okay to be camp. Until that moment, drag queens had performed in burlesque theaters and nightclubs alongside female strippers. Other gay men stigmatized them for not being "masculine."[35]

Meanwhile, the burlesque striptease Tempest Storm did was dead. In 1970, Ann Corio returned *This Was Burlesque*, her nostalgic show about striptease, to New York after a seven-year hiatus. None of her strippers wore G-strings, although, Corio explained, they did wear sheer body stockings. "They have a nude look," she said. "My manager wanted me to see *Oh! Calcutta!* I have no interest in seeing it. I don't see any culture or entertainment values in it. It's strictly for shock effect. . . . The Broadway theatre has sunk to its lowest level in obscenity," she added.[36]

From Las Vegas, where she was stripping in *Minsky's Burlesque 70*, Tempest Storm agreed. "I don't think that pornography and obscenity serve anything. They certainly don't entertain. And that is what I try to do."[37] By the end of the next decade, though, she too was stripping nude.

IN THE SEVENTIES, with the Sexual Revolution in full swing, everyone was. As Stanley Kauffman noted in the *New Republic*, sex had gone public. "For five dollars you can see a live sex show," he wrote. In 1979, Tom Wolfe wrote in *Life* in an essay called "The Sexed-Up, Doped-Up, Hedonistic Heaven of the Boom-Boom Seventies," "It was in the seventies . . . that the ancient wall around sexual promiscuity fell."[38]

Thus striptease came to seem even more old-fashioned. For one, female strippers no longer represented the "bad girl," and so men no longer feared them. Also, other changes were beginning: for the first time, women could watch male strippers. In the academy, perhaps in response to the "Make love not war" mood of the 1960s, sociologists and feminists began to speculate about why women became strippers.[39]

One answer, familiar since the thirties, was that most women did not want to become strippers: they were forced to do so by economic need and patriarchal repression. A survey conducted in 1971 asserted that fewer women wanted to become strippers than be anything else, including janitors, artists' models, and gamblers. "Every stripper we spoke with firmly believed that people regard her work as dirty and immoral," the survey reported. Using jargon like "deviance," other studies returned to the Cold War explanation that abused women and lesbians were more prone to becoming strippers than "normal" women.[40]

Alongside the new leniency, purity campaigns reasserted themselves as conservatives sought to get back to "family values." In his second term in the White House, Richard M. Nixon campaigned against sexual permissiveness in a number of areas, including pornography. In several landmark First Amendment cases, the Nixon Supreme Court gave power to the states and allowed them to determine "community standards."[41] Thus, as in earlier eras, many states and cities left rulings on obscenity to local

"Larry's Ballyhoo." Susan Meiselas/Magnum Photos, from the series *Carnival Strippers*.

officials. In some cities, strippers could still flash the G-string, so long as they kept it on. In other cities, strippers lowered the G-string to the knees or ankles, and in still others they removed it. Carnivals also were disappearing as venues for striptease. By the 1970s, they had become venues for sex shows.

And yet the fact was that while some strip clubs and burlesque theaters produced live sex shows, other strippers continued to perform a more nude version of fifties striptease. And a market remained for some kind of burlesque, although by this point it was pornographic films mixed with live acts. *Newsweek* reported that there were six "burlesque" theaters in New York in 1970. The following year, the eastern burlesque circuit—then also known as the Bryan and Engle circuit—linked eleven theaters in ten cities east of the Mississippi. This circuit served about seven thousand strippers who worked for as little as three- to four-month stretches or as much as forty weeks per year.[42]

Pornography was shifting from the nudie-cutie movies into an industry. The rating X and triple-X were invented. In 1973 the *New York Times* coined the phrase "porno chic" to describe the literati's flirtation with the industry, and two hard-core films, *The Devil in Miss Jones* and *Deep Throat*, were among the top ten moneymakers in Hollywood. And yet in San Francisco, the Mitchell brothers, who had filmed the pornographic classic *Behind the Green Door* in 1969, continued to book burlesque queens from earlier eras at their theaters—the O'Farrell and the Palace—until the end of the 1970s. Blaze Starr stripped at the O'Farrell, "the Carnegie Hall of Sex," in 1975 alongside of triple-X rated films. "Everyone's getting tired of the celluloid nudity of the porno flicks. They want to see real flesh again," Starr said, by way of explanation.[43]

Headliners could add to their salaries by starring in pornographic movies or posing for magazines such as *Playboy*.[44]

By the middle of the decade, while Americans dallied sexually, resentment in Washington against politicians' erotic excesses accrued, as radical feminist and gay rights continued to gain power. In 1974, Larry Flynt, who got his start as a strip club owner in Ohio and Kentucky, founded *Hustler*, a hard-core pornography magazine also depicting violence against women. *Hustler* paved the way for *Screw*, an even more explicit magazine. Women's libbers began to ask when it would stop. That same year, after Fanne Fox, aka Annabella Batistella, a stripper who worked under the name "the Argentinean Bombshell," was discovered to be having an affair with House Ways and Means Committee chair Wilbur Mills, the media reception was considerably less forgiving than it had been twenty years earlier during Earl Long's reign.

When Mills, who was married, crashed his car in the Tidal Basin, Fox was inside. At first he was flippant. Asked what he had learned from the adventure, he said, "Don't go out with foreigners who drink champagne." But in a moment of spectacularly bad judgment, Mills flew a Lear Jet to see Fox at the Pilgrim in Boston, where TV cameras caught him stepping onstage with the stripper, who was costumed in the requisite feather boa and G-string. Even as public opinion turned against him, Mills was proclaiming, "Nothing can ruin me." But Mills's performance forced him out of the Congress and destroyed his marriage.[45]

By the end of the decade, most burlesque theaters, having switched to showing adult films, were put out of business by civic committees. The Folly Burlesque Theatre in Kansas City closed again in 1974. It had outlasted every other theater except for Philadelphia's Trocadero, which would shut its doors four years later. The Folly played adult films until January 23, when it "died a quiet death," after a final, forgettable X-rated movie starring "Chesty Gabor."[46] Sold to a New York property management company and slated to become a parking lot for the new convention center across the street, the theater was destined for the wrecking ball until a group of civic-minded developers stepped in to declare it a historic landmark.[47] When the Folly reopened in 1980, developers referred to its burlesque past as part of a heritage of popular culture. But developers chose John Murray and Albert Boretz's *Room Service*, a thirties comedy, as the entertainment for the theater's premiere. Tempest Storm attended as a guest alongside Walter Cronkite and other luminaries.[48]

Elsewhere, the transformation of strip clubs and burlesque theaters into pornography palaces caught the interest of feminists. In the late seventies, Susan Brownmiller founded Women Against Pornography after her anti-pornography book *Against Our Will: Men, Women, and Rape* was published. The group began to host tours to New York topless and strip bars as part of its campaign. As the feminist movement against pornography expanded, protests against strip clubs increased. Many feminists believed that alongside pornographic movies, strip clubs incited violence against women and that women were coerced into performing in them. In 1978 radical feminists launched the first "Take Back the Night" march in San Francisco as a protest against theater managers' abuse of topless dancers. Thousands of women marched through North Beach.

Male striptease became an industry. *Cosmopolitan* ran its first male nude centerfold in 1970. Male striptease found its way onto television, inspiring the *New York Times* to write articles about the trend of "swatches" of bare male chests.[49] In 1979 an Indian immigrant named Steve Banerjee founded Chippendale's, a franchise peddling heterosexual male striptease. At first Chippendale's presented the raunchy type of stripping seen in strip clubs in previous decades. But the owners soon realized they could make more money by experimenting with romantic and Hollywoodish modes of undressing onstage. Instead of toying with indifference to their own sexuality, or camping it up à la drag, straight male strippers tried to project a super-masculinity beneath which lurked an extreme vulnerability. The macho-man costume with little more than hard hat or handcuffs accentuates the G-string, which is still shocking—a method of feminine display, emphasizing a man's buttocks.[50]

In some ways, male strip clubs like Chippendale's referred back to the elite supper clubs of the fifties, although they reversed the gender roles. A couple of them served women multicourse meals before and the performance. Some of them created "star" male dancers who attracted their own fans. These male strippers made dances such as the hustle part of popular culture. They used humor in their routines, and they did numbers revealing their dreams of fame and fortune that in the end resembled Gypsy Rose Lee's.[51]

Newspaper coverage about male strippers sometimes focused on female audiences' savagery, as if that in and of itself were shocking. "Would men behave as pathetically as women?" one reporter asked. Conclusions varied. Women "shout their encouragement" at the male dancers, another announced. A third described how a mob of women marched into a male strip club and ripped the shirt off of two employees, who ran away. Another ended by averring, "So long as men retain the economic and social power in this culture, male strip shows are not a true reversal . . . but a joke."[52]

Several communities across the country reacted to clubs' adding male strippers by shutting them down. In New York, Chippendale's itself was brought to trial for refusing to admit men.[53] And many women remained as divided about male stripping as they had been about the female version. Some saw the advent of male strippers as part of their expanding voice about things sexual. In 1980, when the feminist Gloria Allred organized a fund-raising event featuring male strippers, other feminists and feminists' organizations, including the National Organization for Women (NOW), rushed to condemn her.[54] But at least some ordinary women leapt at the opportunity to see naked men. "I'm not a women's libber," said Mary Diaz, "but I might be over this."[55]

Although the media coverage of strip clubs in this decade proved that, given the opportunity, women would become wild and crazy consumers of sex at least as often as men, in the popular imagination one difference seemed to be that the male performers were allowed to love the adulation. By contrast, at "gentlemen's clubs," women expressed less exuberance.[56]

In the 1980s, in many American cities, the new generation of "topless and bottomless" strip clubs flourished while the AIDS crisis made ordinary people more fearful of sex than they had been since the 1950s. The corresponding sexual counterrevolution would inspire Americans to be more cautious, even suspicious, of the "liberation" of the two previous decades. And yet in 1980, when Tempest Storm, fifty-two, stripped at the Valley Forge Music Fair, she held a crowd made up of men, women, and children.[57]

# Conclusion

Today, the very scope of sexual possibilities available to women has paradoxically resuscitated a version of old-fashioned burlesque striptease. One idea driving this "movement" is that teasing, in all of its retro varieties, is as sexy as stripping, and possibly more so because it reveals less. One Los Angeles–based group, the Los Angeles Pussycat Dolls, presents "neoburlesque" shows starring Carmen Electra and "guest dolls," like Charlize Theron, who lip-synch routines choreographed by MTV dancer Robin Antin. Their most popular numbers are retro: one is a Tex Guinan type of "Big Spender" dance; another, a fifties-style cigarette-smoking romp set to Henry Mancini's "Pink Panther." Aspiring to legitimacy, the Dolls perform at "celebrity" hangouts like Johnny Depp's Viper Room in LA, and, like many of the strippers who preceded them, describe themselves not as strippers but as "professional dancers" inspired by Bob Fosse, Berlin cabaret, Cyd Charisse, Fred Astaire, and Gene Kelly.[1]

By contrast, TV shows like HBO's *G-String Divas* and *The Sopranos* also reflect renewed interest in stripping, but mostly by using strip clubs as backdrops for illicit activity and by painting strippers as hookers *manquées*. There is often an air of violence in these shows, a boredom with women, the suggestion that decadence and deviant activity go hand in hand with stripping. *G-String Divas*, first aired in 2000 as a part of HBO's "sexploitation" series, offered cable television viewers a chance to peek at the private lives of women at Diva's, a luxurious strip club north of Philadelphia. Among other questions the show asked was how much a stripper's success was based on old-fashioned "tease" and how much on pornography. *G-String Divas* told a more cynical story than pre–Sexual Revolution answers to this question had: Although "teasing" might be provocative, it could not compete with stripping. Customers tended to want to see women take it all off in the VIP rooms. On camera, at least, the strippers appeared to be doing a lot of undressed grinding, and little teasing.[2]

Other television shows and advertising phenomena mostly present stripping, with the tease part happening so quickly that we barely see it. A cartoon show presents a stripper who is a superhero, and something called "cardio striptease" promotes the idea that stripping is now good for you as well as being sexy. The show *Are You Hot or Not?* updates a version of striptease for the twenty-first century by reducing contest participants to hunks of throbbing sex appeal. Unlike reality "talent" shows such as *American Idol*, there is no possibility of smarts or skills intervening in *Are You Hot?* Judges are interested solely in the way contestants project what *Variety* used to call s.a. (sex appeal)—but whereas highbrow critics used to knock striptease for being "no talent" in the twenties and thirties, here we celebrate it.

Although both the Dolls and television shows present an extension of Minskys'-style stripping, neither of them is, in the end, a contemporary version of the striptease I have described in this book. For we live in an age in which tease is irrelevant and stripping is all. This reflects both the social freedoms arrived at in the last quarter century and the fact that we prize instant gratification over anticipation. Stripping itself is so common as to be no longer shocking, except that perhaps it may be the one arena where, beneath everything, women are women and men are men. The real radicalism in stripping today—if there is any—arises from the fact that it glorifies women, even when a commercial impulse drives that glorification.[3]

Meanwhile, neoburlesque striptease remains a minor-league diversion. Neoburlesque, as its performers proclaim, is about neither nudity nor pornography. But it sometimes reveals nostalgia for, among other things, more stable gender roles of earlier eras, even if only for something to react against. Although some neoburlesquers do comic stripteases to rock and roll soundtracks, I have never seen any strips performed to rap or hip-hop. And for the most part, neoburlesque's popularity drives against the great equalizing trend in modern life, which prefers fluidity and androgyny over masculinity and femininity. Neoburlesque's popularity tends to yearn for the fifties—for a time when fewer choices existed—although it also sometimes makes fun of the limitations of those choices. In the 1870s, in the Jazz Age, or in the 1950s, when women taking off their clothes played with and against ideas of male behavior, striptease acts rebelled against the status quo, all the while being less androgynous than, say, fashion.

The ideal of static gender roles no longer carries much weight. Yet popular ideas about commercializing the female body assume that sex is always in some way going on and that it can nonetheless sometimes be subverted. Therefore, journalists, critics, and performers refer to neoburlesque—and even sometimes the stripping in gentlemen's clubs—as "overthrowing" restrictive categories abandoned in previous epochs, as part of an ongoing revolution, and above all as fun. So-called Grrrl feminists—those who proclaim they can be sexy and also be feminist—often use both neoburlesque and stripping to congratulate themselves on how far they've come from the radical feminism of the 1960s and 1970s. Sometimes they do also play at being androgynous or even masculine. The decision to strip is a choice, they argue, not a desperate move driven by need or repression.

And yet this is too simple a story. In terms of stripping, as journalists since the 1920s have documented, many women do enter it out of financial desperation, and some others are coerced into it. Echoing some of the skeptics confronting the claims of the Sexual Revolution in the 1960s, one question to be asked is: What kind of protest is taking off your clothes in front of a group of paying customers? Or, as the feminist scholar Marilyn Yalom puts it in *A History of the Breast*, "Where is the line between the empowerment of an individual woman paid for showing her breasts and the victimization of numerous other women all lumped together as sex objects?" Or, to raise another perhaps unfashionable question of my own: Is it possible for commerce and sexual pleasure ever to not be at odds?[4]

Both stripping and neoburlesque answer these questions in confounding ways, which is what's fascinating about them. Neoburlesque recalls in its origins a mix of protest and commercialism, as well as a dash of ennui tossed together by economic booms. Between World War I and the Sexual Revolution, burlesque striptease flourished, defying economic conditions and reformers and drawing in audiences and hard-up women (and sometimes less-hard-up ones). But if this stripping was "radical" in the sense that it allowed women to climb the economic ladder, it is difficult to accept the idea that either neoburlesque or "gentlemen's club" stripping are radical, except in the vaguest terms.[5]

IN THE MEDIA, the question of whether striptease of any sort denigrates women continues to simmer. In the seventies, that debate arose as part of a larger argument about pornography: was it patriarchal and therefore misogynist, or liberating and feminist? Today, that debate remains unsettled, but strip clubs endure. At the same time, even though more and more women claim stripping to be "fun," men can still lose their jobs and reputations if reporters discover them at a strip club or in a stripper's company.[6]

Meanwhile, the American desire to know what strippers "really" think about what they do drives the publication of memoirs and the producing of movies and miniseries. There is now a book about striptease for every demographic. In the last decade, at least ten memoirs about striptease have been published. One thing separating these memoirs from those of the 1950s and earlier, however, is that although they purport to reveal why women take off their clothes for money, for the most part, by paying little attention to class, they reveal less than they did in the past. Gypsy Rose Lee might have constructed the details of her life in *Gypsy*—she was a great American fake. And yet she was essentially honest about her motive for stripping, which was to hurl herself away from the constraints of her family and her past and into the American dream.

But many of these new memoirs want to have it all ways: They assert that their heroines are virtuous, having fun. Stripping is a dalliance for them—and it is not necessary for them to escape their situations. Yet by the denouement, the writers inevitably discover that stripping makes them feel bad. "For a long time I swore striptease wouldn't affect me deeply because I was working with my body, not my soul," Lili Burana writes in *Strip City*. And then she goes on to say that of course it did.[7]

After the Sexual Revolution, common wisdom dictates that women who strip should have other options. But as these memoirists tell it, their options are as constrained as Lydia Thompson's were. And moreover, they treat the audience in the opposite way than, say, Gypsy did in her day. Gypsy came from nothing and claimed the working class as her audience, all the while courting the elite. These days, one reigning paradigm is the upper class, or even celebrity, strippers who "fall" to take their clothes off —slumming, in other words. A recently published memoir, *Ivy League Stripper*, announces that paradox simply by its title.[8]

These memoirs are confused. First they provoke readers with their very premise: It is impossible in America really to make it as a woman unless one is willing to take off one's clothes for money. *Ivy League Stripper* poses as an indictment of a system requiring working-class women to strip if they want to get together the money to attend an elite college. But *Ivy League Stripper* also poses as an indictment of the sexist abuses wreaked against women in those colleges, which, the writer claims, are more dishonest than anything occurring in strip joints. Finally, although this memoir claims to be turning the tables on men because the "Ivy League Stripper" is taking their money (a not altogether new idea), she also facilely uses the word "empowering" to describe why she strips.

The threads connecting these memoirs to golden age burlesque are both more tenuous and more complicated than these writers admit. There continues to be an economic incentive: Stripping offers uneducated women—and, according to these memoirs, educated ones—a flexible and lucrative way to pay the bills. In other words, stripping allows women to, in the jargon of our times, "take control" of their lives financially, much as burlesque striptease once did. Another (vaguer) constant is that stripping allows working-class women to enter a world whose gender rules seem paradoxically less proscribed than the worlds of Ivy League colleges or nine-to-five work. Still other women find stripping to be a pleasurable realm where gender roles appear to be static and yet different from the outside world's. In other words, one can deviate from the rules of attraction. Perhaps this is why some women report liking the power that stripping seems to offer. They find stripping neither degrading nor enlightening. (Although they do sometimes describe what they do in language that suggests that they are conning the "baldheads" in the audience, there is no sympathy for those baldheads, as there was in earlier eras.)

Taken as a group, the recent memoirs prove that stripping continues to serve a clear function in American society and one that we often prefer not to think about: to titillate. However we make fun of it, stripping still has the power to catapult women—even if just for a moment—outside of conventional boundaries of sex and gender.

IN ITS HEYDAY, the so-called golden age, striptease inspired Americans of all tastes and pleasures with irreverence, and, at its best, wit. Neoburlesque striptease sometimes does the same, even though there is also sometimes something antiseptic about all of the effort put into these acts, a grunting, melancholy foray into the past. The new scene also lacks the particular relationship burlesque created between performer and audience. Although the performer continues to strive for indecorous yet charming ways, encouraged by the feeling of wanting to do something taboo, often what she is doing is hardly more taboo than anything the audience could see on television. This despite what is perhaps the major change—that the majority of audience members for striptease until 1968 were men and now the audience is composed of all genders and sexual preferences.

Then too, whereas the nightclubs where strippers performed in the old days brought audiences right into the heart of a city's underbelly, today that underbelly is harder to find. Even though in the 1990s AIDS made sex a scary phenomenon and allowed striptease subsequently to reassert itself as a cabaret entertainment, this seems out of synch with what is going on in general in American culture. Finally, the major difference between the golden age of striptease in the 1930s and our own era is that so many more varieties of pleasure and so many types of undressing are for sale.

And what about the claim that striptease is an art form? Is this just hype? Our skeptical, modern tendency would have it thus. Striptease is, of course, neither Rembrandt nor Beckett. And yet there is certainly something to be said for the idea that golden age striptease offered its audience more than pornography—it was a popular art. This striptease presented seduction, which is at best a kind of interpretive art, like acting. It was also sentimental, like Norman Rockwell, Hallmark cards, or Tin Pan Alley, and comic, in that it made fun of our obsession with sex, which is what made reformers turn against it as much as its tendency to reveal flesh. It could also be nostalgic, hearkening back to another era. Like other popular arts, striptease inspired imitation, as well as contempt and distress. Even today, it arouses these emotions and clings to our imagination.

I initially wanted to consider striptease as a social force, as a piece of history, as a profession, and as a destination for women on the way up. Also, striptease appeared to flout established ideas about the boundary between pornography and entertainment and to confound ideas that the women performing it are either victims or entrepreneurs. Striptease remains one of the most vivid forms of live entertainment—outside of simple pornography—that revolves almost completely around the phenomenon of human beings' watching each other for pleasure.

Only by looking at striptease as part of popular history can we explain its force and pervasive character, as well as what continues to make it so potent. The meaning of striptease remains fluid and ultimately paradoxical. Although it is impossible to return to the languorous innocence of the golden era of striptease, women taking off their clothes in public continue to evince a primal and primally compelling force. Striptease remains essentially about itself, and as long as the promise of sex is more alluring than the reality, striptease will command our attention.

# Notes

## Abbreviations, Archival Sources

| | |
|---|---|
| AGVA | American Guild of Variety Artists Collection, Robert F. Wagner Labor Archives, Bobst Library, New York University |
| BRTC | Billy Rose Theater Collection, New York Public Library for the Performing Arts |
| BV | Bambi Vawn Papers, Billy Rose Theater Collection, New York Public Library |
| COP | A Century of Progress International Exposition Records, Special Collections Department, Richard J. Daley Library, University of Illinois at Chicago |
| C-Press | Century of Progress International Exposition, New York World's Fair Collection, Manuscripts and Archives Division, Sterling Memorial Library, Yale University |
| 4 A's | Four A's Records, Robert F. Wagner Labor Archives, Bobst Library, New York University |
| FTA | Folly Theatre Archives, Kansas City |
| GRL | Gypsy Rose Lee Papers, Billy Rose Theater Collection, New York Public Library for the Performing Arts |
| HM | Harold Minsky Collection, University of Nevada, Las Vegas, Special Collections |
| HRP | Harold Rome Papers, Irving S. Gilmore Music Library, Yale University |
| HUTC | Harvard University Theater Collection |
| JDM | Jess and Dorothy Mack Collection, University of Nevada, Las Vegas, Special Collections |
| KI | Kinsey Institute |
| LGNS | LaGuardia News Scrapbook, Municipal Archives, Department of Records and Information Services, City of New York |
| MA | LaGuardia Papers, Municipal Archives, Department of Records and Information Services, City of New York |
| MCNY | Museum of the City of New York |
| NYPL | New York Public Library |
| SA | Shubert Archives |
| SRM | Sally Rand Manuscript Collection, Uncatalogued Collection, Chicago Historical Society |

TUNC     Temple University Nudity Collection Clippings Files

UTA      University of Texas at Austin, Harry Ransom Humanities Research
         Center, Striptease Clippings File, New York Journal-American

WHMC     Tamony Collection/Western Historical Manuscript Collection, a
         joint collection of the University of Missouri and the State
         Historical Society of Missouri

## Introduction

1. "The Business of Burlesque, 1935 A.D.," *Fortune*, February 1935, 67.
2. "The Business of Pornography," *U.S. News and World Report*, February 10, 1997, 44, 48. The number of strip clubs doubled between 1987 and 1992. The annual revenue of a strip club can be as much as $5 million. A top porn actress can earn $15,000 a week at one of these clubs.
3. Louis Sobol, *Broadway Heartbeat* (New York, 1953), 257; *The Longest Street: A Memoir* (New York, 1968), 203–4. Gypsy quoted in Jean Charvil, *Histoire et Sociologie du Striptease* (Paris, 1969), 96.
4. Gypsy Rose Lee, "Gypola's Big Illusion," *Variety*, September 6, 1950, 2, 52.
5. Private communication with Alison Lurie, June 15, 2004.
6. Denys Chevalier, *Métaphysique du Striptease* (Paris, 1961), 1.
7. This term comes from John Lahr's book *Automatic Vaudeville: Essays on Star Turns with a New Essay on the Rolling Stones* (New York, 1985).
8. Just a few examples: Guy Trebay, "After Nice, a Return to Vice," *New York Times*, June 8, 2003, Section 9; Debra Sontag, "Fierce Entanglements," *New York Times*, November 18, 2002, Section 6; Adam Fiefield, "Life on Freedom Street," *New York Times*, December 23, 2001, Section 14; Judith Lynn Hannah, "Wrapping Nudity in a Cloak of Law," *New York Times*, Section 2. *Live Nude Girls Unite!*, a 2000 film by Julia Query, documents the efforts of the women at the Lusty Lady Peep Show to unionize.
9. Nor is the revival limited to the coasts. In 2001 a group of women in Columbus, Ohio, formed Miss Kitty's Hot Box, a troupe devoted to old-fashioned burlesque. A Vancouver-based burlesque troupe called the Fluffgirls tours America and Canada. The list goes on and on.
10. Adam Gopnick, "The Naked City," *New Yorker*, July 23, 2001, 30; *Village Voice*, March 5, 2003, 27.
11. Amanda Zeitlin, "American Talkers: The Art of the Sideshow Carnival Pitchman and Other Itinerant Showmen and Vendors," Ph.D. dissertation, University of Pennsylvania, 1992, 166.
12. Walter Kerr, "The Year of Sex," *New York Times*, February 2, 1969.
13. Lewis Erenberg, *Steppin' Out: New York Nightlife and the Transformation of American Culture: 1890–1920* (Chicago, 1981), preface.
14. See, for example, Robert C. Allen, *Horrible Prettiness: Burlesque and American Culture* (Chapel Hill, 1990), 245.
15. Susan Glenn, *Female Spectacle: The Roots of Modern Feminism* (Cambridge, 2000), 7.
16. "Not Dirty, Not Clean, Not Good for Hybrid Stock Burlesque in Pittsburgh," *Variety*, April 29, 1931, 62. This argument was also often made about music hall and variety performers, but it gained a particular intensity—even viciousness— when referring to strippers.

17. Performance historian Jill Dolan argues that burlesque made women "the easy target of men's jokes" and that striptease simply reveals women's "desire to be desired," thus reproducing a conventional power relationship between men and women; Robert C. Allen talks about striptease as an area of negotiation of power but uses the fact that after 1930, the majority of strippers performed in silence to suggest that burlesque is ultimately not "empowering." Allen, 283.

18. Jean Cocteau, *My Journey around the World* (London, 1958), tr. W. F. Strachey, originally published in Paris, 1936, 169; Zeitlin, 129.


**"A Startled Fawn upon the Stage"**

1. Lynn Garafola, *Rethinking the Sylph: New Perspectives on the Romantic Ballet* (Hanover, N.H., 1994), 4.
2. L'Affaire Hutin is recounted in Robert C. Allen, *Horrible Prettiness: Burlesque and American Culture* (Chapel Hill, 1990), 87–89. Circuses and New York in the 1840s comes from T. Allston Brown, *Amphitheaters and Circuses* (San Bernadino, 1994), 23. Alvin Harlow, *The Old Bowery* (New York, 1931); David Nasaw, *Going Out: The Rise and Fall of Popular Amusements* (New York, 1983).
3. Joseph Norton Ireland, *Records of the New York Stage from 1750 to 1860*, Volume 1 (New York, 1866), 528. Some sources say that Mme Hutin was wearing loose, harem-like trousers the first time she performed. Allston claims that she never performed in New York again, but that is contradicted by other sources.
4. Sylvie Chevalley, "Mme Francisque Hutin," *Dance* 31 (April 1957), 40–42, 83–85.
5. Mary Grace Smith, *Belles and Beaux on Their Toes: Dancing Stars in Young America* (Washington, 1980), 24.
6. Quoted in David Grimsted, *Melodrama Unveiled: American Theatre and Culture, 1800–1850* (Chicago, 1995), 26.
7. Christopher Lazare, "That Was New York," *New Yorker*, December 9, 1944, 58–72. Lazare suggests that Hutin was a man, a concept that is interesting given the later history of cross-dressed female performers. George C. D. Odell, *Annals of the New York Stage, 1821–1834* (New York, 1928), 264–65; Allen, 88; Ireland, 528.
8. Lithographs of *La Sylphide* show Taglioni in bare feet, although ballerinas did not really perform barefoot or barelegged until the Trilby craze of 1895 paved the way for Maud Allen's "classical" Oriental dances circa 1908.
9. Allen, 90.
10. Sean Wilentz, *Chants Democratic: New York City and the Rise of the American Working Class* (New York, 1984), 257. This influx of working-class people into New York has been well documented not just by Wilentz but also by Eric Hobsbawm, Lawrence Levine, and Bruce McConachie.
11. Walt Whitman, "The Old Bowery: A Reminiscence of New York Plays and Acting Fifty Years Ago," in *Complete Prose Works* (Boston, 1902), 429.
12. Walt Whitman, *The Journalism, 1846–1848*, Volume 1, ed. Herbert Bergman (New York, 1998), 228. Whitman continued in this vein for several years; Herbert Bergman, *Journalism*, Volume 2 (New York, 1998), 190. George G. G. Foster, *New York in Slices* (New York, 1856), 120, Beinecke Rare Books and Manuscripts Library, Yale University.

Notes to Pages 15-17

13. Johannes Goethe recounts that one afternoon in the spring of 1787, at the home of his friend Sir William Hamilton, the British ambassador to Rome, the ambassador's consort, Emma Hart, a famous British beauty whose amorous liaisons included Lord Nelson, imitated some figures on Greek vases. Wearing a Greek costume, Hart went through the motions displayed on the vases and, Goethe noted excitedly, resembled "the Apollo Belvedere." Goethe was delighted.

14. John Elsom, *Erotic Theater* (New York, 1974), 23.

15. This is well documented, perhaps best in Michael Schudson, *Discovering the News* (New York, 1984), 12–57. Tice Miller, ed., *Bohemians and Critics: American Theatre Criticism in the Nineteenth Century* (Metuchen, N.J., 1981), 4–6, 10–13, 140–41, 160–61.

16. Jack McCullough, *Living Pictures on the New York Stage* (Ann Arbor, 1983), chapters 2 and 3. Sources documenting the Anglo-American rivalry in the 1840s that led to the Astor Place riots in 1849 include David Grimsted and Robert C. Allen.

17. Brooks McNamara, *The New York Concert Saloon: The Devil's Own Nights* (New York, 2002), 83–96; Luc Sante, *Low Life: Lures and Snares of Old New York* (New York, 1991), 104–45.

18. George G. G. Foster, *New York by Gaslight* (New York, 1857), 12–15, Beinecke Rare Books and Manuscripts Library, Yale University.

19. Foster wrote in another one of his underground guides to the city, *New York Naked*: "It is incredible that anything short of goats and satyrs should find such obscene exhibitions of bandy-legged, flabby breasted, and lank deformity enticing," 145. Nor was Foster the only contemporary writer to describe the women in living pictures as bedraggled, desperate, impoverished, and obscene. A caricature of a living picture model from the *Police Gazette* shows another old crone "remembering" her former beauty, as if to imply that she had never attained it. Robert Toll, *On with the Show: The First Century of Show Business in America* (New York, 1976), 208; Foster, *New York by Gaslight*, 81.

20. Foster quoted in Timothy Gilfoyle, *City of Eros: New York City, Prostitution, and the Commercialization of Sex, 1790–1920* (New York, 1992), 128.

21. Quoted in Gilfoyle, 127. Neil Harris, *Humbug: The Art of P. T. Barnum* (Chicago, 1993), 31–59, and Philip B. Kunhardt Jr. et al., *P. T. Barnum: America's Greatest Showman* (New York, 1995), 28–86, both devote extensive time to the American museum's acquisition of male and female curiosities. There was, for example, the Fiji mermaid, a half-woman half-fish. Foster, *New York by Gaslight*, 7–8.

22. "The Police and the Model Artists," *New York Times*, April 10, 1852, 2.

23. Foster, *New York by Gaslight*, 15.

24. In Europe, a similar rise in "depravity" inspired a wave of reform that would extinguish the old bawdy music halls. The new generation of music halls were now featuring plays, operas, and ballets in addition to the regular comic turns. In England, the Lord Chamberlain clamped down with the 1843 Theater Act, which forced the music halls to either become legitimate theaters—and not sell alcohol—or confine themselves to musical numbers and get their customers as drunk as they liked. Women were finally admitted with the idea that they would help reform this genre of entertainment, and so by the 1860s, the craze for music halls had spread to the middle class and many elaborate new halls were built.

Although Paris lacked the repressive Theater Act, there too, music halls became architecturally and theatrically more ornate, as if sex could be made proper with enough gilt on the ceiling. The three oldest theaters—the Café Morel, the Ambassadeurs, and the Pavillon de l'Horloge—guarded either side of the Champs d'Elysées like ferocious lions. But the most elaborate was the El Dorado, the Goncourt brothers' favorite. Built in 1853, the El Dorado by the next decade had been renovated to include the bourgeois glory of "a big circular room with two tiers of boxes all gilt and painted with false marble [and] dazzling chandeliers."

25. Gilfoyle, 110.
26. Patricia Cline Cohen, *The Murder of Helen Jewett* (New York, 2001), 69–79
27. Christine Stansell, *City of Women: Sex and Class in New York, 1780–1860* (Urbana, 1986), 90–95.
28. Alan Nevins and Milton Halsey Thomas, eds., *The Diary of George Templeton Strong* (New York, 1952), Volume 2, 225; Foster, *New York in Slices*, 154; Claudia Johnson, "That Guilty Third Tier: Prostitution in Nineteenth-Century American Theaters," *American Quarterly* (a journal of the American Studies Association) 27 (1975), 575–84.
29. Prostitutes, Gilfoyle, 60; Thomas Nevins, *The Diary of George Templeton Strong*, Volume 1, 114, 217–18, 262, 294; Foster, *New York in Slices*, 154.

## Legs

1. T. J. Clark, *The Painting of Modern Life: Paris in the Art of Manet and His Followers* (Princeton, 1999), 128.
2. There are many books about the development of the department store and its effects on women; see Donald L. Miller, *City of the Century* (New York, 1998), 254–65, and Emile Zola, *Ladies Paradise*, trans. Brian Nelson (New York, 1995), 5, 117.
3. Charles Baudelaire cited in Abigail Solomon-Godeau, "The Legs of the Countess," *October* 39 (1986), 75.
4. Ivor Guest cited in Solomon-Godeau, 85–86.
5. This history is documented in William C. Darrah, *Cartes de Visite in Nineteenth Century Photography* (Gettysburg, Pa., 1981), 54, 55, 126–27. Elizabeth Anne McCauley, *A. A. E. Disderi and the* Carte de Visite *Portrait Photograph* (New Haven, 1985), 85–112.
6. Pierre Apraxine et al., *La Divine Comtesse: Photographs of the Countess de Castiglione* (New Haven and London, 2000), 38. Solomon-Godeau's Feminist-Marxist interpretation of the Countess is also interesting and attributes more agency to her than other sources do.
7. Apraxine, 27.
8. Solomon-Godeau, 76, 77, 80.
9. McCauley, 96, 106–9.
10. This is well documented in Valerie Steele, *Fashion and Eroticism: Ideals in Feminine Beauty from the Victorian Era to the Jazz Age* (New York, 1985), 192–95.
11. The absence of the crotch is only matched in significance by the appearance of pantaloons. Before the nineteenth century, women—except for courtesans and actresses—eschewed underwear, which was considered obscene because it divided their legs.
12. Yvette Guilbert, *The Song of My Life: My Memories* (London, 1929), 74.

13. Heinrich Heine, *The Works of Heinrich Heine*, Volume IV, trans. Charles Godfrey Leland (London, 1893), 356.
14. Solomon-Godeau, 91 (n33).
15. Michel Souvais, *Le Memoir d'un insolante* (Paris, 1998), 16.
16. Gustave Coquiot quoted in "Queens of the Cancan, Dance and Dancers," December 1952, 14–18.
17. Lynn Garafola, "The Travesty Dancer," *Dance Review Theatre Journal* 17, no. 2, 35–40.
18. Born in Louisiana, the Menken had married a Jew, had converted to Judaism, and was possibly one-quarter black.
19. Paul Lewis, *Queen of the Plaza* (New York, 1964), 23. Description of horse, Allen Lesser, *Enchanting Rebel: The Secret of Adah Isaacs Menken* (New York, 1947).
20. Lesser, 8.
21. Wolf Mankowitz, *Mazeppa: The Lives, Loves, and Legends of Adah Isaacs Menken* (New York, 1982), 20.
22. Robert C. Allen, in *Horrible Prettiness: Burlesque and American Culture* (Chapel Hill, 1990), says she was the first.
23. Roy Rosenzweig points out that the spectators for these shows were not primarily blue-collar workers, as they had been in the 1840s: white-collar "sportin' men," as they were called now, represented a good percentage of consumers. *Eight Hours for What We Will: Workers and Leisure in an Industrial City, 1870–1920* (New York, 1983).
24. Ruth Rosen, *The Lost Sisterhood: Prostitution in America, 1900–1918* (Baltimore, 1982), 8–11.
25. Joseph Whitton, *An Inside History of* The Black Crook (New York, 1897), 6.
26. According to Bernard Sobel, in *Burleycue: An Underground History of Burlesque Days* (New York, 1931), *The Black Crook* was also the place where women first performed the cancan in America outside of the brothel.
27. Robert Toll, *On with the Show: The First Century of Show Business in America* (New York, 1976), 215; Allen, 114.
28. There are now a number of critical studies about Lydia Thompson, including Kurt Ganzl, *Lydia Thompson, A Biography, Forgotten Stars of the Musical Theatre* (New York, 2002), chapter 4, and Faye E. Dudden, *Women in the American Theatre: Actresses and Audiences, 1790–1870* (New Haven, 1994), 149–82.
29. Timothy Gilfoyle, *City of Eros: New York City, Prostitution, and the Commercialization of Sex, 1790–1920* (New York, 1992), 129.
30. Alan Nevins and Milton Halsey Thomas, eds., *The Diary of George Templeton Strong* (New York, 1952), Volume 2, 228.
31. Frederick Van Wyck, *Recollections of an Old New Yorker* (New York, 1932), 183–84.
32. Mark Twain, *Travels with Mr. Brown*, ed. Franklin Walker and G. Ezra Dane (New York, 1940), 84–86.
33. Allen, 134–35.
34. Thomas Beer, *The Mauve Decade: America at the End of the Nineteenth Century* (New York, 1926), 36.
35. Olive Logan cited in Allen, 122–27. Olive Logan, *Apropos of Women and Theatres* (New York, 1869), 129.
36. February 24, 1869; this story is cited in Allen, 19–20. This was the first of many such incidents in the history of striptease in which the bad girl won popular support over the forces of authority.

37. Nicola Beisel, *Imperiled Innocents: Anthony Comstock and Family Reproduction in Victorian America* (Princeton, 1997), introduction and chapter 1.

38. Gilfoyle, 161–63. Gilfoyle notes that many of Comstock's descriptions of disrobing acts are full of "ironic" details. The important point is its growing similarity to theatrical entertainments of the day.

39. Ibid.

40. "I departed from the old style minstrel show then composed exclusively of males and substituted a bevy of most talented women," Leavitt wrote in his memoir. *How I Made It in the Theatre* (New York, 1898), 308.

41. Analysis of Rentz Santley posters draws on Allen, 204–21.

42. Quoted in Toll, 122.

43. May Howard Clippings File, NYPL. Douglas Gilbert, *American Vaudeville: Its Life and Times* (New York, 1932), 200–4; Beef Trust, Allen, 176; Susan Glenn, *Female Spectacle: The Roots of Modern Feminism* (Cambridge, 2000), 53, 75. Also see Peter G. Buckley, "The Culture of Leg Work," in *The Mythmaking Frame of Mind: Social Imagination and American Culture*, ed. James Gilbert (Berkeley, 1993) 113–35.

44. Henry T. Sampson, *Blacks in Blackface: A Sourcebook on Early Black Musical Shows* (Metuchen, N.J., 1980), 6.

45. James Weldon Johnson, *Black Manhattan* (New York, 1958), 95.

46. Toll, 222–25.

47. Gilbert, *American Vaudeville: Its Life and Times*, 5. Ralph Allen, *The Best Burlesque Sketches* (New York, 1995); Don Wilmeth, *Variety Entertainment and Outdoor Amusement: A Reference Guide* (Westport, 1980), 154.

48. Gunther Barth, *City People: The Rise of Modern City Culture in Nineteenth-Century America* (New York, 1980), 192–228; Robert Snyder, *The Voice of the City: Vaudeville and Popular Culture in New York* (New York, 1989); Robert C. Allen, "B. F. Keith and the Origins of American Vaudeville," *Theatre Survey* 21 (November 1980), 105–15.

49. Foster Hirsch, *Boys from Syracuse: The Shuberts' Theatrical Empire* (Carbondale, 1998), 35–40; Brooks McNamara, *The Shuberts of Broadway* (New York, 1990), 31–59.

50. Other works describing the burlesque scene of this era include Irving Zeidman, *The American Burlesque Show* (New York, 1967), 60, 78; Allen Churchill, *The Great White Way: A Recreation of Broadway's Golden Era of Theatrical Entertainment* (New York, 1962), 24; William Green, "A Survey of the Development of Burlesque in America," master's thesis, Columbia University, 1950; and William Green, "Strippers and Coochers—The Quintessence of Modern Burlesque," in *Western Popular Theatre*, proceedings of a symposium sponsored by the Manchester University Department of Drama, ed. David Mayer and Kenneth Richards (London, 1977).

**"Yvette Goes to Bed": The First Undressing Acts**

1. This chapter draws on Jerrold Seigel, *Bohemian Paris: Culture, Politics, and the Boundaries of Bourgeois Life, 1830–1930* (Baltimore, 1986), 215–42; and Roger Shattuck, *The Banquet Years: The Arts in France 1885–1918* (New York, 1958), 8–11, 22–23. *Les Can Cans de La Goulue, L'Unique Biographie, Les Premieres de la célèbre danseuse, reconstitute et redigée par Michel Souvais* (Paris, 1992). Although in the case of Dumas fils, it seems unlikely since he would have been

in his seventies. Michel Souvais, *Le Memoir d'un insolante* (Paris, 1998). André Warner, *Les bals de Paris* (Paris, 1922), 159–207.

2. Souvais; F. Berkeley Smith, *The Real Latin Quarter* (New York, 1901), 70–93. Smith focuses on the first *bal* in 1892, but all other details are similar.

3. Jean Emil-Bayard, *The Latin Quarter Past and Present* (New York, 1927), 232.

4. Souvais, 37.

5. M. Delsol, *Paris-Cythere* (Paris, n.d.), 47–52. Other sources, such as Paul Derval, *The Folies Bergere* (London, 1955), call her "Mona"; 47–52.

6. Quoted in Mauriel Oberther, *Cafés and Cabarets of Montmartre* (Salt Lake City, 1984), 85.

7. Yvette Guilbert, *The Song of My Life: My Memories* (London, 1929), 80. Yvette Guilbert, *Struggles and Victories of My Life* (London, 1910), 151–53.

8. Franck Evrard, *Effeuillages Romanesques: Essai sur la representation litteraire et culturele du striptease* (Paris, 1984), 24–25. The story of Cavelli is told in various places, including Jean Charvil, *Histoire et Sociologie du Striptease* (Paris, 1969), 23–24.

9. Charvil, 23–24; Andre Sallee, *Music Hall et Café Concert* (Paris, 1968), 141–42; Cecil Saint-Laurent, *A History of Ladies' Undressing* (London, 1968), 138.

10. T. J. Clark cites the names of these performers in his book. Clark, *The Painting of Modern Life: Paris in the Art of Manet and His Followers* (Princeton, 1999). Alison McMahon, *Alice Guy Blaché: Lost Cinematic Visionary* (New York, 2002). The first woman director, Alice Guy, who worked for the Gaumont film company, may have captured her undressing in a short called *Coucher d'Yvette*. McMahon does not think Guy actually directed this film.

11. Saint-Laurent, 140.

12. Quoted in Cocteau, *Souvenir Portraits: Paris in the Belle Epoque* (New York, 1990), 54–55.

13. Valerie Steele, *The Corset: A Cultural History* (New Haven, 2001), 50; Steele, *Fashion and Eroticism: Ideals in Feminine Beauty from the Victorian Era to the Jazz Age* (New York, 1985), 19, 172; Colin MacDowell, ed., *The Pimlico Companion to Fashion* (London, 1998), 346–47.

14. Charles Castle, *The Folies Bergere* (London, 1982), 94–101. Quote in Paul Derval, *The Folies Bergere* (London, 1955), 10–13. A million postcards and eventually a movie depicted such scenes in the striptease era. See, for example, "Olga Desmond, Real Naked Dancer," *Variety*, March 20, 1909, 10. This article describes a peripatetic "naked" act.

15. Cited in Clark, 244–45. The entry from the *Guide Secret de l'étranger celibataire a Paris* for 1889 advertised "The Folies Bergères, 32 Rue Ricard, famous for its promenoirs, its gardens, its constantly changing attractions, and its public of pretty women." *La Vie Parisienne* quoted in Steele, *Fashion and Eroticism*, 249–50. Elizabeth Ewing, *Dress and Undress: A History of Women's Underwear* (New York, 1978), 89.

16. Gordon Hendricks, *The Kinetoscope: America's First Commercially Successful Motion Picture Exposition* (New York, 1972), 168; Charles Musser, *Thomas A. Edison and His Kinetographic Motion Picture* (New Brunswick, 1995). Musser, in *The Emergence of Cinema: The American Screen to 1907* (New York, 1990), also asserts that the number of female dancer films is way more than is commonly supposed because some of the films were distributed clandestinely. Robert C. Allen, "Vaudeville and Film, 1895–1915: A Study in Media Interactions," EMI dissertations (New York, 1980). Terry Ramsaye, *A Million and One Nights: A History of the Motion Picture*, Volume 1 (New York, 1926), 117.

Kino Video, *Movies Begin: A Treasury of Early Cinema, Volume IV: The Great Train Robbery and Other Primary Works.*

17. *Movies Begin.* In one of these movies, a burlesque dancer tries on new corsets, but is so fat she cannot get the garment on by herself. In *The Troubles of a Manager of a Burlesque Show*, a burlesque soubrette models a union suit for the manager, who then chases her around the table. Quote from Ramsaye, Volume 1, 259.

18. Robert Sklar, *Movie-Made America: A Cultural History of American Movies* (Philadelphia, 1998), 23–24; Musser, *The Emergence of Cinema*, 78–79, 234–35. *Gay Shoe Clerk* in Linda Williams, *Hard Core: Power, Pleasure, and the Frenzy of the Visible* (Berkeley, 1989).

19. Douglas Gilbert, *American Vaudeville: Its Life and Times* (New York, 1932), 16.

20. Olmsted quoted in John F. Kasson, *Amusing the Million: Coney Island at the Turn of the Century* (New York, 1978), 23.

21. *The Dream City: A Portfolio of Photographic Views of the World's Columbian Exposition* (St. Louis, 1893).

22. There's some controversy as to whether Little Egypt "saved the fair." Bernard Sobel claims that she did. But Charles A. Kennedy (in "When Cairo Met Main Street: Little Egypt, Salome Dancers, and the World's Fair of 1893 and 1904," in *Music and Culture in America*, ed. Michael Saffle [New York, 1998]) says that there's no historical evidence of that.

23. Donna Carlton, *Looking for Little Egypt* (Bloomington, Ind., 1994), 46.

24. Carlton, 47–54; "Ministers Hissed by Chorus Girls," *Variety*, December 7, 1927, 39.

25. Marian Shaw, *World's Fair Notes: A Woman Journalist Views Chicago's 1893 Columbian Exposition* (Philadelphia, 1893), 59; Stuart Charles Wade, *The Nutshell: The Ideal Pocket Guide to the World's Fair and What to See There* (Chicago, 1893); Robert Rydell, *World of Fairs: The Century of Progress Expositions* (Chicago, 1993).

26. Sol Bloom, *The Autobiography of Sol Bloom* (New York, 1948), 137.

27. Quoted in Robert Toll, *On with the Show: The First Century of Show Biz in America* (New York, 1976), 225.

28. Nancy Reynolds, *No Fixed Points: Dance in the Twentieth Century* (New Haven, 2003), 4.

29. Bloom, 135; Heywood Broun and Margaret Leech, *Anthony Comstock: Roundsman of the Lord* (New York, 1927), 226–29; Kennedy, 274.

30. Cited in Kennedy, 280.

31. Edo McCullough, *Good Old Coney Island: A Sentimental Journey into the Past; The Most Rambunctious, Scandalous, Rapscallion, Splendiforous, Spectacular, Illusory, Prodigious, Frolicsome Island on Earth* (New York, 1957), 254; William Green, "Strippers and Cootchers: The Quintessence of American Burlesque," in David Meyers and Kenneth Richards, eds., *Western Popular Theatre* (New York, 1977), 157–69.

32. Cited in Robert C. Allen, *Horrible Prettiness: Burlesque and American Culture* (Chapel Hill, 1990), 230; Morton Minsky and Milt Machlin, *Minsky's Burlesque: A Fast and Funny Look at America's Bawdiest Era* (New York, 1986), 75; *National Police Gazette*, October 1, 1896, 2. A chronicle of Sam Jack's working methods appears in M. J. O'Neill, *Sam T. Jack, Twenty Years a King in the Realm of Burlesque: How He Does It* (Chicago, 1895), HUTC.

33. *New York Tribune*, December 22, 25, 27, 29, 31, 1896; Lucius Beebe, "The Awful Seeley Dinner," *New Yorker*, January 16, 1932, 34–40. The same year,

another Little Egypt supposedly jumped out of a Jack Horner pie at Stanford White's lavish party for Diamond Jim Brady high in White's studio in Madison Square Garden, which White was in the middle of redesigning as one of the tallest buildings in America.

34. *National Police Gazette*, January 16, 1897.
35. *New York Tribune*, January 9, 13, 1897; *National Police Gazette*, January 8, 16, 1897. Seeley Dinner is also recounted in Ramsaye, Volume 1, 336–40.
36. Cited in Carlton, 65–67.
37. Joris-Karl Huysmans, À *rebours*, tr. as *Against Nature* by Robert Baldick (Baltimore, 1959), 66; Stéphane Mallarmé, *Herodiade* (New York, 1981), 19.
38. Eva Tanguay Clippings File, BRTC. The Americanization of Salome is well documented, particularly in Glenn, 96–126, and Toni Bentley, *Sisters of Salome* (New Haven, 2002), 27–47.
39. M'Kee cited in Glenn, 103.
40. Ellis cited in Allen, *Horrible Prettiness*, 229.
41. Barbara Grossman, *Funny Woman: The Life and Times of Fanny Brice* (Bloomington, 1992), 28–32; Herbert Goldman, *Fanny Brice: The Original Funny Girl* (New York, 1992), 36–38.
42. Committee of Fourteen Collection, Special Collections, Series V, Investigators' Reports, Box 28, NYPL Manuscripts and Archives Division; *Blue Book Guide to New Orleans*, 1915, Beinecke Rare Book and Manuscript Library, Yale University.

## From Ziegfeld to Minsky:
## Respectable Undressing and the Rise of Burlesque

1. "Beauty Talk," n.d., Anna Held, Robinson Locke Collection of Dramatic Scrapbooks, v. 1–3, BRTC. Anna Held staged a number of undressing "acts" in her private life, such as the one where she took a bath in milk, and newspapers were constantly running features about her, showing how she got dressed and undressed.
2. Eve Golden, *Anna Held and the Birth of Ziegfeld's Broadway* (Lexington, Ky., 1995), 17.
3. Lois Banner, *American Beauty* (New York, 1983), 144–46. In America in 1893 there were one million riders.
4. Golden, 93–95. The cover page of the sheet music shows a Stage Door Johnny peering over the top of a screen and a girl taking off her clothes behind it.
5. Marjorie Farnsworth, *The Ziegfeld Follies* (New York, 1956), 25.
6. Broadway: *The Parisian Model*. Parisian Model Clippings File, NYPL. "Anna Held's Risque Carnival Pleases and Does Not Shock," n.d., Anna Held, Robinson Locke Collection of Dramatic Scrapbooks, v. 2, BRTC.
7. B. F. Keith quoted in *Vaudeville as Seen by Its Contemporaries*, ed. Charles Stein (New York, 1990), 17.
8. William Dean Howells quoted in Stein, 72–73.
9. Robert Snyder, *The Voice of the City: Vaudeville and Popular Culture in New York* (New York, 1989), 130–61.
10. Quoted in Lawrence Senelick, *The Changing Room: Sex, Drag, and the Theatre* (New York, 2000), 296–97. Senelick describes the Romantic fascination with gender bending acrobats.

11. Douglas Gilbert, *American Vaudeville: Its Life and Times* (New York, 1932), 183–96.
12. George Jean Nathan, *Entertainment of a Nation* (New York, 1942), 219–20. The other description of Charmion comes from Tracy Davis, *Actresses as Working Women: Their Social Identity in Victorian Culture* (London, 1991), 122. Here Charmion undresses to white undergarments and then hangs upside down, allowing the audience to see her acrobat's costume. But perhaps this speaks to British conventions vs. American. Or perhaps to the fact that Nathan saw her when he was a boy. In another act, Charmion disrobed in a chair without letting her feet touch the floor, as if any contact with the earth would have broken the illusion that she was an angel, not a flesh-and-blood woman.
13. Caroline Caffin, *Vaudeville* (New York, 1932), 181. Photo in clipping, June 22, 1901, n.d., Charmion, Robinson Locke Collection of Dramatic Scrapbooks, 123–28, BRTC. "She disrobes in a chair," July 13, 1901, *The Standard*, n.d., Charmion, ibid. Other performers of the era used similar strategies to mute their erotic force. Alison Kibler, *Rank Ladies: Gender and Cultural Hierarchy in American Vaudeville* (Chapel Hill, 1999), 130, 147, 246 n16, describes the following three women. Maybelle Meeker opened with a song and dance, then stripped to tights and contorted her body into a pretzel-like shape. Grace DeMar also used this convention in her act, changing costume while hanging suspended by her teeth from a bar. Lala Selbini stripped to tights while riding a bicycle.
14. Clipping, n.d., Charmion, Robinson Locke Collection of Dramatic Scrapbooks.
15. Allen, *Horrible Prettiness*, 195–241.
16. Kneeland quote in Marybeth Hamilton, *When I'm Bad I'm Better: Mae West, Sex, and Popular Culture* (New York, 1999), 22.
17. The fluidity between vaudeville and burlesque performers of this era is documented in Albert McLean, *American Vaudeville as Ritual* (Lexington, Ky., 1965), 46; Irving Zeidman, *The American Burlesque Show* (New York, 1967), 53–56, 65; *Variety*; and other newspapers of the time. As in other burgeoning areas of theater, competition between the theater owners and producers arose so quickly and became so cutthroat that producers booked shows independently to outdo each other. Impresario Jesse Lasky started out in burlesque. Lasky, *I Blow My Own Horn* (New York, 1957), 64, 72.
18. David Dressler, "Burlesque as a Cultural Phenomenon," Ph.D. dissertation, New York University, 1937, 57, notes that the Western wheel became more prurient because it was hard to enforce reform laws in smaller communities in the West.
19. Bernard Sobel, *Burleycue* (New York, 1931), 56–57. Another popular disrobing act of the era, "The Queen of the Moulin Rouge," dramatized the goings-on in a house of ill repute. Here the undressing act took place after the prostitutes were arrested and safely in their prison cells and to the music of a song called "Take That off Too," which had the inmates turning their hats into costumes, redressing themselves, and then somehow busting out of prison.
20. Joe Laurie and Abel Green, *Show Biz from Vaude to Video* (New York, 1951), 74.
21. Zeidman, 69, 137; Sobel, 97, 115; Kibler, 144–48. Miner's cited in McLean, 47. Cootch became a fad. See, for example, "Cootch Race in Philly," *Variety*, April 3, 1909, 8. But Truly Shattuck performed in both vaudeville and burlesque until World War I. Truly Shattuck, Robinson Locke Collection of Dramatic Scrapbooks, v. 427, BRTC.

22. *Variety*, March 14, 1909, 10, describes "the hook."

23. E. L. Hartt, "The Home of Burlesque," *Atlantic Monthly*, January 1908, 68–78.

24. West would always have the stigma of burlesque. Four years later, the magazine was hounding her again. "She just as well might hop out of vaudeville into burlesque," wrote Sime Silverman, the paper's lead critic, in 1916. After she became famous, West struggled to keep her years in burlesque out of her official story even as she drew from its boisterous idiom. Cited in Jill Watts, *Mae West: An Icon in Black and White* (New York, 2001), 29–30, and most other biographies of Mae West. Many white Americans dismissed burlesque because it seemed too close to black culture for comfort. At a rehearsal for the *Follies* of 1910, Abe Erlanger told Fanny Brice, herself a burlesque graduate, not to sing "Lovey Joe" in ragtime because it "sounded like burlesque." What Erlanger meant was that she sounded black.

25. Zeidman, 13–17; Anne Fliotsos, "Gotta Get a Gimmick: The Burlesque Career of Millie De Leon," *Journal of American Culture* 21, no. 4 (Winter 1998), 8–16.

26. Clipping, n.d , Millie De Leon, Robinson Locke Collection of Dramatic Scrapbooks, v. 364, 35–36, BRTC.

27. Ibid.

28. Sobel, 145.

29. I wish to thank Sondra Gilley of Portland, Maine, for several clippings from the *Chicago Herald*, 1904. One reads, "The woman with whom the banker's name had been connected haunted the Corn Exchange Bank for several days after Haas had gone. She generally brought a horsewhip with her and said she wished to chastise the man who deceived her. On one occasion she was ejected from the bank by detectives."

30. *Variety*, March 10, 1906, 7.

31. *Philadelphia North American*, September 16, 1915, in Robinson Locke Collection of Dramatic Scrapbooks, v. 364, BRTC. Also cited in Zeidman, 17.

32. Clipping, n.d., Robinson Locke Collection of Dramatic Scrapbooks, v. 364, BRTC.
    De Leon Clippings File, NYPL.

33. See, for example, *Variety*, March 27, 1909, 6.

34. According to Robert Baral, Ann Pennington posed as September Morn; but according to Richard Ziegfeld it was 1914 and Kay Laurell.

35. *New York Times*, March 22, 1913, 1; May 15, 1913, 7.

36. *New York Dramatic Mirror*, June 18, 1913, 6; *New York Times*, May 21, 1915, c2.

37. Lasky, 86.

38. Kathy Peiss, *Cheap Amusements: Working Women and Leisure in Turn of the Century* New York (Philadelphia, 1986) describes how in the teens, as women gained earning power, they began to demand diversions oriented specifically toward their gratification. *The dansants* catered to middle- and working-class women out shopping or attending theater matinees. In the evening, women might indulge in a "booze dansant," where they would drink and shimmy the night away. Also, David Nasaw, in *Going Out: The Rise and Fall of Popular Amusements* (New York, 1983), describes how more Americans of all classes began going out at the turn of the century.

39. Ethel Waters, *His Eye is on the Sparrow* (New York, 1950), 15. Waters quoted in Marshall Stearns and Jean Stearns, *Jazz Dance: The Story of Vernacular Dance* (New York, 1968), 104. Also see Marshall Stearns, *The Story of Jazz* (New York, 1975), 140–50. There are many stories about the origins of that dance's

name, the most convincing of which is put forth by Gilda Gray, who claimed it came from the word "chemise." Danced between 1910 and 1920, the shimmy first appeared in 1909 in "The Bullfrog Hop," a number by the prolific black songwriter Perry Bradford. Then, it could be found as "the shimmy sha-wabble" on the Theater Owners' Booking Association (TOBA) vaudeville circuit, which brought black performers to black audiences below the Mason-Dixon line. The popular singing and dancing group the Whitman Sisters punctuated their entrances and exits with king-sized hip wiggles. Ethel Waters, having learned how to shimmy from neighborhood whores in the 1930s, parlayed the dance into part of her personal idiom.

40. Robert Toll, *On with the Show: The First Century of Show Business in America* (New York, 1976), 232.

41. The historian Louis Erenberg calls this mingling "public privacy." Cited in Erenberg, *Steppin' Out: New York Nightlife and the Transformation of American Culture: 1890–1920* (Chicago, 1981), xi.

42. *Dance*, March 1927, 56. This practice had been going on for some time. In 1903, Flo Ziegfeld had introduced the old burlesque house trick of having the chorus march around the theater to Broadway.

43. Erenberg, 216–17.

44. Ibid., 220.

45. John Corbin, *New York Times*, November 21, 1915, 18. This complaint was reiterated throughout the war. See, for example, *Variety*, October 12, 1917, 18; Review of Watson's Beef Trust, November 1, 1918, 10.

46. Dressler, 54.

47. Louis Minsky was one of many Jews who were becoming American by producing music hall/popular entertainment. He was also a pioneer in the "Americanized" version of advertising, as Andrew R. Heinze describes in *Adapting to Abundance: Jewish Immigrants, Mass Consumption, and the Search for American Identity* (New York, 1990), 158.

48. H.K. got his J.D. in 1915. *New York Times*, October 25, 1915. Quoted in Irving Howe, *World of Our Fathers: The Journey of the East European Jews to America and the Life They Found and Made* (New York, 1976), 127.

49. Morton Minsky and Milton Machlin, *Minsky's Burlesque: A Fast and Funny Look at America's Bawdiest Era* (New York, 1968), 16–21; "Strip Numbers on Way Out: Minsky to Gradually Eliminate Them at Republic," *Zit's Theatrical Newspaper*, May 21, 1932, 11.

50. Quoted in Diane Cypkin, "Second Avenue: The Yiddish Broadway," Ph.D. dissertation, New York University, 1986, 131, 207.

51. *New York Clipper*, August 7, 14, September 25, 1915, and July 8, 1916, provide details about Ben Kahn's expansion during the war. On October 14, 1916, the *Clipper* notes that "rumors of a new stock house in opposition to the Union Square have not yet materialized." On October 24, 1917, *Variety* reports that the National Winter Garden opened under the Minsky camp.

52. For example, one of *Variety*'s first news items about the National Winter Garden, of March 16, 1917, notes that the Minskys charged fifty cents for a seat, as compared to other burlesque theaters that charged fifteen.

53. In his "Current Comment" on the raid of Minskys' on February 24, 1927, on March 12 of that year, 34. *Billboard*'s Nelse describes this audience as "excitable: Italians, Russians, and Hebrews." Interview with Harold Minsky at Las Vegas, 1975.

54. Minsky and Machlin, 4; Rowland Barber, *The Night They Raided Minskys': A Fanciful Expedition to the Lost Atlantis of Show Business* (New York, 1960), 29–36.

55. Harry Roskolenko, *The Time That Was Then: The Lower East Side, 1900–1914: An Intimate Chronicle* (New York, 1971), 144–45. Nina Warnke has shown how the rise of music halls on the Lower East Side was seen as a way to assimilate. Warnke, "Immigrant Popular Culture as Contested Sphere: Yiddish Music Halls, the Yiddish Press, and the Processes of Americanization, 1900–1910," *Theatre Journal* 48, no. 3 (1996), 321–35. Actually as late as 1928, Yiddish theater was still playing in some burlesque houses. See "Stock Burlesque Supplants Yiddish Drama at Irving Place," *Variety*, April 25, 1928, 43. This article began with the line "East siders know spring is here . . ." because Yiddish theater was giving way to burlesque.

56. Barber, 95; Minsky and Machlin, 3–5.

57. Billy planned to go to Europe, but as far as I can tell never arrived. "Billy Minsky Puts off Trip to Paris," *New York Clipper*, March 9, 1921; "Nick Elliot off for Europe," *Billboard*, July 12, 1924, 33.

58. A pass from 1920 called the National Winter Garden "The Moulin Rouge of America." Passes and Promotions, Folder 34, Burlesque Collection, MCNY.

59. Bernard Sobel, "Voices of Broadway: Down Memory Lane," n.d., Burlesque Clippings, Articles, Etc., Folder 30, Burlesque Collection, MCNY, asserts that Lee Shubert saw Billy Minsky at one of his shows and warned him: Don't let me catch you using any of this stuff." Minsky allegedly replied, "Too late."

60. Farnsworth, 26.

61. Florenz Ziegfeld, "How I Pick Beauties," *Theatre Magazine*, September 1919, 158; Ziegfeld, "Picking out Pretty Girls for the Stage," *American Magazine*, December 1919, 34, 125.

62. These figures are from Frank Thistle, "Burlesque," *Real Magazine*, June 1966, 76, Box 1, Folder 11, HM.

63. Zeidman, 132.

64. E. E. Cummings, *The Dial* 68, no. 12 (January 1920). In fact, Shargel did not speak any English.

65. Minsky and Machlin, 34. *Variety* locates Mae Dix at the Union Square in 1920 when she "came out of retirement." See, for example, September 17, 1920, 10; November 19, 1920, 6, 8. But I could find no record of her performing at the National Winter Garden in the teens in either *Variety* or *Billboard*.

## After the Doughboys Returned:
## Nudity in Burlesque and on Broadway

1. Edmund Wilson, *The Twenties: An Intimate Portrait of the Jazz Age* (New York, 1975), 183.

2. Thus the Sigmund Spaeth book *The Facts of Life in Popular Music*. Kathy Peiss, *Cheap Amusements: Working Women and Leisure in Turn of the Century* New York (Philadelphia, 1986).

3. Bert Lowry, "In the Days of Variety," *American Vaudeville as Seen by Its Contemporaries* (New York, 1984), 8.

4. Edward Bennett Marks, as told to A. J. Liebling, *They All Sang: From Tony Pastor to Rudy Vallee* (New York, 1934), 103. The song was also called "If Only Jack Were Here."

5. Marks, quoted in ibid., 5.

6. Orchestrations of Irving Berlin's song appeared on many burlesque albums in the 1950s and 1960s, including *Music in the Minsky Manor, Strip Along with Us, and How to Strip for Your Husband.*

7. This was already a tradition by 1918. It goes back to 1916 at least.

8. The list of songs used in burlesque in this era comes from *Billboard*'s "Melody Mart" page in the late teens and early twenties. This page listed songs sung on wheel burlesque and stock houses, including the Union Square and the National Winter Garden. "A Pretty Girl Is Like a Melody" was first sung by Wen Miller at the National Winter Garden and reviewed in *Billboard* on March 13, 1920, 28. A typical line-up of songs in January 1921 included Margie Pennetti singing "Timbuktu," "Bright Eyes," and "Scandal." "Swanee River" was also popular. A list of the most-played songs in burlesque appeared in *Billboard*, July 7, 1923, 33. "Winter Garden Show Has Bright Lines and Clever Comedy," *New York Clipper*, April 6, 1921, 27.

9. *New York* Clipper, August 25, 1920, 27; *New York Times*, September 4, 1921, 6.

10. Minsky had other ideas about how to cross over and be a legitimate producer. In 1921, he premiered "Strut Miss Lizzie," a black musical revue starring Bert Williams, before it went to Broadway. He also screened Charlie Chaplin's *The Kid* at the National Winter Garden. "Minsky's Plan Times Square Invasion," *New York Clipper*, February 9, 1921, 14; "Burlesque for Park Theatre," *New York Clipper*, March 8, 1922, 19; "Park Music Hall Prices," *New York Clipper*, September 6, 1922, 19; "Free Women's Matinees," *Variety*, November 22, 1922, 9.

11. "Minsky Burlesque Stock," *Billboard*, September 9, 1922, 32; "Minsky's Making Changes," *Billboard*, October 7, 1922, 57; "Minsky's Burlesques," *Billboard*, November 11, 1922, 34; "Minsky Brothers Change Policy of New Park Music Hall," *Billboard*, December 9, 1922, 34; "Burlesques' New Show at Park Music Hall," *New York Clipper*, September 20, 1922, 19; "Park Closes," *New York Clipper*, February 14, 1923, 19.

12. Frederick Lewis Allen, *Only Yesterday: An Informal History of the 1920s* (New York, 1931), and many other sources.

13. *Billboard*, May 7, 1927, 30.

14. "Wheel Shows to Carry Own Orchestra," *New York Clipper*, April 13, 1921, 14. Scribner also took other steps to keep Columbia clean, as in 1920, when he banned jokes about Prohibition and suffrage. *Variety*, April 4, 1920, 10.

15. During this era, both circuits experimented with how far they could go. *Variety*, September 23, 1921, 10; October 21, 1921, 11; November 11, 1921, 10; November 25, 1921, 10.

16. "Review of *Lid Lifters*," *Variety*, January 27, 1922, 10.

17. At first, it was called the Progressive circuit, then the Number Two circuit, and finally the American Wheel. Under this name it lasted until 1922. Through it all, its headquarters was the Columbia Theater Building on Broadway and Forty-seventh Street, which was also Columbia's flagship.

18. The birth of the Mutual circuit is described in *Variety*, December 1, 1922, 7; December 8, 7; December 22, 7.

19. *Billboard*, December 22, 1923, 34. Many communities across the country began to ban Mutual burlesque from their cities. See for example, "Mayor Bans Mutual, New Carlisle, Pa.," *Billboard*, February 19, 1924, 34.

20. "Henry Ford of Burlesque," *Mutual Burlesquer Newsletter*, September 9, 1929, 2, Box 11, Folder 8, JDM; *Billboard*, December 13, 1924, 18, 237.

21. Irving Zeidman, *The American Burlesque Show* (New York, 1967), 104. Also *Billboard*, November 1, 1924, 34.

22. This phrase comes from Robert Snyder, *The Voice of the City: Vaudeville and Popular Culture in New York* (New York, 1989).

23. Bernard Sobel, in *Burleycue: An Underground History of Burlesque Days* (New York, 1931), 246.

24. Marshall Stearns and Jean Stearns, *Jazz Dance: The Story of Vernacular Dance* (New York, 1968), 104–8.

25. Marybeth Hamilton, *When I'm Bad I'm Better: Mae West, Sex, and Popular Culture* (New York, 1999), 26–27; Jill Watts, *Mae West: An Icon in Black and White* (New York, 2001), 52–54.

26. "Gilbert Seldes review, Follies," 1922, Follies Clipping File, BRTC; Richard and Paulette Ziegfeld, *The Ziegfeld Touch: The Life and Times of Florenz Ziegfeld* (New York, 1993), 254.

27. James Curtis, *W. C. Fields: A Life* (New York, 1990), 209; Ken Murray, *The Body Merchant: The Story of Earl Carroll* (New York, 1973), ix. For Vanities, I also consulted Lee Davis, *Scandals and Follies: The Rise and Fall of the Great Broadway Revue* (New York, 2001).

28. The Midwestern boy who would become notorious for hosting the 1926 back-stage "bathtub" orgy in which showgirls bathed naked in champagne also found time to fix beauty contests and procure for President Harding. "Look at Flo . . ." quoted in Murray, 17.

29. Cited in Anthony Carl Sferrazza, *Florence Harding: The First Lady, the Jazz Age, and the Death of America's Most Scandalous President* (New York, 1998), 298. It should be noted, though, that Sferrazza's source is *True Magazine* from the 1940s. But Carroll was known as a fleshpeddler. In 1926 he served a year in an Atlanta prison for violating the Volstead Act.

30. Murray, *The Body Merchant*, epigraph. According to Murray, this is from Earl Carroll's unpublished autobiography, *Through These Portals Passed*.

31. Undated clipping, Vanities of 1923 Clippings File, BRTC; Vanities of 1924 Clippings File, BRTC; Vanities of 1925 Clippings File, BRTC; Murray, 44, 62; Davis, *Scandals and Follies*. Subsequent editions of the *Vanities* lived up to the first one. The following year, trying to top himself, Carroll choreographed a "peacock dance," in which the 108 chorines paraded across the stage wearing enormous headdresses and carrying peacock fans. Behind the fans, the women, wearing pasties and—as the tiny trademark G-strings were called— "Carroll's chastity belts," gyrated to Ravel's *Bolero*. In 1925, Carroll turned the thousand-seat Earl Carroll Theater into a nightclub, in part by instructing his performers to mingle with the audience, as they did in burlesque. The showgirls got so close that one critic observed that they did everything except "sit down to dinner with you."

32. Maryann Chach, "Artists and Models of 1923," *The Passing Show* (newsletter of the Shubert Archive) 11, no. 2 (Fall 1988), 12–14, n.d., Artists and Models Series, SA; Heywood Broun, "It Seems to Me," *New York World*, August 23, 1923, n.d. Every newspaper in town chimed in pro or con.

33. "Costume of Eve Gives Shubert Review Flavor," Burns Mantle review of 1923 edition of *Artists and Models*, Artists and Models Series, SA; Hirsch, 155.

34. "Promise or Menace?" review of 1923 edition of *Artists and Models*, Artists and Models Series, 1923–42, SA.

35. George Jean Nathan, "Judge Artists and Models Number: What the International Critic George Jean Nathan Says about Artists and Models," September 15, 1923, n.d., Artists and Models Series, SA.
36. "Woods Wins Suit over Demi-Virgin," *New York Times*, February 21, 1922, 16. A year before the Shuberts and Carroll began to produce these shows, A. H. Woods won a suit restricting the power of the license commissioner.
37. *National Police Gazette*, October 13, 1923, 2, WHMC.
38. Clipping, n.d., Artists and Models Series, SA.

**The First Strippers and Teasers**

1. "Hollow bowling alleys" in Edmund Wilson, *The Twenties: An Intimate Portrait of the Jazz Age* (New York, 1975), 275; "Star, B'Klyn, Runway," *Variety*, September 27, 1923 8; "Review of *Moonlight Maids* at the Prospect Theatre, Bronx," *Variety*, October 29, 1924, 11. For another angle on runways and burlesque, see Tara Maginnis, "Fashion Shows, Strip Shows, and Beauty pageants: The Theatre of the Feminine Ideal. Ph.D. dissertation, University of Georgia, 1991.
2. Morton Minsky and Milton Machlin, *Minsky's Burlesque: A Fast and Funny Look at America's Bawdiest Era* (New York, 1968), 33; Rowland Barber, *The Night They Raided Minskys': A Fanciful Expedition to the Lost Atlantis of Show Business* (New York, 1960), 200–201. Trying to get women closer to the audience was nothing new, of course. The Shuberts had gotten a similar effect by installing runways in their theaters since the 1912 Winter Garden revue *Whirl of Society*. They got the idea from *Sumurun*, the Kabuki review that had been in New York the previous year. In *Whirl of Society*, Al Jolson imitated the review. The runway quickly became known as "the bridge of thighs." (According to one story, Jolson suggested the runway, but the Shuberts vetoed the idea at first, arguing it would take up too many seats.) *Billboard's* 1934 "History of Burlesque" attributes the first burlesque runway to either the Minskys or the Raymonds.
3. Minsky and Machlin, 33; "Varicose Alley" in Douglas Gilbert, *American Vaudeville: Its Life and Times* (New York, 1932), 381.
4. The rise of the runway seems associated with the rise of stock burlesque theaters. Theaters like the Olympic and Hurtig and Seamon's began to use illuminated runways at around the same time, so, like many of the Minskys' claims of "firsts," this one is dubious.
5. "Hurtig/Seamon Illuminated Runway," *Variety*, December 17, 1924, 7; "Scribner's Idea of Burlesque Isn't Hurtig and Seamon's," *Variety*, December 27, 1923, 8; "Columbia Bans Bare Legs," *Variety*, August 13, 1924, 1, 22; Bernard Sobel, *Burleycue: An Underground History of Burlesque Days* (New York, 1931), 241.
6. "Isabelle Van and Her Dancing Dolls," *Billboard*, February 13, 1926, 34; "Review of Apollo," *Billboard*, October 10, 1927, 34; Jack Lait, *Chicago Confidential* (Chicago, 1950), 158.
7. The first reference to the word "pasties" in the *OED* is 1961. However, references to something that resembled pasties do appear up to thirty years earlier in *Billboard* and *Variety*.
8. In terms of the precise moment when each of the two acts were introduced into the American vernacular, "strip" seemed to precede "tease" by a few

months, intimating, perhaps, that teasing required a more modern and "liberated" sensibility. But both words continued to be used into the late 1920s. In Rouben Mamoulian's *Applause* (1929), the seedy Hitch talks about a "strip and teaser" number.

9. "Review of *Moonlight Maids*," *Billboard*, November 1, 1924, 35; "Anna Toebe: An Amateur Won Recognition in Rochester and as a Professional One of Best Bets in Burlesque," *Billboard*, January 26, 1924, 34; December 19, 1928, 34; program for *Moonlight Maids*, Programs, Box Two, Folder 7, JDM.

10. "Review of *Moonlight Maids*," *Variety*, October 29, 1924, 11.

11. Ibid. See also other reviews, including "*Moonlight Maids*," *Variety*, November 1, 1923, 8; and "Moonlight Maids," *Variety*, November 11, 1925, 18. Her name is variously spelled Toebe and Tobie; David Dressler, "Burlesque as a Cultural Phenomenon," Ph.D. dissertation, New York University, 1937, 58.

12. "Review of *Moonlight Maids*," *Variety*, June 10, 1925, 16.

13. The first reference to Finnell as the "first" teaser and Toebe as the "first" stripper appears in "The History of Burlesque," *Billboard*, December 29, 1934, 99, 102.

14. "Minsky Brand of Stock pleases," *New York Clippes*, April 23, 1919, 23; "Minsky Brothers National Winter Garden," *Billboard*, June 19, 1920, 27; "National Winter Garden Reopens Burlesque Stock Season," *Billboard*, August 23, 1920, 22; H. M. Alexander, *Striptease: The Vanished Art of Burlesque* (New York, 1938), 44. According to some sources, Finnell also performed in the 1916 *Ziegfeld Follies*.

15. "Carrie Finnell obituary," *Variety*, November 20, 1963, 79.

16. *Kentucky Post Courier*, n.d., 1924, Carrie Finnell Obituaries, BRTC.

17. *Cleveland Plain Dealer*, January 8, 1924, 15.

18. *Cleveland Plain Dealer*, September 15, 1923, 13.

19. Finnell's journey documented in "Chatter from Cleveland," *Billboard*, October 20, 1923, 35; November 3, 1923, 35; December 1, 1923, 35; December 8, 34. The following year she varied her act considerably; for example, January 12, 1924, 35, reports that she added her sister. February 2, 1924, 35; September 6, 1924, 35; and November 1, 1924, 35, report that Finnell had "cleaned up her act" since 1923. *Cleveland Plain Dealer*, September 1923–February 1924. See, for example, *Cleveland Plain Dealer*, September 17, 1923, 14; September 30, 1923, 3; and October 21, 1923, 3.

20. *New York Clipper*, February 16, 1921, 14.

21. *Billboard*, December 2, 1922, 34; "Question of Chorus Dancer's Clothes," *Variety*, December 1, 1922, 9.

22. Clipping, n.d., October 25, 1913; assorted clippings, n.d., Cleveland Historical Society. *The Encyclopedia of Cleveland History*, ed. David D. Van Tassel and John J. Grabowski (Bloomington, 1937), 290; Miles Theater Clippings File, Cleveland Historical Society.

23. *Billboard*, November 4, 1922, 34, Empire Theater Clippings File, Cleveland Historical Society; *Cleveland Plain Dealer*, September 1, 1923, 13; September 10, 1923, 14; September 14, 1923, 13.

24. *New York Herald Tribune* obituary, November 16, 1963, Carrie Finnell Obituaries, BRTC.

25. Picture in Irving Zeidman, *The American Burlesque Show* (New York, 1967), 116; Irene Sharaff, *Broadway and Hollywood* (Cincinnati, 1976), 37.

26. *Variety*, November 22, 1923, 8. According to Barber, 231, "It was also at the Liberty that 'Carrie Fenway' busted a brassiere strap in her first act solo and

*Notes to Pages 83–86*                    361

out it pops, this one like a big vanilla sundae with a cherry on top and Carrie plays it great, bawls it out for getting loose, and Dane screams keep the busted strap in the act."

27. "Nude Photos for Burlesque Stock," *Variety*, November 5, 1924, 11; *Variety*, November 19, 1924, 41.

28. *New York Clipper*, July 27, 1921, 19; December 20, 1923, 19. Scribner also continued to reject undressing acts. See for example, "Scribner's Idea of Burlesque Isn't Hurtig and Seamon's," *Billboard*, December 29, 1923, 34. Scribner is quoted as saying, "We permit no undressing." Scribner maintained this position well into the late twenties. In "Columbia Amusement Company Review," *Billboard*, July 19, 1924, 30, he says, "We are not exploiting nakedness."

29. Douglas Shand Tucci quoted in "Gaiety Theatre Study Report," unpublished paper, Boston Landmarks Commission, City of Boston, 1975, 24.

30. Fred Allen, *Much Ado about Me* (New York, 1950), 85–86; Stewart Holbrook, *Little Annie Oakley and Other Rugged People* (New York, 1948), 122–26. Originally published in the *American Mercury*, April 1944, 411–16.

31. "Always Somethin' Doin'," *Collier's*, September 30, 1950, 22–25; Brooks Atkinson, "Exploration Unrewarded," *Boston Evening Transcript*, May 1, 1922, 9, 12.

32. Al Rose, *Storyville, New Orleans: Being an Authentic, Illustrated Account of a Notorious Red Light District* (Tuscaloosa, 1974), 24, 103; Nat Shapiro and Nat Hentoff, *The Story of Jazz and the Men Who Made It: Hear Me Talkin' to Ya* (New York, 1955), 54; Michael Ondaatje, *Coming Through Slaughter* (London, 1979); Billie Holiday, *Lady Sings the Blues* (New York, 1995), 10–11, 34–35; Herbert Asbury, *The French Quarter* (New York, 1936).

33. *Time*, May 10, 1937, 33–34.

34. Eugene Clinton Elliot, *A History of Variety-Vaudeville in Seattle, from the Beginning to 1914* (Seattle, 1944), 46.

35. Cited in Theodore A. Brown and Lyle Dorset, *K.C: A History of Kansas City* (Boulder, 1978), 195; Nathan Pearson, *Goin' to Kansas City* (Urbana, 1987), 100.

36. Quoted in *Adam* 3, no. 10 (1959), n.d.

37. Gillis Theater Clippings File, April 15, 1974, n.d., Kansas City Public Library.

38. Other sources used in this section include Franklin S. Driggs, "Kansas City and the Southwest," in Nat Hentoff and A. J. McCarthy, eds., *Jazz: Twelve Scholars and Practitioners Talk About It* (New York, 1959), 189–231; Dwight Garwood, *Crossroads of America: The Story of Kansas City* (Kansas City, 1990), 302; Pearson, 100–3. Morton Minsky, "Modern Burlesque" interview, in *American Popular Entertainment: Proceedings of the Conference on the History of Popular Entertainment* (Westport, 1979), 74; William Reddig, *Tom's Town: Kansas City and the Pendergast Legend* (Philadelphia, 1974), 87–91; Maurice Milligan, *Missouri Waltz: The Inside Story of the Pendergast Machine by the Man Who Smashed It* (New York: 1948)

39. "Runway's Song Plugs," *Variety*, November 28, 1928, 41.

40. *Billboard*, September 1, 1928, 34.

41. Pennetti also sang in Yiddish. "Melody Mart" column, *Billboard*, November 29, 1924, p. 35; June 28, 1924, 34. "Pennetti Is Responsible for High Attendance at the National Winter Garden," *Variety*, June 10, 1925, 34, reports that Toebe and Pennetti were responsible for burlesque management's decision to feature female names above male ones. "Review of National Winter Garden," *Billboard*, May 22, 1926, 34, and subsequent ones focus dramatically on female performers.

42. *Variety*, November 3, 1929, 64.
43. *Variety*, February 10, 1926, 36.
44. Zeidman, 126; "Minskys Make Merry at Opening," *Billboard*, September 7, 1929, 33.
45. *Variety*, April 12, 1928, 36.
46. Reviews of Isabelle Van and Her Dancing Dolls, *Billboard*, February 13, 1926, 34; *Billboard*, May 8, 1926, 33.
47. Nancy Cott, *The Grounding of Modern Feminism* (New Haven, 1987), 150. Estelle B Freedman, on the other hand, dismisses some of the gains of the New Woman in *The History of Feminism and the Future of Women* (New York, 2002).
48. "Would Be Reformers after Burlesquers," *Billboard*, March 20, 1926, 64.
49. See, for example, *Billboard*, September 13, 1924; Babe Quinn is described as a Dresden doll. Additionally, as the decade wore on, it was clear that some of these doll acts began to include more stripping. See for example, *Variety*, December 4, 1929, 49: "Review of *Moonlight Maids*" describes Anna Toebe's "mechanical doll" number as "the dirtiest piece of business in the book."
50. *Dial*, January 1920, n.d., Dial Collection, Beinecke Library, Yale University.
51. Allen, 190, 192.
52. Carl Van Vechten, "A Note on Tights," *American Mercury*, July 1924, 432.
53. "Review of the Teaser," *New York Times*, June 15, 1925, 10.
54. Gilbert Seldes, "Fat Ladies," *New Republic*, March 30, 1932, 182.
55. Seldes, *The Seven Lively Arts* (New York, 1924), 251.
56. Cecil Saint-Laurent, *A History of Ladies' Undressing* (London, 1968), 43.
57. Albert McLean, *American Vaudeville as Ritual* (Lexington, Ky., 1965), 6. Zeidman, 142.

**Pansies, Reformers, and a "Frenzy of Congregate Cootchers":
The Birth of Modern Striptease**

1. Georgia Sothern, *My Life in Burlesque* (New York, 1972), 100. Morton Minsky and Milt Machlin, *Minsky's Burlesque: A Fast and Funny Look at America's Bawdiest Era* (New York, 1986), Martin Collyer, *Burlesque: The Story of a Unique American Institution* (New York, 1964), and others.
2. "Minsky Bros New Theatre," *Billboard*, July 12, 1924, 34.
3. The Little Apollo was not the same as the Apollo of swing fame, although they were on the same block. "Minsky Brothers Take Over Apollo," *Variety*, July 9, 1924, 8; "Minskys' Uptown," in "Burlesque Review, Apollo, New York," *Billboard*, September 10, 1927, 32.
4. In other words, Fifi, or Feef, was "a class A shimmier." *Billboard*, June 23, 1923, 34. *Variety* also described her as "unshouldering the burden and unburdening the shoulders." *Variety*, September 17, 1924, 10, 52. "Burlesque Reviews, *Moonlight Maids* (Mutual)," *Variety*, November 11, 1925, 18; Jack Schiffman, *Uptown: The Story of Harlem's Apollo Theatre* (New York, 1971), 47–48; "Burlesque Review, Prospect Theatre, Bronx," *Billboard*, September 6, 1924, 24. The Apollo was also the place where the Minskys began to elaborate on some of their famous "gimmicks," such as sending newspaper editors "personalized season passes" to the theater. "Apollo Press Stunt," *Variety*, September 3, 1924, 10.

5. "Apollo Opening Not Overly Clean," *Billboard*, September 13, 1924, 34, 35; "Review of Apollo," *Variety*, January 14, 1925, 45–46

6. Fifi in *Billboard*, ibid. Rowland Barber, *The Night They Raided Minskys'* (New York, 1960), 345. According to Barber, Mademoiselle Fifi (aka Mary Dawson) a cootch dancer who had also opened at the Apollo, arrived onstage at the National Winter Garden on the night of April 20, 1925, sheathed in skin-tight black net from toe tips to bra. As Barber describes it, "in a delirium," she pulled one of her straps from her shoulder and took off her bra while the orchestra raced through a medley of Puccini, ragtime, and Offenbach's *Gaîté Parisienne*. Sumner arrested her. Whereas there are records of many other arrests from the twenties and thirties in *Billboard* and *Variety*, there is no record of this event on this date in those newspapers or in the *New York Times*. It is retold in Morton Minsky and Milt Machlin, *Minsky's Burlesque: A Fast and Funny Look at America's Bawdiest Era* (New York, 1968), and in an interview with Minsky from the University of Nevada at Las Vegas Collection, August 15, 1975.

7. Alison Parker, *Purifying America: Women, Cultural Reform, and Pro Censorship Activism, 1873–1933* (Urbana, 1997); Paul Boyer, *Purity in Print: The Vice Society Movement and Book Censorship in America* (New York, 1968).

8. Gilbert W. Gabriel, "They Call It Burlesque," *New Yorker*, November 14, 1925, 12–13. Sumner quote cited in Jay. A. Gertzman, *Bookleggers and Smuthounds: The Trade in Erotica, 1920–1940* (Philadelphia, 2002), 105. This argument draws on Gertzman, 103–12, who describes Sumner's public image as a "blueblood censor" and describes how, in the 1930s, this contributed to his ultimate demise.

9. Barber, 503–53; Minsky and Machlin, 73–86. According to Barber, Sumner saw the Minskys' version of burlesque the previous Monday and had warned Billy that he would be in the audience that evening. Ordinarily, Billy would have simply had Fifi do the "clean version" of her act. But at the exact moment that Fifi was taking off her bra, one of the Minsky backers, Joe Weinstock, came into the theater. Billy was put into the position of having to make a choice: should he try to please the backer or the cop? Should he stop the act by flashing the red warning light or let her go on? Billy chose the backer. Not liking what he saw, Sumner had the joint raided. The trial ran for seven weeks. Paul Weintraub, the Minskys' defense lawyer, argued along class lines that uptown Carroll and Ziegfeld revues showed the same amount of flesh. Eventually the Minskys won.

10. George Chauncey, *Gay New York: Gender, Culture, and the Makings of the Gay Male World* (New York, 1998), especially introduction and chapter 9.

11. Jimmy Durante and Jack Kafoed, *Nightclubs* (New York, 1931), 54–55; Frederick Lewis Allen, *Only Yesterday: An Informal History of the Twenties* (New York, 1931).

12. "Impersonator in Chorus," *Variety*, March 30, 1927, 40; *Garden of Allah* recounts how a stripper's balls fell out of his G-string. *Zit's* also reported various incidences of male impersonators' playing in burlesque, including one at the Casino in Pittsburgh.

13. Lawrence Senelick, *The Changing Room: Sex, Drag, and the Theatre* (New York, 2000), 295–312.

14. Edmund Wilson, *The American Earthquake* (New York, 1958), 59–60.

15. *Billboard*, January 6, 1940, 26, 28.

16. Francis Steegmuller, *Cocteau: A Life* (New York, 1970), 364–68; Francis Steegmuller, "Onward and Upward with the Arts: An Angel, A Flower, A Bird," *New Yorker*, September 27, 1969, 130–43; Jean Cocteau, "Le Numero Barbette," *La Nouvelle Revue Français* (July 1926), 33–38.
17. Cocteau, "Le Numero Barbette.» 37.
18. Barbette Clippings File, n.d., BRTC; Janet Flanner, *Paris Was Yesterday* (New York, 1972), 70–71. Years later, Barbette would coach Jack Lemmon and Tony Curtis in *Some Like It Hot*.
19. Flanner, 69. Baker is also described in Phyllis Rose's *Jazz Cleopatra* (New York, 1997), 21.
20. Marshall Stearns and Jean Stearns, *Jazz Dance: The Story of Vernacular Dance* (New York, 1968), 235–38. Quote, 237. Frankel cited in Jack Schiffman, *Harlem Heyday* (Buffalo, 1984), 168.
21. *Variety*, December 25, 1929, 37.
22. According to Gypsy Rose Lee in *Gypsy: A Memoir* (New York, 1957), two tassel twirlers worked in 1929 when she was at the Missouri Theater in Kansas City, 182.
23. Ann Corio, *This Was Burlesque* (New York, 1968), 74. Minsky and Machlin, 51, also asserted that Finnell developed tassel twirling in the early twenties at the National Winter Garden, 51, but I could find no evidence of Finnell's performing in New York until 1927 or so. Review of Carrie Finnell at Le Ruban Bleu, *Variety*, September 24, 1941, 41.
24. Zeidman claims that this song was the children's song "Pop Goes the Weasel." In a more theoretical vein, Erenberg and others talk about how women's girth defused their threatening sexuality.
25. In the 1926 season, Finnell grossed more than any other burlesque performer. Details about Tucker are cited in Lewis Erenberg, *Steppin' Out: New York Nightlife and the Transformation of American Culture: 1890–1920* (Chicago, 1981), 190–200. Sophie Tucker Clippings File, BRTC. Additionally, an article on Finnell in the March 1956 edition of *Cabaret* (20–24) directly compares the two performers, but notes that Finnell had a higher singing voice.
26. Ethel Waters, *His Eye Is on the Sparrow* (New York, 1950), 71.
27. Stearns, 110–12; Waters, 71–91.
28. Cited in Marybeth Hamilton, *When I'm Bad I'm Better: Mae West, Sex, and Popular Culture* (New York, 1999), 47. Description of *Sex* from Jill Watts, *Mae West: An Icon in Black and White* (New York, 2001), and from *Three Plays by Mae West: Sex, The Drag, The Pleasure Man*, ed. Lillian Schissel (New York, 1997), 8–10.
29. Quoted in Watts, 70.
30. Mary Henderson, *The City and The Theater: New York Playhouses from Bowling Green to Times Square* (Clifton, N.J., 1973), 193.
31. In 1924 the burlesque producer Rube Bernstein, soon to be Hinda Wassau's husband, created an all-black burlesque show for a black audience in Harlem. Jimmie Cooper produced another wildly successful black and white burlesque show called *Seven Eleven* for the Columbia circuit. *Seven Eleven* sandwiched a black show inside of a white one. It was one of the most financially successful shows of the season. *Billboard*, May 10, 1924, 10, also reports that Barney Gerard's "All in Fun," a Columbia circuit show, featured Ada Lum, a Chinese American prima donna from New Orleans. "Review of Jimmie Cooper's Black and White Show," *Billboard*, September 18, 1926, 34. *Billboard* also featured a profile of Lum on May 10, 1924, 32.

32. "Columbia and Mutual Effect Consolidation of Burlesque Needs," *Billboard*, January 14, 1928, 34.

33. *Billboard*, June 15, 1929, 39.

34. Henry T. Sampson, *Blacks in Blackface: A Sourcebook on Early Black Musical Shows* (Metuchen, N.J., 1980), 31–32; Irving Zeidman, *The American Burlesque Show* (New York, 1967), 110.

35. Edmund Wilson, *The Shores of Light: A Literary Chronicle of the Twenties and Thirties* (New York, 1952), 275.

36. Angela Latham, "The Right to Bare: Containing and Encoding Women in the 1920s," *Theatre Journal* 49, no. 4 (December 1997), 455–73.

37. Wilson, *The Twenties: An Intimate Portrait of the Jazz Age* (New York, 1975), 198; Brooks Atkinson, "Nothing Serious: Melancholy Reflections about the Burlesque Stage," *New York Times*, September 4, 1927, xi; "Review of *Wine, Women, and Song*," *Billboard*, September 3, 1927, 32.

38. "Review of *Moonlight Maids*," *Variety*, December 19, 1928, 36.

39. "Review of Carrie Finnell Show," *Variety*, February 15, 1928, 39.

40. Joel Harvey, "American Burlesque as Reflected through the Career of Kitty Madison, 1916–37," Ph.D. dissertation, Florida State University, 1980, 100.

41. "Minsky's Novelty," *Billboard*, July 4, 1925, 33. Cozzier (her name is spelled variously throughout the 1920s), is characterized in *Variety* and *Billboard* reviews as a "wild" performer. See, for example, "BandBox Review," *Billboard*, October 20, 1923, 35. On hiring of comics and color scheme at the National Winter Garden, see *Billboard*, September 12, 1925, 33, and September 19, 1925, 32.

42. "Minsky Brothers' National Winter Garden Stock Company," *Billboard*, December 4, 1926, 35.

43. Don Wilmeth, *Variety Entertainment and Outdoor Amusements: A Reference Guide* (Westport, Conn., 1982), 155. Most burlesque shows after 1925 placed strippers right before the curtain went down or in the next-to-last spot. See, for example, Exhibit D, City of New York, Department of Licenses, August 21, 1935, hearing held by the Holly Holding Company, in Minsky and Machlin, 297. Minsky and Machlin, 49–50.

44. Barber, 207–10.

44. "National Winter Garden Company Competing in Contests," *Billboard*, January 30, 1926, 34. Other Minsky antics to compete included giving out twelve-ticket passbooks and circulating rumors that they were going to Paris. See "Minsky's Stock Company Sailing," *Variety*, December 29, 1926, 34; "Stock Burlesque Competish on Lower East Side," *Variety*, September 16, 1926, 34.

45. One of the Minskys' most outrageous stunts occurred right after Rudolph Valentino died. Mort Minsky made Ella Buckley, a bit performer who had appeared in several of Valentino's films, take poison to show her sympathy. "Poison Publicity," *Variety*, August 25, 1926, 11.

46. "Minsky Bros in Brooklyn," *Billboard*, June 19, 1926, 38, 89.

47. "Minsky Re-Opens," *Billboard*, September 4, 1926, 34, 57; "Burlesque Reviews, National Winter Garden Stock Company," *Billboard*, October 30, 1926, 34.

48. Committee of Fourteen Records, 1905–32, Investigators Reports, 1926, Box 33, Special Collections Manuscripts and Archives Division, NYPL.

49. George Jean Nathan, *The Art of the Night* (New York, 1928), 242. It's interesting to note that Nathan's section on burlesque appears in the "vice" section of the book as opposed to the entertainment section. Wilson, *Shores of Light*, 277.

50. "Burlesque Reviews, National Winter Garden Stock Company"; Minsky, 85; Barber, 216.
51. "Minsky's," *Billboard*, December, 4, 1926, 35.
52. Lawrence quoted in Ann Douglas, *Terrible Honesty: Mongrel Manhattan in the 1920s* (New York, 1994), 167.
53. Reprinted in E. E. Cummings, *A Miscellan-y*, ed. George Firm (New York, 1958), 91.
54. E. E. Cummings, *Dial*, August 1927, 54–55, 64–66; Cummings, "The National Winter Garden?" *Dial*, December 1925, 73.
55. Henry Miller, *Black Spring* (Paris, 1936), 189–90.
56. Some of these details appear in an essay on mass culture and modernism: William Solomon, "Burlesque Dreams: American Amusement, Autobiography, and Henry Miller," *Style* 35, no. 4 (Winter 2001), 681. Solomon argues that Crane and other modernists were searching for redemption through popular art. Henry Miller, *Letters to Emil* (New York, 1989), 10, 155.
57. Wilson, *The Twenties*, 257.
58. Wilson, *Shores of Light*, 280.
59. Edmund Wilson, *The Higher Jazz* (Iowa City, 1999), 99.
60. Solomon, 681, argues that burlesque in Crane's view provided not just redemption, but a desolate view of the underworld.
61. Hart Crane, *The Bridge* (London, 1931), 89.
62. Paul Boyer, 162, quotes John Sumner as saying that "aggressive action" was required.
63. According to *Variety*, November 10, 1926, 25, Gus Hill, a burlesque producer, owned 25 percent of the interest in *Sex*, and there were plans to open it at the Columbia burlesque theater.
64. Murray, 67–68. *Billboard*, June 26, 1926, 34; July 12, 1926, 34.
65. Chauncey, 311–12, notes that *The Drag* was the first play in which gay men represented themselves.
66. These trials are thoroughly documented. Also other less likely suspects such as Arthur Miller's *Death of a Salesman* and the *Merchant of Venice* were censored during this time. Anticipating the class argument made in the burlesque hearings of the thirties, the defense attorney cited Aristophanes as the model for popular entertainment; the prosecuting attorney castigated "Greek and French degenerates"; while the plays hosted capacity audiences.
67. This is well documented in Kaier Curtin, *We Can Always Call Them Bulgarians: The Emergence of Lesbians and Gay Men on the Stage* (Boston, 1987), and elsewhere. According to Mort Minsky in Minasky and Machlin, 92, during the months preceding the hearings, advertisements for the National Winter Garden continued to appear in the *New Yorker*, but I could not corroborate this with primary sources. It is possible that Minsky confused this event with the 1932 hearings, when ads for the Republic did appear in the *New Yorker*.
68. *Variety*, March 2, 1927, 27; "Police Stop Performance at National Winter Garden," *Billboard*, March 5, 1927, 40.
69. Section 1140b added that "a person who in any place exposes his person, private parts in presence of two or more persons of the opposite sex . . . or who as owner, manager, lessee, director, promoter, or agent; or who in any other capacity, hires, leases, or permits the land, building or premises of which he is owner, lessee or tenant, or over which he has control, to be used for any such purpose, is guilty of a misdemeanor."

70. Laws about anti-theatricalism and obscenity described in Abe Laufe, *The Wicked Stage: A History of Theater Censorship and Harassment in the United States* (New York, 1978), 60–61; also Morris Ernst and Alexander Linney, *The Censor Marches On: Recent Milestones in the Administration of the Obscenity Law in the United States* (New York, 1940), 65–68.

71. John Sumner, "Padlock Drama," *Theater* 47 (May 1928), 11–12, 62.

72. The law also inspired Billy Minsky to refocus his energies on the Winter Garden. See, for example, "Radical Reorganization at Minsky's Winter Garden," *Billboard*, April 2, 1927, 34. "Parties and Booze in St. Charles Hotel," *Variety*, June 20, 1928, 43.

73. "$125,000 Dropped by Stock Burlesque in Greater New York," *Variety*, June 1, 1927, 41; "Police Raids and Lent Hurt Stock Biz," *Variety*, April 20, 1927, 40; Ernst and Linney, 67.

74. "Legislature Gets Play Padlock Bill," *New York Times*, March 19, 1927, 3; "Indecent Performance Charge Dismissed in Court," *Billboard*, June 4, 1927, 30. LaGuardia Indecent Shows File, February and April 1932, MA; Committee of Fourteen Records, Box 37, Manuscripts and Archives Division, NYPL. *Variety*, June 1, 1927, 41.

75. *Billboard*, November 5, 1927, 32, describes how competition from the movies was making burlesque racier.

76. R. L. Lurie, "Burlesque" *New Republic*, April 8, 1925, 181–82.

77. There are several sources for this. One is Barber, 270.

78. Gabriel, 12.

79. "Jockey Blues" quoted in David Dressler, "Burlesque as a Cultural Phenomenon," Ph.D. dissertation, New York University, 1937?], 70. Different variations of this song emerged in the 1920s and 1930s. One version was sung by Bill Samuels and Lonnie Johnson, both Memphis bluesmen, another by Memphis Minnie. It was first recorded by Johnson in 1931.

80. This story about Wassau in Chicago first emerges in the 1950s. Some early records of it occur in the Burlesque Scrapbook, 1950–59, BRTC. Franklin Thistle, "Striptease, the National Fetish: How the Bump and Grind Became the Biggest Entertainment Draw in History," *Sir Knight* 1, no. 12 (July 1960), HM, claims that it was the Haymarket. Corio, 73, says the State-Congress. Both of these theaters were in operation in 1928 and both, according to ads in the *Chicago Tribune*, hosted amateur shimmy contests; however, there is no mention of Wassau and this story in any newspaper of the time.

81. The Minskys had to cut burlesque performers' salaries. *Billboard*, April 23, 1927, 34; "Theatre Raids in Milwaukee," *Variety*, March 2, 1927, 27; "Stage Decency Drive in Milwaukee Just a Laugh," *Variety*, March 23, 1927, 33; "Mil cleans up Stock: Fines Shimmy Dancer $50," *Variety*, April 13, 1927, 37. There are few records of Wassau's whereabouts in *Variety* or *Billboard* from the spring of 1927 to the summer of 1928. According to Harvey, Wassau performed in Kitty Madison's *Jazztime Review* in 1927; Harvey, 94.

82. Hugues Panassié, *Hot Jazz: The Guide to Swing Music* (New York, 1936), 144–46.

83. "Rialto Stock," *Variety*, July 13, 1927, 35.

84. Allen H. Spear, *Black Chicago: The Making of a Negro Ghetto, 1890–1920* (Chicago, 1967), 129–201; St. Clair Drake and Horace A. Cayton, *Black Metropolis: The Story of Negro Life in a Northern City* (Chicago, 1993); William Howland Kennedy, *Chicago Jazz: A Cultural History*, 1904–1930 (New York, 1987).

85. "Review, Haymarket," *Variety*, February 25, 1925, 14; "Haymarket Raid," *Chicago Tribune*, March 5, 1926, n.d.

86. Louise Berliner, *Tex Guinan: Queen of the Nightclubs* (Austin, 1993); Stanley Walker, *The Nightclub Era* (New York, 1934), 240–45; Texas Guinan Scrapbooks, NYPL. For Club Intime closing, see *Variety*, April 24, 1927. Also see Watts, 114. "Added Attractions," *Billboard*, August 23, 1930, puts Wassau in Chicago "for a three week engagement" at the Academy Theater, at the same time as Guinan was opening the Green Mill Nightclub.

87. "Seen and Heard" column by Nelse, *Billboard*, March 5, 1928, 34, notes the Shubert offer. Advertisements in the *Toledo Blade*, October 26, 1929, 12; March 29, 1930, 12. *Variety*'s "Burlesque Routes" show that the Hindu Belles toured straight from August 22, 1928, to at least February 27, 1929. A January 19 review in *Billboard* notes that Wassau displayed a "self satisfied affectation of staginess." Wassau herself toured on the Mutual circuit until December 4, 1929. Tex Guinan's Salon Royale was open from New Year's Eve 1927 to June 1928, the period when there are no *Variety* or *Billboard* records for Wassau. Tex opened the Club Intime on New Year's Eve 1928.

88. "The Business of Burlesque, a.d. 1935," 148; Richard and Paulette Ziegfeld, *The Ziegfeld Touch: The Life and Times of Florenz Ziegfeld* (New York, 1993), 140, 142, 160, 308.

89. Helen Lawrenson, "Where Sex Was Fun," *Show*, March 1964, 87.

90. Sothern, 25–26; Corio, 72–73; Zeidman, 155–56.

91. *Variety*, October 13, 1931, 60.

92. Barber, 340.

93. "Burlesque Review, *Nite Life in Paris* (Mutual)," *Billboard*, December 1, 1928, 37. "Sex seductive strip teaser" is the first mention of the two words together. The *OED* lists the word striptease as first appearing in 1929.

94. "Burlesque Review, *Nite Life in Paris*," *Billboard*, September 1, 1928, 37; "Review of Isabelle Van and her Dancing Dolls," *Billboard*, February 26, 1928, 33.

95. Allen, 87, discusses how bobbed hair and cosmetics became a sign of modernity. The ur-source for this is F. Scott Fitzgerald, "Berenice Bobs her Hair," *Saturday Evening Post*, May 1, 1920. For trade paper mentions of marcelled hair in burlesque, see, for example, "Burlesque Reviews, Apollo Theatre (Stock)," *Billboard*, September 10, 1927, 32; *Billboard*, December 1, 1923, 34; "Mutual Wheel Listings," *Variety*, December 4, 1929, 46; "Burlesque Reviews, Hindu Belles (Mutual)," *Variety*, January 9, 1929, 45. There was even a Mutual show called the *Bobbed Hair Bandits*.

96. "Burlesque Reviews, Girls from Follies (Mutual)," *Variety*, December 25, 1929, 3; "Hung onto Brassieres for 20 Yrs in Burlesque," *Variety*, December 11, 1929, 49.

## A Pretty Girl Is Like a Melody, Sort Of

1. Clipping, n.d., Burlesque Clippings File, NYPL; clipping, n.d., Tamony Collection, WHMC.

2. Bernard Sobel, *Burleycue: An Underground History of Burlesque Days* (New York, 1931), 247.

3. Leonard Bernstein, *The Joy of Music* (New York, 1955), 166–67.

4. "Burlesque: A Sound of Our Times," *New York Times*, February 6, 1955, n.d., Tamony Collection, WHMC.

5. Georgia Sothern, *My Life in Burlesque* (New York, 1972), and elsewhere.

6. Margie Hart Clippings File, BRTC.

7. Sothern, 197–99.
8. "Dignified savagery" quoted in Martin Collyer, *Burlesque: The Story of a Unique American Institution* (New York, 1964). This is how she was originally billed. Sometimes strippers changed names several times over the course of their career.
9. *Time*, n.d., 1934, Tamony Collection, WHMC.
10. John Bakeless, "The Anatomical Drama: Burlesque Shows and Lesser Wickedness," *Outlook and Independent*, December 31, 1931, 698–99.
11. Gypsy Rose Lee, *The G-String Murders* (New York, 1943), 266.
12. William Green interview with Charles de Milt, 1979, ASTR interviews, Theater on Film and Tape, NYPL.
13. Denys Chevalier, *Métaphysique du Striptease* (Paris, 1961), 21–22.
14. Ibid.
15. Marshall Stearns, *The Story of Jazz* (New York, 1975), 184.
16. Niesen cited in Hugues Panassié, *Hot Jazz: The Guide to Swing Music* (New York, 1936), 183, 188. "Republic, Stock," *Variety*, November 24, 1931, 30. Grover Frankie played a cootch interpretation of "Minnie the Moocher."
17. James Lincoln Collier, *Duke Ellington: The Life and Times of the Restless Genius of Jazz* (London, 1987), 149.
18. Stearns, 104–5.
19. *Variety*, December 15, 1931, 30; June 2, 1931, 50; January 11, 1947, 47.
20. "Burlesque Bits," *Billboard*, March 15, 1952, 45.
21. *Dial*, April 11, 1925, 38.
22. "Irving Place," *Variety*, September 30, 1934, 36.
23. *The Great Soloists, featuring Benny Goodman*, New York Biograph Records, 1972.
24. Robert C. Allen, *Horrible Prettiness: Burlesque and American Culture* (Chapel Hill, 1990), 272.
25. Mary Cass Canfield quoted in *Vaudeville as Seen by Its Contemporaries*, ed. Charles Stein (New York, 1990), 373.
26. Caroline Caffin, *Vaudeville* (New York, 1932), 19.

**The Burlesque Soul of Striptease**

1. Gypsy Rose Lee, *Gypsy: A Memoir* (New York, 1957), 5; clipping, n.d., Gypsy Rose Lee Clippings Folder, Brown and Lyman Collection, NYPL.
2. Irving Zeidman, *The American Burlesque Show* (New York, 1967), 201. Other sources for this chapter include Ralph Allen, "Our Native Theatre: Honkey-Tonk, Minstrel Shows, Burlesque," in *The American Theatre: A Sum of Its Parts*, ed. Henry B. Williams (New York, 1971); Ralph G. Allen, "At My Mother's Knee (and Other Low Joints)," *American Popular Entertainment*, ed. Myron Matlaw (Westport, 1979); Brooks Atkinson, "Casting and Comedy," *New York Times*, September 11, 1927, xi; and Ralph Allen, *Best Burlesque Sketches* (New York, 1995), xxviii.
3. "The Business of Burlesque"; Zeidman, 202.
4. Morton Minsky and Milt Machlin, *Minsky's Burlesque* (New York, 1986), 41.
5. E. E. Cummings, "Burlesque, I Love It!" *Stage*, March 1936, 61.
6. Ibid.
7. Bernard Sobel, *Burleycue: An Underground History of Burlesque Days* (New York, 1931), 274–76.
8. Clipping, n.d., October 29, 1939, TUNC.

9. Blaze Starr, *My Life as Told to Huey Perry* (New York, 1974), 86–98.

10. Rose La Rose described in Martin Collyer, *Burlesque: The Story of a Unique American Institution* (New York, 1964), 48. Georgia Sothern, *My Life in Burlesque* (New York, 1972), 42.

11. Jean Cocteau, *My Journey around the World* (London, 1958), tr. W. F. Strachey, originally published in Paris, 1936, 167.

12. Ibid., 168.

13. Robert Toll, *On with the Show: The First Century of Show Biz in America* (New York, 1976), 228.

14. Alva Johnston, "A Tour of Minskyville," *New Yorker*, May 28, 1932, 34–39.

15. "Burlesque Is Back," *New York World-Telegram*, June 25, 1942, LGNS, Volume 218, 135.

16. H. M. Alexander, *Burlesque: The Vanished Soul of Striptease* (New York, 1938), 36; "Burlesque Queen," *Chicago Daily Tribune*, January 28, 1934, F4.

17. Ann Corio, *This Was Burlesque* (New York, 1968), 90–92; Sothern, 42–43.

18. Caffin cited in Marshall Stearns and Jean Stearns, *Jazz Dance: The Story of Vernacular Dance* (New York, 1968), 129. Joseph Mitchell, *My Ears Are Bent* (New York, 2000), 56; Barbara Stratyner Cohen, "Ned Wayburn and the Dance Routine: From Vaudeville to the Ziegfeld Follies," *Studies in Dance History* 13, Society of Dance History Scholars (New York, 1996), 15.

19. *New York Times Magazine*, June 26, 1966, 190.

20. Mitchell, 55.

21. Joel Harvey, "American Burlesque as Reflected through the Career of Kitty Madison, 1916–37," Ph.D. dissertation, Florida State University, 1980, 147.

22. Personal interview with Kitty Oakes, September 2001.

23. Hugues Panassié talks about "straight" and "hot" or "sweet" in *Hot Jazz: The Guide to Swing Music* (New York, 1936), 122. This book anticipates the way writers like H. M. Alexander talked about striptease, 32.

24. Ever since Constance Rourke published *The American Humor* in 1931, and perhaps before, observers have noted that women are not funny. The scholar Susan Glenn discusses this in detail. Susan Glenn, *Female Spectacle: The Roots of Modern Feminism* (Cambridge, 2000), 42.

25. Ad for Lois De Fee, *Billboard*, December 2, 1939, 39. Robert Bogdan, *Freak Show: Presenting Human Oddities for Amusement and Profit* (Chicago, 1999), 114–16. Bogdan explains that it was a stock carnival practice to advertise "opposing"—fat woman, thin man, etc—types together. Thus the popularity of tattooed and bearded women, who have attributes not associated with conventional femininity.

26. *Variety*, January 5, 1938, n.d., WHMC.

27. Barbara Grossman, *Funny Woman: The Life and Times of Fanny Brice* (Bloomington, 1992), 205–7.

28. *Washington Star*, December 5, 1933. The Countess Dubinsky number by Billy Rose, Ballard MacDonald, and Joseph Meyer was featured in Act I of the *Ziegfeld Follies of 1933–34*, which started out of town. The earliest Winter Garden program is dated January 4, 1934; out-of-town programs for the Boston Shubert, November 6, 1933; Forrest, Philadelphia, November 20; National, Washington, December 4; all in SA.

29. John Cheever, "The Teaser," in *Literature and Liberalism: An Anthology of Sixty Years of the New Republic*, ed. Edward Zwick (New York, 1976), 6. June Sochen, *Women's Comic Visions* (Detroit, 1991), 141–59; Sochen, *From Mae to Madonna: Women Entertainers in the 20th Century* (Lexington, 1999), 41–59.

**"Minskyville"**

1. Brooks Atkinson, "Burlesque with a Ph.D.," *New York Times*, September 7, 1930, 7. Joseph Kaye, "The Last Legs of Burlesque," *Theatre Magazine*, February 1930, 36, discusses how the Broadway revue continued to steal from striptease.
2. *Zit's Theatrical Newspaper*, April 15, 1930, 15; "Minskys Have Classy Show," *Zit's*, September 20, 1930, 15; *Evening Graphic*, November 8, 1930, n.d.
3. "Minskys Make Merry at Garden Opening," *Billboard*, September 7, 1929, 45. The phenomenon of upwardly mobile audiences was not limited to New York. In 1929 the Old Howard had offered a midnight "ladies' show" that gave "unescorted women" the chance to see Ann Corio.
4. Gypsy Rose Lee, *Gypsy: A Memoir* (New York, 1957), 234–37; Master Book, GRL Papers, NYPL.
5. *Zit's Theatrical Newspaper*, March 21, 1931, 15. Actually Gypsy was so popular that when she got arrested that year, she got telegrams from admirers. GRL, Box 7, Folder 1.
6. *Variety*, November 3, 1929, 1, 64. There are many sources documenting Forty-second Street's fall from grace and the Depression's effect. Frederick L. Allen, *Since Yesterday: An Informal History of the Thirties, September 3, 1929–September 3, 1939* (New York, 1986), chapters 1–17. Atkinson notes that in 1929, the number of legitimate productions was 239. One year into the Depression, it had fallen to 187. By 1938 it had dropped to 100. Brooks Atkinson, *Broadway* (New York, 1957), 285.
7. "Burlesque War Brewing between Herk and Minsky," *Zit's Theatrical Newspaper*, February 7, 1931, 15. In New York alone, there were eighteen burlesque houses in 1931. *Billboard*, February 14, 1931, 24.
8. Lee, 198.
9. Margaret Knapp, "A Historical Study of the Legitimate Playhouses on West Forty-Second Street between Seventh and Eight Avenues in New York City," Ph.D. dissertation, City University of New York, 1982, 371; Lee, 251–55; Alva Johnston, "A Tour of Minskyville," *New Yorker*, May 28, 1932, 34.
10. Morton Minsky and Milt Machlin, *Minsky's Burlesque: A Fast and Funny Look at America's Bawdiest Era* (New York, 1968), 133–35; *Zit's Theatrical Newspaper*, February 9, 1931, 30; Brooks Atkinson, "Broadway Sideshow," *New York Times*, April 24, 1932, 23.
11. Lee, 251–54; Irving Zeidman, *The American Burlesque Show* (New York, 1967), 168–71; Minsky, 94–104; Atkinson, "Broadway Sideshow," "Burlesque Houses Called Unsightly," *New York Times*, May 10, 1932, 25. These nude pictures were one of the chief things cited in the 1932 hearings as bringing down the neighborhood. Another was the link to prostitutes.
12. Rowland Barber, *The Night They Raided Minskys'* (New York, 1960), 341; Stanley Walker, *The Nightclub Era* (New York, 1934), 207; Burlesque programs after 1900, MCNY.
13. Barber, 341–42. It would be these barkers who would incite the first trials in 1932. See, for example, "Broadway Sideshow," *New York Times*, April 24, 1932, xi.
14. "Burly Nudes Invade 42nd Street," *Zit's Theatrical Newspaper*, February 24, 1931, 25.
15. "The Killer of Burlesque," *Variety*, February 18, 1937, 47, 78; "Commissioner Moss Keeps after Burlesque," *Billboard*, April 6, 1935, 24.

16. "Burlesque Review, Republic, New York," *Billboard*, February 21, 1931, 24.

17. Brooks Atkinson review of burlesque show at the Republic, *New York Times*, February 13, 1931, 20. Also, it's worth noting that in a follow-up review of the Republic, *Zit's* gave the Minsky show a favorable treatment in "Minsky Hits Public Favor," *Zit's*, February 24, 1931, 25.

18. Cited in Minsky, 105, 108. The Minskys ran a series of ads in the *New Yorker* with captions designed to appeal to the literati. For example, February 21, 1931, 62, advertised the Republic show as "snappier and fresher than ever." The ads ran until the hearings in April and May of 1932.

19. "Review of Stock Burlesque at the Republic," *Variety*, November 24, 1931, 30.

20. This was much debated. "Irving Shows are Drawing Ladies," *Zit's Theatrical Newspaper*, May 20, 1930, 25; "Many Women at Burlesque," *Zit's*, February 24, 1931, 25; Joseph Wood Krutch, "Burlesque," *The Nation*, June 8, 1932, 647; Dressler, "Burlesque as a Cultural Phenomenon," Ph.D. dissertation, New York University, 1937, 83. In the 1932 hearings, though, the prosecution described the audience as mostly working class.

21. Barber, 340. In general, the theater scene was more violent than it is today. For George White punching Billy Minsky, also see *Variety* and *Billboard*.

22. *Zit's Theatrical Newspaper*, February 24, 1931, 25; *Variety*, February 4, 68; "Stock Burlesque Menace," *Variety*, March 4, 1931, 1, 41; "8 Convicted of Dirty Stock Burlesque," *Variety*, March 4, 1931, 41; "Stock Actors Sent to Jail," *Variety*, March 17, 1931, 44. Sumner does not mention the Republic by name in his report, which was published at the end of 1931. But he does mention two burlesque theaters that he had helped to raid.

23. "Eltinge Show Just Rehearsal; Rush to Launch Burlesque Premieres in 42nd Street Harmful," *Zit's Theatrical Newspaper*, March 14, 1931, 22.

24. Description of "Yetta Lostit from Bowling," Lee, 252–53. According to Rowland Barber, this was the first horse appearing in burlesque since *Mazeppa*. "Best Show Ever at Republic," *Zit's Theatrical Newspaper*, April 23, 1931, 11.

25. Lee, 252; Kathy Peiss, *The Making of America's Beauty Culture* (New York, 2002), 197. Billy Minsky seems to have been responsible for a lot of decisions about the way Depression-era strippers looked. When Georgia Sothern arrived at the Republic in 1931, Billy made her dye her hair red.

26. "Unofficial Burlesque Censor Will Advise on Indecency," *Zit's Theatrical Newspaper*, May 16, 1931, 22; "Cops Step in on Stock Burlesque on 42nd Street," *Variety*, April 10, 1931, 50.

27. *New York Press*, April 29, 1931, 4, WHMC; "Sumner Fails to Convict Stock Burlesque People," *Variety*, May 13, 1931, 69.

28. Alfred Kazin, *Starting Out in the Thirties* (New York, 1989), 87.

29. Frank Thistle, "Burlesque," *Real Magazine*, June 1966, 40, Box 1, Folder 11, HM. The idea that the economic situation has something to do with burlesque was also expressed on the op-ed page of the *New York Times*, May 17, 1933, 16.

30. "Burlesque Goes into the Republic," *Zit's Theatrical Newspaper*, February 24, 1931, 24; "Intimate Burlesque," *Billboard*, February 21, 1931, 24.; Zeidman, 168–71.

31. "Burlesque Men Get Together," *Zit's Theatrical Newspaper*, April 4, 1931, n.d.

32. Zeidman, 168–72.

33. *Variety*, February 4, 1931, 68.

34. *Variety*, October 6, 1931, 39.

35. Walker, 206–7.
36. Walker, 199; "Billy Minsky Dies; Producer of Burlesque," *New York Herald Tribune*, June 13, 1932, n.d., BRTC; "Billy Minsky Passes Away," *Zit's Theatrical Newspaper*, June 18, 1932, 11.
37. "Find Obscene Books on Increase Here," *New York Times*, April 6, 1932, 40. At the bottom of this article is a paragraph about burlesque in which Sumner argues that the rights given to actors allowed to do obscene performances are "unconstitutional." Cited in Jay A. Gertzman, *Bookleggers and Smuthounds: The Trade in Erotica, 1920–1940* (Philadelphia, 2002), 62.
38. For how the Depression created a backlash against the Jazz Age, see James D. Horan, *The Desperate Years: A Pictorial History of the Depression* (New York, 1962), and Cabell Phillips, *From the Crash to the Blitz: 1929–1939* (New York, 1969). Cited in James Peterson, *The Century of Sex* (New York, 2000), 114.
39. Paul Boyer, *Purity in Print: The Vice Society Movement and Book Censorship in America* (New York, 1968), 142; Allen, 250.
40. This is Robert C. Allen's assertion, 251.
41. "Review of *Burleycue*," *New York Times*, January 24, 1932, 12; Gypsy Rose Lee, *The G-String Murders* (New York, 1943), 274–78.
42. Sobel, *Burleycue: An Underground History of Burlesque Days* (New York, 1931), 262–74.
43. Zeidman, 117, 164; "What's Doing in Burlesque" column, *Zit's Theatrical Newspaper*, May 12, 1930, 15; "Strip Numbers on Way Out," *Zit's*, May 21, 1932, 11. In the 1932 hearings, the prosecution described that one stripper took off her bra "with delight." Testimony from prosecution, April 26, 1932, 200, Indecent Show Files, MA.
44. "High Priced Teasers Leaving the Wheel," *Variety*, November 10, 1931, 35.
45. Herbert Mitgang, *The Man Who Rode the Tiger: The Life of Judge Samuel Seabury and the Story of the Greatest Investigation of Corruption in this Century* (New York, 1963), 204–5.
46. Horan, 39–40. Seabury himself was put into office by Roosevelt after the stripper Vivian Gordon was murdered by one of her famous clients. Mitgang, 245–65. H; Paul Jeffers, *The Napoleon of New York* (New York, 2002), 141–48.
47. "Hottest Show Not Hot, *Zit's* Finds: Irving Place, Owned by District Attorney Crain, Target of City Dailies," *Zit's Theatrical Newspaper*, April 26, 1932, 11.
48. This history is described in much greater detail in Mitgang, *The Man Who Rode the Tiger*; Mitgang, *Once Upon a Time in New York: Jimmy Walker, Franklin Roosevelt, and the Last Great Battle of the Jazz Age* (New York, 2000); and George Welsh, *Gentleman Jimmy Walker: Mayor of the Jazz Age* (New York, 1974), 253–327. Walker, 224–34.
49. Probably the first indication in the press that there would be intensified activity against burlesque is "Open Drive to End Broadway Rackets," *New York Times*, January 1, 1932, 25. These were immediately followed with efforts to shut down burlesque shows (and vaudeville shows) on Sunday. *New York Times*, January 27, 1932, 19.
50. NYSSV Fifty-Eighth Annual Report (New York, 1931), 11.
51. Ibid., 12.
52. A couple of days before the hearings started, Brooks Atkinson wrote a piece about how burlesque had forced Forty-second Street to degenerate. *New York Times*, April 24, xi. In that article, he called burlesque "ugly, monstrous, and obscene."

53. The events leading up to the 1932 hearings, and the property owners' role in it, is documented in the *New York Times*, March 17, 23; March 25, 22; April 7, 29; April 12, 20; and April 21, 1932, 23. "Civic Groups Rush 42nd Street Clean Up," *New York Times*, April 26, 1932, 23. The trial began on April 27 and was covered in the *New York Times* on April 28, 23; April 29, 17; April 30, 19; May 5, 33; and May 7, 11. The hearings ended on May 12. Testimonies, April 26, Indecent Shows Files, MA.

54. Testimony of Louis Fehr and others, April 25, 26, Indecent Show Hearing on Before Commissioner of License, Box WJJ-242, James Walker Collection, MA. The hearing went on through May 9.

55. "Old Actress Backs Burlesque Shows," *New York Times*, April 27, 1932, 19; "Mother" Annie Elms Testimony, Indecent Show Hearing on Before Commissioner of License, Box WJJ-243, James Walker Collection, MA.

56. Atkinson cited in *New York Herald*, May 6, 1932, n.d. MCNY Burlesque Collection, Folder 32, Burlesque Raids, Trials, etc. Brooks Atkinson Testimony, May 5, Indecent Show Hearing on Before Commissioner of License, James Walker Collection, MA. Other testimonies early in May included that of Charles Feldheimer, who wrote the "Uno" column in *Billboard*.

57. The Cowl telegram and discovery of its fakeness is documented in the *New York Times*, May 6, 1932, 17; May 7, 1932, 11; and May 10, 1932, 25. Apparently the legitimate theater producers fabricated it to help their case. Cowl incident in cited in Andrea Friedman, "The Habitats of Sex-Craved Perverts: Campaigns against Burlesque in Depression-Era new York City," *Journal of the History of Sexuality* 7 (October 1996), 203–38. The event is also documented in the Burlesque Hearing Transcript, 1022–24, 1088–89, 1090, 1192, Indecent Show Hearing on Before Commissioner of License, James Walker Collection, MA.

58. *New York Times*, September 21, 1932, 20.

59. "Republic Gets License Back," *Zit's Theatrical Newspaper*, October 15, 1932, 11; *New York Times*, October 12, 1932, 25.

59. *Billboard*, October 29, 1932, 12.

## "I Never Made Any Money until I Took My Pants Off": Fans and Bubbles around the Nation

1. "McKee Demands Clean Up of Burlesque," *New York Times*, September 18, 1932, 1; "McKee Closes Two Burlesques in 42nd Street," *New York Times*, September 20, 1932, 3.

2. O'Brien, "O'Brien For Clean Stage," *New York Times*, May 17, 1933, 15. Clipping, n.d., Burlesque Clippings File, 1940, MCNY.

3. "Burlesques Told to End Obscenity," *New York Times*, May 16, 1933, 19; "Strip Songs Must Be Out," *Zit's Theatrical Newspaper*, May 21, 1933, 7; "No-Strip Ruling Forces Talent S.O.S.," *Variety*, May 23, 1933, 1, 54.

4. Cabell Phillips, *From the Crash to the Blitz: 1929–1939* (New York, 1969), 99–105; James Peterson, *The Century of Sex* (New York, 2000), 109–53.

5. "Boston Censors to Close Old Howard," *New York Times*, January 22, 1933, E7; cited in David Kruh, *Always Something Doin'* (Boston, 1991), 68. Michael James Curley, *I'd Do It Again! A Record of My Uproarious Years* (New York, 1957), 255–56, 321.

6. "Always Somethin' Doin'" at Boston's Old Howard," *Collier's*, September 30, 1950, 22, 23. This is not to imply that Boston was liberal in regard to burlesque, but rather that Curley was. The license commissioner at the time, John Casey, was as inflexible as Moss. Eliot Norton, *Broadway Down East* (Boston, 1972), 84.

7. This is documented in all the theatrical trade papers of the time.

8. "Loop Burlesques Mainly Nudes," *Zit's Theatrical Newspaper*, April 15, 1936, 30; *Billboard*, June 10, 1933, 11.

9. See, for example, society-page photo in the *Chicago Daily Tribune*, February 8, 1931, 5. At the height of the Depression, wealthy women carried luxurious accessories such as fans. "Evening Accessories Show Luxurious Trend," *Chicago Daily Tribune*, January 15, 1930, n.d.

10. "In Nudity, A Girl Reporter Finds What It's About," *Chicago Daily Times*, n.d., Folder 14-315, COP. Other stories claim that Bacon first did the dance in Miami. In any case the salient point is that Bacon is on the record as doing it first. Additionally, a letter dated March 10, 1930, from the SRM places Rand in New York, where she might have seen the fan dance at the Vanities. Richard and Paulette Ziegfeld, *The Ziegfeld Touch: The Life and Times of Florenz Ziegfeld* (New York, 1993), 264. Ziegfeld program, *Ziegfeld Follies of 1931*, BRTC. The account of the obscenity trial of the 1930 *Vanities* appears in the *New York Times*, July 9, 10, 11, 12, 13, 16, 17, 18, 20, 23, 30; August 7, 13.

11. Clipping, n.d., Faith Bacon Clippings File, TUNC. "Legitimate Review, Earl Carroll's Vanities, 1932," *Billboard*, September 24, 1932, 13; Murray, 164–65. Many critics found Carroll offensive. In an essay titled "The Woman's Age," Percy Hammond noted that his shows combined "beauty and mire." That essay is found in *This Atom in the Audience: A Digest of Reviews and Comment* (New York, 1940), 257–61.

12. Faith Bacon Clippings File, n.d., TUNC. Bacon quote in "In Nudity."

13. *Chicago Tribune*, February 25, 1925, 17.

14. In the Jazz Age, Rand also appeared in other films, including *Bachelor Brides*, *Gigolo*, and *Golf Widows*.

15. On Rand's departure from the movies, see "The Life of Sally Rand," *Chicago Daily News*, August 10, 1926. This article claims that DeMille propositioned her. Holly Knox, *Sally Rand: From Film to Fans* (New York, 1974), 18. A letter suggests that she was intimate with the MGM executive Paul Bern, who later married Jean Harlow and tragically killed himself. March 10, 1930, SRM. She headlined at the Palace in Chicago in September 1928, *Chicago Daly Tribune*, September 5, 1928, 31; September 8, 1928, 14. After that she toured and went to New York, where, in 1930, she was in the chorus of *Luana*, an illfated Rudolf Friml musical produced by Arthur Hammerstein. When Rand came back to Chicago in 1932, she also appeared in a play, *The World Between*, which ran for about a month. *Chicago Daily Tribune*, September 11, 1932. She began to perform in nightclubs and speakeasies in December. See, for example, *Chicago Daily Tribune*, December 4, 1932, F5, and December 11, 1932, F5.

16. Rand tells the story of how she brought the fans from New York to a *Tribune* reporter in 1933, COP Records. It's reiterated in Joseph Mitchell, *My Ears Are Bent* (New York, 2000), 81. Knox, 20, tells a story that made Rand look virtuous in the Depression, which was that she bought two fans and a toga for ten dollars in an antique show and wore nothing underneath because she had no money to buy a costume.

17. Studs Terkel, *Hard Times: An Oral History of the Great Depression* (New York, 1970), 168–74.
18. The *Chicago Daily Tribune* provides documentation that the Lady Godiva ride actually took place. In fact, there was a long history of controversy surrounding the appearance of Godiva at the Beaux Arts Ball. In 1927, for example, the year that Rand first came to Chicago, there was enormous controversy over whether a Godiva figure should appear at all and if she should be "draped" or undraped. See, for example, *Chicago Daily Tribune*, November 26, 1927, 1. In 1928, the Florenz Ziegfeld revue *Whoopee* featured five Lady Godivas, *Chicago Daily Tribune*, December 16, 1928, H1. But by 1933, things had changed considerably. See *Chicago Daily Tribune*, May 28, 1933, 9, which reports that at the Beaux Arts Ball, a Lady Godiva appeared undraped; *Chicago Daily Tribune*, June 4, 1933, fl, reports that some people were "shocked."
19. Terkel, 102.
20. "Rand is quicker than the eye," press release, SRM. Several reporters mentioned this wig. In Chicago, Rand was having difficulty paying for it. "Court Refuses Attachment for Salary of Sally Rand," *Chicago Daily Tribune*, August 18, 1933, 6; Mitchell, 78; Robert C. Allen, *Horrible Prettiness: Burlesque and American Culture* (Chapel Hill, 1990), 99.
21. Nelson Algren, *Somebody in Boots* (New York, 1935), 220.
22. "World's Fair Shows Profit," *Billboard*, November 10, 1934, 1, cites the figure earned in the second year of the fair as $300,000. The most conservative estimates place the amount of money Rand made at around $160,000. Rand herself claimed to have grossed on average $56,000 a week for eleven weeks. Personal letter, April 29, 1935, SRM.
23. Century of Nudity pamphlet, n.d., 1933, 1, Chicago Historical Society; "Fair Officials Clamp Ban on Scanty Shows," *Chicago Daily News*, July 20, 1933, 4.
24. Century of Nudity pamphlet, 8.
25. Folder 1-8459, COP; "Dancer Gets Year, Gangster Six Months," *Chicago Reader*, September 25, 1933, n.d., TUNC.
26. Kelly quoted in Emmett Dedmon, *Fabulous Chicago: A Great City's History and People* (New York, 1953), 336.
27. "Mayor Asks Fan Dancers to Cover Up," *Chicago Daily News*, August 2, 1933, 23.
28. "Sally Dances to Yawns," *Chicago Daily News*, August 7, 1933, 4.
29. Rand did have a tendency to bite people. In 1938 she bit someone who tried to photograph her and was fined a hundred dollars. "Sally Rand Fined $25," *Chicago Daily News*, August 8, 1938, 1. "In Nudity"; "'Fan Dance' Sally Tells Thrills of Lake 'Bath,'" *Chicago Daily Times*, August 14, 1933, Folder 14-315, COP; "Sally Takes Bath in Lake," *Chicago Tribune*, August 14, 1933. An advertisement in *Variety*, August 15, 1933, 56, claimed that she smashed the records of Al Jolson, Eddie Cantor, and others at the Chicago Theater. Records of her fight with Sam Belkin, the Paramount Club owner, are found in "S.R. and Club Head Fight Teeth and Fist," *Chicago Tribune*, September 18, 1933; "S.R., Ex Employer Absent Trials Postponement," *Chicago Tribune*, September 29, 1933; "Sally, Ex Boss Drop Mutual Assault Case," *Chicago Tribune*, September 30, 1933; "Sally Rand, Given Year in Jail for Fan Dancing Act, *Philadelphia Inquirer*, September 24, 1933, n.d., TUNC. During the trial, one of the jurors sought to recuse himself because he had a headache. "Juror Had Pain in Head," *Philadelphia Evening Bulletin*, October 5, 1933, n.d., TUNC.
30. "Sally Rand's Fan Not Enough for Gotham, Either," *New York Herald Tribune*, October 12, 1933, TUNC; "New Official's Verdict," *New York Times*, October 12, 1933, 3.

31. "Sally Rand Fan Dance Puts Her in Movies," *New York American*, September 11, 1933, TUNC.

32. "An Ambitious Dancer," February 20, 1934, n.d., TUNC; "Review, *Bolero*," *Variety*, February 20, 1934, n.d., in Variety *Film Reviews, 1934–39*, Volume 5 (New York, 1980).

33. According to Mike Todd and others, the mob was involved in getting Rand back at the fair. Michael Todd Jr. and Susan McCarthy Todd, *A Valuable Property: The Life Story of Michael Todd* (New York, 1983), 32–33. Knox also asserts mob involvement, and given the events of the summer and fall of 1933, it is not unlikely.

34. Rand quoted in Knox, 38.

35. Mitchell, 73–76, reports that Royce invented it.

36. Ibid.

37. Ibid.

38. "Daily Notes," July 12 and July 30, 1934, Italian Village, COP; "Sally's Balloon Goes Boo-oom and Not a Fan to Hide," *New York American*, July 17, 1934, TUNC. According to Holly Knox, 37–38, this may have been mob related, as Sally was caught in the middle of a fight about where she could perform.

39. In June 1936, at the San Diego exposition, Rosita Royce arrived claiming Sally Rand stole her bubble dance.

40. Todd, 33. Mitchell, 74–76, suggests that one of these women was Rosita Royce.

41. Chicago was also the place where Todd met Carrie Finnell, whom he would later cast at the World's Fair and in *Star and Garter*.

42. "Review of *Bolero*," February 17, 1934, in New York Times *Film Reviews*, Volume 2, (New York, 1970), n.d. According to Knox, Rand got the role in *Bolero* because of her Chicago gangster connections.

43. "Sally Rand Fans 500 Salesmen's Selling Spark," *New York Herald Tribune*, February 12, 1935, Sally Rand Clippings Folder, TUNC.

44. *Chicago Tribune*, February 25, 1925, 17.

45. "Nudists Picket Sally Rand: It Looks Like a Good Show," *San Diego Star Telegram*, April 12, 1936, n.d., Sally Rand Clippings Folder, TUNC.

46. "Stubby hair" quoted in San Diego Fair Files, Sally Rand Clippings Folder, n.d. *San Diego Star Evening Telegram*, May 11, 1936, TUNC. "One journalist" quoted in Stephen Nelson, *Only a Paper Moon: The Theatre of Billy Rose* (Ann Arbor, 1987), 112. *San Diego Star Morning Telegram*, April 8, 1936, n.d.; November 6, 1938, n.d.; Fort Worth Exposition Files, the University of Texas at Arlington, Special Collections Division.

47. Anne Hollander, *Sex and Suits: The Evolution of Modern Dress* (New York, 1994), 40–41; Paul Fussell, *Uniforms: Why We Are What We Wear* (New York, 2002).

48. "Nudies Ogle Coin," *Variety*, October 24, 1933, 63; *New York Post*, September 10, 1956, 37. This chapter also draws on Robert Rydell, *World of Fairs: The Century of Progress Expositions* (Chicago, 1993), 92–93, 136–38.

**"Temporary Entertainment for Morons and Perverts":**
**LaGuardia Kicks Striptease out of New York**

1. "Again after Burlesque," *Variety*, January 2, 1934; "Review of the Apollo," *Variety*, November 13, 1934, 63; undated clipping, Burlesque Clippings File,

MCNY; "Two Burlesque Houses Face License Ban," *New York Times*, October 26, 1933, 25; Four More Burlesques Face Ban by Levine," *New York Times*, October 29, 1933, 21; "Cleanup of Stage Ordered by Moss," *New York Times*, January 21, 1934, 1. "Levine Is Out, Paul Moss Sets License Post," *New York Times*, January 16, 1934, LGNS, Volume 3, 57; "Levine Fired Moss in License Chair," n.d., January 19,1934, LGNS, Volume 3, 67; "Moss Won't Be a Sissy in Censoring Theatre," *Brooklyn Eagle*, January 21, 1934, LGNS, Volume 3, 84.

2. Quoted in David Gelernter, *The Lost World of the Fair* (New York, 1995), 2.
3. H. Paul Jeffers, *The Napoleon of New York: Mayor Fiorello LaGuardia* (New York, 2002), 249.
4. Cabell Phillips, *From the Crash to the Blitz: 1929–1939* (New York, 1969), 233.
5. Louis Sobol, *The Longest Street: A Memoir* (New York, 1968), 204; Ward Morehouse, *Matinee Tomorrow: Fifty Years of New York Theatre* (New York, 1949), 260.
6. George Chauncey, *Gay New York: Gender, Culture, and the Makings of the Gay Male World* (New York, 1998), 195. This is also cited in David Dressler, "Burlesque as a Cultural Phenomenon," Ph.D. dissertation, New York University, 1937, 161, 204, 210.
7. Advertisement in *Zit's Theatrical Newspaper*, December, n.d., 1932, 11, shows Margie at the Trocadero. *Zit's* also reviews her in January 1933, at the Troc. Joseph Mitchell, *My Ears Are Bent* (New York, 2000), 48; Irving Zeidman, *The American Burlesque Show* (New York, 1967), 152; "Low Brow's Garbo," n.d., November 16, 1939, Margie Hart Clippings File, TUNC. The first time her name appears in *Billboard* is in the 1933 year-end issue. According to Sherry Britton, Hart incited LaGuardia to shut down burlesque in New York on New Year's Eve of 1937 or 1938. There are several primary sources connecting Hart to burlesque shutdowns in 1935. "Burlesque Show Raided," *New York Times*, April 6, 1935, 11, describes a raid at the Republic. There is no record of shutdowns on New Year's Eve of either of those years.
7. John D'Emilio and Estelle Freedman, *Intimate Matters: A History of Sexuality in America* (New York, 1988), 280.
8. This fact would be much mentioned by the Minsky brothers in the 1936–37 trial proceedings against them.
9. "Moss Won't Be a Sissy," 84 .
10. Clippings, op. cit., LGNS, Volume 3; *Time*, May 10, 1937, 33–34; *Time*, March 12, 1945, 58; *Billboard*, March 3, 1934, 24.
11. I say alleged because although burlesque was linked to organized crime from 1932, it also was linked to ordinary ruffians. Clipping, n.d., WHMC. Clippings, op. cit., LGNS, Volume 3.
12. "Seven New York Burly Theatres in Move to Clean Up Shows," *Billboard*, February 24, 1934, 22; "Commissioner Moss Keeps After Burlesque," *Billboard*, April 6, 1935, 24.
13. "New York Decides to preserve Public Morality," *Newsweek*, May 8, 1937, 21; "New York Censor Threat Dies," *Billboard*, April 20, 1935, 24; "Striptease Held Indecent," *New York Times*, April 9, 1937, 23. The chronicle of the death of striptease in New York was covered by the *New York Times* beginning on April 10, and continuing on April 16, April 22, April 30, and May 1, and on into the summer. It was also covered by *Billboard*, *Variety*, and *Zit's Theatrical Newspaper*.

14. The shift from 1931 and 1932 is covered in many places, most effectively in James Horan, *The Desperate Years: A Pictorial History of the 1930s* (New York, 1962). "A Code for Burleycue, Maybe a Union for Strippers," *Variety*, November 7, 1933, 63. "Burlesque Men Plan Separate Code," *New York Times*, August 19, 1933, 14; "Burlesque Hits Snag in Framing Code," *New York Times*, August 22, 1933, 20. This last documents how burlesque impresarios walked out of the room when performers asked for set salaries.

15. Letter from Thomas Phillips to Frank Gilmore, October 25, 1933, Guide to the Associated Actors and Artistes of America, 4 A's, 1909–1916, Box 6, Folder 122, "BAA: 1933–39," Robert F. Wagner Labor Archives, Bobst Library, NYU; "Burlesquers Organizing," *Zit's*, June 23, 1933, 11; "Burly Actors Preparing for Drive against Dirt," *Billboard*, February 9, 1935, 24. Attempts to get chorus girls a minimum wage of seventeen dollars per week continued to flop throughout the mid-thirties. Philip Sterling, "Burlesque," *New Theatre* (July 1936), 18, 19, 36, 37.

16. A "Burly Briefs" item, *Billboard*, September 9, 1933, 20, said that if BAA officials had their way, "striptease would be a thing of the past." Letter, November 9, 1934, Series 7, 4 A's.

17. Letters from Thomas Phillips to Frank Gilmore, November 2, December 23, 1933, Box 6, Folder 122, 4 A's; BAA Charter, January 12, 1934, Box 6, Folder 122, 4 A's.

18. The most famous strike of 1934 in New York was the taxi drivers' strike, which Clifford Odets then dramatized in *Waiting for Lefty* the following year. "Closed Shop for Burlesque," *Zit's Theatrical Newspaper*, March 17, 1934. Although the 1934 clean-up met with some success, for example in the removal of some runways, it was not sufficient for New York authorities. "BAA Resolves to Clean Up Burly," *Billboard*, April, 13, 1935, 29.

19. *Billboard*, May, 12, 1934, 22.

20. "I. Herk Named Code Advisor," *Zit's Theatrical Newspaper*, November, n.d., 1933, 7.

21. "BAA Protests to NRB on Actors' Working Conditions," *Billboard*, February 10, 1934, 22; *Zit's*, February n.d., 7.

22. "Burlesque Review, Republic, New York"; "Burlesque Review, Irving Place, New York"; and "B.A.A. to Defend Cast Pinched in Irving Place Raid," *Billboard*, February 17, 1934, 22; "Phillips Outlines BAA Activities," *Billboard*, May 25, 1935, 24.

23. *Billboard*, April 15, 1934, 22. Margie was one of ten performers arrested at the Irving Place in February.

24. "Burlesque Still Impossible with Routine Comedians and Strippers, But Here's 1 Comic Who Stops 'Em," *Variety*, September 5, 1933, 85; "Herk Severs Connection with Minskys to Do Job," *Variety*, January 1, 1935, 150.

25. "Coast Burley House Defies Code Rules," *Billboard*, March 30, 1935, 24. This was not just boasting. A 1935 newspaper article reveals that the Minskys did not pay their rent for several months during this time.

26. Herk, April 13, 29; December 14, 1921, 19, *New York Clipper*, 8; "Rosenblatt Urges LaGuardia to Let Burley Theaters Do Own Censoring," *Variety*, February 27, 1934, 62; "NRA Refuses to Regulate Burlesque's Morals," *Variety*, April 7, 1934, 63.

27. "BAA Tie-up with Unions Not Set," *Billboard*, March 9, 1935, 24; "BAA Gathers in Full Force," *Billboard*, March 16, 1935, 24; "BAA Resolves to Clean Up Burly," *Billboard*, April 13, 1935, 29; "200 Attend BAA Meeting in New York," *Billboard*, May 18, 1935, 24.

28. "Burlesque Code Is Due to Be Shelved," *Billboard*, March 23, 1935, 24; "Chisel as Code Dies," *Billboard*, June 22, 1935, 25.

29. "Burlesque Code Dies," *Billboard*, May 25, 1935; "Events of Year in Burlesque," *Billboard*, December 28, 1935, 71. The story of the Burlesque Artists' Association strike is told in the *New York Times*, September 6, 1935, 19; September 7, 1935, 19; September 8, 1935, 9; and September 9, 21; as well as in *Billboard*. "Burlesque Strike Settled," *Billboard*, September 11, 1935, 1, 23; "EBMA Promises Cleaner Shows," *Billboard*, October 5, 1935, 24; "NRA Refuses to Cook Burlesque Morals," *Variety*, October 10, 1935, 63.

30. John Sumner, *Half and Half*, unpublished memoir, n.d., Indiana University Library, Bloomington, Indiana, 13. Even *Zit's* noted that "something should be done to curtail gun molls . . . from classifying themselves as former burlesque choristers." "Not Burlesquers," *Zit's*, n.d., July 20, 1935.

31. "Minskys Plan Heavy Season," *Billboard*, June 22, 1935, 25. Nor were the Minskys the only ones to investigate Miami. That same year, the Weinstocks also visited Florida, presumably for the purpose of starting their own burlesque theater. *Billboard*, January 5, 1935, 25.

32. Foster Hirsch, *Boys from Syracuse: The Shuberts' Theatrical Empire* (Carbondale, 1998), 176–77.

33. "Hollywood House to open," *Billboard*, July 6, 1935, 25. "U-Notes," item, *Billboard*, July 13, 1935, 21; "Burlesque Review, Minsky's Music Hall, Hollywood," *Billboard*, July 27, 1935, 24; "Minsky Shows Go to Hollywood," *Zit's Theatrical Newspaper*, June 29, 1935, 7; "Minsky Caravan en Route," *Zit's*, July n.d., 1935, n.d.; "Hollywood Goes Minsky," *Zit's*, July, n.d., 1935.

34. "Burlesque Review, Minsky's Music Hall, Hollywood," *Billboard*, 24.

35. The question of how much strippers took off in the thirties has been much debated. In trials and testimonies, whenever strippers were called to discuss this, they would claim that they were not naked, but wearing layers of tights and bras, rubber, net, and powder. But this is a theater manager argument dating back to the nineteenth century and seems spurious to me. In the 1932 burlesque hearings, the prosecution claimed to have been at burlesque theaters where strippers took off all their clothes. The defense claimed the women wore rubber pants. Some newspapers of the day document nudity. "Burlesque Mug's Lowdown on Strippers," *Variety*, December 12, 1933, 1. On four vs. three strippers: "Burly Battle on Broadway," *Billboard*, March 2, 1935, 24; "Burlesque Review, Gaiety Theater, New York," *Billboard*, September 19, 1936, 24. On no G-strings: "Burlesque Review, New Gotham, New York," *Billboard*, March 23, 1935, 24. On the Republic in 1935: transcripts from August 21, 1935, hearing of *Police Department and Department of Licenses vs. Holly Holding Corporation* in Morton Minsky and Milt Machlin, *Minsky's Burlesque: A Fast and Funny Look at America's Bawdiest Era* (New York, 1986), Appendix C, 292–99. Margie Hart wore "a spangled arrangement to match her hair at the pelvic region."

36. Stanley Walker, *The Nightclub Era* (New York, 1934), 94–99.

37. Lewis Erenberg, "Impresarios of Broadway Nightlife," in *Inventing Times Square: Culture at the Crossroads of the World*, ed. William Taylor (New York, 1992), 173; Nils T. Granlund, *Blondes, Brunettes, and Bullets* (New York, 1957), 234–35. "Nightclub Review: Paradise," *Billboard*, May 26, 1934, 13. "Nightclub Review: Paradise," *Billboard*, July 9, 1934. *Variety*, October 16, 1935, 53, also describes Pat Paree stripping at the Paradise.

38. Granlund, 202–3; Georgia Sothern, *My Life in Burlesque* (New York, 1972), 209–11, 220–40. Another stripper who worked at the Casino de Paree was Hinda Wassau. By 1933, Wassau's act had become considerably more raucous. According to *Billboard*, she stripped down to a loincloth and to "considerable abandon." *Billboard*, October 10, 1936, 24. An ad for Rose La Rose says that she's "back in burlesque after a post graduate course at Leon and Eddie's."

39. George Jean Nathan, *The Theatre of the Moment* (New York, 1937), 169. According to *Billboard*, the first burlesque show in a nightclub occurred in Sully's Showboat in the Village. "Offers Burley Show," *Billboard*, December 7, 1935, 12.

40. Nathan, 174.

41. Some strippers who had been big stars in burlesque did less well in nightclubs. In the *New York Times*, November 6, 1937, 9, Margie Hart is quoted as saying that she "missed the wisecracks" of the burlesque audience. Interestingly, the *Times* claimed that Hart's performances in nightclubs were too "timid." But *Zit's* thought that her nightclub performances benefited her burlesque appearances. "Margie Hart's New Style, Hit," *Zit's Theatrical Newspaper*, February 9, 1935, n.d. "Burlesque Review, Club Frolics, Miami," *Billboard*, December 12, 1946, 40. Margie Hart performed at the Mirador and the Apollo. *Billboard*, March 13, 1937, 24.

42. H. M. Alexander, *Striptease: The Vanished Art of Burlesque* (New York, 1938), 40; *Zit's Theatrical Newspaper*, February 22, 1936, 1.

43. *Oxford English Dictionary*, online edition, dates the first usage of B-girl to 1936.

44. Favorable reviews about the Irving Place appear in *Zit's*, December 18, 1934, 7; *Zit's*, January 13, 1934, 7; and *Zit's*, January 20, 1934, 7,

45. Miccio as mobster in "Strip to Fame," *Collier's*, December 19, 1936, 47. H. M. Alexander also implies Miccio and his partner were associated with the mob. Miccio took over the Irving Place in the fall of 1935, as reported in "Irving Place, People's Bow out of EBMA," *Billboard*, October 19, 1935, 24. On Irving Place as "highbrow," see "Irving Place Doing Well," *Zit's Theatrical Newspaper*, May 13, 1933, 11.

46. June Havoc, *More Havoc* (New York, 1980), 94–97.

47. Geoffrey Gorer, *Hot Strip Tease and Other Notes on American Culture* (London, 1937), 48–55.

48. Havoc, 94.

49. "Gilbert's Numbers Score in Irving Place Show," *Zit's*, November 11, 1933, 7; "Clever, Eye Filling Show at Irving Place Theatre," *Zit's*, December 18, 1933, 8. Gilbert actually defends striptease in an editorial in *Billboard*, where he says that "the right use of nudity and strip acts" is desirable and that six strip acts "are not too much if your strippers are varied as to techniques." *Billboard*, December 26, 1936, n.d., Gypsy Rose Lee Clippings folder, Chamberlain and Lyman Brown Collection, BRTC.

50. Alexander, 28; "Burlesque Review, Irving Place, New York," *Billboard*, September 28, 1935, 23. It also got around Paul Moss's anti-runway edict, and three other theaters followed suit. "Four Burlesque Houses Build Stairs," *Billboard*, November 9, 1935, 25.

51. "Burlesque Review, Irving Place, New York," *Billboard*, September 28, 1935, 23; Allen Gilbert Clippings File, September 1938, n.d., NYPL.

52. "Burlesque Review, Irving Place, New York," *Variety*, October 2, 1935, 63.

53. "Burlesque Review, Irving Place, New York," *Variety*, October 2, 1934, 86; "Irving Place Burlesque Sets New High in Beauty," *Zit's*, September 16, 1933,

7. "Packed House Greets Show at Irving Place Theatre," *Zit's*, January 20, 1934, 7. *Billboard*, May 2, 1936, 22.

54. Alexander, 6–13.

55. Letter dated January 29, 1935, in *Selected Letters of E. E. Cummings*, ed. F. W. Dupell and George Stade (New York, 1969), 135.

56. James T. Farrell, *Judgement Day* (New York, 1935), 383–86; John Dos Passos, *The Big Money* (New York, 1936), 198.

57. This section owes much to the Ph.D. dissertation of Marilyn Cohen, "Reginald Marsh: An Interpretation of His Art," New York University, 1987. Cohen lists about ten works by Marsh depicting burlesque scenes. Norman Sasowky, *The Prints of Reginald Marsh* (New York, 1976). Phillips, 407–9. Ellen Wiley Todd, "Kenneth Hayes Miller and Reginald Marsh on Fourteenth Street, 1920–1940," *Gender and American History since 1890* (New York, 1993), 127–55. Todd points out that many of Marsh's "non-striptease" paintings, such as his department store ones, showed women stripping.

58. Marsh quoted in Sasowky, 10. Marsh gave Minsky one of his drawings in 1931.

59. The major works on Hopper's drawings and paintings of burlesque figures are Lloyd Goodrich, *Edward Hopper: An Exhibition and Catalogue* (New York, 1964); Gail Levin, *Edward Hopper: An Intimate Biography* (New York, 1984), 310, 348; Robert Silberman, "Hopper and the Theatre of the Mind," in *On the Edge of Your Seat: Popular Theater and Film in Early 20th-Century Art*, ed. Patricia Mcconnel et al. (New York, 2002), 138–40; Vivian Green Fryd, *Art and the Crisis of Marriage: Edward Hopper and Georgia O'Keeffe* (Chicago, 2003), 87–114; Gail Levin, *Edward Hopper: The Art and the Artist* (New York, 1980), 54–55.

60. Working conditions at some burlesque theaters continued to be deplorable as burlesque performers went without being paid for fear that they would be blacklisted. At other theaters, performers worked eighty-hour weeks. "Nudity Legislation Perils Burlesque Strippers, Night Club Shows, and Musicals," *Zit's Theatrical Newspaper*, February 16, 1935, 1.

61. Robert Caro, *The Power Broker: Robert Moses and the Fall of New York* (New York, 1996), 441–43.

62. "Burlesque Review, Star, Brooklyn," *Variety*, October 21, 1936, 63.

63. "Burlesque, If You're Interested: 12 Best Strippers," *Variety*, January 6, 1937, 233. *Time*, May 10, 1937, 33–34; *Variety*, March 3, 1937, 59. In January 1937, Alfred Kinsey visited New York and attended some striptease performances. About them he wrote, "Burlesque at Broadway has the most gorgeously thrilling girls I ever expect to see—and they stop at nothing. The g-strings to which they finally strip are half as wide as your little finger and not a button wider at the strategic spot. When the audience insists strenuously enough, she will remove even the string—slipping a finger in place (to live up to the law) with more damaging effect than the complete exposure of a nudist camp." Cited in Jonathan Gathorne-Hardy, *Sex: The Measure of All Things: A Life of Alfred C. Kinsey* (London, 1998), 86.

64. *Promoting Public Decency: The Society for the Suppression of Vice Yearly Report*, 1936, 12–13.

65. Sumner quoted in "Sumner Doubts Burlesque Code," clipping, n.d., Burlesque Clippings File, 1930–39, NYPL.

66. Three years earlier, the brothers had tried to buy the Adams burlesque house in Newark. Their attempt backfired when the church across the street blocked the sale. (In 1942 the brothers would succeed.)

67. "Bel Geddes May Do Scenery, Sanford to Stage Minskys' Classy Byway Burly," *Variety*, November 25, 1936, 63; "The Minsky Kids," *Collier's*, March 6, 1937, 15, 16, 17.

68. Clipping, n.d., Red, Hot, and Nude Clippings File, BRTC.

69. "Living Minskys Drop Dud on B'Way in Classy Burlesque Try," *Variety*, December 29, 1936, 54.

70. "H.M. goes to Red, Hot, and Blue in Boston," *Billboard*, October 18, 1936, 24; "Minskys' High Hat Stem Start Combines Vaude, Review, Burly," *Billboard*, January 3, 1937 1; Barber, 347.

71. The 1937 closing of burlesque houses is documented in the *New York Times* from April 9 to May 7, and in LGNS, Volumes 83–86, April–May 1937.

72. "Minsky University," *Billboard*, March 13, 1937, 35; "Washington Critics Plan to Aid Burly," *Billboard*, February 27, 1937, 24, Burlesque Critics Clippings File, BRTC.

73. "Burlesque Theatres Resent Copping of Strippers by Vaude and Cafes," *Variety*, March 24, 53, 1, 32. "Burlesque Reviews, Gotham, New York," *Variety*, March 24, 1937, 59.

74. *Variety*, April 21, 1937, 62.

75. "Striptease Held Indecent by Court," *New York Times*, April 9, 1937, 23. *Billboard*, April 17, 24; April 24, 24.

76. "Gotham Loses Its License," *New York Times*, April 16, 1937, 27; "Minsky's Fined $500 in strip-Tease Case," *New York Times*, April 17; "Burlesque Owner Charges a Plot," *New York Times*, May 1, 1937.

77. This section of the book also draws on Andrea Friedman, "The Habitats of Sex-Crazed Perverts": Campaigns against Burlesque in Depression-Era New York City," *Journal of the History of Sexuality* 7 (October 1996), 203–38. "Gotham Burly Won't Reopen 'Til Fall," *Variety*, April 21, 1937, 62. *Variety* re-ran its "Killer of Burlesque" column, which first appeared in 1931 when the Minskys took over Broadway. Also, it's interesting to learn that while LaGuardia moved to shut down burlesque, the "elite" crowd continued to crave it. On April 17, 1937, hundreds of New Yorkers attended a "burlesque ball" at which celebrities staged a burlesque of burlesque. See *New York Times*, April 17, 1937, 20.

78. *Journal-American*, April 24, 1937, n.d., MCNY Burlesque Collection.

79. "Moss Weighs Ban on 14 Burlesques," *New York Times*, April 30, 1937, 1.

80. Ibid. On sex crimes, see "Albany Acts to End Sex Crimes," *Brooklyn Eagle*, March 23, 1937, LGNS, Volume 83, 138; "Propose Curb for Sex Crimes," *New York News Mirror*, March 24, 1937, LGNS, Volume 83, 147; "Doctors Join in War on Sex Criminals," *New York News Mirror*, March 27, 1937, LGNS, Volume 84, 17; "Bail Ban Urged for Sex Crimes," *New York Post*, LGNS, Volume 84, 79; "New York Burlesque Cleaning Up," *Billboard*, April 24, 1937, 1. "Sex crimes increase 43.6 percent," n.d., LGNS, Volume 84, 85.

81. "Burlesque Houses of the City Shut as a Public Menace," *New York Times*, May 2, 1937, 27.

82. Ibid.; *Variety*, April 21, 1937, 39. "N.Y. Burly Closed Down," *Billboard*, May 8, 1, 10, reports thirteen, not fourteen theaters. "No Chance for NY Burly: Out of Town Fares Better," *Billboard*, May 15, 1937, 1, 15. Also it's worth noting that LaGuardia's action set off a nationwide anti-burlesque crusade. "Panicky Burly People Look to Mountain Jobs and Night Clubs," *Billboard*, May 15, 1937, 36.

83. "Moss Leases New Broadway House," *Zit's Theatrical Newspaper*, September 7, 1935, n.d.

84. Brooks Atkinson, "On the State of Burlesque," *New York Times*, May 9, 1937, IV, 7.
85. "2 of the Minskys Strike Their Flag," *New York Times*, May 6, 1937, 26. In this article, the Minskys are quoted as saying, "We tried to elevate burlesque and look where it got us."
86. "Burlesque Bows in Its New Attire," *New York Times*, July 13, 1937, 22; "Minskys are Turned Down Cold," *New York Sun*, June 4, 1937, Burlesque Clippings folder, BRTC; "Moss Talks on Theatre," *New York Times*, June 18, 1937, 25; "Minsky Theatre May be Reopened," *New York Times*, June 29, 1937, 18.
87. "New York Theaters to Be Permitted under Cleanup Rules," *Billboard*, June 26, 1937, 1; Brooks Atkinson, *Broadway Scrapbook* (New York, 1947), 70–73.
88. In "Undressing for Cash," *Zit's Theatrical Newspaper*, June 16, 1937, n.d., headliner Ann Corio suggested that striptease should fight censors by returning to its proletariat roots: "Stripping does not belong in night clubs or on Broadway," she wrote. "It belongs in burlesque."
89. Lyrics of "Mr. Striptease Is Dead," in Laguardia News Scrapbook 1937, MA.
90. Ann Corio, "Mr. Striptease Is Dead," number mentioned in "It's Ladies Day," *Life* 61 (September 16, 1966), 128–29, 132–33, and cited in Robert Toll, *On with the Show: The First Century of Show Business in America* (New York, 1976), 238. "Burlesque Review, Apollo, New York," *Billboard*, June 24, 1937, 22. "Burlesque Bows in Its New Attire," *New York Times*, July 13, 1937, 22, also reports that the Republic featured a striptease in reverse, and a Carrie Finnell–like number in which the strippers got undressed offstage. The nightclubs also responded to LaGuardia with toned-down stripteases. For example, the Harlem Uproar House nightclub dedicated a whole evening to the "funeral of striptease." *New York Times*, May 8, 1937, 22.
91. NYSSV Annual Report (New York, 1937), 11.
92. "Midwest Burly Brassiered; Biz N.S.G.," *Variety*, March 27, 1935, 38.
93. "Miccio Plans N.Y. Showboat," *Billboard*, April 9, 1938, 22. Dave Rosen also tried this idea. *Variety*, January, 1939, 49. "Burlesque Reviews, Triboro, New York," *Variety*, September 28, 1938, 50; "Burlesque Reviews, Triboro, New York," *Variety*, April 26, 1939, 45.
94. *New York Times*, January 23, 1938, II, 2.
95. Brooks McNamara, "The Entertainment District at the End of the 1930s," in *Inventing Times Square*, 185.

## Gypsy

1. Ziegfeld Follies of 1936 Folder, SA.
2. Gypsy did give in and participate in a farewell for Columbia seniors. *New York Daily Mirror*, November 1, 1936, n.d., GRL.
3. Gypsy Rose Lee, *Gypsy: A Memoir* (New York, 1957), 181.
4. Series X, Photos, Box 73, Folders 1–5, GRL; Box 78, Folders 8–10, GRL; Box 79, Folders 1–2, GRL; Scrapbook, Volume 1, n.d., Volume 2, 1936–37, GRL.
5. Lee, 226–48. Lyrics to "Powder My Back," 230. *Variety* confirms that the *Girls from the Follies* toured the Midwest in the 1929–30 season. Also, *Zit's Theatrical Newspaper* notes that Gladys Clark took a rest for the summer on May 12, 1930. On May 24, Clark rejoined the show in Cleveland. There is no

mention of *Girls* in *Zit's* for this date. *Zit's* lists *Girls from the Follies* as running in Philadelphia from December 8 to December 13, 1930. *Zit's* also lists *Girls from the Follies* as being in Chicago on February 6, 1931. However, Chicago papers do not list Gypsy as a headliner. This doesn't necessarily invalidate Gypsy's claim, however, since before the late thirties, very few strippers would have gotten headliner billing in local papers. And in general, *Gypsy* checks out factually.

6. Lee, 152, photo insert.
7. The song was written by Erwin Gilbert, who later became a Hollywood screenwriter. Obviously it was also inspired by Fanny Brice's Countess Dubinsky number and by the other Broadway shows mentioned. Subseries 2, General Correspondence, Box 14, Folders 7–8, GRL.
8. *Zit's*, March 19, 1932, 11.
9. Patricia Higham, *Ziegfeld* (New York, 1954), 211–15; Richard and Paulette Ziegfeld, *The Ziegfeld Touch: The Life and Times of Florenz Ziegfeld* (New York, 1993), 162–64. *New York Sun*, n.d., June 28, 1936, Burlesque Collection, MCNY; "Legitimate Review, *Hot-Cha*," *Billboard*, March 19, 1932, 16; "More of the Same," *New Yorker*, March 19, 1932, 28–29.
10. Sobol, *Broadway Heartbeat* (New York, 1953), 128–33.
11. "Minsky's Brooklyn Theatre Puts on Marvelous Show," *Zit's Theatrical Newspaper*, November 24, 1932, 11 ; Nelson, 23–25 ; Polly Rose Gottlieb, *The Nine Lives of Billy Rose* (New York, 1968), 184; "Gypsy Rose Lee Left Casino de Paree and Went into Burly Friday," *Billboard*, June 30, 1934, 24; *Billboard*, May 5, 1934, 22. "Nightclub Review: Casino de Paree, New York," *Billboard*, July 28, 1934, 12, announced that it would reopen without Gypsy Rose Lee but with Georgia Sothern. On August 11, Gypsy was back at the Irving Place. A "Burly Brief" item in *Billboard*, August 25, 22, announced she would leave.
12. Clippings, n.d., GRL; "Burlesque Review, Irving Place, New York," *Billboard*, September 28, 1935, 23. "Burlesque Review, Irving Place, New York, " *Billboard*, November 23, 1935, 24.
13. Lee, 296; *Zit's Theatrical Newspaper*, April 7, 1931, 15; *Billboard*, December 26, 1931, 15.
14. *Zit's Theatrical Newspaper*, 1935, n.d.; Lee, 296.
15. Dwight Fiske, *Without Music*, ed. Robert Benchley (New York, 1933), 3–8. George Davis, "The Dark Young Pet of Burlesque," *Vanity Fair*, February 1936, 50–52; Irving Drutman, *Good Company: A Memoir, Mostly Theatrical* (New York, 1997), 103–5.
16. Fiske, 3–8.
17. "Burlesque Review, Irving Place, New York," *Billboard*, April 20, 1935, 24.
18. 1934 Irving Drutman handwritten note, n.d., GRL, General Correspondence Series, Box 53, Folder 7, says, "She sings Ida the Wayward Sturgeon, Mrs. Pettibone, and Anthony and Cleopatra." Another source for Gypsy's ideas about her act was her married lover at the time, the socialite Eddie Braun.
19. Brooks Atkinson, "On the State of Burlesque," *New York Times*, May 9, 1937, 15.
20. "Leonard Silliman signs her for "new faces," *New York Herald Tribune*, September 13, 1935. GRL. List of the opening shows in *Variety*, throughout 1935. Also, it is not in Robert Baral's *Revue: A Nostalgic Reprise of the Great Broadway Period* (New York, 1962), which lists all of the shows that opened on Broadway between the 1920s and the 1950s, or in Lee Davis, *Scandals and Follies: The Rise and Fall of the Great Broadway Revue* (New York, 2001), or in the New York Times Online.

21. *Vanity Fair*, February 1936, 51–53.

22. "No Hits, Several Errors," *New Yorker*, October 26, 1935, 32.

23. Herrman, *The Body Beautiful*, program, SA. The Body Beautiful Clippings File, BRTC. "Legitimate Review, *The Body Beautiful*," *Billboard*, November 9, 1935, 20.

24. Quoted in Lee, 290–91. O. O. McIntyre, *New York Day by Day* (New York, 1935).

25. Quoted in Lee, 290.

26. Ziegfeld, 172.

27. "Strip to Fame," *Collier's*, December 19, 1936, 45, 47; Lee, 289, cites this figure as $250. Elsewhere it's $300.

28. Richard Rodgers, *Musical Stages: An Autobiography* (New York, 2002), 171–76; Ethan Mordden, *Rodgers and Hammerstein* (New York, 1992), 33; Tamara Geva, *Split Seconds* (New York, 1972), 358–59.

29. *Newsweek*, April 25, 1936, 28–29. Geva quoted in Richard Buckle, *Balletmaster: The Life of Balanchine* (New York, 1999), 100.

30. I wish to thank the dance scholar Lynn Garafola for this idea.

31. In the October 26, 1936, program, Act I, Scene 13, a note says, "Miss Lee's number by Edwin Gilbert." *Ziegfeld Follies of 1936* script, Shubert Archive Script Series 51.

32. *Billboard*, March 3, 1934, 22.

33. See note 30. This version of "A Stripteaser's Education" is from the second *Ziegfeld Follies of 1936*, which opened on September 21, 1936, and closed in January. Gypsy is in all of the programs from September 21, 1936, on. The program credits list Gershwin and Duke as the lyricist/composers. On September 21, Gypsy is listed in Scene 8 as singing "The Economic Situation"; she is listed in Scene 13 by name only—this would have been her specialty number. In Act II, Scene 8, she and Bobby Clark perform "I Can't Get Started with You." Gypsy appears in other sketches. There are numerous typos in this version, including Susanne for Cezanne, Rossine for Racine, etc. Shubert Archive Script Series 51.

34. GRL. Erik Preminger, *Gypsy and Me: At Home and on the Road with Gypsy Rose Lee* (New York, 1984), 15–17.

35. *Variety*, June 4, 1941, 40. Brooks Atkinson, "Abbott and Costello and Gypsy Rose Lee in the Streets of Paris," *New York Times*, May 20, 1940.

36. "Dark Pet of Burlesque," *Vanity Fair*; "Minsky's Strip to Fame," *Collier's*, March 6, 1937, 15.

37. Clipping, n.d., Gypsy Rose Lee Files, SA.

38. Wolcott Gibbs, "Crime without Punishment," *New Yorker*, September 26, 1936, 25.

39. Cited in Lee, 306.

40. Telegram inviting Gypsy to party, December 7, 1936, General Correspondence File, GRL.

41. The kudos Gypsy was awarded in the popular press are impressive. Clipping, n.d., *New York Post*, 1936, GRL.

42. *New York Post*, September 15, 1936, SA.

43. A quarter of the movies Zanuck made in the thirties were set between 1890 and 1920.

44. Correspondence, Subseries 2, Business 1936–1964, Box 4, Folder 2, GRL.

45. Letter releasing Gypsy from her contract with the Shuberts, SA; Series 1, Correspondence, Box 4, Folder 2, Twentieth Century Fox Contract, GRL.

46. *New York Post*, June 29, 1937, n.d.

47. Review of *You Can't Have Everything*, *New York Times*, August 4, 1937, 15; *Variety*, July 28, 1937; Reviews of *Ali Baba*, *New York Times*, October 23, 14; *Variety*, October 20, 1937; reviews of *Sally, Irene, and Mary*; *New York Times*, February 26, 1938, 9; *Variety*, March 2, 1938; reviews *of Battle of Broadway*, *New York Times*, April 25, 1938, 19; *Variety*, April 27, 1938; reviews of *My Lucky Star*, *New York Times*, September 10, 1938, 20; *Variety*, September 14, 1938. All *Variety* reviews from *Variety Film Reviews*, Volume 7 (New York, 1983), n.d.

48. *New York Times*, May 17, 11; May 30, 1937, X, 3.

49. Clipping, *New York World Telegram*, n.d., 1937, GRL; Frank Walsh, *Sin and Censorship: The Catholic Church and the Motion Picture Industry* (New Haven, 1996), 152–54; *New York Times* film reviews, see note 47.

50. Clipping, *New York World Telegram*, n.d., 1937, GRL.

51. *Variety*, November 2, 1938, 48; *Variety*, December 7, 1938, 41.

52. Clipping, n.d. April 13, 1942, GRL.

53. McCullers quoted in Rachel Shteir, "Everybody Slept Here," *New York Times Book Review*, November 10, 1996, 71.

54. Dorothy J. Farman, *Auden in Love* (New York, 1984), 53; Humphrey Carpenter, *W. H. Auden: The Life of a Poet* (London, 1981), 309–11; Shteir, 71.

55. But it was difficult for her to write. In 1940, George Davis, then an editor at *Vanity Fair*, who was helping her, wrote about the manuscript she had sent: "I like the 10 pp very much—they're lively, the talk is natural, and the weed business seems fine to me. I'll start work on them tomorrow." A few days later, perhaps intimidated by the writers around her, Gypsy gave up. "I've decided not to go on with my book. I simply am not one of those people who must write. Carson is. Wyston is. I'm not." Davis replied, "Obviously, the surprise and real kick of your book should be that you have managed to turn out a book that abides by the rules, given that, plus the publicity angles." Correspondence, Subseries 3, General Correspondence, Box 7, Folder 4, GRL; Series VI, Writings 5, Box 45, Folder 18, GRL.

56. *Daily Worker*, October 22, 1941, in GRL. According to *Life*, December 14, 1942, 92–93, in November 1941 her first book had sold thirty thousand copies. *Sun Mirror*, n.d., GRL. "Strippers Who Write," *New York World Telegram*, n.d., GRL.

57. Series VII, Serials, ca. 1930–1969, Burlesque Routines, Box 46, GRL. She bought songs from Ed Ziman, including "The Chastity Belt" and "Let's Play Dr." Another songwriter she used was Bernie Weissman. And she did not always warm to Lit Strip numbers when they were pitched to her. For example, upon receiving one number, "That's How a Stripper Was Born," she wrote the songwriter that it was "déclassé."

58. Routines and Sketches, Boxes 53 and 56, Folder 22, GRL.

## From Literary Strippers to Queens of Burlesque

1. "Undressing for Cash," *Zit's Theatrical Newspaper*, June 16, 1937; "Ann Corio Guest of Nobility," "Do You Know That" column, *Zit's*, January 23, 1937, n.d. In "Proof Ann Corio Knows How to Get Publicity," *Billboard*, September 28, 1940, 35, Corio complained, "Why, stripteasers have taken the place of Mexicans and men with moustaches as villains."

2. "Faith Bacon, First of the Fan Dancers," *San Francisco Examiner*, December 14, 1938, 8; "Sally Rand Will Tell Harvards a Few Things," *Baltimore Star Telegram*, May 4, 1938.

3. Joseph Mitchell, *My Ears Are Bent* (New York, 2000), 76–79.

4. *Variety*, January 27, 1937, 59.

5. Sherrie Tucker, *Swing Shift: All Girl Bands of the 1940s* (Raleigh, 2001), 260–73.

6. Mort Cooper, "Profile of a Character: Sally Rand," 33–34, 55–36, *Modern Man*, January 1960, KI.

7. Mencken, *The American Language* (New York, 1936), 586.

8. Alexander, *Striptease: The Vanished Art of Burlesque* (New York, 1938), x.

9. Clipping, n.d., GRL.

10. C. F. Zittel obituary, *Variety*, February 3, 1943, 33; Douglas Gilbert, *American Vaudeville: Its Life and Times* (New York, 1932), 380.

11. "How Burlesque Declined," *Variety*, December 29, 1931, 22.

12. Bernard Sobel, *Burleycue: An Underground History of Burlesque Days* (New York, 1931), 274–77.

13. Mitchell, 45–86.

14. Cited in James Peterson, *The Century of Sex* (New York, 2000), 126. The woman who posed for this pictorial spread, June St. Clair, was a stripper who performed mostly in LA. *Billboard*, September 25, 1937, 22.

15. Mark Gabor, *The Pin Up* (New York, 2000), 76–77; Joanne Meyerowitz, "Women, Cheesecake, and Borderline Material: Responses to Girlie Pictures in the Mid-Twentieth Century U.S.," *Journal of Women's History* 8, no. 3 (Fall 1996); Hugh Merrill, *Esky: The Early Years at* Esquire (New Brunswick, 1995).

16. John Erskine, "Burlesque Ritual," *Stage*, October 1936, 58; "The History of Burlesk," *Pic*, August 1937, n.d., WHMC; Laurence Bell, "Striptease as a National Art," *American Mercury*, September 1937, 56–64. Probably the first of these articles to take striptease seriously as a phenomenon is "The Business of Burlesque: Striptease, A.D. 1935," which appeared in February of that year in *Fortune*. Also Alva Johnston, "Onward and Upward with the Arts: The Billboard, Miscellaneous Entertainment," *New Yorker*, September 12, 1936, 31–36, told the story of this newspaper.

17. "Not Burlesquers," *Zit's Theatrical Newspaper*, tk.

18. Westbrook Pegler, "Fair Enough," syndicated column, February 27, 1937, WHMC; George Weller, "Striptease," *Atlantic Monthly*, July 1940, 50–55.

19. Bell, 58.

20. "That Cowhand Sweetheart Ain't Roped Our Sally Yet," *American Weekly*, November 2, 1941, 143; "The 1890 Stripper—in a Museum Now," *American Weekly*, September 26, 1943, WHMC; "The Gentle Art of Strip-Teasing," syndicated column, WHMC.

21. George Shute, "Strip Girls," *Easy Money*, June 1936, n.d., WHMC; Walter Winchell, "The Gentle Art of Strip-Teasing," *San Francisco Call Bulletin*, January 19, 1937, n.d., WHMC.

22. Mencken, Supplement, 586. In 1945, Mencken published an addendum to *The American Language* in which he added to striptease's lexicon, intending, perhaps, to make some of its words as well known as Broadway slang of the 1920s. This vocabulary both eroticizes and ridicules anything reasonable, especially anything borrowed from legitimate realms of show business.

23. Helen Lawrenson, "Where Sex Was Fun," *Show*, March 1964, 63, 65, 88, JDM.

24. David Dressler, "Burlesque as a Cultural Phenomenon," Ph.D. dissertation, New York University, 1937. This is not to say that Dressler was neutral toward burlesque. He is quoted in 1937 as describing its "amazing abnormality." *NYWT*, June 9, 1937, LaGuardia Personal Correspondence, MA. On the other hand, he also said that "burlesque doesn't breed social vices," *New York Post*, July 28, 1937, n.d., Folder 30, Clippings, Articles, Etc., Burlesque Collection, MCNY. The most politically relevant section of the thesis, though, describes how burlesque theaters arose in neighborhoods where other types of crime occurred.

25. Dressler, 180.

26. The actual percentage of women attending burlesque varies according to who is talking. In the 1932 burlesque hearings, for example, defense testimonies put it at about 20 percent. Dressler is more cautious and observes women "here and there." Ann Corio says they attended sometimes.

27. Frederick L. Allen, *Since Yesterday: An Informal History of the Thirties, September 3, 1929–September 3, 1939* (New York, 1986), 136–39.

28. Robert Friedel, *Zipper: An Exploration in Novelty* (New York, 1986), 213.

29. Alexander, x.

30. "Striptease: It's Done with Snaps," n.d., March 11, 1937, UTA Collection.

31. Irving Zeidman, *The American Burlesque Show* (New York, 1967), 152–53; Corio, *This Was Burlesque* (New York, 1968), 90; *Variety*, January 6, 1937, 233. DuPont introduced nylon stockings in 1940. Irene Sharaff, *Broadway and Hollywood* (Cincinnati, 1976), 36–38; "Police Confiscate Margie Hart Robes," *Billboard*, January 13, 1940, 35.

32. In the early 1940s, fashion imitated striptease. See, for example, "New Stripper Fashions," *Harper's Bazaar*, June 1949.

33. *Variety*, April 31, 1934, 50. Later like many who worked in burlesque in the thirties, Guyette went on to pornography, selling fetish paraphernalia in New York and in Europe. "Burlesque Is Dead," *Collier's*, November 27, 1943, 14–15, 39. Also Robert Bienvenu III, *American Fetish*, unpublished dissertation, University of Maryland, 1999, 71–72.

34. *Oxford English Dictionary*, On Line Edition, cites 1936 as the year the word G-string first entered the English language.

35. *Random House Dictionary of American Slang*, Volume I (New York, 1993), 851, 908.

36. Alexander, 120; William Safire, "Ode on a G-String," *New York Times*, August 4, 1991, VI, 12.

37. Gypsy Rose Lee, *The G-String Murders* (New York, 1941), 87.

38. Joyce Wadler, "Public Lives" column, *New York Times*, July 24, 1998, B2.

39. For center of striptease shifting out of New York, see "Burlesque Is Dead." "Men Who Make G-Strings," *Modern Man*, June 1955, 36–40, 44–45, KI.

40. "Flash" in *Vaudeville as Seen by Its Contemporaries*, ed. Charles Stein (New York, 1990), 174; Marshall Stearns and Jean Stearns, *Jazz Dance: The Story of Vernacular Dance* (New York, 1968), 190–91, 276–82; for "bump and grind," see *The American Language*, Supplement II, 694. (Although this last also seems to have been descended from the English slang for "cop.")

41. Nathan, *Entertainment of a Nation* (New York, 1942), 221.

42. "Discussing Alien Actors and Such," *New York Times*, April 5, 1937, IV, 6. Westbrook Pegler, in "Fair Enough," syndicated column in the *San Francisco News*, February 27, 1937, 11, asked, "Hasn't Congress anything better to do than hear burlesque defense?"

43. *New York Times*, February 25, 1937, 10; "House Committee in DC Gets an Earful from Minsky," *Variety*, March 3, 1937, 59.

44. Henri Champli, *Coloured Men, White Women* (Paris, 1936), 96.

45. *Variety*, November 20, 1929, 51.

46. Stearns and Stearns, 84–90; Nadine Graves George, *The Royalty of Negro Vaudeville: The Whitman Sisters and the Negotiation of Race, Gender, and Class in African American Theatre, 1900–1940* (New York, 2000), 33, 45; Henry Sampson, *Blacks in Blackface* (Metuchen, N.J., 1980).

47. The first mention of a black stripper performing in a burlesque house appears in the 1932 New York burlesque hearings. On April 26, Wilbur Clemens, a member of the Greater New York Federation of Churches, testified that he saw "a mulatto dancing around the Republic theatre." Burlesque hearing on Before Commissioner of License, Box WJJ-2423, Folder 8, 290.

48. Algren, *Somebody in Boots* (New York, 1935), 228.

49. "U-Notes," *Billboard*, January 9, 1937, 24. It seems like the *Star* might have attracted a mixed audience during the Depression. Paterfamilias Sam Raymond began at the Union Place Theater in the Jazz Age, but by the Crash he had turned the running of the theaters over to his sons, Harold and Leonard.

50. Zeidman, 177–79.

51. "Review of the Century," *Variety*, January 13, 1937. Zita, a "sepia" dancer at the Old Howard, in *Variety*, April 12, 1937, 24.

52. In addition to Valda, there were also Lovey Lane and Sajey; and Irvin Miller's Brownskin Models, a troupe that at the very least included black cootch dancers, ran at the Hudson and the Century theaters in New York during this time. "U-Notes," *Billboard*, January 30, 1937, 19. Valda Clippings File, NYPL; "Review of Century Burlesque," *Variety*, February 10, 1937, 58; "Keen Interest in Colored Unites for Burly Theatres," *Billboard*, April 24, 1937, 24; "Hirst Unit Review, Hindu Belles," *Billboard*, January 24, 1940, 19.

53. "Negro Show along Burly Lines Set at Lincoln, Philly," *Billboard*, December 28, 1940, 51.

54. George Jean Nathan remarks on the "Striptease of All Nations" effect in *Entertainment of a Nation* in 1942.

55. *Billboard*, March 17, 1934, 22.

56. "Ming Toya Novelty Hit," *Zit's Theatrical Newspaper*, April 27, 1935, 7. Also in this section other sources used include Judy Yung, ed., *Unbound Voices: A Documentary History of Chinese American Women in San Francisco* (Berkeley, 1999), 273–81, 319–29; Judy Yung, *Unbound Feet: A Social History of Chinese Women in San Francisco* (Berkeley, 1995); Lorraine Dong, *The Forbidden City Legacy and Its Chinese American Women* (San Francisco, 1992), 125–48; Thomas Chinn, ed., *Bridging the Pacific: San Francisco Chinatown and Its People* (San Francisco, 1989), 218–20; Gloria Chung, *Of Orphans and Warriors: Inventing Chinese American Culture and Identity* (New Brunswick, 2000); *Forbidden City, USA*, a video by Arthur Dong (1989).

57. Low quoted in Dong, 146.

58. J. A. Val Alst, *Chinese Music* (New York, 1966), 176.

59. Orpheum Theater Program, *Amy Fong and Her Oriental Dolls*, January 3, 1940, MS-22, Box 11, Folder 7, JDM. *Billboard*, January 16, 1937, 24. Asian women could strip next to white women as well. For example, "Burlesque Review, Casino Pittsburgh," *Variety*, October 5, 1938, 50, lists Fong as one of three peelers.

60. For many of these women, it was the only way they could earn money. Toy was at UC Berkeley during the Depression, for example. *Billboard*, November 9, 1940, 27; October 25, 1941, 26. Chang Lee, or Princess Chiyo, whose Japanese "cherry blossom" specialty number got her acclaim, performed at Chicago's Rialto Theater on South State Street.

61. "Ming Toi Not Ming Toya," *Billboard*, March 9, 1935, 24; "Burlesque Review, Rialto, Chicago," *Billboard*, February 15, 1936, 22; February 7, 1937, 22; see for example, "Burlesque Notes," *Billboard*, October 11, 1941, 25 places Amy Fong at the Rialto. Noel Toy played in *Wine, Women and Song* in New York in 1942. Source tk, 4 A's.

## "Clamouring for a Table and Pounding for an Encore": Striptease at the World's Fair

1. Wells quoted in *Trylon and Perisphere: The 1939 New York World's Fair*, ed. Barbara Cohen, Seymour Chwast, and Steve Heller (New York, 1989), 39.

2. Brooks McNamara, "The Entertainment District at the End of the 1930s," in *Inventing Times Square: Culture and Commerce at the Crossroads of the World*, Russell Sage Foundation, New York, 1996, 178–91; Polly Rose Gottlieb, *The Nine Lives of Billy Rose* (New York, 1968), 88, 96; "*Let's Play Fair* on Tuesday," *New York Times*, January 16, 1938, 152; "*Let's Play Fair* Opens at the Casa Manana," *New York Times*, January 19, 1938, 26.

3. Quoted in Stephen Nelson, *Only a Paper Moon: The Theatre of Billy Rose* (Ann Arbor, 1987), 81–83.

4. "The Business of Burlesque, 1935 A.D.," *Fortune*, February 1935. Rand had also worked with Rose at the Fort Worth exposition in 1936. According to *Fortune*, Fanny Brice, still Rose's wife, had seen Wassau when she was on tour with her 1931 show *Crazy Quilt* and convinced Rose to hire her.

5. Nelson, 83–84.

6. Let's Play Fair Clippings File, BRTC; Irving Zeidman, *The American Burlesque Show* (New York, 1967), 156, 244.

7. Nelson, 83–84; press releases, July 2, 1938, and Jan 31, 1938, Series II, Box 37, C-Press; "Wassau Cannot Dance, Rand Can," *Chicago Tribune*, January 28, 1938, n.d.; "News Notes of the Nightclubs," *New York Times*, January 13, 152; Horan, 257–59. According to some sources, the Aquacade grossed thirty thousand dollars a day.

8. Joseph Mitchell, *My Ears Are Bent* (New York, 2000), 62; Robert Rydell, *World of Fairs: The Century of Progress Expositions* (Chicago, 1993), 142; Series I, Box 3, News Release Folder, C-Press.

9. *Variety*, February 22, 1939, 55.

10. "Sally Rand Cannot Dance," *Chicago Tribune*, November 20, 1938, n.d.

11. Holly Knox, *Sally Rand: From Film to Fans* (New York, 1974), 53; Sally Rand Clippings File, Fiorello LaGuardia News Scrapbooks, no. 40, n.d., MA. Also 1939 New York World's Fair Collection, 1939–1940, Minutes, March 13, 1939, July 13, 1939, Box 378. Complaints, Boxes 375–76, Manuscripts and Archives Division, NYPL.

12. "Happy Nude Year for Sally Rand," *Philadelphia Bulletin*, January 2, 1939, n.d., TUNC.

13. "Corio to Picket Whalen if Fair Plan Is Unfair," n.d., February 14, 1939, TUNC.

14. "Dancer and Faun Publicity Martyrs," *New York Times*, April 24, 1939, 2.
15. "Sally's Nude Ranch Banned by N.Y. Fair," *Philadelphia Inquirer*, March 8, 1939, n.d., TUNC; *Variety*, February 22, 1939, 55.
16. *New Yorker*, April 29, 1939, 10; May 6, 10; May 13, 10. *Variety*, May 3, 1939, 1.
17. "Official Fair Guidebook," 47–75, 1939 World's Fair, C-Press.
18. Gill cited in *Trylon and Perisphere*, 53.
19. Rydell, 135–48; David Gelernter, *1939: The Lost World of the Fair* (New York, 1998), chapter 7; *Life*, July 3, 1939, 66; *Variety*, May 31, 1939, 35; Atkinson, *Broadway Scrapbook* (New York, 1947), 123–25.
20. *Billboard*, February 8, 1941, 25.
21. *Variety*, May 10, 1939, 1.
22. *Variety*, May 1, 1940, 43.
23. "Review of Florentine Gardens," *Variety*, May 15, 1940, 41; *New Yorker*, May 12, 1940, 14–16.
24. Michael Todd Jr. and Susan McCarthy Todd, *A Valuable Property: The Life Story of Michael Todd* (New York, 1983), 62–63; Brooks Atkinson review of *Streets of Paris*, *New York Times*, May 20, 1940, n.d., SA.
25. Streets of Paris Clippings File, SA.
26. "Someone Pinks Rosita's Doves," *New York Sun*, July 2, 1940, Tirza Scrapbook, author's personal collection.
27. Tirza Scrapbook, author's personal collection.
28. Personal interview with Tirza, September 2, 2001.
29. Burlesque Scrapbooks, 1952–1956, BRTC; personal interview with Tirza.
30. *Dallas Morning News*, January 6, 1948. The license commissioner had approved Tirza's number because there was no bumping or grinding.
31. "Burlesque Notes," *Billboard*, November 15, 1941, 15.
32. "Burlesque Notes," *Billboard*, December 26, 1942, 15.

**Striptease during Wartime**

1. Joe Laurie and Abel Green, *Show Biz from Vaude to Video* (New York, 1951), 507; "Burlesque Ties up G-Strings," *Variety*, September 9, 1941, 1, 18. As in the Depression, burlesque theater managers essentially created a monopoly to prevent star strippers from getting the high salaries they demanded.
2. "Burlesque Incorporates Vaudeville Acts," *Variety*, September 18, 1940, 37; Ann Corio, "The Whirly-Girly Burly," *Variety*, January 8, 1941, 145.
3. "Cafes Use Them, Vaude, Burlesque, Face Scarcity," *Billboard*, August 16, 1941, 25.
4. "Hirst Wheel Held Back by Shortage of Chorus Girls," *Billboard*, August 25, 1941, 25.
5. *Billboard*, February 21, 1942, 16.
6. "H.K. Minsky Hypos Detroit with Strip and Dance Comics, Cab Driver Tie-Ups, Punchy Ads," *Billboard*, June 22, 1940, 25. Also, an ad in *Billboard*, October 20, 1941, 39, shows Diane Ross doing a strip based on a "faithful" but "modernized" impersonation of Mae West.
7. Mencken, *The American Language* (New York, 1936), Supplement I, 584. According to Mencken, her agent, Maurice Zolotov, wrote this letter.
8. Ibid., 584–85.
9. Ibid., 587. In "My Burlesque Customers," an article published in the *American Mercury* in November 1942, 548–62, Gypsy talks about how her custom-

ers at the Irving Place Theater in the 1930s were identical to those at uptown cafés in the 1940s.

10. Lee, "My Burlesque Customers," 588.

11. "Strip, Strip Tease or Exotic Dancing, and the Difference," *Billboard*, October 10, 1942, 15. The *Oxford English Dictionary* cites "exotic" as first coming to the general vocabulary in 1954. *Oxford English Dictionary*, Volume VIII, 419, 1961. However, I have found usages of it much earlier.

12. Cited in James Peterson, *The Century of Sex* (New York, 2000), 161.

13. Sheila Van Damm, *We Never Closed: The Windmill Story* (London, 1967), 62–70; "Strip, Strip Hooray," *Time*, April 15, 1940, 29.

14. Clipping, n.d., 1940, Burlesque Clippings File, 1939–1949, BRTC.

15. In Britain, as in America, Jane's striptease inspired a certain amount of censorship at the official level. Writing about her, Douglas Reed drew a dramatic parallel between Weimar Germany and World War II England. "Are we going to tread the whole path that Berlin trod and have palaces of sexual perversion with electric signs outside advertising the wares? To anyone who remembers the appalling conditions in Berlin between 1918 and 1930, the present trend of affairs in London is terrifying." Reed's protest subsided, however, as the Allies began to win.

16. Advertisement for Josette, Burlesque Clippings File, 1939–1949, n.d., BRTC.

17. "Margie Hart from Missouri Strips for 40 cents as the Poor Man's Garbo," *Life* 8, no. 26 (1940), 49–50, 51, WHMC. John Costello, *Virtue under Fire: How World War II Changed Our Social and Sexual Attitudes* (New York, 1985), reports how Boeing sent home women for wearing tight sweaters and how that event became a cause célèbre.

18. *Time*, October 7, 1940, 21.

19. Cited in Costello, 215.

20. *New York Times*, August 17, 1941, n.d., TUNC.

21. These films were all panned. See, for example, the following reviews: Reviews of *Swamp Woman*, *New York Times*, December 27, 1941, 15; *Variety*, December 31, 1941. Review of *Jungle Siren*, *New York Times*, October 1942, 10. Review of *Sarong Girl*, *New York Times*, June 18, 1943, 16; *Variety*, June 23, 1943. All *Variety* reviews from Variety *Film Reviews 1940–49*, Volume 8 (New York, 1983).

22. "Burlesque Notes," *Billboard*, August 22, 1942, 15; October 31, 1942, 15; December 19, 1942, 15.

23. "Review of Ann Corio," *New York Times*, August 17, 1941, X, 2; "Corio Outstrips Femme Cop in Her Backstage Room," *Variety*, September 11, 1940, 55. Corio made eleven thousand dollars in one night in that year. *Variety*, November 27, 1940, 37; "Corio's Skin Some Tondelayo in White Cargo Big B.O. despite the (Leg)it Art," *Variety*, May 28, 1941, 49.

24. *Time*, December 3, 1934, 25, WHMC; "Striptease . . . It's Done with Snaps," n.d., Ann Corio Clippings Folder, TUNC. Lamarr also recommended being feminine, so it's possible that Corio stole the idea from her.

25. "New York Burly Ops Get Strong Support," *Billboard*, March 7, 1942, 3, 19.

26. Harold Clurman, *The Fervent Years: The Group Theatre and The Thirties* (New York, 1988), 156; *New York Times*, March 30, 1942; Letter, Box 3629, Indecent Show Files, MA.

27. See Lindsay Crouse, "A Munich in Censorship of Burlesque," *New York World Telegram*, February 27, 1942, LGNS, Volume 212, 57.

28. Letter from Frank Gilmore, president, Associated Actors and Artists of America, to Paul Moss, in BAA Correspondence File, 1939–49, AGVA.

29. *San Francisco Examiner*, October 1, 1942, n.d., WHMC. Winchell's column was syndicated, so it would've first appeared in New York slightly earlier.

30. Molly Minsky letter, March 3, 1942, Box 3629, LaGuardia Correspondence Files, Mayor Fiorello LaGuardia Collection, MA. On bankruptcy, see "Minsky Files for Bankruptcy," *New York Times*, May 13, 1942, 14; "H. M. Minsky Files Bankruptcy, *Variety*, May 13, 1942, 47. Molly Minsky quoted in "Battle of Burlesque," *New York World Telegram*, March 19, 1942, LGNS, Volume 213, 41.

31. Letters, Box 3629, *Bonserk v. the City of New York*, Box 3629, Licenses 1942, Mayor Fiorello LaGuardia Collection, MA.

32. "New York Shutters 2 Times Square Burleys," *Variety*, February 4, 1942, 41. "Rumpus in City Hall," *New York Times*, March 22, 1942, xi, describes Morris Ernst's failed attempts to appeal. "New Prohibition," *Billboard*, April 15, 1942, 45.

33. "West Coast Burly Seen as Stepping Stone to Films," *Billboard*, March 8, 1942, 16.

34. Stanwyck herself was a chorus girl in the late twenties. In 1941 she had also starred in *Dance, Girl, Dance*, about a rivalry between a classical dancer and a burlesque queen. In other words, she was perfect for the role. Leonard J. Leff, *The Dame in the Kimono* (New York, 1990), 130, also reports that the "G-string" song had to be altered for the movie version.

35. *New York Times*, May 14, 1943, 17; *Variety*, April 29, 1943, in Variety *Film Reviews*, Volume 8 (New York, 1983), n.d.

36. Frederick Nolan, *Lorenz Hart: A Poet on Broadway* (New York, 1994), 274, 278, 308. Also Gerald Gardner, *The Censorship Papers: Movie Censorship Letters from the Hays Years, 1934–1968* (New York, 1987), 16–19, 114, 169, detail some of the reasons why it took fifteen years for the movie version of *Pal Joey* to be made, including the fact that the play treated adultery, homosexuality, and striptease without punishing the characters.

37. Richard Rodgers, *Musical Stages: An Autobiography* (New York, 2002), 199–202. The cast included the sophisticated Vivienne Segal and Gene Kelly, as well as Gypsy Rose Lee's sister, June Havoc, in a small part.

38. June Havoc played Gladys Bump, Joey's girlfriend. In the 1957 Hollywood version of the musical, however, it is Vera who sings the song. Played by Rita Hayworth, Vera is exposed by Joey at a benefit auction in front of her society friends. Joey takes control of the auction and gets the bids up to five thousand dollars to see the wealthy woman do a striptease. As a result, she has to sing "Zip" and do a *Gilda*-like number.

39. This fact is often mentioned in histories of sexuality in America.

40. The lyrics are from the published version of *Pal Joey* (New York, 1952), 86–88. The song was not copyrighted until 1961.

41. Ethan Mordden, *Rodgers and Hammerstein* (New York, 1992); *New York Theatre Critics' Reviews*, Volume 3, no. 33 (1940), 172–74. By contrast, *Oklahoma!*, which also opened in 1943, ran for over two thousand performances.

42. *Billboard*, January 31, 1942, 26.

43. Philip Furia, *The Poets of Tin Pan Alley* (New York, 1990), 264; Victor Green, *A Passion for Polka: Old Time Ethnic Music in America* (Berkeley, 1992).

44. Mercer in advertisement, *San Francisco Call Bulletin*, March 26, 1943, WHMC. The initial bars of Frank Sinatra's rendition of "Fly Me to the Moon" lurches

forward with the kind of blood-rushing antic beat that a stripper needs to go onstage.

45. *Time*, October 12, 1942, 72; "'Strip Polka' Gets Spot at Liberty," *San Francisco Call Bulletin*, March 26, 1943, WHMC; John Sforza, *Swing It: The Andrews Sisters Story* (Lexington, Ky., 2001), 67. In the 1944 movie *Follow the Boys*, Patty begins to do a striptease during the performance of "Strip Polka," but her sisters rush on the stage and stop her.

46. "4.40 Burley planned by Todd," *Variety*, February 11, 1942, 2.

47. GRL; Series V, Programs, Star and Garter, Folder 83/13, MSS 49, HRP; clippings, Series VII, Star and Garter, Folder 90/23, HRP.

48. Review of *Star and Garter*, *New York Times*, June 25, 1942, 26.

49. Cited in Toni Bentley and Lincoln Kirstein, *Costumes by Karinska* (New York, 1995), 52; Irene Sharaff, *Hollywood and Broadway* (Cincinnati, 1976), 36–37. Series I, Correspondence, Star and Garter, Box 6, Folders 19, 20, GRL.

50. Review of *Star and Garter*, *New York Times*.

51. Clipping, n.d., Carrie Finnell, Obituaries, BRTC.

52. Biographical information from *Star and Garter* program, author's personal collection. Lamberti description from various sources, including Collyer, full cite tk, 78–79. A few years later, Lamberti would perform a watered-down version of this number in the movie *Tonight and Every Night* with Rita Hayworth.

53. June 28, 1942, n.d., TUNC.

54. Clipping, n.d., Star and Garter Clippings File, SA; reviews of *Star and Garter*, *New York Theatre Critics' Reviews*, Volume 3, no. 33 (September 1942), 262–64; George Jean Nathan, *Theatre Book of the Year*, 1942–43 (New York, 1943), 21–23.

55. Michael Todd Jr. and Susan McCarthy Todd, *A Valuable Property: The Life Story of Michael Todd* (New York, 1983), 76–81. It is difficult to calculate the earnings of *Star and Garter*, but everyone agrees it was a winner. In the first three weeks, according to *Variety*, the show grossed $26,000, $24,000, and $24,000. *Variety*, July 1, 50, 1942; July 8, 50; July 15, 52. In the fall, after it had been running for three months, according to the *New York Times*, Todd himself was taking home about $7,000 a week. *New York Times*, September 13, 1942.

56. Reviews of *Strip for Action*, *New York Theatre Critics' Reviews*, Vol. 3, no. 33, 1942; Nathan, *Theatre Book of the Year*, *1942–43*, 83–85; Dorothy Kilgallen, "The Voice of Broadway," *New York World Telegram*, September 11, 1942, LGNS, Volume 224, 114, also noted that striptease was conquering Broadway.

57. Quoted in Irving Zeidman, *The American Burlesque Show* (New York, 1967), 38–44, 60–61.

58. Reviews of *Wine, Women, and Song*, *New York Theatre Critics' Reviews*, Vol. 3, no. 23, 226–27.

59. Ibid. It's worth noting that the show was doing very well financially at this point. However, after the trial started, according to Atkinson, it hit 95 percent of estimated grosses. Nathan, *Theatre Book of the Year*, 1942–43. Brooks Atkinson, "Burlesque at Vaudeville Prices," *New York Times*, September 29, 1942, 18. *Variety*, November 4, 1942, reported the week's gross as $11,000, and *Variety*, November 18, at $15,000.

60. *Daily Mirror*, November 3, 1942, LGNS, Volume 224.

61. The *Wine, Women, and Song* trial is documented in the *New York Times*, September 14, 12; September 15, 18; September 29, 18; October 12, 13; December 1,

27; December 2, 27; and December 3, 27. This account also draws from LGNS, Volumes 225–28.

62. "Closing Statements," *New York Daily News*, December 3, 1942, 104, LGNS, Volume 228, 104.

63. Clipping, December 17, n.d., LGNS, Volume V.

64. *New York Theatre Critics' Reviews*, Volume 2, no. 33, 15; "The Conviction of Herk," *Billboard*, December 11, 1942, 15; Nathan, *Theatre Book of the Year, 1942–43*, 74–78.

65. A letter to LaGuardia from John Golden, March 18, 1943, says that Lee Shubert had no idea what was happening. Illicit Show Files, 1943, MCNY. On the other hand, in *The Shuberts of Broadway* (New York, 1990), 200, Brooks McNamara posits that he did. Also Herk's obituary in *Variety*, July 12, 1944, 37, expresses this position.

66. Laurie, 508; *New York Theatre Critics' Reviews*, Volume 2, no. 33, 236–38.

67. GRL, 1910–1970, Series VI, Writings, The Naked Genius, Box 44, Folders 8, 9; *Naked Genius* Clippings File, BRTC; Nathan, *Theatre Book of the Year, 1942–43*, 94–96. *Life* called it "inept."

68. Revues using striptease in the 1940s include *Artists and Models of 1943*. Nathan, *Theatre Book of the Year, 1942–43*, 119–21. The 1946 revival of *Show Boat*, *Are You With It?* and *Around the World*. "Good Night, Ladies," *Life*, September 6, 1943, 69; *San Francisco Chronicle*, June 22, 1947, 18, WHMC.

69. Author's interview with Betty Comden, September 2002.

70. "Burlesque Notes," *Billboard*, January 3, 1942, 28. In a new act she did at the Oriental Theater in Chicago, Gypsy plugged similar themes. Titled "When Men Get What They Want, What Have They Got?" the act told of the love affairs of Aristotle, Omar Khayyam, Plato, and Errol Flynn. Gypsy made fun of herself more aggressively, talking about her hat and furs—"You've seen enough of these"—and made fun of striptease more aggressively, telling the audience, "We can't all have talent." *Variety*, March 14, 1945, 49.

71. Harry Henderson and Sam Shaw, "Burlesque Is Dead," *Collier's*, November 27, 1943, 15, 39–40.

72. Clipping, n.d., WHMC.

73. "Downtown Chis Back to Burlesque Policy after Folding Vaudefilm Try," *Variety*, March 27, 1945, 49; *Life*, September 18, 1944, 53, WHMC.

74. "Rialto, Chi, Reopens for Vaude; 29 Years Burley," *Variety*, September 6, 1944, 6; "Burly Fall B.O. Lusty; G.I.'s and Firemen Have $$," *Billboard*, September 8, 1945, 38.

**The Private Lives of Strippers**

1. Cited in Joseph Mitchell, *My Ears Are Bent* (New York, 2000), and many others.

2. Britton's sentiments come from Martin Collyer, *Burlesque: The Story of a Unique American Institution* (New York, 1964), 84. The examples of this are endless. In "At the Top of the Best Undressed List," *New York Times*, May 23, 1967, 4, Lili St. Cyr says, "I wanted to be a fashion designer."

3. "The Business of Burlesque, 1935 A.D.," *Fortune*, February 1935, 143.

4. Interview with Kitty Oakes, August 14, 2002.

5. "Razelle Roland Ex Burlesque Girl to Marry Millionaire," *Zit's Theatrical Newspaper*, March n.d., 1935, n.d.

6. Joyce Wadler, "Public Lives" column, *New York Times*, July 24, 1998, B2.

7. This phenomenon is well documented in Ruth Rosen, *The Lost Sisterhood: Prostitution in America, 1900–1918* (Baltimore, 1982).

8. *New York Herald Tribune* obituary, November 16, 1963, n.d.

9. Clipping, n.d., Rose La Rose Clippings File, BRTC; Betty Rowland, "I Strip for Cash and Like It," *National Police Gazette* 144, no. 28 (August 1939), 2, WHMC.

10. H. M. Alexander, *Striptease: The Vanished Art of Burlesque* (New York, 1938), 90.

11. "The Business of Burlesque"; Joel Harvey, "American Burlesque as Reflected through the Career of Kitty Madison, 1916–37," Ph.D. dissertation, Florida State University, 1980, 144–45.

12. These facts come from "The Business of Burlesque," 70; Alexander, 54.

13. "Her Daring Dance: Turbulent Torso Flinging of Beautiful Charmaine," *National Police Gazette*, May 1941, 2.

14. Is this Gypsy Rose Lee, *Gypsy: A Memoir* (New York, 1957), 201, 226.

15. *Variety*, May 27, 1931. At the People's Theater, one of the low-end burlesque theaters, a striptease performer could earn thirty dollars a week.

16. *Billboard*, January 20, 1940, 25.

17. Jane Addams, *The Spirit of Youth and the City Streets* (New York, 1912), 6.

18. Georgia Sothern, *My Life in Burlesque* (New York, 1972), 19.

19. Nat Morton advertisement in Irving Zeidman, *The American Burlesque Show* (New York, 1967), insert.

20. *Variety*, October 23, 1934, 1.

21. *Billboard*, February 4, 1933, 6–10; clipping, November 19, 1941, n.d., TUNC. "Milkmen Make Riot at Republic," *Billboard*, January 11, 1936, 24; "Two Burly Houses Treated to Gas and Stench Bombs," *Billboard*, November 2, 1935, 24.

22. "Films Ruined It for Burlesque: You See More on Wide Screen," *Variety*, March 4, 1951, 48; burlesque film ads, *San Francisco Examiner* and *San Francisco Chronicle*, n.d., WHMC.

23. Rachel Shteir, "Big Town Biography," Kiki Roberts, *New York Daily News*, May 12, 1999, 13.

24. Kiki Roberts Clippings File, NYPL; Shteir, ibid.; "What's Doing in Burlesque" column, *Zit's Theatrical Newspaper*, n.d., 15.

25. *New York Mirror*, November 8, 1954, Burlesque Scrapbook, 1950–59, BRTC.

26. Clipping, Faith Bacon Clippings File, n.d., TUNC.

27. *Toledo Blade*, February 24, 1937, n.d., Faith Bacon Clippings File, TUNC; *Zit's Theatrical Newspaper*, March 6, 1937, n.d.

28. "Faith Bacon's Faith Needs Resurrecting," *Chicago Tribune* obituary, September 26, 1956.

29. "Loretta Miller Dies," *Variety*, December 1, 1954, 66.

30. On breast implants, see A. W. Stencell, *Girl Shows: Into the Canvas World of Bump and Grind* (Toronto, 1999), 92. *New York Herald Tribune*, May 20, 1955, Burlesque Scrapbooks, BRTC.

31. About being cast as Margaret in *Cat on a Hot Tin Roof* in 1954, Corio joked, "They came to see me, not hear me." Ann Corio, *This Was Burlesque* (New York, 1968), 78.

32. "Boston Bans Burlesque, Revokes Licenses of Two Theaters," *New York Times*, November 13, 24; 6; *Boston Globe*, November 6, 1, 3; November 8, 1953, 3.

33. "The Business of Striptease," 67, 69, 140–53; Helen Lawrenson, "Where Sex Was Fun," *Show*, March 1964, 63, 65, 88, JDM, 87; "Take Offs Get Pay Offs;

Strippers Salaries High: Heavy Demand for Names, Novelties; Ann Corio's $800–$1000 Is Tops," *Variety*, January 10, 1941, 15, 25.

34. St. Cyr could pull in about twenty-five thousand dollars a week in the 1950s, according to *Variety*. Holly Knox, *Sally Rand: From Film to Fans* (New York, 1974), 52.

35. These items are from the morgue of the *Kentucky Post*. "Covington Girl with $100,000 Legs Weds," *Kentucky Post*, February 13, 1924; *Kentucky Post* column by Jim Reis; "If You Want," *Cincinnati Post*, October 10, 1963, n.d.

36. *Billboard*, January 11, 1941, 25.

37. Alfred N. Bernheim, "The Facts of Vaudeville," in *Vaudeville as Seen By Its Contemporaries*, ed. Charles Stein (New York, 1983), 128. Movie facts quoted in Larry May, *Screening Out the Past* (Chicago, 1990), 164–65.

38. Committee of Fourteen Papers; "The Business of Burlesque," 67. "Burlesque Faces Grand Jury Drive," *New York Times*, May 1, 1937, says burlesque employs about 400 strippers and serves 400,000 people weekly.

39. Neal Gabler, *Walter Winchell* (New York, 1994) 242–49; Louis Sobol, *The Longest Street: A Memoir* (New York, 1968); Bernard Sobel, *Broadway Heartbeat* (New York, 1953); "Burlesque Stock Spurt Windfall for Agents," *Variety*, February 26, 1930, 58.

40. Details about Schuster from letters from the 1940s and 1950s in the Folly Theater Clippings File, FTA.

41. Eddie Jaffe obituaries, *Variety*, April 11, 2003, 22; *New York Times*, March 27, 2003, 9. It wasn't until the fifties that agents such as Dave Cohn, who booked only strippers, entered the scene.

42. *Variety*; July 12, 1939, n.d., GRL; letter from Eddie Jaffe, GRL, 1910–1970, Series I, Correspondence, Subseries 2, Business, Boxes 1–5.

43. "Gypsy Rose Lee Talks Three Agents into the Price of One," n.d., Folder 32, Burlesque Clippings, Burlesque Collection, MNCY.

44. Ann Corio Clippings, File, September 1958, n.d., TUNC.

45. Sothern, 141–44.

46. Letter, Sally Rand Manuscript Collection, n.d., Chicago Historical Society.

47. Knox, 60–61.

48. Dorothy Kilgallen, clipping, n.d., Paul Valentine Clippings Folder, BRTC; Rose La Rose clipping, n.d., Burlesque Scrapbooks, 1952–1956, BRTC.

49. Alfred Kinsey, *Male Sexual Behavior* (New York, 1948), 388–89; Karen Anderson, *Wartime Women: Sex Roles, Family Relations, and the Status of Women during World War Two* (Westport, 1981).

## Stripty-Second Streets

1. *PM*, February 24, 1946, n.d., Burlesque Clippings File 1940–49, BRTC; "New Burly Season Finds N.Y. Only Key City Not on List," *Variety*, August 30, 1947, 41.

2. "Just One More Chance," *Time*, March 4, 1946, 56. Alfred Kinsey continued to visit burlesque theaters in Chicago and Boston for his research. Cited in Jonathan Gathorne-Hardy, *Sex: The Measure of All Things: A Life of Alfred C. Kinsey* (Bloomington, 2000), 234. "Equity's Pitch to New York's Mayor O'Dwyer for Burlesque OK Excites Strippers," *Variety*, February 6, 1946, 55.

3. "Burlesque Circuit Grinds Profitably Despite Talent Raids by Vaude, Video," *Variety*, October 11, 1950, 51; Louis Sobol, *The Longest Street: A Memoir* (New York, 1968), 203.

4. "Burlesque Bits," *Billboard*, June 21, 1951, 43; *Swank*, September 1962, n.d., JDM.

5. *Music in the Minsky Manor*, Jubilee Records, 1953, Gilbert Milstein liner notes.

6. "Burley Back to K.C. After 8 Years," *Variety*, December 24, 1941, 44; "Review, Folly, Kansas City," *Billboard*, December 10, 1942, 15. Another famous burlesque theater to open at this moment was the President Follies in San Francisco. "President Follies Will Open Tonight," *San Francisco Examiner*, December 25, 1941, 25.

7. Clippings, n.d., Folly Theater Clippings File, FTA.

8. Ibid.

9. Rose La Rose Clippings File, Kansas City Public Library; "Backstage at the Folly," *Kansas City News Press*, n.d., circa 1949, Folly Theater Clippings Files, FTA; Martin Collyer, *Burlesque: The Story of a Unique American Institution* (New York, 1964), 44–52.

10. Tom McElfresh, "Gayety Reminiscence," *Cincinnati Enquirer*, April 5, 1970, n.d.

11. *Cincinnati Times-Star*, March 17, 1951, 5; "Youngstown, Ohio, Theatre HQ for 7-House Burley Loop," *Variety*, September 10, 1952, 47. Details on Cincinnati nightlife quoted in Michael Binstein and Charles Bowden, *Trust Me: Charles Keating and the Missing Millions* (New York, 1993), 84n. George Palmer, "Going, Going, Gone Are the Days," *Cincinnati Enquirer*, April 5, 1970, 18–25, JDM.

12. "*Life* Spends Saturday Night in Calumet City," *Life*, January 20, 1941, 74–82.

13. "Sin City," *Expose*, 1955, n.d., Burlesque Scrapbooks, 1952–1956; Jesse Alson Smith, *Syndicate City: The Chicago Crime Cartel and What to Do about It* (Chicago, 1954), 183.

14. "Burley Needs Special Concessions to Survive," *Variety*, December 16, 1953, 47.

15. Cited in J. J. Farrell, "The Crossroads of Bikini," *Journal of American Culture* 10 (Summer 1987), 57.

16. James Peterson, *The Century of Sex* (New York, 2000), 184. But the bikini was not really widely worn until the late 1950s. In 1959, Anne Cole, a major U.S. swimsuit designer, said about the bikini, "It's nothing more than a G-string. It's at the razor's edge of decency."

17. James Gavin, *Intimate Nights: The Golden Age of New York Cabaret* (New York, 1991), 10.

18. Jan Morris, *Manhattan '45* (New York, 1987), 196–99.

19. "National Pleasure Jag," *Variety*, January 5, 1944, 207; "The Swing on Swing Street Is from Be-Bop to Be-Pretty," *Billboard*, November 15, 1947, 37; "New York Letter to a Pal," Louis Sobol, syndicated column, *San Francisco Examiner*, November 17, 1948, 22–28, WHMC. . "The Short Happy Life of 52nd Street," *Cabaret*, November 1955, n.d., Burlesque Scrapbooks, 1952–1956, BRTC.

20. Britton in *Billboard*, November 25, 1946, 40. Jazz musician quoted in Erin Clune, "The Stripper's Union: Sexuality, Deviance, and the Politics of Distancing in the American Guild of Variety Artists, 1948–1962," 6, unpublished 1994 seminar paper, housed in the Robert F. Wagner Labor Archives, New York University. Clune's research influenced this section.

21. "Some Cafés to Experiment with Burlesque Units to Bolster Biz," *Variety*, September 20, 1950, 48; Miles Davis, *Miles: The Autobiography* (New York, 1989), 108.

22. Allen Churchill, "The Private Lives of Strip Alley," n.d., WHMC; Robert Sylvester, *No Cover Charge: A Backward Look at Nightclubs* (New York, 1956), 89, 267–69.

23. "Rum and Coca Cola" was another song made popular by the Andrews Sisters. Stanley Walker, "Not for Debutantes," *Stage*, February 1937, 58–59.

24. "Burley Strippers Bumping Hot Combos, Torch Chirpers off N.Y.'s Swing St.," *Variety*, November 12, 1947, 52.

25. *Variety*, March 14, 1945, 45.

26. Jack Lait and Lee Mortimer, *New York Confidential!* (New York, 1948), 48. Their cynicism was not warranted. Georgia Sothern stripped to rosettes. "Cops' Crackdown on Georgia Sothern Put Strippers under Wraps," *Variety*, March 10, 1948, 52.

27. "Wants AGVA stripped of strippers," "AGVA Enlisted to Clean up Midwest Strip Joints," *Variety*, June 22, 1947, 47; "New York 52nd Street Swings as Cops Strip Streets of Strippers," *Variety*, July 20, 1949, 1: Arnold Shaw, *The City That Never Slept* (New York, 1971), 335–41.

28. *Variety*, September 29, 1954; *Cabaret* 1, no. 6 (October 1955), 32–38.

29. "Gayety, Montreal," *Variety*, January 27, 1943, 38; "Gayety, Montreal," *Variety*, December 19, 1945, 42.

30. "Throttle Wide Open in Miami," *Billboard*, January 8, 1944, 23; Jack Kofoed, "The Palaces of Strip," *Cabaret* 5 (1956), 62–69, KI; *Variety*, January 4, 1938, 200.

31. "Balto Gayety Closing Best Season in Recent Years," *Billboard*, May 33, 1943, 15. Noah Sarlat, ed., *America's Cities of Sin* (New York, 1951), chapter 3; Vincent Dantini, *The Star Spangled City: Our Baltimore*, n.d., n.p. "Baltimore: Vice Capital," *USA*, Fotorama, February 1955; "The Bush Leagues of Baltimore," *Cabaret*, July 1956, n.d., Burlesque Scrapbooks, 1952–1956, BRTC.

32. Bruce met his wife, the stripper "Hot" Honey Harlow, in Baltimore. Program from Club Charles, n.d., WHMC. "Sin City," *New York Times*, September 21, 1967, 26.

33. "Strips, Tired Comics in Honky Tonks all That's Left in Balto's Night Spots," *Variety*, September 21, 1949, 50.

34. Christine Wiltz, *The Last Madame: A Life in the New Orleans Underworld* (New York, 2000), 7.

35. "New Orleans Joint Opens," *Zit's Theatrical Newspaper*, November 7, 1932, 11; "Pansy Joints Tabooed by Mayor of New Orleans in Vice Clean Up," *Zit's*, February 23, 1935, 1; Michael T. Marsden, "New Orleans' Bourbon Street: Evolution of an Entertainment District," in *Cultures of Celebration*, ed. Michael Marsden and Ray B. Brown (Bowling Green, Ohio, 1994), 185–200; "Women Who Shocked America," *Stag*, n.d., 1955, 12, KI. "New Orleans: America's Most Exotic City," *Cabaret*, March 1956, Burlesque Scrapbooks 1952–1956, BRTC.

36. "N.O. French Quarter Coming Back to Life," *Variety*, October 16, 1940, 53; "New Orleans War Boom Harvest Makes City 'Paris of the New World,'" *Variety*, April 21, 1943, 48.

37. "Strip Splurge in New Orleans," *Billboard*, November 8, 1947, 37; Alfred Felig, *Weegee by Weegee* (New York, 1978), 111–12.

38. Quoted in Hugues Panassié, *Hot Jazz: The Guide to Swing Music* (New York, 1936), 159.

39. *Variety*, September 15, 1942, 47.

40. Jean Charvil, *Histoire et Sociologie du Striptease* (Paris, 1969), 123–27. Technically, Christine was not a stripper, but an exotic.

41. Clipping, n.d., Burlesque Clippings Files, 1940–49, BRTC; "Royale Flush," *Life*, November 28, 1949, 127, WHMC.

42. Mortimer Lait, *U.S.A. Confidential* (New York, 1952), 79; "N.O. Liquor Board Files Report on Cleaning Up Lewd Joints, *Variety*, June 15, 1949, 47; "New Orleans Cracks Clubs," *Billboard*, July 5, 1952, 19; "N.O. Judge Cites French Quarter Cafes for Lewd Shows and Ballyhoos, *Variety*, August 10, 1949, 51; Wiltz, 78–81.

43. Britton, "Burlesque Up Front," *Fortnight*, November 10, 1952, 46; Rowland, *Billboard*, March 18, 1944, 32. Other areas of the country also saw women become managers during and directly after the war. In Detroit the stripper Frances Parks took over the Gayety around 1945. She continued to be the manager for several years. Tempest Storm, *The Lady Is a Vamp* (Atlanta, 1987), 94. In Miami, Helene Kayfetz changed her name to Helene Polka and managed the Jungle Club. *Variety*, March 1, 1944, 46.

44. Ads for St. Cyr at the Samoa nightclub in New York, Burlesque Scrapbooks, 1952–1956, BRTC. The lute act was slightly later, around 1954. This section was also informed by Lili St. Cyr Clippings Folder, TUNC.

45. "Night Club Reviews: Latin Quarter, Miami Beach," *Variety*, January 12, 1944, 57. As with many *Variety* reviews, it's difficult to tell what comprised "good taste." It's possible that she took off too much for the censors or that she bumped and ground excessively.

46. "St. Cyr Makes Easy Jump from 52nd Street to Park Avenue," *Variety*, February 24, 1954, 55.

47. Nils T. Granlund, *Blondes, Brunettes, and Bullets* (New York, 1957), 284–86. Her name is sometimes spelled van Schacht. According to Granlund, St. Cyr's mother first brought her daughter to his attention.

48. "Sally Rand at Florentine Gardens," *Variety*, January 24, 1940, 38; *Variety*, January 13, 1943, 46; Jim Heimann, *Out with the Stars: Hollywood Nightlife in the Golden Era* (New York, 1985), 171–76.

49. Lili St. Cyr, *Ma Vie De Stripteaseuse* (Montreal, 1950), 118.

50. Ibid., 119.

51. Ibid., 120, 128.

52. "Servicemen Pack 3-a-Night Burly Shows in San Diego," *Billboard*, January 9, 1943, 19; "Stem Grosses Still Big in San Diego," *Billboard*, April 24, 1943, 18.

53. St. Cyr, 125; "A Bump, a Grind, and a Gimmick," *Playboy*, August 1954, 40, 43; *Cabaret*, March 1955, 46, KI Special Collections.

54. St. Cyr, 152; "Burlesque in the 1955 Manner," *Suppressed*, January 1955, WHMC; "Paul Valentine Rates as Charming Villain," clipping n.d., Paul Valentine Clippings File, BRTC.

55. *Frolic*, 1951, n.d., WHMC.

56. "Nightclub Notes," *Variety*, February 6, 1946, 56, places her at Leon and Eddie's doing a "sexy cootch." "Gayety, Montreal," *Variety*, April 10, 1946, 64.

57. "Review of Leon and Eddie's," *Billboard*, February 9, 1946, 38.

58. *CCNY Mercury*, March 22, 1950, 20–22, JDM.

59. St. Cyr, 168; *Pic*, March 1950, n.d.; Al Palmer, quoted in William Weintraub, *City Unique: Montreal Days and Nights in the 1940s and 1950s* (New York, 1997), 116–20. Granlund notes that in St. Cyr's Chinese Empress act, she was carried across the stage completely naked.

60. St. Cyr, 132.

61. Clipping, n.d., WHMC.

62. St. Cyr, 170.

63. Weintraub; uncited clippings, WHMC.

64. Ted Jordan, *My Secret Life with Norma Jean* (New York, 1989), 92–94, 104–5, 181–84, 193, 195, 197, 200–1, 203–4. Jordan was also briefly married to St. Cyr in 1954. *Variety* noted acidly that if he changed his name to St. Cyr, it would have helped him professionally. Ted Jordan Clippings File, n.d., NYPL.

65. Leonard Michaels, "The Zipper," in *Best American Essays*, ed. Susan Sontag (New York, 1992), 248.

66. "9 Burly Houses in California," *Billboard*, March 2, 1940, 33; "Carroll's New H'Wood Spot Opens," *Variety*, December 21, 1938, 55; "Nitery Reviews, Earl Carroll's, Hollywood," *Variety*, January 4, 1939, 168; Ken Murray, *The Body Merchant: The Story of Earl Carroll* (New York, 1973), 208–10; Sheila Weller, *Dancing at Ciro's: A Family's Loss, Love, and Scandal on Sunset Strip* (New York, 2003), 103–8.

67. "L.A. Inns, Niteries Face Talent Battle," *Billboard*, August 18, 1951, 34; clipping, n.d., Ciro's Clippings File (Miami, Chicago, New Orleans), BRTC; "Herman Hover obituary," Burlesque Scrapbooks, 1952–1956, BRTC; Heimann, 183–85. Weller, 119–20, 152–60, 224–27.

68. The battle over Lili St. Cyr's performance at Ciro's is covered in *Variety* and *Billboard* in the spring of 1951. "Ban Strips but They Like 'Em," *Variety*, April 7, 1951, 42. This article tells of how the sheriff watched St. Cyr at Ciro's even while cracking down on the Follies, Strip City, and Last Call. Articles in *Billboard* from the same era tell of the shutdown. For example, "Strippers Bow out of Hollywood Last Call," *Billboard*, April 14, 1951, 33; "Coast Ops Fight Anti-Strip Edict," *Billboard*, April 21, 33; "AGVA Promised Strip Hearings," *Billboard*, April 28, 33. For news about St. Cyr's visit to Montreal, see "Montreal Morals Group Hits Lili St. Cyr," *Variety*, June 13, 1951, 51, and "Montreal Cops Haul St. Cyr to Court," *Variety*, June 20, 1951, 53.

69. There's some discrepancy in descriptions of the physical appearance and clientele of Strip City. According to Albert Goldman, in *Ladies and Gentlemen, Lenny Bruce* (New York, 1965), 141–90, during the week, slumming movie stars such as Marlon Brando, Joan Collins, and Elizabeth Taylor spent time there. In *How to Talk Dirty and Influence People* (New York, 2002), 82, Lenny Bruce himself claims that Hedy Lamarr was a customer, as well as B-level TV and movie people. That is contradicted by Ronald K. L. Collins and David M. Skover, *The Trials of Lenny Bruce: The Fall and Rise of an American Icon* (Naperville, Ill., 2002), 80–94. In general, it's fair to say that by the fifties, the area had become more dilapidated.

70. "Man It's Like Satire," *New York Times Sunday Magazine*, May 3, 1959, 28. "Burlesque House," *Lenny Bruce Live at Carnegie Hall*, 1961.

71. Lenny Bruce, 52, 82, 93; Goldman, 274; Honey Bruce, *Honey! The Lives and Loves of Lenny's Shady Lady* (Chicago, 1976), 213–16.

72. *Billboard*, June 15, 1940, 25; Walter Winchell column, *San Francisco Call Bulletin*, November n.d., 1957; *San Francisco Chronicle*, October 11, 1961, WHMC.

73. Personal interviews with Art Hess, several dates in the fall and winter of 2001 and 2002. "Chicago after Dark," *Fotorama*, n.d., 1955, Burlesque Scrapbooks, 1952–1956, BRTC.

74. One story claims that Frank Sinatra had a hand in this effort, and Maurice Chevalier and Bing Crosby also take credit.

75. Bernadin cited in André Sallée and Philippe Chaveau, *Music Hall et Café Cabaret* (Paris, 1985), 58.

76. Ibid.

77. "Jap Burley and Legit Tease Yen: How? Via Yen for Tease," *Billboard*, October 11, 1947, 51.

78. *Cavalcade of Burlesque* 1, no. 2 (Winter 1951), 44–45, BV; "Tokyo's Biggest Industry: Sex," n.d., "Tokyo," *Cabaret*, May 1956, n.d., Burlesque Scrapbooks 1952–1956, BRTC; "Burlesque in Tokyo," *Playboy*, December 1955, 40.

79. Robert Garland, "Low Gags, Tall Gals, and Middling Scenes," Review of *Peep Show, New York Journal American*, June 29, 1950; clippings, Series VII, Michael Todd's Peep Show Folder 87/27, HRP. The celebration of these girls was to the license commissioner Edward T. McCaffrey's chagrin.

80. Michael Todd Jr. and Susan McCarthy Todd, *A Valuable Property: The Life Story of Michael Todd* (New York, 1983), 197–202; George Jean Nathan, *Theatre Book of the Year, 1950–51* (New York, 1951), 17–20.

81. Charvil, 123–27; "Review of Basin Street, NY," *Variety*, October 7, 1953, 69; *New York News*, October 7, 1953, n.d., Burlesque Scrapbooks, 1952–1956, BRTC.

82. *New York Theatre Critics' Reviews*, Volume 31, no. 29, 285.

83. Nathan, *Theatre Book of the Year, 1950–51*, 17–20; Daniel Blum, ed., *Theatre World*, 1950 (New York, 1950), 10–11. *Peep Show* was also one of the top moneymakers of the year, grossing about $50,000 weekly. For a while it was at the top of the musicals. According to *Variety*, July 5, 1950, 51, for example, it earned $55,000.

**The Seamy Sides of Striptease**

1. *Billboard*, May 26, 1934, 30; *Billboard*, July 20, 1940, 25; *Billboard*, June 21, 1941, 52; George Jean Nathan, *Entertainment of a Nation* (New York, 1942), 282.

2. "Wine, Women, and a Thousand Pounds of Plumbing," *Sir*, n.d., "New York Cavalcade," *New York Journal American*, November 3, 1947, 23. Both in Tirza Scrapbook, author's personal collection. Burlesque Scrapbooks, 1952-1956, BRTC.

3. "*Billboard*, July 14, 1945, 52.

4. "Films Ruined It for Burlesque: You See More on Wide Screen," *Variety*, March 4, 1951, 48.

5. *Billboard* began to run a "roadshow" page around 1942.

6. Eric Schaefer, *Bold! Daring! Shocking! True!: A History of Exploitation Films* (Durham, 1999), 303–24; St. Cyr quoted in Schaefer, 55–56. Eddie Muller and Daniel Farris, *Grindhouse: The Forbidden World of Adults Only Cinema* (New York, 1996), 34–54, 56. "Canned Burlesque," *Time*, April 16, 1951, 104.

7. *Cavalcade of Burlesque* 1, no. 3 (May 1952), BV.

8. *Burlesque in Harlem*, produced by William Alexander, directed by Joseph Tuller, released in 1949.

9. The explosion of gay life in nightclubs during and after World War II is documented in many places, including Lawrence Senelick, *The Changing Room: Sex, Drag, and the Theatre* (New York, 2000), 380–81. Elizabeth Lapovsky Kennedy and Madeline D. Davis, *Boots of Leather, Slippers of Gold: The History of a Lesbian Community* (New York, 1994), 39–40; Allen Berube, *Coming Out Under Fire: The History of Gay Life in World War Two* (New York, 1990), 73–75, 113–15; John D'Emilio and Estelle Freedman, *Intimate Matters: A History of Sexuality in America* (New York, 1988), 288–95; John D'Emilio, *Sexual Politics, Sexual Communities: The Making of a Gay Minority in the United States* (Chicago, 1983); Elizabeth Drorbaugh, "Sliding Scales: Notes on Storme

DeLarverie and the Jewel Box Revue, the Cross-Dressed Woman on the Contemporary Stage, and the Invert," in Lesley Ferris, ed., *Crossing the Stage: Controversies on Cross Dressing* (New York, 1993); Anthony Slide, *Great Pretenders: A History of Female and Male Impersonation in the Performing Arts* (Lombard, Ill., 1986); "Female Impersonators," *Jet*, 1954, n.d., Burlesque Scrapbooks , 1952–1956, BRTC.

10. Rae Bourbon's song "Strip Queen" is track 11 on *Ladies of Burlesque*.

11. Don Paulson with Roger Simpson, *An Evening at the Garden of Allah: A Gay Cabaret in Seattle* (New York, 2000), xi, 14.

12. Paulson, 8, 24. But in many other places female impersonators continued to be banned as often as strippers were. See for example, *Variety*, March 28, 1951, 44; *Variety*, April 5, 1950, 51. On the other hand, female impersonators continued to draw audiences throughout the 1950s. See for example, "Femme Impersonators Whooping Up Biz on Pittsburgh's Saloon Circuit," *Variety*, August 2, 1950, 47.

13. Paulson, 132.

14. Ibid., 128, 150.

15. *Focus,* January 20, 1954, n.d., Burlesque Scrapbooks, 1952–1956, BRTC. Also Christine Jorgensen, *Christine Jorgensen: A Personal Autobiography* (New York, 1967). "Christine Tops $7,000 at the Latin Quarter," *Billboard*, February 6, 1954, 18.

16. Jorgensen, 67.

17. Lillian Faderman, *Naked in the Promised Land* (New York, 2003), 238–41, 247–66. Numerous articles link gay life and striptease.

18. "Carnivals to Take to Rails in '37," *Variety*, November 25, 1936, 63.

19. Sound portrait of James E. Strates carnival, Library of Congress Archives, Winter 1941.

20. Amanda Zeitlin, "American Talkers: The Art of the Sideshow Carnival Pitchman and Other Itinerant Showmen and Vendors," Ph.D. dissertation, University of Pennsylvania, 1992, 129.

21. Sally Rand, "With It and for It," *Billboard*, July 31, 1948, 53.

22. *Billboard* forecast that 1948 would be a great year in the carnival. *Billboard*, December 23, 1947, 53. A. W. Stencell, *Girl Shows: Into the Canvas World of Bump and Grind* (Toronto, 1999); Charles Fish, *Blue Ribbons and Burlesque* (Woodstock, 1998), 235–65. The feeling was that men might cut it to peek in or throw bottles at the lights outside.

23. "Hennie's Sign Sally Rand," *Billboard*, February 8, 1947, 53; "Name Acts Supplement Carnival's Cootch and Corn," *Variety*, September 29, 1948, 66. Rand's earnings for Hennie's cited in Stencell, 71. Also *Variety*, September 22, 1948, 42, says she made $42,000 in ten days. *Carnival Magazine*, December 1953, n.d., Burlesque Scrapbooks, 1952–1956, BRTC. The requirements for what strippers had to wear in this era varied widely. In Florida a stripper had to wear a bra and panties; in Illinois, however, anything went. *Variety*, September 8, 1948, 47. The following year, Rand got business of almost a million dollars.

24. *Billboard*, August 23, 1952, 47.

25. "Sex Shows Bumped for Mpls Fair," *Variety*, August 17, 1949, 51.

26. "Nudity Run Riot, Iowans Say," *Chicago Tribune*, August 29, 1951, 1.

27. *Variety*, August 31, 1949, 50

28. In an article in *Flair*, she describes it. Later, Royal American Carnival would also hire Yvette Dare.

29. Stencell, 81.
30. "CBS Blew My Fuse," *Variety*, December 29, 1948, 1. There were several shows promoting burlesque comics in the 1950s, however.
31. Stan Corwin, *Betty Page Confidential* (New York, 1996), 27–29; Karen Essex and James L. Swanson, *Betty Page: Life of a Pin Up Legend* (New York, 1996). "Klaw Movie Still Monarch, *New York Times*, November 6, 1947, x5. "Senators Start Morals Hearings," *New York Times*, May 25, 1955, 35. "Rise in Spread of Pornography," June 1, 1955, *New York Times*, 35.
32. Lait and Mortimer, *New York Confidential!* (New York, 1948), 158.
33. Ibid., 297.
34. Bureau of National Affairs, McClellan Committee Hearings, 1962.
35. *Show World* 1, no. 1 (July 1952), Burlesque Scrapbook, 1950–59, BRTC; "Sin City," *Expose*, 1955, n.d., Burlesque Scrapbooks, 1952–1956, BRTC.
36. Robert C. Ruark, "Strip Row," *San Francisco News*, October 26, 1950, 27, WHMC; *Variety*, February 24, 1954, 51.
37. But this endeavor failed until 1961, when the citizens of Cal City elected a cleanup mayor, who in turn convened a national committee to investigate. Before that year, even a delegation of five hundred citizens waving a copy of the *Life* article proclaiming Cal City's decrepitude failed to shame mobsters and strippers into decency. After a day or two, the strip bars returned to normal as far as vice and striptease were concerned. Thus although the Kefauver hearings shocked the nation, they failed to shut down nightclubs.
38. "M & L Switch Moves Ciro's Booking Sked," *Billboard*, September 22, 1951, 49. According to Jerry Giesler, St. Cyr's attorney, the bathtub was transparent. Jerry Giesler, *The Jerry Giesler Story* (New York, 1960), 179.
39. According to Ted Jordan, St. Cyr flashed her nipple onstage. "Tease on the Strip," *Fortnight*, November 12, 1951, 17, WHMC. The account of the trial is taken from the *L.A. Times*, December 6, 12; December 7, 12; December 8, 3; December 10, 14; December 12, 5.
40. "Ban Strips but They Like 'Em," *Billboard*, April 7, 1951, 42; *Billboard*, May 5, 1951, 42.
41. St. Cyr, chapter 9.
42. Giesler, 5. The jury was composed of ten women and two men.
43. St. Cyr, 213; "The Law vs. Lili," *Life*, December 17, 1951, 53; "Mouthpiece of the Stars," *Argosy*, June 1955, n.d., Burlesque Scrapbooks, 1952–1956, BRTC. According to Giesler, the inexperienced prosecuting attorney bears some responsibility for St. Cyr's acquittal. Giesler had called the tough Los Angeles newspaperwoman Florabel Muir to testify. Muir, who had been first on the scene at Bugsy Siegel's murder and who was at Ciro's on the night in question, did not agree that Lili had done anything wrong. In cross-examining her, the prosecutor kept calling her "Madam," and Muir finally leaned forward and warned him to stop. He slunk away. Giesler, 177–81.
44. *Look Magazine*, February 12, 1952, n.d., Burlesque Scrapbooks, 1952–1956, BRTC; *Variety*, October 29, 1952, 58.

## Striptease Confidential

1. Letter, May 10, 1952, Series I, Correspondence, Box 1, Folder 13, GRL.
2. Goldman, *Ladies and Gentlemen, Lenny Bruce* (New York, 1965), 141–46.
3. "Capital Nightclub Review," *Billboard*, April 21, 1951, 44.

4. WHMC.

5. "Tempest in a C-Cup," *Playboy*, July 1955, 47. Storm performed almost exclusively on the West Coast in her early career. See "Burlesque Bits," *Billboard*, November 15, 1952, 64, and "Burlesque Bits," *Billboard*, April 4, 1953, 50, for example.

6. According to one story, Storm once complained to Follies manager Lillian Hunt that her breasts were too big; Hunt replied, "God didn't make boobs too big for my business." Tempest Storm, *The Lady Is a Vamp* (Atlanta, 1987), 100.

7. Ibid., 121–22.

8. "San Francisco Night Club King," *Cabaret*, October 1955, 4–11.

9. Hirsch quote from author's interview with Hirsch, n.d., summer 2000. "A Tempest in the World of Burlesque," n.d., WHMC; Morton Cooper, "Harold Minsky Picks the Twelve Best Strippers," *Cabaret*, April 1956, JDM; Harold Minsky, "Striptease Goes West, *See*, March 1950, 15–17.

10. *Adam* magazine, n.d., 1954, KI.

11. Ad for Tempest Storm and Herb Jeffries, *San Francisco Chronicle*, May 13, 1959, 6, WHMC.

12. Earl Wilson quoted in Martin Collyer, *Burlesque: The Story of a Unique American Institution* (New York, 1964), 153.

13. West quote in Collyer, 130. "One Gibson Coming Up," *Esquire*, December 12, 1955, 8, WHMC.

14. *Time*, June 29, 1959, 54. See also "Paris Syndicates," *Variety*, January 1, 1955, 64.

15. Denys Chevalier, *Metaphysique du Striptease* (Paris, 1961), chapter 3.

16. Jean Charvil, *Histoire et Sociologie du Striptease* (Paris, 1969), 45.

17. "Put It On," *Newsweek*, January 7, 1957, 48–49; Charvil, 129–32; Art Buchwald, *I'll Always Have Paris: A Memoir* (New York, 1997), 199–209.

18. *Cabaret*, October 1955, 15–21; Charvil, 140–47.

19. Charvil, 41; *Modern Man*, September 1955, 38–41, 48; *Time*, January 2, 1956, 19.

20. Roland Barthes, "Striptease," in *Mythologies*, trans. Annette Lavers (New York, 1984), 84.

21. Chevalier, 105.

22. Umberto Eco, *Misreadings* (New York, 1962), 27–33.

23. Lenny Bruce quoted in Ronald K. L. Collins and David M. Skover, *The Trials of Lenny Bruce: The Fall and Rise of an American Icon* (Naperville, Ill., 2002), 91. *Cabaret*, December 1956, 5. The nightlife guide lists seven clubs and performers, including Zorita and her snake and Dixie Evans, the self-proclaimed Marilyn Monroe of Burlesque.

24. "Sin's Last Stand in Miami," *Cabaret*, December 1955, n.d., Burlesque Scrapbooks, 1952–1956, BRTC.

25. Jesse Alson Smith, *Syndicate City: The Chicago Crime Cartel and What to Do about It* (Chicago, 1954), 182–94.

26. "B-Belles of Burlesque: You Get Striptease with Your Beer in Baltimore," *Esquire*, February 1954, 55–60. Prior to this, in September 1953, Blaze Starr had been featured in *Cavalcade of Burlesque* 2, no. 4 (September 1953), KI.

27. "'Worst' Nitery with 'World's Lousiest Shows,' Going into 14th Yr. in Balto," *Variety*, January 25, 1939, 50.

28. Blaze Starr, *My Life as Told to Huey Perry* (New York, 1974), 52.

29. "All Burlesque Parodies Aren't Necessarily Hits," *New York Herald Tribune*, December 11, 1963, TUNC. Thomas Morgan, "Blaze Starr in Nighttown," *Esquire*, July 1964, 58.

30. "At Top of the Best (Un)dressed List," *New York Times*, May 23, 1967. L'affair Rizzo didn't explode onto the front page until twenty years later—in 1974—when Starr's autobiography was published. Starr did perform at the Black Cat Café in February 1955. Rizzo always denied the affair. Blaze Starr Clippings Folder, TUNC.

31. Description of her act drawn from Morgan, 59–60; "Blaze Starr," *Modern Man*, November 1955, n.d., KI; Blaze Starr, *Gala*, July 1956; "Blaze Starr, *Follies*, September 1958.

32. "That's My Desire" was written in 1959.

33. Starr quoted in Morgan, 1964, 61.

34. "Why Agnew Quit," syndicated column, *New York Post*, April 19, 1974, Blaze Starr Clippings Folder, TUNC, alludes to Agnew's "spicy" private life.

35. Alfred Kinsey quoted in James Peterson, *The Century of Sex* (New York, 2000), 223. John D'Emilio and Estelle Freedman, *Intimate Matters: A History of Sexuality in America* (New York, 1988), 285–87.

36. *Top Secret Magazine*, n.d., UNLV Collection.

37. *Modern Man*, September 1955, 9–14. Interview with West in Collyer, 130–40. Also "How Burlesque Became Respectable," *Cabaret*, June 1955, 25–29, compares Minsky to Kinsey: "In presenting its own Kinsey report on the women of the world . . . the revue probes into the sexual behavior of the human female." Another finding of *Sexual Behavior in the Human Female* was that striptease aroused men more than women, even though the number of women in the audience had increased since the 1930s. *Sexual Behavior in the Human Female* (Philadelphia, 1953), 658, 660.

38. See, for example, "Strip Game," *Playboy*, December 1953, 10; "Paris Hotspots," *Playboy*, February 1954, 37; "A Bump, a Grind, and a Gimmick," *Playboy*, August 1954, 40–44. *Playboy*, October 1954, 41; December 1954, 41; October 1955, 1; November 1955, 40; December 1955, 40.

39. "How Hugh Hefner Makes Millions from the Myth of *Playboy*'s Bunnies," *Saturday Evening Post*, April 23, 1966, 96–101. Launched by straight man Jess Mack, *Cavalcade of Burlesque* was designed to promote burlesque, by then a failing industry.

40. "Mr. Playboy of the Western World," *Saturday Evening Post*, April 23, 1966, 100; Jean Cocteau, *My Journey around the World* (London, 1958), 160.

41. Quoted in Peterson, 228.

42. Quoted in "A Bump, a Grind, and a Gimmick," 40.

43. Spillane quoted in David Halberstam, *The Fifties* (New York, 1993), 59–61.

44. "Chris Owens," Burlesque Scrapbooks, 1952–1956, BRTC.

45. Cited in Eric Schaefer, *Bold! Daring! Shocking! True! A History of Exploitation Films* (Durham, 1999), 311. There are many other feature-length roadshow burlesque films in each genre.

46. Ibid., 56.

47. *A Night in Hollywood* (1953).

48. Schaefer, 307; *Swank*, September 1962, 70, UNLV Collection.

49. Hunt directed *Strip Strip Hooray* (1950), with Tempest Storm; *Bedroom Fantasies*; and *The ABCs of Love* (1950), with Lili St. Cyr. Cited in Schaefer, 307.

50. Michael Atkinson, "Manic Regression," *The Village Voice*, May 16, 2001, 5.

51. Frank Walsh, *Sin and Censorship: The Catholic Church and the Motion Picture Industry* (New Haven, 1996), 267, discusses how Hughes pushed the censors in the making of *Son of Sinbad*. *The Naked and the Dead* publicity book, author's personal collection. *Film Quarterly* 12, no. 1 (1958).

52. The list of these movies goes on and on. *What's New, Pussycat?*, for which Woody Allen wrote the screenplay, had Paula Prentiss doing a striptease, which was cut from the film. "What's Nude, Pussycat," *Playboy*, April 1968, 99, 100, 102–3.

53. Simone de Beauvoir, *The Lolita Syndrome* (New York, 1971), 20.

54. Interestingly, this film appears to have stolen its title from the 1950 burlesque film of the same name. This may in part account for its scandalous quality. Legion of Decency inspector quoted in Walsh, 165. "Best of Mansfield," *Playboy*, February 1960, 72.

55. Tom Wolfe, "Public Lives, *Confidential Magazine*: Reflections in Tranquility by the former owner, Robert Harrison, Who Managed to Get Away with It," *Esquire*, April 1964, 152–53. Having previously published pinup magazines with such salacious titles as *Titter*, Harrison got the idea for a gossip magazine about sex, celebrities, and politics from the Kefauver hearings in 1951. *Confidential* lasted until 1958, when the Supreme Court closed it for obscenity.

56. This story is widely reported, particularly in "Monica Kaufman: Closeups," WSB-TV, December 15, 1987, Museum of Television and Radio Archives, n.d.; Storm, 122.

57. "The Man Who Could Tap 100,000 Telephone Lines," *Philadelphia Bulletin*, December 18, 1955; "Ann Corio's Phone Tapped; 7 Other N.Y. Victims Listed," *Philadelphia Evening Bulletin*, February 21, 1955; TUNC. "Listening Toms," *Wall Street Journal*, February 25, 1955, 8.

58. *Billboard*, September 11, 1954, 59.

59. Costume Folder, n.d., SRM. There are several magazine covers of Marilyn and Jane Manfield. A striptease "battle" took place in Vegas between Marlene Dietrich and Terry Moore, a stripper. "Las Vegas Skin Game," *Playboy*, December 1954, 40.

60. *Cabaret* 1, no. 6 (October 1955), 38–49.

61. Harold Minsky, "Harold Minsky Picks the Ten Best Strippers," n.d., HM.

62. Philip Furia, *The Poets of Tin Pan Alley* (New York, 1990), 235. As Furia points out, Brown "never ventured beyond the tritest romantic clichés." He and his writing partner Arthur Freed were West Coast songwriters who wrote primarily for movie musicals with simple rhythms and harmonies. As important was the fact that in 1952, this song was used in the movie musical *Singin' in the Rain* and would have been known to the entire country.

63. *Cabaret*, October 1955, 48. Interview with Dixie Evans in the June 22, 1999, Velvet Hammer souvenir program, n.d.

64. Jelke acts were popular in nightclubs as well. Cited in Neal Gabler, *Walter Winchell* (New York, 1994), 459–61.

65. Al Silverman, *Climax*, n.d., JDM.

66. Barbara Land and Myrnick Land, *A Short History of Las Vegas* (Reno, 1999).

67. Cited in Peterson, 241.

68. *Cabaret*, August 1955, n.d., Burlesque Scrapbooks, 1952–1956, BRTC.

69. Burlesque Scrapbooks, 1952–1956, BRTC. This was hardly a rock-solid point of view. Meyerowitz recounts how women wrote in to protest.

70. *Ebony*, March 1953, n.d., Burlesque Scrapbooks, 1952–1956, BRTC.

71. "The White Entertainer in Negro Clubs," *Jet*, September 1953, n.d., Burlesque Scrapbooks, 1952–1956, BRTC.

72. Charvil, 38; "Associated Actors and Artists of America Withdraw Charter of BAA," *New York Times*, June 26, 1957, 27; "Agva Opens Drive to Sign Burlesque Performers," *New York Times*, September 12, 1957.

73. "Newark Ended in Burly Ban," *Billboard*, March 9, 1953, 45.

74. "Burlesque a Form of Speech, N.J. Court Finds in Ruling," April 27, 1953, n.d., TUNC; "Burlesque Closes in Newark as Police Press Arrests," clipping, n.d., TUNC; *Variety*, February 6, 1957, 57; "Two Newark Theatres Will Ask Supreme Court Review," *New York Times*, January 12, 1957, 37; "Minsky to Quit Newark," *New York Times*, February 7, 1957, 21; "Hudson Burlesque Dies: Union City Theatre, Balked by Law, Turns in License," *New York Times*, October 15, 1957, 38.

75. "Industry Leaders, Others, Urge Commissioner McCaffrey to Restore 'Clean, Old Fashioned Burlesque' for License to Open Show at Orpheum Theater, Brooklyn," *New York Times*, February 24, 1955, 29.

76. "City Bars Burlesque in Any Shape and Manner," *New York Mirror*, April 21, 1955, Burlesque Scrapbooks, 1952–1956, BRTC.

77. "'Welcome Exile' Out in Cold," *New York Times*, December 27, 1955, 22; "Show Closes, Speculation on Reasons," *New York Times*, December 31, 1956, 9; "Decision on Brooklyn Burlesque under Wraps after Third Hearing," *New York Times*, April 16, 1955, 21; "NYS Supreme Court Reserves Decision on Burlesque License for Phillips," *New York Times*, May 17, 1955, 32; "NYS Supreme Court Sanctions Return of Modified Burlesque by Approving Phillips Appeal for License," *New York Times*, May 20, 1955, 1; "City to Appeal Ruling that Backs Burlesque," *New York Times*, May 27, 1955, 46; "City Will Permit Burlesque Again, but Striptease, Bumps and Grinds Will Be Missing under New License," *New York Times*, December 10, 1956, 31; "License Approved Minus Burlesque," *New York Times*, November 26, 1955, 37.

78. GRL, 1910–1970, Series IV, Writing, Gypsy Correspondence, Box 43, Folder 7, 1959. This remark was widely quoted.

**You Gotta Get a Gimmick**

1. Kofoed quoted in Don Ediger, *Miami Herald*, August 20, 1967, n.d., WHMC.

2. Garry Wills, *Jack Ruby* (New York, 1967), 1–9; Gary Cartwright, "Bad Girl of the Century," *Texas Monthly*, December 1999, 155.

3. Wills, 10; Diana Hunt, *Jack Ruby's Girls* (Atlanta, 1970). Additional data on Jada thanks to fact sheet given to me by Mark Coulter and in Gerald Posner, *Case Closed* (New York, 1993), 350–65. One of the stories told in Posner's book has to do with Jack and Barney Weinstein's using mob connections to get amateur and professional strippers to work in the same club in 1963. This was against union rules at the time since amateur strippers could be paid less.

4. "Truculent Texan," *New York Times*, October 6, 1966, 31, describes Ruby as "semi-literate" and a "bad boss." These details and others are also found in the *Report of the Warren Commission* (New York, 1964), 700–18.

5. *Naughty Dallas*, directed by Breck Wall, produced by Larry Buchanan, 1964. According to Gary Cartwright, Jada was a drug courier for the mob. Cartwright, "Who Was Jack Ruby?" in *Confessions of a Washed Up Sportswriter* (Austin, 2000), 35–58.

6. Wills, 64.

7. Story about Judge Joe Brown in *New York Times*, February 18, 1964, 24. Wills, 67.

8. *Dallas Morning News*, October 27, 4; October 28, 4.

9. *Dallas Morning News*, February 14, 1958, 1, 9; February 15, 1958, 1. Also, Gary Cartwright, "Candy: Taking the Wrapper off a Texas Legend," *Texas Monthly*, December 1976, 99–103, 187–90; John Bainbridge, *The Super-Americans* (New York, 1961), 250–56; Wills, 68; Cartwright, "Who Was Jack Ruby?" 38–40; Candy Barr Clippings Folder, TUNC.

10. Postcard from author's personal collection.

11. Barbara Landes, *A Short History of Las Vegas* (New York, 1996); Ovid Demaris and Ed Reid, *The Green Felt Jungle* (New York, 1991); Sally Denton and Roger Morris, *The Money and the Power: The Making of Las Vegas and Its Hold on America* (New York, 2001); Mike Tronnes, ed., *Literary Las Vegas: The Best Writing about America's Most Fabulous City* (New York, 1995). Taylor Howell, *Las Vegas: City of Sin?* (New York, 1963), 97.

12. Burlesque Scrapbooks, 1952–1956, BRTC.

13. *Variety*, January 30, 1957, 50; Ted Jordan, *My Secret Life with Norma Jean* (New York, 1989), 193. Other strippers also benefited from Vegas, including Sally Rand, who did her fan dance at the big, plush Last Frontier Hotel, the Hacienda, and the Silver Slipper. Sherry Britton also played El Rancho.

14. "Minsky University, New Golden Reno," *Variety*, September 17, 1952, 62.

15. "Minsky in Vegas: French Flavored Burleycue Sears the Desert Sands," *Playboy*, April 1958, 40–44.

16. *Las Vegas Sun*, January 31, 1951, UNLV Collection.

17. Howell, *Las Vegas*.

18. Ibid., 75.

19. Gilbert Milstein, "Cloud on Las Vegas Silver Lining," *New York Times*, March 18, 1956, X, 17, 63, 64.

20. Thomas R. Fuller, "Life Begins for Harold," *Sir Knight* 1, no. 5, 1960, 12–15, Clippings File, HM.

21. "How Minsky Chooses Showgirls," clipping, n.d., HM.

22. Clipping, n.d., Burlesque Scrapbooks, 1952–1956, BRTC; "Las Vegas," *Look*, November 4, 1952, 57–69.

23. Minsky quoted in Fuller, 12.

24. A. J. Liebling, *The Earl of Louisiana* (New York, 1961), 235.

25. "Singing the Blues for Burlesque," *Philadelphia Enquirer*, n.d., Tempest Storm Clippings Folder, TUNC.

26. These were actual numbers from the early 1950s.

27. *New York Theatre Critics' Reviews*, Volume 20, no. 26 (1959), 300–303. The musical ran for 702 performances and made hundreds of thousands of dollars.

28. Brooks Atkinson, "Merman in Gypsy," *New York Times*, May 31, 1959, ii, 1.

29. Kenneth Tynan, *Curtains* (New York, 1961), 320; Walter Kerr, "First Night Report," *Herald Tribune*, in *New York Theatre Critics' Reviews*, Volume 20, no. 26 (1959), 16.

30. Quoted in Keith Garabian, *The Making of Gypsy* (Toronto, 2002), 107–14. This account is also informed by Arthur Laurents, *Original Story: A Memoir of Broadway and Hollywood* (New York, 2002), 375–400.

31. There's some dispute as to how old Starr was when she had the affair with Long. Some say she was twenty-three. Also, regarding Long's erratic behavior, scholars have recently ventured that Long was bipolar or that he had had several strokes. *The Saga of Uncle Earl* is one of the books that use mental illness to explain Long's behavior.

32. Blaze Starr, *My Life as Told to Huey Perry* (New York, 1974), 103–54.

33. Quoted in Richard B. McCaughan, *Socks on a Rooster: Louisiana's Earl K. Long* (New Orleans, 1998), 186. Starr is quoted in "Louisiana Story the End of a Chapter," *New York Times Sunday Magazine*, September 27, 1959, 32, 34, 39.

34. *Life*, July 13, 1959, 80; Michael Kurtz and Morgan J. Peoples, *Earl K. Long: The Saga of Uncle Earl and Louisiana Politics* (Baton Rouge, 1990), 215, 256; Stan Opotowsky, *The Longs of Louisiana* (New York, 1960), 186.

35. *Life*, ibid.

36. *Time*, June 15, 1959, 17; June 29, 1959, 13–14; July 6, 1959, 17.

37. *New Orleans Times Picayune*, July 13, 1959, 1.

38. Additional details about Long's travel and unstable behavior in July 1959 come from the *Times Picayune*, July 3, 1; July 6, 2; July 8, 2; July 11, 5; July 12, 1; and July 14, 1. Also "Louisiana Story the End of a Chapter." McCaughan reports that at the end of the month he took a drive with someone else. Also *Philadelphia Daily News*, n.d., TUNC.

39. Liebling, 242.

40. Statistic on premarital sex cited in John D'Emilio and Estelle Freedman, *Intimate Matters: A History of Sexuality in America* (New York, 1988), 334–35. Leslie Fiedler, "A Night with Mr. Teas," *Show*, October 1961, 118–19; Eddie Muller and Daniel Farris, *Grindhouse: The Forbidden World of Adults Only Cinema* (New York, 1996), 82–84.

41. Kenneth Turan and Stephen F. Zito, *Sinema: American Pornographic Films and the People Who Make Them* (New York, 1974,), 11–13.

42. Gloria Steinem, "I Was a Playboy Bunny," in *Outrageous Acts and Everyday Rebellions* (New York, 1983), 29–70. Barbara Ehrenreich, *The Hearts of Men: American Dreams and the Flight from Commitment* (New York, 1983), 44.

43. Dave Cohn quoted in *Show*, March 1956, n.d., Burlesque Scrapbooks, 1952–1956, BRTC. "He Books the Stripper," *Star*, October 1954, n.d., Burlesque Scrapbooks, 1952–1956, BRTC.

44. "Striptease, the National Fetish," *Sir Knight* 1, no. 12 (1960), University of Nevada at Las Vegas Collection.

45. Ann Corio, *Variety*, August 13, 1941, 2; clipping, n.d., Dave Cohn Clippings File, NYPL.

46. Gayety Clippings File, Detroit Public Library. The following year, the city council called the building an "eyesore" and proposed building a garage there. Two years later, with the Gayety still open, a fire swept through the theater.

47. David Kruh, *Always Something Doin'* (Boston, 1991), 78–80.

48. "Strippers Retreat: Closing of Rialto," *Time*, January 11, 1954, 73. "Gayety Burns," *Billboard*, January 15, 1953, 14.

49. See Erin Clune's unpublished 1994 seminar paper "The Stripper's Union: Sexuality, Deviance, and the Politics of Distancing in the American Guild of Variety Artists, 1948–1962," housed in the Robert F. Wagner Labor Archives, New York University. Additionally, a memo from Jackie Bright dated November 10, 1948, AGVA, is devoted to the problem of the burlesque field. The AGVA National Board Meeting Notes, February 16–18, 1959, AGVA, show that Candy Barr was a subject of concern. "Staid Senators Learn about B-Girls," *New York Herald Tribune*, June 10, 1962, UTA; "Hardy Band of Strip Teasers is Keeping Old Burlesque Alive," *Journal American*, April 23, 1961, UTA; postcard, 1970, author's personal collection.

50. AGVA Hearings, 1962, Permanent Subcommittee of Investigations of the Committee on Government Operations, 16, Robert F. Wagner Labor Archives; "Congress to Bare Strip-Tease Kick Backs," *New York Journal American*, June 10, 1962, UTA; other clippings, June 14–20, 1962, UTA.

51. "Senators Hear of B-Girls' Role; Witness Accuses Artists' Guild," *New York Times*, June 12, 1962, UTA; *San Francisco Examiner*, June 10, 1962, WHMC.

52. AGVA Hearings, 1962, 18, 30.

53. Ibid., 38.

54. Ibid., 49.

55. Ibid., 134, 171, 232.

56. Ibid., 104–6. Additionally, an anecdote about Chicago is told in David Friedman's memoir, *A Youth in Babylon: Confessions of a Trash Film King*, in which a young "college educated" organizer tries to get Dwain Esper, by all accounts the sleaziest of burlesque producers and carnival guys, to sign AGVA contracts. In this story, which may be apocryphal, the organizer goes to Esper's sleazy South Loop joint and is seduced and rolled by a stripper. He wakes up without his clothes and escapes only through the mercy of a kind older woman.

57. Quoted in Jesse Alson Smith, *Syndicate City: The Chicago Crime Cartel and What to Do about It* (Chicago, 1954), 190.

58. AGVA hearings, 160, 164.

59. *New York Times*, June 12, 1962, n.d., WHMC.

60. Howard Lucraft, "David Rose: Hollywood Film Composer," *Crescendo & Jazz Music* 36, no. 1 (February–March 1999), 6.

61. Stripper ad in *New York Times*, July 29, 1962, 35.

62. "I am really just a prude" quoted in *Courier*, September 19, 1966. "*This Was Burlesque* at Casino East, Narrated by Ann Corio," *New York Times*, March 7, 1962, 9. *This Was Burlesque* also grossed eight million dollars in ten years, according to the *New York Times*, January 20, 1970, 48, and, according to the *New York Times*, March 18, 1965, 18, offered a profit-sharing plan to performers in the show. *This Was Burlesque* was revived in 1970.

63. *Time*, November 10, 1961, n.d., WHMC.

64. August 28, 1970, clipping, TUNC.

65. "Striptease Names," WHMC, listing names of strippers in 1950s and 1960s. "An Able Seeman Observes College Navel Maneuvers," *Daily News*, September 16, 1964, n.d., UTA.

## Topless Dancing

1. "Go Go Go," *Esquire*, February 1964, 200.

2. In 1965, Saigon would ban the twist. See *New York Times*, April 15, 1965, 9.

3. "Swim Madness is Observed with Caution," *San Francisco Examiner*, March 24, 1964, 26. In 1966, the *New Yorker* asked Gypsy what she thought of the swim and she seemed unimpressed. "Bumps and grinds are less offensive with kids than with the older ones," she told them.

4. Cited in John D'Emilio and Estelle Freedman, *Intimate Matters: A History of Sexuality in America* (New York, 1988), 306.

5. In 1953, Ethel Gant, the wife of the president of a North Carolina textile mill, discovered that her pregnancy prevented her from wearing stockings because she couldn't put on a girdle and garters to hold them up. Instead, Mrs. Gant got the idea of sewing stockings to a pair of panties. Eventually, designers figured out how to make a single nylon garment, but the product didn't become de rigueur until the mid-1960s, when it was worn on fashion runways by the English model Twiggy, beneath another new—and equally torturous, from a feminine point of view—invention, the miniskirt, whose brevity put severe limitations upon what could be worn beneath it.

6. "The Nude Is Here Today," *San Francisco Examiner*, June 12, 1964, 27; Peggy Moffitt, *The Rudi Gernreich Book* (New York, 1963), 18–22; Gloria Steinem, "Gernreich's Progress or Eve Unbound," *New York Times Magazine*, January 31, 1965, 18–24.

7. Tom Wolfe, *The Pump House Gang* (New York, 1968), 83; Nan Almilla Boyd, *Wide Open Town: A History of Queer San Francisco to 1965* (Berkeley, 2003).

8. Wolfe, 10.

9. Arthur Berger, "Varieties of Topless Experience," *Journal of Popular Culture* I, no. 2 (1970); "Topless," *Playboy*, August 1966, 160–67; Andrew Blake, *Topless* (New York, 1969), 414–24.

10. Stanley Kauffman, "Review of *Head*," *New Republic*, December 7, 1968, 24.

11. "I'm Really a Housewife at Heart," *San Francisco Examiner*, March 30, 1964.

12. "Two Burlesque Shows in Downtown Bow," *New York Times*, December 12, 1963, 48.

13. "Block Seat of Baltimore's Libido Awaits Bulldozer," *New York Times*, April 13, 1970, 18. This was really the first moment when city officials made a concentrated effort to shut down the block.

14. Wolfe, *San Francisco Chronicle*, August 17, 1975, n.d., WHMC.

15. Quoted in Moffitt, 20. "London Town Bare Bosoms," *San Francisco Examiner*, June 22, 1964, 3; "Topless in San Mateo," *San Francisco Examiner*, June 23, 1964, 3; "The Bare Legalities," *San Francisco Examiner*, June 25, 1964, 18; "The Topless Swimsuit," letter, *San Francisco Examiner*, date tk, 34; advertisement, *San Francisco Examiner*, June 28, 1964, 12; Earl Wilson, "The Almost Topless Gown," *San Francisco Examiner*, June 29, 1964, 16.

16. "Topless Waitresses Put Inns in Stew," *New York World*, April 1, 1965, UTA.

17. "North Beach Raid—Dancers Arrested," *San Francisco Examiner*, April 23, 1965, 1–7; "No Nudes with Frisco Food: Clubs Raided; Too Much French Dressing," *San Francisco Examiner*, April 24, 1965, 1; clipping, n.d., UTA; "Topless at Noon, New Raid," *San Francisco Examiner*, April 27, 1965, 1, 5; "North Beach Has New Troubles," *San Francisco Examiner*, April 28, 1965, 5; "Test Case for Bare Bosoms," *San Francisco Chronicle*, March 5, 1965, n.d., WHMC.

18. "A Race for Nudie Trials," *San Francisco Examiner*, April 29, 1965, 14.

19. San Francisco Chamber of Commerce figure cited in Marilyn Yalom, *A History of the Breast* (New York, 1997), 194. Earl Wilson, *Show Business Laid Bare* (New York, 1974), 110–29, reports that almost immediately after Doda, strippers were performing bottomless. Herbert Gold, "Those Frisky Friscotheques," *Playboy*, April 1965, 73.

20. Cited in James Peterson, *The Century of Sex* (New York, 2000), 262–63. Also, Herb Caen, *San Francisco Chronicle*, August 12, 1965, 25.

21. Caen, ibid. The same story is told in a slightly different fashion in Tom Wolfe, "What if He's Right?" in *The Pump House Gang*, 30.

22. Laura Kipnis, *Bound and Gagged* (New York, 1990), 124–25; Larry Flynt, *An Unseemly Man* (Los Angeles, 1996).

23. Harold Minsky quoted in "Topless No Threat to Strip," *Variety*, June 2, 1965, 1, 70.

## 1969: Who Killed Striptease?

1. *Kansas City Star*, December 28, 1969, 1.

2. George Palmer, "Gayety Fire, Baltimore," *Marquee Postcard Collection* (New York, 1970).

3. Clipping, n.d., 1960, TUNC; "CBS Blew My Fuse Again," Gypsy Rose Lee, *Variety*, December 29, 1948, 1.

4. Items in *San Francisco Chronicle*, May 12, 19, 1969, WHMC.

5. "Queen of a Dying Art, Tempest Storm, Likes the Money, not the Job," *Wall Street Journal*, August 15, 1969. In 1973, at Le Crazy Spot, she wore a skin-tight white rhinestone dress and a feathered boa. Her soundtrack roamed from the theme from *Mutiny on the Bounty* to the theme from *Mission Impossible*. "A Tempest in the World of Burlesque," n.d., WHMC.

6. "It's Ladies' Day at the Burleycue," *Life*, n.d., 1966, WHMC; "Gypola's Carney Tour," *Variety*, December 29, 1948, 48.

7. "Behind Those Fans, Sally's Still Sexy at 68," undated clipping, n.d., TUNC; Mel Gussow, "Stage Burlesque Returns," *New York Times*, February 12, 1970. "Ann Corio is immortal," Gussow concludes.

8. Clipping, n.d., Lili St. Cyr Clippings File, BRTC. "Lili St. Cyr, 80, Burlesque Star Famous for Her Bubble Baths," obituary, *New York Times*, February 6, 1999, C16.

9. "Stripper Bounces Back," *San Francisco Chronicle*, June 6, 1975, WHMC; "The Superstar Is a Lady," *San Francisco Chronicle*, June 11, 1975, WHMC.

10. David Allyn, *Make Love Not War: The Sexual Revolution, An Unfettered History* (New York, 2000), chapter 10, although his focus is wider, inspired this section of the book; John Tytell, *The Living Theatre: Art, Exile, and Outrage* (New York, 1994), 225–50.

11. "*Sweet Eros* and *Witness*: A Terrence McNally Double Bill Opens," *New York Times*, November 22, 1968, 38; Dan Sullivan, "Nudity Moves into Center Stage; Trend to Nakedness Linked to Candor of Other Media," *New York Times*, April 25, 1968, 51; Martin Esslin, "Nudity: Barely the Beginning," *New York Times*, December 15, 1968, 18.

12. *New York Theatre Critics' Reviews*, Volume 28, no. 5 (1967), 343–46.

13. "Of Course There Were Some Limits," *New York Times*, May 19, 1968, II, 1, 3; *New York Theatre Critics' Reviews*, Volume 29, no. 13 (1968), 268, 279. "Topless and No Bottoms Either," *New York Times*, April 28, 1968, D1, notes that the sheer blouse is obsolete.

14. Martin Gottfried, *Opening Nights: Theatre Criticism of the Sixties* (New York, 1969), 103–5.

15. Anderson quoted in *New York Theatre Critics' Reviews*, Volume 30, no. 17 (1969), 207–13; Gottfried quoted in Gillian Hanson, *Original Skin: Nudity and Sex in Cinema and Theatre* (New York, 1970), 126.

16. Tytell, 247–48; Elenore Lester, "Or Is Futz the Wave of the Future?" *New York Times*, June 30, 1968, D1; Guy Flatley, "Is This Strip Necessary?" *New York Times*, January 26, 1969, D12.

17. Gottfried, 353–66. The opening and censuring of *Che* is documented in the *New York Times*, March 24, 56; March 25, 41; and April 25, 35.

18. "Tynan Plans a Stage Tribute to Eros," *New York Times*, April 9, 1969, 54; Stefan Brecht, "Review of *Dionysus in 69*," *The Drama Review* 13, no. 3 (Spring 1969), 56.

19. *Oh! Calcutta!* chronicled in the *New York Times* from April 19, 1969, through February 15, 1970. "Porn—Is That Bad?" *New York Times*, June 15, 1969, 1. Kathleen Tynan, *The Life of Kenneth Tynan* (New York, 1987), 365–68.

20. Mort Minsky, Letter to the Editor, *New York Times*, June 29, 1969, D9.

21. *New York Times*, December 19, 1969, 23.

22. Bruce Williamson, "Oh! Calcutta!" *Playboy*, October 1969, 166–72, 242–43; Clive Burns, *"Oh! Calcutta!* Almost Innocent Dirty Show," *New York Times*, June 18, 1969.

23. *"Oh! Calcutta!* to be Back," *New York Times*, July 22, 1969, 35; "2 'Oh! Calcutta!' Rows go to $25 a seat September 9," *New York Times*, July 29, 1969, II, 9.

24. Keating quoted in Allyn, 122.

25. Levy quoted in Allyn, 123. "Jacques Levy Testified for Chicago 7," *New York Times*, February 15, 1970, 168.

26. Tytell, 227; Julian Beck and Judith Malina, *Paradise Now* (New York, 1969), 17–19.

27. *New York Times*, September 28, 1968, 27.

28. "History Now," interview with Julian Beck, Judith Malina, and Robert Brustein, *Yale/Theatre* vol. 2, no. 1 (Spring 1969), 23. In interviews at the time, Schechner used the same argument against his critics that the Minskys and other burlesque impresarios had used thirty years earlier: "If you think it's obscene, you have a dirty mind." Bernard Dick, "Is It Hip to Strip?" in "Drama Mailbag," *New York Times*, August 17, 1969, argued that to reduce theater to striptease simplifies theater.

29. "The Final Decline and Total Collapse of the American Avant-Garde," *Esquire*, May 1969, 143–50.

30. Walter Kerr, "What Can They Do for an Encore?" *New York Times*, February 2, 1969, VI, 24.

31. James Riardon, *Break on Through: The Life and Death of Jim Morrison* (New York, 1996), 289, 290, 299; James Miller, *Flowers in the Dustbin: The Rise of Rock and Roll* (New York, 1999), 290–93; Joan Didion, *The White Album* (New York, 1976), 22–25.

32. *New York Times* coverage of the 1968 Miss America protest shows the origins of the bra-burning myth, at least in part. Asked whether the Atlantic City government had objected to the protest, Robin Morgan told a reporter the mayor had been worried about fire safety, but said, "We told him we wouldn't do anything dangerous—just a symbolic bra-burning." This article made clear that no fires were set, but by September 28 the *Times* refers to bra burnings as if they had happened. There are many other accounts of this event, including Marcia Cohen, *The Sisterhood* (New York, 1999), 149–53.

33. Todd Gitlin, *The Sixties: Years of Hope, Days of Rage* (New York, 1987), 363; Ellen Willis, "Up From Radicalism: A Feminist Journal," *Us*, January 1969; conversation with Willis, spring 2000.

34. Anne Hollander, *Sex and Suits: The Evolution of Modern Dress* (New York, 1995), 174–75.

35. Esther Newton, *Mother Camp: Female Impersonators in America* (Chicago, 1972), preface. As late as 1965, Newton recounts that drag queens who impersonated women in clubs were unable to go out in public in their makeup. At Harlem's Apollo Theater in the late fifties , male performers were still emphasizing their fake femininity, just as female strippers would remove oranges from their bras and reveal hard, un-made-up features in their acts' final moments.

36. Corio File, various dates including 1966 and 1970, TUNC.

37. "'I Am Not a Nude,' Stripper Storm Cool on Calcutta," *Las Vegas Review-Journal*, April 29, 1970, Tempest Storm Clippings Folder, TUNC.

38. Tom Wolfe cited in James Peterson, *The Century of Sex* (New York, 2000), 322. Carolyn See, *Blue Money: Pornography and the Pornographers—A Look at the Two Billion Dollar Fantasy* (New York, 1974).

39. This has been well documented. See Alex Comfort, Erica Jong, Marabel Morgan, etc.

40. James K. Skipper and Charles H. McCaghy, "The Stripper," *Sexual Behavior* 1, no. 3 (June 1971), 78–81. This team turned out several articles with similar theses, including "Lesbian Behavior as an Adaptation to the Occupation of Stripping," *Social Problems* 17, no. 2 (Fall 1969), 262–70. Gale Miller, *Odd Jobs: The World of Deviant Work* (Saddle River, N.J., 1978), 159–91; "The Stripteaser," *Social Problems* 17, no. 3 (Winter 1970), 391–405.

41. John D'Emilio and Estelle Freedman, *Intimate Matters: A History of Sexuality in America* (New York, 1988), chapter 14.

42. *Newsweek* cited in Peterson, 323. James K. Skipper and Charles H. McCaghy, "The Stripper," *Sexual Behavior* 1, no. 3 (June 1971), 80.

43. Kenneth Turan, *Sinema: American Pornographic Films and the People Who Make Them* (New York, 1974), ix; "Stripper Bounces Back," *San Francisco Chronicle*, June 6, 1975, WHMC. Tempest Storm stripped at the O'Farrell as late as 1980. John Hubner, *Bottom Feeders: From Free Love to Hard Core: The Rise and Fall of Counterculture Heroes Jim and Artie Mitchell* (New York, 1993); David McCumber, *X-Rated: The Mitchell Brothers: A True Story of Sex, Money, and Death* (New York, 1992); "The Faithful Flock to See Strip's Legends," *San Francisco Examiner*, March 6, 1979.

44. Skipper and McCaghy, 79.

45. Some of this story is recounted in Fanne Fox, *Fanne Fox* (New York, 1975).

46. *Kansas City Star*, January 24, 1974.

47. Folly Theater Clippings File, FTA.

48. Folly Theater program, author's personal collection.

49. "And Now for the Women in the Audience," *New York Times*, March 19, 1978, D37.

50. Troy Kline and Joe Bice, *Chippendale's: The Naked Truth* (New York, 1998).

51. The USA Network movie *The Chippendale's Murder* told the story of how Indian immigrant and founder Steve Banerjee spiraled into murder, blackmail, and mob activity.

52. UPI, January 12, 1980, WHMC; "Musings on the Male Stripper," *San Francisco Sunday Examiner & Chronicle*, December 7, 1980; "For Starters, an Exploitable Story of a Male Stripper," *San Francisco Chronicle*, October 21, 1981; Herb Caen column, *San Francisco Chronicle*, March 31, 1980; "Not Just Another Pretty Face," *San Francisco Examiner*, October 23, 1981.

53. "Nightclub for Women Charged with Bias," *New York Times*, February 23, 1984, B4. Eventually it was found that treating male and female strip clubs differently was not bias.

54. "Male Strip Clubs," n.d., TUNC; "Ogling Men: They're not Eye to Eye," UPI, May 8, 1980, TUNC.

55. Cheering on Fremont's Male Strippers," *San Francisco Chronicle*, February 29, 1980, 2.

56. Katherine Liepe-Levinson, *Strip Show: Performances of Gender and Desire* (London, 2000), 38–41.

57. "She's a Tempest at 52 and Still a-Peeling," *Philadelphia Bulletin*, July 13, 1980, TUNC.

**Conclusion**

1. "21st Century Burlesque," *Interview*, November 2002, 116.
2. See also "Dancing in the Lap of Luxury: At New Upscale Strip Clubs, Stripping Is a Dirty Word," *New York Times*, May 12, 2004.
3. Certainly teasing is no longer relevant in the lingerie industry. In the past five years, the Ohio-based chain Victoria's Secret has opened multilevel megastores all over America. Mannequins writhe in the windows in their merry widows and thongs. The thong—an undergarment derived from the stripper's G-string—is today the fastest-selling kind of underwear and accounts for 40 percent of Victoria's Secret's sales.
4. Marilyn Yalom, *A History of the Breast* (New York, 1997), 161.
5. This is an argument made by many others, including David Allyn in *Make Love Not War: The Sexual Revolution, An Unfettered History* (New York, 2000).
6. There are many examples of female producers of porn. On the other hand, coach Mike Price was recently fired from a ten-million-dollar contract for carousing at a strip club. "Coach at Alabama Has No Intention of Quitting," *New York Times*, May 3, 2003, 2.
7. Lili Burana, *Strip City* (New York, 1998), 123.
8. It turned out that the "Ivy League" Stripper was from a working-class family and couldn't afford college. Other titles include Yvette Paris, *Queen of Burlesque* (New York, 1990); Elizabeth Eaves, *Bare: On Women, Dancing, Sex, and Power* (New York, 2002); Jake Frankman, *Being Frank* (London, 1988); Andrea Stuart, *Showgirls* (London, 1996); Lucinda Jarrett, *Stripping in Time: A History of Erotic Dancing* (London, 1997); Jessica Glasscock, *Striptease: From Gaslight to Spotlight* (New York,, 2003); Sylvia Plachy and James Ridgeway, *Red Light: Inside the Sex Industry* (New York, 1996), 139–97; Lynn Snowden, *Nine Lives: From Stripper to Schoolteacher: My Yearlong Odyssey in the Work World* (New York, 1994), 185–218.

# Acknowledgments

Writing a book, one incurs innumerable debts. My first is to the many people who shared their memories of burlesque and striptease with me and made the book richer, especially, but not limited to, Art Hess and "Tirza the Wine Girl." They are not responsible for any omissions or errors.

This book could not have been completed without my incredible editor, Peter Ginna, tireless provider of "tough love" notes on the manuscript. Furaha Norton, also at Oxford, was always full of sensible advice and good cheer, especially at the photo-wrangling stage. Maryann Zissimos and Barbara Fillon displayed endless enthusiasm for the project. Joellyn Ausanka and copyeditor Diana Gavales were steadily terrific. I could not have asked for a better team. My wonderful agent, Denise Shannon, took a chance on the proposal, and then hung in there and believed in the book, while continuing to take me out to lunch.

My parents, who even though they only lately have understood what I was doing, nonetheless rooted for me. Since 2000, DePaul University has granted me a course load reduction, a Humanities Fellowship, creative leaves, and a travel stipend to give conference talks on various sections of the book. For allowing me to try out some of those sections at conferences, I am grateful to the American Society for Theatre Research, the Oral History Society at Columbia University, the Gotham Center Conference on New York History, the American Popular Culture Association, Eileen Mackevich and the Chicago Humanities Festival, the DePaul Humanities Center, the International Society of Humor, Bobbi Kwall and the Law and Humanities Lecture Series at DePaul, and the Kinsey Institute for Research in Sex and Gender. I am particularly grateful to Thom Gunn at the Mass Culture Workshop at the University of Chicago, whose response to my take on film in an early draft of the manuscript made me rethink.

David Krasner and Dorothy Chansky each, in different ways, probably without knowing it, influenced my thinking on various sections of the book and also were models of patience when essays I had promised them were inexcusably late. Marc Robinson was stern and said smart things about the manuscript.

Many editors endured my obsession on the subject of striptease over the years and published excerpts or riffs. I thank especially Jim O'Quinn at *American Theatre magazine*, Katherine Bouton at the *New York Times Book Review*, Emily Eakin at *Lingua Franca*, Dick Babcock at *Chicago*, Art Winslow at the *Nation*, Tim Bannon at the *Chicago Tribune*, and Ken Emerson and Jennifer Krauss at the late *New York Newsday*. Jonathan Black let me peruse hard-to-find copies of *Playboy* from the 1950s and lent me his books.

My research assistants at DePaul University, Caitlin Parrish, Rob Cohn, Karen Kobb, Adam Simon, and especially Josh Saletnik, rose to the occasion and assisted me tracking down footnote citations. Josh helped me secure rights and permissions and was calm in the face of what often seemed like a tangle of insurmountable deadlines. Friends and colleagues, including Lisa Portes, Carlos Murillo, Lenora Brown, Dean Corrin, and, most of all, Rishona Zimring, were supportive when I was rewriting. Rina Rinalli and Wendy Rohm read drafts and answered questions about practical details. David Zivan was interested.

The idea for this book began, albeit in much different form, as my doctoral thesis at the Yale School of Drama. From that era, I wish to thank my much-admired teacher Erika Munk, who one day, over lunch at Kavanaugh's, noted that I seemed to have a feel for writing about striptease and encouraged me to write about it more. "Wednesday" Martin, by becoming a stripper, made me curious. By their examples as writers, my other teachers, Gordon Rogoff and Dick Gilman, provided inspiration.

The late Debra Bernhardt, as well as Andy Davis, Brooks McNamara, and Steve Zeitlin, each provided input about striptease, burlesque, popular culture, and folk-lore in the book's early stages. Librarians at the New York Public Library and else-where were indefatigable in their attempts to track down images I wanted to use. The New York Public Library gave me a room in the initial stages of writing. Jeremy McGrew and Louise Martzinek at NYPL, Faye Haun at MCNY, Jane Klain at MTVR, Suzanne Eggleston at Yale, and especially Maryann Chach at the Shubert Archives were generous with time and resources. Ralph Pugh at the Chicago Historical Society not only let me view uncatalogued material from the Sally Rand Manuscript Collection, he accompanied me down to the basement to get it.

Ellen Lange, Maria Leveton, and Frank Torok each helped with technical difficulties.

Finally, there is no way these acknowledgments would be complete without my thanking Mitchell Korn, who inspired me in many ways over the last several years. That will all be difficult, if not impossible, to repay.

# Credits

# Index